MW01050387

Introduction to Electrical Power System Technology

Introduction to Electrical Power System Technology

Theodore R. Bosela
Youngstown State University

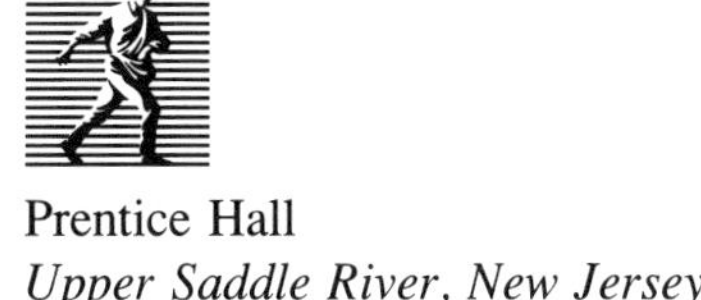

Prentice Hall
Upper Saddle River, New Jersey   *Columbus, Ohio*

Library of Congress Cataloging-in-Publication Data
Bosela, Theodore R.
Introduction to electrical power system technology / Theodore R. Bosela.
p. cm.
Includes index.
ISBN 0-13-186537-4
1. Electric power systems. I. Title.
TK1001.B67 1997
621.31--dc20 96-33742
CIP

Cover art/photo: PhotoBank
Editor: Charles E. Stewart, Jr.
Editorial/production supervision: Gretchen K. Chenenko
Production Editor: Sheryl Glicker Langner
Design Coordinator: Julia Zonneveld Van Hook
Cover Designer: Scott Rattray
Production Manager: Patricia A. Tonneman
Marketing Manager: Debbie Yarnell
Electronic Text Management: Karen L. Bretz

This book was set in Times Roman by The Clarinda Company
and was printed and bound by Book Press, Inc., a Quebecor America Book Group Company.
The cover was printed by Phoenix Color Corp.

Printed in the United States of America

10 9 8 7 6 5 4 3 2 1

ISBN: 0-13-186537-4

Prentice-Hall International (UK) Limited, *London*
Prentice-Hall of Australia Pty. Limited, *Sydney*
Prentice-Hall of Canada, Inc., *Toronto*
Prentice-Hall Hispanoamericana, S. A., *Mexico*
Prentice-Hall of India Private Limited, *New Delhi*
Prentice-Hall of Japan, Inc., *Tokyo*
Simon & Schuster Asia Pte. Ltd., *Singapore*
Editora Prentice-Hall do Brasil, Ltda., *Rio de Janeiro*

Dedication

This book is dedicated to
my lovely wife Christine,
for her patience and understanding
during the preparation of the manuscript,
and to my beautiful children,
Stephen and Emily.

Preface

This textbook is designed to be used in an upper-level electrical engineering technology course or sequence of courses covering electrical power systems. However, the material covered in the text may also be suitable for upper-level electrical engineering courses in utility power systems as well. Necessary prerequisites would be a one-year electrical circuits sequence of courses, applied calculus, direct current machines, and alternating current machines.

The text focuses on electrical power systems from an electrical utility perspective. The main emphasis of the text is on the application of codes and standards in the design, analysis, and operation of electrical utility power systems. Many of the topics discussed in the text are also applicable to large commercial and industrial power systems.

Chapters 1 and 2 provide the necessary review of alternating current circuits and machines. This review will provide all students with a common level of competence before moving on to the more advanced topics.

Chapter 3 provides the student with a broad overview of electric utility power systems. The actual layout of the power system, including generation, transmission, and distribution facilities, is discussed. Here the student is provided with an understanding of the overall function of the power system, rather than the functions of the individual components.

Chapter 4 discusses the nature and modeling of electrical loads in the power system. The metering of electrical power and billing calculations are also discussed.

Chapter 5 introduces the per unit system as applied to both single-phase and three-phase systems. Transformer representation in the per unit system is also discussed. The per unit system is used extensively when performing short-circuit and voltage-drop calculations.

Chapter 6 involves the application of transformers to electrical utility distribution systems. Basic construction, connections, winding voltage designations, and standard ratings are discussed. Loading calculations and sizing are presented to enable proper selection of transformer ratings. Autotransformers, distribution substation, grounding, and network transformers are also discussed.

Line and cable characteristics are discussed in Chapter 7. The various types of overhead and underground cables used for power distribution are presented. Special considerations for cable splicing and terminations are discussed. The modeling of the electrical characteristics of lines and cables using the equivalent circuit approach is also presented.

Voltage drop and voltage regulation on electrical power systems are discussed in Chapter 8. The discussion focuses on radial distribution circuits and services. Voltage regulation by means of transformer taps and step voltage regulators is presented. Voltage drop due to motor starting is also discussed.

Chapter 9 presents a discussion of the application of capacitors to electrical power systems. Basic capacitor construction, standard ratings, and connections are presented. The use of capacitors to correct power factor, improve line voltage, and reduce line losses is discussed. Capacitor switching and operation at off-nominal voltages and frequencies are covered.

Chapters 10 and 11 introduce the method of symmetrical components. The basic concepts of the symmetrical component method and system modeling are discussed in Chapter 10. The use of the symmetrical component method to perform short-circuit calculations is presented in Chapter 11, and the use of current-limiting inductors to limit short-circuit currents to an acceptable level is also covered in Chapter 11.

Chapter 12 involves the overcurrent protection of distribution lines, transformers, and capacitors. The characteristics of fuses, breakers, reclosers, sectionalizers, and time overcurrent relays are discussed. The proper coordination of these overcurrent devices as applied to radial distribution systems is discussed.

The topic of power system harmonics is introduced in Chapter 13. Sources of harmonic currents, resonance problems, and harmonic filter design are discussed. The application of IEEE Standard 519 to determine acceptable harmonic limits is also covered.

Acknowledgments

I would like to express my appreciation to Mr. Donald R. Slanina, Youngstown State University, for his thorough review, valued suggestions, and constructive criticism during the preparation of the manuscript.

I would also like to thank the reviewers: John Reeves, DeVry Institute of Technology; Laverne Hardy, Milwaukee School of Engineering; Steve Berk, DeVry Institute of Technology; and Roy Powell, Chattanooga State Technical College.

Contents

1

Review of Alternating Current Circuits

1-1 General

This chapter provides a review of the concepts and laws related to single-phase and three-phase alternating current (ac) circuits. This review is presented to refresh the student's understanding of basic circuit analysis techniques. Since virtually all electrical utility power systems use alternating current, the discussion will concentrate on ac circuits.

The review begins with a discussion of phasor or vector representation of alternating current waveforms. Representation of resistance, inductance, and capacitance as complex impedances in steady-state ac circuits is presented. Several steady-state analysis techniques, such as Nodal and Mesh analyses, are presented next. Network theorems such as Thevenin's, Norton's, and the superposition theorem are discussed. Balanced and unbalanced three-phase circuits are also reviewed along with wye–delta and delta–wye conversions. Finally, the concepts of active, reactive, and apparent power in single- and three-phase circuits are discussed.

1-2 Sinusoidal Waveforms and Phasor Representation

To be able to perform power system calculations, a thorough understanding of sinusoidal waveforms and phasor representation of these waveforms is essential.

Consider the sinusoidal waveform shown in Fig. 1-1. Since the waveform has no direct current (dc) offset, the maximum positive value E_M and maximum negative value $-E_M$ of the waveform have the same absolute value. The peak to peak value of the waveform, E_{PP}, is equal to the sum of the absolute values of the maximum positive and maximum negative peaks. The period of the waveform is designated T and represents the time duration of each cycle of the waveform. The waveform thus repeats itself every T seconds. The frequency of the waveform is designated f and is a measure of how many times the waveform repeats itself every second. Therefore, the frequency is the reciprocal of the period of any periodic waveform. The instantaneous value of the waveform is the magnitude at any instant in time. For the waveform shown in Fig. 1-1, the instantaneous value is given by

$$e(t) = E_M \sin(\alpha) \tag{1.1}$$

To simplify operations such as addition, subtraction, multiplication, and division of sinusoidal functions, it is desirable to express these waveforms in terms of a rotating vector or phasor. Consider the sinusoidal waveform of Fig. 1-1 and observe the vertical projection of a vector rotating counterclockwise in a circular fashion, as shown in Fig. 1-2. When $\alpha = 0$, the vertical projection of the rotating vector has a magnitude of zero.

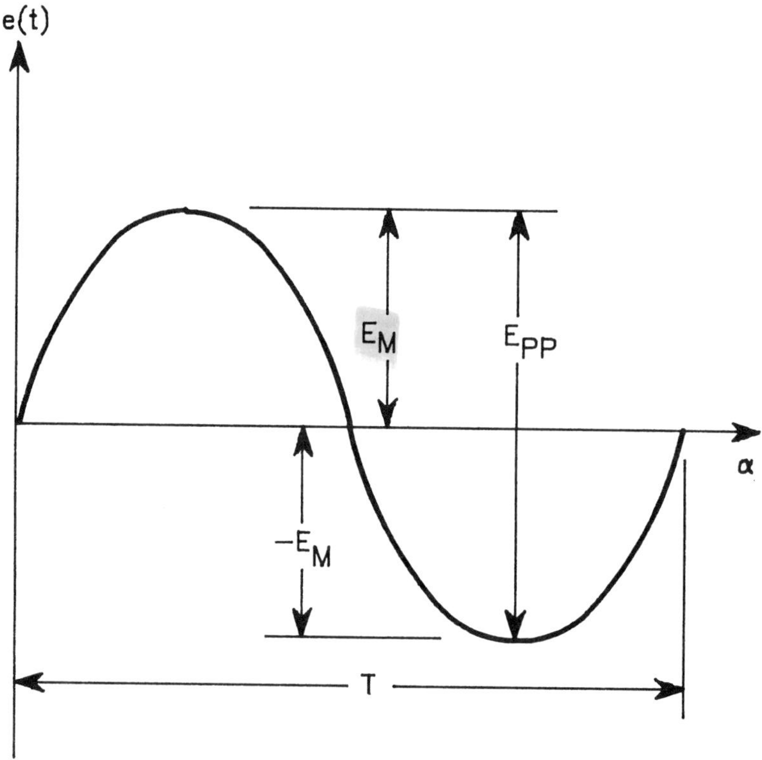

Figure 1-1 Sine wave definitions.

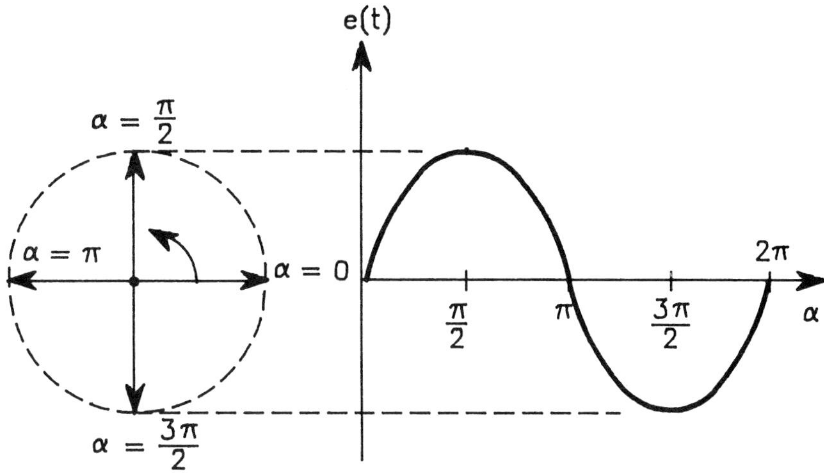

Figure 1-2 Phasor development.

Likewise, the sinusoidal waveform has an instantaneous value of zero when $\alpha = 0$. The vertical projection of the rotating vector will have its maximum positive value when $\alpha = \pi/2$ radians. Likewise, the sinusoidal waveform will have its maximum positive value at $\alpha = \pi/2$ radians. The same analogy would apply for any value of α between 0 and 2π radians for sinusoidal waveforms. (Note that this analogy between a rotating vector and a time-varying function is true only for sinusoidal waveforms).

One complete cycle of the sine wave is obtained after the vector has rotated 2π radians or 360°. The vector rotates at an angular velocity ω given by

$$\begin{aligned}\omega &= \frac{\text{distance in degrees or radians}}{\text{time in seconds}} \\ &= \frac{\alpha}{t}\end{aligned} \tag{1.2}$$

Solving Eq. (1.2) for α results in

$$\alpha = \omega t \tag{1.3}$$

The angular distance covered in one revolution is 2π radians. Also, the time required to complete one cycle of the waveform is equal to the period of the waveform, T. In addition, the period of the waveform is equal to the reciprocal of the frequency, $T = 1/f$. Therefore,

$$\begin{aligned}\omega &= \frac{2 \cdot \pi}{T} \\ &= \frac{2 \cdot \pi}{1/f} \\ &= 2\pi f\end{aligned} \tag{1.4}$$

Furthermore, since $\alpha = \omega t$,

$$\alpha = 2\pi f t \tag{1.5}$$

Using the results of Eqs. (1.3) and (1.5), the sine wave shown in Fig. 1-1 can be described mathematically as

$$\begin{aligned} e(t) &= E_M \sin(\omega t) \\ &= E_M \sin(2\pi f t) \end{aligned} \tag{1.6}$$

The sine wave shown in Fig. 1-1 had an instantaneous value of zero at time $t = 0$ seconds. In actual sinusoidal steady-state circuit analysis calculations, the sine waves will be displaced either by virtue of impedance voltage drops or by generator design. Figure 1-3 shows several examples of sine waves displaced from the vertical axis. Also shown are the corresponding phasor representations of each of the displaced sine waves.

In Fig. 1-3a, the sine wave is delayed by an angle θ from the vertical axis. The mathematical expression for this sine wave is

$$e(t) = E_M \sin(\omega t - \theta) \tag{1.7a}$$

Note that the minus sign on θ indicates that the waveform is delayed. The corresponding phasor representation of this delayed waveform will show the phasor rotated clockwise by an angle of θ from the real axis.

Figure 1-3b shows a sine wave that is advanced by an angle θ from the vertical axis. The expression for this waveform is

$$e(t) = E_M \sin(\omega t + \theta) \tag{1.7b}$$

In this case, the plus sign on θ indicates that the waveform is advanced in time. In the phasor diagram, the phasor is shown rotated counterclockwise by an angle θ to indicate the advance in phase angle.

A special case is shown in Fig. 1-3c, where the waveform is advanced by $\pi/2$ radians. The expression for this waveform is

$$\begin{aligned} e(t) &= E_M \sin\left(\omega t + \frac{\pi}{2}\right) \\ &= E_M \cos(\omega t) \end{aligned} \tag{1.7c}$$

Note that in this special case the waveform is actually a cosine wave rather than a sine wave. Thus, a cosine wave may be thought of as merely a sine wave advanced by $\pi/2$ radians, or 90°. A cautionary note is in order. When applying Eqs. (1.7), care must be taken to ensure that the same units are used for ωt and θ. Typically, ωt is expressed in radians. If θ is expressed in degrees, then you must convert θ to radians before evaluating these equations. Failure to do so will result in gross errors.

The phasor representation of the sinusoidal waveforms previously discussed used phasors that had a magnitude equal to the peak amplitude E_M of the sine wave. These phasors are often referred to as *magnitude phasors.* Since the voltage and current ratings of electrical power system apparatus are given in terms of *root mean square* (rms) quantities, it is common practice to use phasors that have a magnitude equal to the rms value

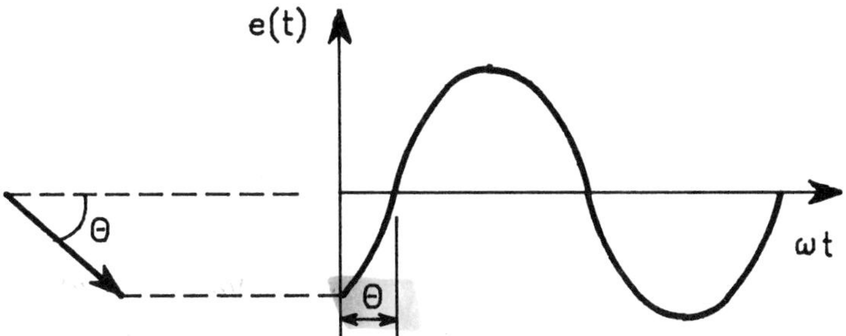

(a) Waveform Delayed by Angle Θ.

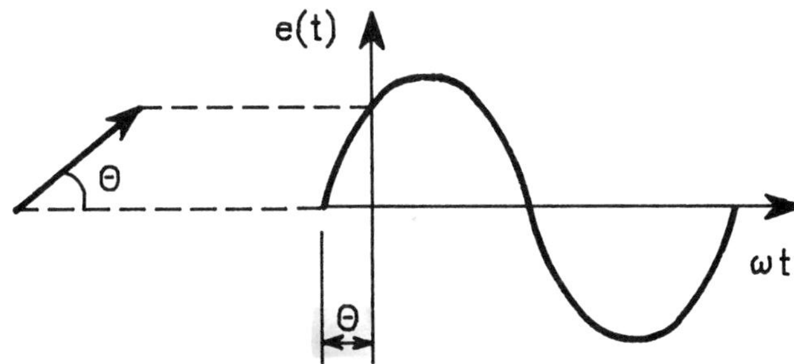

(b) Wavefrom Advanced by Angle Θ.

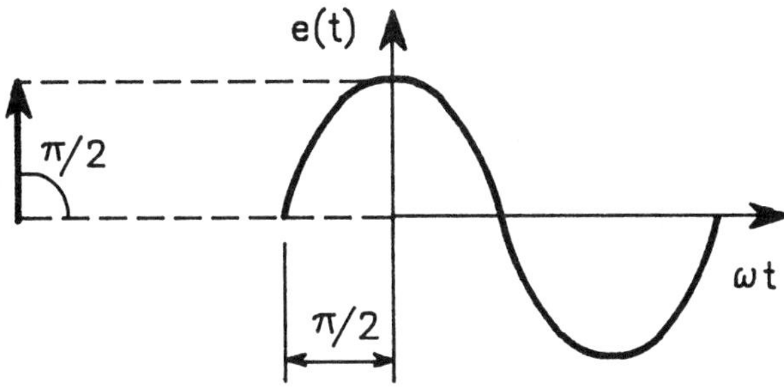

(c) Waveform Advanced by π/2 rad.

Figure 1-3 Phasor representation of phase-shifted sine waves.

of the waveform. For sinusoidal waveforms, the rms value is equal to the peak value divided by $\sqrt{2}$. Mathematically,

$I = \frac{I_m}{\sqrt{2}}$

$$E = \frac{E_M}{\sqrt{2}} \tag{1.8}$$

The hand held meter shows this

The phasors used throughout this text will have a magnitude equal to the rms value of the sinusoidal waveform that they represent.

The rest RMS. →

EXAMPLE 1-1

Determine the rms phasor representation of the following:

a. $e(t) = 391.7 \sin(377t - 30°)$ V
b. $i(t) = 230.5 \sin(377t + 85°)$ A
c. $v(t) = 169.7 \sin(377t - 23°)$ V

Solution

a. $\mathbf{E} = 277.0\angle{-30°}$ V
b. $\mathbf{I} = 163.0\angle 85°$ A
c. $\mathbf{V} = 120.0\angle{-23°}$ V

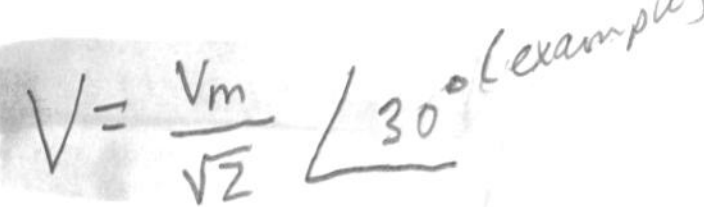

Representation of Phasors in the Complex Plane

In the previous discussion, it was determined that sinusoidal waveforms can be represented by a rotating vector or phasor. These phasors had both magnitude and phase angle associated with them. Thus a phasor can be represented in *polar* form as follows:

$$\mathbf{V} = V\angle\theta \tag{1.9}$$

where V is the magnitude of the phasor, and θ is the phase angle of the phasor with respect to the reference axis. The phasor can be represented in the complex plane as shown in Fig. 1-4. The horizontal and vertical axes are referred to as the *real* and *imaginary* axes respectively. The imaginary axis is also referred to as the j axis. In this context, the j operator is introduced, which serves to rotate a phasor by 90° counterclockwise in the complex plane. This is the same as advancing the phasor by 90°.

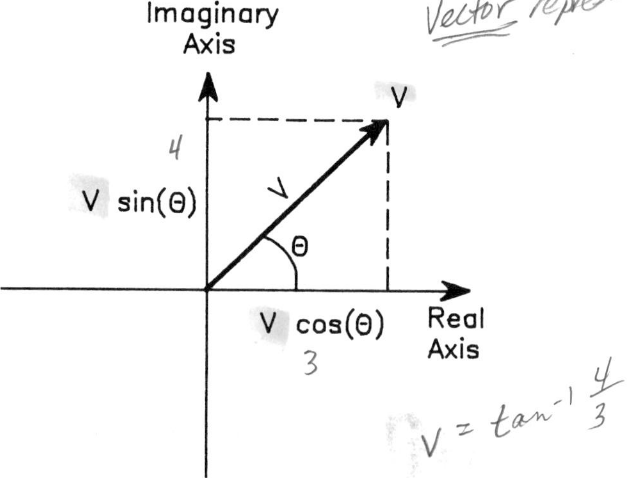

Figure 1-4 Phasor representation in the complex plane.

The phasor as given by Eq. (1.9) can also be expressed in rectangular form by resolving the phasor into real and imaginary components as follows:

$$\mathbf{V} = \text{Re}(\mathbf{V}) + j\,\text{Im}(\mathbf{V}) \tag{1.10}$$

where

$$\text{Re}(\mathbf{V}) = V\cos(\theta) \tag{1.11}$$

$$\text{Im}(\mathbf{V}) = V\sin(\theta) \tag{1.12}$$

The conversion of the phasor from polar to rectangular form is accomplished by direct application of Eqs. (1.11) and (1.12).

It is also possible to convert a phasor from rectangular to polar form. The magnitude of the phasor is determined by applying the following equation:

$$\text{Mag}(V) = [\text{Re}(\mathbf{V})^2 + \text{Im}(\mathbf{V})^2]^{1/2} \tag{1.13}$$

To determine the phase angle of the phasor, it is advisable to sketch the phasor in the complex plane and determine which quadrant the phasor is located in. The following equations can then be applied to determine the phase angle.

Quadrant	**Re(V)**	**Im(V)**	θ	
I	>0	>0	$\tan^{-1}[\text{Im}(\mathbf{V})/\text{Re}(\mathbf{V})]$	**(1.14a)**
II	<0	>0	$180° + \tan^{-1}[\text{Im}(\mathbf{V})/\text{Re}(\mathbf{V})]$	**(1.14b)**
III	<0	<0	$180° + \tan^{-1}[\text{Im}(\mathbf{V})/\text{Re}(\mathbf{V})]$	**(1.14c)**
IV	>0	<0	$360° + \tan^{-1}[\text{Im}(\mathbf{V})/\text{Re}(\mathbf{V})]$	**(1.14d)**

Complex Algebra

In many instances it is necessary to add, subtract, multiply, and divide complex numbers. For the purposes of this discussion, consider the following complex numbers:

$$\mathbf{X} = A + jB = X\angle\theta_x$$

$$\mathbf{Y} = C + jD = Y\angle\theta_y$$

The complex numbers **X** and **Y** are expressed in both rectangular and polar form.

If addition or subtraction of two complex numbers is desired, it is necessary to express the two complex numbers in rectangular form. The sum of the complex numbers **X** and **Y** is

$$\mathbf{X} + \mathbf{Y} = (A + C) + j(B + D) \tag{1.15}$$

The difference between two complex numbers is the difference between the respective real and imaginary parts:

$$\mathbf{X} - \mathbf{Y} = (A - C) + j(B - D) \tag{1.16}$$

If it is necessary to multiply or divide two complex numbers, it is desirable to use the polar form. The product of the complex numbers **X** and **Y** is

$$\mathbf{X} \cdot \mathbf{Y} = X \cdot Y\angle(\theta_x + \theta_y) \tag{1.17}$$

The quotient of **X** ÷ **Y** is

$$\frac{\mathbf{X}}{\mathbf{Y}} = \frac{X}{Y}\angle(\theta_x - \theta_y) \tag{1.18}$$

To obtain the complex conjugate of a complex number expressed in rectangular form, the sign of the imaginary part must be reversed. In polar form, the sign of the angle is reversed.

$$\mathbf{X}^* = A - jB = X\angle-\theta_x \tag{1.19}$$

$$\mathbf{Y}^* = C - jD = Y\angle-\theta_y \tag{1.20}$$

EXAMPLE 1-2

Given the two complex numbers $\mathbf{X} = 3 + j4$ and $\mathbf{Y} = 5 + j12$, determine the following in both polar and rectangular form:

a. $\mathbf{X} + \mathbf{Y}$
b. $\mathbf{X} - \mathbf{Y}$
c. $\mathbf{X} \cdot \mathbf{Y}$
d. $\mathbf{X} \div \mathbf{Y}$
e. $\mathbf{X} \cdot \mathbf{Y}^*$

Solution

a. $\mathbf{X} + \mathbf{Y} = (3 + j4) + (5 + j12) = 8 + j16 = 17.89\angle 63.4^\circ$
b. $\mathbf{X} - \mathbf{Y} = (3 + j4) - (5 + j12) = -2 - j8 = 8.25\angle 256^\circ$
c. $\mathbf{X} \cdot \mathbf{Y} = (3 + j4) \cdot (5 + j12) = (5\angle 53.13^\circ) \cdot (13\angle 67.38^\circ)$
$= 65\angle 120.5^\circ = -32.99 + j56.01$
d. $\mathbf{X} \div \mathbf{Y} = (3 + j4) \div (5 + j12)$
$= (5\angle 53.13^\circ) \div (13\angle 67.38^\circ)$
$= 0.385\angle -14.3^\circ = 0.3731 - j0.0951$
e. $\mathbf{X} \cdot \mathbf{Y}^* = (3 + j4) \cdot (5 + j12)^*$
$= (5\angle 53.13^\circ) \cdot (13\angle -67.38^\circ)$
$= 65\angle -14.3^\circ = 62.99 - j16.05$

1-3 Complex Impedances

The concept of a complex impedance is used extensively in sinusoidal steady-state circuit analysis. Basically, the concept of a complex impedance is derived by investigating the effect that various circuit elements have on voltage and current waveform phase shifting. The three passive circuit elements to be discussed are the resistor, inductor, and capacitor.

Resistor

Consider the resistive circuit element shown in Fig. 1-5a. Let the voltage applied to the resistor be defined as

$$v(t) = V_M \sin(\omega t)$$

From Ohm's law the current through the resistor is given by

$$\begin{aligned} i(t) &= \frac{v(t)}{R} \\ &= \frac{V_M \sin(\omega t)}{R} \\ &= \frac{V_M}{R} \sin(\omega t) \\ &= I_M \sin(\omega t) \end{aligned} \tag{1.21}$$

where

$$I_M = \frac{V_M}{R} \tag{1.22}$$

Equation (1.22) is solved for V_M, resulting in the following:

$$V_M = I_M R \tag{1.23}$$

Note that the magnitude of the voltage across the resistor is equal to the magnitude of the current through the resistor multiplied by R. Also, note that there is no phase shift between the voltage and current in a resistive element. That is, the voltage and current through the resistor are in phase with each other. The phasor diagram in Fig. 1-5a shows

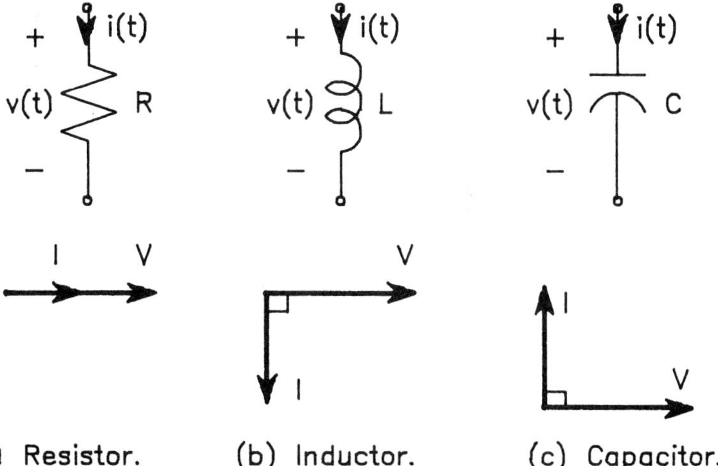

Figure 1-5 Circuit elements.

the phase relation between the voltage and current in the resistor. The complex impedance of a resistor is equal to

$$\begin{aligned}\mathbf{Z}_R &= R + j0 \\ &= R\angle 0°\ \Omega\end{aligned} \qquad \textbf{(1.24)}$$

Examination of Eq. (1.24) indicates that the resistive element produces no phase shift between the voltage across and the current through the element.

Inductor

The circuit symbol for the inductor is shown in Fig. 1-5b. As in the case of the resistor, the voltage across the inductor is given by

$$v(t) = V_M \sin(\omega t)$$

From Ohm's law, the current through the inductor is

$$\begin{aligned}i(t) &= \frac{1}{L}\int v(t)\,dt \\ &= \frac{1}{L}\int V_M \sin(\omega t)\,dt \\ &= -\frac{1}{\omega L} V_M \cos(\omega t) \\ &= \frac{V_M}{\omega L}\sin\left(\omega t - \frac{\pi}{2}\right) \\ &= I_M \sin\left(\omega t - \frac{\pi}{2}\right)\end{aligned} \qquad \textbf{(1.25)}$$

where

$$I_M = \frac{V_M}{\omega L} \qquad \textbf{(1.26)}$$

Solving Eq. (1.26) for V_M results in the following:

$$V_M = I_M \omega L \qquad \textbf{(1.27)}$$

Inspection of Eq. (1.25) indicates that there is a phase shift between the current and voltage in an inductor. In particular, the current lags the voltage by $\pi/2$ radians or 90°. Note also from Eq. (1.27) that the magnitude of the voltage across the inductor is equal to the magnitude of the current through the inductor multiplied by the term ωL. The term ωL is referred to as the *inductive reactance* of the element and is often designated X_L. The inductive reactance is a function of frequency, whereas the inductance is not. Note that the current phasor is shown lagging the applied voltage phasor by 90° in the phasor diagram of Fig. 1-5b.

The complex impedance of an inductor is

$$\begin{aligned} \mathbf{Z}_L &= 0 + j\omega L \\ &= jX_L \qquad\qquad \textbf{(1.28)} \\ &= X_L\angle 90^\circ\ \Omega \end{aligned}$$

Note that the complex impedance of the inductor has a magnitude that is a function of frequency and a phase angle of 90°. Multiplying the complex current through the inductor by the complex impedance of the inductive element will produce a voltage that is shifted ahead of the current by 90°. Therefore, the complex current lags the voltage in an inductor by 90°.

Capacitor

The circuit symbol for the capacitor is shown in Fig. 1-5c. As in the previous cases, let the voltage across the capacitor be given by

$$v(t) = V_M \sin(\omega t)$$

From Ohm's law, the current through the capacitor is

$$\begin{aligned} i(t) &= C\frac{dv(t)}{dt} \\ &= C\frac{d}{dt}V_M \sin(\omega t) \\ &= \omega C V_M \cos(\omega t) \qquad\qquad \textbf{(1.29)} \\ &= \omega C V_M \sin\left(\omega t + \frac{\pi}{2}\right) \\ &= I_M \sin\left(\omega t + \frac{\pi}{2}\right) \end{aligned}$$

where

$$I_M = \omega C V_M \qquad\qquad \textbf{(1.30)}$$

Solving Eq. (1.30) for V_M results in the following:

$$V_M = \frac{1}{\omega C} I_M \qquad\qquad \textbf{(1.31)}$$

frequency dependent

Inspection of Eq. (1.29) indicates that there is a phase shift between the current and voltage in a capacitor. In particular, the current leads the voltage by $\pi/2$ radians, or 90°. Equation (1.31) shows that the magnitude of the voltage across the capacitor is equal to the magnitude of the current through the capacitor multiplied by $1/\omega C$. The quantity $1/\omega C$ is referred to as the *capacitive reactance* of the capacitor and is designated X_C.

Similarly to the inductive reactance, the capacitive reactance is a function of frequency. The phasor diagram shows the current leading the applied voltage by 90°.

The complex impedance of a capacitor is given by

$$\begin{aligned}\mathbf{Z}_C &= 0 - j\frac{1}{\omega C} \\ &= -jX_C \\ &= X_C\angle -90^\circ\ \Omega\end{aligned} \qquad \textbf{(1.32)}$$

The representation of the complex impedance as given by Eq. (1.32) takes into account both the change in magnitude and the 90° phase shift produced by the capacitive element. If the complex current through the capacitor is multiplied by the capacitive reactance, the resultant voltage will be delayed by 90° with respect to the current. Thus, the complex current through the capacitor will lead the voltage across the capacitor by 90°.

EXAMPLE 1-3

Determine the complex impedances for the following:

a. A 100-μF (microfarad) capacitor at 60 Hz (hertz)
b. A 100-μF capacitor at 300 Hz
c. A 535-μH (microhenry) inductor at 60 Hz
d. A 535-μH inductor at 420 Hz

Solution

a. $X_C = \dfrac{1}{2 \cdot \pi \cdot 60 \cdot 100 \times 10^{-6}} = 26.525\ \Omega$

$\mathbf{Z}_C = -j26.525\ \Omega$

b. $X_C = \dfrac{1}{2 \cdot \pi \cdot 300 \cdot 100 \times 10^{-6}} = 5.305\ \Omega$

$\mathbf{Z}_C = -j5.305\ \Omega$

c. $X_L = 2 \cdot \pi \cdot 60 \cdot 535 \times 10^{-6} = 0.2017\ \Omega$

$\mathbf{Z}_L = j0.2017\ \Omega$

d. $X_L = 2 \cdot \pi \cdot 420 \cdot 535 \times 10^{-6} = 1.4118\ \Omega$

$\mathbf{Z}_L = j1.4118\ \Omega$

1-4 Steady-State Circuit Analysis

This section will discuss the application of the concept of phasor representation to steady-state circuit analysis. Transformation of a circuit from the time domain to the phasor domain, series and parallel combinations of impedances, application of Ohm's law, voltage- and current-divider rules, and Kirchhoff's current and voltage laws will be reviewed. The application of these basic steady-state circuit analysis concepts is extremely important in many power system applications. Advanced topics such as voltage drop, short-circuit calculations, transformer loading calculations, and capacitor applications are all based on these fundamental principles.

Circuit Transformation from Time Domain to Phasor Domain

The first step in sinusoidal steady-state ac circuit analysis is to transform the circuit from the time domain to the phasor domain. This transformation involves converting all voltage and current sources to rms phasors. In addition, all passive circuit elements such as resistors, inductors, and capacitors must be converted to complex impedances. Since the inductive and capacitive reactances are a function of frequency, it is necessary to ensure that all sources are operating at the same frequency. If sources of different frequency are present, then the circuit must be analyzed at each frequency and the results combined. This situation occurs frequently when analyzing a circuit in the presence of harmonic current injecting equipment such as solid-state, variable-speed motor drives. The subject of harmonics will be taken up in greater detail in Chapter 13. For the purposes of this section, all sources are assumed to operate at the same frequency.

EXAMPLE 1-4 For the circuit shown in Fig. 1-6a, convert all sources and impedances to the phasor domain.

Solution The voltage source operates at a frequency of 377 radians per second, or 60 Hz. The rms value of the voltage source is

$$170 \div \sqrt{2} = 120.2 \text{ V}$$

The phase angle of the voltage source is $-30°$. Therefore, the source voltage can be represented by

$$\mathbf{V}_S = 120.2\angle -30° \text{ V}$$

The complex impedances of the inductors and capacitor are calculated by applying Eqs. (1.28) and (1.32):

$$\begin{aligned}\mathbf{Z}_{LT} &= j(377)(30.6 \times 10^{-6}) \\ &= j11.536 \times 10^{-3}\ \Omega \\ \mathbf{Z}_{LL} &= j(377)(5 \times 10^{-3}) \\ &= j1.885\ \Omega\end{aligned}$$

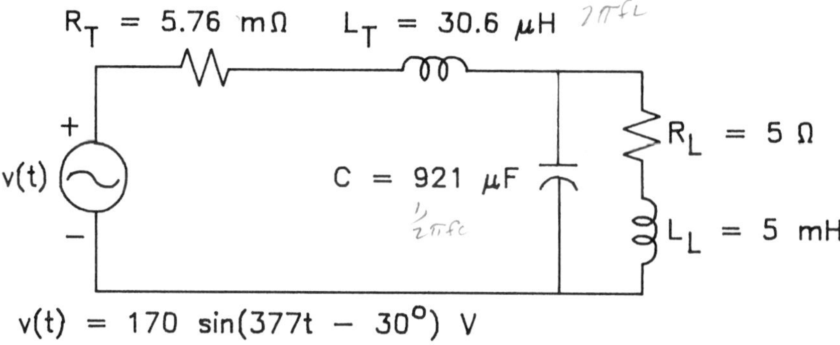

(a) Circuit in Time Domain.

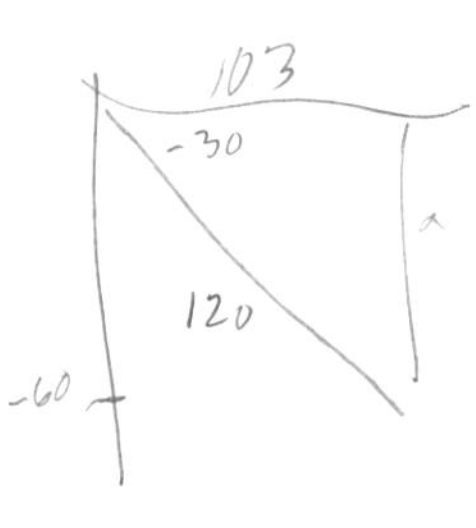

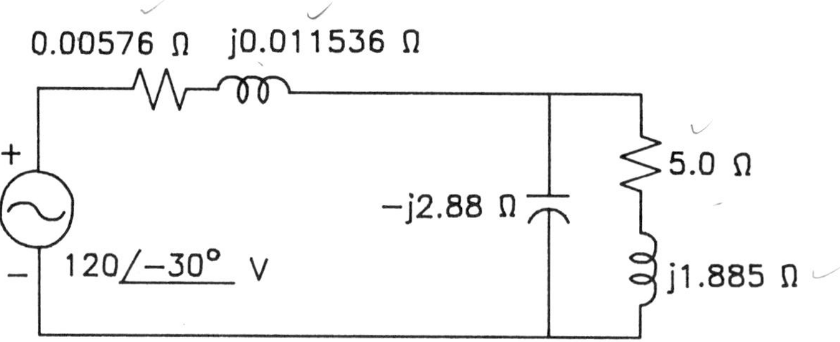

(b) Circuit Transformed to Phasor Domain.

Figure 1-6 Circuit for Example 1-4.

$$\mathbf{Z}_C = -j\frac{1}{(377)(921 \times 10^{-6})}$$
$$= -j2.88\ \Omega$$

The circuit is redrawn in Fig. 1-6b showing all sources and impedances converted to the phasor domain.

Series and Parallel Combinations of Complex Impedances

The rules for combining series and parallel resistors in a dc circuit are applicable to ac circuits containing complex impedances. That is, series complex impedances add, and parallel complex admittances add. Recall that the complex admittance is the reciprocal of a complex impedance. When combining series or parallel complex impedances, it is extremely important that the calculations be carried out with regard to both real and imaginary components, as well as magnitude and phase angle.

EXAMPLE 1-5

Calculate the resultant complex impedance for the following series and parallel combinations:

a. A 10.0-Ω resistor in series with a 5.0-Ω inductive reactance
b. A 5.0-Ω resistor in series with a 5.0-Ω capacitive reactance
c. A 3.0-Ω resistor, 5.0-Ω inductive reactance, and 2.0-Ω capacitive reactance all in series
d. A 20.0-Ω resistor and 5.0-Ω inductive reactance in parallel
e. A 5.0-Ω resistor and 5.0-Ω capacitive reactance in parallel
f. A 3.0-Ω resistor, 5.0-Ω inductive reactance, and 2.0-Ω capacitive reactance all in parallel

Solution

a. $\mathbf{Z} = 10.0 + j5.0\ \Omega = 11.18\angle 26.6^\circ\ \Omega$

b. $\mathbf{Z} = 5.0 - j5.0\ \Omega = 7.071\angle -45^\circ\ \Omega$

c. $\mathbf{Z} = 3.0 + j5.0 - j2.0$

$= 3.0 + j3.0$

$= 4.243\angle 45^\circ\ \Omega$

d. $$\mathbf{Z} = \frac{(20.0\angle 0^\circ)(5.0\angle 90^\circ)}{20.0 + j5.0}$$

$$= \frac{100.0\angle 90^\circ}{20.616\angle 14^\circ}$$

$$= 4.851\angle 76^\circ\ \Omega$$

e. $$\mathbf{Z} = \frac{(5.0\angle 0^\circ)(5.0\angle -90^\circ)}{5.0 - j5.0}$$

$$= \frac{25.0\angle -90^\circ}{7.071\angle -45^\circ}$$

$$= 3.536\angle -45^\circ\ \Omega$$

f. For three or more parallel complex impedances, it is desirable to convert each impedance to a complex admittance and then add the complex admittances to determine the equivalent admittance. The equivalent impedance is equal to the reciprocal of the equivalent admittance.

$$\mathbf{Y}_R = \frac{1}{\mathbf{Z}_R} = \frac{1}{3.0\angle 0^\circ} = 0.3333\angle 0^\circ = 0.3333 + j0.0000\ \text{S}$$

$$\mathbf{Y}_L = \frac{1}{\mathbf{Z}_L} = \frac{1}{5.0\angle 90^\circ} = 0.2\angle -90^\circ = 0.0000 - j0.2000\ \text{S}$$

$$\mathbf{Y}_C = \frac{1}{\mathbf{Z}_C} = \frac{1}{2.0\angle -90^\circ} = 0.5\angle 90^\circ = 0.0000 + j0.5000\ \text{S}$$

The equivalent admittance is

$$\mathbf{Y}_{EQ} = \mathbf{Y}_R + \mathbf{Y}_L + \mathbf{Y}_C = 0.3333 + j0.3000$$
$$= 0.4484\angle 42^\circ \text{ S}$$

The equivalent impedance is

$$\mathbf{Z}_{EQ} = \frac{1}{\mathbf{Y}_{EQ}} = \frac{1}{0.4484\angle 42^\circ} = 2.2302\angle -42^\circ\ \Omega$$

Application of Ohm's Law to Complex Impedance Elements

Ohm's law states that the voltage across an impedance is equal to the current through the impedance multiplied by the ohmic value of the impedance:

$$\mathbf{V} = \mathbf{I} \cdot \mathbf{Z} \tag{1.33}$$

In ac circuits, all calculations must be carried through using complex algebra.

EXAMPLE 1-6

Calculate the following:

a. The voltage across an impedance of $3 + j4\ \Omega$ if the current is

$$\mathbf{I} = 10.0\angle -36.87^\circ \text{ A}$$

b. The current through an impedance of $5 + j3\ \Omega$ if the applied voltage is

$$\mathbf{V} = 277\angle 120^\circ \text{ V}$$

Solution

a. $\mathbf{V} = \mathbf{I} \cdot \mathbf{Z}$

$$= (10.0\angle -36.87^\circ)(3 + j4) = 50.0\angle 16.26^\circ \text{ V}$$

b. Solving Eq. (1.33) for **I**,

$$\mathbf{I} = \frac{\mathbf{V}}{\mathbf{Z}}$$
$$= \frac{277\angle 120^\circ}{5 + j3}$$
$$= 47.5\angle 89^\circ \text{ A}$$

Current Divider

In many instances it is necessary to calculate the current in one element of a group of elements connected in parallel. The current-divider rule states that the current in one element of a parallel group of elements is equal to the total current flowing into the group, multiplied by the admittance of the element, and divided by the equivalent parallel admittance of the elements. Mathematically,

$$\mathbf{I}_i = \mathbf{I}_T \frac{\mathbf{Y}_i}{\mathbf{Y}_{EQ}} \tag{1.34}$$

where

$\mathbf{I}_i$ = current in the ith element

$\mathbf{I}_T$ = total current flowing into the parallel group

$\mathbf{Y}_i$ = admittance of the ith element

$\mathbf{Y}_{EQ}$ = equivalent admittance of the parallel group

---

EXAMPLE 1-7

The following elements are connected in parallel:

$$\mathbf{Z}_1 = 2 + j3\ \Omega, \qquad \mathbf{Z}_2 = 4 + j6\ \Omega, \qquad \mathbf{Z}_3 = 2 - j5\ \Omega$$

The total current flowing into the parallel group is 120∠25° A. Calculate the current in each element using the current-divider rule.

Solution First, it is necessary to calculate the equivalent admittance and equivalent impedance of the parallel group.

$$\mathbf{Y}_1 = \frac{1}{\mathbf{Z}_1} = \frac{1}{2 + j3} = 0.2774\angle -56.3^\circ = 0.1539 - j0.2308\ \text{S}$$

$$\mathbf{Y}_2 = \frac{1}{\mathbf{Z}_2} = \frac{1}{4 + j6} = 0.1387\angle -56.3^\circ = 0.0770 - j0.1154\ \text{S}$$

$$\mathbf{Y}_3 = \frac{1}{\mathbf{Z}_3} = \frac{1}{2 - j5} = 0.1857\angle 68.2^\circ = 0.0690 + j0.1724\ \text{S}$$

$$\begin{aligned}\mathbf{Y}_{EQ} &= \mathbf{Y}_1 + \mathbf{Y}_2 + \mathbf{Y}_3 = 0.2999 - j0.1738 \\ &= 0.3466\angle -30.1^\circ\ \text{S}\end{aligned}$$

Next, the current-divider rule is applied to determine the current in each element.

$$\mathbf{I}_1 = 120\angle 25^\circ \frac{0.2774\angle -56.3^\circ}{0.3466\angle -30.1^\circ} = 96.0\angle -1.2^\circ\ \text{A}$$

$$\mathbf{I}_2 = 120\angle 25^\circ \frac{0.1387\angle -56.3^\circ}{0.3466\angle -30.1^\circ} = 48.0\angle -1.2^\circ\ \text{A}$$

$$\mathbf{I}_3 = 120\angle 25^\circ \frac{0.1857\angle 68.2^\circ}{0.3466\angle -30.1^\circ} = 64.3\angle 123.3^\circ\ \text{A}$$

It is desirable to check the results of these calculations. The sum of the three currents should equal the total current flowing into the parallel group:

$$\mathbf{I}_1 + \mathbf{I}_2 + \mathbf{I}_3 = 96.0\angle -1.2^\circ + 48.0\angle -1.2^\circ + 64.3\angle 123.3^\circ$$
$$= 120\angle 25^\circ \text{ A}$$

Voltage Divider

The voltage-divider rule states that the voltage across an individual element in a series connection of several elements can be determined by multiplying the voltage applied to the total series group by the impedance of the element and then dividing by the sum of the series-connected impedances. Mathematically,

$$\mathbf{V}_i = \mathbf{V}_{\text{IN}} \frac{\mathbf{Z}_i}{\mathbf{Z}_1 + \mathbf{Z}_2 + \cdots + \mathbf{Z}_N} \tag{1.35}$$

where

$\mathbf{V}_i$ = voltage across i^{th} element in the group

$\mathbf{V}_{IN}$ = voltage applied to series group

$\mathbf{Z}_i$ = complex impedance of ith element in the group

---

EXAMPLE 1-8 The following elements are connected in series

$$\mathbf{Z}_1 = 7 + j10\ \Omega, \qquad \mathbf{Z}_2 = 4 - j15\ \Omega$$

The voltage applied to the series group is

$$\mathbf{V} = 120\angle 0^\circ \text{ V}$$

Using the voltage-divider rule, calculate the voltage across each element.

Solution Direct application of Eq. (1.35) results in the following:

$$\mathbf{V}_1 = 120\angle 0^\circ \cdot \frac{7 + j10}{(7 + j10) + (4 - j5)}$$
$$= 121.2\angle 30.6^\circ \text{ V}$$

$$\mathbf{V}_2 = 120\angle 0^\circ \cdot \frac{4 - j5}{(7 + j10) + (4 - j5)}$$
$$= 63.6\angle -75.7^\circ \text{ V}$$

As a check, the sum of the voltages across the series-connected elements must equal the applied voltage.

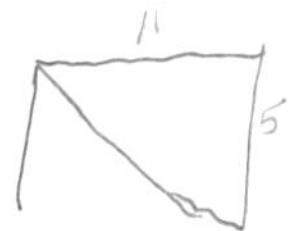

$$\mathbf{V}_1 + \mathbf{V}_2 = 121.2\angle 30.6° + 63.6\angle -75.7°$$
$$= 120\angle 0° \text{ V}$$

Kirchhoff's Current Law

Kirchhoff's current law (KCL) states that the sum of all currents entering a node must equal the sum of all currents leaving a node. Since complex quantities are involved in the calculations, both the real and imaginary parts must add up to zero. Kirchhoff's current law can be stated mathematically as

$$\sum \mathbf{I}_{in} = \sum \mathbf{I}_{out} \qquad (1.36)$$

EXAMPLE 1-9

A certain node or *bus* in a power system has three lines terminating on it. The line currents in two of the lines are

$$\mathbf{I}_1 = 127\angle -10° \text{ A}, \qquad \mathbf{I}_2 = 150\angle 90° \text{ A}$$

Calculate the current in the third line. Assume that positive current flow is into the bus.

Solution From Kirchhoff's current law,

$$\mathbf{I}_1 + \mathbf{I}_2 + \mathbf{I}_3 = 0$$

Solving for $\mathbf{I}_3$,

$$\mathbf{I}_3 = -(\mathbf{I}_1 + \mathbf{I}_2)$$
$$= -(127\angle -10° + 150\angle 90°)$$
$$= -(125.1 - j22.1 + j150)$$
$$= -(125.1 + j127.9)$$
$$= 178.9\angle -134.4° \text{ A}$$

If the positive direction of current flow for $\mathbf{I}_3$ were assumed to be away from the bus, then $\mathbf{I}_3$ would be given by

$$\mathbf{I}_3 = +(\mathbf{I}_1 + \mathbf{I}_2)$$
$$= 178.9\angle 45.6° \text{ A}$$

Notice that the magnitude of $\mathbf{I}_3$ has not changed, but that the phase angle has been rotated by 180°. It is extremely important to designate the assumed positive direction of current flow when applying Kirchhoff's current law.

Kirchhoff's Voltage Law

Kirchhoff's voltage law (KVL) states that the summation of all voltage rises around a closed loop is equal to the summation of all voltage drops around the same loop. Mathematically,

$$\sum \text{voltage rises} = \sum \text{voltage drops} \tag{1.37}$$

EXAMPLE 1-10 Consider the circuit shown in Fig 1-7. Calculate the voltage across the load terminals by applying KVL.

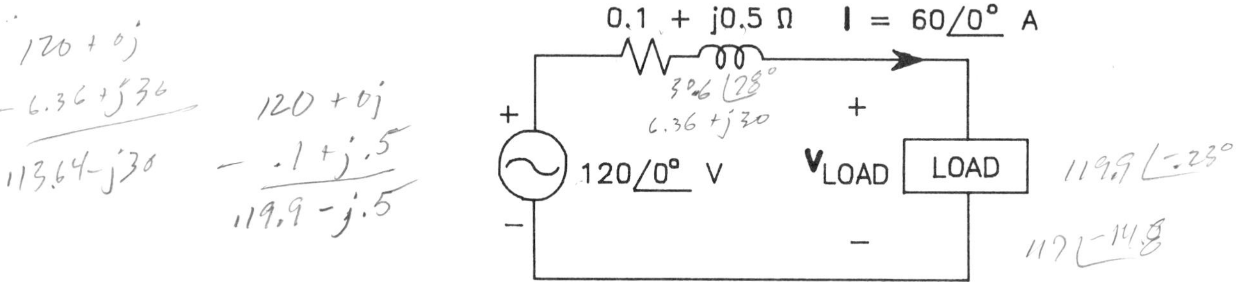

Figure 1-7 Circuit for Example 1-10.

Solution Note that the positive current flow is assumed to be out of the source and into the load. This is the common convention for sources and loads using conventional current flow. Summing the voltages around the loop,

$$120\angle 0^\circ = (60\angle 0^\circ)(0.1 + j0.5) + \mathbf{V}_{\text{LOAD}}$$

Solving for $\mathbf{V}_{\text{LOAD}}$,

$$\begin{aligned}\mathbf{V}_{\text{LOAD}} &= 120\angle 0^\circ - (60\angle 0^\circ)(0.1 + j0.5)\\ &= 120\angle 0^\circ - 30.6\angle 78.7\\ &= 114.1 - j30.0\\ &= 117.9\angle -14.7^\circ \text{ V}\end{aligned}$$

Source Conversions

A voltage source in series with a complex impedance may be converted to a current source in parallel with the same impedance by application of Ohm's law. The value of the current source is equal to

$$\mathbf{I} = \frac{\mathbf{V}}{\mathbf{Z}} \tag{1.38}$$

Likewise, a current source in parallel with an impedance can be converted to a voltage source in series with the same impedance. The voltage source is determined by direct application of Eq. (1.33).

1-5 Nodal Analysis

Nodal analysis involves the calculation of node voltages at each node or bus in a network. The solution is determined by simultaneously applying Ohm's law and Kirchhoff's current law to each node in the network. A set of simultaneous equations results. The number of equations will equal the number of nodes in the network.

The first step in nodal analysis is to label all nodes in terms of their node voltage: $\mathbf{V}_1$, $\mathbf{V}_2$, $\mathbf{V}_3$, and so on. Next, Ohm's law is applied to each node, with all currents assumed to be leaving the node. The ground or reference node need not be considered in the equations since the voltage at this node is zero. When equations have been written for each node, a system of simultaneous equations will result. The simultaneous equations are then solved for the unknown voltages.

EXAMPLE 1-11 Apply nodal analysis to the system shown in Fig. 1-8 to determine the voltages $\mathbf{V}_1$ and $\mathbf{V}_2$.

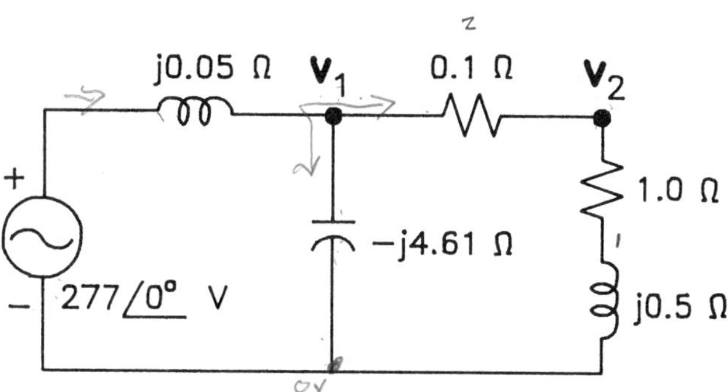

Figure 1-8 Circuit for Example 1-11.

Solution The nodal equations for the system are

$$\text{Node 1:} \quad \frac{\mathbf{V}_1 - 277\angle 0^\circ}{j0.05} + \frac{\mathbf{V}_1}{-j4.61} + \frac{\mathbf{V}_1 - \mathbf{V}_2}{0.1} = 0.0$$

$$\text{Node 2:} \quad \frac{\mathbf{V}_2 - \mathbf{V}_1}{0.1} + \frac{\mathbf{V}_2}{1.0 + j0.5} = 0.0$$

Simplifying the system of equations results in

$$\text{Node 1:} \quad -j20.0(\mathbf{V}_1 - 277\angle 0^\circ) + j0.2169\mathbf{V}_1 + 10.0(\mathbf{V}_1 - \mathbf{V}_2) = 0.0$$

$$\text{Node 2:} \quad 10.0(\mathbf{V}_2 - \mathbf{V}_1) + \mathbf{V}_2(0.8944\angle -26.6^\circ) = 0.0$$

Arranging the equations in matrix format,

$$\begin{bmatrix} 10.0 - j19.7831 & -10.0 \\ -10.0 & 10.8 - j0.4 \end{bmatrix} \begin{bmatrix} \mathbf{V}_1 \\ \mathbf{V}_2 \end{bmatrix} = \begin{bmatrix} -j5540 \\ 0.0 \end{bmatrix}$$

The system is solved using Cramer's rule.

$$\Delta = 217.66\angle -90^\circ, \qquad \Delta_1 = 59{,}873.0\angle 267.0^\circ, \qquad \Delta_2 = 55{,}400.0\angle -90^\circ$$

The node voltages are

$$\mathbf{V}_1 = \frac{\Delta_1}{\Delta} = 275.1\angle -2.1^\circ \text{ V}, \qquad \mathbf{V}_2 = \frac{\Delta_2}{\Delta} = 254.5\angle 0.0^\circ \text{ V}$$

1-6 Mesh Analysis

Mesh analysis is an application of Kirchhoff's voltage law applied to each closed loop or mesh in a circuit. The equations are written for each mesh in the loop, resulting in a system of equations to be solved. When writing the mesh equations, the voltage rises are treated as negative values, while the voltage drops are treated as positive values. As in nodal analysis, it is extremely important to assign a convention for voltage drops and voltage rises and to use this convention throughout the analysis.

When applying mesh analysis to a circuit, it is desirable to have all sources represented as voltage sources. Also, it is desirable to designate all mesh currents as flowing in a clockwise direction around each mesh. The voltage across each impedance element is treated as a drop when writing the equation for that particular mesh. Voltage sources are considered as a rise if the assigned mesh current leaves the positive terminal of the source. Likewise, if the assigned mesh current leaves the negative terminal of the voltage source, the source is to be treated as a drop.

EXAMPLE 1-12

For the circuit shown in Fig. 1-9, calculate the following:

a. Mesh currents $\mathbf{I}_1$ and $\mathbf{I}_2$
b. The current $\mathbf{I}$ through load 1
c. Voltages across load 1 and load 2 by applying Ohm's law

Solution

a. The mesh equations for this circuit are

$$\text{Mesh 1:} \quad -120\angle 0^\circ + \mathbf{I}_1(j0.1) + (\mathbf{I}_1 - \mathbf{I}_2)(4 + j3) = 0$$
$$\text{Mesh 2:} \quad (\mathbf{I}_2 - \mathbf{I}_1)(4 + j3) + \mathbf{I}_2(j0.05 + 2 + j1.0) = 0$$

Gathering terms and simplifying,

$$\mathbf{I}_1(4 + j3.1) + \mathbf{I}_2(-4 - j3) = 120\angle 0^\circ$$
$$\mathbf{I}_1(-4 - j3) + \mathbf{I}_2(6 + j4.05) = 0$$

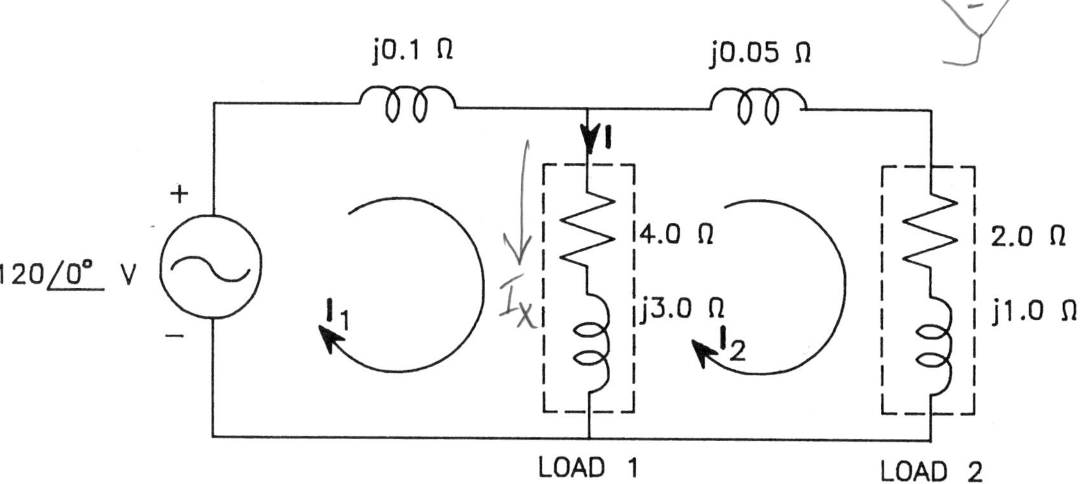

Figure 1-9 Circuit for Example 1-12.

Expressing the mesh equations in matrix form,

$$\begin{bmatrix} 4 + j3.1 & -4 - j3 \\ -4 - j3 & 6 + j4.05 \end{bmatrix} \begin{bmatrix} \mathbf{I}_1 \\ \mathbf{I}_2 \end{bmatrix} = \begin{bmatrix} 120\angle 0^\circ \\ 0.0 \end{bmatrix}$$

The system of equations is solved using Cramers rule. The following results:

$$\begin{aligned} \Delta &= (4 + j3.1)(6 + j4.05) - (-4 - j3)(-4 - j3) \\ &= 11.68\angle 67.6^\circ \\ \Delta_1 &= (120\angle 0^\circ)(6 + j4.05) = 868.7\angle 34^\circ \\ \Delta_2 &= -(-4 - j3)(120\angle 0^\circ) \\ &= 600.0\angle 36.87^\circ \end{aligned}$$

The mesh currents are

$$\mathbf{I}_1 = \frac{\Delta_1}{\Delta} = 74.4\angle -33.6^\circ \text{ A}$$

$$\mathbf{I}_2 = \frac{\Delta_2}{\Delta} = 51.4\angle -30.7^\circ \text{ A}$$

b. The current **I** is equal to

$$\begin{aligned} \mathbf{I} &= \mathbf{I}_1 - \mathbf{I}_2 \\ &= 74.4\angle -33.6^\circ - 51.4\angle -30.7^\circ \\ &= 23.5\angle -40^\circ \text{ A} \end{aligned}$$

c. The voltage across each load is determined by direct application of Ohm's law.

$$\mathbf{V}_{\text{load 1}} = \mathbf{I}(4 + j3) = (23.5\angle -40^\circ)(4 + j3) = 117.5\angle -3.13^\circ \text{ V}$$
$$\mathbf{V}_{\text{load 2}} = \mathbf{I}_2(2 + j1) = (51.4\angle -30.7)(2 + j1) = 115.1\angle -5.13^\circ \text{ V}$$

1-7 Thevenin's Theorem

An understanding of Thevenin's theorem is extremely important when performing short-circuit calculations in electrical power systems. It is a common practice to represent a large power network by a voltage source in series with the equivalent system impedance. The voltage source in this equivalent system representation is the Thevenin voltage, and the equivalent system impedance is the Thevenin impedance ''looking into'' the system from a certain point.

To determine the Thevenin equivalent voltage at a particular bus, it is necessary to analyze the circuit with no load connected to the bus. The open-circuit voltage that appears at the bus is equal to the Thevenin equivalent voltage. In electrical power systems, it is common practice to equate the Thevenin equivalent voltage to the nominal system voltage at the point of interest.

The Thevenin equivalent impedance, or equivalent system impedance, is determined by setting all sources in the system equal to zero. This means replacing all voltage sources with a short and all current sources with an open. The rules of series and parallel combinations can then be applied to determine the Thevenin equivalent impedance.

EXAMPLE 1-13

For the circuit shown in Fig. 1-10, determine the Thevenin equivalent representation looking into the network from the load bus. Note that the two voltage sources are essentially connected in parallel to the load bus.

Solution The Thevenin equivalent impedance is calculated by replacing the two voltage sources with a short circuit. The impedance looking into the system from the load bus is

$$\begin{aligned}\mathbf{Z}_{\text{sys}} &= (0.5 + j4) \parallel (0.7 + j5) + (1.0 + j1.5) \\ &= 3.93\angle 71.6^\circ\ \Omega\end{aligned}$$

The Thevenin equivalent voltage at the load bus is determined by assuming an open circuit at the load bus and calculating the resultant voltage. The circuit for no-load or open-circuit conditions is redrawn in Fig. 1-10b. Note that since the load current is zero under no load conditions the voltage drop across the $(1 + j1.5)\ \Omega$ impedance is equal to zero. Thus, the load voltage is equal to the voltage at the bus where the two voltage sources are paralleled. This voltage is designated $\mathbf{V}_{\text{bus}}$ in Fig. 1-10b. The circulating current in the circuit is

$$\begin{aligned}\mathbf{I}_{\text{circ}} &= \frac{14{,}400\angle 0^\circ - 14{,}400\angle -15^\circ}{0.5 + j4 + 0.7 + j5} \\ &= \frac{490.7 + j3727}{1.2 + j9} \\ &= 414\angle 0.1^\circ\ \text{A}\end{aligned}$$

The voltage across the open-circuit load terminals is

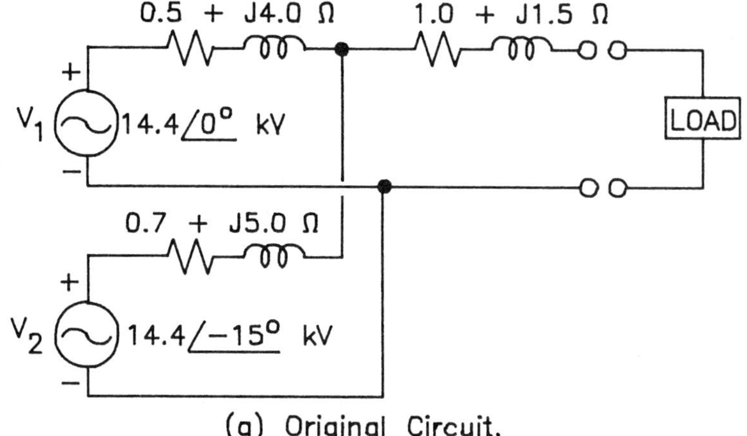

(a) Original Circuit.

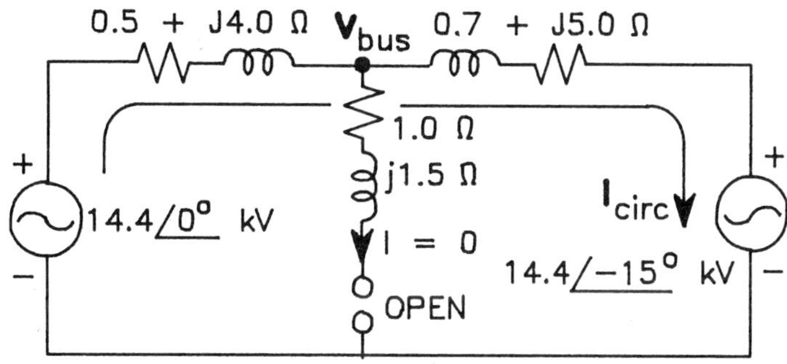

(b) Original Circuit Redrawn.

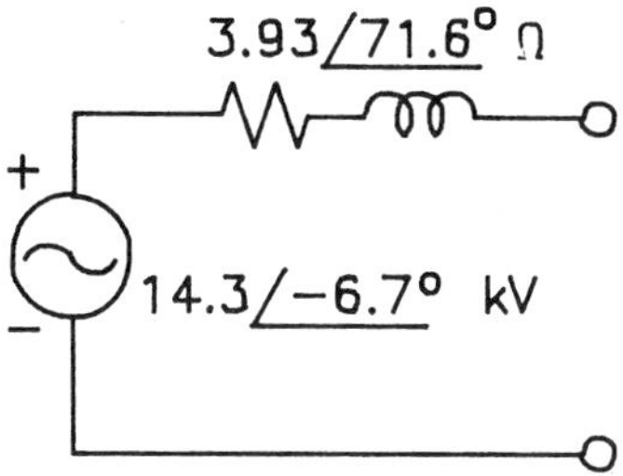

(c) Thevenin Equivalent Circuit.

Figure 1-10 Circuit for Example 1-13.

$$\begin{aligned}\mathbf{V}_{\text{bus}} &= 14{,}400\angle 0^\circ - (414\angle 0.1^\circ)(0.5 + j4)\\ &= 14{,}400 - 1669\angle 83^\circ\\ &= 14{,}197 - j1657 = 14{,}293\angle -6.7^\circ \text{ V}\end{aligned}$$

The Thevenin equivalent circuit for the system is shown in Fig. 1-10c.

1-8 Norton's Theorem

Like Thevenin's theorem, Norton's theorem is used to reduce a complex network to a simplified equivalent representation. The Norton equivalent circuit consists of the Norton equivalent system impedance in parallel with the Norton equivalent current source. The Norton equivalent system impedance is determined in the same manner as the Thevenin equivalent system impedance. The Norton equivalent current source is determined by replacing the load with a short circuit at the load terminals and calculating the resulting short-circuit current. This short-circuit current is equal to the Norton equivalent current source.

EXAMPLE 1-14

Determine the Norton equivalent circuit for the circuit of Example 1-13.

Solution The Norton equivalent impedance is equal to the Thevenin equivalent impedance.

$$\mathbf{Z}_{sys} = 3.93\angle 71.6°\ \Omega$$

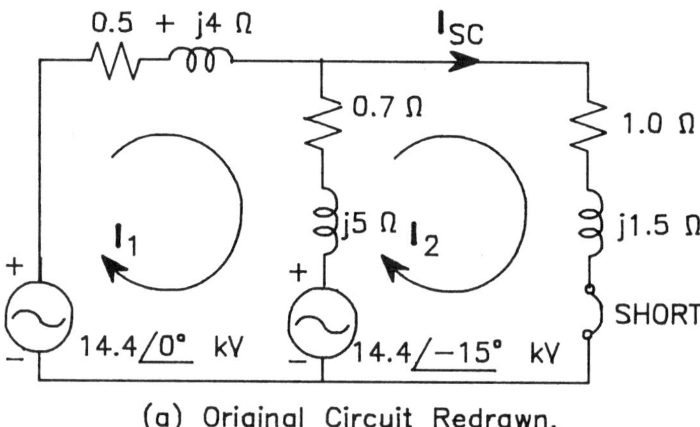

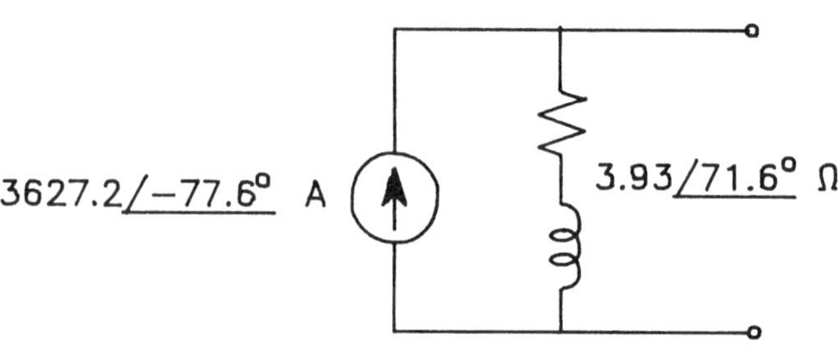

Figure 1-11 Circuit for Example 1-14.

The Norton equivalent current source is determined by replacing the load with a short circuit and calculating the short-circuit current. The system for these conditions is shown in Fig. 1-11a. Note that the system has been redrawn in order to facilitate the application of mesh analysis. The short-circuit current $\mathbf{I}_{sc}$ is equal to mesh current $\mathbf{I}_2$. Therefore, it is necessary to solve only for mesh current $\mathbf{I}_2$.

The mesh currents are as follows:

$$\text{Mesh 1:} \quad -14{,}400\angle 0° + \mathbf{I}_1(0.5 + j4) + (\mathbf{I}_1 - \mathbf{I}_2)(0.7 + j5) + 14{,}400\angle -15° = 0$$

$$\text{Mesh 2:} \quad -14{,}400\angle -15° + (\mathbf{I}_2 - \mathbf{I}_1)(0.7 + j5) + \mathbf{I}_2(1 + j1.5) = 0$$

Simplifying and arranging in matrix form,

$$\begin{bmatrix} 1.2 + j9 & -0.7 - j5 \\ -0.7 - j5 & 1.7 + j6.5 \end{bmatrix} \begin{bmatrix} \mathbf{I}_1 \\ \mathbf{I}_2 \end{bmatrix} = \begin{bmatrix} 3759.2\angle 82.5° \\ 14{,}400\angle -15° \end{bmatrix}$$

The current $\mathbf{I}_2$ is solved for using Cramers rule as follows:

$$\Delta = -31.95 + j16.1 = 35.78\angle 153.3°$$

$$\Delta_2 = 31{,}953.9 + j125{,}784.8 = 129{,}780.1\angle 75.7°$$

The short circuit current is

$$\mathbf{I}_{sc} = \mathbf{I}_2 = \frac{\Delta_2}{\Delta} = 3627.2\angle -77.6° \text{ A}$$

The Norton equivalent circuit is shown in Fig. 1-11b.

1-9 Superposition Theorem

The superposition theorem states that a circuit containing several sources can be analyzed with one source active at a time with all other sources set to zero. To determine the actual value of a particular voltage or current, the results of the calculations with each source energized one at a time are added together. The superposition theorem arises frequently in the study of power system harmonics when a circuit has to be analyzed at several different frequencies. This topic is covered in more detail in Chapter 13.

EXAMPLE 1-15 Repeat Example 1-13 using the superposition theorem.

Solution With $\mathbf{V}_1$ in the circuit and $\mathbf{V}_2$ set equal to zero (shorted), the voltage-divider rule can be applied.

$$\mathbf{V}'_{bus} = 14{,}400\angle 0° \frac{0.7 + j5}{0.5 + j4 + 0.7 + j5} = 8008.8\angle -0.4° \text{ V}$$

Likewise, with $\mathbf{V}_2$ in the circuit and $\mathbf{V}_1$ set equal to zero,

$$\mathbf{V}''_{bus} = 14{,}400\angle -15° \frac{0.5 + j4}{0.5 + j4 + 0.7 + j5} = 6391.2\angle -14.6° \text{ V}$$

The actual bus voltage with both sources in the circuit is

$$\begin{aligned}\mathbf{V}_{\text{bus}} &= \mathbf{V}'_{\text{bus}} + \mathbf{V}''_{\text{bus}} \\ &= 8008.8\angle -0.4° + 6391.2\angle -14.6° \\ &= 14{,}291\angle -6.7° \text{ V}\end{aligned}$$

This result agrees favorably with Example 1-13.

1-10 Balanced Three-Phase Circuits

The vast majority of power transmission and distribution lines are operated as three-phase circuits. There are a few high-voltage dc transmission lines in operation throughout the world. It is therefore extremely important that the concepts related to three-phase circuits be understood by the power system engineer and technologist. This section is limited to a discussion of balanced three-phase circuits.

Balanced Three-Phase Voltage Sources

Balanced three-phase voltages are generated by synchronous alternators located in utility power plants. These alternators generate voltages that are sinusoidal, equal in magnitude, and displaced from each other by 120°. Since the generated voltages are sinusoidal in nature, they can be represented as voltage sources using phasor representation. Each of the three voltage sources will have the same rms magnitude, and there will be a 120° phase displacement between the sources. The three voltage sources are shown in Fig 1-12a. The voltage sources shown can be connected either in a wye configuration, as shown in Fig. 1-12b, or in a delta configuration, as shown in Fig. 1-12c. The wye connection is the most common connection for electric utility generators.

In the wye connection of Fig. 1-12b, terminals designated a', b', and c' are connected together and form a common node referred to as the neutral and designated n. The terminals designated a, b, and c are referred to as the line terminals. The line to neutral voltages are equal to the individual source voltages.

$$\mathbf{V}_{an} = E\angle 0° \text{ V} \tag{1.39a}$$

$$\mathbf{V}_{bn} = E\angle -120° \text{ V} \tag{1.39b}$$

$$\mathbf{V}_{cn} = E\angle 120° \text{ V} \tag{1.39c}$$

The line to line voltages are determined by applying Kirchhoff's voltage law around each loop.

$$\begin{aligned}\mathbf{V}_{ab} &= \mathbf{V}_{an} - \mathbf{V}_{bn} \\ &= E\angle 0° - E\angle -120° \\ &= \sqrt{3}E\angle 30° \text{ V}\end{aligned} \tag{1.40a}$$

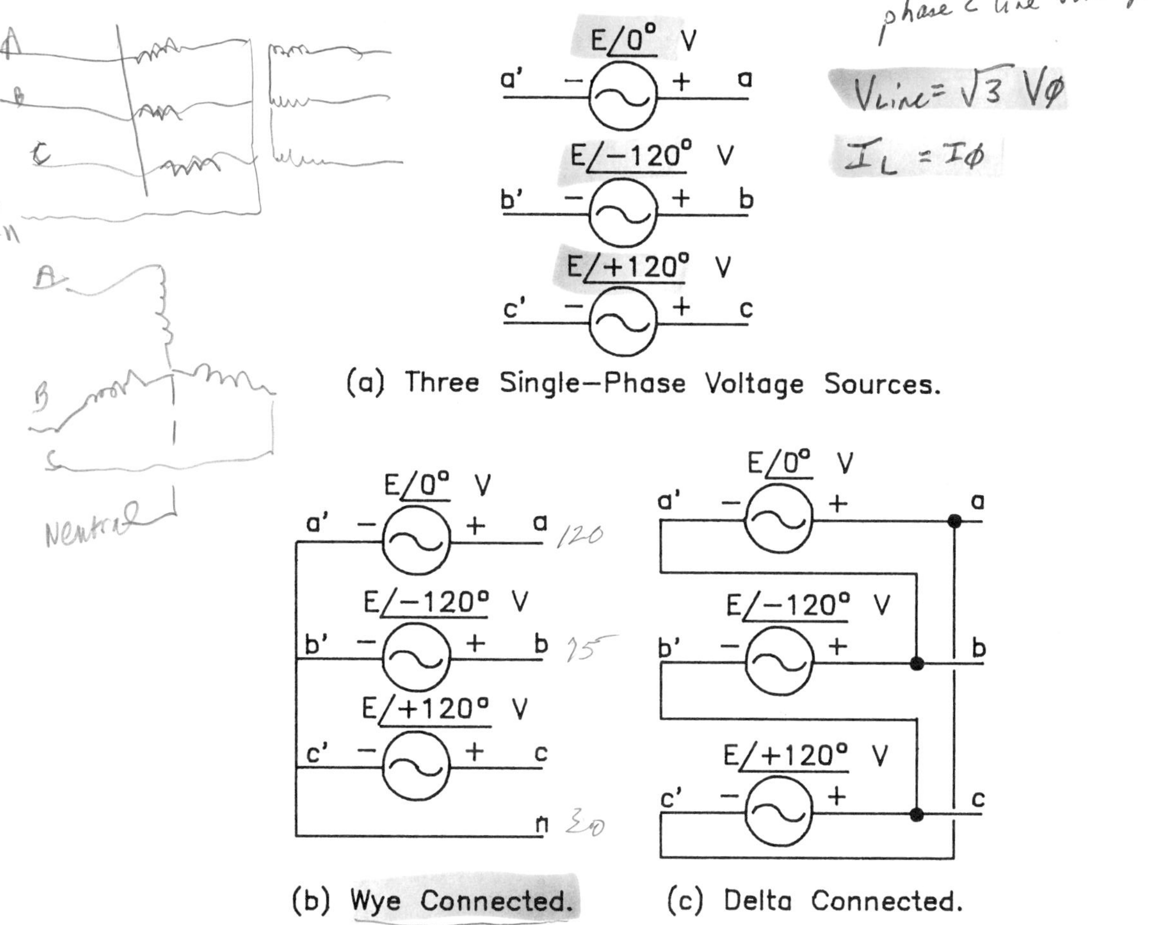

Figure 1-12 Balanced three-phase voltage sources.

$$\begin{aligned}\mathbf{V}_{bc} &= \mathbf{V}_{bn} - \mathbf{V}_{cn} \\ &= E\angle -120^\circ - E\angle 120^\circ \\ &= \sqrt{3}E\angle 270^\circ \text{ V}\end{aligned} \tag{1.40b}$$

$$\begin{aligned}\mathbf{V}_{ca} &= \mathbf{V}_{cn} - \mathbf{V}_{an} \\ &= E\angle 120^\circ - E\angle 0^\circ \\ &= \sqrt{3}E\angle 150^\circ \text{ V}\end{aligned} \tag{1.40c}$$

These voltages are shown in the phasor diagram of Fig. 1-13a. Note that in the wye connection the magnitude of the line to line voltage is equal to the magnitude of the line to neutral voltage multiplied by $\sqrt{3}$. There is also a phase shift between the line to line and line to neutral voltages, as indicated on the phasor diagram.

In the delta connection, terminal a' is connected to b, b' is connected to c, and c' is connected to a to form a closed delta. The delta connection of the three voltage sources

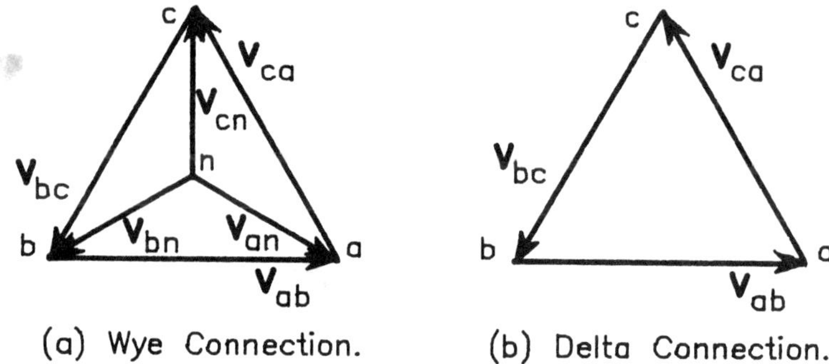

Figure 1-13 Phasor diagrams of three-phase voltage sources.

is shown in Fig. 1-12c. It is extremely important to connect the negative terminal of one source to the positive terminal of another source. Incorrect connection between any two sources will result in a short circuit, with short-circuit current flowing around the closed delta path.

The line to line voltages are equal to the voltage sources in each phase.

$$\mathbf{V}_{ab} = E\angle 0^\circ \text{ V} \tag{1.41a}$$

$$\mathbf{V}_{bc} = E\angle -120^\circ \text{ V} \tag{1.41b}$$

$$\mathbf{V}_{ca} = E\angle 120^\circ \text{ V} \tag{1.41c}$$

In the delta connection there is no common point between the three sources; therefore, there is no neutral connection to the generator windings. As such, no line to neutral voltage will be present. However, a line to ground voltage may be present due to the presence of line to ground capacitance from each phase to ground. The phasor diagram for the delta connection is shown in Fig. 1-13b.

Balanced Three-Phase Loads

Similarly to the balanced three-phase voltage sources previously discussed, balanced three-phase loads may be either delta or wye connected. If wye connected, the common point may be either solidly grounded or ungrounded. The solidly grounded or delta connection of loads is desirable since these connections will result in a fixed voltage applied across each phase of the load.

The balanced wye-connected load is shown in Fig. 1-14a. The voltages applied to each impedance are equal to the line to neutral system voltages as given by Eqs. (1.39). The phase currents in each element are calculated using Ohm's law.

$$\mathbf{I}_a = \frac{\mathbf{V}_{an}}{\mathbf{Z}_{an}} \tag{1.42a}$$

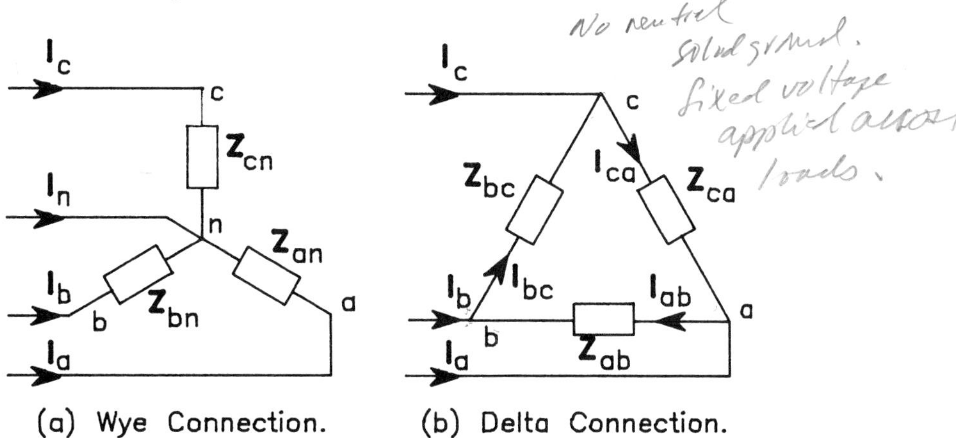

Figure 1-14 Balanced three-phase loads.

$$\mathbf{I}_b = \frac{\mathbf{V}_{bn}}{\mathbf{Z}_{bn}} \tag{1.42b}$$

$$\mathbf{I}_c = \frac{\mathbf{V}_{cn}}{\mathbf{Z}_{cn}} \tag{1.42c}$$

In a balanced three-phase load, the three impedances are equal. Therefore, the three phase currents will be equal in magnitude and rotated 120° in phase from each other. Also, in the wye connection the line currents are equal to the phase currents, both in magnitude and phase. Applying Kirchhoff's current law to the neutral results in

$$\mathbf{I}_n = -(\mathbf{I}_a + \mathbf{I}_b + \mathbf{I}_c) \tag{1.43}$$

The neutral current for a balanced three-phase, wye-connected load is equal to zero.

Figure 1-14b shows the connection for the balanced three-phase delta load. The voltages applied to each of the impedances are now equal to the line to line system voltages. The phase currents are equal to

$$\mathbf{I}_{ab} = \frac{\mathbf{V}_{ab}}{\mathbf{Z}_{ab}} \tag{1.44a}$$

$$\mathbf{I}_{bc} = \frac{\mathbf{V}_{bc}}{\mathbf{Z}_{bc}} \tag{1.44b}$$

$$\mathbf{I}_{ca} = \frac{\mathbf{V}_{ca}}{\mathbf{Z}_{ca}} \tag{1.44c}$$

Again, since the load is balanced, the three load impedances are equal. Therefore, the three phase currents will be equal in magnitude and displaced by 120° from one another.

To determine the line currents in a delta connection, it is necessary to apply Kirchhoff's current law to nodes a, b, and c of Fig. 1-14b.

$$\begin{aligned}
\mathbf{I}_a &= \mathbf{I}_{ab} - \mathbf{I}_{ca} \\
&= \frac{\mathbf{V}_{ab}}{\mathbf{Z}_{ab}} - \frac{\mathbf{V}_{ca}}{\mathbf{Z}_{ca}} \\
&= \frac{\mathbf{V}_{ab} - \mathbf{V}_{ca}}{\mathbf{Z}_{ab}} \\
&= \frac{\sqrt{3}\angle -30^\circ\ \mathbf{V}_{ab}}{\mathbf{Z}_{ab}} \\
&= \sqrt{3}\angle -30^\circ\ \mathbf{I}_{ab}
\end{aligned} \qquad \textbf{(1.45a)}$$

$$\begin{aligned}
\mathbf{I}_b &= \mathbf{I}_{bc} - \mathbf{I}_{ab} \\
&= \frac{\mathbf{V}_{bc}}{\mathbf{Z}_{bc}} - \frac{\mathbf{V}_{ab}}{\mathbf{Z}_{ab}} \\
&= \frac{\mathbf{V}_{bc} - \mathbf{V}_{ab}}{\mathbf{Z}_{bc}} \\
&= \frac{\sqrt{3}\angle -30^\circ\ \mathbf{V}_{bc}}{\mathbf{Z}_{bc}} \\
&= \sqrt{3}\angle -30^\circ\ \mathbf{I}_{bc}
\end{aligned} \qquad \textbf{(1.45b)}$$

$$\begin{aligned}
\mathbf{I}_c &= \mathbf{I}_{ca} - \mathbf{I}_{bc} \\
&= \frac{\mathbf{V}_{ca}}{\mathbf{Z}_{ca}} - \frac{\mathbf{V}_{bc}}{\mathbf{Z}_{bc}} \\
&= \frac{\mathbf{V}_{ca} - \mathbf{V}_{bc}}{\mathbf{Z}_{ca}} \\
&= \frac{\sqrt{3}\angle -30^\circ\ \mathbf{V}_{ca}}{\mathbf{Z}_{ca}} \\
&= \sqrt{3}\angle -30^\circ\ \mathbf{I}_{ca}
\end{aligned} \qquad \textbf{(1.45c)}$$

Examination of Eqs. (1.45) indicates that the magnitude of the line current is equal to the magnitude of the phase current multiplied by $\sqrt{3}$. There is also a phase displacement of -30° between the line and phase currents, as indicated in Eqs. (1.45).

Phase Sequence

The phase sequence of a three-phase voltage source is extremely important in determining the direction of rotation of three-phase motors. Phase sequence can be thought of as the order in which the phasors pass through the 0° reference axis. (Recall that the phasor representation of sinusoidal waveforms involves the concept of a vector rotating in the counterclockwise direction). For the voltage phasors shown in Fig. 1-13, the phase sequence will be *a–b–c*. If any two of the voltage sources were reversed, the opposite phase sequence, *a–c–b*, would result. Reversal of phase sequence will cause three-phase motors to reverse direction of rotation. The consequences are obvious!

1-11 Unbalanced Three-Phase Circuits

When analyzing unbalanced three-phase loads connected to three-phase sources, it is first necessary to determine the magnitude and phase angle of the voltages applied across each impedance. This is true regardless of whether the load is delta or wye connected. Next, the phase current through each element is calculated by direct application of Ohm's law. Finally, the line currents can be calculated using Kirchhoff's current law.

EXAMPLE 1-16

A three-phase, delta-connected load consists of the following impedances:

$$\mathbf{Z}_{ab} = 3 + j4\ \Omega$$

$$\mathbf{Z}_{bc} = 5\ \Omega$$

$$\mathbf{Z}_{ca} = -j5\ \Omega$$

The voltage source is a balanced three-phase source with a line to line voltage of 480 V. Assume an *abc* phase sequence and determine the following:

a. Phase voltages
b. Phase currents in the load
c. Line currents

Solution

a. The voltage reference will be selected as

$$\mathbf{V}_{ab} = 480\angle 0^\circ \text{ V}$$

The other two phase voltages will be

$$\mathbf{V}_{bc} = 480\angle -120^\circ \text{ V}, \qquad \mathbf{V}_{ca} = 480\angle 120^\circ \text{ V}$$

b. The phase currents are

$$\mathbf{I}_{ab} = \frac{\mathbf{V}_{ab}}{\mathbf{Z}_{ab}} = \frac{480\angle 0^\circ}{3 + j4} = 96\angle -53.13^\circ \text{ A}$$

$$\mathbf{I}_{bc} = \frac{\mathbf{V}_{bc}}{\mathbf{Z}_{bc}} = \frac{480\angle -120^\circ}{5} = 96\angle -120^\circ \text{ A}$$

$$\mathbf{I}_{ca} = \frac{\mathbf{V}_{ca}}{\mathbf{Z}_{ca}} = \frac{480\angle 120^\circ}{-j5} = 96\angle 210^\circ \text{ A}$$

c. The line currents are

$$\mathbf{I}_a = \mathbf{I}_{ab} - \mathbf{I}_{ca} = 96\angle{-53.13^\circ} - 96\angle 210^\circ = 143.7\angle{-11.6^\circ}\ \text{A}$$

$$\mathbf{I}_b = \mathbf{I}_{bc} - \mathbf{I}_{ab} = 96\angle{-120^\circ} - 96\angle{-53.13^\circ} = 105.8\angle 183.4^\circ\ \text{A}$$

$$\mathbf{I}_c = \mathbf{I}_{ca} - \mathbf{I}_{bc} = 96\angle 210^\circ - 96\angle{-120^\circ} = 49.7\angle 135^\circ\ \text{A}$$

EXAMPLE 1-17

A three-phase, wye-connected load consists of the following impedances:

$$\mathbf{Z}_{an} = 3 + j4\ \Omega$$

$$\mathbf{Z}_{bn} = 5\ \Omega$$

$$\mathbf{Z}_{cn} = -j5\ \Omega$$

The voltage source is a 208-V (line to line) three-phase source. Assume an *acb* phase sequence and determine the following:

a. Phase voltages
b. Line and phase currents
c. Neutral current

Solution

a. The magnitude of the line to neutral voltages is

$$V_{ln} = V_{ll} \div \sqrt{3} = 208 \div \sqrt{3} = 120\ \text{V}$$

The voltage from *a* to *n* will be selected as the reference

$$\mathbf{V}_{an} = 120\angle 0^\circ\ \text{V}$$

The line to neutral voltages of the other two phases are

$$\mathbf{V}_{bn} = 120\angle 120^\circ\ \text{V}$$

$$\mathbf{V}_{cn} = 120\angle{-120^\circ}\ \text{V}$$

Note the phase angles for the *acb* phase sequence.

b. The phase currents are

$$\mathbf{I}_{an} = \frac{\mathbf{V}_{an}}{\mathbf{Z}_{an}} = \frac{120\angle 0^\circ}{3 + j4} = 24\angle{-53.13^\circ}\ \text{A}$$

$$\mathbf{I}_{bn} = \frac{\mathbf{V}_{bn}}{\mathbf{Z}_{bn}} = \frac{120\angle 120^\circ}{5} = 24\angle 120^\circ\ \text{A}$$

$$\mathbf{I}_{cn} = \frac{\mathbf{V}_{cn}}{\mathbf{Z}_{cn}} = \frac{120\angle{-120^\circ}}{-j5} = 24\angle{-30^\circ}\ \text{A}$$

The phase and line currents are equal in a wye connection.

c. The neutral current is

$$\begin{aligned}\mathbf{I}_n &= -(\mathbf{I}_{an} + \mathbf{I}_{bn} + \mathbf{I}_{cn})\\ &= -(24\angle -53.13^\circ + 24\angle 120^\circ + 24\angle -30^\circ)\\ &= -(23.2 - j10.4)\\ &= 25.43\angle 155.9 \text{ A}\end{aligned}$$

It is interesting to note that the phase currents in Example 1-16 have the same magnitude. The load is unbalanced, however, since the phase displacements between the three-phase currents are not equal to 120°. The resulting line currents in the unbalanced delta connection have different magnitudes, thereby indicating an unbalanced load. In Example 1-17, the line and phase currents had the same magnitude, but a different phase angle. Also, the neutral current was not equal to zero for the unbalanced wye-connected load. The following observations can be made:

1. In general, the line current magnitudes in an unbalanced delta-connected load will differ.
2. In general, the neutral current will be nonzero in an unbalanced wye-connected load.

1-12 Wye–Delta and Delta–Wye Conversions

It is often desirable to convert a wye-connected load to an equivalent delta-connected load, or vice versa. Figure 1-15 shows the delta and wye connections. To determine the conversion equations, equate the impedance "looking in" to like terminals of the delta and wye.

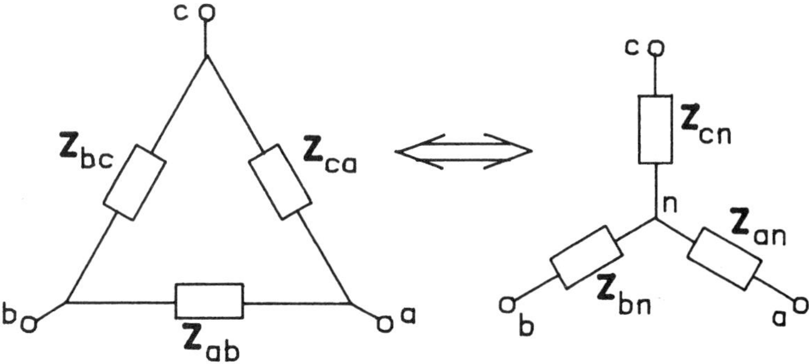

Figure 1-15 Delta–wye and wye–delta conversions.

Delta-to-Wye Conversion

When converting from a delta connection to an equivalent wye, the following equations are used:

$$\mathbf{Z}_{an} = \frac{\mathbf{Z}_{ab}\mathbf{Z}_{ca}}{\mathbf{Z}_{ab} + \mathbf{Z}_{bc} + \mathbf{Z}_{ca}} \tag{1.46}$$

$$\mathbf{Z}_{bn} = \frac{\mathbf{Z}_{ab}\mathbf{Z}_{bc}}{\mathbf{Z}_{ab} + \mathbf{Z}_{bc} + \mathbf{Z}_{ca}} \tag{1.47}$$

$$\mathbf{Z}_{cn} = \frac{\mathbf{Z}_{bc}\mathbf{Z}_{ca}}{\mathbf{Z}_{ab} + \mathbf{Z}_{bc} + \mathbf{Z}_{ca}} \tag{1.48}$$

Note that the denominators of Eqs. (1.46), (1.47), and (1.48) are the same. Therefore, it is necessary to calculate the denominator only once and use this value for all three equations. When converting from a delta to an equivalent wye, the neutral point of the equivalent wye representation must not be connected to the source neutral.

Wye-to-Delta Conversion

When converting from a wye to equivalent delta, the following equations are used:

$$\mathbf{Z}_{ab} = \frac{\mathbf{Z}_{an}\mathbf{Z}_{bn} + \mathbf{Z}_{bn}\mathbf{Z}_{cn} + \mathbf{Z}_{an}\mathbf{Z}_{cn}}{\mathbf{Z}_{cn}} \tag{1.49}$$

$$\mathbf{Z}_{bc} = \frac{\mathbf{Z}_{an}\mathbf{Z}_{bn} + \mathbf{Z}_{bn}\mathbf{Z}_{cn} + \mathbf{Z}_{an}\mathbf{Z}_{cn}}{\mathbf{Z}_{an}} \tag{1.50}$$

$$\mathbf{Z}_{ca} = \frac{\mathbf{Z}_{an}\mathbf{Z}_{bn} + \mathbf{Z}_{bn}\mathbf{Z}_{cn} + \mathbf{Z}_{an}\mathbf{Z}_{cn}}{\mathbf{Z}_{bn}} \tag{1.51}$$

Note that the numerators of Eqs. (1.49), (1.50), and (1.51) are the same. Therefore, it is necessary to calculate the value of the numerator only once and then use this value for all three equations.

In the case of a balanced delta-connected load, $\mathbf{Z}_{ab} = \mathbf{Z}_{bc} = \mathbf{Z}_{ca}$. Equations (1.46), (1.47), and (1.48) reduce to the following:

$$\mathbf{Z}_{an} = \frac{\mathbf{Z}_{ab}\mathbf{Z}_{ab}}{\mathbf{Z}_{ab} + \mathbf{Z}_{ab} + \mathbf{Z}_{ab}} = \tfrac{1}{3}\mathbf{Z}_{ab} \tag{1.52}$$

$$\mathbf{Z}_{bn} = \frac{\mathbf{Z}_{ab}\mathbf{Z}_{ab}}{\mathbf{Z}_{ab} + \mathbf{Z}_{ab} + \mathbf{Z}_{ab}} = \tfrac{1}{3}\mathbf{Z}_{ab} \tag{1.53}$$

$$\mathbf{Z}_{cn} = \frac{\mathbf{Z}_{ab}\mathbf{Z}_{ab}}{\mathbf{Z}_{ab} + \mathbf{Z}_{ab} + \mathbf{Z}_{ab}} \tag{1.54}$$

$$= \tfrac{1}{3}\mathbf{Z}_{ab}$$

Equations (1.52), (1.53), and (1.54) indicate that the equivalent wye-connected impedances of a balanced delta-connected load are equal to one-third times the delta-connected impedance.

For a balanced wye-connected load, $\mathbf{Z}_{an} = \mathbf{Z}_{bn} = \mathbf{Z}_{cn}$, and Eqs. (1.49), (1.50), and (1.51) are reduced as follows:

$$\mathbf{Z}_{ab} = \frac{\mathbf{Z}_{an}\mathbf{Z}_{an} + \mathbf{Z}_{an}\mathbf{Z}_{an} + \mathbf{Z}_{an}\mathbf{Z}_{an}}{\mathbf{Z}_{an}} \tag{1.55}$$

$$= 3\mathbf{Z}_{an}$$

$$\mathbf{Z}_{bc} = \frac{\mathbf{Z}_{an}\mathbf{Z}_{an} + \mathbf{Z}_{an}\mathbf{Z}_{an} + \mathbf{Z}_{an}\mathbf{Z}_{an}}{\mathbf{Z}_{an}} \tag{1.56}$$

$$= 3\mathbf{Z}_{an}$$

$$\mathbf{Z}_{ca} = \frac{\mathbf{Z}_{an}\mathbf{Z}_{an} + \mathbf{Z}_{an}\mathbf{Z}_{an} + \mathbf{Z}_{an}\mathbf{Z}_{an}}{\mathbf{Z}_{an}} \tag{1.57}$$

$$= 3\mathbf{Z}_{an}$$

Equations (1.55), (1.56), and (1.57) indicate that the equivalent delta-connected impedances for a balanced wye-connected load are equal to three times the wye-connected impedances.

1-13 Power Concepts In Single- and Three-Phase Circuits

The concept of active, reactive, and apparent power is important in the study of load characteristics, power factor correction, conductor sizing, and voltage-drop calculations in electric utility power systems. This section will review the fundamental power concepts related to single-phase and balanced three-phase loads. In addition, power concepts related to single-phase and balanced three-phase sources will be discussed.

Single-Phase and Balanced Three-Phase Loads

The schematic representation for a single-phase load is shown in Fig. 1-16a. The load is represented as an impedance **Z**, the voltage across the impedance is designated **V**, and the current through the impedance is designated **I**. Note that the impedance, voltage, and current are all phasor quantities having both magnitude and phase angle. The complex apparent power dissipated in the load is

$$\mathbf{S} = \mathbf{V} \cdot \mathbf{I}^* \tag{1.58}$$

active reactive

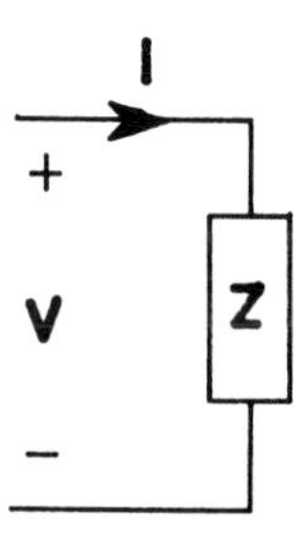

(a) Single Phase.

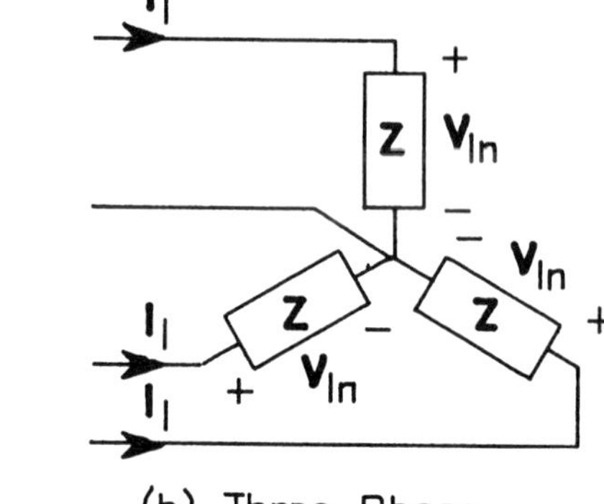

(b) Three Phase.

Figure 1-16 Power concepts for single-phase and balanced three-phase loads.

The apparent power given by Eq. (1.58) is a complex number having both magnitude and phase angle. The apparent power can also be expressed in rectangular form as

$$\mathbf{S} = P + jQ \tag{1.59}$$

where P is the active power dissipated in the load, given by

$$P = VI\cos(\theta) \tag{1.60}$$

and Q is the reactive power dissipated in the load, given by

$$Q = -VI\sin(\theta) \tag{1.61}$$

In Eqs. (1.60) and (1.61), θ is the phase angle between the voltage and current. The angle θ is negative if the current lags the voltage and positive if the current leads the voltage. Note that the reactive power is negative if the current leads the voltage and positive if the current lags the voltage. The apparent power has units of volt-amperes (VA), the active power has units of watts (W), and the reactive power has units of volt-amperes-reactive (VAR).

The magnitude of the apparent power is equal to

$$S = VI \tag{1.62}$$

In terms of the active and reactive power, the magnitude of the apparent power is

$$S = (P^2 + Q^2)^{1/2} \tag{1.63}$$

The power factor (PF) of the load is defined to be the ratio of the magnitude of the active power to the magnitude of the apparent power.

$$\begin{aligned} \text{PF} &= \frac{P}{S} \\ &= \frac{VI\cos(\theta)}{VI} \\ &= \cos(\theta) \end{aligned} \tag{1.64}$$

The power factor is lagging if the current lags the voltage (negative θ) and leading if the current leads the voltage (positive θ). In a lagging power factor load, the reactive power is absorbed from the system, while in a leading power factor load the reactive power is supplied to the system.

In a similar fashion, the reactive factor (RF) is defined to be the ratio of the magnitude of the reactive power to the magnitude of the apparent power.

$$\begin{aligned} \text{RF} &= \frac{Q}{S} \\ &= \frac{VI\sin(\theta)}{VI} \\ &= \sin(\theta) \end{aligned} \tag{1.65}$$

The circuit diagram for a balanced three-phase, wye-connected load is shown in Fig. 1-16b. Again the load impedance is designated **Z** in each phase. The magnitude of the line to neutral voltages is designated V_{ln}, and the magnitude of the line currents is designated I_l. The magnitude of the total apparent power dissipated in the load for all three phases is

$$S_{3\Phi} = 3\, V_{ln}\, I_l \tag{1.66}$$

In a balanced three-phase, wye-connected load, the magnitude of the line to neutral voltage is equal to the magnitude of the line to line voltage divided by $\sqrt{3}$. Applying this relationship to Eq. (1.66) results in

$$\begin{aligned} S_{3\Phi} &= 3\left(V_{ll} \div \sqrt{3}\right)I_l \\ &= \sqrt{3}\, V_{ll}I_l \end{aligned} \tag{1.67}$$

In a similar manner, the magnitudes of the active and reactive power dissipated in all the phases are equal to

$$P_{3\Phi} = \sqrt{3}\, V_{ll}I_l \cos(\theta) \tag{1.68}$$

$$Q_{3\Phi} = -\sqrt{3}\, V_{ll}I_l \sin(\theta) \tag{1.69}$$

where θ is the phase angle between the line current and line to neutral voltage in each phase. Since the load is assumed to be balanced, θ is the same for all three phases. The power factor and reactive factors are given by Eqs. (1.64) and (1.65), respectively.

Single-Phase and Balanced Three-Phase Sources

The equations developed for the apparent, active, and reactive powers apply also to single- and three-phase sources, with some minor differences in sign conventions. The representation of single- and three-phase sources is shown in Fig. 1-17. Notice that the current is now assumed to be leaving the instantaneously positive terminal.

The active and reactive power can be calculated using Eqs. (1.60) and (1.61). A positive active power indicates that the source is supplying active power to the load, while a negative active power indicates that the source is absorbing active power from

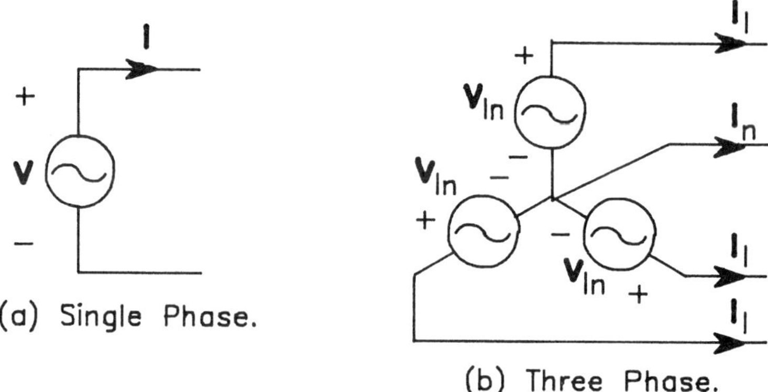

Figure 1-17 Power concepts for single-phase and balanced three-phase sources.

the system. Likewise, a positive reactive power indicates that the source is supplying reactive power to the load, and a negative reactive power indicates that the source is absorbing reactive power from the system. Therefore, a source or generator that is operating at a lagging power factor is actually supplying reactive power to the system. A source that is operating at a leading power factor is absorbing reactive power from the system. Note that the concept of leading and lagging power factors for sources is opposite to that for loads.

1-14 Single-Phase Analysis of Balanced Three-Phase Systems

Many portions of the electrical utility power system are operated at balanced or very nearly balanced conditions. To simplify the calculations, the balanced three-phase system can be thought of as three separate single-phase systems. The voltages and currents in each of the three phases are equal in magnitude. The phase angles of the voltages and currents in each of the other phases will differ by 120° and 240° from the reference quantities. Therefore, it is necessary to analyze only one phase of the balanced three-phase system to determine the desired quantities and to recognize that the voltages and currents in the other two phases will differ in phase angle only. Voltage drop, three-phase short circuit, load flow, economic dispatch, and state estimation are examples of calculations performed using the assumption of balanced three-phase conditions.

Consider the balanced three-phase system shown in Fig. 1-18a. The three-phase voltage source is represented by three single-phase voltage sources of equal magnitude and 120° phase displacement. The impedances in each of the three-phase conductors are designated $R_{\Phi} + jX_{\Phi}$ and are equal. The impedance of the neutral conductor is designated $R_N + jX_N$. In general, the impedance of the neutral conductor will exceed that of the phase conductors. The load is represented by three equal complex impedances designated Z_L connected in a wye configuration. If the impedances were actually connected in delta, a delta–wye conversion would have to be made to determine the equivalent wye.

Inductive- P(+), Q(+) Power Factor lag
Capacitive- P(-), Q(-) Power Factor lead

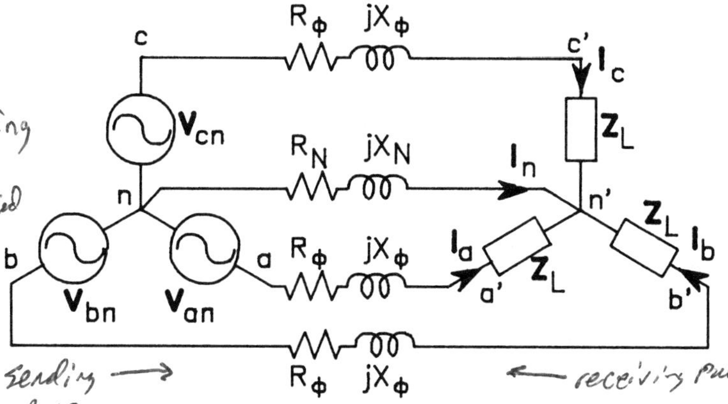

(a) Original Circuit Model.

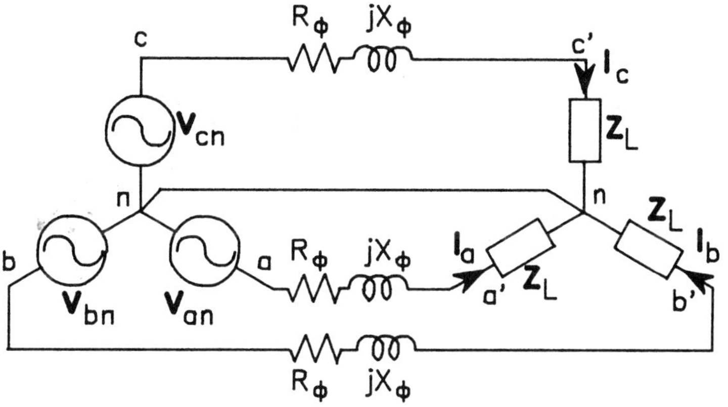

(b) Simplified Circuit Model.

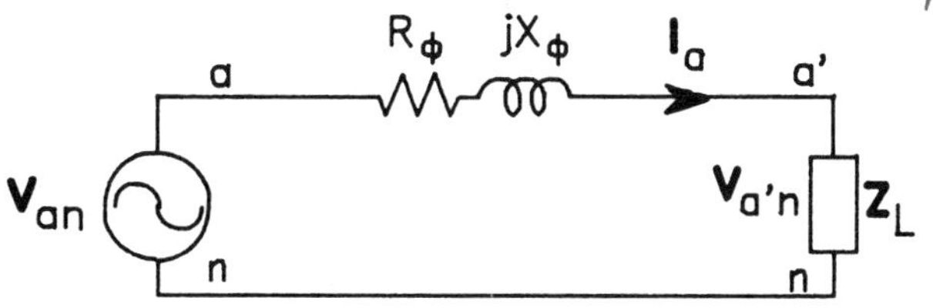

(c) Single Phase Equivalent.

Figure 1-18 Balanced three-phase system.

Applying Kirchhoff's current law to node n results in the following:

$$\mathbf{I}_a + \mathbf{I}_b + \mathbf{I}_c + \mathbf{I}_n = 0 \qquad \textbf{(1.70)}$$

Since the system is balanced, $\mathbf{I}_a + \mathbf{I}_b + \mathbf{I}_c = 0$. Therefore, from Eq. (1.70) the neutral current $\mathbf{I}_n$ is also zero. Since the neutral current is zero, the voltage drop across the neutral conductor impedance is also zero. Thus, nodes n and n' are at the same electrical potential and can be modeled as a common node, as shown in Fig. 1-18b. It is obvious from Fig. 1-18b that each phase of the three-phase system is identical. Analysis of any one phase will produce results that are similar for the other two phases. It is common practice to select phase a as the phase on which to perform the necessary calculations. The single-phase equivalent circuit representation of the balanced three-phase system is shown in Fig. 1-18c. The phase quantities for the b and c phases will be delayed by 120° and 240°, respectively, from the phase a results, assuming an abc phase sequence. Example 1-18 demonstrates the simplicity in using the line to neutral equivalent circuit approach when analyzing balanced three-phase systems.

EXAMPLE 1-18

A balanced three-phase load is connected to a 4.16-kV three-phase, four-wire, grounded-wye dedicated distribution feeder. The load can be modeled by an impedance of $Z_L = 5 + j13\ \Omega$/phase, wye connected. The impedance of the phase conductors is $R_\Phi + jX_\Phi = 0.3 + j0.8\ \Omega$. Using the phase a to neutral voltage as a reference, calculate the following:

a. Line currents for phases a, b, and c
b. Line to neutral voltages for all three phases at the load
c. Apparent, active, and reactive power dissipated per phase and for all three phases in the load
d. Active power losses per phase and for all three phases in the phase conductors

Solution

a. The reference voltage is selected as

$$\mathbf{V}_{an} = \frac{4160}{\sqrt{3}} \angle 0° \text{ V} = 2400\angle 0° \text{ V}$$

The total impedance for phase a is

$$\begin{aligned}\mathbf{Z}_a &= 0.3 + j0.8 + 5.0 + j13.0 \\ &= 5.3 + j13.8\ \Omega\end{aligned}$$

The line current in phase a is

$$\mathbf{I}_a = \frac{2400\angle 0°}{5.3 + j13.8} = 162.35\angle -69° \text{ A}$$

The line current in phase b lags the current in phase a by 120°:

$$\mathbf{I}_b = 162.35\angle -189° \text{ A}$$

The line current in phase c lags the current in phase a by 240°:

$$\begin{aligned}\mathbf{I}_c &= 162.35\angle -309^\circ \\ &= 162.35\angle 51^\circ \text{ A}\end{aligned}$$

b. The phase a to neutral voltage at the load is determined by application of Kirchhoff's voltage law.

$$\begin{aligned}\mathbf{V}_{a'n} &= \mathbf{V}_{an} - \mathbf{I}_a \cdot (R_\Phi + jX_\Phi) \\ &= 2400\angle 0^\circ - (162.35\angle -69^\circ)(0.3 + j0.8) \\ &= 2400\angle 0^\circ - 138.71\angle 0.44^\circ \\ &= 2261.29 - j1.07 \\ &= 2261.29\angle -0.03^\circ \text{ V}\end{aligned}$$

The phase b to neutral voltage at the load is

$$\mathbf{V}_{b'n} = 2261.29\angle -120.03^\circ \text{ V}$$

The phase c to neutral voltage at the load is

$$\mathbf{V}_{c'n} = 2261.29\angle -240.03^\circ \text{ V}$$

c. Using the phase a quantities as a reference, the apparent power dissipated per phase in the load is

$$S_{1\Phi} = V_{a'n} \cdot I_a = 2261.29 \cdot 162.35 = 367.12 \text{ kVA}$$

The total apparent power dissipated in all three phases is equal to

$$S_{3\Phi} = 3 \cdot S_{1\Phi} = 1101.36 \text{ kVA}$$

The active power dissipated per phase is

$$P = V_{a'n} \cdot I_a \cdot \cos(\theta)$$

where θ is the angle between the line to neutral voltage and line current at the load. Therefore,

$$\theta = -0.03^\circ - (-69^\circ) = 68.97^\circ$$

The active power is therefore

$$\begin{aligned}P_{1\Phi} &= 2261.29 \cdot 162.35 \cdot \cos(68.97^\circ) \\ &= 131.74 \text{ kW}\end{aligned}$$

The total active power dissipated in all three phases is equal to

$$P_{3\Phi} = 3 \cdot P_{1\Phi} = 395.2 \text{ kW}$$

The reactive power dissipated per phase is equal to

$$\begin{aligned}Q &= V_{a'n} \cdot I_a \cdot \sin(\theta) \\ &= 2261.29 \cdot 162.35 \cdot \sin(68.97^\circ) \\ &= 342.67 \text{ kVAR}\end{aligned}$$

The total reactive power dissipated in all three phases is equal to

$$Q_{3\Phi} = 3 \cdot Q_{1\Phi} = 1028.01 \text{ kVAR}$$

d. The line losses per phase are

$$\begin{aligned} P_{\text{loss},1\Phi} &= I^2 \cdot R_\Phi \\ &= 162.35^2 \cdot 0.3 \\ &= 7907.3 \text{ W} \end{aligned}$$

The total line loss for all three phases is

$$P_{\text{loss},3\Phi} = 3 \cdot P_{\text{loss},1\Phi} = 23{,}722 \text{ W}$$

Problems

1.1. Express the following sinusoidal functions in terms of rms phasors.

a. $v(t) = 10{,}182 \sin(377t - 30°)$ V

b. $v(t) = 3394 \cos(377t + 120°)$ V

c. $i(t) = 500 \sin(377t - 56.8°)$ A

d. $i(t) = 230 \sin(377t + 34°)$ A

1.2. Given the two complex numbers $\mathbf{A} = 34 + j16$ and $\mathbf{B} = 78 - j67$, perform the following operations:

a. $\mathbf{A} + \mathbf{B}$

b. $\mathbf{A} - \mathbf{B}$

c. $\mathbf{A} \cdot \mathbf{B}$

d. $\mathbf{A} \div \mathbf{B}$

e. $\mathbf{AB}^*$

1.3. Determine the complex impedance for the following elements:

a. $L = 45$ mH (millihenries) at 60 Hz (hertz)

b. $L = 565$ μH (microhenries) at 400 Hz

c. $C = 45$ μF (microfarads) at 60 Hz

d. $C = 1$ mF (millifarad) at 60 Hz

e. $R = 15$ Ω at 60 Hz

1.4. For the circuit shown in Fig. 1-19, perform the following:

a. Transform the circuit from the time domain to the phasor domain.

b. Calculate the source current $\mathbf{I}_S$ by reducing the network to an impedance in series with the source and applying Ohm's law.

c. Calculate the capacitor current $\mathbf{I}_C$ and the load current $\mathbf{I}_{\text{load}}$ using the current-divider rule.

d. Calculate the voltage across the capacitor and load by applying Ohm's law to each of these impedances. Are the results the same?

1.5. For the circuit shown in Fig. 1-20, solve for the node voltages $\mathbf{V}_1$ and $\mathbf{V}_2$ using nodal analysis.

1.6. For the circuit shown in Fig. 1-21, solve for the mesh currents $\mathbf{I}_1$ and $\mathbf{I}_2$ using mesh analysis. Calculate the current through and the voltage across the 5-Ω resistor.

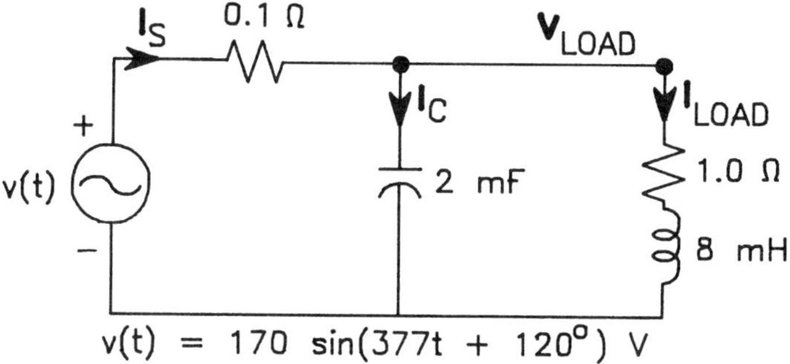

Figure 1-19 Circuit for Problem 1-4.

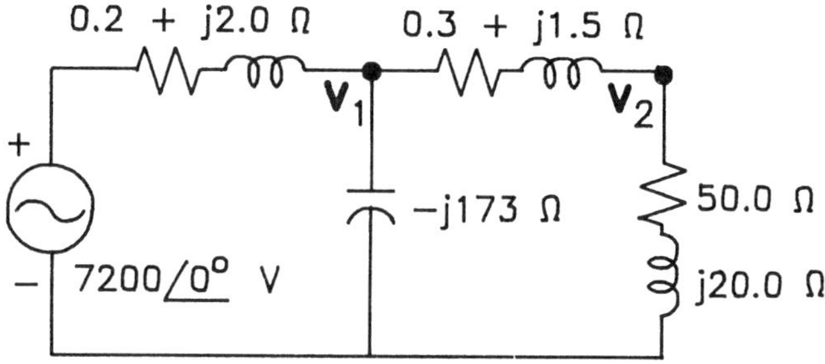

Figure 1-20 Circuit for Problem 1-5.

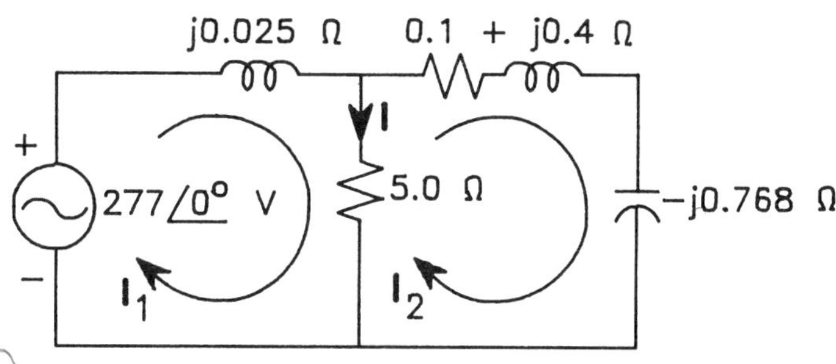

Figure 1-21 Circuit for Problem 1-6.

1.7. For the circuit shown in Figure 1-22, determine the Thevenin equivalent circuit "looking into" the system from the load terminals.

1.8. Calculate the line and phase currents for the following unbalanced delta-connected impedances:

$$\mathbf{Z}_{ab} = 3 + j3\ \Omega, \qquad \mathbf{Z}_{bc} = 10 + j0\ \Omega, \qquad \mathbf{Z}_{ca} = 1 - j5\ \Omega$$

The voltage source is a balanced three-phase system, 480-V line to line. Assume an *abc* phase sequence and use $\mathbf{V}_{ab}$ as the reference phasor.

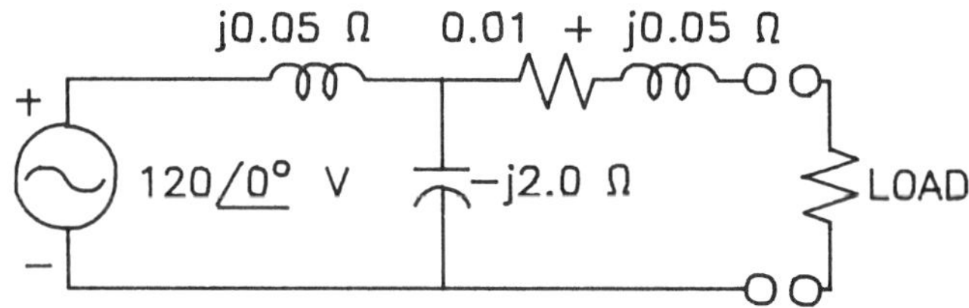

Figure 1-22 Circuit for Problem 1-7.

1.9. Calculate the line and neutral currents for the following unbalanced wye-connected impedances:

$$\mathbf{Z}_{an} = 2 + j5\ \Omega, \qquad \mathbf{Z}_{bn} = 8 + j0\ \Omega, \qquad \mathbf{Z}_{cn} = 1 - j12\ \Omega$$

The voltage source is a balanced three-phase system, 208 V line to line. Assume an *abc* phase sequence and use $\mathbf{V}_{an}$ as the reference phasor.

1.10. Convert the following wye-connected impedances to an equivalent delta.

$$\mathbf{Z}_{an} = 5 + j12\ \Omega, \qquad \mathbf{Z}_{bn} = 13 + j0\ \Omega, \qquad \mathbf{Z}_{cn} = 1 - j15\ \Omega$$

1.11. Convert the following delta-connected impedances to an equivalent wye.

$$\mathbf{Z}_{ab} = 5 + j3\ \Omega, \qquad \mathbf{Z}_{bc} = 9 + j0\ \Omega, \qquad \mathbf{Z}_{ca} = 2 - j8\ \Omega$$

1.12. An impedance of $10 + j6\ \Omega$ has an applied voltage of $277\angle 0°$ V. Calulate the following:

a. Complex current
b. Complex apparent power
c. Apparent, active, and reactive powers
d. Power factor
e. Reactive factor

1.13. A balanced three-phase load consists of three wye-connected impedances equal to $\mathbf{Z} = 5 + j13\ \Omega$ per phase. The voltage source is a balanced three-phase, 480-V system. Assume an *abc* phase sequence and use $\mathbf{V}_{an}$ as the reference phasor. Calculate the following:

a. Complex line currents
b. Complex apparent power for the total load
c. Total apparent, active, and reactive powers
d. Power factor
e. Reactive factor

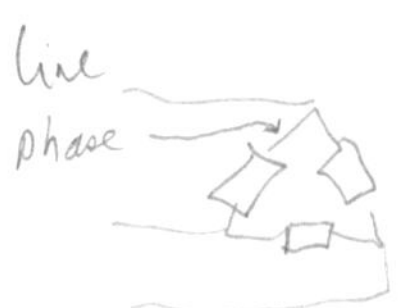

1.14. A balanced three-phase load consists of three delta-connected impedances equal to $10 + j2\ \Omega$ per phase. The voltage source is a balanced three-phase, 208-V system. Assume an *abc* phase sequence and use $\mathbf{V}_{ab}$ as the reference phasor. Calculate the following:

a. Complex phase currents
b. Complex line currents
c. Complex apparent power for the total load
d. Total apparent, active, and reactive powers
e. Power factor
f. Reactive factor

1.15. Calculate the line current of a 480-V, 300-kW, 0.8 lagging power factor three-phase load.

1.16. Calculate the line current of a 12.47-kV, 3-MW, 0.9 lagging power factor three-phase load.

 Probably Test

1.17. A balanced three-phase load consisting of an impedance of $30 + j30\ \Omega$/phase is connected to a 12.47-kV three-phase, four-wire, wye-connected source. A power factor correction capacitor bank having an impedance of $-j74\ \Omega$/phase is connected to the load bus in parallel with the load. The feeder supplying this load has an impedance of $1.5 + j4.0\ \Omega$/phase. Calculate the following:

a. Line current in phases A, B, and C of the feeder with and without the capacitor connected

b. Line to neutral voltage of phase A at the load with and without the capacitor connected

c. Apparent, active, and reactive power consumed at the load bus with and without the capacitor connected

d. Active power loss per phase occurring in the feeder with and without the capacitor connected

2

Review of Alternating Current Machines

2-1 General

This chapter presents a review of the alternating current machinery commonly used as the building blocks of electrical power systems. Single-phase and three-phase transformers are disscussed from a per phase equivalent circuit perspective. The starting and running characteristics of single- and three-phase induction motors are also reviewed. The per phase equivalent circuit representation of synchronous motors and generators is presented, as well as the power factor control capabilities of these synchronous machines. The chapter concludes with a discussion of the effect of changes in field excitation and prime mover power input on the active and reactive power output of three-phase synchronous generators.

2-2 Single-Phase Transformers

Single-phase transformers are used to supply residential and small commercial establishments. For larger commercial and industrial customers, two or three single-phase transformers may be connected in a *bank* to provide three-phase service. The equivalent circuit for a single-phase transformer is shown in Fig. 2-1.

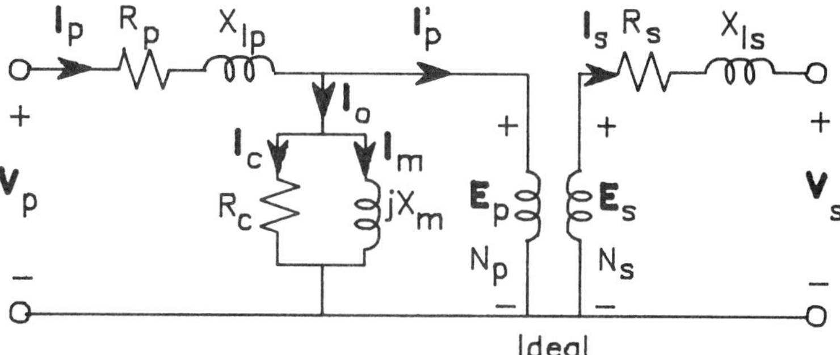

Figure 2-1 Single-phase transformer equivalent circuit.

No-Load Conditions

When voltage is applied to the primary winding with no load connected to the secondary, a small no-load current will flow. This current is designated $\mathbf{I}_o$ and consists of two components, $\mathbf{I}_c$ and $\mathbf{I}_m$. $\mathbf{I}_c$ is referred to as the core loss component of excitation current and represents the active or real power loss due to hysteresis and eddy current losses in the core. Since the core loss component of excitation current represents real power losses, it will be in phase with the applied voltage, $\mathbf{V}_p$. Therefore, the equivalent circuit component required to model core loss is a resistor. This resistor is designated R_c in the equivalent circuit. The magnetizing component of the excitation current is designated $\mathbf{I}_m$ and represents the component of current required to create magnetic flux in the iron core. The magnetizing component of the excitation current lags the applied voltage by 90° and is modeled by the magnetizing reactance X_m.

Since the primary and secondary windings surround the core, a voltage will be induced in the primary and secondary windings according to Faraday's law:

$$e_p(t) = N_p \frac{d\phi(t)}{dt} \tag{2.1a}$$

and

$$e_s(t) = N_s \frac{d\phi(t)}{dt} \tag{2.1b}$$

Equations (2.1a) and (2.1b) express the induced voltages in instantaneous form. For a sinusoidal flux, the rms value of the voltages induced in the primary and secondary can be expressed as

$$E_p = 4.44 N_p \phi_{\max} f \tag{2.2a}$$

and

$$E_s = 4.44 N_s \phi_{\max} f \tag{2.2b}$$

where f is the frequency of the flux waveform, ϕ_{max} is the peak amplitude of the flux waveform, and N_p and N_s are the number of turns on the primary and secondary windings, respectively.

The transformer turns ratio can be obtained by dividing Eq. (2.2a) by (2.2b). The result is:

$$\begin{aligned} a &= \frac{E_p}{E_s} \\ &= \frac{4.44N_p\phi_{max}f}{4.44N_s\phi_{max}f} \\ &= \frac{N_p}{N_s} \end{aligned} \qquad \textbf{(2.3)}$$

Therefore, the ratio of induced voltages is equal to the turns ratio of the transfomer.

It is important to mention that the induced voltages are approximately equal to the terminal voltages under no-load conditions. The transformer designer will use the ratio of the rated terminal voltages to establish the required turns ratio. If it is necessary to calculate the transformer turns ratio, rated terminal voltages should be used. The actual terminal voltages under load conditions will vary substantially from rated due to the impedance drops in the transformer windings. The important point to remember is that the transformer turns ratio is a constant.

The transformer windings are constructed of several turns of copper or aluminum conductor. As such, the windings will have a certain resistance associated with them. These resistances are designated R_p and R_s for the primary and secondary windings respectively. Also, in a real transformer, not all the flux that links the primary coil links the secondary coil. The difference in flux linkages is due to a certain amount of flux leaking or escaping from the iron core. This leakage flux contributes to a reduction or drop in the induced voltages in the transformer windings. To model the voltage drop due to leakage flux, the leakage reactances X_{lp} and X_{ls} are introduced into the circuit model. The voltage drops across these fictitious reactances closely model the voltage drop produced by leakage flux.

The impedances of the high-voltage winding may be reflected to the low-voltage side, or vice versa. When reflecting impedances from high voltage to low voltage, the high-side impedances are divided by the turns ratio squared. Likewise, when reflecting from the low-voltage side to the high-voltage side, the low-side impedances are multiplied by the turns ratio squared.

Load Conditions

Since a voltage $\mathbf{E}_s$ is induced in the secondary winding, a voltage $\mathbf{V}_s$ will appear at the transformer secondary terminals. When a load impedance is connected to the transformer secondary, a load current $\mathbf{I}_s$ will flow. This current will produce a magnetomotive force (mmf) equal to N_sI_s ampere turns in the secondary. To balance the mmf of the secondary, an mmf equal to N_pI_p will be produced in the primary. Equating the mmf of the primary and secondary,

$$N_pI'_p = N_sI_s \tag{2.4}$$

The current I'_p is often referred to as the load component of primary current and flows only when load is connected to the transformer.

In reference to the equivalent circuit, the primary current $\mathbf{I}_p$ is equal to

$$\mathbf{I}_p = \mathbf{I}'_p + \mathbf{I}_o \tag{2.5}$$

Typically, the no-load current of a power transformer is equal to approximately 1% to 6% of the full-load current rating. As such, the load component of primary current is much greater than the no-load current. Mathematically,

$$\mathbf{I}'_p >> \mathbf{I}_o \tag{2.6}$$

Substituting the results of Eq. (2.6) into (2.5) and rearranging,

$$\mathbf{I}'_p \approx \mathbf{I}_p \tag{2.7}$$

Solving Eq. (2.4) for the ratio of primary to secondary currents and applying Eq. (2.7) results in

$$\frac{I_p}{I_s} = \frac{N_s}{N_p} \tag{2.8}$$

Combining Eqs. (2.3) and (2.8) and rearranging results in

$$\frac{I_p}{I_s} = \frac{1}{a} \tag{2.9}$$

Equation (2.9) states that the ratio of primary to secondary current is equal to the reciprocal of the turns ratio.

EXAMPLE 2-1

A 50-kVA, 14,400–240-V, single-phase transformer has the following equivalent circuit parameters:

$$R_p = 20.7\ \Omega, \quad R_s = 0.008\ \Omega, \quad R_c = 400\ \text{k}\Omega$$

$$X_{lp} = 40.5\ \Omega, \quad X_{ls} = 0.015\ \Omega, \quad X_m = 200\ \text{k}\Omega$$

The transformer is supplying rated load at 0.9 lagging power factor and 240 V. Calculate the following:

a. Turns ratio

b. Secondary current

c. Induced secondary voltage
d. Induced primary voltage
e. Excitation current
f. Load component of primary current
g. Primary current
h. Applied primary voltage
i. Equivalent circuit with all parameters referred to the low-voltage side
j. Equivalent circuit with all parameters referred to the high-voltage side

Solution

a. The turns ratio is

$$a = \frac{14{,}400}{240} = 60$$

b. The magnitude of the secondary load current is

$$I_s = \frac{50{,}000}{240} = 208.3 \text{ A}$$

The phase angle of the secondary load current is $\cos^{-1}(0.9) = 25.84°$. The load voltage will be selected as the reference:

$$\mathbf{V}_s = 240\angle 0° \text{ V}$$

Therefore, the load current is

$$\mathbf{I}_s = 208.3\angle -25.84° \text{ A}$$

c. The induced secondary voltage is determined by applying KVL around the secondary loop:

$$\begin{aligned}\mathbf{E}_s &= \mathbf{V}_s + \mathbf{I}_s(R_s + jX_{ls}) \\ &= 240\angle 0° + (208.3\angle -25.84°)(0.008 + j0.015) \\ &= 240\angle 0° + 3.54\angle 36.1° \\ &= 242.86 + j2.1 = 242.9\angle 0.5° \text{ V}\end{aligned}$$

d. The induced primary voltage is

$$\mathbf{E}_p = a\mathbf{E}_s = 60(242.9\angle 0.5°) = 14{,}574\angle 0.5° \text{ V}$$

e. The excitation current is

$$\mathbf{I}_o = \frac{\mathbf{E}_p}{R_c \parallel jX_m}$$
$$= \frac{14{,}574\angle 0.5°}{400{,}000 \parallel j200{,}000}$$
$$= 0.0815\angle -62.94° \text{ A}$$

f. The load component of the primary current is

$$\mathbf{I}'_p = \frac{1}{a}\mathbf{I}_s$$
$$= \frac{1}{60}(208.3\angle -25.84°)$$
$$= 3.47\angle -25.84° \text{ A}$$

g. The total primary current is

$$\mathbf{I}_p = \mathbf{I}'_p + \mathbf{I}_o$$
$$= 3.47\angle -25.84° + 0.0815\angle -62.94°$$
$$= 3.16 - j1.59 = 3.54\angle -26.7° \text{ A}$$

h. The applied primary voltage is obtained by applying KVL to the primary loop:

$$\mathbf{V}_p = \mathbf{E}_p + \mathbf{I}_p(R_p + jX_{lp})$$
$$= 14{,}574\angle 0.5° + (3.54\angle -26.7)(20.7 + j40.5)$$
$$= 14{,}574\angle 0.5° + 161\angle 36.2°$$
$$= 14{,}703.4 + j222.3 = 14{,}705.1\angle 0.9° \text{ V}$$

i. The high-side impedances referred to the low side are

$$R'_p = 20.7 \cdot \frac{1}{(60)^2} = 0.00575\ \Omega$$

$$X'_{lp} = 40.5 \cdot \frac{1}{(60)^2} = 0.01125\ \Omega$$

$$R'_c = 400{,}000 \cdot \frac{1}{(60)^2} = 111.11\ \Omega$$

$$X'_m = 200{,}000 \cdot \frac{1}{(60)^2} = 55.55\ \Omega$$

The values for R_s and X_{ls} are already referred to the low-voltage side. The equivalent circuit of the transformer with all values referred to the low-voltage side is shown in Fig. 2-2a.

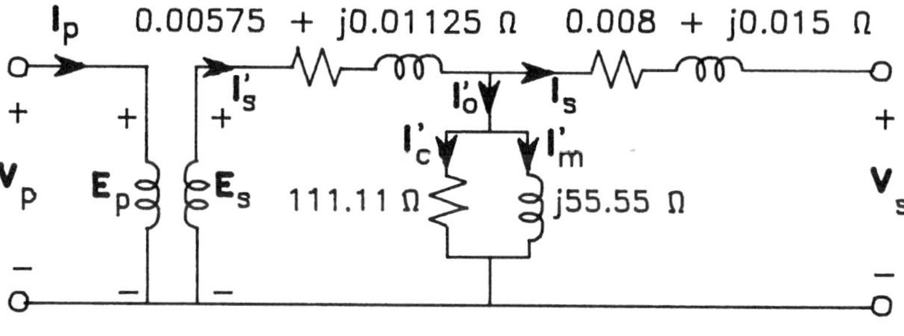

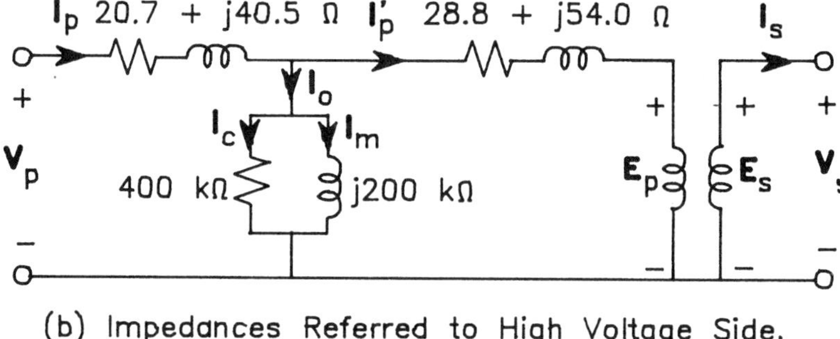

Figure 2-2 Circuits for Example 2-1.

j. The low-side impedances referred to the high side are

$$R'_s = 0.008 \cdot 60^2 = 28.8\ \Omega$$

$$X'_{ls} = 0.015 \cdot 60^2 = 54.0\ \Omega$$

The equivalent circuit with all values referred to the high-voltage side is shown in Fig. 2-2b.

2-3 Three-Phase Transformers

When analyzing three-phase transformers, the equivalent circuit diagram shown in Fig. 2-1 may be used. It must be understood that the model shown in Fig. 2-1 will represent the single-phase line to neutral equivalent circuit of the three-phase transformer. All parameters in the equivalent circuit will correspond to the per phase values. The total three-phase apparent power will be three times the per phase apparent power. The most common connections for three-phase transformers are the delta–delta, delta–wye, wye–delta, and wye–wye.

EXAMPLE 2-2

A three-phase transformer has an apparent power rating of 500 kVA, a rated line to line high-side voltage of 12,470 V, and a rated line to line low-side voltage of 480 V. The windings are delta connected on the high side and grounded wye connected on the low side. Calculate the following:

a. Rated line and phase current magnitude on the high side
b. Rated line and phase current magnitude on the low side

Solution

a. The apparent power rating per phase is

$$S_\phi = \frac{500{,}000}{3} = 167{,}000 \text{ VA}$$

The phase voltage is equal to the line to line voltage in a delta connection:

$$V_\phi = 12{,}470 \text{ V}$$

The rated phase current is

$$I_\phi = \frac{S_\phi}{V_\phi} = \frac{167{,}000}{12{,}470} = 13.4 \text{ A}$$

Since the high side is delta connected, the magnitude of the line current is equal to

$$I_l = \sqrt{3} I_\phi = 23.2 \text{ A}$$

b. Since the low side is wye connected, the magnitude of the line and phase currents are equal. The magnitude of the phase voltage is equal to

$$V_\phi = V_l \div \sqrt{3}$$
$$= 480 \div \sqrt{3} = 277 \text{ V}$$

The magnitude of the line and phase current is

$$I_l = I_\phi = \frac{S_\phi}{V_\phi}$$
$$= \frac{167{,}000}{277}$$
$$= 602.9 \text{ A}$$

2-4 Induction Motors

Polyphase and single-phase induction motors are used extensively in residential, commercial, and industrial establishments. An understanding of the starting and running characteristics of these motors is essential in the design and operation of electrical power systems.

Three-Phase Induction Motors

The three-phase induction motor is the predominant source of mechanical power in many commercial and industrial establishments. Typical voltage ratings are 200, 220, and 460 V in the lower voltage class to 13.2 kV in the medium voltage class. The horsepower ratings for three-phase induction motors range from fractional horsepower to several thousand horsepower.

All three-phase induction motors may be treated as balanced three-phase devices for the purposes of analysis. It is therefore necessary to analyze only one phase of the motor and realize that the other two phases will be identical. The per phase equivalent circuit of the polyphase induction motor is shown in Fig. 2-3a. Note the similarities to the single phase transformer equivalent circuit.

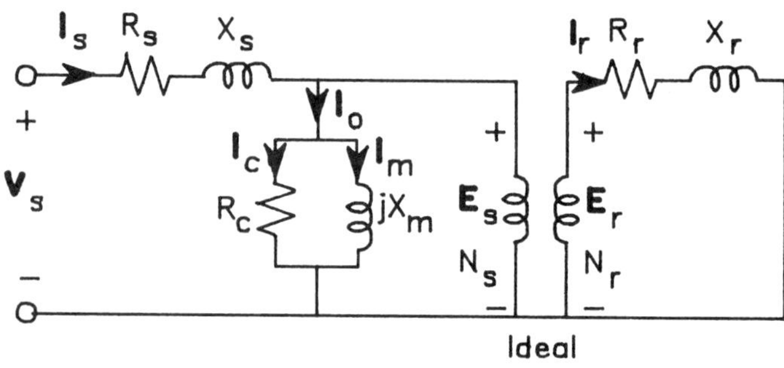

(a) Original Equivalent Circuit.

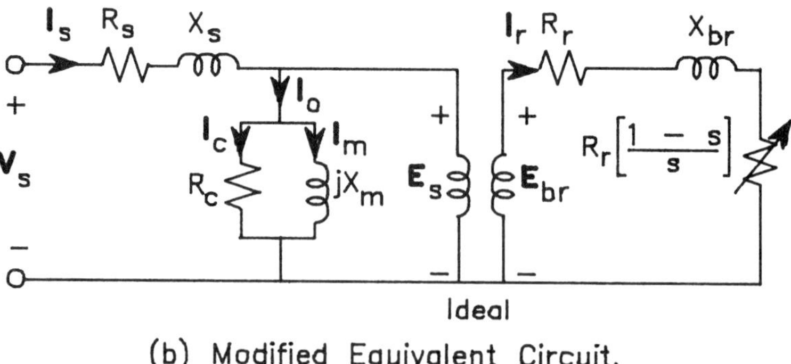

(b) Modified Equivalent Circuit.

Figure 2-3 Per phase equivalent circuit of three-phase induction motor.

When a balanced set of three-phase voltages is applied to the stator of the three-phase induction motor, a rotating flux is produced. This flux rotates at a speed equal to the synchronous speed of the motor:

$$n_s = \frac{120f}{P} \tag{2.10}$$

where

f = source frequency

P = number of poles

The synchronous speed of the motor is constant as long as the applied frequency remains constant and the number of poles is not changed. A countervoltage $\mathbf{E}_s$ is also induced in the stator as a result of the flux produced.

The stator conductor resistance and reactance are designated R_s and X_s respectively. The core loss and magnetizing components of current are modeled by the core loss resistance R_c and magnetizing reactance X_m in much the same fashion as the transformer.

As the motor rotates, the rotating flux cuts the rotor conductors and induces a voltage, $\mathbf{E}_r$, in the rotor circuit. The frequency of the induced rotor voltage is designated f_r. The rotor resistance and inductance are designated R_r and L_r, respectively. The rotor reactance is given by

$$X_r = 2\pi f_r L_r \tag{2.11}$$

Equation (2.11) shows that the rotor reactance is directly proportional to the rotor frequency.

As a result of the voltage induced in the rotor conductors, rotor currents will flow. These rotor currents produce a flux that interacts with the stator flux to produce rotation. For a voltage to be induced in the rotor circuit, there must be relative motion between the stator flux and the rotor. This relative motion is referred to as the *slip* of the motor and is usually expressed as a percentage of the synchronous speed, as follows:

$$s = \frac{n_s - n_r}{n_s} \cdot 100 \tag{2.12}$$

where n_r is the actual speed of the rotor. The slip will have a value of 100% or 1.0 at standstill and 0% at sychronous speed. Most squirrel-cage induction motors will operate with a full load slip of between 3% and 5%.

The magnitude and frequency of the voltage induced in the rotor are also functions of slip. As the rotor accelerates, the magnitude of both the induced rotor voltage $\mathbf{E}_r$ and rotor frequency f_r will decrease. Corresponding to the decrease in rotor frequency will be a decrease in the rotor reactance.

At standstill or blocked rotor conditions, the rotor voltage, rotor frequency, and rotor reactance are designated E_{br}, f_{br}, and X_{br}, respectively. These blocked rotor parameters are constant for a given machine. The blocked rotor frequency will be equal to the supply frequency. Due to the stator to rotor turns ratio, the magnitude of the blocked rotor voltage will be

$$E_{br} = E_s \frac{N_r}{N_s} \tag{2.13}$$

It can be shown that the induced rotor voltage, frequency, and reactance at any speed are related to the corresponding blocked rotor values and slip by the following relationships:

$$E_r = sE_{br} \tag{2.14}$$

$$f_r = sf_{br} \tag{2.15}$$

$$X_r = sX_{br} \tag{2.16}$$

A simplified rotor equivalent circuit can be determined by applying Ohm's law to the rotor circuit of Fig. 2-3a. The equation for the rotor current in terms of the rotor voltage and impedance is

$$\mathbf{I}_r = \frac{\mathbf{E}_r}{R_r + jX_r} \tag{2.17}$$

Dividing numerator and denominator by s and applying Eqs. (2.14) and (2.16) results in

$$\begin{aligned} \mathbf{I}_r &= \frac{\mathbf{E}_r/s}{(R_r/s) + (jX_r/s)} \\ &= \frac{\mathbf{E}_{br}}{(R_r/s) + (jX_{br})} \end{aligned} \tag{2.18}$$

The term R_r/s in Eq. (2.18) is often separated into two components, as follows:

$$\frac{R_r}{s} = R_r + R_r\left(\frac{1-s}{s}\right) \tag{2.19}$$

The equivalent rotor circuit is now modified to reflect the results of Eqs. (2.18) and (2.19). This modifed equivalent circuit is shown in Fig. 2-3b.

The term R_r in the equivalent circuit of Fig. 2-3b represents the actual resistance of the rotor conductors. The term $R_r(1 - s)/s$ models electrically the mechanical load on the motor. Under starting conditions, the slip is equal to 1.0, and the total rotor resistance is equal to R_r. Recall that under normal operating conditions the slip is in the range of 3% to 5% for most squirrel-cage motors. For a given slip, the total rotor resistance is calculated using Eq. (2.19).

To simplify the analysis of the induction motor under various load conditions, the rotor impedances are reflected from the rotor to stator in a manner similar to reflecting impedances from one side of a transformer to another. The rotor resistance and reactance are reflected from the rotor to the stator using the following relationships:

$$R'_r = \left(\frac{N_s}{N_r}\right)^2 \frac{R_r}{s} \qquad \textbf{(2.20)}$$

$$X'_r = \left(\frac{N_s}{N_r}\right)^2 X_{br} \qquad \textbf{(2.21)}$$

With all impedances referred to the stator, the equivalent circuit can be reduced to a simple series circuit. The stator current can then be calculated for the specified conditions. An example will illustrate the procedure.

EXAMPLE 2-3

A 50-hp, 60-Hz, 460-V, 1728-rpm, four-pole, three-phase, squirrel-cage induction motor has the following equivalent circuit parameters:

$X_s = 0.30\ \Omega \qquad R_r = 0.015\ \Omega$

$R_s = 0.06\ \Omega \qquad X_{br} = 0.07\ \Omega$

$R_c = 60.0\ \Omega \qquad \dfrac{N_s}{N_r} = 2:1$

$X_m = 4.5\ \Omega$

Calculate the following:

a. Stator current, apparent power, and power factor at starting
b. Stator current and power factor under normal running conditions

Solution

a. At start, the per unit slip is 1.0. The rotor resistance referred to the stator is

$$R'_r = (2)^2 \frac{0.015}{1.0} = 0.06\ \Omega$$

The rotor reactance referred to the stator is

$$X'_r = (2)^2\ (0.07) = 0.28\ \Omega$$

The equivalent circuit with all parameters referred to the stator is shown in Fig. 2-4a.

The rotor impedance referred to the stator is

$$\mathbf{Z}'_r = 0.06 + j0.28 = 0.2864\angle 77.9°\ \Omega$$

The parallel impedance of the excitation branch is

$$\mathbf{Z}_0 = 60 \parallel j4.5 = \frac{60(j4.5)}{60 + j4.5}$$
$$= 4.49\angle 85.7° = 0.3367 + j4.48\ \Omega$$

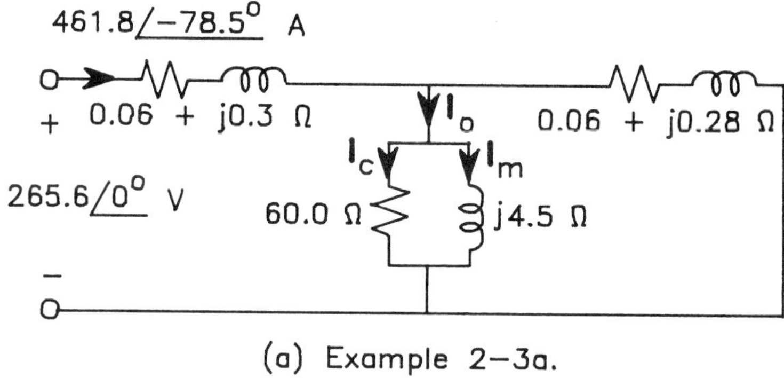

(a) Example 2–3a.

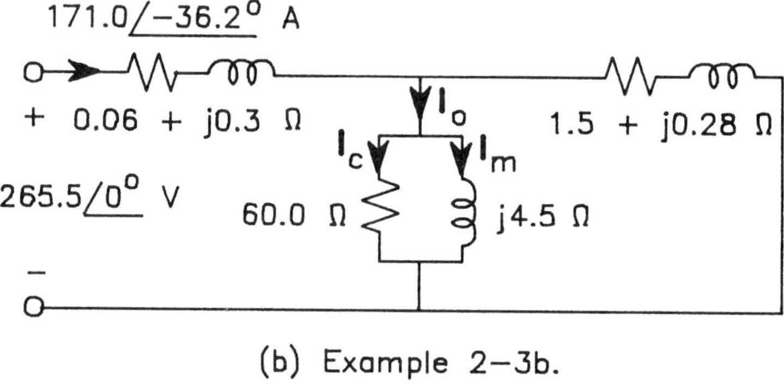

(b) Example 2–3b.

Figure 2-4 Equivalent circuits for Example 2-3.

The impedance of the motor looking into the stator terminals is

$$\begin{aligned}\mathbf{Z}_{\text{in}} &= 0.06 + j0.3 + \mathbf{Z}_r' \parallel \mathbf{Z}_0 \\ &= 0.06 + j0.3 + \frac{(0.2864\angle 77.9°)(4.49\angle 85.7°)}{0.06 + j0.28 + 0.3367 + j4.48} \\ &= 0.5752\angle 78.5°\ \Omega\end{aligned}$$

The stator current is equal to the applied voltage per phase divided by the equivalent impedance looking into the stator terminals:

$$\mathbf{I}_s = \frac{\left(460 \div \sqrt{3}\right)\angle 0°}{0.5752\angle 78.5°} = 461.8\angle -78.5°\ \text{A}$$

The apparent power for all three phases is

$$S_{\text{in}} = \sqrt{3}(460)(461.8) = 367.9\ \text{kVA}$$

The kVA per horsepower during starting is

$$\frac{\text{kVA}}{\text{hp}} = \frac{367.9}{50} = 7.358$$

The power factor at starting is

$$\text{PF} = \cos(78.5°) = 0.2 \text{ lagging}$$

b. At full load the per unit slip is equal to

$$s = \frac{1800 - 1728}{1800} = 0.04$$

The rotor resistance referred to the stator is

$$R_r' = (2)^2 \frac{0.015}{0.04} = 1.5\ \Omega$$

The rotor reactance referred to the stator remains as in part a. The equivalent circuit with all parameters referred to the stator is shown in Fig. 2-4b. The rotor impedance referred to the stator is

$$\mathbf{Z}_r' = 1.5 + j0.28 = 1.526\angle 10.6°\ \Omega$$

The parallel impedance of the excitation branch remains the same as in part a. The impedance of the motor looking into the stator terminals is

$$\begin{aligned}\mathbf{Z}_{\text{in}} &= 0.06 + j0.3 + \mathbf{Z}_r' \parallel \mathbf{Z}_0\\ &= 0.06 + j0.3 + \frac{(1.526\angle 10.6°)(4.49\angle 85.7°)}{1.5 + j0.28 + 0.3367 + j4.48}\\ &= 1.5528\angle 36.2°\ \Omega\end{aligned}$$

The full-load stator current is

$$\mathbf{I}_s = \frac{\left(460 \div \sqrt{3}\right)\angle 0°}{1.5528\angle 36.2°} = 171.0\angle -36.2°\ \text{A}$$

The apparent power for all three phases is

$$S_{\text{in}} = \sqrt{3}(460)(171.0) = 136.2\ \text{kVA}$$

The power factor is

$$\text{PF} = \cos(36.2°) = 0.81 \text{ lagging}$$

Several observations can be made from Example 2-4 with regard to induction motor behavior.

1. The starting and running power factors are both lagging.
2. The starting power factor is less than the running power factor.
3. The motor can be represented during starting and running as a simple series *RL* circuit.
4. It is possible to calculate the kVA/hp under starting conditions.

Table 2-1 Locked Rotor kVA/hp

Code Letter	*kVA/hp*	*Code Letter*	*kVA/hp*
A	0.0–3.15	L	9.0–10.0
B	3.15–3.55	M	10.0–11.2
C	3.55–4.0	N	11.2–12.5
D	4.0–4.5	P	12.5–14.0
E	4.5–5.0	R	14.0–16.0
F	5.0–5.6	S	16.0–18.0
G	5.6–6.3	T	18.0–20.0
H	6.3–7.1	U	20.0–22.4
J	7.1–8.0	V	22.4 and up
K	8.0–9.0		

Values for kVA/hp during starting are determined by referring to the code letter of the motor. The inrush kVA of the motor is determined by multiplying the motor horsepower by the kVA/hp value pertaining to the particular code letter. Table 2-1 shows the locked rotor kVA/hp values for the different code letters.

EXAMPLE 2-4 A 100-hp, 60-Hz, 460-V, 1728-rpm, four-pole, code letter G, squirrel-cage induction motor is operating at rated conditions. The motor efficiency is 90%, and the power factor is 0.85 lagging. Calculate the following:

a. Power output in watts at full load
b. Active power input at full load
c. Apparent power input at full load
d. Input line current magnitude at full load
e. Synchronous speed and slip at full load
f. Inrush current during starting at rated voltage

Solution

a. $P_{out} = 100 \text{ hp} \cdot 746 \text{ W/hp} = 74{,}600 \text{ W}$

b. $P_{in} = \dfrac{P_{out}}{\text{efficiency}} = \dfrac{74{,}600}{0.90} = 82{,}889 \text{ W}$

c. $S_{in} = \dfrac{P_{in}}{\text{PF}} = \dfrac{82{,}889}{0.85} = 97{,}516 \text{ VA}$

d. $I_l = \dfrac{97{,}516}{\sqrt{3} \cdot 460} = 122.4 \text{ A}$

e. $n_s = \dfrac{120 \cdot 60}{4} = 1800 \text{ rpm}$

$$s = \frac{1800 - 1728}{1800} \cdot 100\%$$
$$= 4.0\%$$

f. For code letter G, the inrush kVA/hp varies between 5.6 and 6.3. A value of 6.3 will be used for worst-case conditions. The inrush kVA is

$$\text{Inrush kVA} = (\text{kVA/hp})(100 \text{ hp})$$
$$= 6.3 \cdot 100 = 630 \text{ kVA}$$

The inrush current with rated voltage applied is

$$I_s = \frac{630{,}000}{\sqrt{3} \cdot 460} = 790.7 \text{ A}$$

Single-Phase Induction Motors

The single-phase induction motor is used to a large extent in residential and small commercial applications where three-phase service is not available. The most commom voltage ratings for single-phase motors are 115 and 230 V. Typical horsepower ratings range from fractional horsepower to approximately 10 hp. Mechanical power requirements that exceed 10 hp are usually supplied by three-phase induction motors.

Most single-phase induction motors are equipped with an auxiliary or starting winding in addition to the main or run winding. A phase splitting circuit is used to produce a phase displacement between the currents in the start and run windings. The interaction of the fluxes produced by the start and run winding currents produces a rotating magnetic field similar to that produced in the three-phase induction motor. This rotating flux cuts the rotor conductors and induces a voltage in the rotor circuit. These rotor currents produce a flux that interacts with the stator flux and causes rotation. Once the rotor is rotating, the start winding may be switched out of the circuit by use of a centrifugal switch or other means. Rotation will continue because there is relative motion between the rotating stator flux and the rotor conductors. The synchronous speed and slip of the single-phase induction motor are given by Eqs. (2.10) and (2.12).

Single-phase induction motors use a variety of methods to produce the required phase displacement between the start and run winding currents. The different types of single-phase motors available include permanent split capacitor, split phase start–induction run, capacitor start–induction run, and capacitor start–capacitor run. Equivalent circuits for single-phase motors employing separate start and run windings are shown in Fig. 2-5. The choice of starting and running method depends on specific load torque and speed requirements.

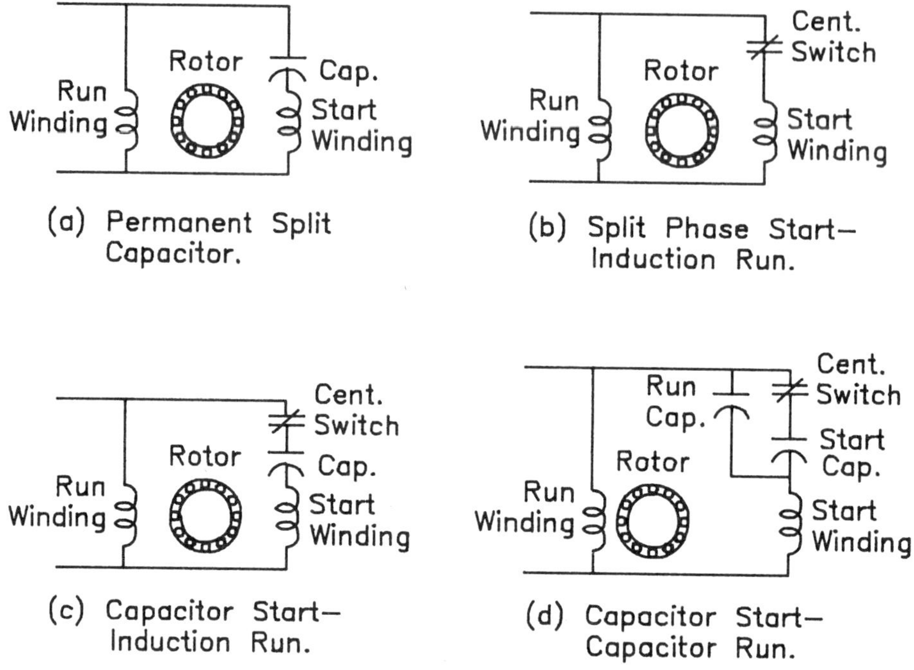

Figure 2-5 Single-phase induction motors.

The shaded pole motor is also used in low starting torque applications. A cross-sectional view of shaded pole motor construction is shown in Fig. 2-6. Shaded pole motors use a shading coil placed around a portion of the main field pole. The shading coil produces a sweeping of flux from the unshaded to the shaded portions of the main field poles. This flux cuts the rotor conductors and causes rotation of the rotor.

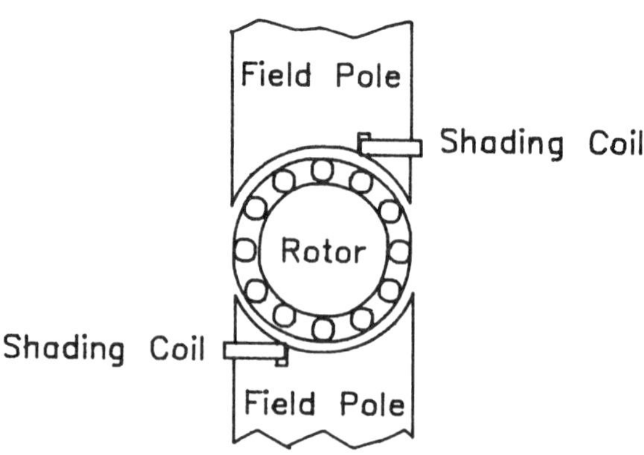

Figure 2-6 Shaded pole motor.

EXAMPLE 2-5

A 3/4-hp, 230-V, 1725-rpm, 60-Hz, four-pole, capacitor start motor draws a line current of 5.8 A and has a power factor of 0.83 lagging when operating at full load. Calculate the following:

a. Apparent power input
b. Active or real power input
c. Reactive power input
d. Real power output
e. Overall efficiency

Solution

a. $S_{in} = V \cdot I = 230 \text{ V} \cdot 5.8 \text{ A} = 1334 \text{ VA}$
b. $P_{in} = \text{PF} \cdot S_{in} = 0.83 \cdot 1334 = 1107.2 \text{ W}$
c. $Q_{in} = (S_{in}^2 - P_{in}^2)^{1/2} = (1334^2 - 1107.2^2)^{1/2} = 744.1 \text{ VAR}$
d. $P_{out} = \text{hp} \cdot 746 = 3/4 \cdot 746 = 559.5 \text{ W}$
e. $\text{Efficiency} = \dfrac{P_{out}}{P_{in}} \cdot 100\% = \dfrac{559.5}{1107.2} \cdot 100\% = 50.53\%$

2-5 Polyphase Synchronous Motors

Polyphase synchronous motors are used primarily for constant-speed, high-power requirements. The stator of the polyphase synchronous motor is constructed similarly to the polyphase induction motor. As in the case of the induction motor, a three-phase voltage is applied to the stator to produce a rotating flux. The rotor of a polyphase synchronous motor employs a dc field winding to produce distinct north and south field poles on the rotor. Once the motor is started, it is synchronized to the line, thereby locking in the north and south poles of the rotating stator flux to the south and north poles of the rotor field. Once synchronized, the motor will run at a constant speed equal to the synchronous speed of the motor. The synchronous speed of the motor is given by Eq. (2.10).

The per phase equivalent circuit of the polyphase synchronous motor is shown in Fig. 2-7. The stator winding resistance and synchronous reactance are designated R_s and X_s respectively. The countervoltage produced in the motor is designated $\mathbf{E}_f$. The magnitude of the countervoltage is controlled primarily by varying the dc field excitation voltage V_F. By adjusting the magnitude of the field excitation voltage, the operating power factor of the synchronous motor may also be controlled. The sychronous motor is typically operated at a power factor between unity and 0.8 leading. The synchronous motor can be used to improve overall system power factor as well as to provide voltage support.

Typically, the terminal voltage is selected as the phase reference at an angle of 0°. The phase angle of the countervoltage is then expressed in reference to the terminal voltage. The phase angle of the countervoltage is referred to as the *torque angle* of the

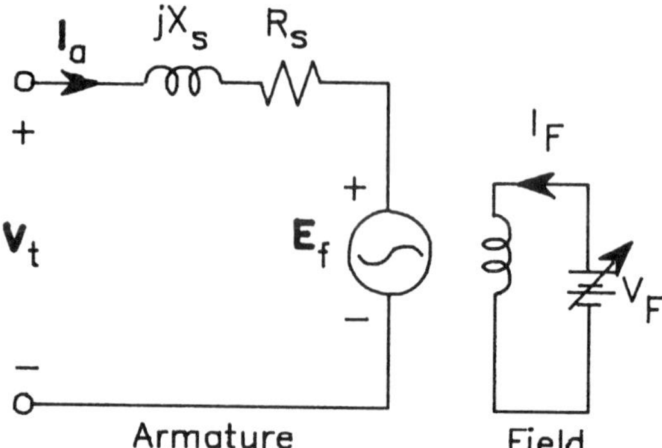

Figure 2-7 Synchronous motor per phase equivalent circuit.

motor. The torque angle is an indication of the mechanical loading on the motor. The torque angle will increase as the load is increased, and vice versa.

Smaller single-phase synchronous reluctance and hysteresis motors are used for constant-speed applications requiring lower starting and running torque. Typical applications include tape players, VCRs, and clocks.

EXAMPLE 2-6

A 2000-hp, 900-rpm, 4-kV, three-phase, 60-Hz, wye-connected, synchronous motor draws an armature current of 300 A and operates at 0.8 leading power factor with rated load applied. The stator winding resistance is 1.0 Ω per phase, and the synchronous reactance is 5.0 Ω per phase. Calculate the countervoltage $\mathbf{E}_f$.

Solution The reference voltage will be selected as

$$\mathbf{V}_t = \frac{4000}{\sqrt{3}} \angle 0° = 2309.5\angle 0° \text{ V}$$

The magnitude of the armature current was given as 300 A. The phase angle of the armature current with respect to the selected reference voltage is

$$\theta = \cos^{-1}(0.8) = 36.87°$$

Therefore, the armature current is

$$\mathbf{I}_a = 300\angle 36.87° \text{ A}$$

The countervoltage can be determined by applying KVL to the circuit of Fig. 2-7 as follows:

$$\begin{aligned}\mathbf{E}_f &= \mathbf{V}_t - \mathbf{I}_a(R_s + jX_s)\\ &= 2309.5\angle 0° - (300\angle 36.87°)(1 + j5)\\ &= 2309.5\angle 0° - 1529.7\angle 115.6°\\ &= 2969.5 - j1380 = 3274.5\angle -24.9° \text{ V}\end{aligned}$$

The torque angle is 24.9° at this load condition.

EXAMPLE 2-7

For the motor in Example 2-6, assume that the dc field is adjusted such that the magnitude of the countervoltage and applied voltage are equal. Assume that the torque angle at this new operating condition is 36.7°. Calculate the following:

a. Armature current
b. Apparent, active, and reactive power input
c. Power factor

Solution

a. The countervoltage is now equal to

$$\mathbf{E}_f = 2309.5\angle{-36.7^\circ}\ \text{V}$$

The armature current can be calculated by applying KVL to the circuit shown in Fig. 2-7 and solving for $\mathbf{I}_a$. The result is

$$\begin{aligned}\mathbf{I}_a &= \frac{\mathbf{V}_t - \mathbf{E}_f}{R_s + jX_s}\\ &= \frac{2309.5\angle 0^\circ - 2309.5\angle{-36.7^\circ}}{1 + j5}\\ &= \frac{457.8 + j1380.2}{1 + j5}\\ &= 285.2\angle{-7.0^\circ}\ \text{A}\end{aligned}$$

b. The total three-phase apparent power input is

$$\begin{aligned}S_{\text{in}} &= 3V_t I_a^* = 3(2309.5\angle 0^\circ)(285.2\angle 7.0^\circ)\\ &= 1{,}976{,}008.2\angle 7.0^\circ\ \text{VA}\\ &= 1976\angle 7.0^\circ\ \text{kVA}\end{aligned}$$

The active power input is

$$P_{\text{in}} = 1976\cos(7.0^\circ) = 1961.3\ \text{kW}$$

The reactive power input is

$$Q_{\text{in}} = 1976\sin(7.0^\circ) = 240.8\ \text{kVAR}$$

c. The power factor is

$$\text{PF} = \cos(7.0^\circ) = 0.9925\ \text{lagging}$$

Notice that the power factor changed from 0.8 leading in Example 2-6 to 0.9925 lagging in this example by decreasing the dc field excitation.

2-6 Polyphase Synchronous Generators

The polyphase synchronous generator is the primary source of generation in electric utility systems. The construction of the polyphase synchronous generator is similar to the polyphase synchronous motor. The per phase equivalent circuit of the polyphase synchronous generator is shown in Fig. 2-8a. Note the similarities of this equivalent circuit to the synchronous motor equivalent circuit.

The frequency of the generated voltage is determined by solving Eq. (2.10) for f:

$$f = \frac{P \cdot n}{120} \tag{2.22}$$

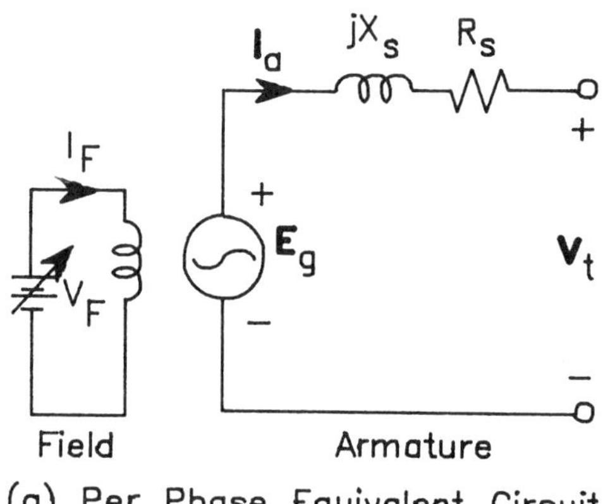

(a) Per Phase Equivalent Circuit.

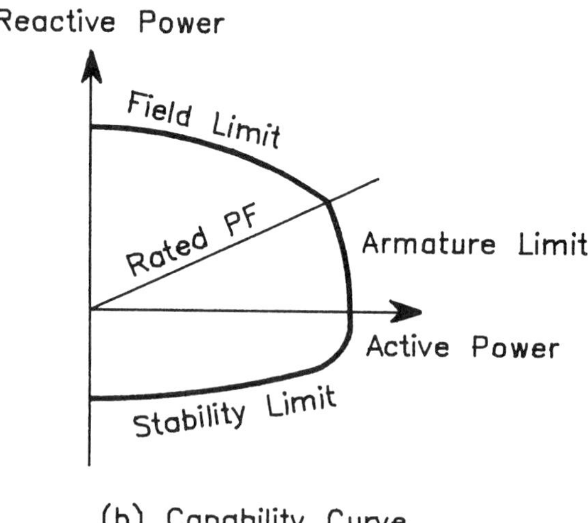

(b) Capability Curve.

Figure 2-8 Synchronous generator.

If the frequency is to be constant, the speed of the generator must also be constant. To generate 60-Hz voltage, a two-pole machine must rotate at 3600 rpm, a four-pole machine at 1800 rpm, and so on. Automatic generation control regulates the speed and output power of the generators in the system to ensure that a constant system frequency is maintained.

Effect of DC Field Excitation

The magnitude of the generated voltage $\mathbf{E}_g$ is controlled by regulating the dc field excitation. As the magnitude of the dc field excitation is increased, the terminal voltage and reactive power output of the generator will increase. A limit on the reactive output power capability of the generator is reached when the dc field current is at its maximum permissible value. When the generator is supplying reactive power to the system, the generator is operating at a lagging power factor. If the magnitude of the generated voltage exceeds the terminal voltage, the generator is operating in the overexcited mode.

As the dc field excitation is decreased, the magnitude of the generated voltage will decrease until it equals the magnitude of the terminal voltage. Under these conditions, the generator is said to be operating at normal excitation and approximately unity power factor.

If the dc field excitation is decreased further, the generator will begin to absorb reactive power from the system. The generator will be operating at a leading power factor under these conditions. At this point, the magnitude of the generated voltage is less than the terminal voltage, and the generator is operating in the underexcited mode. The ability of the generator to maintain synchronism under these conditions is weakened. Also, overheating of the rotor may occur when operating at a leading power factor.

Effect of Mechanical Power Input

To increase the active power output of the generator, the mechanical power input to the generator must be increased. As the mechanical input power is increased, the generator will momentarily accelerate. This acceleration causes an increase in the phase angle between the generated and terminal voltages. The angle between the generated and terminal voltages is referred to as the *power angle* of the generator. Note that the power angle of the generator is analogous to the torque angle of the synchronous motor. If the terminal voltage is selected as the phase reference, the power angle is equal to the angle of the generated voltage $\mathbf{E}_g$ in the per phase equivalent circuit model.

In large generators, the stator resistance is much smaller than the synchronous reactance. Therefore, the resistance is usually neglected when calculating the active power output of the generator. In reference to Fig. 2-8a, it can be shown that the active power output of the generator is given by

$$P_{\text{out}} = \frac{E_g V_t}{X_s} \sin \delta \tag{2.23}$$

where δ is the power angle of the generator.

Generator Capability Curve

The operating limits of a synchronous generator are presented in graphic form on the generator capability curve. A representive capability curve is shown in Fig. 2-8b. The armature limit curve is indicative of the maximum armature current permitted due to thermal limitations of the armature conductors. For a given voltage and maximum armature current, the armature limit curve represents the maximum apparent power output capability of the generator.

The field limit curve indicates the capability of the generator when the field current is at maximum permissible value due to thermal limitations of the field windings. The stability limit curve indicates the maximum reactive power absorption capabilities of the generator when operating at a leading power factor. Decreases in field excitation may cause operation in the unstable region and must be avoided.

EXAMPLE 2-8

A three-phase wye-connected synchronous generator in a power plant has the following ratings: 1075 MVA, 18 kV, 0.85 power factor. The synchronous reactance is 0.3 Ω per phase, and the resistance is negligble. The generator is operating at 0.9 lagging power factor and supplies 700 MW at rated voltage. Calculate the following:

a. Rated current

b. Generated voltage at the specified load conditions

Solution

a. The rated armature current is

$$I_a = \frac{1{,}075{,}000{,}000}{\sqrt{3} \cdot 18{,}000} = 34{,}482 \text{ A}$$

b. The apparent power output for the specified load conditions is

$$S_{\text{out}} = \frac{P_{\text{out}}}{\text{PF}} = \frac{700{,}000{,}000}{0.9} = 777.8 \text{ MVA}$$

The line current magnitude for the specified load conditions is

$$I_a = \frac{777.8 \times 10^6}{\sqrt{3} \cdot 18{,}000} = 24{,}948 \text{ A}$$

The reference voltage is selected as

$$\mathbf{V}_t = \left(18{,}000 \div \sqrt{3}\right)\angle 0° = 10{,}393\angle 0° \text{ V}$$

At 0.9 lagging power factor, the phase a line current lags the phase a reference voltage by 25.84°. Therefore, the line current is

$$\mathbf{I}_a = 24{,}948\angle -25.84° \text{ A}$$

From the equivalent circuit shown in Fig. 2-8a, the generated voltage is

$$\begin{aligned}
\mathbf{E}_g &= \mathbf{V}_t + \mathbf{I}_a(R_s + jX_s) \\
&= 10{,}393\angle 0° + (24{,}948\angle -25.84°)(0 + j0.3) \\
&= 10{,}393\angle 0° + 7484.4\angle 64.2° \\
&= 13{,}655.1 + j6736.1 \\
&= 15{,}226.2\angle 26.3° \text{ V}
\end{aligned}$$

The power angle is 26.3°. Note that the power angle is positive, indicating that the generated voltage leads the terminal voltage. In the synchronous motor, the torque angle was negative indicating that the countervoltage lagged the terminal voltage.

Problems

2.1. A 25-kVA, 7200–240-V, single-phase transformer has the following equivalent circuit parameters:

$$R_p = 12.5\ \Omega \qquad R_s = 0.014\ \Omega \qquad R_c = 173\ \text{k}\Omega$$

$$X_{lp} = 16.0\ \Omega \qquad X_{ls} = 0.018\ \Omega \qquad X_m = 135\ \text{k}\Omega$$

The transformer is supplying rated load at 0.95 lagging power factor and 240 V. Calculate the following:

a. Turns ratio
b. Secondary current
c. Induced secondary voltage
d. Induced primary voltage
e. Excitation current
f. Load component of primary current
g. Primary current
h. Applied primary voltage
i. Equivalent circuit with all parameters referred to the low-voltage side
j. Equivalent circuit with all parameters referred to the high-voltage side

2.2. Calculate the rated high-side and low-side currents for the following single-phase transformers:

a. 10 kVA, 7200–240 V
b. 25 kVA, 2400–240 V
c. 167 kVA, 4800–277 V
d. 75 kVA, 19,920–240 V

2.3. Calculate the rated line and phase currents for both high and low sides for the following three-phase transformers:

a. 225 kVA, 34,500GrdY/19,920–480Y/277 V, wye–wye connected
b. 500 kVA, 4160–208Y/120 V, delta–wye connected
c. 750 kVA, 13,800–480 V, delta–delta connected

2.4. A 75-hp, 60-Hz, 460-V, 1785-rpm, four-pole, three-phase, squirrel-cage induction motor has the following equivalent circuit parameters:

$X_s = 0.22\ \Omega$ $\quad R_r = 0.012\ \Omega$

$R_s = 0.04\ \Omega$ $\quad X_{br} = 0.063\ \Omega$

$R_c = 50.0\ \Omega$ $\quad N_s/N_r = 2.4:1$

$X_m = 3.5\ \Omega$

Calculate the following:

a. Stator current, apparent power, and power factor at starting

b. Stator current and power factor under normal running conditions

2.5. A 150-hp, 460-V, 1790-rpm, 60-Hz, four-pole, three-phase, code letter H, premium efficiency motor has a full-load current rating of 166 A and a NEMA nominal efficiency of 95.8%. Calculate the following:

a. Active, apparent, and reactive power input

b. Power factor

c. Inrush kVA and inrush current during full-voltage starting

2.6. A 5-hp, 230-V, single-phase, two-pole, 60-Hz, code letter G, capacitor start motor has a full-load current rating of 21.5 A. The NEMA nominal efficiency is 85%. Calculate the following:

a. Active, apparent, and reactive power input

b. Power factor

c. Inrush kVA and inrush current during full-voltage starting

2.7. A 200-hp, 600-rpm, 460-V, three-phase, 60-Hz, synchronous motor draws an armature current of 255 A when operating at rated load and 0.8 leading power factor. The synchronous reactance is 0.7 Ω/phase and the stator winding resistance is 0.2 Ω/phase. Calculate the following:

a. Armature current in complex form

b. Countervoltage

c. Torque angle

2.8. The motor in Problem 2.7 is disconnected from the load. Assume that the magnitude of the countervoltage $\mathbf{E}_f$ remains constant and that the torque angle at no load is −5°. Calculate the armature current and power factor under these conditions.

2.9. A 300-MVA, 14-kV, two-pole, 60-Hz, wye-connected, three-phase synchronous generator is supplying rated load at 0.85 lagging power factor. The synchronous reactance is 0.75 Ω/phase, and the stator resistance is negligible. Calculate the armature current, generated voltage and power angle for the specified load conditions.

2.10. The generator of Problem 2.9 is now operating at rated load and 0.9 leading power factor. Calculate the armature current, generated voltage, and power angle for this load condition. Compare the results to Problem 2.9.

3

Introduction to Electric Utility Power Systems

3-1 General

This chapter provides a general overview of the design and operation of electrical utility power systems. The development and operation of the interconnected systems in the United States are discussed. Typical generating plant, transmission, distribution, and substation topologies are presented.

3-2 Operating Voltage Levels

The electric power network is operated at several different voltage levels. Figure 3-1 is a diagram of a simple power system showing typical voltage levels from generation to utilization.

Generation at utility power plants is typically at voltage levels ranging from 14 to 24 kV for large three-phase synchronous generators. The source of mechanical power to drive the generators is primarily from hydraulic (water power) or steam turbines. Gas combustion turbines are also used to provide additional generation during peak load conditions.

The output voltage of the generator is stepped up to transmission levels in the generating plant substation. Transmission voltage levels typically range from 138 to 765 kV. The bulk transmission network is used to transmit power between utilities and from the generating plants to the major load centers.

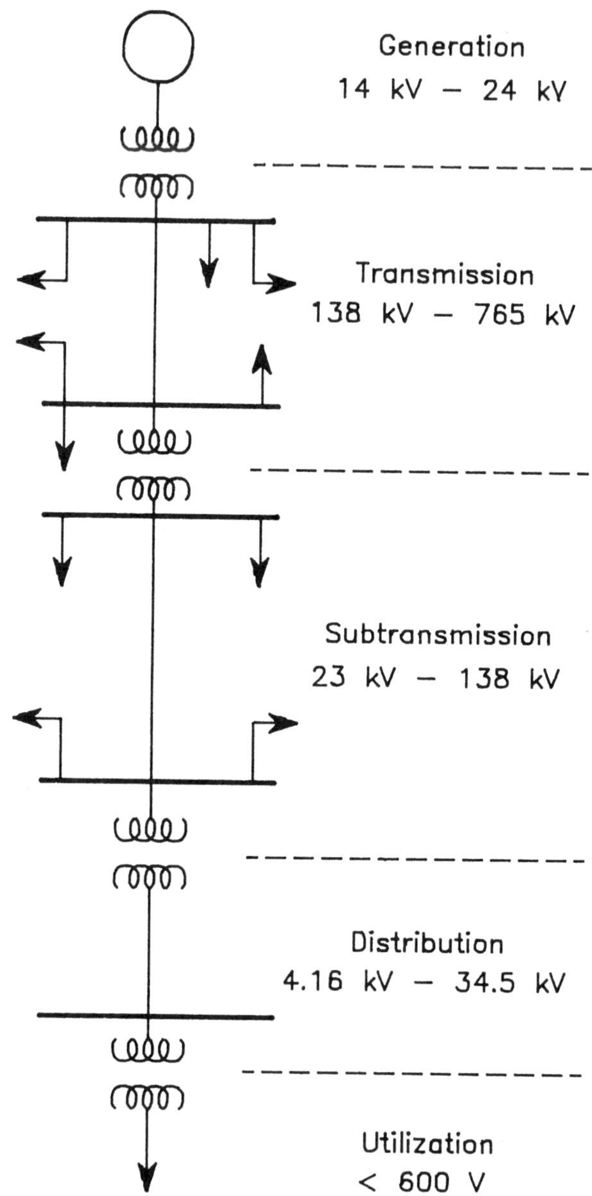

Figure 3-1 Operating voltage levels.

Table 3-1 Typical Power System Voltage Levels

Transmission	*Subtransmission*	*Distribution*	*Utilization*
765 kV	138 kV	34.5 kV 3Φ 4W	480 V 3Φ 4W
500 kV	115 kV	24.94 kV 3Φ 4W	208 V 3Φ 4W
345 kV	69 kV	22.86 kV 3Φ 4W	240 V 3Φ 4W
230 kV	23 kV	13.2 kV 3Φ 4W	600 V 3Φ 3W
		12.47 kV 3Φ 4W	480 V 3Φ 3W
		8.32 kV 3Φ 4W	240 V 3Φ 3W
		4.16 kV 3Φ 4W	120/240 V 1Φ 3W
		13.8 kV 3Φ 3W	
		4.16 kV 3Φ 3W	

The subtransmission network receives power from the bulk transmission network at various transmission substations. Typical voltage levels for the subtransmission network range from 23 to 138 kV. The subtransmission network is used to distribute power to the distribution substations throughout the system and to supply large industrial loads.

The distribution system is used to distribute power on a local level in urban and rural areas. Power is supplied to the distribution system at distribution substations. Typical voltage levels for distribution circuits are 4.16 to 34.5 kV. The most common distribution system voltage level is 12.47 kV line to line.

Utilization or secondary voltage is used to supply residential, commercial, and industrial systems. The utilization voltage for large commercial and industrial facilities may be at the medium voltage distribution levels previously discussed.

Some of the more common nominal voltage levels for electrical power systems are shown in Table 3-1. Generally, voltage levels exceeding 230 kV are classified as extra high voltage (EHV). Voltages between 100 and 230 kV are classified as high voltage (HV), and voltages between 1000 V and 100 kV are medium voltage (MV). Utilization voltages below 1000 V are generally classified as low-voltage (LV) systems.

3-3 Interconnected Systems

In the early days of the electric utility industry, many systems were operated as isolated systems. These systems were located primarily in the larger urban areas of the country. Generation was often at low voltage utilization or medium voltage distribution voltage levels. As these systems expanded, it became necessary to provide additional generation capacity to supply the additional load and to provide reliability in the event of an outage. Many of these isolated systems grew to include several generating plants and several miles of distribution circuits.

Eventually, power systems in neighboring areas were interconnected with one another for reasons of reliability and economics. For example, if the generation in one area was lost due to an outage, power could be transmitted from another system to supply the load. Also, as newer power generating plants were constructed, the cost of generation decreased. In some instances, it became more economical to purchase power from a neighboring system that used newer, more efficient generation than to generate within the system. Figure 3-2 shows an example of interconnected power systems.

The operation of interconnected utility systems is much more complicated than that of an isolated system. Some of the problems associated with transmitting large amounts of power over long distances include excessive line I^2R power losses, excessive voltage drop, and maintenance of synchronization between systems. Many of these problems were minimized by transmitting power at higher voltage levels. Also, as computer technology developed, control of large-scale interconnected systems became feasible. Economic generation dispatch, control of area power interchanges, and regulation of voltage levels on the bulk transmission system are controlled by an energy management system (EMS). The EMS uses real-time measurements of voltage, active and reactive power flows, generation, load, and current to determine system operating conditions. Discussion of these control functions is beyond the scope of this text.

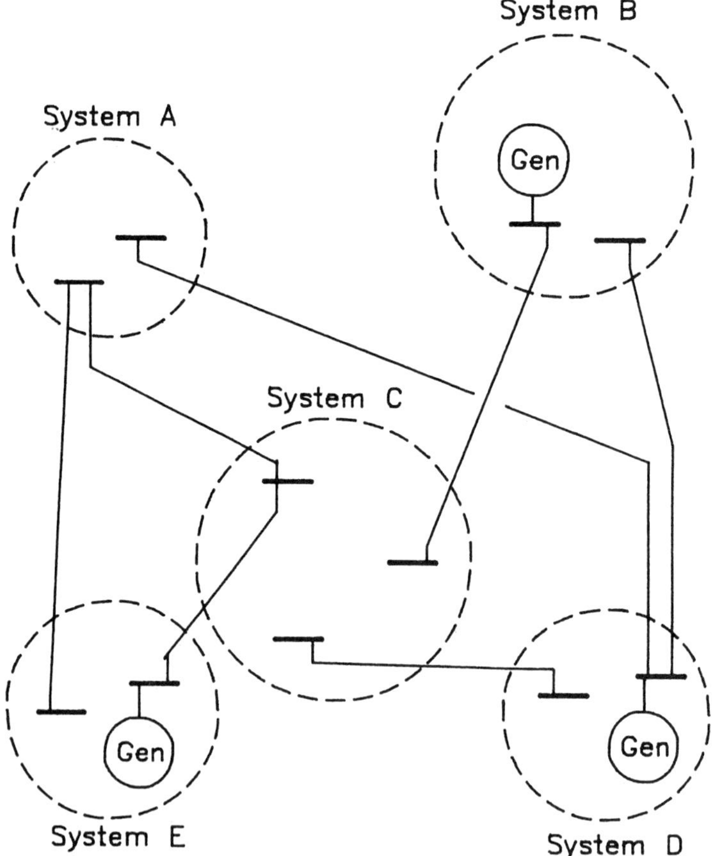

Figure 3-2 Interconnected power systems.

3-4 Three-Line, One-Line, and Impedance Diagrams

The three-line diagram is often used to represent each phase of a three-phase system. A representive three-line diagram for a circuit exit of a subtransmission substation is shown in Fig. 3-3. Major equipment, relaying, and conductor size for each phase of the three-phase system are shown on the three-line diagram.

The three-line diagram becomes rather cluttered for large substations and systems. A shorthand version of the three-line diagram is referred to as the one-line diagram. Similar to the three-line diagram, the one-line diagram shows all major equipment and relaying. A one-line diagram for the substation circuit exit of Fig. 3-3 is shown in Fig. 3-4.

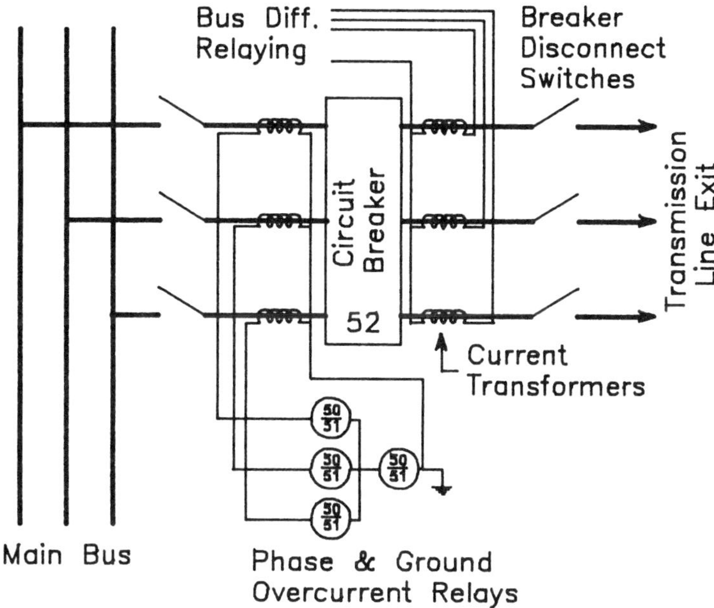

Figure 3-3 Three-line diagram.

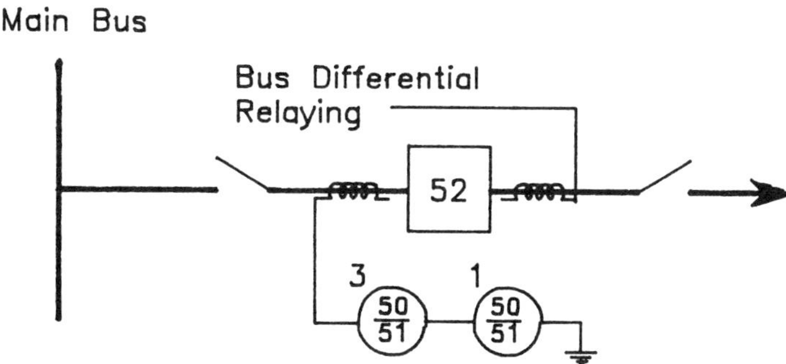

Figure 3-4 One-line diagram.

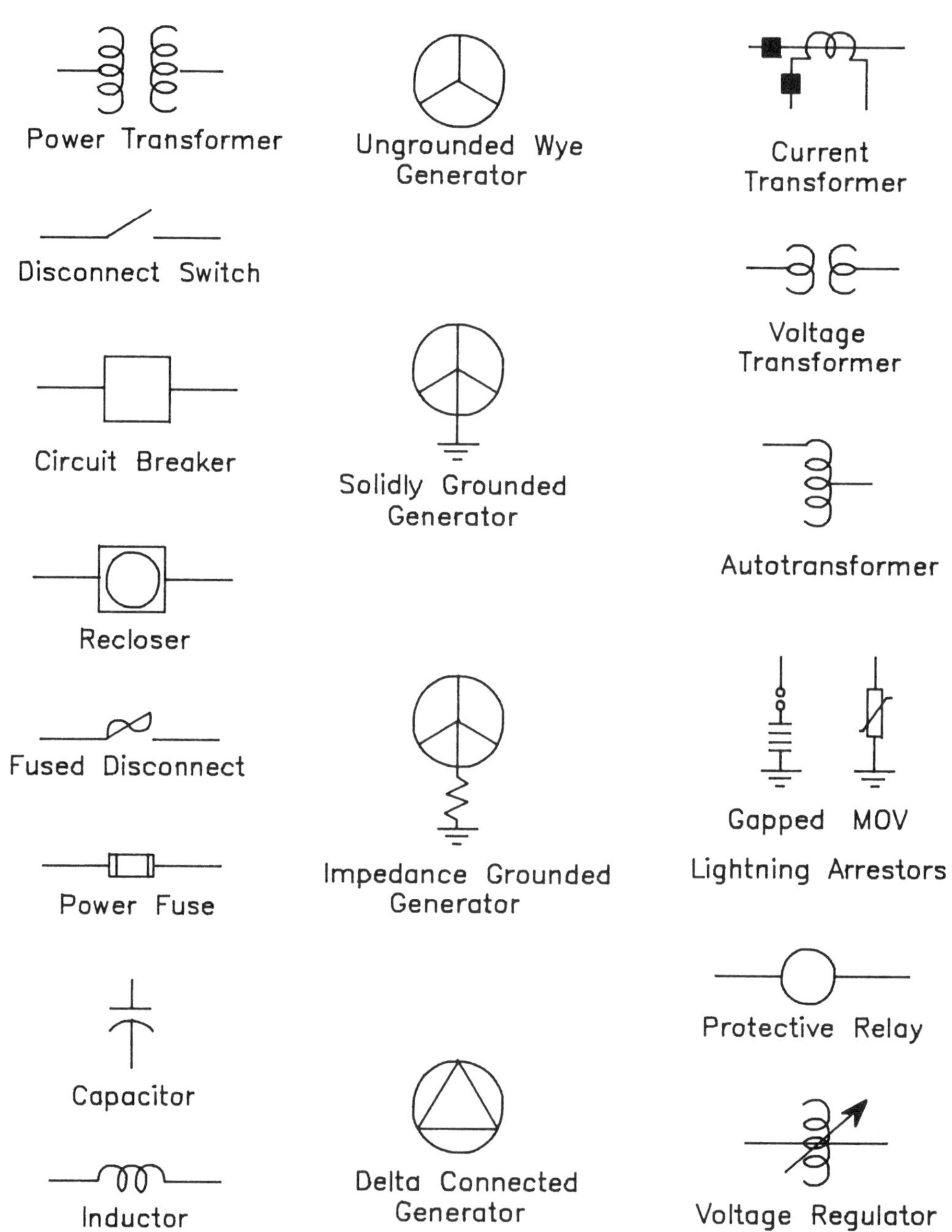

Figure 3-5 Common one-line diagram symbols.

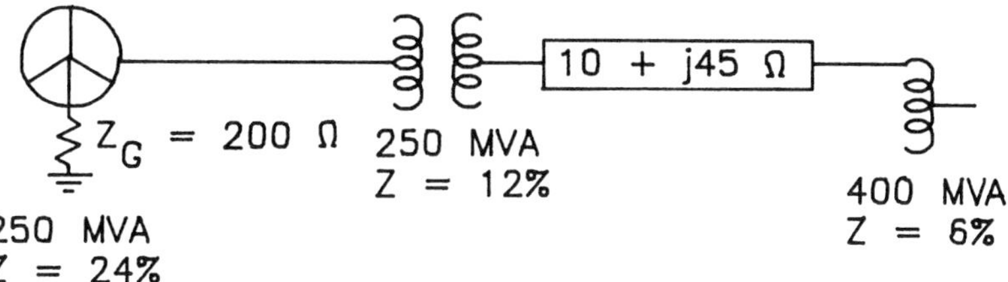

Figure 3-6 Impedance diagram.

The standard symbols used to represent various equipment will vary somewhat among different electric utility companies. Some of the standard symbols for one- and three-line diagrams are shown in Fig. 3-5.

The impedance diagram shown in Fig. 3-6 is used to record the impedance data of generators, lines, transformers, regulators, capacitors, cables, and the like. This impedance data are used for voltage-drop, short-circuit, load transfer, and circuit loading calculations. It is extremely important that these impedance data be kept up to date as system conditions are changed.

3-5 Generating Plant Layout

Generating plants represent the largest single portion of capital investment made by the electrical utility industry. Therefore, it is extremely important that provisions be made to ensure reliability and flexibility of operation to minimize outages and downtime. Although each generating plant has its own distinct electrical layout, a basic layout will be presented here. A one-line diagram for a typical generating plant is shown in Fig. 3-7.

In the majority of power plants, the generator windings are connected in a wye configuration. The neutral point of the wye-connected winding is usually connected to ground through an impedance. By grounding the neutral through an impedance, the short-circuit current for line to ground faults is minimized.

Typically, the stator of the generator is connected directly to the generator step-up transformer and auxiliary power transformers through isolated phase bus duct. Each phase of this bus duct consists of a single-phase conductor supported by insulators and surrounded by an enclosure. Since each phase is isolated from the other phases, the possibility of a short circuit involving two or more phases is minimized. The most probable short circuit that may occur is a line to ground fault between the bus conductor and the bus duct enclosure. Cooling air is typically forced through the enclosure to cool the bus conductor.

The main generator step-up transformer is either a single three-phase unit or three single-phase units connected in a three-phase configuration. The transformer is usually connected delta on the low-voltage side and solidly grounded wye on the high-voltage side. By connecting the low-voltage side of the generator step-up transformer in delta,

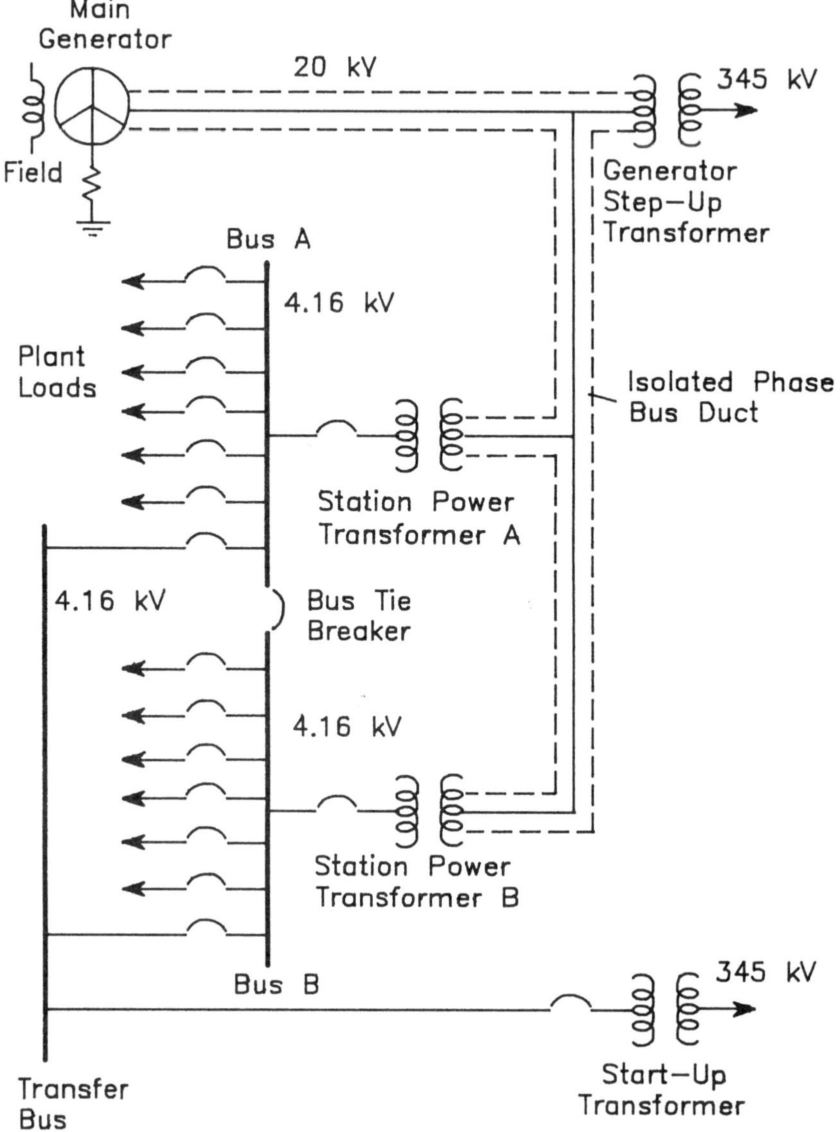

Figure 3-7 Typical generating plant one-line diagram.

the contribution of short-circuit current from the system in the event of a line to ground fault in the isolated phase bus duct will be zero. Also, the rated phase current of the low-voltage, delta-connected transformer winding will be less than that of a comparable wye-connected winding. (Recall that the phase current in a delta connection is equal to the line current divided by $\sqrt{3}$). Therefore, a smaller total cross-sectional area of coil conductor is required in the low-voltage delta connection as compared to the wye connection.

(However, the delta-connected winding will require $\sqrt{3}$ more turns as compared to a wye-connected winding of the same line to line voltage rating.)

The high-voltage winding is connected solidly grounded wye and connects to the high-voltage grounded wye transmission system through a set of power circuit breakers. The grounded wye-connected high-voltage winding is more economical to insulate than a delta-connected high-voltage winding having the same voltage rating. Thus, the delta grounded wye connection for the generator step-up transformer provides the most desirable electrical characteristics and may also be the most economical to construct.

The station power transformers are also connected directly to the stator terminals of the generator. These station power transformers may consist of a three-phase transformer, or three single-phase transformers connected in a three-phase bank. These transformers provide power to the auxiliary equipment, such as pumps, fans, and controls, required to operate the main generator. The windings of the station power transformers are usually connected delta on the high-voltage (generator) side and either delta or grounded wye on the low side. Typical low-voltage ratings are 4.16 and 13.8 kV. Notice in Fig. 3-7 that the low-voltage station power buses, *A* and *B*, are connected through transfer breakers to at least two different sources. This provides improved reliability in the event of a transformer failure. Note also that the station auxiliary power transformers are connected directly to the generator isolated phase bus duct.

The start-up, or cranking transformer as it is sometimes referred to, is used to provide power to the station auxiliary equipment during initial start-up of the main generator. The cranking transformer is usually grounded wye connected on the high- and low-voltage sides. The high-voltage side is connected to the transmission system, and the low-voltage side is connected to the station auxiliary buses.

During start-up, the high-voltage side of the main generator step-up transformer is disconnected from the transmission system. In addition, all station auxiliary power transformers are disconnected from the station auxiliary power buses. The generator is brought up to speed and synchronized with the system. Once synchronized, the generator breaker(s) on the high-voltage side of the generator step-up transformer are closed to connect the generator to the system. The station power auxiliary transformers are now connected to the station power buses, and the cranking transformer is disconnected. The active power output and terminal voltage of the generator are adjusted to the desired operating conditions.

3-6 Transmission System Layout

Bulk Transmission System

The bulk transmission system is used to transmit large amounts of power from the generating plants to major load centers and to facilitate interchange of power between utilities. Similarly to the generating plants, the bulk transmission system is designed for maximum reliability and flexibility of operation. Several transmission lines connect between transmission substations, generating plant locations, and neighboring utility systems. The system is designed such that a single line outage will not adversely affect overall system operation. A representive one-line diagram of a bulk power transmission system is shown in Fig. 3-8. Notice that generator *A* is connected to the 345-kV transmission system, while generator *B* is connected to the 138-kV portion of the system. Figure 3-9 shows a 345-kV transmission line used to transmit bulk power from re-

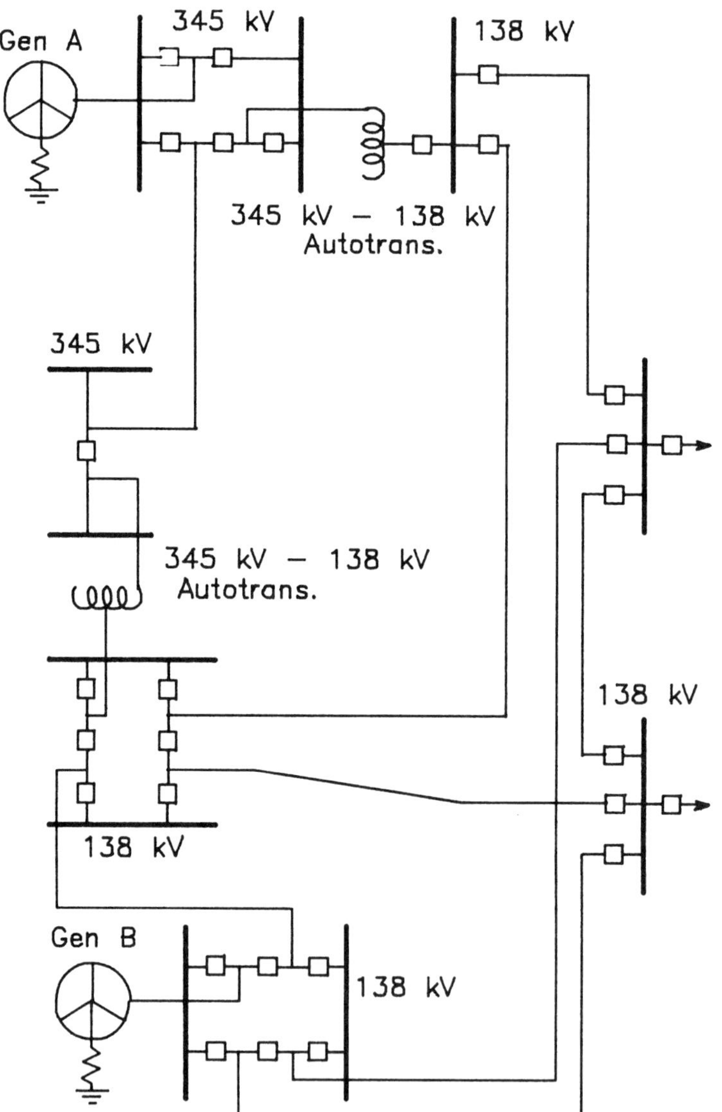

Figure 3-8 Bulk power transmission system.

Figure 3-9 345-kV transmission line. (Photo Courtesy of Ohio Edison Company)

mote generating plants to the system load centers. Note that there are two conductors per phase.

Subtransmission System

The subtransmission system may be designed in a network, loop, or radial configuration depending on the degree of reliability desired. The network configuration is the most reliable and most expensive to construct, while the simple radial system is the least expensive and least reliable. Many portions of the subtransmission system are designed in a loop configuration, but operated as a radial system. Figure 3-10 shows a 69-kV subtransmission line used for transmitting power from the subtransmission substations to the distribution substations.

Figure 3-11 shows the one-line diagram of a subtransmission line constructed in a loop configuration, with distribution substations located at various points along the line. The line in this figure is operating at a nominal voltage of 69 kV and is supplied from transmission substations *A* and *B*. At each distribution substation tap point, there is a set

Figure 3-10 69-kV subtransmission line. (Photo Courtesy of Ohio Edison Company)

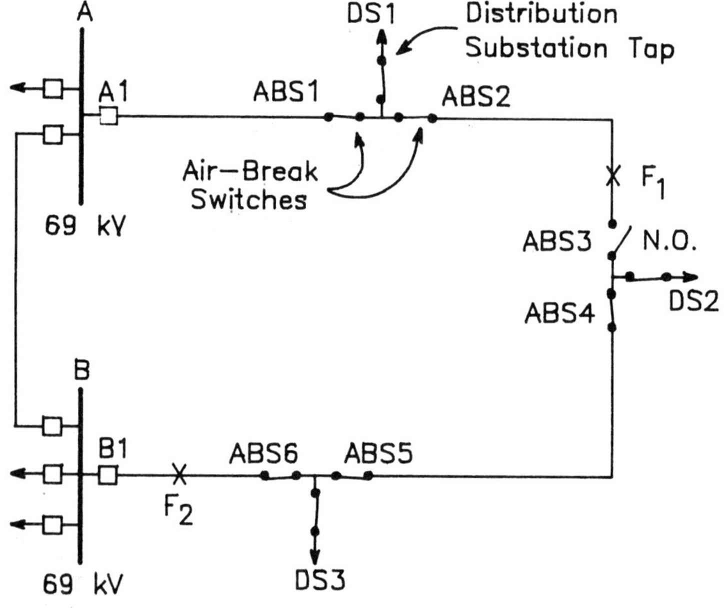

Figure 3-11 Subtransmission system one-line diagram.

of air-break switches to isolate the line sections and substation taps. Typically, these air-break switches are not designed to interrupt load or fault current. Their only purpose is to provide a means of isolating lines and equipment. Therefore, before attempting to operate any of these air-break switches, the circuit must be de-energized by tripping the respective circuit breaker or other load break device. A typical air-break switch installation is shown in Fig. 3-12.

Note that opening the line at two or more points would leave a section of line de-energized during normal operation. If a fault occurs on this de-energized section of line, no fault current will flow, and none of the breakers will trip. Therefore, the system operator will not be aware of the fault until the de-energized section of line is energized. Thus, the faulted section of line will not be available for service when it is needed. It is common practice to keep all lines and buswork energized to enable detection of faulted conditions.

In the subtransmission loop shown in Fig. 3-11, if a fault occurs at point F_1, only breaker *A*1 will trip since the line is open at *ABS*3. Distribution substation *DS*1 is now without a source of power. Air break switch *ABS*2 could be opened since the line is already de-energized by the tripping of breaker *A*1. Breaker *A*1 can now be reclosed to restore power to distribution substation *DS*1. The faulted section of line between *ABS*2 and *ABS*3 has now been isolated, and power is restored to all distribution substations. Repair of the faulted line section can now be performed at a convenient time.

For a fault at F_2, only breaker *B*1 will trip since the loop is open at *ABS*3. Distribution substations *DS*2 and *DS*3 will now be without power. This faulted section of line can be isolated by performing the following switching order:

1. Open *ABS*6
2. Trip breaker *A*1

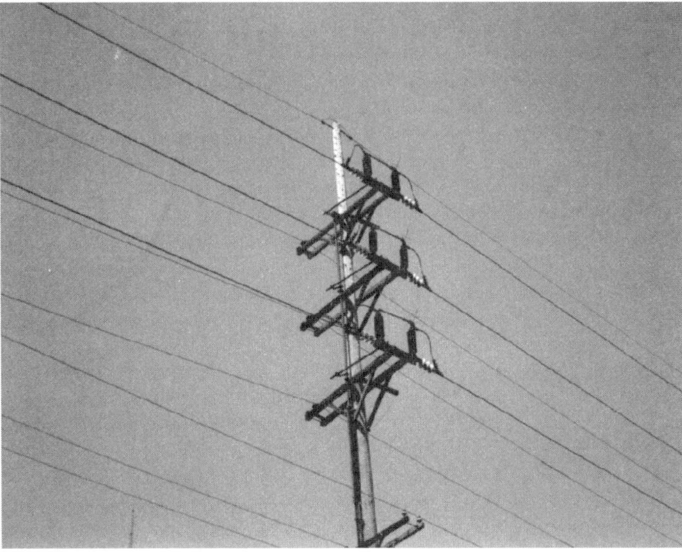

Figure 3-12 69-kV air-break switch installation. (Photo Courtesy of Ohio Edison Company)

3. Close *ABS*3
4. Reclose breaker *A*1

Note that it is necessary to trip breaker *A*1 *before* closing *ABS*3, since the air-break switches must *not* be operated under load conditions. Under these operating conditions, all three distribution substations are supplied from substation *A* through breaker *A*1.

3-7 Substation Layout

Transmission and distribution substations are also designed for maximum reliability and flexibility of operation. The ability to switch equipment out of service for either scheduled or unscheduled outages while maintaining service is essential for reliable system operation. Several different substation bus layouts are used by electric utilities to accomplish reliable and flexible system operation. Some of these same layouts are also used in large commercial and industrial power systems. Figure 3-13 is an overall view of a large power substation supplying both transmission and subtransmission circuits.

Breaker and a Half

The breaker and a half scheme shown in Fig. 3-14 is used primarily in bulk transmission substations at voltage levels above 100 kV. In this substation bus layout, there are two main buses, with three breakers connecting the two buses as shown. The transmission lines terminate at a point electrically between any two of the breakers.

Figure 3-13 Overall view of transmission substation. (Photo Courtesy of Ohio Edison Company)

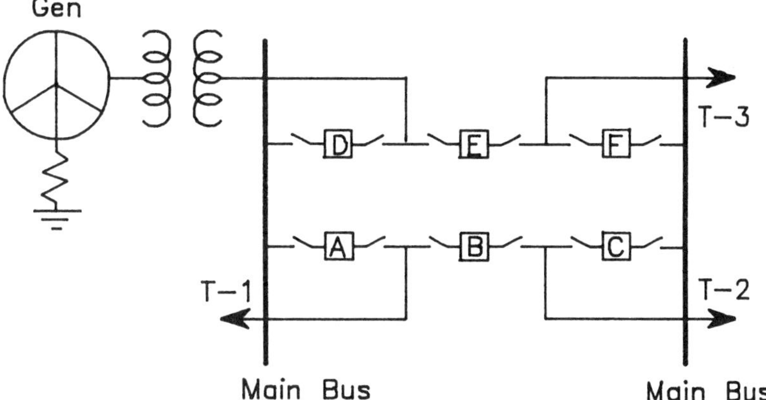

Figure 3-14 Breaker and a half scheme.

A high degree of reliability is achieved since any one breaker may be removed from service while keeping all transmission lines energized. For example, if breaker *A* fails or is removed from service for scheduled maintenance, transmission line *T*-1 will remain energized through breaker *B*. If breaker *B* is removed from service, line *T*-1 will be energized through breaker *A,* line *T*-2 will remain energized through breaker *C,* and so on. Note also that the generator is connected to the transmission substation in the same manner as the transmission lines. Again, this is for reasons of reliability. If either breaker *D* or *E* is removed from service, the generator will remain connected to the power grid. Synchronization of the generator to the power grid is accomplished through breakers *D* or *E,* or both.

It is common practice to install disconnect switches on both sides of each breaker in the substation as shown. As in the case of the transmission line air-break switches, these disconnect switches are not designed for load breaking duty. The breaker must first be tripped out of service; then the disconnects on each side of the breaker are opened to isolate the breaker. Once the breaker is isolated, *each* pole of the breaker is grounded on *both sides* of the breaker for safety purposes. The desired maintenance can now be performed on the breaker.

The name "breaker and a half" probably comes from the fact that there are three breakers for every two transmission lines, or one and a half breakers per line. The middle breaker is actually shared by the two lines. For substations with more than four transmission line terminations, additional rows or *bays* of breakers are installed, with the lines terminated similarly to Fig. 3-14.

Ring Bus

In the ring bus scheme shown in Fig. 3-15, the number of breakers is equal to the number of lines terminating in the station. The ring bus is a more economical design than the breaker and a half scheme, but offers less reliability and flexibility of operation. The

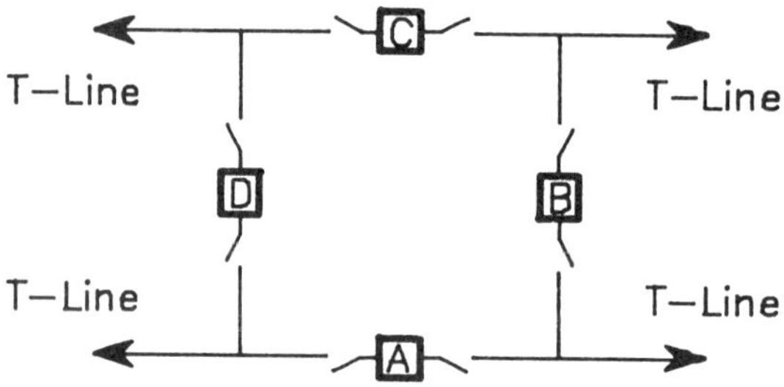

Figure 3-15 Ring bus.

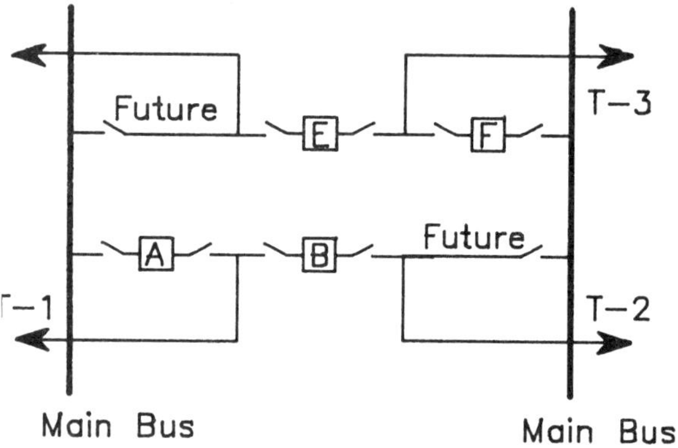

Figure 3-16 Future breaker and a half operating as a ring bus.

name "ring bus" comes from the fact that the breakers and buswork form a ring electrically. The transmission lines terminate at the buswork between the breakers as shown.

In some instances, a substation may be designed for a breaker and a half scheme and operated as a ring bus by leaving out two of the breakers, as shown in Fig. 3-16. When system conditions require additional reliability, the other two breakers can be added.

Transfer Bus

In the transfer bus arrangement, each transmission line is connected to the main bus through a breaker, as shown in Fig. 3-17. In addition, the line side of each line breaker is connected to the transfer bus by means of a disconnect switch. The transfer bus is connected to the main bus via the transfer breaker. The transfer bus and breaker thus serve as the alternative supply for any one of the transmission lines. Under normal operation, the transfer bus and main bus are energized.

If it is required to remove one of the line breakers from service, the following switching order may be performed:

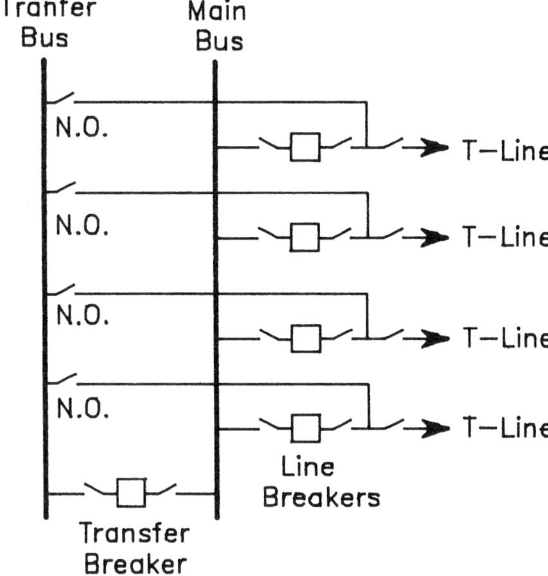

Figure 3-17 Transfer bus scheme.

1. Trip transfer breaker.
2. Close transfer bus switch on affected line.
3. Reclose transfer bus breaker.
4. Trip line breaker on affected line.
5. Open line breaker disconnect switches to isolate breaker.

The actual switching order to be performed depends on the substation layout and utility operating procedures. This switching order is only one possibility.

Radial

The radial scheme shown in Fig. 3-18 is the most economical layout in terms of equipment requirements. Note that there is only one breaker for each line termination, with no provision for supplying a line from another bus within the substation. Thus, the radial configuration offers the lowest operating flexibility. Most subtransmission substations have the radial bus configuration.

Distribution Substation Layout

An overall view of a distribution substation with circuit exits at 4.16 and 12.47 kV is shown in Fig. 3-19. The bus configuration of a typical distribution substation is shown

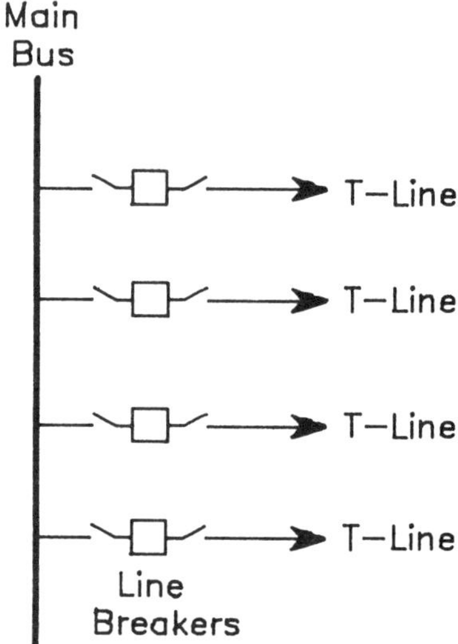

Figure 3-18 Radial bus scheme.

Figure 3-19 Overall view of distribution substation. (Photo Courtesy of Ohio Edison Company)

in Fig. 3-20. Also included is a portion of the subtransmission system feeding the distribution substation, indicating the location of the high-voltage air-break switches. These air-break switches may be mounted on transmission line structures outside the substation or located on the substation structure itself. The high-voltage substation disconnect switch is usually located on the substation structure. The substation disconnect provides a means to de-energize and isolate the entire substation from the system.

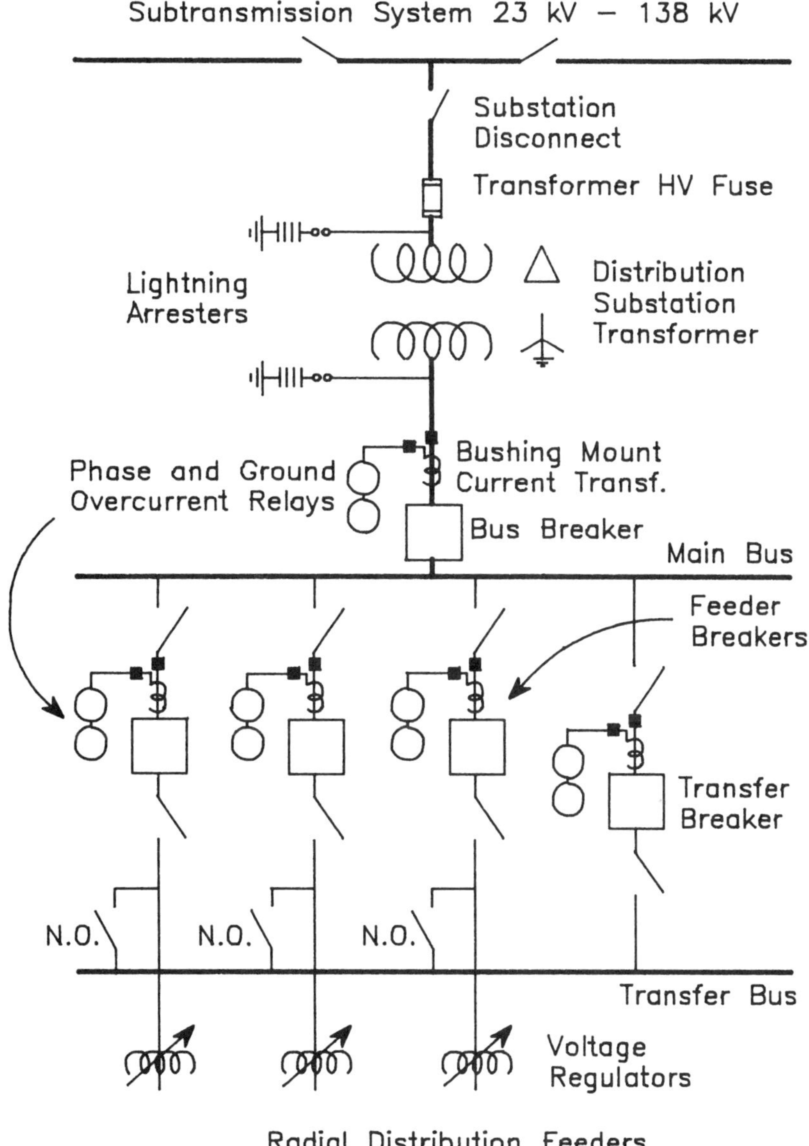

Figure 3-20 Distribution substation one-line diagram.

The distribution substation transformer steps down the voltage from subtransmission levels to distribution levels. The transformer may be protected by fuses or circuit breakers on the high-voltage side. Lightning arresters are applied on both the high- and low-voltage sides of the transformer to protect against overvoltages. The transformer windings are usually connected in delta on the high-voltage side and in solidly grounded wye on the low-voltage side. Taps are generally provided on the high-voltage side to allow adjustment of the bus voltage on the low side. These taps may be fixed or adjusted by an automatic load tap changing mechanism. The more common application is to use fixed taps at nominal, ±2.5%, and ±5% levels.

The low-voltage side of the transformer may be connected to the substation bus directly or through a circuit breaker, as shown in Fig. 3-20. Distribution feeders are tapped from the low-voltage bus and protected by reclosers or circuit breakers. In some designs, a bypass fuse is used to allow for the removal of the recloser or breaker. In other designs, a transfer bus scheme may be used to allow bypassing the recloser or breaker.

Voltage regulators are used to regulate the voltage on the distribution circuit. These regulators are typically tapped autotransformers that provide a certain amount of increase or decrease in the voltage in discrete steps. In some utilities, the entire substation bus is regulated, rather than the individual feeders, as shown in Fig. 3-20. The subject of voltage regulation will be discussed in more detail in Chapter 8.

3-8 Distribution System Layout

The distribution system consists of the overhead lines, underground cables, and distribution transformers used to distribute power from the distribution substations to the user. The distribution system typically operates as a multigrounded neutral system, with the neutral solidly grounded at the distribution substation transformer low-voltage side. In addition, the neutral is grounded at each major equipment location and at regular intervals along the line. The vast majority of distribution feeders are operated in a radial configuration, with provisions for transferring load between substations if required.

A representive distribution circuit one-line diagram is shown in Fig. 3-21. The distribution feeders originate from the distribution substation as a three-phase, four-wire system. The hash marks indicate the number of phase conductors. The phase designations, along with the number, size, and type of phase conductor or cable, are also indicated on the one line. The size of the neutral conductor may also be indicated. One-, two-, or three-phase conductors and the neutral may be tapped from the main feeder at various points to supply loads. At locations where there is a change in conductor size, or number of phases, an × is placed. The sizes and locations of all distribution transformers, capacitors, fuses, reclosers, and switches are indicated on the one-line diagram. Note also that in some configurations it is possible to provide a tie to another distribution feeder to allow for switching between circuits if required.

3-9 Secondary System Layout

The secondary system is used to distribute power at utilization voltage from the distribution transformers to the end users. The radial, network, and spot network secondary systems are the most common types of secondary systems in use.

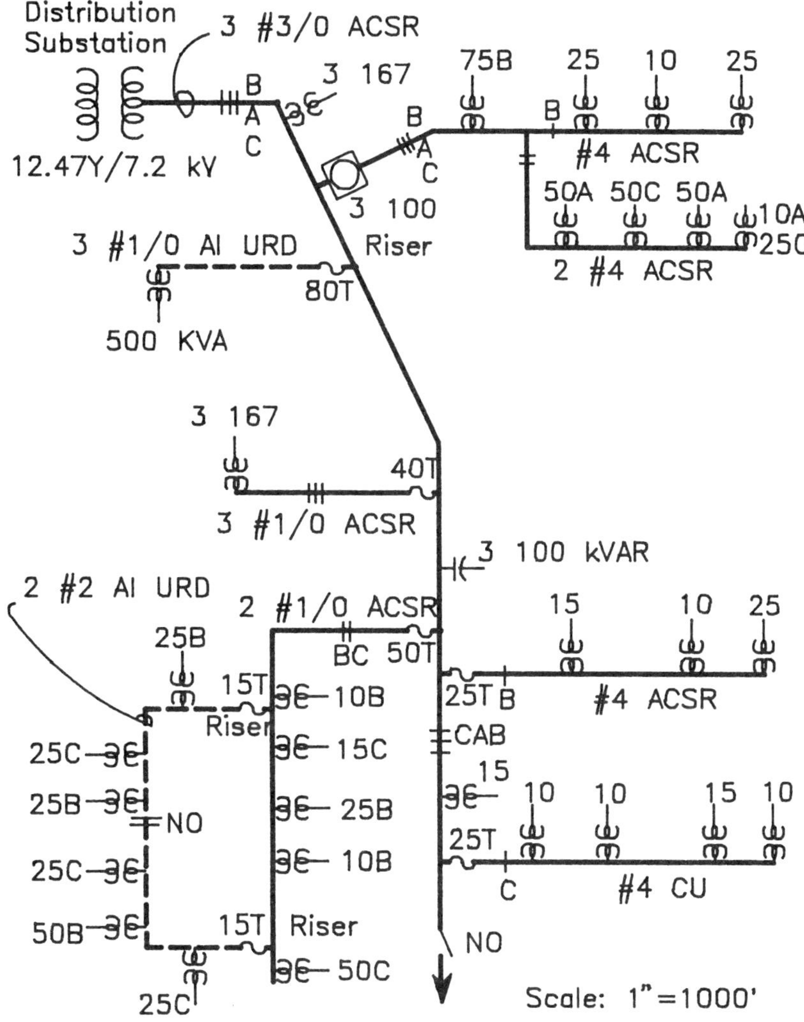

Figure 3-21 Distribution circuit one-line diagram.

Radial Secondary System

The most common form of secondary distribution system is the radial system. A representive secondary layout for a residential development is shown in Fig. 3-22. Low-voltage secondaries and service drops are made to each user in a radial manner, with no provision for alternative sources. Radial secondary systems are installed either overhead or underground.

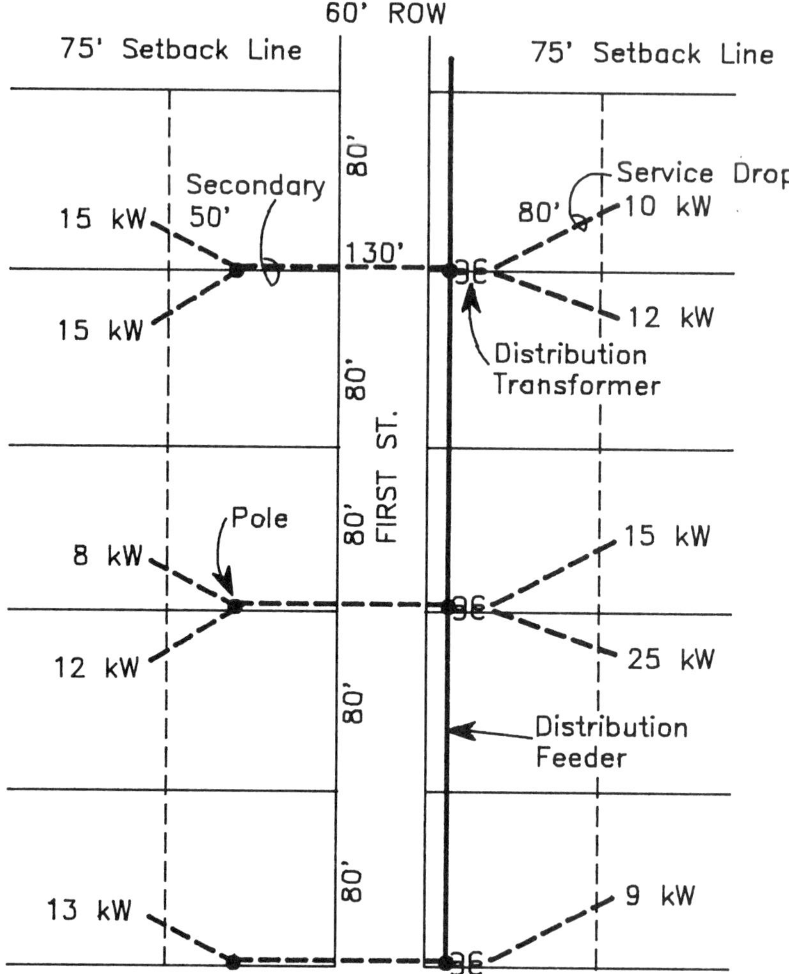

Figure 3-22 Overhead secondary distribution system one-line diagram.

Secondary Network System

The secondary network system is used primarily in large urban areas to supply commercial loads. A one-line diagram of a typical network system is shown in Fig. 3-23a. A distinguishing feature of the network system is that the secondary cables are connected in the form of a grid or network. A special type of fuse referred to as a *cable limiter,* is used to protect and isolate the secondary cables in the event of a fault. These cable limiters are installed in each conductor at major junction points in the secondary network system. The cable limiter will isolate only the faulted cable, thereby allowing service to be maintained. Individual services are tapped from the network at various points to supply loads in the area. Typical nominal voltage levels for network systems are 208Y/120 V and 480Y/277 V, three phase, four wire.

The secondary network is supplied at various points by means of network transformers. Figure 3-23b shows a one-line diagram of a typical network transformer in-

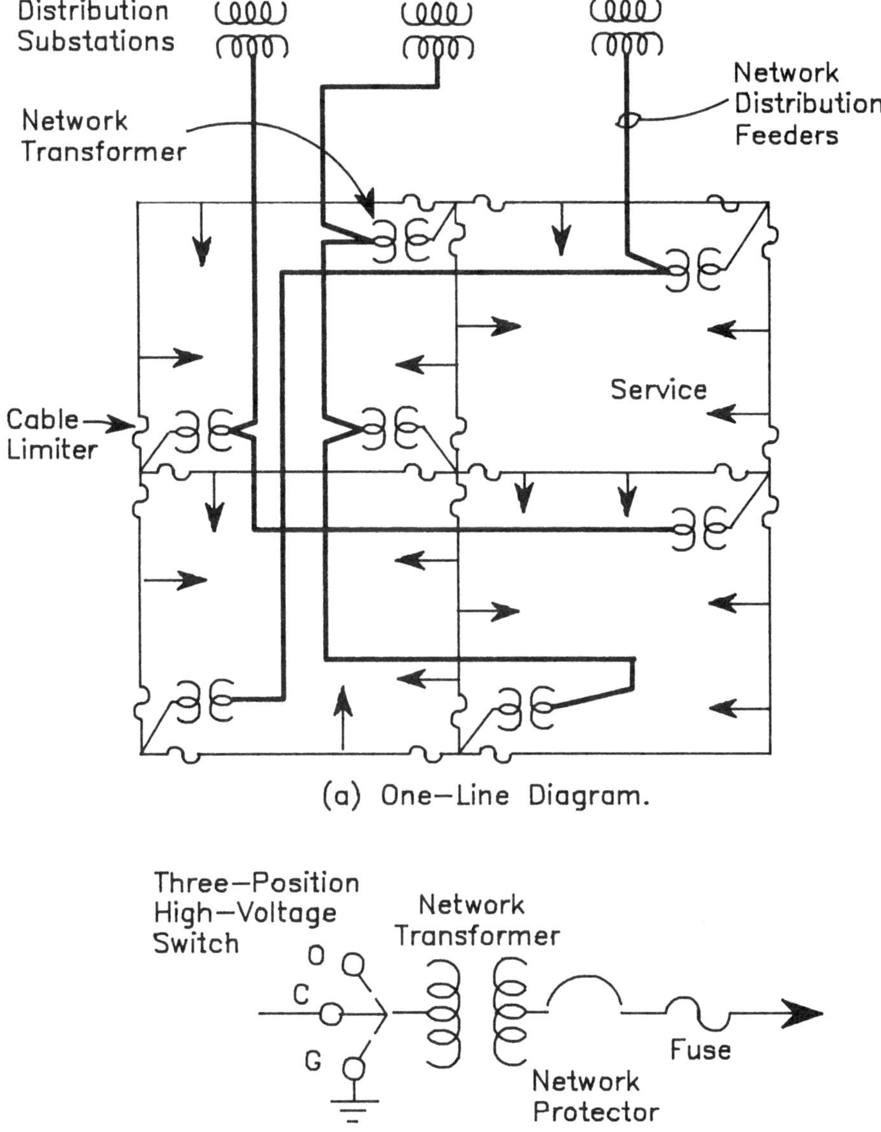

Figure 3-23 Secondary network system.

stallation. The functions of the various network transformer components will be discussed in Chapter 6. These network transformers receive power from the primary distribution feeders at voltages between 4.16 and 34.5 kV. These feeders are usually dedicated network feeders that supply power only to the network transformers from one or more distribution substations. Since the network is typically supplied from several distribution substations, the loss of any one distribution substation, feeder, or network transformer will not cause an outage on the network.

Spot Network System

Spot network systems are similar in nature to the network systems previously described, but supply isolated load centers in a particular location. For example, individual spot

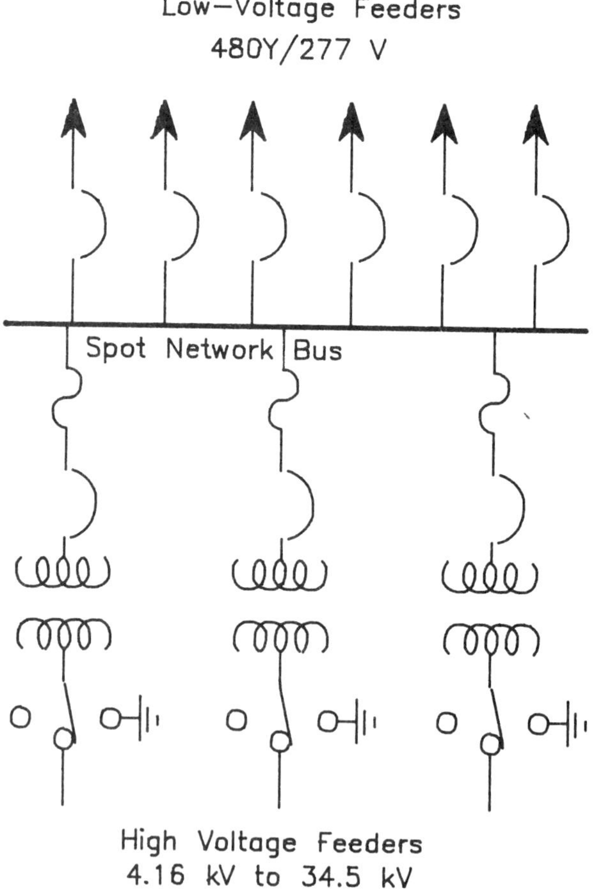

Figure 3-24 Spot network system.

networks may be designed to supply several floors of a high-rise building. In the spot network system, several network transformer secondaries are connected to the spot network bus. The network transformer primaries are connected to various feeders in a manner similar to the secondary network system previously discussed. Individual loads or feeders are tapped off this network bus. Figure 3-24 shows a one-line diagram of a typical spot network installation supplying several floors of a high-rise building.

4

Load Characteristics, Modeling, and Metering

4-1 General

An understanding of the concept of a load in an electrical power system is of significant importance in performing various electrical calculations. In general, the loads in an electrical power system are not constant, but vary depending on certain factors. Consider, for example, your own residence. The electrical power consumed is not constant throughout the day, but varies depending on the amount of activity, time of day, season, temperature, and so forth. Since an electrical power system or portion of a power system is made up of several different types of loads, the overall load on the system will tend to be random in nature. Electrical loads are typically grouped into categories having the same general characteristics, such as residential, commercial, or industrial. Although the individual loads in these categories are unique, the group as a whole will have certain predictable characteristics. This chapter deals with the characterization, modeling, metering, and rate calculations of electrical loads.

4-2 Definitions [1]

The electrical power consumed by a load is generally quantified by two terms: *usage* and *demand*. Demand refers to the instantaneous electrical power drawn by the load and is typically specified in terms of active power, apparent power, reactive power, or a combination of these quantities. Real or active power demand is typically expressed in terms of kilowatts (kW) or megawatts (MW), depending on the size of the load. Likewise, apparent power is expressed in terms of kilovolt-amperes (kVA) or megavolt-amperes (MVA), depending on the size of the load. Reactive power is expressed either in terms of kilovolt-amperes-reactive (kVAR) or megavolt-amperes-reactive (MVAR).

Usage refers to the amount of energy consumed by a load over a specified time interval. Typically, usage is expressed in terms of kilowatt-hours (kWH) or megawatt-hours (MWH). The units indicate that the usage is the product of the demand multiplied by the time during which the demand occurs. For example, a demand of 100 kW lasting for 1 minute (min) will consume 1.67 kWH, whereas a demand of 100 kW lasting for 60 min will consume 100 kWH of energy. Note that in both instances the demands were equal, but the time duration of the demands differed.

The variable nature of electrical loads is quantified by use of several defining terms. Consider the daily load profile shown in Fig. 4-1. Although this load profile is shown for a 24-hr time period, other time periods may also be used. For example, hourly, seasonal, and yearly load profiles may also be plotted. Furthermore, the variable shown in Fig. 4-1 is the active or real power demand of the load. It is also possible to plot load profiles using apparent power, reactive power, or a combination thereof.

The *instantaneous demand* is the actual demand at any given time. The *maximum instantaneous demand* is the maximum demand that occurs over the specified time interval of interest. The *average demand* is the average value of the instantaneous demand taken over a specified time interval. This time interval is referred to as the *demand*

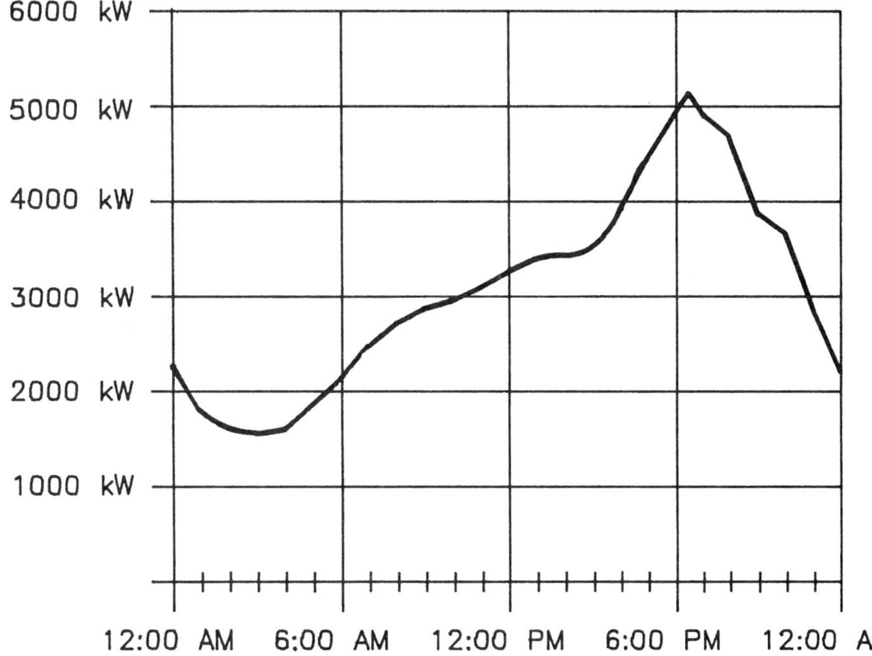

Figure 4-1 Load profile for Example 4-1.

interval. The maximum average demand is the maximum that occurs during a given time period. Most thermal demand meters have a typical demand interval of 15 min. When discussing average demand, it is important to specify the demand interval as well. The average demand will be a function of the demand interval for all time-varying loads. The *load factor* is a ratio of the average demand to the maximum average demand for the same time interval. Typically, the load factor is calculated on a daily, monthly, or yearly basis.

EXAMPLE 4-1

For the load profile shown in Fig. 4-1, assume that the demand is shown for a 15-min demand interval and determine the following:

a. Average daily demand
b. Maximum average demand using a 1-hour (hr) demand interval
c. Maximum average demand using a 15-min demand interval
d. Daily load factor

Solution

a. From the load profile, approximate average demands for selected time intervals can be determined. The area under the load profile curve can be determined by multiplying

Table 4-1

Time	*Demand (kW)*	*kWH*
12 AM–1 AM	2000	2000
1 AM–3 AM	1700	3400
3 AM–4 AM	1600	1600
4 AM–5 AM	1800	1800
5 AM–6 AM	2000	2000
6 AM–7 AM	2200	2200
7 AM–8 AM	2500	2500
8 AM–9 AM	2700	2700
9 AM–10 AM	2900	2900
10 AM–11 AM	3000	3000
11 AM–12 PM	3200	3200
12 PM–1 PM	3300	3300
1 PM–2 PM	3400	3500
2 PM–3 PM	3500	3400
3 PM–4 PM	3800	3800
4 PM–5 PM	4200	4200
5 PM–6 PM	4700	4700
6 PM–7 PM	5000	5000
7 PM–8 PM	4800	4800
8 PM–9 PM	4200	4200
9 PM–10 PM	3800	3800
10 PM–11 PM	3200	3200
11 PM–12 AM	2500	2500
	Total	73,700

the approximate demands by their respective time intervals. The result will be the total kilowatt-hours (kWH) consumed during the time interval. The total amount of kWHs consumed during the day is equal to the sum of the kWHs for the individual time intervals. The average daily demand is then found by dividing the total daily kWHs by the time interval of 24 hr. Table 4-1 shows the average demand for selected time intervals and a computation of the kWHs consumed during each time interval.

The average 24-hr demand is equal to

$$\text{Average demand} = \frac{73{,}700 \text{ kWH}}{24 \text{ hr}} = 3070.8 \text{ kW}$$

b. The maximum 1-hr demand is approximately 5000 kW and occurs between 6:00 PM and 7:00 PM.

c. The maximum 15-min demand is approximately 5300 kW and occurs between 6:15 PM and 6:30 PM.

d. For this example, the daily load factor is the ratio of the average daily demand to the maximum instantaneous demand. The maximum 15-min average demand is 5300 kW, and the daily average demand is 3070.8 kW as determined in part a. The daily load factor is computed as

$$\text{Daily load factor} = \frac{3070.8 \text{ kW}}{5300 \text{ kW}} = 0.5794$$

Note that the load factor is a unitless quantity and can never be greater than unity.

In several types of power system calculations, it is necessary to determine the loading on a certain portion of the system with respect to the installed capacity. For example, when performing voltage-drop calculations on a distribution feeder, the loading on the individual distribution transformers can be estimated by multiplying the transformer apparent power rating by the *utilization factor*. Mathematically, the utilization factor is a ratio of the actual demand on a system or subsystem to the capacity of the system or equipment. When calculating the utilization factor, it is customary to express the actual demand and system capacity using the same units. For example, if the load profile of Fig. 4-1 represented the loading on a 7500-kVA distribution substation transformer, the utilization factor would be (assuming unity power factor)

$$\text{Utilization factor} = \frac{5300 \text{ kVA}}{7500 \text{ kVA}} = 0.7067$$

Thus, the transformer is operating at approximately 70.7% of rated capacity during peak load conditions.

The random nature of several independent loads connected to the same circuit or transformer must be quantified in order to perform loading and voltage-drop calculations. For example, several residences may be connected to the same distribution transformer or several distribution transformers connected to the same distribution circuit, and so on. The individual demands of each load generally will not occur at the same time, but rather in a random nature independent of one another.

The *diversity factor* is defined as the ratio of the sum of the individual peak demands divided by the peak demand of the group as a whole. Since the sum of the individual peak demands will always be equal to or exceed the peak demand of the group as a whole, the diversity factor will always be greater than or equal to unity. The larger the diversity factor is, the greater the nonsimultaneous occurrence of the peak demand for each load. The *coincidence factor* is defined as the ratio of the peak demand to the sum of the individual peak demands. From this definition, it can be seen that the coincidence factor is the reciprocal of the diversity factor and will therefore be less than or equal to unity. The smaller the coincidence factor is, the greater the nonsimultaneous occurrence of the peak demand of each load.

The *demand factor* is defined to be the ratio of peak demand to total connected load. The total connected load is the sum of the apparent power rating of all connected equipment. The demand factor is used extensively to determine loading on circuits and equipment when planning electrical systems. The apparent power ratings of all connected electrical equipment are added and multiplied by a suitable demand factor to determine the estimated peak demand. This estimated demand is used to size cables, conductors, and transformers and to perform voltage-drop and circuit coordination studies. Unlike the diversity and coincidence factors, the demand factor uses the equipment ratings rather than the demands on the connected equipment, since the actual demands will not be known in the planning stages. Generally, the demand factor will be less than the coincidence factor. Also, the demand factor will decrease as the number of loads increases.

EXAMPLE 4-2

A distribution transformer supplies the following loads:

Load	*Demand (kVA)*	*Connected Load (kVA)*
1	9	15
2	14	20
3	8	12
4	22	25

Calculate the following:

a. Demand factor for each load
b. Estimated peak demand on the distribution transformer if the demand factor for the four loads as a whole is 0.65
c. Diversity factor for all four loads
d. Coincidence factor for all four loads

Solution

a. The demand factor for each load is the ratio of the demand divided by the connected load. The results are tabulated as follows:

Load	*Demand Factor*
1	0.6
2	0.7
3	0.67
4	0.88

b. Estimated peak demand = demand factor · total connected load
= 0.65 · (15 + 20 + 12 + 25) = 46.8 kVA

c. The diversity factor is the ratio of the sum of the individual demands divided by the peak demand of the entire group of loads.

$$\text{Diversity factor} = \frac{9 + 14 + 8 + 22}{46.8} = 1.1325$$

d. The coincidence factor is the reciprocal of the diversity factor.

$$\text{Coincidence factor} = \frac{1}{\text{diversity factor}} = \frac{1}{1.1325} = 0.8830$$

4-3 Load Modeling

Electrical loads in a power system may be modeled in one of three ways: constant impedance, constant power, or constant current sink. The choice of modeling depends on the degree of accuracy required. For example, in distribution circuit voltage-drop and loading calculations, the loads are typically modeled as constant current sinks. In transmission system load flow and voltage-drop calculations, the constant power model is commonly used. For certain voltage unbalance and motor starting calculations, the constant impedance representation may be used.

Constant Impedance Representation

The constant impedance representation of loads is developed assuming that all three-phase loads are balanced. Recall from Chapter 1 that a balanced three-phase load may be analyzed on a single-phase line to neutral equivalent basis. Consequently, the constant impedance representation involves the determination of equivalent line to neutral connected impedances. This representation applies regardless of whether the load is wye or delta connected.

Consider a balanced three-phase load that consumes a certain amount of active power $P_{3\Phi}$ and reactive power $Q_{3\Phi}$ at a line to line voltage magnitude of V_{ll}. The line current magnitude of the three-phase load is I_l. The total active and reactive powers dissipated in the load are given by

$$P_{3\Phi} = 3 \cdot I_l^2 \cdot R_\Phi \tag{4.1}$$

$$Q_{3\Phi} = 3 \cdot I_l^2 \cdot X_\Phi \tag{4.2}$$

where R_Φ and X_Φ are the equivalent resistance and reactance of the three-phase load representation. Solving Eqs. (4.1) and (4.2) for R_Φ and X_Φ results in

$$R_\Phi = \frac{P_{3\Phi}}{3 \cdot I_l^2} \tag{4.3}$$

$$X_\Phi = \frac{Q_{3\Phi}}{3 \cdot I_l^2} \tag{4.4}$$

The line current magnitude I_l can be calculated by applying Eq. (1.67).

EXAMPLE 4-3

A three-phase, 50-hp, 460-V, induction motor operates at 75% rated load. At this load the efficiency is 90%, and the power factor is 0.85 lagging. Determine the constant impedance representation of this load.

Solution The active power output of the motor is

$$P_{\text{out}} = 0.75 \cdot (50 \text{ hp}) \cdot (746 \text{ W/hp}) = 27{,}975 \text{ W}$$

The active power input to the motor is

$$P_{3\Phi} = \frac{P_{\text{out}}}{\text{efficiency}} = \frac{27{,}975}{0.9} = 31{,}083 \text{ W}$$

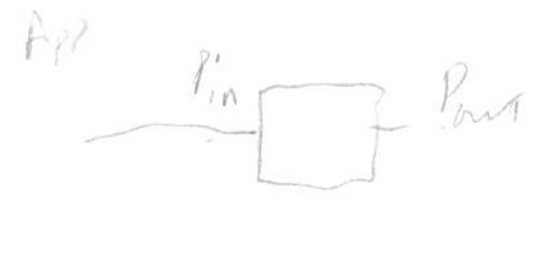

The apparent power input is

$$S_{3\Phi} = \frac{P_{3\Phi}}{\text{power factor}} = \frac{31{,}083}{0.85} = 36{,}569 \text{ VA}$$

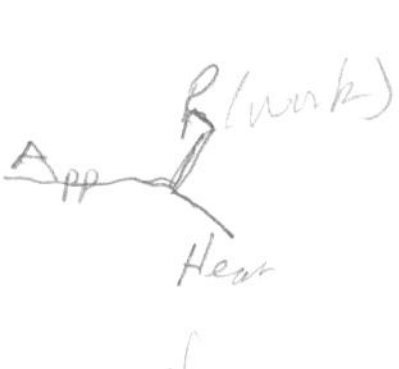

The reactive power input is

$$Q_{3\Phi} = (S_{3\Phi}^2 - P_{3\Phi}^2)^{1/2} = (36{,}569^2 - 31{,}083^2)^{1/2} = 19{,}265 \text{ VAR}$$

The line current magnitude is

$$I_l = \frac{S_{3\Phi}}{\sqrt{3} \cdot V_{ll}} = \frac{36{,}569}{\sqrt{3} \cdot 460} = 45.9 \text{ A}$$

The equivalent resistance per phase is

$$R_\Phi = \frac{31{,}083}{3 \cdot (45.9)^2} = 4.92\ \Omega$$

The equivalent reactance per phase is

$$X_\Phi = \frac{19{,}265}{3 \cdot (45.9)^2} = 3.05\ \Omega$$

EXAMPLE 4-4

Determine the equivalent reactance of a 500-kVAR, 480-V, three-phase, delta-connected capacitor bank.

Solution The rated line current of the capacitor bank is

$$I_l = \frac{500{,}000 \text{ VA}}{\sqrt{3} \cdot 480 \text{ V}} = 601.4 \text{ A}$$

The active power absorbed by the capacitor bank is negligible compared to the reactive power and will be neglected. Therefore, the equivalent resistance of the capacitor bank is zero. The equivalent reactance is

$$X_\Phi = \frac{500{,}000}{3 \cdot (601.4)^2} = 0.4608 \ \Omega$$

For single-phase loads, the equivalent resistance and reactance are given by

$$R_\Phi = \frac{P_{1\Phi}}{I_l^2} \quad \textbf{(4.5)}$$

$$X_\Phi = \frac{Q_{1\Phi}}{I_l^2} \quad \textbf{(4.6)}$$

The line current magnitude for the single-phase load can be calculated by applying Eq. (1.62).

EXAMPLE 4-5

A ¾-hp, 230-V, 1725-rpm, single-phase motor has an efficiency of 94.3% and a power factor of 0.87 lagging when operating at rated conditions. Determine the constant impedance representation for this motor at rated conditions.

Solution The active power output of the motor is

$$P_{\text{out}} = (3/4 \text{ hp}) \cdot (746 \text{ W/hp}) = 559.5 \text{ W}$$

The active power input to the motor is

$$P_{1\Phi} = \frac{P_{\text{out}}}{\text{efficiency}} = \frac{559.5}{0.943} = 593.3 \text{ W}$$

The apparent power input is

$$S_{1\Phi} = \frac{P_{1\Phi}}{\text{power factor}} = \frac{593.3}{0.87} = 682 \text{ VA}$$

The reactive power input is

$$Q_{1\Phi} = (S_{1\Phi}^2 - P_{1\Phi}^2)^{1/2} = (682^2 - 593.3^2)^{1/2} = 336.3 \text{ VAR}$$

The line current magnitude is

$$I_l = \frac{S_{1\Phi}}{V_{ll}} = \frac{682 \text{ VA}}{230 \text{ V}} = 3.0 \text{ A}$$

The equivalent resistance per phase is

$$R_\Phi = \frac{593.3}{3.0^2} = 65.92 \ \Omega$$

The equivalent reactance per phase is

$$X_\Phi = \frac{336.3}{3.0^2} = 37.37 \ \Omega$$

Constant Power Representation

In the constant power representation of a load, the apparent, active, and reactive powers consumed by the load are assumed to remain constant regardless of the actual voltage applied to the load. The current and voltage will be allowed to vary in order to maintain constant power conditions.

EXAMPLE 4-6 A three-phase load is to be modeled using the constant power representation. The load consumes 1000 kW, 400-kVAR, lagging power factor. The nominal system voltage is 12.47 kV. Calculate the complex line current necessary to maintain this constant power condition for the following applied voltages:

a. 12.1 kV
b. 13.1 kV

Use a reference voltage phase angle of 0° for parts a and b.

Solution Phase *A* will be selected as the reference for this problem. Both parts will be analyzed using the single-phase line to neutral equivalent method developed in Chapter 1. The magnitude of the apparent power consumed by the load will remain constant and is given by

$$S_{3\Phi} = (1000^2 + 400^2)^{1/2} = 1077 \text{ kVA}$$

a. The magnitude of the line current at 12,100 V is

$$I_l = \frac{1{,}077{,}000 \text{ VA}}{\sqrt{3} \cdot 12{,}100 \text{ V}} = 51.39 \text{ A}$$

The phase angle of the phase *A* line current is

$$\theta = \tan^{-1}(\text{kVAR/kW}) = 21.8°$$

The phase *A* current in complex form is

$$\mathbf{I}_l = 51.39\angle -21.8° \text{ A}$$

b. The magnitude of the line current at 13,100 V is

$$I_l = \frac{1{,}077{,}000 \text{ VA}}{\sqrt{3} \cdot 13{,}100 \text{ V}} = 47.47 \text{ A}$$

The phase angle of the phase *A* line current remains the same as in part a since the same reference voltage will be used. The phase *A* current in complex form is

$$\mathbf{I}_l = 47.47\angle -21.8° \text{ A}$$

From Example 4-6, notice that the current magnitude will decrease as the voltage magnitude increases to maintain constant apparent power magnitude.

Constant Current Representation

In the constant current representation of loads, both the magnitude and the phase angle of the load current are assumed to remain constant regardless of the applied voltage. This assumption results in a change in the apparent, active, and reactive powers consumed by the load, but provides sufficient accuracy for most calculations. Typically, when determining the constant current representation of a load, the nominal system voltage at the load is used.

EXAMPLE 4-7

A three-phase load of 500 kW, 0.85 lagging power factor is supplied from a 4.16-kV, three-phase, four-wire, multigrounded neutral system.

a. Determine the constant current representation of the load.

b. Calculate the apparent, active, and reactive powers if the actual system voltage is 4.4 kV at the point of supply.

Solution

a. The apparent power magnitude is

$$S_{3\Phi} = \frac{P_{3\Phi}}{\text{power factor}} = \frac{500{,}000}{0.85} = 588{,}235 \text{ VA}$$

The line current magnitude is

$$I_l = \frac{588{,}235 \text{ VA}}{\sqrt{3} \cdot 4{,}160 \text{ V}} = 81.64 \text{ A}$$

The phase angle of the phase *A* line current will be determined by selecting the phase *A* voltage as a reference. The phase angle is

$$\theta = \cos^{-1}(0.85) = 31.8°$$

Therefore, the constant current representation of this load is

$$\mathbf{I}_l = 81.64\angle -31.8° \text{ A}$$

Note that the current lags the reference voltage due to the lagging power factor of the load.

b. The load current as calculated in part a remains constant with this type of load representation. The complex apparent power at a voltage of 4.4 kV is

$$\begin{aligned}\mathbf{S}_{3\Phi} &= \sqrt{3} \cdot 4400 \cdot (81.64\angle -31.8°)^* \\ &= 622{,}162\angle 31.8° \text{ VA} \\ &= 528{,}771 + j327{,}852 \text{ VA}\end{aligned}$$

Therefore,

$$P_{3\Phi} = 528.8 \text{ kW}, \qquad Q_{3\Phi} = 327.9 \text{ kVAR}$$

4-4 Electric Metering

Measurement of electrical quantities in electrical power systems is done for several reasons. The metering of electrical power is used for revenue billing, energy management, and transaction purposes. The quantities measured include active power, reactive power, apparent power, power factor, watthours, varhours, current, voltage, and others. Metering may be done directly at low voltage or through voltage and current transformers for higher-voltage and higher-current systems. Either single-phase or total three-phase quantities may be metered.

Two types of electric meters are available: self-contained and transformer rated. The self-contained meter is directly connected to the service entrance conductors. The current rating of the meter must be sufficient to carry the maximum current drawn by the load. The meter class designation indicates the maximum continuous current rating of the meter. Self-contained meters are typically available in classes 100 and 200. Some manufacturers offer meters in classes 320 and 400 as well. Likewise, the voltage rating of the meter must be equal to the service voltage. Typical self-contained voltage ratings are 120, 240, 277, and 480 V.

Transformer rated meters are typically used for services of 400 A and above. These meters require the use of current transformers (CTs) to step down the current to a level that is suitable for metering. Since current transformers are used, the class designation for these meters is typically 10 or 20. In addition to current transformers, voltage or potential transformers (PTs) are required for high-current, high-voltage services. The purpose of the voltage transformers is to step down the high voltage to a lower voltage suitable for metering.

Induction Disc Watthour Meter

The induction disc watthour meter uses the principle of induction to produce a torque on a small rotating disc. This torque is produced by the interaction of the magnetic flux produced by the stator(s) in the meter. Each stator of the meter has a voltage coil and one or more current coils. The torque produced by the stator causes rotation of the disc at a speed proportional to the amount of energy consumed by the load. For polyphase watthour meters, as many as three stators may be acting independently to produce torque on the rotating disc. Therefore, the amount of energy used in all three phases will be measured and recorded.

In the conventional dial-type register, the mechanical rotation of the disc causes several dials to rotate, thereby recording the amount of energy being used. These dial registers are read from right to left, with the dial on the far right having units of 1's. The next dial to the left has units of 10's, and so on. Typically, units of 1's, 10's, 100's, 1000's, and 10,000's are indicated. To read the meter, start at the left dial. If the dial pointer is between two numbers, read the lower number. If a certain dial pointer appears to be exactly on a number, it is necessary to check the next dial to the right. If the next dial pointer has not yet reached 0, then read the lower number. If the reading of the next dial is past 0, then read the number as indicated. For example, consider the dial register shown in Fig. 4-2. The left dial appears to be directly on 4. However, the dial to the right has not yet rotated past 0, so the number is recorded as 3. The remaining dials are read as 9, 4, and 7, respectively. Therefore, the meter reading is 3947. The previous reading is subtracted from the present reading to determine the amount of kWHs consumed.

In the cyclometer type of meter register, the mechanical rotation of the induction disc causes the indicating register to advance. The cyclometer display is similar to the odometer found in an automobile. The readings are taken directly from the indicating wheels, in a manner similar to the indicating dial type.

In addition to measuring energy usage, it is also possible to obtain an estimate of the demand of the load from a watthour meter. As previously discussed, the rotational speed of the disc is proportional to the amount of energy used. The number of watthours per revolution is referred to as the meter constant and is usually designated K_h. Therefore, the demand in kilowatts can be calculated from:

$$\text{Demand} = \frac{3.6 \cdot (\text{no. of disc revolutions}) \cdot (K_h)}{\text{time in seconds}} \text{ (kW)} \tag{4.7}$$

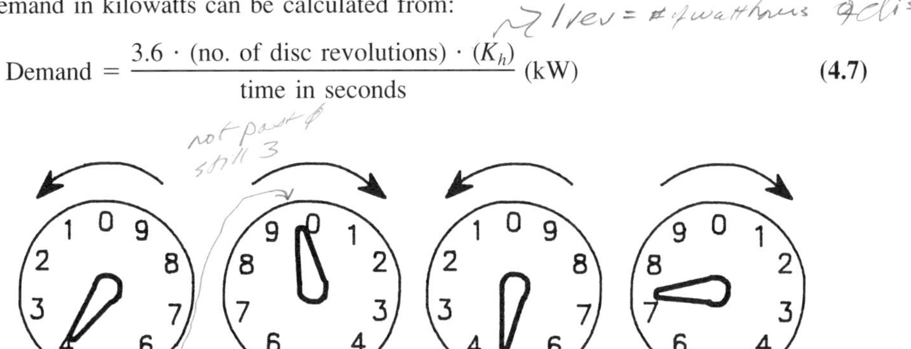

Figure 4-2 Dial register of induction watthour meter.

For example, assume that the disc rotates 20 revolutions in 130 seconds (sec) and that the meter constant is 7.2. The average demand is

$$\text{Demand} = \frac{3.6 \cdot (20) \cdot (7.2)}{130} = 4.0 \text{ kW}$$

Equation (4.7) applies to self-contained meters that are connected directly to the service entrance conductors without the use of instrument transformers. If the meter is connected to a high-voltage or high-current service through instrument transformers, the demand as well as kWH usage must be modified to include the instrument transformer turns ratios, as follows:

$$\text{Demand} = \frac{3.6 \cdot (\text{no. of revolutions}) \cdot (K_h) \cdot (\text{CT ratio}) \cdot (\text{PT ratio})}{\text{time in seconds}} \quad \textbf{(4.8)}$$

EXAMPLE 4-8

A three-phase induction disc watthour meter is connected to a 12.47-kV, three-phase, four-wire system through instrument transformers. The PTs are connected in a wye–wye configuration, with a voltage rating of 7200–120 V. The CTs are wye connected and have a turns ratio of 400:5 A. The polyphase meter has a meter constant K_h of 1.8. Determine the estimated demand if the disc rotates 5 revolutions in 120 sec.

Solution

$$\text{Demand} = \frac{3.6 \cdot (5) \cdot (1.8) \cdot (400/5) \cdot (7200/120)}{120} = 1296 \text{ kW}$$

In addition to measuring energy usage, many induction disc watthour meters are equipped with a demand register to measure peak energy consumption. This register records the peak average demand for a specified demand interval. Typically, demand intervals of 15 or 30 min are used. Certain utility rate structures are designed to include the peak demand in the rate calculations. The reason for including the peak demand in the rate calculations is that the utility must design and construct power generation, transmission, and distribution facilities to meet peak demands on the system. A user with a high peak demand and low kWH (energy) consumption is generally penalized for having a poor load factor.

The instantaneous demand of a load may be measured directly by use of an indicating wattmeter. A permanent record of the instantaneous demand may be obtained by use of a strip chart, circular disc, magnetic tape, or other type of recording medium. The maximum demand may then be determined by referring to the recorded data and reading the appropriate value. In metering installations using magnetic tape, the tape is removed from the recorder and taken to a magnetic tape reader where the billing information is obtained.

The integrating demand register operates by counting the number of disc revolutions for a specified demand time interval. Since the demand interval is a fixed value, the maximum demand occurs in the time interval with the greatest number of disc revolutions. At the end of each time interval, the register is reset to zero and the process repeated. A separate register will store the maximum demand until manually reset to zero.

The thermal or lagged type of demand meter is the most common for small services. In the thermal type of demand meter, the thermal element produces heat, which is proportional to the amount of energy being used at a given time. The heat energy is used to drive an indicating pointer that indicates the instantaneous demand. A friction pointer is also advanced by the indicating pointer to indicate the maximum demand. As the indicating pointer advances, the friction pointer advances along with it. If the demand decreases, however, the friction pointer remains at the maximum value until manually reset. In most meters, the indicating pointer is black and the friction pointer is red. The friction pointer is reset after each meter reading.

Solid-State Metering

The use of solid-state, microprocessor-based metering is becoming more and more widespread in the utility industry. Multifunction meters are able to replace several induction disc-type meters for various metering schemes. For example, many solid-state meters can be programmed to measure and display quantities such as polyphase and single-phase watthours (WH), varhours (VH), and volt-ampere hours (VAH); watts, vars, and volt-amperes delivered and received; peak demand, time of peak, and minimum demand; power factor, and so on. In addition to measuring and displaying electrical quantities, solid-state meters have the capability of storing the information in memory. The stored information can then be downloaded to a computer for billing calculations or load analysis. The downloading can be done either on site by direct connection to the meter or by remote communication through the use of a built-in modem. Fiber-optic, power line carrier, radio, or telephone channels may be used as the communication link between the meter and the computer.

Metering Connections

This section will show some of the more common connections for the metering of electric power. The diagrams are simplified to show only one meter connection. In some instances, it is desirable to meter other electrical quantities as well. The instrument trans-

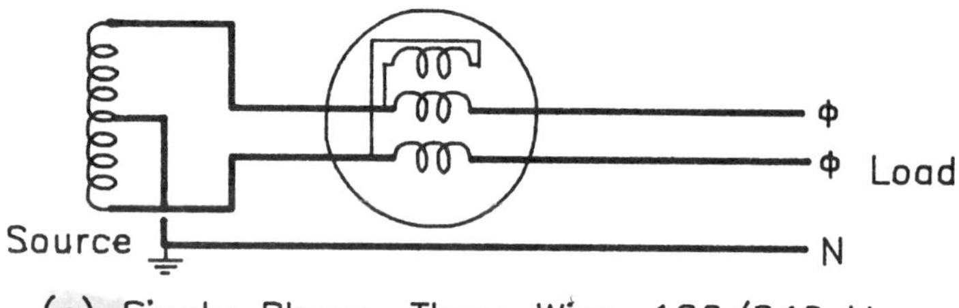

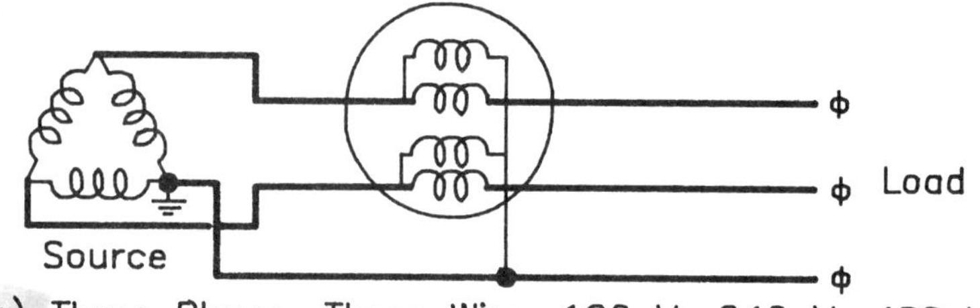

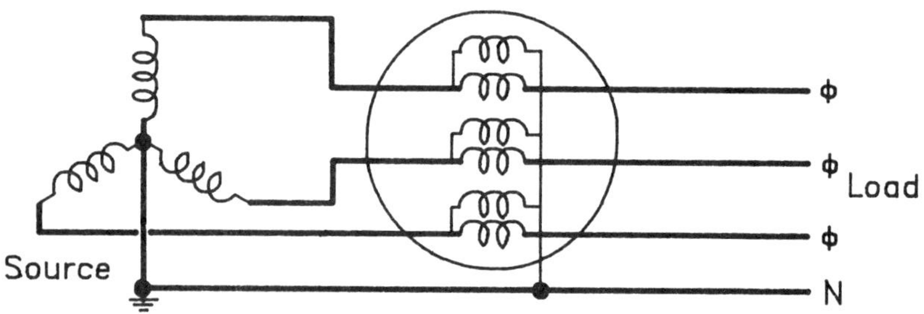

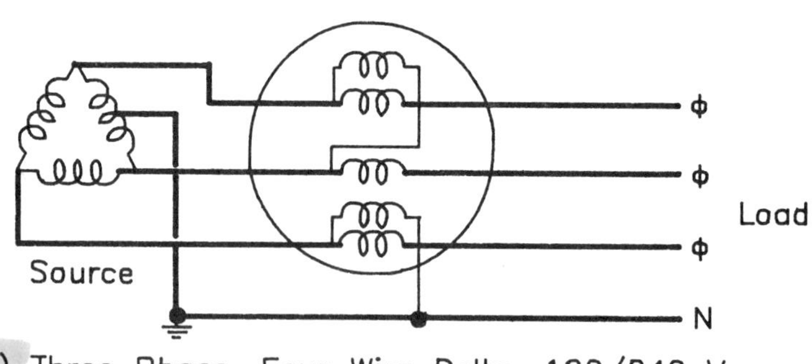

Figure 4-3 Self-contained watthour meter connections.

formers and meters are usually furnished by the utility and installed by the customer's electrician.

The metering schematics shown in Fig. 4-3 are for self-contained meters that do not require instrument transformers. Figure 4-3a shows the connection for a typical 120/240-V, single-phase, three-wire system. This is the common service voltage for residential and small commercial establishments. The stator consists of one voltage coil and two current coils. Since the voltage coil is connected between the two ''hot'' conductors, the voltage rating of the meter is 240 V. The current or class rating of the meter must be sufficient to carry the maximum load current. Figure 4-4 shows a typical single-phase, three-wire meter installation.

The circuit shown in Fig. 4-3b shows the metering connections for three-phase, three-wire services. Typical service voltages are 120, 240, and 480 V. The metering in this situation is similar to the two-wattmeter method used for three-phase, three-wire loads. Note that the meter has two stators, with voltage coils connected from phase to phase. Therefore, the voltage rating of the meter must be equal to the phase to phase voltage of the service.

Three-phase, four-wire services are typically metered using the configuration shown in Fig. 4-3c. Service voltages are either 480Y/277 V or 208Y/120 V. The meter shown has three stators, with each stator having one potential coil and one current coil. Since the voltage coils are connected from phase to neutral, the voltage rating of the meter coils is either 277 V for 480Y/277-V services or 120 V for 208Y/120-V services.

Three-phase, four-wire, delta-connected services are metered by the configuration shown in Fig. 4-3d. Two stators are used, with one of the stators having two current coils and one voltage coil and the other stator having one current coil and one voltage coil. The meter has a voltage rating of 240 V for this type of service.

Figure 4-4 Single-phase, three-wire, induction-disc watthour meter installation. (Photo Courtesy of Ohio Edison Company)

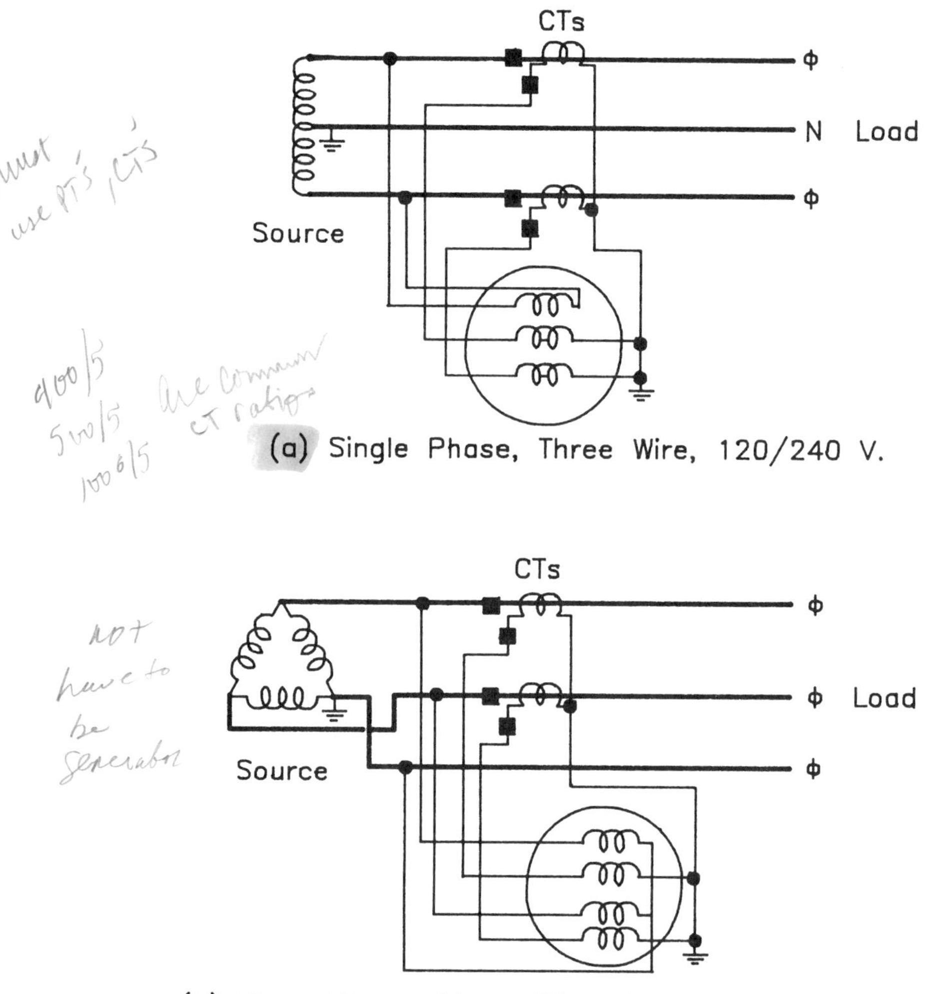

(a) Single Phase, Three Wire, 120/240 V.

(b) Three Phase, Three Wire, 120 V, 240 V, 480 V.

Figure 4-5 Connection diagrams for transformer rated watthour meters, low-voltage services.

The metering connections shown in Fig. 4-5 are for transformer rated meters. The meter connections shown are for high-current, low-voltage services. For example, on a 480Y/277-V, 2000-A, three-phase, four-wire service, current transformers are required to step down the current from 2000 to 5 A. Generally, the primary rating of the CT is selected to match the ampacity of the service. The secondary rating of the CTs is typically 5 A. As a result, it is common to use class 10 or 20 meters for these configurations. The meter voltage rating is selected to match the voltage ratings of the services, as was done for the metering configurations in Fig. 4-3.

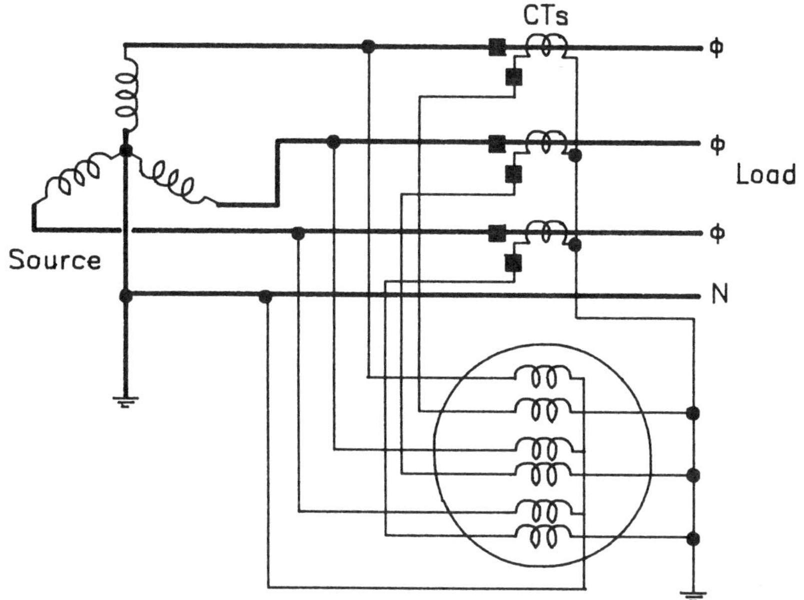

(c) Three Phase, Four Wire, 208Y/120 V, 480Y/277 V.

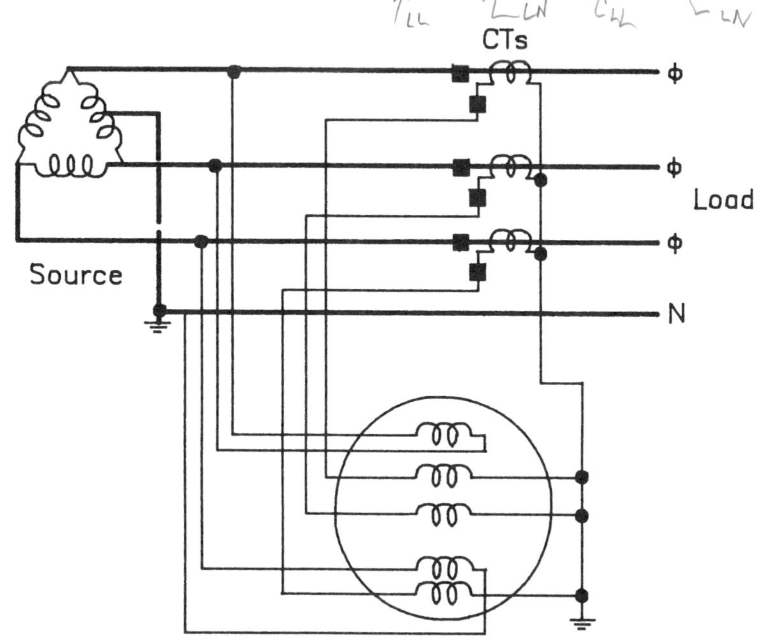

(d) Three Phase, Four Wire, 120/240 V.

Figure 4-5 (Cont.)

Figure 4-6 CT-metered, low-voltage service. (Photo Courtesy of Ohio Edison Company)

The current transformers are typically of the window type with the service conductor passing through the CT window. Essentially, the primary of the CT has one turn, that of the service conductor itself. For overhead services, the CTs are typically mounted on the exterior building wall near the service drop location. In underground services, the CTs may be mounted in a cabinet near the service entrance or over the secondary terminals of the pad mount distribution transformer supplying the service. Figure 4-6 shows a typical low-voltage CT metered service. Note the CT enclosure to the right of the service mast.

For high-voltage, high-current services, voltage transformers as well as current transformers are required. Figure 4-7a shows the metering connections for three-phase, four-wire services. Figure 4-7b shows the connections for the three-phase, three-wire service. These services are common among larger commercial and industrial establishments. These connections would be typical for service voltages above 600 V. Figure 4-8 shows a typical primary metering installation for service at 12.47 kV.

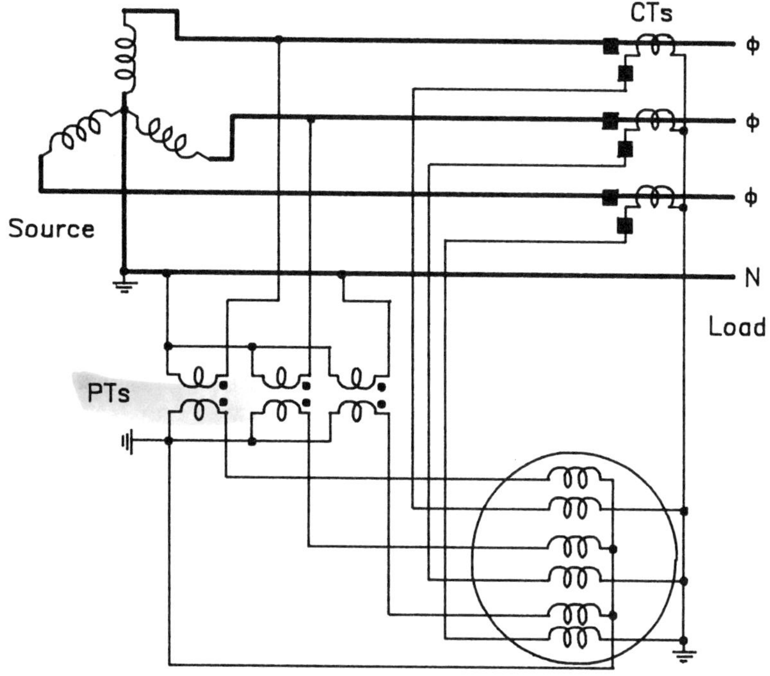

(a) Three Phase, Four Wire, Wye Service.

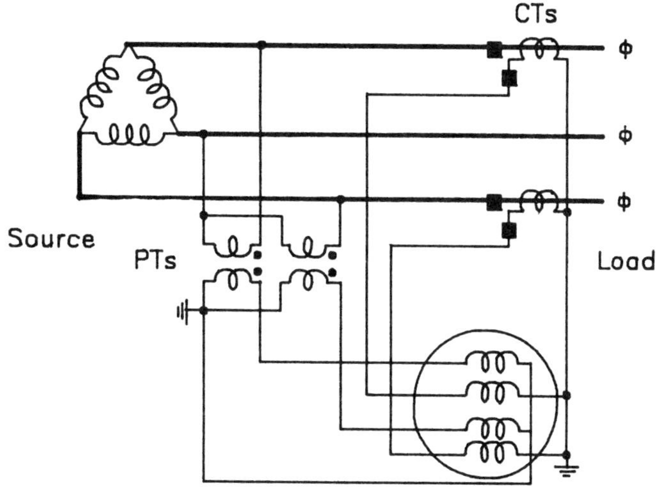

(b) Three Phase, Three Wire, Delta Service.

Figure 4-7 Transformer rated meter connections for high-voltage, high-current service.

Figure 4-8 Primary metering installation for 12.47-kV service. (Photo Courtesy of Ohio Edison Company)

4-5 Rates and Billing

Utility rate schedules vary considerably among utilities nationwide. The rates vary depending on the type of generation, geographic location, size and voltage of the load being served, customer class, and other factors. All rate schedules include a certain charge per kWH used. Other rate schedules include charges related to peak demand, power factor, time of day usage, interruptible services, and so forth. Special rates are offered by utilities for street lighting, water heating, private outdoor lighting, traffic signals, and other services.

The cost of generating power is directly related to the type of energy source used to drive the utility generators. Geographic location will have an impact on the type of prime mover used in the generating plants, as well as on the nature of the electrical load to be supplied. Inexpensive hydroelectric power constitutes the largest percentage of the total generation mix for utilities in the northwestern United States and Canada. Relatively expensive oil-fired steam power plants represent a substantial portion of utility generation in the eastern United States. In the midwestern region of the United States, coal-fired steam power plants make up the largest percentage of generation mix.

Rates are usually lower for customers supplied from utility medium- and high-voltage systems. For example, a large steel mill supplied at 138 kV will be charged a lower amount per kWH than the typical residential user. This is because it costs the utility less to supply the steel mill than a residential customer. The steel mill will have to operate and maintain the transformers and switchgear necessary to transform the voltage from 138 kV down to utilization voltage levels. There is also an economy of scale since the steel mill will use such a large amount of power compared to the average residential user.

Most utilities separate the customer base into three major classes: residential, commercial, and industrial. Within each class there may be several rate structures. For example, within the residential class, there may be a rate schedule for basic kWH metering, as well as a rate schedule for load demand metering. The customer will usually have a choice between the two schedules. Rates for residential water heating may apply if the water heater is connected to a separate meter and timed for certain hours of operation. Special rates for residential outdoor lighting are offered by some utilities. Within the commercial and industrial class, different rate schedules may apply for small, medium, or large establishments, depending on the demand and amount of energy consumed.

The following example illustrates rate calculation for a small commercial establishment. The rate schedule shown in the example has been derived for purposes of illustration. Rate schedules for your area can be readily obtained from the local utility.

EXAMPLE 4-9 Load data for a commercial establishment indicate a peak demand of 167 kW and that 45,890 kWH were used last month. Using the following rate schedule, calculate the monthly billing.

Rate Schedule for Example 4-9

Demand charge:	\$17.32 per kW for first 100 kW
	\$13.56 per kW for remaining kW
Energy charge:	\$0.0856 for first 200 kWH per kW of billing demand
	\$0.0474 for all kWH over 200 kWH per kW of billing demand
Fuel cost adjustment:	\$0.0035 per kWH

Solution

Demand:	100 kW · \$17.32 per kW =	\$1732.00
	67 kW · \$13.56 per kW =	\$ 908.52
Energy:	200 kWH per kW of demand is	
	167 kW · 200 = 33,400 kWH at \$0.0856 per kWH =	\$2859.04
	The remaining kWH is	
	45,890 − 33,400 = 12,490 kWH at \$0.0474 per kWH =	\$ 592.02
Fuel cost adjustment:		
	45,890 kWH at \$0.0035 per kWH =	\$ 160.62
	Total	\$6252.20

References

[1] Reprinted from IEEE Standard 100-1972, *IEEE Standard Dictionary of Electrical and Electronics Terms*, © 1972 by the Institute of Electrical and Electronics Engineers, Inc. This is an

archived document which has been superceded. The IEEE disclaims any responsibility or liability resulting from the placement and use of this publication. Information is reprinted with the permission of the IEEE.

Problems

4.1. The load profile shown in Fig. 4-9 represents the daily load on a 12-MVA distribution substation transformer. The average power factor is 0.95 lagging. Calculate the following:

a. Average daily demand in kVA

b. Maximum instantaneous demand in kVA

c. Daily load factor

d. Utilization factor for the substation transformer

4.2. A distribution transformer is required to serve the following connected loads:

Load 1: 10 kW, 0.95 lagging power factor
Load 2: 11 kW, 0.95 lagging power factor
Load 3: 15 kW, 0.95 lagging power factor

Determine the minimum required apparent power rating of the transformer, assuming a demand factor of 0.73 for three loads.

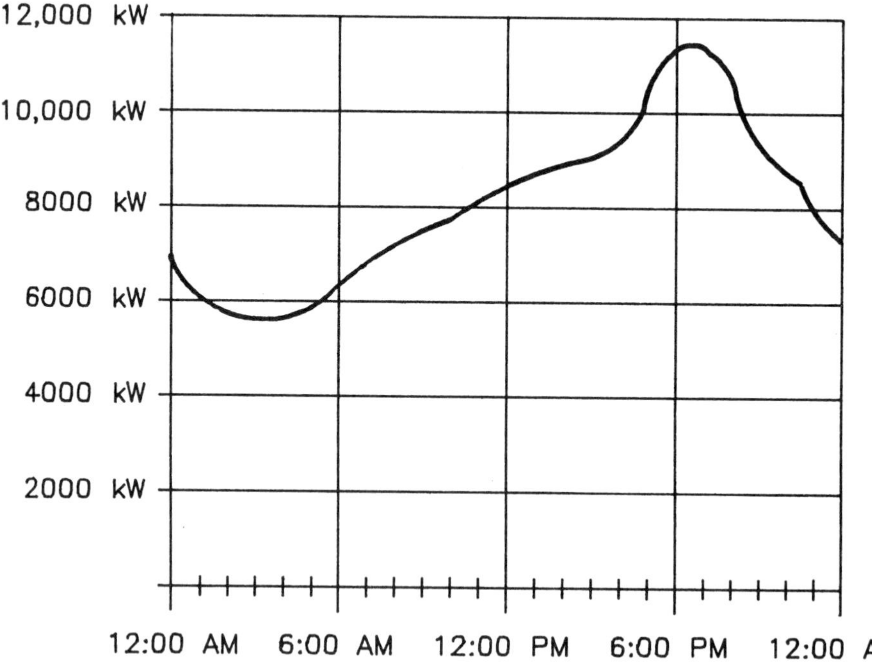

Figure 4-9 Load profile for Problem 4-1.

4.3. A 12.47-kV distribution feeder experiences a maximum peak demand of 4300 kVA. The following distribution transformers are installed on the circuit:

Single Phase	*Three Phase*
30 at 10 kVA	
42 at 15 kVA	3 at 112.5 kVA
57 at 25 kVA	2 at 150 kVA
33 at 50 kVA	4 at 225 kVA
21 at 75 kVA	5 at 300 kVA
14 at 100 kVA	1 at 500 kVA
13 at 167 kVA	1 at 750 kVA

Determine the total installed distribution transformer capacity and the utilization factor for the distribution transformers as a group.

4.4. The following peak demands were read from five residences connected to a distribution transformer:

Load 1:	10 kW	Load 4:	5 kW
Load 2:	13 kW	Load 5:	7 kW
Load 3:	9 kW		

If the diversity factor is 1.7 for a group of five loads, determine the peak demand on the distribution transformer. What is the coincidence factor?

4.5. A large three-phase load is supplied at 4.16 kV from a three-phase, four-wire distribution circuit. The loading is 567 kW at a power factor of 0.91 lagging. Determine the following:

a. Constant active and reactive power representation
b. Constant impedance representation
c. Constant current representation

4.6. Determine the constant impedance representation for the following motor at locked rotor conditions:

100 hp, 460 V, three phase, 60 Hz, 1725 rpm, code H

Assume a locked rotor power factor of 0.30 lagging.

4.7. Determine the constant impedance representation for the following motor operating at full-load rated conditions:

50 hp, 460 V, three phase, 60 Hz, 1725 rpm, code H
FLA = 62 A, full-load efficiency = 90%, full-load power factor = 0.89 lagging

4.8. A polyphase induction disc watthour meter is connected to a 480 V, three-phase, four-wire service using current transformers having a 1000:5 A ratio. The voltage rating of the meter stator elements is 277 V. The meter constant is 1.8. It is observed that the disc rotates six revolutions in 28 sec. Determine the estimated demand.

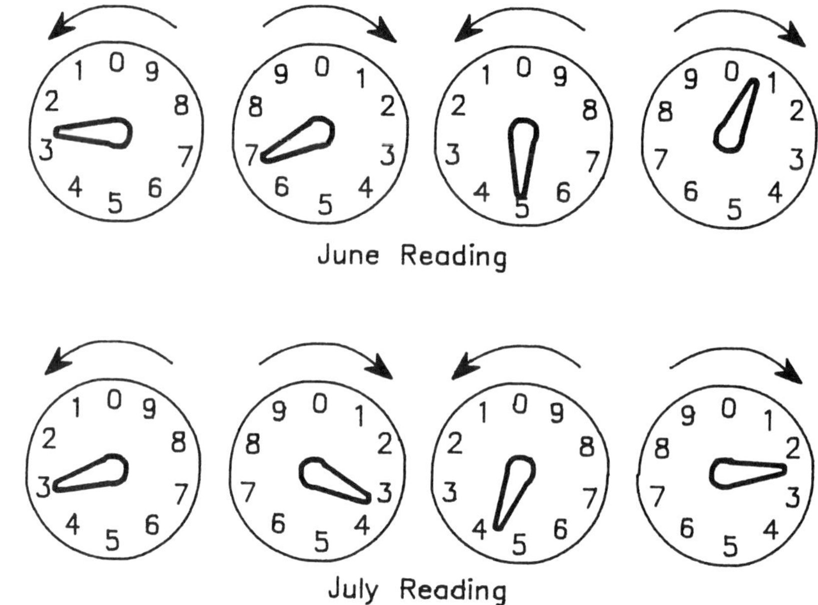

Figure 4-10 Dial register readings for Problem 4-9.

4.9. The meter readings shown in Fig. 4-10 were taken for the months of June and July. The peak demand as recorded on the meter was 5 kW. Using the following rate schedule, calculate the monthly bill.

Rate Schedule for Problem 4.9

Customer charge:	\$6.00 per month
Demand charge:	\$2.75 per kW
Energy charge:	\$0.1000 for first 100 kWH per kW of billing demand
	\$0.0675 for all kWH over 100 kWH per kW of billing demand
Fuel cost adjustment:	\$0.0057 per kWH

5

The Per Unit System

5-1 General

The per unit system is used extensively in electrical power system calculations. Essentially, the per unit system is a system of measurement in which various electrical quantities are normalized with respect to a specified base value. The per unit system is also used to some extent in everyday life. Consider for example the following statement: "The gas tank is half full." This could be interpreted as saying, "The gas tank has 0.5 per unit." If the gas tank can hold 20 gallons, then 0.5 per unit would correspond to 0.5 multiplied by 20 gallons, or 10 gallons. In this example, the *base* quantity is 20 gallons, the *per unit* quantity is 0.5, and the *actual* quantity is 10 gallons. If, on the other hand, the gas tank had a capacity of 15 gallons, then 0.5 per unit would correspond to 7.5 gallons. Here the *base* quantity is 15 gallons and the *actual* quantity is 7.5 gallons. In both examples, the per unit value is the same, even though the actual quantities are different. By definition, the per unit value of a certain quantity is the ratio of the actual value to some base value. Therefore, it is important when working in the per unit system to specify the required base values. Otherwise, per unit values have no real meaning.

This section presents the method used to perform electrical power system calculations using the per unit system. The selection of appropriate base quantities will be discussed. Electrical quantities such as voltage, current, impedance, and power will be converted to per unit values. Calculations will be performed on both single- and three-phase systems. Recall from Chapter 1 that a *balanced* three-phase system can be analyzed on an equivalent single-phase basis.

5-2 Single-Phase System

The use of the per unit system in performing calculations on a single-phase system is presented. The results of this section will apply to *balanced* three-phase systems as well. Consider the single-phase circuit element shown in Fig. 5-1. The current in the element is calculated from Ohm's law:

$$\mathbf{I} = \frac{\mathbf{V}}{\mathbf{Z}} \tag{5.1}$$

Also, the apparent power dissipated in the element is given by

$$\mathbf{S} = \mathbf{V} \cdot \mathbf{I}^* \tag{5.2}$$

Examination of Eqs. (5.1) and (5.2) reveals that four electrical quantities are involved: voltage, current, impedance, and apparent power. It should also be recognized that specification of any two of the electrical quantities will enable calculation of the remaining two. For example, if the voltage and impedance are specified, the current can be calculated from Eq. (5.1). This value of current is then substituted into Eq. (5.2) to yield the apparent power. Although Eqs. (5.1) and (5.2) are shown for actual electrical quantities, these same equations can be used to express the relationship between base quantities. Thus, Eqs. (5.1) and (5.2) can be rewritten as follows:

$$\mathbf{I}_{\text{base}} = \frac{\mathbf{V}_{\text{base}}}{\mathbf{Z}_{\text{base}}} \tag{5.3}$$

$$\mathbf{S}_{\text{base}} = \mathbf{V}_{\text{base}} \cdot \mathbf{I}_{\text{base}} \tag{5.4}$$

In electrical power systems calculations, the base values selected have magnitude only, not magnitude and phase angle. Thus, the base quantities are real numbers, not complex. Typically, a base apparent power S_{base} and base voltage V_{base} are specified, and the base impedance Z_{base} and base current I_{base} are calculated. To calculate the base current, Eq. (5.4) is solved for I_{base} as follows:

$$I_{\text{base}} = \frac{S_{\text{base}}}{V_{\text{base}}} \tag{5.5}$$

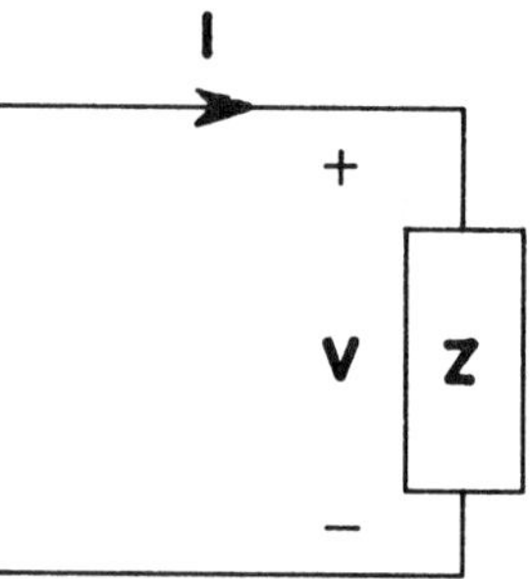

Figure 5-1 Single-phase circuit element.

The base impedance can be calculated using Eq. (5.3) as follows:

$$Z_{\text{base}} = \frac{V_{\text{base}}}{I_{\text{base}}} \tag{5.6}$$

Substituting Eq. (5.5) into (5.6) results in the following:

$$Z_{\text{base}} = \frac{V_{\text{base}}^2}{S_{\text{base}}} \tag{5.7}$$

Equations (5.5) and (5.7) are frequently used to calculate the base impedance and base current when the base apparent power and base voltage are specified.

EXAMPLE 5-1

Calculate the base impedance and base current for a single-phase system if the base voltage is 7.2 kV and the base apparent power is 10 MVA.

Solution

$$Z_{\text{base}} = \frac{7200^2}{10{,}000{,}000}$$
$$= 5.184\ \Omega$$

$$I_{\text{base}} = \frac{10{,}000{,}000}{7200}$$
$$= 1388.9\ \text{A}$$

EXAMPLE 5-2

A series circuit consists of an impedance of $3.50\angle 20°\ \Omega$, with an applied voltage of $7000\angle 30°$ V. Using a base voltage of 7200 V and a base apparent power of 10 MVA, calculate the following:

a. Actual current
b. Actual complex power
c. Per unit voltage
d. Per unit impedance
e. Per unit current
f. Per unit complex power

Solution

a. $\mathbf{I} = \dfrac{7000\angle 30°}{3.50\angle 20°}$

$= 2000\angle 10°$ A

b. $\mathbf{S} = \mathbf{V} \cdot \mathbf{I}^*$

$= (7000\angle 30°)(2000\angle 10°)^*$
$= (7000\angle 30°)(2000\angle -10°)$
$= 14{,}000{,}000\angle 20°$ VA
$= 13{,}155{,}697 + j4{,}788{,}282$ VA
$= 13.156 + j4.788$ MVA

c. $$\mathbf{V}_{pu} = \frac{\mathbf{V}_{act}}{V_{base}} = \frac{7000\angle 30°}{7200} = 0.9722\angle 30° \text{ pu}$$

d. $$\mathbf{Z}_{base} = \frac{V_{base}^2}{S_{base}} = 5.184\ \Omega$$

$$\mathbf{Z}_{pu} = \frac{\mathbf{Z}_{act}}{Z_{base}} = \frac{3.5\angle 20°}{5.184} = 0.6752\angle 20° \text{ pu}$$

e. $$\mathbf{I}_{pu} = \frac{\mathbf{V}_{pu}}{\mathbf{Z}_{pu}} = \frac{0.9722\angle 30°}{0.6752\angle 20°} = 1.4399\angle 10° \text{ pu}$$

f. $$\mathbf{S}_{pu} = \mathbf{V}_{pu} \cdot \mathbf{I}_{pu}^{*} = (0.9722\angle 30°)(1.4399\angle 10°)^{*} = 1.4\angle 20° \text{ pu} = 1.3156 + j0.4788 \text{ pu}$$

5-3 Three-Phase System

In a three-phase system, the base quantities are selected for both line to line and line to neutral voltages. Likewise, base quantities for total three phase apparent power and apparent power per phase are specified. Balanced three-phase operation is assumed in the specification of base quantities for a three-phase system. As such, the following relationships apply:

$$V_{base,ll} = \sqrt{3} \cdot V_{base,lN} \quad \textbf{(5.8)}$$

$$S_{base,3\Phi} = 3 \cdot S_{base,1\Phi} \quad \textbf{(5.9)}$$

Typically, in power system calculations, a line to line base voltage and total three-phase base apparent power are selected. For large power systems, a base apparent power of 100 MVA is usually chosen. Likewise, for smaller industrial power systems, a base apparent power of 10 or 1 MVA may be chosen.

The base current and base impedance are calculated on a per phase basis. Therefore, Eqs. (5.5) and (5.6) become

$$I_{base} = \frac{S_{base,1\Phi}}{V_{base,lN}} \tag{5.10}$$

$$Z_{base} = \frac{V_{base,lN}}{I_{base}} \tag{5.11}$$

Applying the relationships given by Eqs. (5.8) and (5.9) to Eq. (5.10) results in the following:

$$\begin{aligned} I_{base} &= \frac{S_{base,3\Phi}/3}{V_{base,ll}/\sqrt{3}} \\ &= \frac{S_{base,3\Phi}}{\sqrt{3} \cdot V_{base,ll}} \end{aligned} \tag{5.12}$$

Substituting Eq. (5.10) into (5.11) and applying the relationships given by Eqs. (5.8) and (5.9) result in the following:

$$\begin{aligned} Z_{base} &= \frac{(V_{base,lN})^2}{S_{base,1\Phi}} \\ &= \frac{(V_{base,ll}/\sqrt{3})^2}{S_{base,3\Phi}/3} \\ &= \frac{(V_{base,ll})^2}{S_{base,3\Phi}} \end{aligned} \tag{5.13}$$

EXAMPLE 5-3

Calculate the base current and base impedance for a three-phase power system if the three-phase base apparent power is 100 MVA and the line to line base voltage is 345 kV.

Solution

$$\begin{aligned} I_{base} &= \frac{100{,}000{,}000 \text{ VA}}{\sqrt{3} \cdot 345{,}000 \text{ V}} \\ &= 167.35 \text{ A} \end{aligned}$$

$$\begin{aligned} Z_{base} &= \frac{345{,}000^2}{100{,}000{,}000} \\ &= 1190.3\ \Omega \end{aligned}$$

In the previous discussion and examples, the calculations were performed using units of volts, ohms, amperes, and volt-amperes. The calculations become rather cumbersome when using these units to analyze larger power systems. More convenient forms of Eqs. (5.12) and (5.13) can be obtained by recognizing the following:

$$\text{Kilovolts} = \frac{\text{volts}}{1000} \tag{5.14}$$

$$\text{Kilovolt-amperes} = \frac{\text{volt-amperes}}{1000} \tag{5.15}$$

$$\text{Megavolt-amperes} = \frac{\text{volt-amperes}}{10^6} \tag{5.16}$$

Solving Eq. (5.14) for volts and Eqs. (5.15) and (5.16) for volt-amperes results in the following:

$$\text{Volts} = \text{kilovolts} \cdot 1000 \tag{5.17}$$

$$\text{Volt-amperes} = \text{kilovolt-amperes} \cdot 1000 \tag{5.18}$$

$$\text{Volt-amperes} = \text{megavolt-amperes} \cdot 10^6 \tag{5.19}$$

For medium-size industrial power systems and utility distribution systems, it is customary to work with units of kilovolts (kV) for voltage and kilovolt-amperes (kVA) for apparent power. Substituting Eqs. (5.17) and (5.18) into Eqs. (5.12) and (5.13) results in the following:

$$\begin{aligned} I_{\text{base}} &= \frac{\text{kVA}_{\text{base},3\Phi} \cdot 1000}{\sqrt{3} \cdot \text{kV}_{\text{base},ll} \cdot 1000} \\ &= \frac{\text{kVA}_{\text{base},3\Phi}}{\sqrt{3} \cdot \text{kV}_{\text{base},ll}} \end{aligned} \tag{5.20}$$

$$\begin{aligned} Z_{\text{base}} &= \frac{(\text{kV}_{\text{base},ll} \cdot 1000)^2}{\text{kVA}_{\text{base},3\Phi} \cdot 1000} \\ &= \frac{1000(\text{kV}_{\text{base},ll})^2}{\text{kVA}_{\text{base},3\Phi}} \end{aligned} \tag{5.21}$$

For large-scale industrial power systems and utility transmission systems, the calculations are typically carried out using units of kilovolts, and megavolt-amperes. Substituting Eqs. (5.17) and (5.19) into Eqs. (5.12) and (5.13) results in the following:

$$\begin{aligned} I_{\text{base}} &= \frac{\text{MVA}_{\text{base},3\Phi} \cdot 10^6}{\sqrt{3} \cdot \text{kV}_{\text{base},ll} \cdot 1000} \\ &= \frac{\text{MVA}_{\text{base},3\Phi} \cdot 1000}{\sqrt{3} \cdot \text{kV}_{\text{base},ll}} \end{aligned} \tag{5.22}$$

$$\begin{aligned} Z_{\text{base}} &= \frac{(\text{kV}_{\text{base},ll} \cdot 1000)^2}{\text{MVA}_{\text{base},3\Phi} \cdot 10^6} \\ &= \frac{\text{kV}^2_{\text{base},ll}}{\text{MVA}_{\text{base},3\Phi}} \end{aligned} \tag{5.23}$$

EXAMPLE 5-4

Calculate the base current and base impedance for a three-phase power system having a nominal voltage of 69 kV line to line. Use a three-phase apparent power base of 100 MVA.

Solution

$$I_{\text{base}} = \frac{100 \text{ MVA} \cdot 1000}{\sqrt{3} \cdot 60 \text{ kV}}$$

$$= 836.8 \text{ A}$$

$$Z_{\text{base}} = \frac{(69 \text{ kV})^2}{100 \text{ MVA}}$$

$$= 47.61\ \Omega$$

EXAMPLE 5-5

A large industrial plant is supplied from the utility 138-kV system. The actual plant load is 65 MW, 0.91 lagging power factor, at 134 kV. Using a base voltage of 138 kV and a base apparent power of 100 MVA, calculate the following:

a. Plant load in MVA
b. Plant reactive power consumption in MVAR
c. Line current in amperes
d. Base current
e. Line current in per unit
f. Per unit voltage
g. Real power consumption in per unit
h. Reactive power consumption in per unit
i. Apparent power consumption in per unit

Solution

a.
$$\text{Apparent power} = \frac{\text{real power}}{\text{power factor}}$$

$$= \frac{65 \text{ MW}}{0.91}$$

$$= 71.43 \text{ MVA}$$

b.
$$\text{Power factor angle} = \cos^{-1}(0.91)$$

$$= 24.5°$$

$$\text{Reactive factor} = \sin(\text{power factor angle})$$

$$= \sin(24.5°)$$

$$= 0.4146$$

$$\text{Reactive power} = \text{apparent power} \cdot \text{reactive factor}$$

$$= 0.4146 \cdot 71.43 \text{ MVA}$$

$$= 29.61 \text{ MVAR}$$

c.
$$I_{\text{line}} = \frac{71.43 \text{ MVA} \cdot 1000}{\sqrt{3} \cdot 134 \text{ kV}}$$

$$= 307.8 \text{ A}$$

d. $I_{base} = \dfrac{100 \text{ MVA} \cdot 1000}{\sqrt{3} \cdot 138 \text{ kV}}$
$= 418.4 \text{ A}$

e. $V_{pu} = \dfrac{134 \text{ kV}}{138 \text{ kV}}$
$= 0.971 \text{ pu}$

f. $I_{pu} = \dfrac{307.8 \text{ A}}{418.4 \text{ A}}$
$= 0.7357 \text{ pu}$

g. $P_{pu} = \dfrac{65 \text{ MW}}{100 \text{ MVA}}$
$= 0.65 \text{ pu}$

h. $Q_{pu} = \dfrac{29.61 \text{ MVAR}}{100 \text{ MVA}}$
$= 0.2961 \text{ pu}$

i. $S_{pu} = \dfrac{71.43 \text{ MVA}}{100 \text{ MVA}}$
$= 0.7143 \text{ pu}$

5-4 Transformer Representation in the Per Unit System

The advantage of using the per unit system in making certain power system calculations will become evident in this section. It will be shown that the transformer turns ratio is essentially eliminated from the calculations if the per unit system is used. As such, transformer representation will consist merely of a series per unit impedance.

When working with transformers, it is necessary to select base voltages for both the high and low side of the transformer. The base voltages are related by the transformer turns ratio. Let the turns ratio be defined as

$$\text{Turns ratio} = a = \frac{\text{rated high-side voltage}}{\text{rated low-side voltage}} \tag{5.24}$$

Then

$$V_{base,HS} = a \cdot V_{base,LS} \tag{5.25}$$

Likewise,

$$V_{base,LS} = \frac{1}{a} \cdot V_{base,HS} \tag{5.26}$$

The base apparent power will be the same for both the high side and low side. Therefore, once a base voltage is selected for the high or low side, the base voltage on the other side can be established by applying either Eq. (5.25) or (5.26). Equations (5.25) and (5.26) were derived for a single-phase transformer. However, these same equations can be used to calculate base voltages on either side of a three-phase transformer bank as well. In the case of a three-phase transformer bank, the line to line voltage bases are related by the equivalent line to line voltage turns ratio.

EXAMPLE 5-6

A single-phase 25-kVA, distribution transformer has a high-voltage rating of 13.2 kV and a low-voltage rating of 277 V. Determine the low-side base voltage for the following high-side base voltages:

a. 15.0 kV
b. 13.2 kV

Solution The transformer turns ratio is given by

$$a = \frac{13{,}200}{277}$$
$$= 47.653$$

a. $$V_{\text{base,LS}} = \frac{1}{47.653} \cdot 15{,}000$$
$$= 314.8 \text{ V}$$

b. $$V_{\text{base,LS}} = \frac{1}{47.653} \cdot 13{,}200$$
$$= 277 \text{ V}$$

EXAMPLE 5-7

A 400-MVA, three-phase power transformer has a rated high-side voltage of 336.4 kV line to line and a rated low-side voltage of 138 kV line to line. Calculate the base voltage on the high side for the following low-side base voltages:

a. 132 kV
b. 138 kV
c. 140 kV

Solution The transformer line to line turns ratio is

$$a = \frac{336.4 \text{ kV}}{138 \text{ kV}}$$
$$= 2.4377$$

a. $$V_{\text{base,HS}} = 2.4377 \cdot 132 \text{ kV}$$
$$= 321.8 \text{ kV}$$

b. $$V_{\text{base,HS}} = 2.4377 \cdot 138 \text{ kv}$$
$$= 336.4 \text{ kV}$$

c. $$V_{\text{base,HS}} = 2.4377 \cdot 140 \text{ kV}$$
$$= 341.3 \text{ kV}$$

In Examples 5-6 and 5-7, it should be noted that, if the voltage base on either side of the transformer is selected to be equal to the rated transformer voltage, then the base voltage on the other side of the transformer will correspond to the rated voltage. If the transformer has rated voltage applied to either the high- or low-side winding, the voltage induced in the other winding will be equal to rated voltage under no-load conditions. In terms of per unit voltages, the voltage applied to the transformer will be equal to 1.0 per unit, and the voltage induced will also be equal to 1.0 per unit. Therefore, the per unit turns ratio will be equal to 1.0 per unit. When working in the per unit system, base voltages can be selected such that the per unit turns ratio of most transformers in the system is equal to 1:1. Examples of proper selection of base voltages and system analysis in the per unit system are covered in Section 5-4.

The internal impedances of a transformer can also be expressed in per unit. Recall from Chapter 2 the transformer equivalent circuit. This equivalent circuit is redrawn in Fig. 5-2, with the excitation branch neglected. Neglecting the transformer excitation branch will introduce negligible error if the transformer is operating at approximately 25% rated load or above. The resistance and reactance on the high side of the transformer may be reflected to the low side of the transformer by dividing the high side resistance and reactance by the transformer turns ratio squared. The result is then added to the low-side resistance and reactance to obtain the equivalent impedances referred to the low side. Expressed as an equation,

$$R_{\mathrm{LS,eq}} = R_{\mathrm{LS}} + \frac{1}{a^2} \cdot R_{\mathrm{HS}} \tag{5.27}$$

$$X_{\mathrm{LS,eq}} = X_{\mathrm{LS}} + \frac{1}{a^2} \cdot X_{\mathrm{HS}} \tag{5.28}$$

In a similar manner, if it is desired to determine the transformer impedances referred to the high side, the following equations may be used:

$$R_{\mathrm{HS,eq}} = R_{\mathrm{HS}} + (a^2) \cdot R_{\mathrm{LS}} \tag{5.29}$$

$$X_{\mathrm{HS,eq}} = X_{\mathrm{HS}} + (a^2) \cdot X_{\mathrm{LS}} \tag{5.30}$$

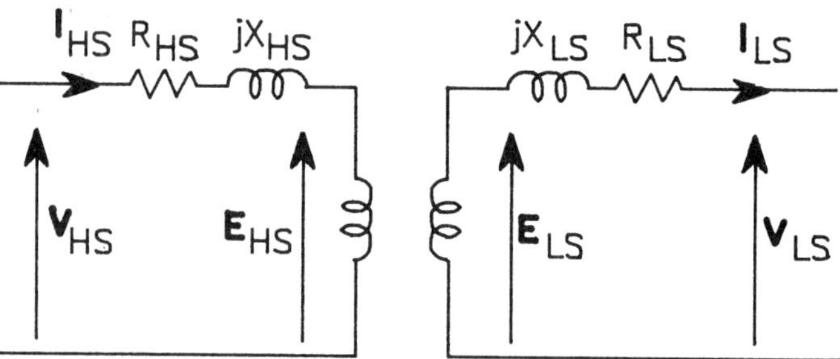

Figure 5-2 Transformer simplified equivalent circuit.

It is also possible to calculate the equivalent low-side resistance and reactance from the equivalent high-side resistance and reactance as follows:

$$R_{\text{LS,eq}} = \frac{1}{a^2} \cdot R_{\text{HS,eq}} \tag{5.31}$$

$$X_{\text{LS,eq}} = \frac{1}{a^2} \cdot X_{\text{HS,eq}} \tag{5.32}$$

Likewise, the equivalent high-side resistance and reactance are related to the equivalent low-side resistance and reactance by the following equations:

$$R_{\text{HS,eq}} = (a^2) \cdot R_{\text{LS,eq}} \tag{5.33}$$

$$X_{\text{HS,eq}} = (a^2) \cdot X_{\text{LS,eq}} \tag{5.34}$$

EXAMPLE 5-8

A single-phase, 50-kVA distribution transformer has a high-side voltage rating of 7.2 kV and a low-side voltage rating of 240 V. The equivalent impedance of the transformer referred to the high-voltage side is $10 + j20\ \Omega$. Determine the equivalent impedance referred to the low-voltage side.

Solution The transformer turns ratio is

$$a = \frac{7200\ \text{V}}{240\ \text{V}}$$

$$= 30$$

$$R_{\text{LS,eq}} = \frac{1}{30^2} \cdot 10\ \Omega$$

$$= 0.0111\ \Omega$$

$$X_{\text{LS,eq}} = \frac{1}{30^2} \cdot 20\ \Omega$$

$$= 0.0222\ \Omega$$

Transformer impedances may be expressed in per unit instead of ohmic values. To calculate the transformer per unit impedance, it is necessary to calculate the base impedance of the transformer. The question arises as to which base apparent power and which base voltage should be selected. An obvious choice for the base apparent power is the apparent power rating of the transformer. Base voltages can also be chosen equal to the rated voltages of the transformer. Therefore, two base impedances will be calculated: one for the high-voltage side and one for the low-voltage side. The per unit impedances can be calculated by dividing the equivalent high- or low-side impedance by the respective high- or low-side base impedance. It is important to remember that you cannot mix high- and low-side values. That is, it would be incorrect to divide the equivalent high-side impedance by the low-side base impedance to determine the per unit impedance.

EXAMPLE 5-9

Calculate the percent resistance and percent reactance for the distribution transformer of Example 5-8. Do this for both the high side and low side and compare the results.

Solution Starting with the high side, the base impedance is calculated:

$$Z_{\text{base,HS}} = \frac{1000 \cdot (7.2 \text{ kV})^2}{50 \text{ kVA}}$$
$$= 1036.8\ \Omega$$
$$R_{\text{pu,HS}} = \frac{10\ \Omega}{1036.8\ \Omega}$$
$$= 0.0096 \text{ pu}$$
$$= 0.96\%$$
$$X_{\text{pu,HS}} = \frac{20\ \Omega}{1036.8\ \Omega}$$
$$= 0.0193 \text{ pu}$$
$$= 1.93\%$$

For the low-voltage side,

$$Z_{\text{base,LS}} = \frac{240^2}{50{,}000}$$
$$= 1.152\ \Omega$$
$$R_{\text{pu,LS}} = \frac{0.0111\ \Omega}{1.152\ \Omega}$$
$$= 0.0096 \text{ pu}$$
$$= 0.96\%$$
$$X_{\text{pu,LS}} = \frac{0.0222\ \Omega}{1.152\ \Omega}$$
$$= 0.0193 \text{ pu}$$
$$= 1.93\%$$

From Example 5-9, it can be seen that the per unit impedance of a transformer is the *same* regardless of whether the calculation is performed on the low- or high-voltage side. Typically, transformer impedances are specified by the manufacturer in per unit or percent, based on the rated apparent power and voltage of the transformer.

The transformer equivalent circuit can be modeled in the per unit system as shown in Fig. 5-3. Note that the turns ratio has been eliminated by proper selection of the voltage bases. Also, all electrical quantities pertaining to this circuit must be specified in per unit, using the same apparent power and voltage bases.

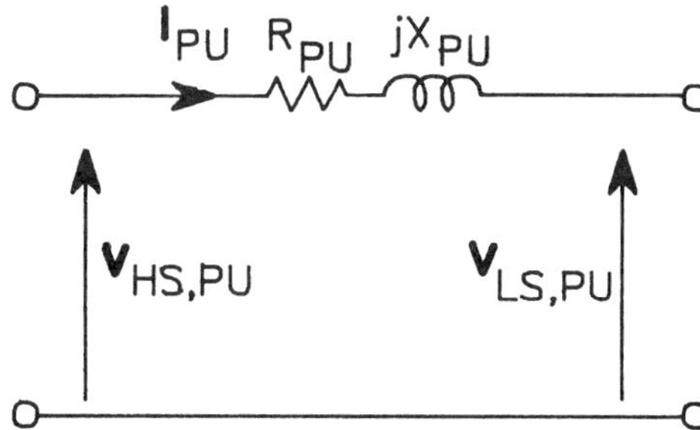

Figure 5-3 Transformer per unit equivalent circuit.

In the case of balanced three-phase transformer connections, the per unit impedances are based on a per phase line to neutral equivalent circuit. It will be shown by example that the per unit impedances of a transformer bank are the same regardless of whether the transformers are wye or delta connected.

EXAMPLE 5-10

Three identical single-phase transformers are to be connected to form a three-phase transformer bank. Each transformer has an apparent power rating of 25 kVA, a high-voltage rating of 2400 V, a low-voltage rating of 277 V, and an equivalent impedance referred to the high side of $3.5 + j5.5\ \Omega$. Calculate the per unit impedance for the following:

a. Transformers wye connected on the high-voltage side
b. Transformers delta connected on the high-voltage side

Solution

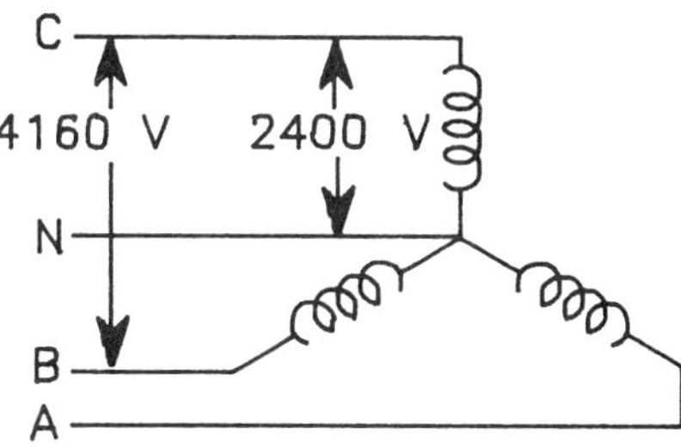

Figure 5-4 Wye-connected high-voltage windings.

a. The high-side wye connection is shown in Fig. 5-4. Note that the line to neutral voltage is equal to 2400 V, which means that the line to line voltage is equal to $\sqrt{3} \cdot 2400 = 4160$ V. The base voltage is selected to be the nominal line to line system voltage. Since the transformer bank is comprised of three 25-kVA transformers, the total three-phase apparent power rating would be 75 kVA. The base impedance is

$$Z_{base} = \frac{1000 \cdot (4.16\ \text{kV})^2}{75\ \text{kVA}}$$
$$= 230.4\ \Omega$$
$$R_{pu} = \frac{3.5\ \Omega}{230.4\ \Omega}$$
$$= 0.0152\ \text{pu}$$
$$X_{pu} = \frac{5.5\ \Omega}{230.4\ \Omega}$$
$$= 0.0239\ \text{pu}$$

b. The high-side delta connection is shown in Fig. 5-5. In the case of the delta connection, the voltage impressed on each of the three transformers is equal to 2400 V. As such, the line to line base voltage is 2400 V. The total three-phase base apparent power remains equal to 75 kVA as in part a. Therefore, the base impedance is

$$Z_{base} = \frac{1000 \cdot (2.4\ \text{kV})^2}{75\ \text{kVA}}$$
$$= 76.8\ \Omega$$

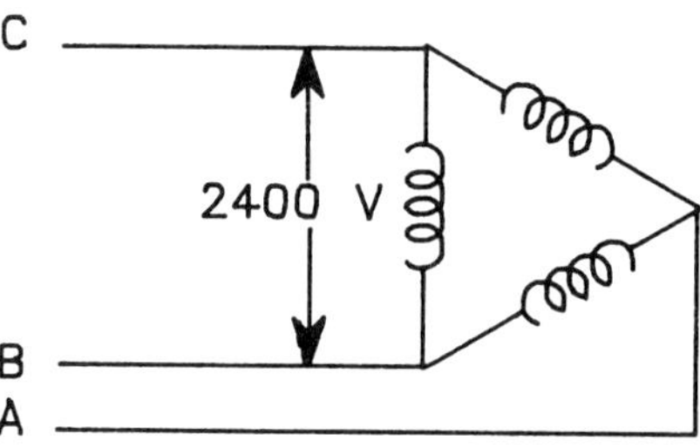

Figure 5-5 Delta-connected high-voltage windings.

Since all calculations are performed on a line to neutral equivalent, it is necessary to convert the delta-connected impedances to an equivalent wye. The equivalent wye resistance is

$$R_{eq,wye} = \frac{R_{eq,delta}}{3}$$
$$= \frac{3.5}{3}$$
$$= 1.167\ \Omega$$

Likewise, the equivalent wye reactance is

$$X_{eq,wye} = \frac{X_{eq,delta}}{3}$$

$$= \frac{5.5}{3}$$

$$= 1.833\ \Omega$$

The corresponding per unit transformer impedances for the line to neutral equivalent circuit are

$$R_{pu} = \frac{1.167\ \Omega}{76.8\ \Omega}$$

$$= 0.0152\ \text{pu}$$

$$X_{pu} = \frac{1.833\ \Omega}{76.8\ \Omega}$$

$$= 0.0239\ \text{pu}$$

Example 5-10 illustrates that the per unit impedance of a *balanced* three-phase transformer bank is equal to the per unit impedance of each transformer in the bank. Furthermore, the per unit impedance is the same regardless of whether the transformers are wye or delta connected.

In summary, this section has shown that the per unit impedances of a transformer are the same whether the impedances are reflected to the high- or low-voltage side. Also, if the base voltages on each side of a transformer are selected equal to the transformer rated voltages, the per unit turns ratio will be equal to unity. The transformer can be represented as a simple series circuit consisting of per unit impedances. Representation of balanced three-phase transformer banks using the line to neutral equivalent circuit is the same as the representation for single-phase transformers.

5-5 System Analysis in the Per Unit System

Most power system calculations are performed using per unit quantities. This section will demonstrate power system calculations using the per unit system. The selection of appropriate base voltages and three-phase base apparent power will be discussed. Also, the conversion of per unit impedances to common system bases will be presented. Examples of three-phase short-circuit and voltage-drop calculations performed in per unit will be presented.

The first step in analyzing a power system in per unit is the selection of an appropriate base apparent power. Any base apparent power may be selected. However, once a power base has been selected, it applies to the entire power system regardless of voltage level. The base voltages for the different voltage levels on the system are determined by selecting a base voltage for a particular portion of the system and then calculating base voltages for other portions of the system by utilizing transformer turns ratios. Base voltages are selected so that the per unit transformer turns ratios are unity.

EXAMPLE 5-11

For the power system shown in Fig. 5-6, determine the appropriate base voltages for the system. As a starting point, select a base voltage equal to 18 kV at the generator terminals.

Solution A base voltage of 18 kV is selected as the reference point. The base voltage on the 345-kV system is calculated as

$$V_{\text{base},345\text{ kV}} = 18\text{ kV} \cdot \frac{345\text{ kV}}{18\text{ kV}}$$

$$= 345\text{ kV}$$

The base voltage for the 230-kV system is calculated as

$$V_{\text{base},230\text{ kV}} = 345\text{ kV} \cdot \frac{230\text{ kV}}{345\text{ kV}}$$

$$= 230\text{ kV}$$

Finally, the base voltage for the 138-kV system is calculated as

$$V_{\text{base},138\text{ kV}} = 345\text{ kV} \cdot \frac{138\text{ kV}}{345\text{ kV}}$$

$$= 138\text{ kV}$$

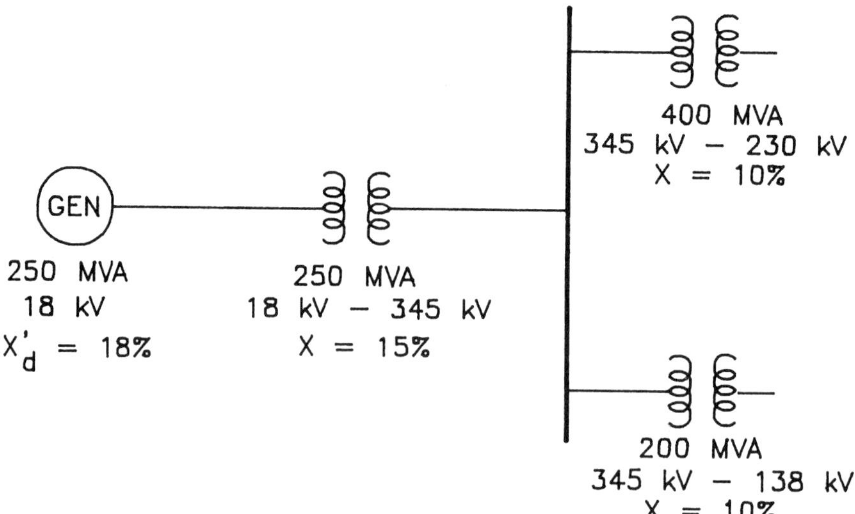

Figure 5-6 System for Example 5-11.

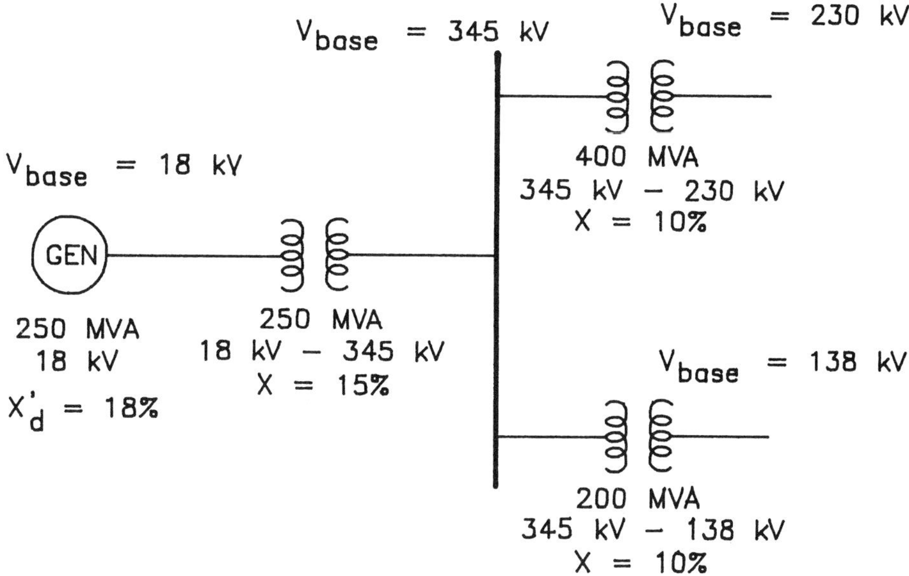

Figure 5-7 System of Example 5-11 indicating base voltages.

The system one-line diagram is redrawn as shown in Fig. 5-7, indicating the base voltages for the entire system.

Example 5-11 demonstrates the proper selection of base voltages for a power transmission system. It is good practice to indicate the base voltage in each portion of the power network on the one-line diagram.

A base apparent power must also be selected for the entire system. It was mentioned in Section 5-4 that the transformer nameplate impedances are specified in percent or per unit, using a base apparent power equal to the transformer nameplate apparent power and base voltages equal to the transformer rated or nominal high- and low-side voltages. The base apparent power selected for the entire system will therefore differ from the transformer nameplate apparent powers. It is necessary to convert or place the specified transformer and generator impedances on a common base. For any piece of electrical equipment, it must be understood that the *ohmic* impedance will be the same regardless of selected voltage or apparent power bases. Let the subscript 1 designate the base impedance and per unit impedance calculated on the equipment nameplate ratings. Then

$$\mathbf{Z}_{\text{act}} = \mathbf{Z}_{\text{pu},1} \cdot Z_{\text{base},1} \tag{5.35}$$

In a similar fashion, let the subscript 2 designate the base impedance and per unit impedance calculated on the new base quantities. The actual ohmic impedance in terms of the new bases is therefore given by

$$\mathbf{Z}_{\text{act}} = \mathbf{Z}_{\text{pu},2} \cdot Z_{\text{base},2} \tag{5.36}$$

Since the actual ohmic impedance of the device is independent of the selected base values, Eqs. (5.35) and (5.36) may be equated to one another:

$$\mathbf{Z}_{\text{pu},1} \cdot Z_{\text{base},1} = \mathbf{Z}_{\text{pu},2} \cdot Z_{\text{base},2} \tag{5.37}$$

Equation (5.37) is solved for the new per unit impedance based on the new base quantities as follows:

$$\mathbf{Z}_{\text{pu},2} = \mathbf{Z}_{\text{pu},1} \cdot \frac{Z_{\text{base},1}}{Z_{\text{base},2}} \tag{5.38}$$

The base impedances were given by Eqs. (5.21) and (5.23). Substituting Eq. (5.21) into (5.38) results in a more convenient form.

$$\begin{aligned}\mathbf{Z}_{\text{pu},2} &= \mathbf{Z}_{\text{pu},1} \cdot \frac{\dfrac{1000 \cdot [(\text{kV}_{\text{base},ll})_1]^2}{(\text{kVA}_{\text{base},3\Phi})_1}}{\dfrac{1000 \cdot [(\text{kV}_{\text{base},ll})_2]^2}{(\text{kVA}_{\text{base},3\Phi})_2}} \\ &= \mathbf{Z}_{\text{pu},1} \cdot \frac{[(\text{kV}_{\text{base},ll})_1]^2}{[(\text{kV}_{\text{base},ll})_2]^2} \cdot \frac{(\text{kVA}_{\text{base},3\Phi})_2}{(\text{kVA}_{\text{base},3\Phi})_1}\end{aligned} \tag{5.39}$$

Likewise, substituting Eq. (5.23) into (5.38) results in the following:

$$\begin{aligned}\mathbf{Z}_{\text{pu},2} &= \mathbf{Z}_{\text{pu},1} \cdot \frac{\dfrac{[(\text{kV}_{\text{base},ll})_1]^2}{(\text{MVA}_{\text{base},3\Phi})_1}}{\dfrac{[(\text{kV}_{\text{base},ll})_2]^2}{(\text{MVA}_{\text{base},3\Phi})_2}} \\ &= \mathbf{Z}_{\text{pu},1} \cdot \frac{[(\text{kV}_{\text{base},ll})_1]^2}{[(\text{kV}_{\text{base},ll})_2]^2} \cdot \frac{(\text{MVA}_{\text{base},3\Phi})_2}{(\text{MVA}_{\text{base},3\Phi})_1}\end{aligned} \tag{5.40}$$

Equations (5.39) and (5.40) are frequently used to convert per unit impedances from one base to another.

EXAMPLE 5-12 For the system shown in Example 5-11, place all impedances on a common power base of 100 MVA. Use the voltage bases for each part of the system as calculated in Example 5-11.

Solution Base impedances must be calculated for each voltage level in the system. For the 18-kV generator, the per unit impedance converted to the new system base values is

$$\begin{aligned}\mathbf{Z}_{\text{pu},2} &= \mathbf{Z}_{\text{pu},1} \cdot \frac{[(\text{kV}_{\text{base},ll})_1]^2}{[(\text{kV}_{\text{base},ll})_2]^2} \cdot \frac{(\text{MVA}_{\text{base},3\Phi})_2}{(\text{MVA}_{\text{base},3\Phi})_1} \\ &= j0.18 \text{ pu} \cdot \frac{(18 \text{ kV})^2}{(18 \text{ kV})^2} \cdot \frac{100 \text{ MVA}}{250 \text{ MVA}} \\ &= j0.072 \text{ pu} \\ &= j7.2\%\end{aligned}$$

Likewise, for the 18-kV–345-kV, 250-MVA generator step-up transformer,

$$\mathbf{Z}_{pu,2} = j0.15 \text{ pu} \cdot \frac{(18 \text{ kV})^2}{(18 \text{ kV})^2} \cdot \frac{100 \text{ MVA}}{250 \text{ MVA}}$$

$$= j0.06 \text{ pu}$$

$$= j6.0\%$$

For the 345-kV–230-kV, 400-MVA transformer,

$$\mathbf{Z}_{pu,2} = j0.10 \text{ pu} \cdot \frac{(345 \text{ kV})^2}{(345 \text{ kV})^2} \cdot \frac{100 \text{ MVA}}{400 \text{ MVA}}$$

$$= j0.025 \text{ pu}$$

$$= j2.5\%$$

Finally, for the 345-kV–138-kV, 200-MVA transformer,

$$\mathbf{Z}_{pu,2} = j0.10 \text{ pu} \cdot \frac{(345 \text{ kV})^2}{(345 \text{ kV})^2} \cdot \frac{100 \text{ MVA}}{200 \text{ MVA}}$$

$$= j0.05 \text{ pu}$$

$$= j5.0\%$$

Note that even though the 345-kV–230 kV and 345-kV–138 kV transformers have the same nameplate percent impedance, the per unit impedances on common voltage and apparent power bases are different. The system one-line diagram with all impedances in per unit on the common base apparent power of 100 MVA is shown in Fig. 5-8.

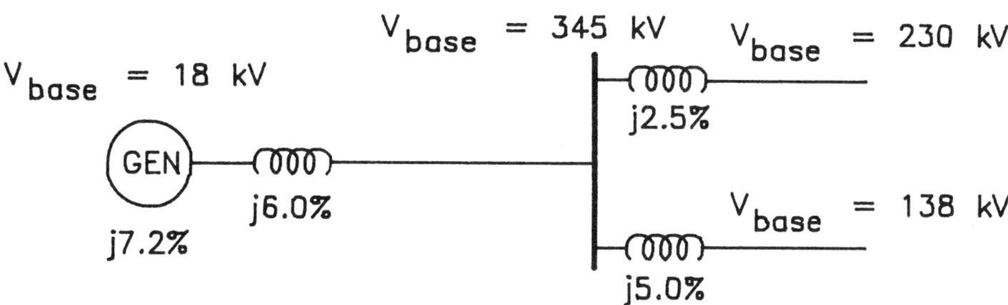

Figure 5-8 System for Example 5-12.

EXAMPLE 5-13

For the power system shown in Example 5-12, calculate the three-phase symmetrical fault current in per unit and amperes for a fault on the 230-kV bus. Assume that the generator is actually operating at 20 kV. Use the same base apparent power and base voltages from Examples 5-11 and 5-12. Also, calculate the currents flowing in the 345- and 18-kV portions of the system due to the fault on the 230-kV bus.

Solution The system impedances have already been placed on common apparent power and voltage bases. The base voltage for the generator was selected as 18 kV. Using the generator voltage as a reference, the per unit generator voltage is

$$\mathbf{V}_{\text{gen}} = \frac{20\angle 0^\circ \text{ kV}}{18 \text{ kV}}$$
$$= 1.111\angle 0^\circ \text{ pu}$$

The impedance diagram for this situation is shown in Fig. 5-9.

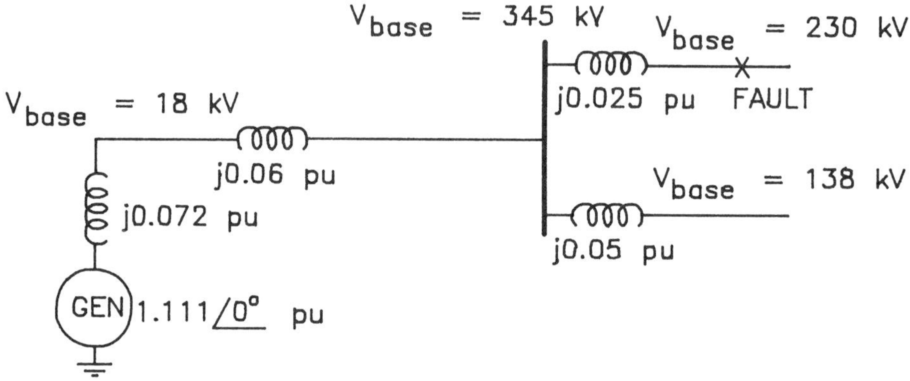

Figure 5-9 System for Example 5-13.

The total impedance between the fault and the generator source is equal to the sum of the generator impedance, generator step-up transformer impedance, and 345-kV–230-kV step-down transformer:

$$\begin{aligned} \mathbf{Z}_{\text{fault}} = {} & j0.072 \quad \text{(generator)} \\ & +j0.060 \quad \text{(step-up transformer)} \\ & +j0.025 \quad \text{(345-kV–230-kV transformer)} \\ \hline & j0.157 \text{ pu} \end{aligned}$$

The per unit fault current is equal to the per unit source voltage divided by the per unit fault impedance:

$$\mathbf{I}_{\text{fault}} = \frac{1.111\angle 0^\circ \text{ pu}}{j0.157 \text{ pu}}$$
$$= 7.076\angle -90^\circ \text{ pu}$$

The base current for the 230-kV system is

$$I_{\text{base},230\text{ kV}} = \frac{100{,}000\text{ kVA}}{\sqrt{3}\cdot 230\text{ kV}}$$
$$= 251.0\text{ A}$$

Therefore, the actual fault current in amperes is

$$\mathbf{I}_{\text{fault},230\text{ kV}} = (7.076\angle -90°)(251.0)$$
$$= 1776.3\angle -90°\text{ A}$$

The per unit fault current is the same in each part of this network, since it is a simple series circuit. The base currents, however, are different in each portion of the network. To calculate the fault currents in other portions of the network, it is necessary to calculate the base currents in these portions of the network. For the 345-kV portion, the base current is

$$I_{\text{base},345\text{ kV}} = \frac{100{,}000\text{ kVA}}{\sqrt{3}\cdot 345\text{ kV}}$$
$$= 167.4\text{ A}$$

Therefore, the actual fault current in amperes is

$$\mathbf{I}_{\text{fault},345\text{ kV}} = (7.076\angle -90°)(167.4)$$
$$= 1184.2\angle -90°\text{ A}$$

For the 18-kV generator, the base current is

$$I_{\text{base},18\text{ kV}} = \frac{100{,}000\text{ kVA}}{\sqrt{3}\cdot 18\text{ kV}}$$
$$= 3207.6\text{ A}$$

Therefore, the actual generator fault current in amperes is

$$\mathbf{I}_{\text{fault},18\text{ kV}} = (7.076\angle -90°)(3207.6)$$
$$= 22{,}697\angle -90°\text{ A}$$

EXAMPLE 5-14

For the power system shown in Example 5-13, assume that the load on the 138-kV bus can be modeled as a constant impedance equal to $95 + j45\ \Omega$ per phase. Assume that the 345-kV–230-kV transformer is out of service. Calculate the voltage on the 138-kV bus in per unit and actual volts for this condition.

Solution It is necessary to convert the actual ohmic impedance of the load to per unit on the same apparent power and voltage bases as before. Therefore,

$$Z_{\text{base},138\text{ kV}} = \frac{(138\text{ kV})^2}{100\text{ MVA}}$$

$$= 190.44\ \Omega$$

$$\mathbf{Z}_{\text{load}} = \frac{95 + j45\ \Omega}{190.44\ \Omega}$$

$$= 0.4988 + j0.2363\text{ pu}$$

The system with this constant impedance load is modeled as shown in Fig. 5-10.

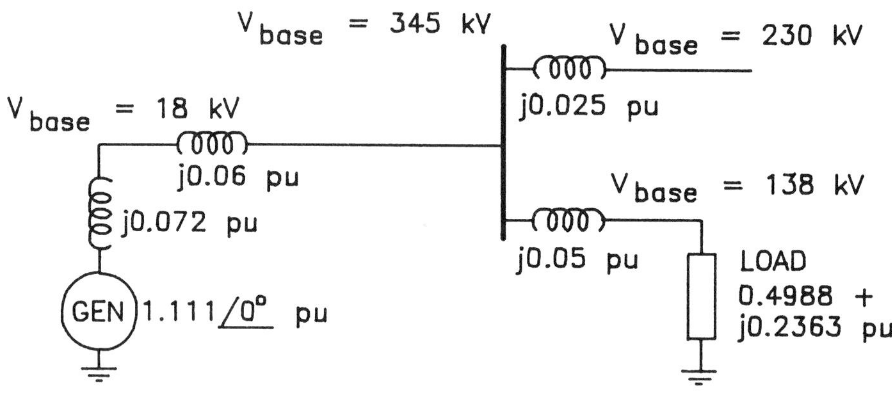

Figure 5-10 System for Example 5-14.

The voltage across the load may now be calculated using a simple voltage divider.

$$\mathbf{V}_{\text{load}} = \frac{(1.111\angle 0°) \cdot (0.4988 + j0.2363)}{0.4988 + j(0.2363 + 0.072 + 0.06 + 0.05)}$$

$$= \frac{(1.111\angle 0°) \cdot (0.4988 + j0.2363)}{0.4988 + j0.4183}$$

$$= \frac{0.6132\angle 25.4°}{0.6510\angle 40°}$$

$$= 0.9420\angle -14.6°\text{ pu}$$

The actual bus voltage in volts is found by multiplying the per unit voltage by the base voltage.

$$V_{\text{act}} = 138\text{ kV} \cdot 0.9420$$

$$= 130.0\text{ kV}$$

Examples 5-13 and 5-14 have demonstrated the use of the per unit system in calculating short-circuit currents and voltage drop in a power system containing different voltage levels. In both of these examples, the transformer turns ratios did not enter into the calculations once the impedances were placed on common power and voltage bases.

5-6 Transformers with Off-Nominal Turns Ratios

In Section 5.3 it was demonstrated that the per unit transformer turns ratio is equal to unity if the base voltages are selected equal to the transformer rated voltages. This section will introduce the situation in which the voltage rating of the transformer does not correspond to the selected base voltages. This situation can occur if there are transformers in a power system connected in a loop or, more likely, if the transformer is equipped with taps to regulate the voltage.

Consider the situation when two transformers are connected in parallel with different turns ratios, as shown in Fig. 5-11. If a base voltage of 12.47 kV is selected on the low-voltage side, the corresponding base voltage on the high-voltage side can be calculated using the turns ratio from either transformer. If the transformer *A* turns ratio is used, the base voltage on the high side is

$$V_{\text{base,HS}} = \frac{69\text{ kV}}{12.47\text{ kV}} \cdot 12.47\text{ kV}$$
$$= 69\text{ kV}$$

If, on the other hand, transformer *B* is chosen, the base voltage on the high-voltage side is

$$V_{\text{base,HS}} = \frac{70.73\text{ kV}}{12.47\text{ kV}} \cdot 12.47\text{ kV}$$
$$= 70.73\text{ kV}$$

It is impossible to have two different base voltages for a given portion of a power system. Usually, the base voltages are chosen to be equal to the nominal system voltages in a power system. In this particular example, a base voltage of 69 kV on the high side and

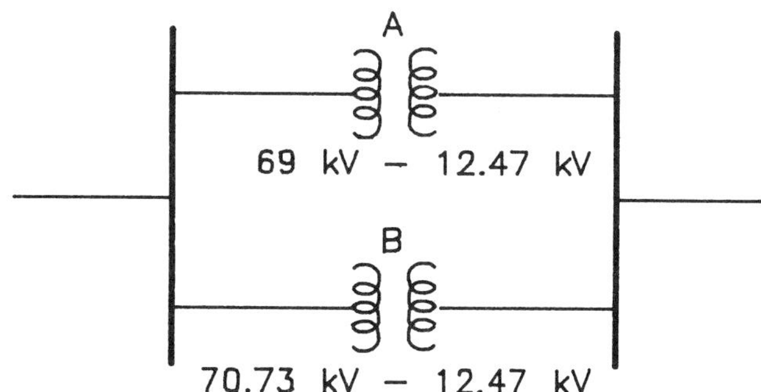

Figure 5-11 Parallel transformers with different turns ratios.

a base voltage of 12.47 kV on the low side correspond to standard nominal voltage ratings for power systems. Thus, the base voltage on the high side is selected as 69 kV. Transformer A therefore has a per unit turns ratio equal to 1:1. The per unit turns ratio of transformer B is then

$$\begin{aligned} a_{pu} &= \frac{V_{rated,HS}/V_{base,HS}}{V_{rated,LS}/V_{base,LS}} \\ &= \frac{70.73/69}{12.47/12.47} \\ &= \frac{1.025}{1.0} \\ &= 1.025:1 \end{aligned} \tag{5.41}$$

The relation between high-side and low-side per unit voltage is given by

$$\mathbf{V}_{pu,HS} = a_{pu} \cdot \mathbf{V}_{pu,LS} \tag{5.42}$$

Likewise, the relation between high-side and low-side per unit current is

$$\mathbf{I}_{pu,HS} = \mathbf{I}_{pu,LS}/a_{pu} \tag{5.43}$$

It is also necessary to account for per unit turns ratios other than 1:1 when reflecting impedances from one side of the transformer to the other. With the per unit turns ratio as defined in Eq. (5.41), the per unit low-side resistance and reactance are related to the per unit high-side resistance and reactance as follows:

$$R_{LS,pu} = \frac{1}{a_{pu}^2} \cdot R_{HS,pu} \tag{5.44}$$

$$X_{LS,pu} = \frac{1}{a_{pu}^2} \cdot X_{HS,pu} \tag{5.45}$$

Likewise, the per unit high-side resistance and reactance are related to the per unit low-side resistance and reactance by the following equations:

$$R_{HS,pu} = a_{pu}^2 \cdot R_{LS,pu} \tag{5.46}$$

$$X_{HS,pu} = a_{pu}^2 \cdot X_{LS,pu} \tag{5.47}$$

EXAMPLE 5-15

For the two transformers shown in Fig. 5-12, calculate the per unit current and apparent power loading on each transformer and the per unit load voltage. Assume that the load is represented by a constant impedance of $14.0 + j6.0\ \Omega$ per phase. Use a base voltage of 69 kV on the high side, a base voltage of 12.47 kV on the low side, and a base apparent power of 10 MVA. Assume that the actual voltage on the high side is 70.0 kV.

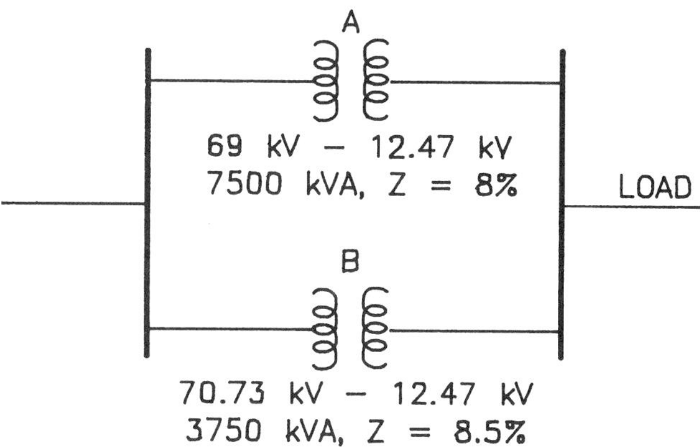

Figure 5-12 System for Example 5-15.

Solution First, it is necessary to convert all quantities to per unit on a common base. The base impedance on the 12.47-kV side is calculated:

$$
\begin{aligned}
Z_{\text{base},12.47\ \text{kV}} &= \frac{(12.47\ \text{kV})^2}{10\ \text{MVA}} \\
&= 15.55\ \Omega
\end{aligned}
$$

The per unit impedance of the load is

$$
\begin{aligned}
\mathbf{Z}_{\text{pu,LOAD}} &= \frac{14.0 + j6.0\ \Omega}{15.55} \\
&= 0.9 + j0.3858\ \text{pu}
\end{aligned}
$$

The transformer impedances must be placed on the same power and voltage bases. Since both transformers have the same low-side voltage rating, the impedances will be placed in per unit on the low-voltage side:

$$
\begin{aligned}
\mathbf{Z}_{A,\text{pu}} &= j0.08 \cdot \frac{(12.47\ \text{kV})^2}{(12.47\ \text{kV})^2} \cdot \frac{10\ \text{MVA}}{7.5\ \text{MVA}} \\
&= j0.1067\ \text{pu} \\
\mathbf{Z}_{B,\text{pu}} &= j0.085 \cdot \frac{(12.47\ \text{kV})^2}{(12.47\ \text{kV})^2} \cdot \frac{10\ \text{MVA}}{3.75\ \text{MVA}} \\
&= j0.2267\ \text{pu}
\end{aligned}
$$

The per unit turns ratio of transformer A is equal to

$$
\begin{aligned}
a_{A,\text{pu}} &= \frac{69\ \text{kV}/69\ \text{kV}}{12.47\ \text{kV}/12.47\ \text{kV}} \\
&= \frac{1.0}{1.0} \quad \text{or} \quad 1{:}1
\end{aligned}
$$

Likewise, the per unit turns ratio of transformer B is

$$a_{B,\text{pu}} = \frac{70.73\text{ kV}/69\text{ kV}}{12.47\text{ kV}/12.47\text{ kV}}$$

$$= \frac{1.025}{1.0} \quad \text{or} \quad 1.025:1$$

The actual voltage on the high side must also be converted to a per unit value. The high-side voltage will also be selected as the reference for this problem.

$$\mathbf{V}_{\text{HS}} = \frac{70.0\angle 0^\circ\text{ kV}}{69.0\text{ kV}}$$

$$= 1.0145\angle 0^\circ\text{ pu}$$

The per unit equivalent circuit with all quantities placed on common voltage and apparent power bases is shown in Fig. 5-13.

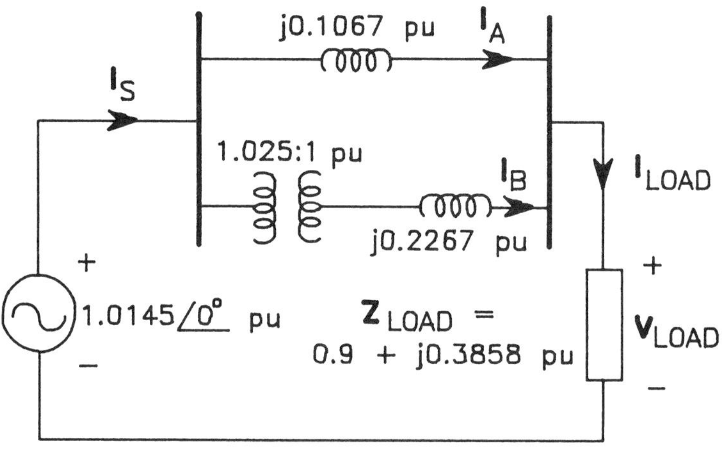

Figure 5-13 Per unit equivalent circuit, Example 5-15.

The source voltage of $1.0145\angle 0^\circ$ pu is applied to both transformers. Since the per unit turns ratio of transformer A is equal to 1:1, the per unit value of the induced secondary voltage will be equal to the per unit value of the applied voltage. Transformer B, however, has a per unit turns ratio of 1.025:1. It is necessary to calculate the per unit induced secondary voltage of transformer B using the applied source voltage and the per unit turns ratio.

$$\mathbf{V}_{B,\text{LS}} = \frac{1.0145\angle 0^\circ}{1.025}$$

$$= 0.9898\angle 0^\circ\text{ pu}$$

The system model is redrawn as shown in Fig. 5-14.

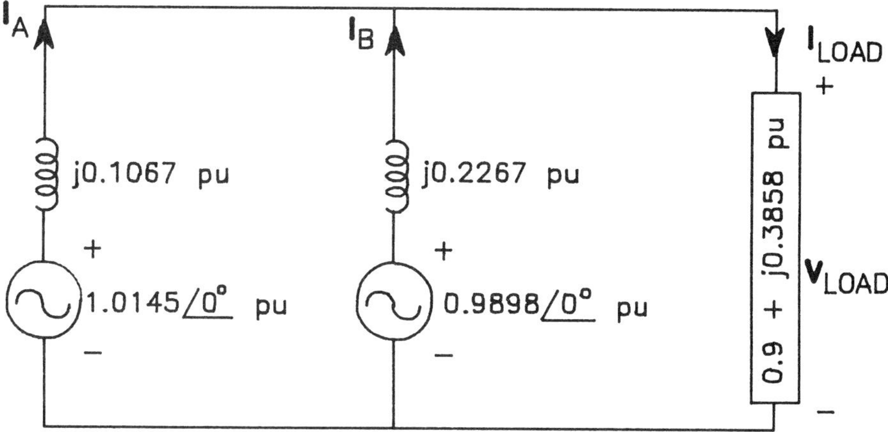

Figure 5-14 System for Example 5-15.

The currents and voltages can be calculated using several different circuit analysis techniques. Mesh analysis involving two mesh currents may be used, as well as the superposition theorem. For this example, a source conversion followed by nodal analysis will be used. Performing a source conversion on the two voltage sources results in the equivalent circuit shown in Fig. 5-15.

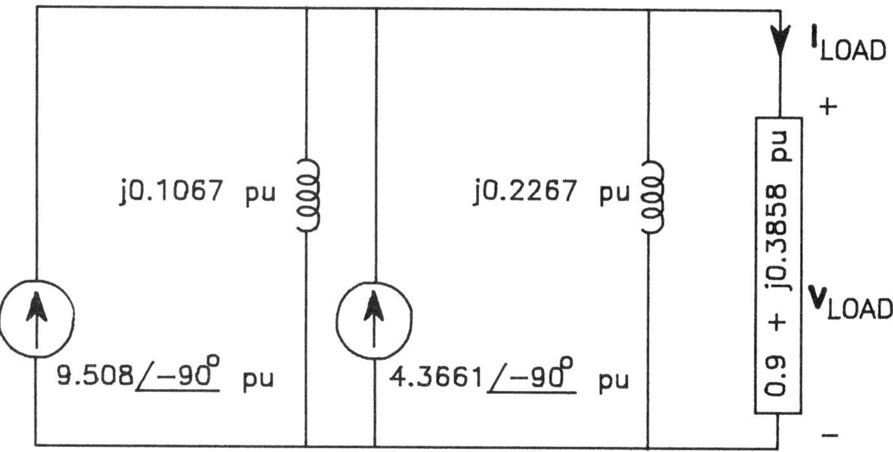

Figure 5-15 System for Example 5-15.

Using nodal analysis, we obtain the following equation:

$$\mathbf{V}_{\text{LOAD}} \cdot \left| \frac{1}{j0.1067} + \frac{1}{j0.2267} + \frac{1}{0.9 + j0.3858} \right| = 9.508\angle -90^\circ + 4.3661\angle -90^\circ$$

Solving for $\mathbf{V}_{\text{LOAD}}$ yields

$$\mathbf{V}_{\text{LOAD}} = 0.9759\angle -3.8° \text{ pu}$$

The load current is

$$\mathbf{I}_{\text{LOAD}} = \frac{0.9759\angle -3.8°}{0.9 + j0.3858}$$
$$= 0.9966\angle -27° \text{ pu}$$

The current in each transformer can be calculated as follows:

$$\mathbf{I}_A = \frac{1.0145\angle 0° - 0.9759\angle -3.8°}{j0.1067}$$
$$= 0.7164\angle -32.17°$$
$$= 0.6064 - j0.3814 \text{ pu}$$
$$\mathbf{I}_B = \frac{0.9898\angle 0° - 0.9759\angle -3.8°}{j0.2267}$$
$$= 0.2939\angle -13.9°$$
$$= 0.2853 - j0.0706 \text{ pu}$$

The apparent power loading on each transformer is

$$\mathbf{S}_{A,\text{pu}} = 0.9759\angle -3.8° \cdot (0.7164\angle -32.17°)^*$$
$$= 0.6991\angle 28.37° \text{ pu}$$
$$\mathbf{S}_{B,\text{pu}} = 0.9759\angle -3.8° \cdot (0.2939\angle -13.9°)^*$$
$$= 0.2868\angle 10.1° \text{ pu}$$

The actual apparent power loading on each transformer is found by multiplying the per unit apparent power by the base apparent power of 10 MVA, as follows:

$$\mathbf{S}_A = 10 \text{ MVA} \cdot 0.6991\angle 28.37°$$
$$= 6.991\angle 28.37° \text{ MVA}$$
$$\mathbf{S}_B = 10 \text{ MVA} \cdot 0.2868\angle 10.1°$$
$$= 2.868\angle 10.1° \text{ MVA}$$

EXAMPLE 5-16

Repeat Example 5-15 if both transformers have a rated high voltage of 69 kV.

Solution Since both transformers have the same high- and low-side voltage ratings, the per unit turns ratio will be equal to 1:1 for both transformers. The simplified equivalent circuit is shown in Fig. 5-16.

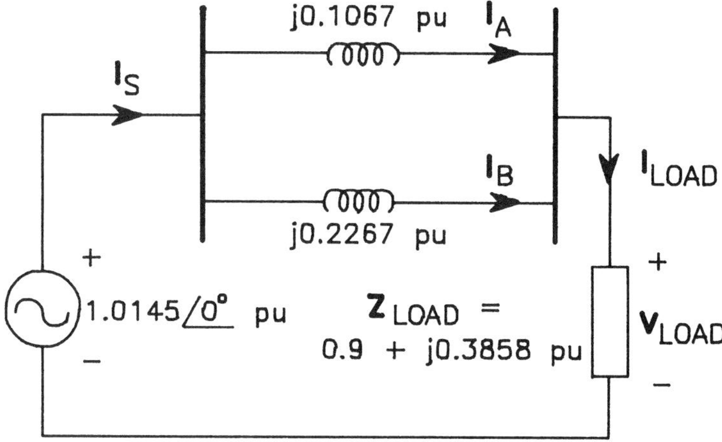

Figure 5-16 System for Example 5-16.

The impedance looking into the system from the source is

$$\begin{aligned}\mathbf{Z}_{\mathrm{IN}} &= j0.1067 \parallel j0.2267 + 0.9 + j0.3858 \\ &= 0.9 + j0.4584 \\ &= 1.01\angle 27^\circ \text{ pu}\end{aligned}$$

Since the resulting circuit is a series circuit, the load current is equal to the source current.

$$\begin{aligned}\mathbf{I}_S = \mathbf{I}_{\mathrm{LOAD}} &= \frac{1.0145\angle 0^\circ}{1.01\angle 27^\circ} \\ &= 1.0045\angle -27^\circ \text{ pu}\end{aligned}$$

The load voltage is

$$\begin{aligned}\mathbf{V}_{\mathrm{LOAD}} &= 1.0045\angle -27^\circ \cdot (0.9 + j0.3858) \\ &= 0.9836\angle -3.8^\circ \text{ pu}\end{aligned}$$

The current divider rule is used to calculate the per unit current in the transformers.

$$\begin{aligned}\mathbf{I}_A &= 1.0045\angle -27^\circ \cdot \frac{j0.2267}{j0.1067 + j0.2267} \\ &= 0.6830\angle -27^\circ \text{ pu}\end{aligned}$$

$$\begin{aligned}\mathbf{I}_B &= 1.0045\angle -27^\circ \cdot \frac{j0.1067}{j0.1067 + j0.2267} \\ &= 0.3215\angle -27^\circ \text{ pu}\end{aligned}$$

The apparent power loading on each transformer is

$$\mathbf{S}_{A,\text{pu}} = 0.9836\angle -3.8° \cdot (0.6830\angle -27°)^*$$
$$= 0.6718\angle 23.2° \text{ pu}$$
$$\mathbf{S}_{B,\text{pu}} = 0.9836\angle -3.8° \cdot (0.3215\angle -27°)^*$$
$$= 0.3162\angle 23.2° \text{ pu}$$

The actual apparent power loading on each transformer is found by multiplying the per unit apparent power by the base apparent power of 10 MVA, as follows:

$$\mathbf{S}_A = 10 \text{ MVA} \cdot 0.6718\angle 23.2°$$
$$= 6.718\angle 23.2° \text{ MVA}$$
$$\mathbf{S}_B = 10 \text{ MVA} \cdot 0.3162\angle 23.2°$$
$$= 3.162\angle 23.2° \text{ MVA}$$

Example 5-15 demonstrates the technique used to model transformers that have voltage ratings that do not correspond to the selected base voltages for the power system. In Example 5-16, the voltage ratings of the two transformers corresponded to the selected base voltages for the system. As such, the per unit turns ratio for each transformer was equal to 1:1, which greatly simplified the calculations.

5-7 Summary

This chapter has introduced the concept of the per unit system of measurement as applied to electrical power systems. It was demonstrated by example that a significant advantage of the per unit system is the elimination of transformer turns ratios for many system conditions. In summary, the following steps are performed when analyzing a power system using the per unit system.

1. Select an appropriate base voltage at some point in the system.
2. Calculate the base voltages for the remainder of the power system using transformer turns ratio relationships.
3. Select an appropriate base apparent power that will apply to the *entire* power system.
4. Convert all ohmic impedances to per unit impedances on the selected voltage and apparent power bases.
5. Convert all per unit impedances to per unit on the new voltage and apparent power bases selected for the system.
6. Perform all calculations in per unit using traditional circuit analysis techniques, such as mesh and nodal analysis, superposition, and source conversions.
7. If required, convert the calculated per unit values to actual values (volts, ohms, amperes, volt-amperes, watts, and vars).

Several examples illustrated the simplification of voltage-drop and fault current calculations if performed in the per unit system. Short-circuit calculations involving only symmetrical three-phase faults were also briefly discussed. The subject of short-circuit analysis will be discussed in greater detail in Chapters 10 and 11. Finally, a brief introduction to voltage-drop calculations was given. Voltage-drop and load flow techniques will be expanded on in Chapter 8.

Problems

5.1. Calculate the base impedance and base current for a single-phase power system using a base voltage of 240 V and a base apparent power of 10 kVA.

5.2. For the circuit shown in Fig. 5-17, calculate the following using a base apparent power of 5000 kVA and a base voltage of 2400 V.

a. Per unit impedances in each branch
b. Per unit source voltage
c. Per unit current in each branch
d. Per unit current supplied by the source
e. Per unit apparent, active, and reactive power dissipated in each branch
f. Per unit apparent, active, and reactive power supplied by the source
g. Compare the total active and reactive power consumed by the loads with the active and reactive power supplied by the source.

5.3. Repeat Problem 2 using actual values (that is, volts, ohms, and amperes).

5.4. Calculate the base impedance and base current using the specified voltage and apparent power bases for the following three-phase power systems.

a. $V_{\text{base},ll} = 765$ kV, $S_{\text{base},3\Phi} = 100$ MVA
b. $V_{\text{base},ll} = 500$ kV, $S_{\text{base},3\Phi} = 100$ MVA
c. $V_{\text{base},ll} = 345$ kV, $S_{\text{base},3\Phi} = 100$ MVA
d. $V_{\text{base},ll} = 138$ kV, $S_{\text{base},3\Phi} = 100$ MVA
e. $V_{\text{base},ll} = 69$ kV, $S_{\text{base},3\Phi} = 100$ MVA
f. $V_{\text{base},ll} = 23$ kV, $S_{\text{base},3\Phi} = 100$ MVA

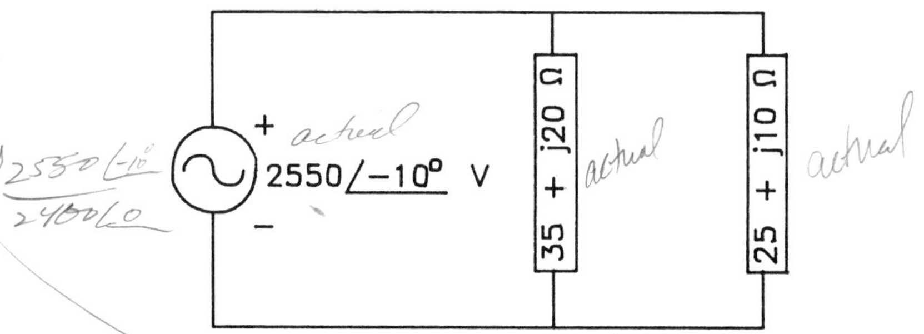

Figure 5-17 Circuit for Problem 5-2.

g. $V_{\text{base},ll} = 12.47$ kV, $S_{\text{base},3\Phi} = 10$ MVA
h. $V_{\text{base},ll} = 8.32$ kV, $S_{\text{base},3\Phi} = 10$ MVA
i. $V_{\text{base},ll} = 4.16$ kV, $S_{\text{base},3\Phi} = 10$ MVA

5.5. A single-phase distribution transformer is rated at 50 kVA, 7.2 kV–240 V, and has a resistance of 1.8% and a reactance of 2.4%. Calculate the following:
a. Ohmic resistance and reactance referred to the low-voltage side
b. Ohmic resistance and reactance referred to the high-voltage side
c. Sketch the equivalent circuit for parts a and b.

5.6. A three-phase power transformer is rated at 7500 kVA, 69 kV–12.47/7.2 kV, and has a resistance of 1.0% and a reactance of 7.0%. The transformer is delta connected on the high-voltage side and wye connected on the low-voltage side. Using the single-phase, line to neutral equivalent circuit concept, calculate the following:
a. Ohmic resistance and reactance referred to the low-voltage side
b. Ohmic resistance and reactance referred to the high-voltage side
c. Sketch the equivalent circuit for parts a and b.

5.7. A three-phase power transformer is rated at 400 MVA, 345 kV–132 kV, and has an impedance of 7.0%. Express the impedance in terms of an apparent power base of 100 MVA and a voltage base of 138 kV on the low-voltage side.

5.8. For the three-phase power system shown in Fig. 5-18, calculate the three-phase symmetrical fault current at points F_1 and F_2. Express your answer in per unit and in actual amperes. Use a base voltage of 69 kV at the high-voltage side of the main transformer and a base apparent power of 10 MVA. Assume that the prefault voltage on the high side is 69 kV. The equivalent system impedance is specified in percent on a base apparent power of 100 MVA and a base voltage of 69 kV.

5.9. An industrial plant is presently served by a 3750 kVA, 69-kV–4.16Y/2.4-kV transformer having an impedance of 7.5%. Due to plant expansion, the electrical load is expected to increase to 6000 kVA at 0.92 lagging power factor. The rating of a new transformer required to supply this load would be 7500 kVA, 69-kV–4.16Y/2.4 kV, $Z = 8\%$. A spare transformer rated at 2500 kVA, 69-kV–4.16Y/2.4 kV, 6.0% impedance, is also available. Rather than

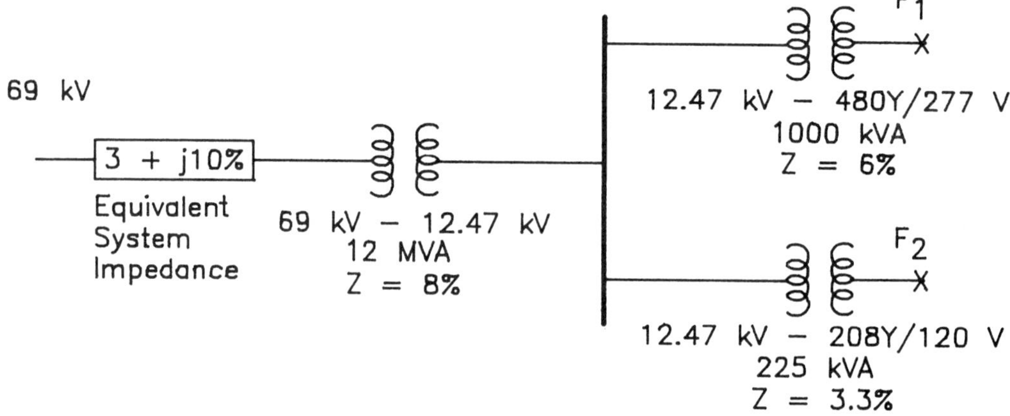

Figure 5-18 System for Problem 5-8.

purchasing a new transformer of sufficient capacity to serve this load, it has been proposed that the spare transformer be placed in parallel with the existing transformer to supply total plant load. Assume that the source voltage is 69 kV and that the plant load for the new condition can be modeled as a constant impedance of $2.8839 + j1.1304\ \Omega$/phase. Calculate the following:

a. Actual apparent power load on each transformer if the 3750- and 2500-kVA transformers are paralleled

b. Total available symmetrical three-phase fault current at the 4.16-kV bus (1) under the existing conditions, (2) with the 3750- and 2500-kVA transformers paralleled, and (3) with a new 7500-kVA transformer installed

c. (1) Load voltage at the 4.16-kV bus with the 3750- and 2500-kVA transformers paralleled and (2) with a new 7500-kVA transformer installed

d. Discuss the loading on each transformer with regard to nameplate apparent power ratings if the 3750- and 2500-kVA transformers are paralleled.

e. Discuss the fault current availability for the three conditions examined in part b.

f. Discuss the load voltage variations for the two conditions examined in part c.

6

Transformer Applications

6-1 General

This chapter will discuss the application of transformers in electrical power systems. Equivalent circuits and standard connections for single- and three-phase transformers were reviewed in Chapter 2. Specific information on transformer testing is assumed to have been covered in a prerequisite course in electrical machinery. Basic transformer construction for both overhead and underground transformers will be discussed.

6-2 Construction

The basic construction of power and distribution transformers can be separated into two major groups: overhead and underground. Overhead transformers are designed primarily for pole mounting, while underground transformers are designed for either pad mounting or installation in underground vaults. The high- or low-side terminals on underground transformers may be designed for either live front or dead front connectors. The dead front type of high-voltage connection typically uses insulated separable connectors such as load break elbows for connection to the high-voltage bushings.

Overhead distribution transformers are available in standard apparent power ratings of 500 kVA and less. The high-voltage rating for distribution transformers is 34,500 V and less. The low-voltage rating is limited to 7970 V and less. Transformers that do not fall into this broad category are classified as power transformers.

Single-Phase Overhead Transformer

The basic construction features and schematic diagram for a single-phase overhead transformer are shown in Fig. 6-1. This type of transformer has one high-voltage bushing designated *H*1. This bushing is located on the left-hand side of the transformer when

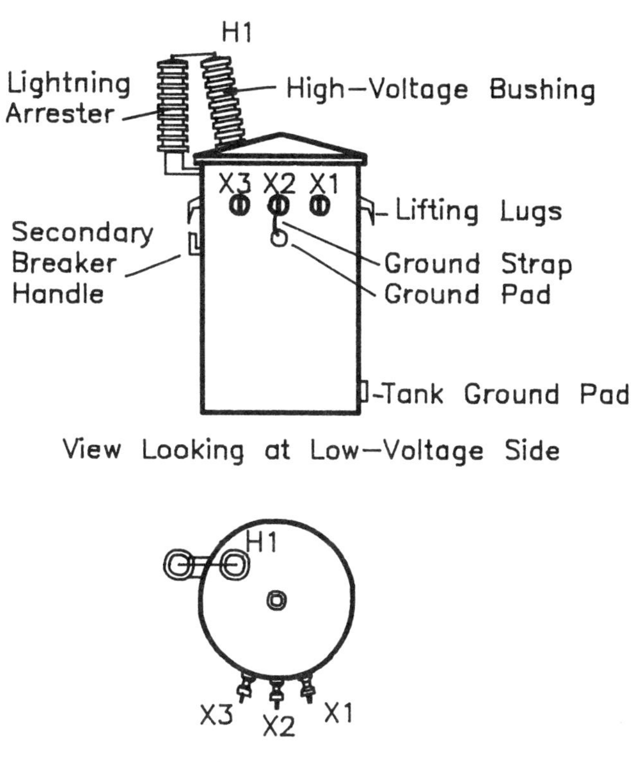

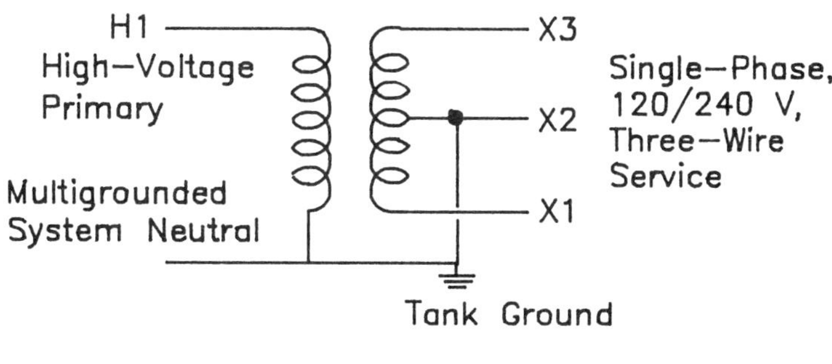

Figure 6-1 Single-bushing overhead transformer.

viewed from the low-voltage side. This type of transformer is to be connected from line to solidly grounded neutral. The *H*2 terminal of the high-voltage winding is connected to the tank ground internally by the manufacturer to complete the electrical circuit. The multigrounded system neutral (MGN) is externally connected to the tank ground. Figure 6-2 shows a typical single-phase overhead transformer installation supplying several single-phase, three-wire services.

If the transformer is to be connected between phases, such as in a delta connection or in a floating-wye configuration, two high-voltage bushings (*H*1 and *H*2) are required. The *H*2 bushing is located to the right of *H*1 as viewed from the low-voltage side. The construction features and schematic diagram of this type of transformer are shown in Fig. 6-3.

In both Figs. 6-1 and 6-3, the low-voltage bushings are designated *X*1, *X*2, and *X*3. This low-voltage bushing configuration applies to transformers that have center-tapped secondary windings for single-phase, three-wire services. Transformers that have a single-voltage secondary will have two secondary bushings marked *X*1 and *X*2. Figures 6-1 and 6-3 show the low-voltage terminal arrangements for additive polarity. If the transformer has subtractive polarity, the low-voltage bushings are designated *X*1, *X*2, and *X*3 left to right as viewed from the low-voltage side. In accordance with ANSI® standards, distribution transformers rated 200 kVA and less, with a high-voltage rating of 8660 V and below, have additive polarity. All other distribution transformers have subtractive polarity. The secondary ground strap is used to connect the *X*2 low-voltage bushing to ground. This is the common connection for a single-phase, 120/240-V, three-wire service requirement. In certain three-phase connections, the grounding strap must be removed from one or two of the transformers in the bank.

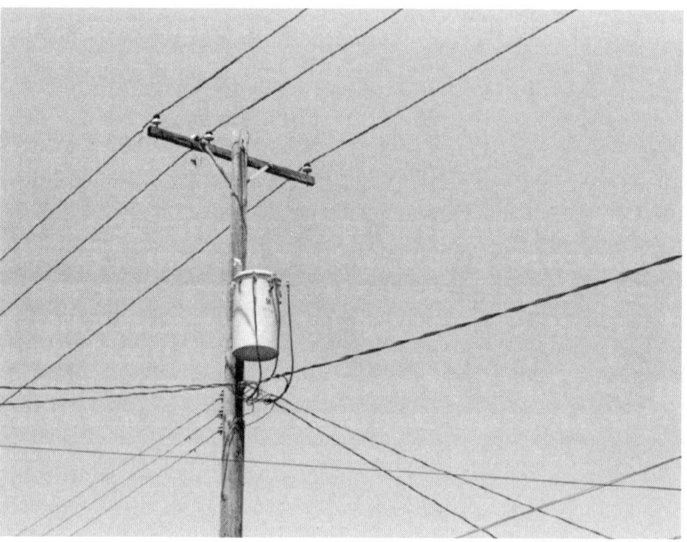

Figure 6-2 Single-phase overhead transformer installation. (Photo Courtesy of Ohio Edison Company)

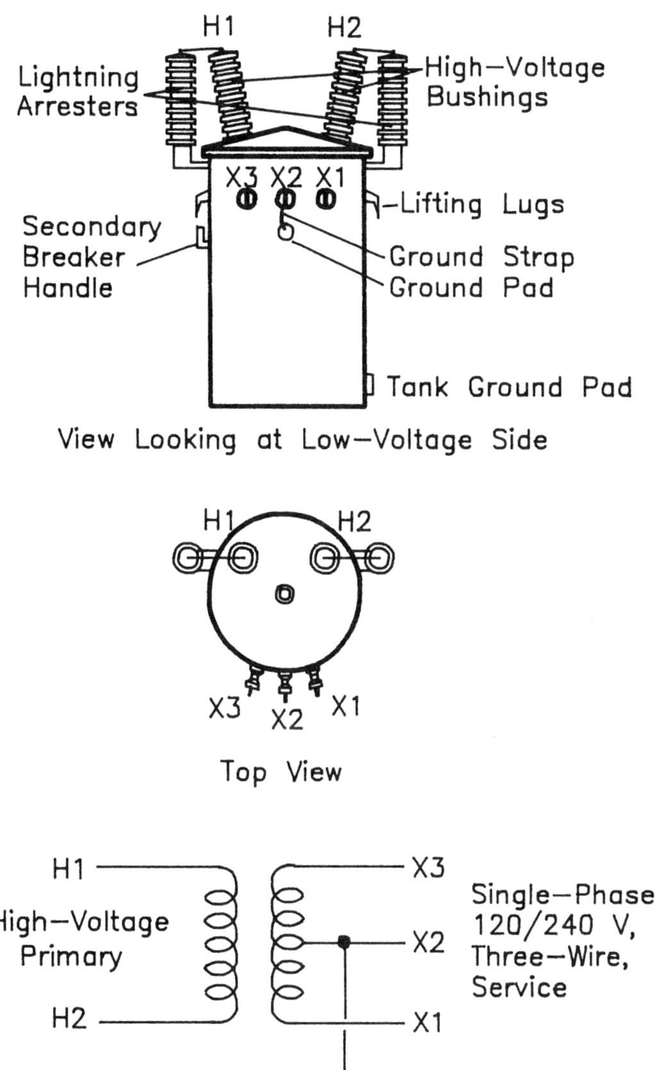

Figure 6-3 Two-bushing overhead transformer.

The single-phase overhead transformers shown in Figs. 6-1 and 6-3 are equipped with a high-voltage lightning arrester, low-voltage circuit breaker, and an internal high-voltage fuse link (not shown). This type of transformer is referred to as a *completely self-protected* (CSP) transformer. A conventional transformer does not have any of these protective devices. Usually, a high-voltage fused cutout and lightning arrester are supplied and installed by the user to protect the conventional transformer.

Three-Phase Overhead Transformers

Three-phase overhead transformers are also available to supply three-phase services. Typically, three-phase services are supplied by connecting two or three single-phase overhead transformers in a bank, rather than use one three-phase overhead transformer. The three-phase service may also be supplied by a three-phase underground transformer. Figure 6-4 shows a bank of three single-phase transformers used to supply a small three-phase service. For additional information regarding three-phase overhead transformers, the reader is referred to ANSI® C57-12.20.

Single-Phase Underground Transformers

Single-phase underground pad mount transformers are designed to be installed on a multigrounded neutral primary system. These transformers are typically used in new residential developments where an underground primary distribution system is required by law. Construction features and the schematic diagram for this type of transformer are shown in Fig. 6-5. Note that the transformer high-voltage bushings are designated $H1A$

Figure 6-4 Bank of three single-phase transformers supplying a three-phase service. (Photo Courtesy of Ohio Edison Company)

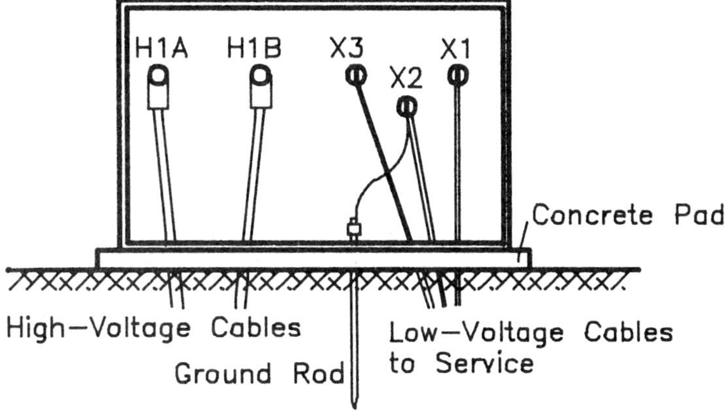

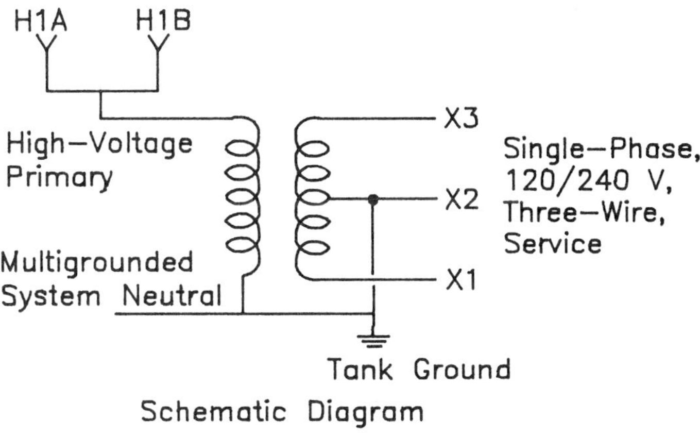

Figure 6-5 Single-phase pad mount transformer.

and *H1B* and are located in the left-hand side of the transformer compartment. For safety, a high-voltage barrier may be placed between the high- and low-voltage compartments. Figure 6-6 shows a typical single-phase pad mount transformer installation supplying a single-phase, three-wire service.

High-voltage bushings *H1A* and *H1B* connect to the same end of the high-voltage coil. The other end of the high-voltage coil is connected to the multigrounded system neutral, which is typically the concentric neutral of the high-voltage cable. The two high-voltage bushings allow for the loop feed capability of these transformers. The incoming high-voltage cable from the source typically terminates on the *H1A* bushing. Connection to transformers on the load side is made through a high-voltage cable connected to the *H1B* bushing. It is therefore possible to daisy-chain these transformers together to form an underground loop system. A *parking stand* is available to terminate a high-voltage cable where it is desirable to form an open in the loop. The high-voltage cable remains

Figure 6-6 Single-phase pad mount transformer installation. (Photo Courtesy of Ohio Edison Company)

energized, but does not connect to the transformer high-voltage winding when connected to the parking stand.

The low-voltage terminals may be either spade type or eyebolt and are designated $X1$, $X2$, and $X3$, similarly to the overhead transformers. These low-voltage terminals are located on the right-hand side of the transformer compartment. The $X2$ terminal is normally connected to a ground rod and the concentric neutral of the high-voltage cable. This ground establishes the neutral for a 120/240-V, single-phase, three-wire service.

Three-Phase Underground Transformers

The construction features of a three-phase underground pad mounted transformer are similar to the single-phase underground pad mounted transformers previously described. Three-phase pad mount transformers are available with either radial or loop feed capability. Figures 6-7 and 6-8 show features and schematic diagrams for three-phase pad mounted transformers having radial and loop feed capability. Figure 6-9 shows a three-phase pad mount transformer installation supplying a small commercial load.

Three-phase underground pad mount transformers with loop feed capability can be used to form an underground loop similar to the single phase pad mount units. This underground loop is desirable in a commercial or industrial area where reliability and operating flexibility are desired. Parking stands are provided for each single-phase power cable entering the high-voltage compartment. If a cable fault develops in a loop feed system, the faulted section of cable can be isolated for repair, while maintaining continuity of service to other customers on the system.

In both single- and three-phase underground transformers, a high-voltage under-oil fuse link may be provided by the manufacturer for overcurrent protection. It is also possible to have an under-oil lightning arrester to protect the transformer against overvoltages.

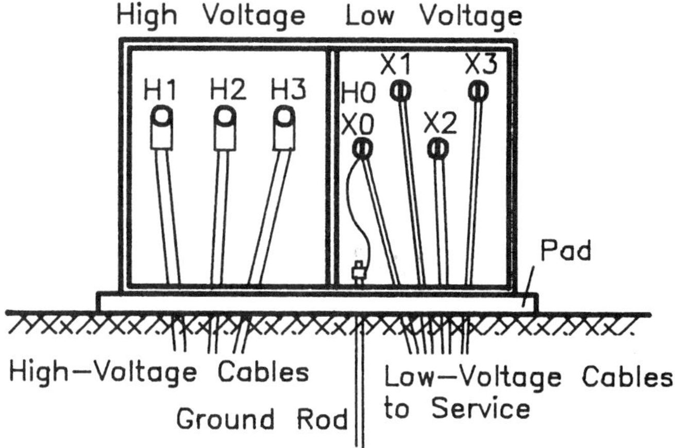

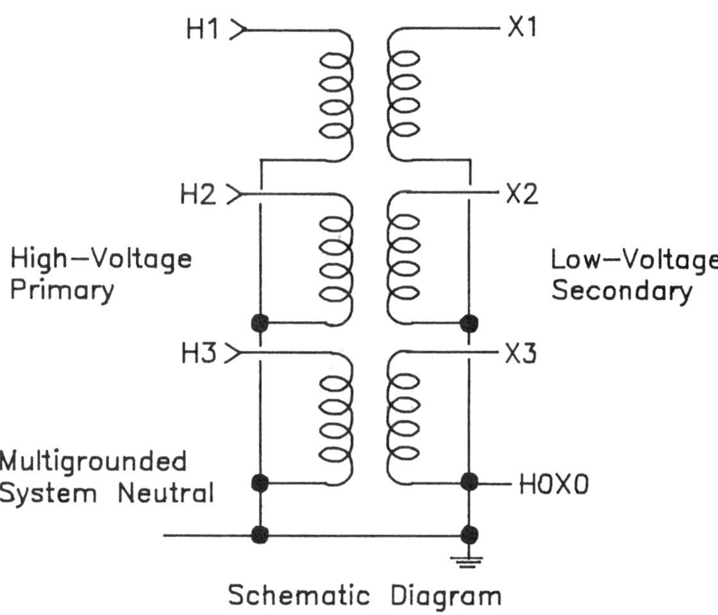

Figure 6-7 Three-phase radial feed pad mount transformer.

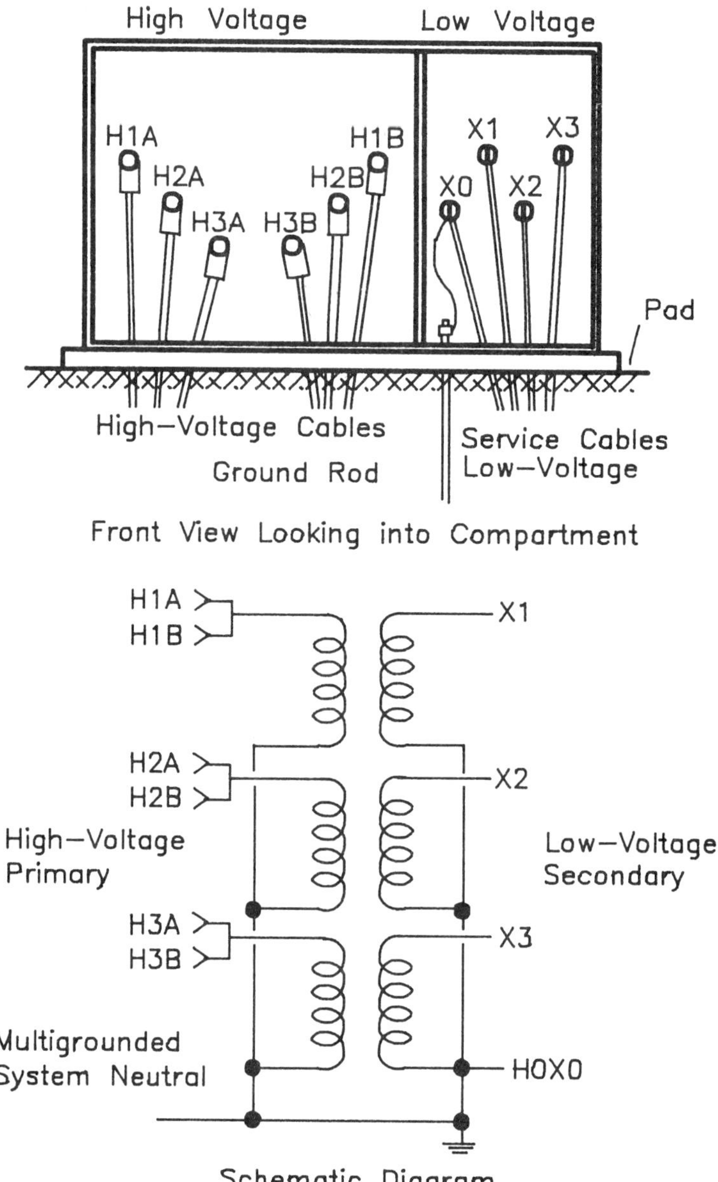

Figure 6-8 Three-phase loop feed pad mount transformer.

Figure 6-9 Three-phase pad mount transformer installation. (Photo Courtesy of Ohio Edison Company)

6-3 Connections and Winding Voltage Designations

Single-Phase Winding Voltage Designations

Single-phase overhead transformers may be connected either as a single unit to supply single-phase loads or in a three-phase bank to supply three-phase loads. In general, a transformer winding can be connected in only two ways in a three-phase system: phase to neutral or phase to phase. The first step in determining the proper voltage designation is to determine what the applied voltage to the winding will be. It is then necessary to determine how the transformer high side will be connected; that is, single phase, wye grounded, floating wye, open wye, open delta, or delta.

A high-voltage winding with a voltage designation of E volts will be suitable for phase to phase connection on an E-volt system. This transformer will have two high-voltage bushings and two lightning arresters if of the CSP type. Figure 6-10 shows examples of the high-voltage connections for this designation.

The E/E_1Y designation is for a winding rated at E volts. This transformer may be connected phase to phase on an E-volt system or phase to neutral on an E_1-volt system. This transformer will have two high-voltage bushings for connection to the primary. If the transformer is a CSP transformer to be connected phase to phase, then two high-voltage lightning arresters and two high-voltage fuse links are required. For a floating-wye connection, only one high-voltage lightning arrester and one high-voltage fuse link are required on the $H1$ bushing. Examples of the high-voltage connections for this winding designation are shown in Fig. 6-11.

The E_1GRDY/E designates a winding rated at E volts with reduced insulation at the neutral end. It is designed to be installed phase to neutral on an E_1-volt system, where

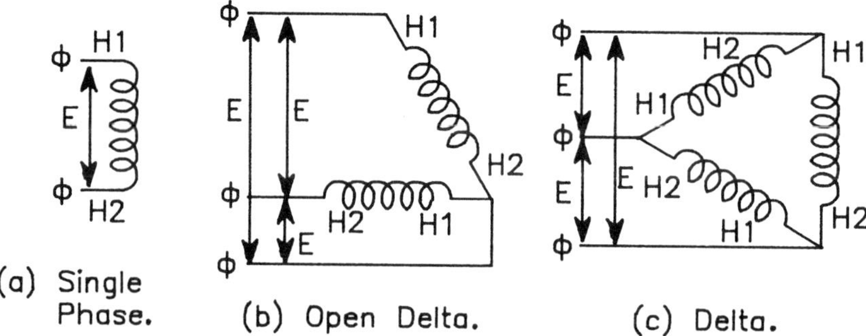

Figure 6-10 High-voltage connections for *E* winding voltage designation.

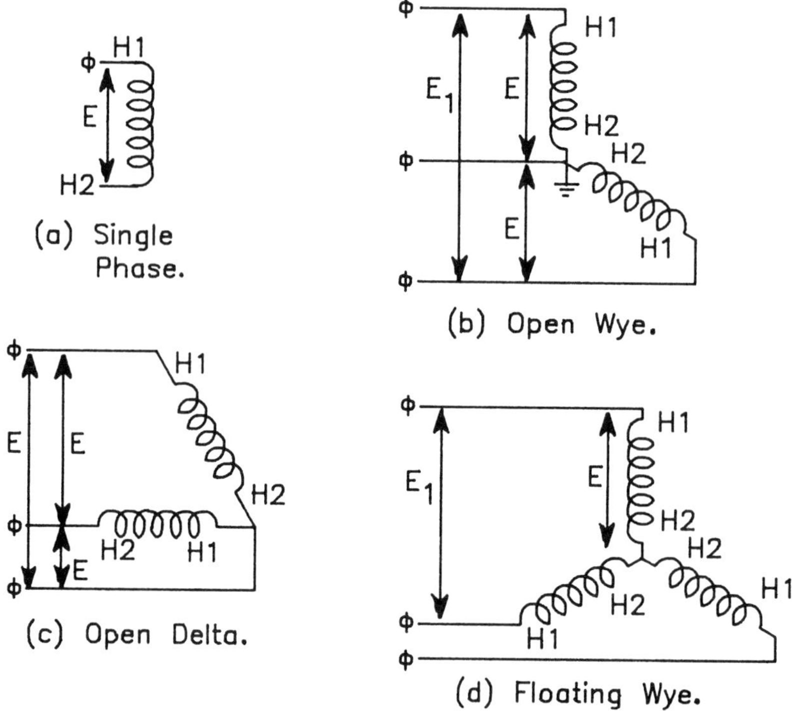

Figure 6-11 High-voltage connections for E/E_1Y winding voltage designation.

the neutral is solidly grounded. This transformer will have a single high-voltage bushing for the phase connection. Normally, the *H*2 lead of the high-voltage winding is connected to the tank ground internally by the manufacturer. Standard connections are shown in Fig. 6-12.

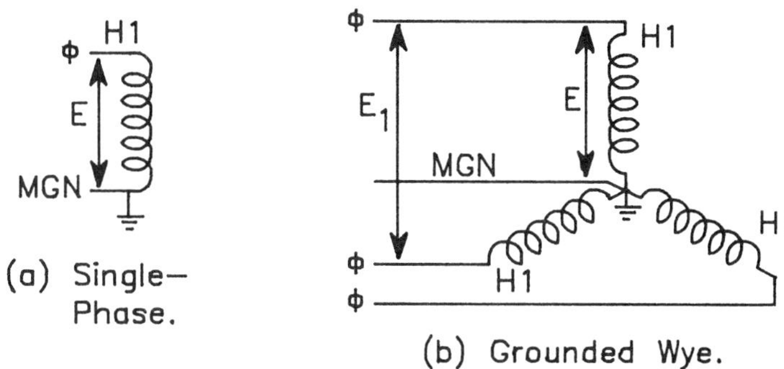

Figure 6-12 High-voltage connections for E_1GrdY/E winding voltage designation.

A winding voltage designation of *E*/2*E* indicates a two-section winding with each section rated at *E* volts. The two sections may be connected in parallel for operation at *E* volts or in series for operation at 2*E* volts. In addition, the windings may be placed in series with a center-point tap between the windings for single-phase, three-wire operation. The center point would normally be connected to ground and forms the neutral of the three-wire system. The currents in the individual winding sections may be unbalanced. This is the common voltage designation used in the low-voltage windings for single-phase, three-wire, 120/240-Vservices. The two winding sections are connected in parallel for a 208Y/120, three-phase, four-wire grounded wye connection. Figure 6-13 shows common connections for this winding voltage designation.

The 2*E*/*E* designation indicates a center-tapped winding that has 2*E* volts across the coil and *E* volts from the extreme terminals to the center tap. This is the common designation used in single-phase pad mounted transformers to supply single-phase, three-wire services. Each section of this winding has one-half the full rated kVA of the entire

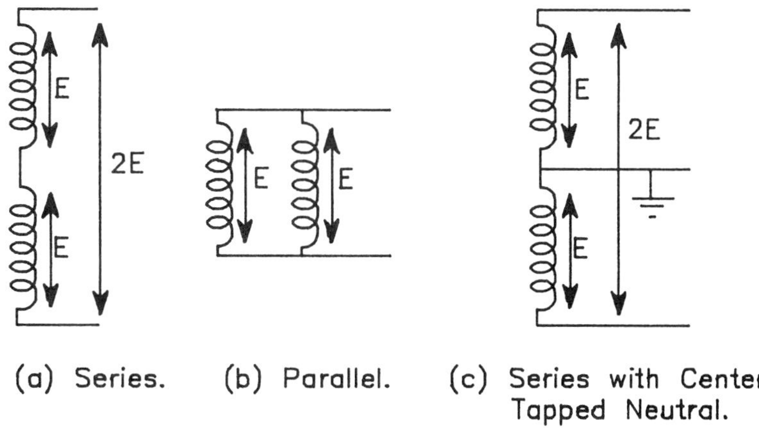

Figure 6-13 Connections for *E*/2*E* winding voltage designation.

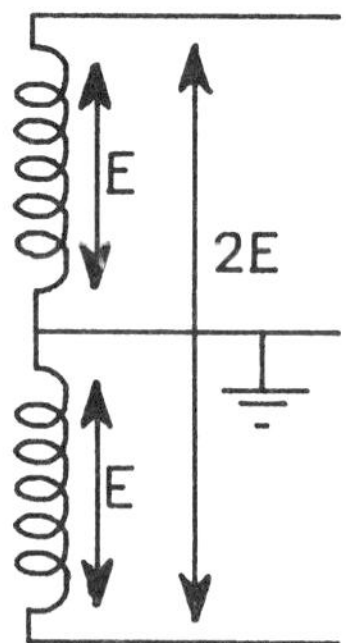

Figure 6-14 Connections for $2E/E$ winding voltage designation.

winding. As in the previous winding designation, the currents in each half of this winding may be unbalanced. The individual coil sections cannot be connected in parallel. Figure 6-14 shows the coil connection for this designation.

The EXE_1 designation indicates a two section winding in which the sections may be connected in series for $2E$-volt operation or in parallel for E-volt operation. This winding is not suitable for three-wire, center-tapped operation. The currents in the two coil sections must be balanced. Figure 6-15 shows the coil connections for this designation.

Three-Phase Transformer Winding Voltage Designations

Three-phase transformers may have their high- and/or low-voltage windings connected in wye or delta. Windings suitable for floating-wye connection have a neutral that is fully insulated and brought out to a bushing for external connection if desired. In a

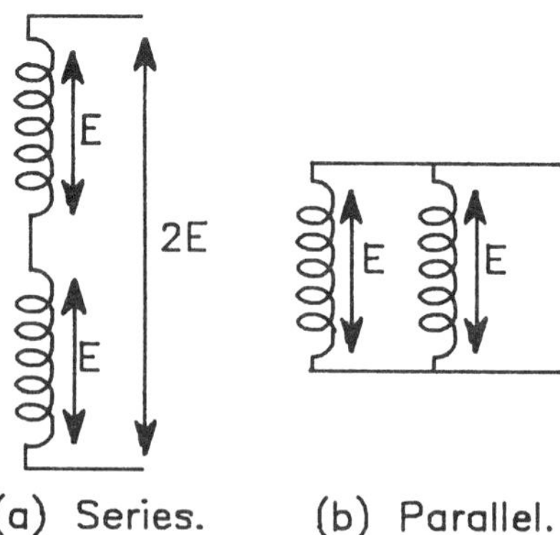

Figure 6-15 Connections for EXE_1 winding voltage designation.

winding specifically designed for a grounded wye connection, reduced winding insulation may be used. The neutral may be connected to the tank ground internally or may be brought out to a neutral bushing for permanent connection to ground.

The E-volt designation as applied to three-phase transformers designates a permanently delta connected winding for use on an E-volt system. The rated coil voltage for each of the three coils is E volts.

The E_1Y designation is for a permanently connected floating-wye winding suitable for use on an E_1-volt system. Each coil has a rated voltage of $E_1/\sqrt{3}$. There is no connection to the neutral.

The E_1Y/E designation is for a permanently wye connected winding with a fully insulated neutral connection. Each coil has a voltage rating of E volts, for connection on an E_1-volt system.

The E_1GRDY/E volt designation is for a permanently connected grounded wye winding suitable for use on an E_1-volt system. Each coil has a voltage rating of E volts. The neutral connection of the winding is brought out to a bushing and permanently grounded. This type of winding may also have a reduced insulation system.

6-4 Standard Ratings

Overhead Pole-Type Transformers

Standard apparent power ratings for single- and three-phase pole-type transformers are shown in Table 6-1. Voltage ratings for pole-type transformers are shown in Table 6-2.

Table 6-1 Standard kVA Ratings for Overhead Transformers

Single Phase	*Three Phase*
10	30
25	45
37.5	75
50	112.5
75	150
100	225
167	300
250	500
333	
500	

Source: This material is reproduced from American National Standard C57.12.20-1988, copyright 1988 with permission by the American National Standards Institute. Copies of this standard may be purchased from American National Standards Institute, 11 West 42nd Street, New York, NY 10036.

Table 6-2 Standard Voltage Ratings for Overhead Transformers

Single Phase	*Three Phase*
2400/4160Y	2400
4800/8320Y	4160Y/2400
7200/12,470Y	4160Y
12,470GrdY/7200	4160
7620/13,200Y	4800
13,200GrdY/7620	8320Y/4800
12,000	7200
13,200/22,860Y	12,000
13,200	12,470Y/7200
13,800GrdY/7970	12,470Y
13,800/23,900Y	13,200Y/7620
13,800	13,200Y
14,400/24,940Y	13,200
24,940GrdY/14,400	13,800
16,340	13,800GrdY/7970
34,500GrdY/19,920	24,940GrdY/14,400
34,500	34,500GrdY/19,920
120/240	208Y/120
277	240
240/480	480
	240X480
	480Y/277

Source: This material is reproduced from American National Standard C57.12.20-1988, copyright 1988 with permission by the American National Standards Institute. Copies of this standard may be purchased from American National Standards Institute, 11 West 42nd Street, New York, NY 10036.

Pad Mounted Transformers

The standard kVA ratings for single- and three-phase pad mounted distribution transformers are shown in Table 6-3. Standard voltage ratings for single- and three-phase distribution transformers are shown in Table 6-4.

Power Transformers

Transformers not classified as distribution transformers fall into the broad classification of power transformers. Additional standard kVA and line to line voltage ratings are shown in Table 6-5.

Table 6-3 Standard kVA Ratings for Pad Mount Transformers

Single Phase	Three Phase
25	75
37.5	112.5
50	150
75	225
100	300
167	500
	750
	1000
	1500
	2000
	2500

Source: This material is reproduced from American National Standard C57.12.21-1980, copyright 1980, and American National Standard C57.12.26-1987, copyright 1987, with permission by the American National Standards Institute. Copies of these standards may be purchased from American National Standards Institute, 11 West 42nd Street, New York, NY 10036.

Table 6-4 Standard Voltage Ratings for Pad Mount Transformers

Single Phase	Three Phase
4160GrdY/2400	2400
8320GrdY/4800	4160
12,000GrdY/6930	4800
12,470GrdY/7200	7200
13,200GrdY/7620	12,000
13,800GrdY/7970	12,470
16,340GrdY/9430	13,200
22,860GrdY/13,200	13,800
23,900GrdY/13,800	16,340
24,940GrdY/14,400	22,860GrdY/13,200
34,500GrdY/19,920	23,900GrdY/13,800
	24,940GrdY/14,400
	34,500GrdY/19,920
240/120	208Y/120
	240
	480
	480Y/277

Source: This material is reproduced from American National Standard C57.12.21-1980, copyright 1980, and American National Standard C57.12.26-1987, copyright 1987, with permission by the American National Standards Institute. Copies of these standards may be purchased from American National Standards Institute, 11 West 42nd Street, New York, NY 10036.

Table 6-5 Additional Standard Ratings for Power Transformers

kVA Single Phase	*kVA Three Phase*	*kV Line Voltage*
3,333	3,750	46.0
5,000	5,000	69.0
6,667	7,500	115.0
8,333	10,000	138.0
10,000	12,000	161.0
12,500	15,000	230.0
16,667	20,000	345.0
20,000	25,000	500.0
25,000	30,000	765.0
33,333	37,500	
	50,000	
	60,000	
	75,000	
	100,000	

Source: Derived from IEEE Std C57.12.00-1987 IEEE Standard General Requirements for Liquid Immersed Distribution, Power and Regulating Transformers, Copyright © 1987 by the Institute of Electrical and Electronics Engineers, Inc. This document is an archived standard which has been superceded.

Cooling Class

Virtually all the transformers used in utility power systems are liquid immersed. The liquid is usually some form of insulating oil or silicone fluid. The temperature rise above ambient for most liquid-immersed transformers is 65°C. In some instances, dry-type transformers may be employed that have a temperature rise of up to 180°C above ambient. In either case, the temperature rise is limited by the amount of heat that the insulating material can withstand. The ANSI® standards have specified the following cooling classes for liquid-immersed transformers:

Class OA: Self-cooled
Class OA/FA: Self-cooled/forced air cooled
Class OA/FA/FA: Self-cooled/forced air cooled/forced air cooled
Class OA/FA/FOA: Self-cooled/forced air cooled/forced liquid cooled
Class OA/FOA/FOA: Self-cooled/forced liquid cooled/forced liquid cooled
Class OW: Water cooled
Class OW/A: Water Cooled/self-cooled

6-5 Loading Calculations and Sizing

Loading calculations are necessary to determine the actual apparent power load to be expected so that the proper kVA rating may be specified. In the case of single-phase,

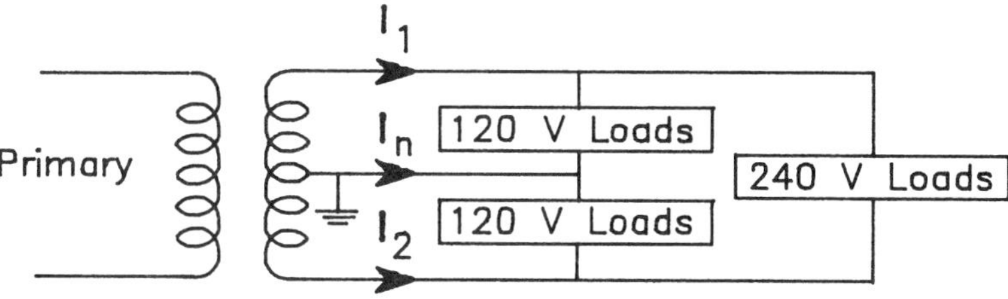

Figure 6-16 Schematic diagram for single-phase transformer loading calculations.

three-wire services, the transformer loading is determined by summing the connected loads and applying the appropriate demand factors. For three-phase, four-wire wye services, the loading on the transformer(s) is easily determined since the three-phase load is assumed to be balanced, and the single-phase load is assumed to be balanced among the three phases. Load calculations for the three-phase, four-wire delta secondary connections are much more difficult. This section will present methods that can be used to calculate the apparent power loading on transformers in single- and three-phase connections. In addition, rules of thumb will be introduced that will enable approximate but rapid determination of transformer loading for most situations.

Single Phase

Single-phase overhead or underground transformers may be used to supply single-phase, three-wire services. Figure 6-16 shows the schematic diagram and connections required to supply a single-phase, three-wire service.

In reference to Fig. 6-16, the single-phase loads are assumed to be balanced from each phase to neutral. This being the case, the current in the neutral conductor will be zero. The total loading on the transformer will then be equal to the estimated total connected load (demand) multiplied by the appropriate demand factor. Recall from Chapter 4 that the demand factor is a function of the total number of individual loads connected to the transformer. The required kVA rating of the transformer used to supply these loads will be the next *larger* standard size available according to Tables 6-1 and 6-3. In some instances, it may be possible to select the next smaller standard size if it is permissible to slightly overload the transformer for short periods of time.

EXAMPLE 6-1

A single-phase pad mount transformer is to be used to supply the following estimated loads:

Load 1: 7 kW, 0.9 lagging power factor
Load 2: 12 kW, 0.9 lagging power factor
Load 3: 5 kW, 0.9 lagging power factor
Load 4: 23 kW, 0.8 lagging power factor

The service voltages are 120/240 V, single phase, three wire. The primary distribution circuit consists of one phase of a 12.47-kV, three-phase MGN circuit. Assume that the demand factor for the four loads is 0.72. Determine the appropriate winding voltage designation for the high- and low-voltage sides and the kVA rating for this transformer.

Solution The voltage impressed on the high-voltage winding is equal to the line to neutral voltage of the system.

$$E = \frac{12{,}470}{\sqrt{3}}$$
$$= 7200 \text{ V}$$

Therefore, the correct winding voltage designation from Table 6-4 is 12,470GrdY/7200 V. The winding voltage designation for the low-voltage side is 240/120 V.

The total demand on the transformer is equal to the sum of the apparent power loads multiplied by the demand factor. Since the four loads have different power factors, it is necessary to separate the real and reactive components of each load, as follows:

Load 1: $P = 7$ kW, $Q = 3.4$ kVAR
Load 2: $P = 12$ kW, $Q = 5.8$ kVAR
Load 3: $P = 5$ kW $Q = 2.4$ kVAR
Load 4: $P = 23$ kW $Q = 17.25$ kVAR

The total real, reactive, and apparent powers are 47 kW, 28.9 kVAR, and 55.1 kVA, respectively. The demand on the transformer is

$$\text{Demand} = 55.1 \cdot 0.72$$
$$= 39.7 \text{ kVA}$$

Therefore, a 50-kVA transformer is required.

EXAMPLE 6-2

A single-phase overhead transformer is used to supply the following loads:

Load 1: 7 kW, 0.9 lagging power factor
Load 2: 12 kW, 0.9 lagging power factor
Load 3: 20 kW, 0.8 lagging power factor

The transformer is to be supplied from a 24.94-kV, three-phase, MGN primary distribution circuit. The service voltage is 120/240 V, single phase, three wire. Assume that the demand factor for these three loads is 0.8. Determine the appropriate kVA rating and winding voltage designations for this transformer.

Solution The transformer will be connected line to neutral on the high voltage side. The line to neutral voltage of this system is

$$E = \frac{24{,}940}{\sqrt{3}}$$
$$= 14{,}400 \text{ V}$$

The winding voltage designation for the high-voltage winding is 24,940GrdY/14,400 V. Only one fully insulated high-voltage bushing is required in this case, since the other end of the high-voltage winding is to be connected to the multigrounded neutral of the primary distribution circuit.

An optional winding voltage designation for the high-voltage winding would be 14,400/24,940Y V. A transformer with this voltage designation would have two fully insulated high-voltage bushings. Since the *H*2 bushing is to be connected to the MGN, it is not necessary to require a fully insulated bushing. Therefore, this choice would not be economical due to the added cost of the second high-voltage bushing.

The winding voltage designation for the low-voltage side is 120/240 V.

The total real, reactive, and apparent powers are 39 kW, 24.2 kVAR, and 45.9 kVA, respectively. The demand on the transformer is

$$\begin{aligned}\text{Demand} &= 0.8 \cdot 45.9 \\ &= 36.7 \text{ kVA}\end{aligned}$$

Therefore, a 37.5-kVA transformer is required.

EXAMPLE 6-3 Repeat Example 6-2 if the primary distribution circuit is a 13,800-V, three-phase, three-wire delta system.

Solution The loading on the transformer does not change. Therefore, a 37.5-kVA transformer is required.

Since the transformer is to be connected to a delta system, the high-voltage winding will be connected line to line. The rated line to line voltage is 13,800 V. Therefore, the winding voltage designation for the high-voltage winding will be 13,800 V. Note that two fully insulated high-voltage bushings are required in this situation. The winding voltage designation for the low-voltage winding will be 120/240 V.

Grounded Wye–Grounded Wye Connection

The grounded wye–grounded wye connection is used to supply a three-phase, four-wire load from a three-phase, four-wire primary distribution system. Single-phase loads may be connected from line to neutral on the low-voltage side. Three-phase loads will involve connection to all three phases. In performing loading calculations, the single-phase loads are assumed to be divided equally between the three phases, and the three-phase load is assumed to be balanced. Thus, each transformer in the bank will be loaded equally. The loading on each transformer will be equal to one-third of the total three-phase load plus one-third of the total single-phase load. Figure 6-17 shows the schematic and connection diagrams for the grounded wye–grounded wye connection.

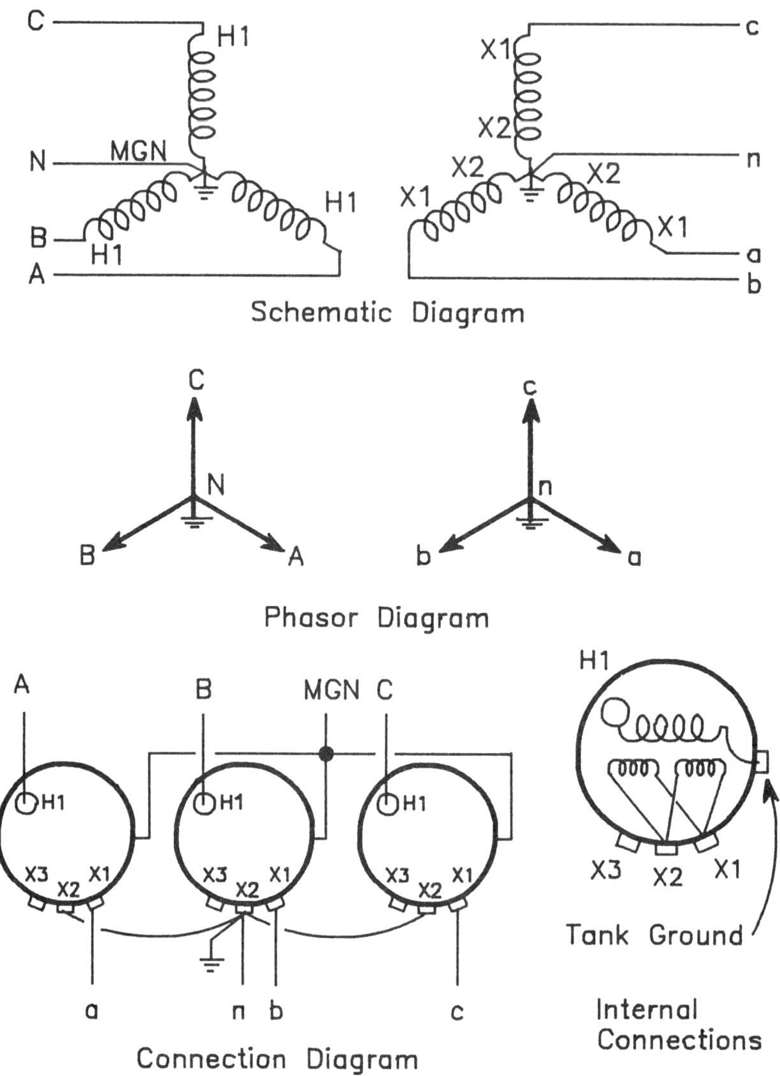

Figure 6-17 Grounded wye–grounded wye connection.

EXAMPLE 6-4 A commercial establishment is to be supplied service at 208Y/120 V, three phase four wire. The utility primary distribution circuit is a 12.47-kV, three-phase, MGN system. The total estimated single-phase load is 30 kW at 0.95 lagging power factor. The total estimated three-phase load is 150 kW at 0.8 lagging power factor. A grounded wye–grounded wye connection of three single-phase transformers is to be used to supply this service. Determine the apparent power ratings and winding voltage designations for each of the three transformers in the bank.

Solution Since the power factors of the three-phase and single-phase loads are different, each load must be expressed in terms of real and reactive power and then added together.

$$\text{Single-phase load} = 30 \text{ kW}, \quad 9.9 \text{ kVAR}$$
$$\text{Three-phase load} = 150 \text{ kW}, \quad 112.5 \text{ kVAR}$$

The loading on each transformer is

$$\begin{aligned} \text{Loading} &= \tfrac{1}{3}(30 + 150) + j\tfrac{1}{3}(9.9 + 112.5) \text{ kVA} \\ &= 60 + j40.8 \\ &= 72.6\angle 34.2^\circ \text{ kVAR} \end{aligned}$$

Therefore, three 75-kVA transformers are required. The winding voltage designations for each of the three transformers are 12,470GrdY/7200–120/240 V. As an alternative, a winding voltage designation of 7200/12,470Y V may be used (two high-voltage bushings).

EXAMPLE 6-5

An industrial plant is to be supplied service at 480Y/277 V, three phase, four wire. The utility primary distribution circuit is a 24.94-kV, three-phase, MGN system. The total estimated single-phase load is 30 kW at 0.95 lagging power factor. The total estimated three-phase load is 300 kW at 0.7 lagging power factor. A grounded wye–grounded wye connection of three single-phase transformers is to be used to supply this service. Determine the apparent power ratings and winding voltage designations for each of the three transformers in the bank.

Solution Expressing the loads in terms of real and reactive powers,

$$\begin{aligned} \text{Single-phase load} &= 30 + j9.9 \text{ kVA} \\ \text{Three-phase load} &= \underline{300 + j306.1 \text{ kVA}} \\ \text{Total load} &= 330 + j316.0 \text{ kVA} \end{aligned}$$

The loading on each transformer is

$$\begin{aligned} \text{Loading} &= \tfrac{1}{3}(330) + j\tfrac{1}{3}(316) \text{ kVA} \\ &= 110 + j105.3 \\ &= 152.3\angle 43.7^\circ \text{ kVA} \end{aligned}$$

Therefore, three 167-kVA transformers are required. The winding voltage designations for each of the three transformers are 24,940GrdY/14,400–277 V. As an alternative, a winding voltage designation of 14,400/24,940Y V may be used (two high-voltage bushings).

Delta–Grounded Wye Connection

The loading calculations for the delta–grounded wye connection are the same as for the grounded wye–grounded wye connection. Figure 6-18 shows the schematic and connec-

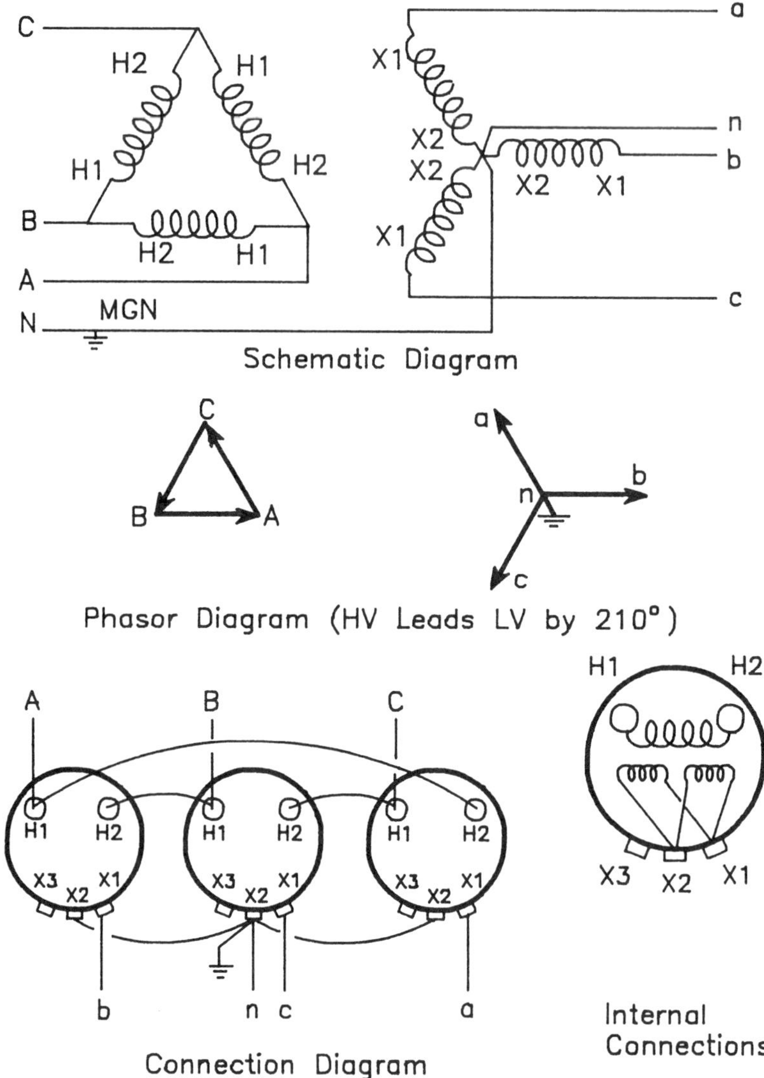

Figure 6-18 Delta–grounded wye connection.

tion diagrams for the delta–grounded wye connection. For the connection shown in Fig. 6-18, the high voltage leads the low voltage by 210°.

EXAMPLE 6-6 Repeat Example 6-5 if the utility primary distribution circuit is a 13.2-kV, three-phase, MGN system. A delta–grounded wye connection of three single-phase transformers is to be used to supply this service. Determine the apparent power ratings and winding voltage designations for each of the three transformers in the bank.

Solution The loading on each transformer is 152.3 kVA, as calculated in Example 6-5. Therefore, three 167-kVA transformers are required. The winding voltage designations for each of the three transformers are 13,200–277 V. Each transformer will have two fully insulated high-voltage bushings since it will be connected line to line. The primary system neutral will be connected to the secondary neutral in this case.

Floating Wye–Delta Connection

In the floating wye–delta connection, the transformer high-voltage sides are connected in a wye configuration with the transformer bank neutral floating; that is, not connected to the primary system neutral. The transformer low-voltage sides are connected in a delta configuration. This connection can be used to supply both 120/240-V single-phase, three-wire loads and 240-V delta, three-phase, three-wire loads. The schematic and connection diagrams are shown in Fig. 6-19. Note that there is a 30° phase shift between the high- and low-voltage sides. For the connection shown in Fig. 6-19, the high-side line voltages lead the low-side line voltages by 210°.

The electrical schematic corresponding to the high-voltage floating-wye primary and low-voltage delta secondary is shown in Fig. 6-20, with all currents and voltages indicated. The voltages designated $\mathbf{V}'_{ab}$, $\mathbf{V}'_{bc}$, and $\mathbf{V}'_{ca}$ represent the induced voltages in the secondary winding. The currents designated $\mathbf{I}_A$, $\mathbf{I}_B$, and $\mathbf{I}_C$ are the currents in the high-voltage windings. The currents designated $\mathbf{I}'_{ab}$, $\mathbf{I}'_{bc}$, and $\mathbf{I}'_{ca}$ represent the corresponding secondary winding currents.

Applying Kirchhoff's current law to the high-voltage windings results in

$$\mathbf{I}_A + \mathbf{I}_B + \mathbf{I}_C = 0 \tag{6.1}$$

If the turns ratio for each transformer is defined as in Eq. (5.24), then the secondary phase currents are given by the following:

$$\mathbf{I}'_{ab} = a \cdot \mathbf{I}_A \tag{6.2}$$

$$\mathbf{I}'_{bc} = a \cdot \mathbf{I}_B \tag{6.3}$$

$$\mathbf{I}'_{ca} = a \cdot \mathbf{I}_C \tag{6.4}$$

Adding Eqs. (6.2), (6.3), and (6.4),

$$\begin{aligned}\mathbf{I}'_{ab} + \mathbf{I}'_{bc} + \mathbf{I}'_{ca} &= a\mathbf{I}_A + a\mathbf{I}_B + a\mathbf{I}_C \\ &= a(\mathbf{I}_A + \mathbf{I}_B + \mathbf{I}_C)\end{aligned} \tag{6.5}$$

Applying Eq. (6.1) to (6.5) results in

$$\mathbf{I}'_{ab} + \mathbf{I}'_{bc} + \mathbf{I}'_{ca} = a \cdot (0) = 0 \tag{6.6}$$

Kirchhoff's current law is applied to each of nodes a, b, and c of Fig. 6-20.

$$\mathbf{I}'_{ab} = \mathbf{I}'_a + \mathbf{I}'_{ca} \tag{6.7}$$

$$\mathbf{I}'_{bc} = \mathbf{I}'_b + \mathbf{I}'_{ab} \tag{6.8}$$

$$\mathbf{I}'_{ca} = \mathbf{I}'_c + \mathbf{I}'_{bc} \tag{6.9}$$

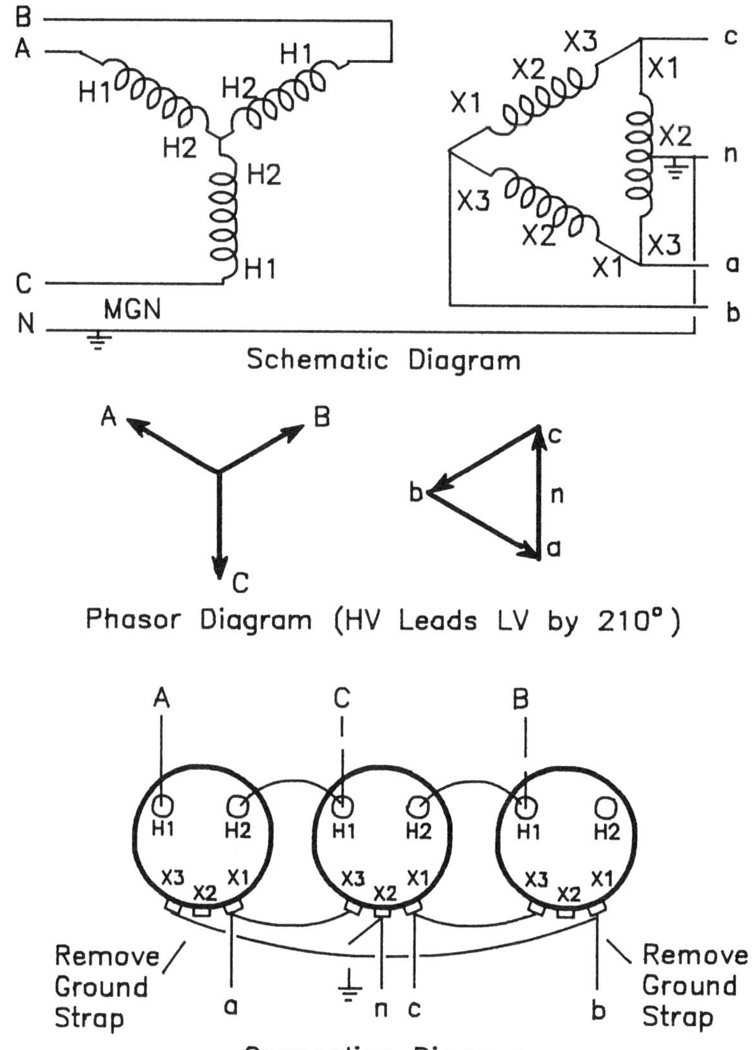

Figure 6-19 Floating wye–delta connection.

Substituting Eqs. (6.8) and (6.9) into (6.6) results in

$$\mathbf{I}'_{ab} + \mathbf{I}'_{b} + \mathbf{I}'_{ab} + \mathbf{I}'_{c} + \mathbf{I}'_{bc} = 0 \tag{6.10}$$

Substituting Eq. (6.8) into (6.10),

$$\mathbf{I}'_{ab} + \mathbf{I}'_{b} + \mathbf{I}'_{ab} + \mathbf{I}'_{c} + \mathbf{I}'_{b} + \mathbf{I}'_{ab} = 0 \tag{6.11}$$

Solving Eq. (6.11) for $\mathbf{I}'_{ab}$,

$$\mathbf{I}'_{ab} = \frac{-\mathbf{I}'_{b} - \mathbf{I}'_{c} - \mathbf{I}'_{b}}{3} \tag{6.12}$$

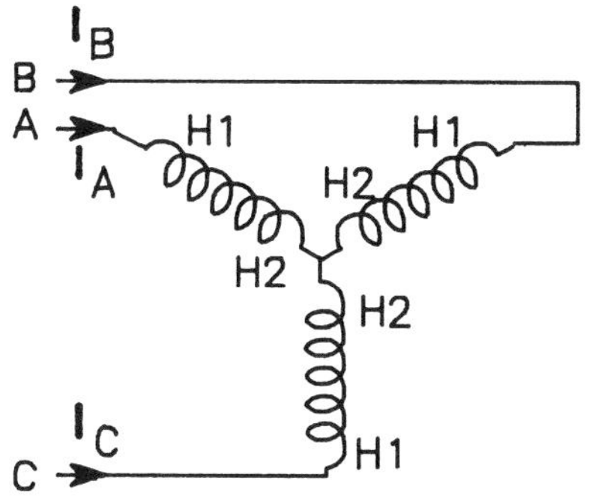

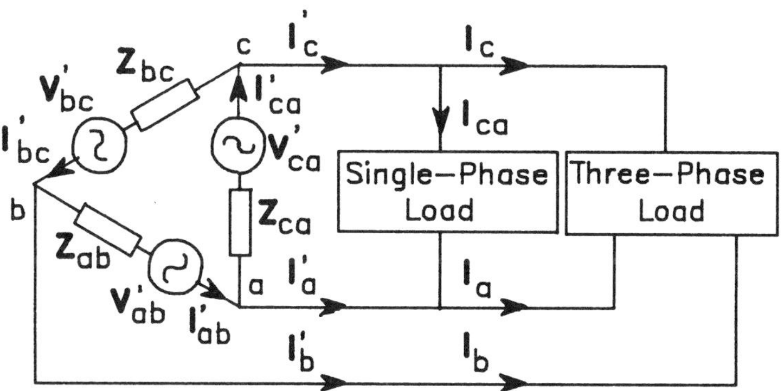

Figure 6-20 Floating wye–delta equivalent circuit.

Furthermore since $\mathbf{I}'_a = -\mathbf{I}'_b - \mathbf{I}'_c$, Eq. (6.12) reduces to

$$\mathbf{I}'_{ab} = \frac{\mathbf{I}'_a - \mathbf{I}'_b}{3} \tag{6.13}$$

Substituting Eqs. (6.7) and (6.9) into (6.6) results in

$$\mathbf{I}'_a + \mathbf{I}'_{ca} + \mathbf{I}'_{bc} + \mathbf{I}'_c + \mathbf{I}'_{bc} = 0 \tag{6.14}$$

Substituting Eq. (6.9) into (6.14),

$$\mathbf{I}'_a + \mathbf{I}'_c + \mathbf{I}'_{bc} + \mathbf{I}'_{bc} + \mathbf{I}'_c + \mathbf{I}'_{bc} = 0 \tag{6.15}$$

Solving Eq. (6.15) for $\mathbf{I}'_{bc}$,

$$\mathbf{I}'_{bc} = \frac{-\mathbf{I}'_a - \mathbf{I}'_c - \mathbf{I}'_c}{3} \tag{6.16}$$

Since $\mathbf{I}'_b = -\mathbf{I}'_a - \mathbf{I}'_c$, Eq. (6.16) reduces to

$$\mathbf{I}'_{bc} = \frac{\mathbf{I}'_b - \mathbf{I}'_c}{3} \tag{6.17}$$

Finally, to find the current in the transformer connected between the c and a phases, Eqs. (6.7) and (6.8) are substituted into (6.6), resulting in

$$\mathbf{I}'_a + \mathbf{I}'_{ca} + \mathbf{I}'_b + \mathbf{I}'_{ab} + \mathbf{I}'_{ca} = 0 \tag{6.18}$$

Substituting Eq. (6.7) into (6.18),

$$\mathbf{I}'_a + \mathbf{I}'_{ca} + \mathbf{I}'_b + \mathbf{I}'_a + \mathbf{I}'_{ca} + \mathbf{I}'_{ca} = 0 \tag{6.19}$$

Solving Eq. (6.19) for $\mathbf{I}'_{ca}$,

$$\mathbf{I}'_{ca} = \frac{-\mathbf{I}'_a - \mathbf{I}'_b - \mathbf{I}'_a}{3} \tag{6.20}$$

Since $\mathbf{I}'_c = -\mathbf{I}'_a - \mathbf{I}'_b$, Eq. (6.20) reduces to

$$\mathbf{I}'_{ca} = \frac{\mathbf{I}'_c - \mathbf{I}'_a}{3} \tag{6.21}$$

The currents $\mathbf{I}'_a$, $\mathbf{I}'_b$, and $\mathbf{I}'_c$ are given by

$$\mathbf{I}'_a = \mathbf{I}_a - \mathbf{I}_{ca} \tag{6.22}$$

$$\mathbf{I}'_b = \mathbf{I}_b \tag{6.23}$$

$$\mathbf{I}'_c = \mathbf{I}_c + \mathbf{I}_{ca} \tag{6.24}$$

To determine the currents $\mathbf{I}_a$, $\mathbf{I}_b$, and $\mathbf{I}_c$, the phasor diagram shown in Fig. 6-21 is used. The phasor diagram of Fig. 6-21 is drawn assuming an *abc* phase sequence. The power factor angle of the single-phase load is designated $\theta_{1\phi}$, and the power factor angle of the three-phase load is designated $\theta_{3\phi}$. Both power factor angles are assumed positive for lagging power factor loads and negative for leading power factor loads. Furthermore, since the three-phase load is assumed to be balanced, the currents $\mathbf{I}_a$, $\mathbf{I}_b$, and $\mathbf{I}_c$ are equal in magnitude and displaced 120° from one another. The single-phase load is assumed to be connected across phases c and a and is also assumed to be balanced.

Substituting Eq. (6.22) and (6.23) into (6.13) results in

$$\mathbf{I}'_{ab} = ⅓(\mathbf{I}_a - \mathbf{I}_{ca} - \mathbf{I}_b) \tag{6.25}$$

From the geometry of the phasor diagram, Eq. (6.25) can be simplified to

$$\mathbf{I}'_{ab} = ⅓\left[\sqrt{3}\left|\mathbf{I}_a\right|\angle -\left(30° + \theta_{3\phi}\right) + \left|\mathbf{I}_{ca}\right|\angle -\left(90° + \theta_{1\phi}\right)\right] \tag{6.26}$$

Substituting Eqs. (6.23) and (6.24) into (6.17) results in

$$\mathbf{I}'_{bc} = ⅓(\mathbf{I}_b - \mathbf{I}_c - \mathbf{I}_{ca}) \tag{6.27}$$

From the geometry of the phasor diagram, Eq. (6.27) can be simplified to

$$\mathbf{I}'_{bc} = ⅓\left[\sqrt{3}\left|\mathbf{I}_b\right|\angle -\left(150° + \theta_{3\phi}\right) + \left|\mathbf{I}_{ca}\right|\angle -\left(90° + \theta_{1\phi}\right)\right] \tag{6.28}$$

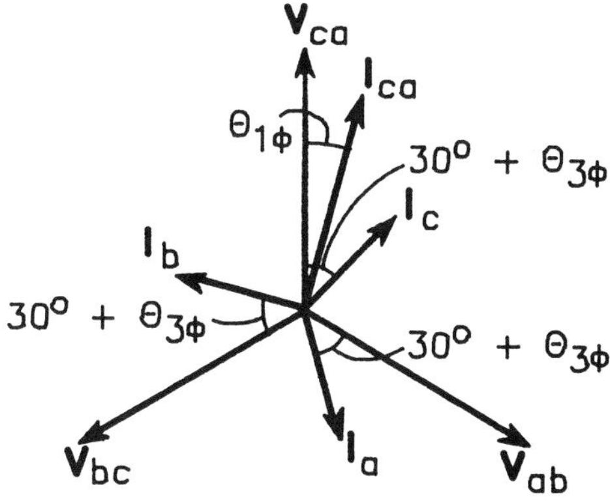

(a) Phasor Diagram Showing Load Currents and Phase Voltages.

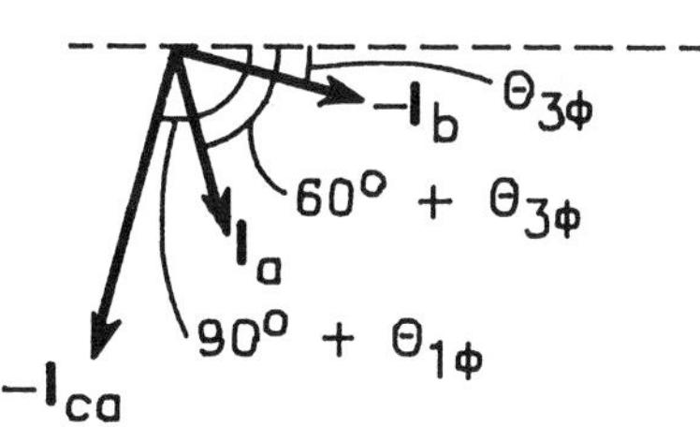

(b) Phasor Diagram for Determination of Current in Phase a'b'.

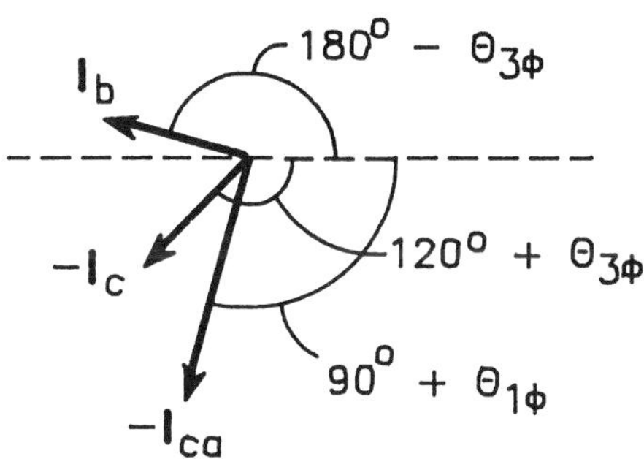

(c) Phasor Diagram for Determination of Current in Phase b'c'.

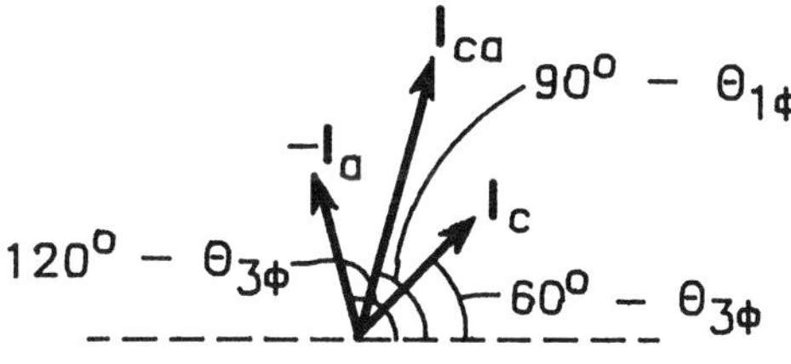

(d) Phasor Diagram for Determination of Current in Phase c'a'.

Figure 6-21 Phasor diagrams for floating wye–delta connection.

Substituting Eqs. (6.22) and (6.24) into (6.21) results in

$$\mathbf{I}'_{ca} = \tfrac{1}{3}(\mathbf{I}_c + \mathbf{I}_{ca} - \mathbf{I}_a + \mathbf{I}_{ca}) = \tfrac{1}{3}(\mathbf{I}_c - \mathbf{I}_a + 2\mathbf{I}_{ca}) \qquad \textbf{(6.29)}$$

From the geometry of the phasor diagram, Eq. (6.29) can be simplified to

$$\mathbf{I}'_{ca} = \tfrac{1}{3}\left[\sqrt{3}|\mathbf{I}_a|\angle(90^\circ - \theta_{3\phi}) + 2|\mathbf{I}_{ca}|\angle(90^\circ - \theta_{1\phi})\right] \qquad \textbf{(6.30)}$$

It is interesting to note that the transformer impedances do not enter into the loading equations. The following list summarizes the procedure used to calculate the loading on each transformer in the floating wye–delta bank:

1. Calculate the magnitude of the single- and three-phase load currents.

2. Calculate the power factor angles of the single- and three-phase loads. A positive angle is assigned to a lagging power factor load; a negative angle is assigned to a leading power factor load.
3. Calculate the transformer currents using Eqs. (6.26), (6.28), and (6.30).
4. Calculate the apparent power loading on each transformer by multiplying the transformer coil current by the coil voltage.

EXAMPLE 6-7

Three single-phase transformers are to be connected floating wye–delta to supply the following loads:

Single-phase load: 30 kW, 0.95 lagging PF, 120/240 V, three wire
Three-phase load: 100 kW, 0.8 lagging PF, 240 V, three wire

The utility primary distribution circuit is a 4.16-kV MGN system. Determine the apparent power ratings and winding voltage designations for each of the three transformers in the bank.

Solution First, it is necessary to calculate the magnitude of the single- and three-phase load currents, as follows:

$$|\mathbf{I}_a| = |\mathbf{I}_b| = \frac{100{,}000/0.8}{\sqrt{3}\cdot 240} = 300.7 \text{ A}$$

$$|\mathbf{I}_{ca}| = \frac{30{,}000/0.95}{240} = 131.6 \text{ A}$$

The power factor angles for the single- and three-phase loads are calculated.

$$\theta_{1\phi} = \cos^{-1}(0.95) = 18.2^\circ$$

$$\theta_{3\phi} = \cos^{-1}(0.80) = 36.9^\circ$$

The transformer coil currents are calculated.

$$\begin{aligned}
\mathbf{I}'_{ab} &= \tfrac{1}{3}\left[\sqrt{3}\left|\mathbf{I}_a\right|\angle -\left(30^\circ + \theta_{3\phi}\right) + \left|\mathbf{I}_{ca}\right|\angle -\left(90^\circ + \theta_{1\phi}\right)\right] \\
&= \tfrac{1}{3}\left[\sqrt{3}\cdot 300.7\angle -\left(30^\circ + 36.9^\circ\right) + 131.6\angle -\left(90^\circ + 18.2\right)\right] \\
&= \tfrac{1}{3}(520.8\angle -66.9^\circ + 131.6\angle -108.2^\circ) \\
&= 54.5 - j201.3 \\
&= 208.6\angle -74.9^\circ \text{ A}
\end{aligned}$$

$$\begin{aligned}
\mathbf{I}'_{bc} &= \tfrac{1}{3}\left[\sqrt{3}\left|\mathbf{I}_b\right|\angle -\left(150^\circ + \theta_{3\phi}\right) + \left|\mathbf{I}_{ca}\right|\angle -\left(90^\circ + \theta_{1\phi}\right)\right] \\
&= \tfrac{1}{3}(520.8\angle -186.9^\circ + 131.6\angle -108.2^\circ) \\
&= -186.0 - j20.8 \\
&= 187.2\angle 186.4^\circ \text{ A}
\end{aligned}$$

$$\mathbf{I}'_{ca} = \tfrac{1}{3}\left[\sqrt{3}\left|\mathbf{I}_a\right|\angle\left(90^\circ - \theta_{3\phi}\right) + 2\left|\mathbf{I}_{ca}\right|\angle\left(90^\circ - \theta_{1\phi}\right)\right]$$
$$= \tfrac{1}{3}(520.8\angle 53.1^\circ + 263.2\angle 71.8^\circ)$$
$$= 131.6 + j222.2$$
$$= 258.2\angle 59.4^\circ \text{ A}$$

The apparent power loading on each transformer is

$$S_{ab} = 240 \cdot 208.6 = 50{,}064 \text{ VA}$$
$$S_{bc} = 240 \cdot 187.2 = 44{,}928 \text{ VA}$$
$$S_{ca} = 240 \cdot 258.2 = 61{,}968 \text{ VA}$$

Therefore, the lighting leg transformer (that is, the transformer connected to the single-phase load) will have an apparent power rating of 75 kVA, and each power leg transformer will be rated at 50 kVA. It is customary to size the two power leg transformers alike in this connection.

The winding voltage designations for all three transformers are 2400/4160Y–120/240 V. Each transformer will have two fully insulated high-voltage bushings.

Delta–Delta Connection

The schematic and connection diagrams for the delta–delta connection are shown in Fig. 6-22. Note that both the transformer high- and low-voltage sides are connected in delta. The equivalent circuit for the delta–delta connection is shown in Fig. 6-23 with all voltages and currents labeled.

In reference to Fig. 6-23, the transformer impedances referred to the low-voltage side are designated $\mathbf{Z}'_{ab}$, $\mathbf{Z}'_{bc}$, and $\mathbf{Z}'_{ca}$. The induced voltages in the transformer low-voltage coils are designated $\mathbf{V}'_{ab}$, $\mathbf{V}'_{bc}$, and $\mathbf{V}'_{ca}$. Finally, the currents flowing in each of the transformer low-voltage coils are designated $\mathbf{I}'_{ab}$, $\mathbf{I}'_{bc}$, and $\mathbf{I}'_{ca}$. On the high-voltage side, the applied voltages to the transformer windings are designated $\mathbf{V}_{AB}$, $\mathbf{V}_{BC}$, and $\mathbf{V}_{CA}$, with an assumed *abc* phase sequence.

Applying Kirchhoff's voltage law to the high-voltage side results in the following:

$$\mathbf{V}_{AB} + \mathbf{V}_{BC} + \mathbf{V}_{CA} = 0 \tag{6.31}$$

The induced secondary voltages are related to the applied primary voltages by the turns ratio of each transformer, as follows:

$$a \cdot \mathbf{V}'_{ab} = \mathbf{V}_{AB} \tag{6.32}$$
$$a \cdot \mathbf{V}'_{bc} = \mathbf{V}_{BC} \tag{6.33}$$
$$a \cdot \mathbf{V}'_{ca} = \mathbf{V}_{CA} \tag{6.34}$$

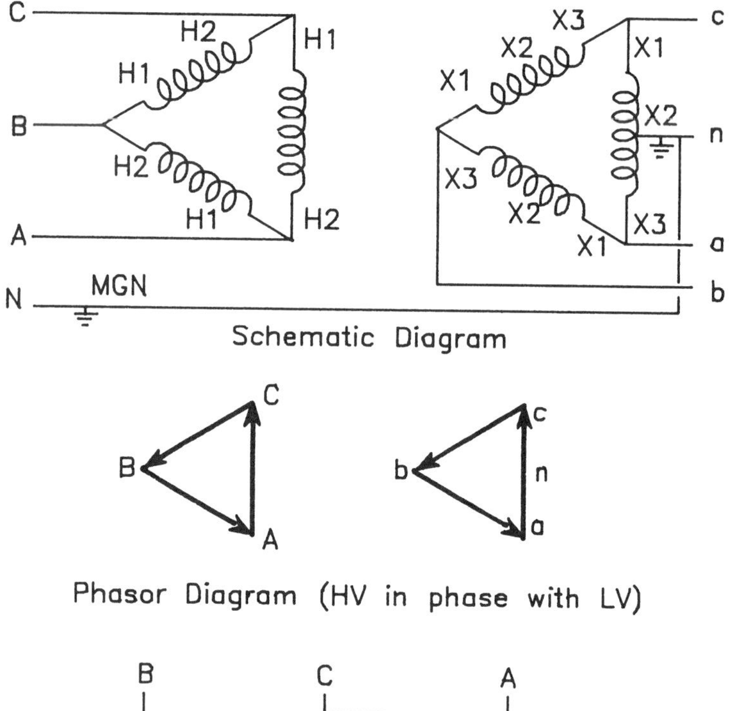

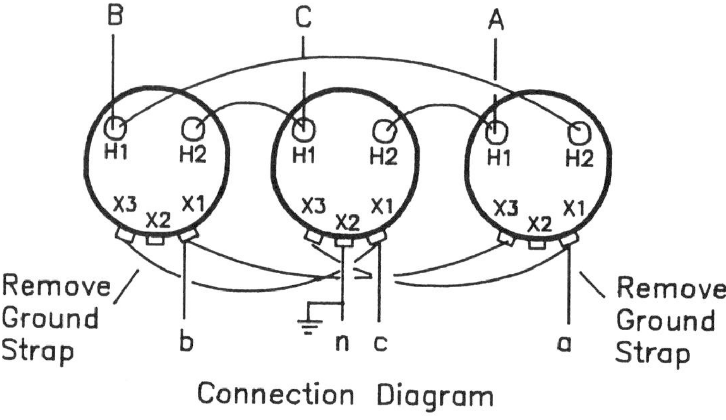

Figure 6-22 Delta–delta connection.

Substituting Eqs. (6.32), (6.33), and (6.34) into (6.31) results in the following:

$$\mathbf{V}'_{ab} + \mathbf{V}'_{bc} + \mathbf{V}'_{ca} = \frac{1}{a}(\mathbf{V}_{AB} + \mathbf{V}_{BC} + \mathbf{V}_{CA}) = \frac{1}{a} \cdot 0 = 0 \tag{6.35}$$

Applying Kirchhoff's voltage-law to the closed delta secondary results in

$$\mathbf{V}'_{ab} + \mathbf{V}'_{bc} + \mathbf{V}'_{ca} - \mathbf{I}'_{ab}\mathbf{Z}'_{ab} - \mathbf{I}'_{bc}\mathbf{Z}'_{bc} - \mathbf{I}'_{ca}\mathbf{Z}'_{ca} = 0 \tag{6.36}$$

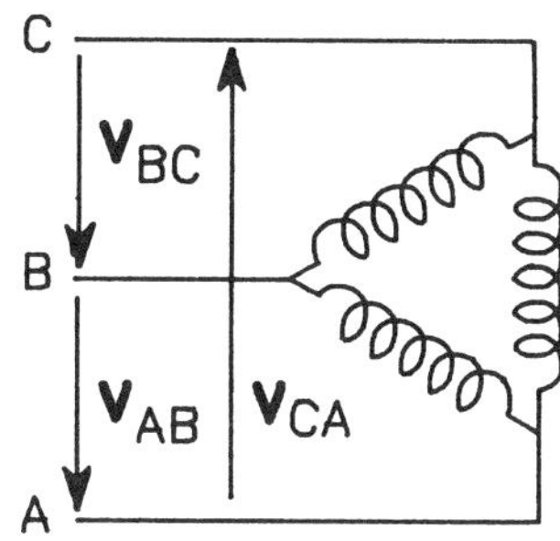

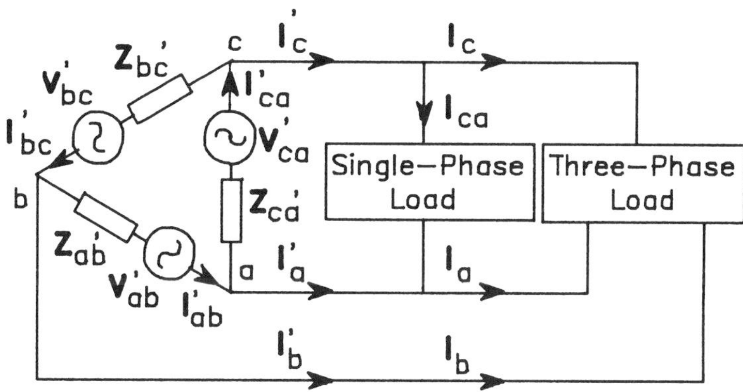

Figure 6-23 Delta–delta equivalent circuit.

Substituting the results of Eq. (6.35) into (6.36) and rearranging yields

$$\mathbf{I}'_{ab}\mathbf{Z}'_{ab} + \mathbf{I}'_{bc}\mathbf{Z}_{bc} + \mathbf{I}'_{ca}\mathbf{Z}'_{ca} = 0 \qquad \textbf{(6.37)}$$

Kirchhoff's current law applied to nodes *a, b,* and *c* results in the following equations:

$$\mathbf{I}'_{ab} = \mathbf{I}'_{a} + \mathbf{I}'_{ca} \qquad \textbf{(6.38)}$$

$$\mathbf{I}'_{bc} = \mathbf{I}_{b} + \mathbf{I}'_{ab} \qquad \textbf{(6.39)}$$

$$\mathbf{I}'_{ca} = \mathbf{I}_{c} + \mathbf{I}'_{bc} \qquad \textbf{(6.40)}$$

Substituting Eqs. (6.39) and (6.40) into (6.37) results in

$$\mathbf{I}'_{ab}\mathbf{Z}'_{ab} + (\mathbf{I}'_{b} + \mathbf{I}'_{ab})\mathbf{Z}'_{bc} + (\mathbf{I}'_{c} + \mathbf{I}'_{bc})\mathbf{Z}'_{ca} = 0 \qquad \textbf{(6.41)}$$

Substituting Eq. (6.39) into (6.41) yields

$$\mathbf{I}'_{ab}\mathbf{Z}'_{ab} + (\mathbf{I}'_b + \mathbf{I}'_{ab})\mathbf{Z}'_{bc} + (\mathbf{I}'_c + \mathbf{I}'_b + \mathbf{I}'_{ab})\mathbf{Z}'_{ca} = 0 \tag{6.42}$$

Solving Eq. (6.42) for $\mathbf{I}'_{ab}$,

$$\mathbf{I}'_{ab} = \frac{-\mathbf{I}'_b\mathbf{Z}'_{bc} - \mathbf{I}'_c\mathbf{Z}'_{ca} - \mathbf{I}'_b\mathbf{Z}'_{ca}}{\mathbf{Z}'_{ab} + \mathbf{Z}'_{bc} + \mathbf{Z}'_{ca}} \tag{6.43}$$

Since $\mathbf{I}'_a = -\mathbf{I}'_b - \mathbf{I}'_c$, Eq. (6.43) reduces to

$$\mathbf{I}'_{ab} = \frac{\mathbf{I}'_a\mathbf{Z}'_{ca} - \mathbf{I}'_b\mathbf{Z}'_{bc}}{\mathbf{Z}'_{ab} + \mathbf{Z}'_{bc} + \mathbf{Z}'_{ca}} \tag{6.44}$$

In a similar manner, the current in transformer *b–c* calculated by substituting Eqs. (6.38) and (6.40) into (6.37), resulting in

$$(\mathbf{I}'_a + \mathbf{I}'_{ca})\mathbf{Z}'_{ab} + \mathbf{I}'_{bc}\mathbf{Z}'_{bc} + (\mathbf{I}'_c + \mathbf{I}'_{bc})\mathbf{Z}'_{ca} = 0 \tag{6.45}$$

Substituting Eq. (6.40) into (6.45) yields

$$(\mathbf{I}'_a + \mathbf{I}'_c + \mathbf{I}'_{bc})\mathbf{Z}'_{ab} + \mathbf{I}'_{bc}\mathbf{Z}'_{bc} + (\mathbf{I}'_c + \mathbf{I}'_{bc})\mathbf{Z}'_{ca} = 0 \tag{6.46}$$

Solving Eq. (6.46) for $\mathbf{I}'_{bc}$,

$$\mathbf{I}'_{bc} = \frac{-\mathbf{I}'_a\mathbf{Z}'_{ab} - \mathbf{I}'_c\mathbf{Z}'_{ab} - \mathbf{I}'_c\mathbf{Z}'_{ca}}{\mathbf{Z}'_{ab} + \mathbf{Z}'_{bc} + \mathbf{Z}'_{ca}} \tag{6.47}$$

Since $\mathbf{I}'_b = -\mathbf{I}'_a - \mathbf{I}'_c$, Eq. (6.47) reduces to

$$\mathbf{I}'_{bc} = \frac{\mathbf{I}'_b\mathbf{Z}'_{ab} - \mathbf{I}'_c\mathbf{Z}'_{ca}}{\mathbf{Z}'_{ab} + \mathbf{Z}'_{bc} + \mathbf{Z}'_{ca}} \tag{6.48}$$

Substituting Eqs. (6.38) and (6.39) into (6.37) results in

$$(\mathbf{I}'_a + \mathbf{I}'_{ca})\mathbf{Z}'_{ab} + (\mathbf{I}'_b + \mathbf{I}'_{ab})\mathbf{Z}'_{bc} + \mathbf{I}'_{ca}\mathbf{Z}'_{ca} = 0 \tag{6.49}$$

Substituting Eq. (6.38) into (6.49) yields

$$(\mathbf{I}'_a + \mathbf{I}'_{ca})\mathbf{Z}'_{ab} + (\mathbf{I}'_b + \mathbf{I}'_a + \mathbf{I}'_{ca})\mathbf{Z}'_{bc} + \mathbf{I}'_{ca}\mathbf{Z}'_{ca} = 0 \tag{6.50}$$

Solving Eq. (6.50) for $\mathbf{I}'_{ca}$,

$$\mathbf{I}'_{ca} = \frac{-\mathbf{I}'_a\mathbf{Z}'_{ab} - \mathbf{I}'_b\mathbf{Z}'_{bc} - \mathbf{I}'_a\mathbf{Z}'_{bc}}{\mathbf{Z}'_{ab} + \mathbf{Z}'_{bc} + \mathbf{Z}'_{ca}} \tag{6.51}$$

Since $\mathbf{I}'_c = -\mathbf{I}'_a - \mathbf{I}'_b$, Eq. (6.51) reduces to

$$\mathbf{I}'_{ca} = \frac{\mathbf{I}'_c\mathbf{Z}'_{bc} - \mathbf{I}'_a\mathbf{Z}'_{ab}}{\mathbf{Z}'_{ab} + \mathbf{Z}'_{bc} + \mathbf{Z}'_{ca}} \tag{6.52}$$

The currents $\mathbf{I}'_a$, $\mathbf{I}'_b$, and $\mathbf{I}'_c$ are calculated using Eqs. (6.22), (6.23), and (6.24). Note that with the delta-connected primary the transformer impedances have an impact on the individual transformer loadings. The actual apparent power loading on each transformer is determined by calculating the transformer currents using Eqs. (6.44), (6.48), and (6.52) and multiplying by the transformer coil voltage.

Rule of Thumb for Determining Loading in Closed Delta Secondaries A rule of thumb is applicable in the determination of transformer loading in banks where the secondaries are connected in closed delta configuration. As an approximation, the lighting leg transformer will carry two-thirds of the single-phase load plus one-third of the three-phase load. The power leg transformers will each carry one-third of the single-phase load plus one-third of the three-phase load. When calculating transformer loading in the delta–delta or floating wye–delta connections, this rule should be applied to determine initial transformer ratings. The loading equations can then be applied to determine actual loading if desired.

Important Application Note: The use of CSP transformers for either the delta–delta or floating wye–delta connections is not recommended. Tripping of the secondary circuit breaker in the lighting leg transformer would create a floating neutral to the load. This floating neutral would most likely lead to overvoltages across the 120-V loads. Conventional transformers are recommended for these connections, with an external high voltage fuse link and lightning arrester furnished and installed by the user.

EXAMPLE 6-8

Three single-phase transformers are to be connected delta–delta to supply the following loads:

Single-phase load: 50 kW, 0.95 lagging PF, 120/240 V, three wire
Three-phase load: 120 kW, 0.8 lagging PF, 240 V, three wire

The utility primary distribution circuit is a 13.8-kV, MGN system. Determine the apparent power ratings and winding voltage designations for each of the three transformers in the bank. Assume that the standard resistance and reactance values for distribution transformers are 1% and 2%, respectively.

Solution As an initial approximation, the rule of thumb will be applied. The three-phase load is equal to 120/0.8 = 150 kVA, and the single-phase load is equal to 50/0.95 = 52.6 kVA. Therefore, the lighting leg transformer will carry approximately 85 kVA, and the two power leg transformers will carry approximately 67.5 kVA. The apparent power rating of the lighting leg transformer will be selected as 100 kVA, and the two power leg transformers will have a rating of 75 kVA for this load condition.

Since the equations for loading in a delta–delta transformer connection involve the transformer impedances, it is necessary to calculate the equivalent transformer impedances referred to the low-voltage side. For the 100-kVA lighting leg transformer,

$$
\begin{aligned}
\mathbf{Z}'_{ca} &= (0.01 + j0.02)\,\frac{240^2}{100{,}000} \\
&= 0.00576 + j0.01152\ \Omega \\
&= 0.01288\angle 63.4^\circ\ \Omega
\end{aligned}
$$

For the two 75-kVA power leg transformers,

$$\mathbf{Z}'_{ab} = \mathbf{Z}'_{bc} = (0.01 + j0.02)\frac{240^2}{75{,}000}$$
$$= 0.00768 + j0.01536\ \Omega$$
$$= 0.01717\angle 63.4°\ \Omega$$

The sum of the three transformer impedances is

$$\mathbf{Z}'_{ca} + \mathbf{Z}'_{ab} + \mathbf{Z}'_{bc} = 0.02112 + j0.04224$$
$$= 0.04723\angle 63.4°\ \Omega$$

The line current magnitudes for the single- and three-phase loads are

$$I_{3\phi} = \frac{120{,}000/0.8}{\sqrt{3}\cdot 240}$$
$$= 360.9\ \text{A}$$
$$I_{1\phi} = \frac{50{,}000/0.95}{240}$$
$$= 219.3\ \text{A}$$

The power factor angles of the single- and three-phase loads are

$$\theta_{1\phi} = \cos^{-1}(0.95) = 18.2°$$
$$\theta_{3\phi} = \cos^{-1}(0.80) = 36.9°$$

In reference to the phasor diagram of Fig. 6-21a, the line currents for the three-phase load are

$$\mathbf{I}_a = 360.9\angle -96.9°\ \text{A}$$
$$\mathbf{I}_b = 360.9\angle -216.9°\ \text{A}$$
$$\mathbf{I}_c = 360.9\angle 23.1°\ \text{A}$$

The load current for the single-phase load is

$$\mathbf{I}_{ca} = 219.3\angle 71.8°\ \text{A}$$

The currents $\mathbf{I}'_a$, $\mathbf{I}'_b$, and $\mathbf{I}'_c$ are calculated from Eqs. (6.22), (6.23), and (6.24).

$$\mathbf{I}'_a = 360.9\angle -96.9° - 219.3\angle 71.8°$$
$$= -111.9 - j566.6$$
$$= 577.6\angle 258.8°\ \text{A}$$
$$\mathbf{I}'_b = 360.9\angle -216.9°\ \text{A}$$
$$\mathbf{I}'_c = 360.9\angle 23.1° + 219.3\angle 71.8°$$
$$= 400.05 + j349.9$$
$$= 531.8\angle 41.1°\ \text{A}$$

The current in each transformer is found by applying Eqs. (6.44), (6.48), and (6.52).

$$\mathbf{I}'_{ab} = \frac{\mathbf{I}'_a\mathbf{Z}'_{ca} - \mathbf{I}'_b\mathbf{Z}'_{bc}}{\mathbf{Z}'_{ab} + \mathbf{Z}'_{bc} + \mathbf{Z}'_{ca}} \tag{6.44}$$

$$= \frac{(577.6\angle 258.8°)(0.01288\angle 63.4°) - (360.9\angle -216.9°)(0.01717\angle 63.4°)}{0.04723\angle 63.4°}$$

$$= 244.8\angle -72.3° \text{ A}$$

$$\mathbf{I}'_{bc} = \frac{\mathbf{I}'_b\mathbf{Z}'_{ab} - \mathbf{I}'_c\mathbf{Z}'_{ca}}{\mathbf{Z}'_{ab} + \mathbf{Z}'_{bc} + \mathbf{Z}'_{ca}} \tag{6.48}$$

$$= \frac{(360.9\angle -216.9°)(0.01717\angle 63.4°) - (531.8\angle 41.4°)(0.01288\angle 63.4°)}{0.04723\angle 63.4°}$$

$$= 214.4\angle 184.6° \text{ A}$$

$$\mathbf{I}'_{ca} = \frac{\mathbf{I}'_c\mathbf{Z}'_{bc} - \mathbf{I}'_a\mathbf{Z}'_{ab}}{\mathbf{Z}'_{ab} + \mathbf{Z}'_{bc} + \mathbf{Z}'_{ca}} \tag{6.52}$$

$$= \frac{(531.8\angle 41.4°)(0.01717\angle 63.4°) - (577.6\angle 258.8°)(0.01717\angle 63.4°)}{0.04723\angle 63.4°}$$

$$= 382.1\angle 60.9° \text{ A}$$

The apparent power loadings on each transformer are

$$S_{ab} = 244.8 \cdot 240 = 58{,}752 \text{ VA} \quad \text{or} \quad 58.8 \text{ kVA}$$

$$S_{bc} = 214.4 \cdot 240 = 51{,}456 \text{ VA} \quad \text{or} \quad 51.5 \text{ kVA}$$

$$S_{ca} = 382.1 \cdot 240 = 91{,}704 \text{ VA} \quad \text{or} \quad 91.7 \text{ kVA}$$

Therefore, the apparent power rating of the two power leg transformers must be 75 kVA if no overloads are permitted. Likewise, the apparent power rating of the lighting leg transformer must be 100 kVA. As in the floating wye–delta connection, it is customary to use the same-sized power leg transformers in the delta–delta connection.

The winding voltage designations for all three transformers is 13,800–120/240 V. Each transformer will have two fully insulated high-voltage bushings.

Open Delta–Open Delta and Open Wye–Open Delta Leading Connection

The loading equations for the open delta–open delta and open wye–open delta are identical. Obviously, the connections on the transformer high side are different for the two connections. The connections on the low-voltage side are identical. In the loading calculations, the single- and three-phase loads are assumed to be balanced. The schematic and connection diagrams for the open delta–open delta transformer connection are shown in Fig. 6-24, and the schematic and connection diagrams for the open wye–open delta connection are shown in Fig. 6-25.

A schematic diagram and low-voltage phasor diagram corresponding to both the open delta–open delta and open wye–open delta leading connection are shown in

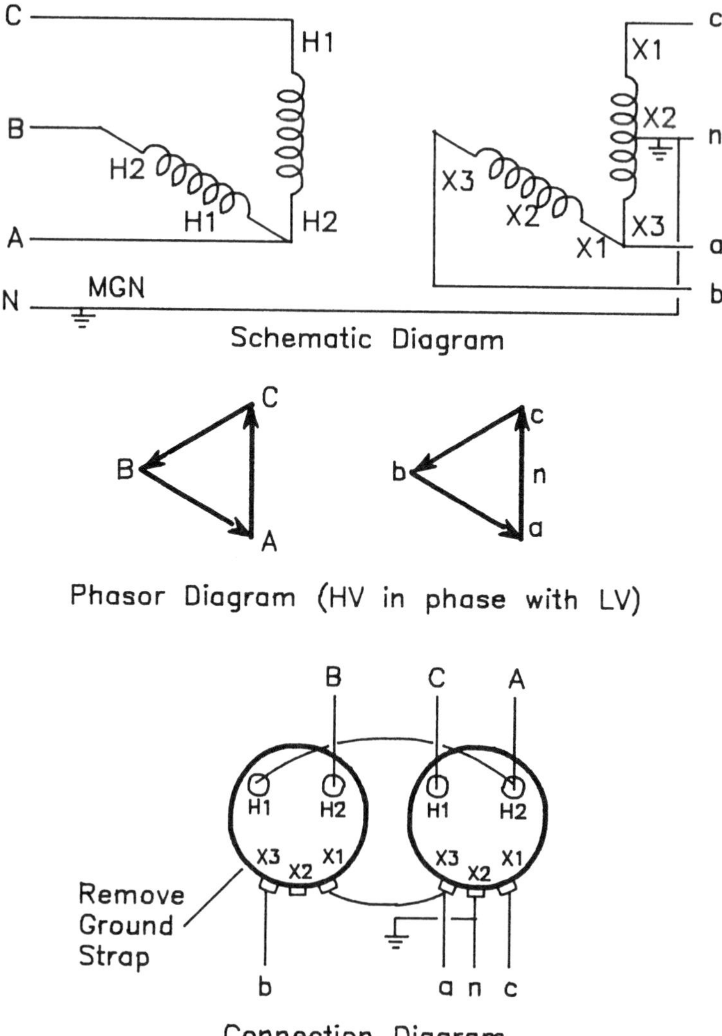

Figure 6-24 Open delta–open delta leading connection.

Fig. 6-26. In the leading connection, the transformer that supplies the single-phase load is connected to the phase voltage that leads the phase voltage supplying the power leg transformer. This is evident from the schematic and phasor diagrams of Fig. 6-26. From the schematic diagram the following relations result:

$$\mathbf{I}'_{ca} = \mathbf{I}_{ca} + \mathbf{I}_{c} \tag{6.53}$$

$$\mathbf{I}'_{ab} = -\mathbf{I}_{b} \tag{6.54}$$

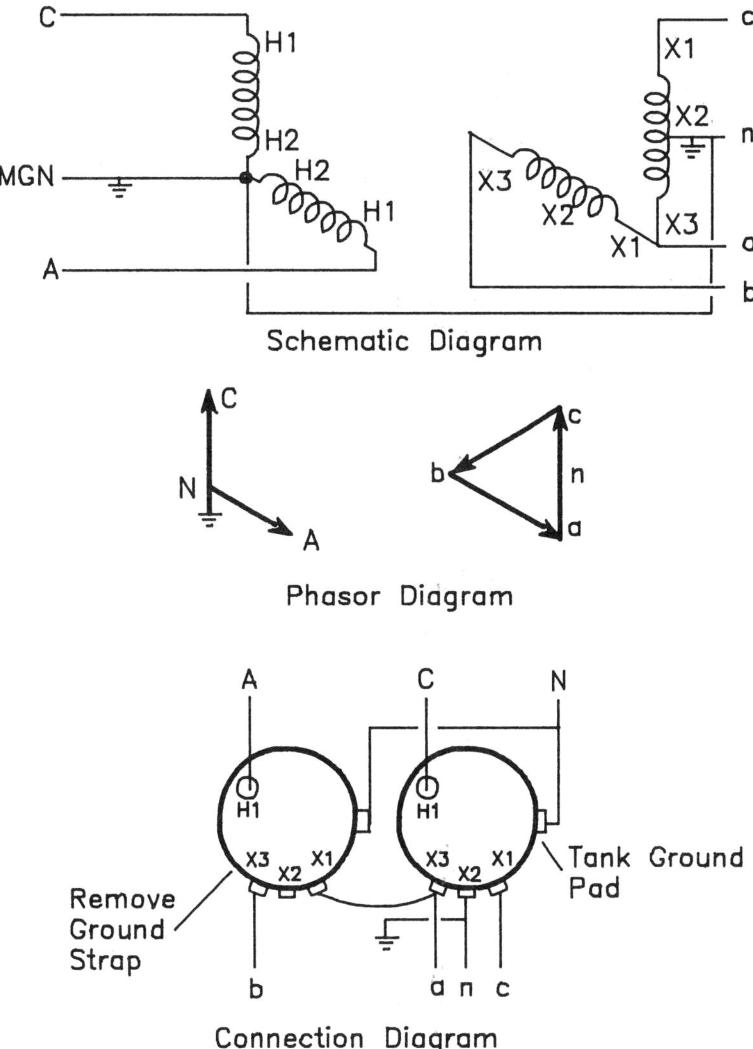

Figure 6-25 Open wye–open delta leading connection.

The apparent power loading on the lighting leg transformer (between phases c and a) is equal to the magnitude of the current $\mathbf{I}'_{ca}$ multiplied by the magnitude of $\mathbf{V}_{ca}$. Likewise, the apparent power loading on the power leg transformer is equal to the magnitude of $\mathbf{I}'_{ab}$ multiplied by the magnitude of $\mathbf{V}_{ab}$. If the transformers are connected to different phases, the same relationships can be used, with a corresponding change in the phase designations.

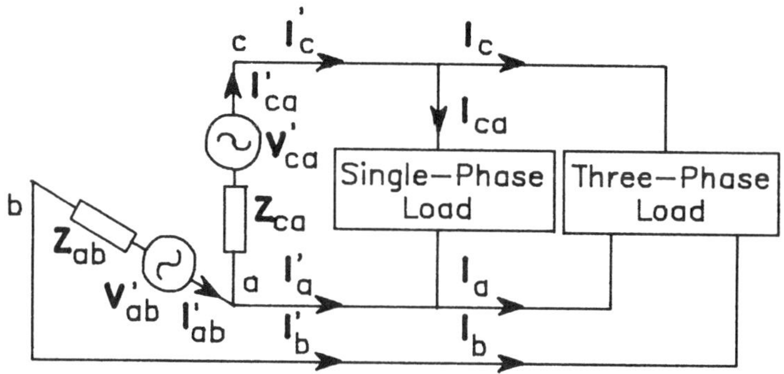

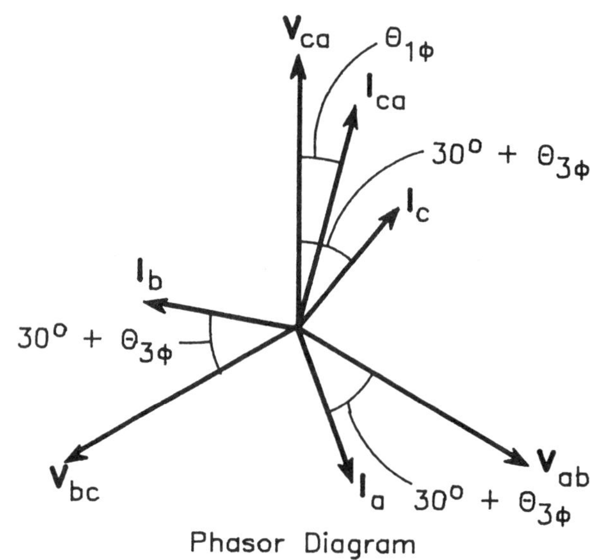

Figure 6-26 Open delta leading–secondary equivalent circuit.

EXAMPLE 6-9

A commercial establishment is to be supplied service from an open wye–open delta leading transformer bank. The single- and three-phase loads are

Single-phase load: 100 kW, 0.90 lagging PF, 120/240 V, three wire
Three-phase load: 20 kW, 0.85 lagging PF, 240V, three wire

The utility primary distribution circuit consists of two phases of a 12.47-kV, three-phase MGN system. Determine the apparent power and voltage ratings for the transformers required to serve this load.

Solution The magnitudes of the single- and three-phase load currents are:

$$I_{1\phi} = \frac{100{,}000/0.90}{240}$$
$$= 463.0 \text{ A}$$
$$I_{3\phi} = \frac{20{,}000/0.85}{\sqrt{3} \cdot 240}$$
$$= 56.6 \text{ A}$$

The power factor angles of the single- and three-phase loads are:

$$\theta_{1\phi} = \cos^{-1}(0.90) = 25.8°$$
$$\theta_{3\phi} = \cos^{-1}(0.85) = 31.8°$$

From the phasor diagram of Fig. 6-26, the line currents for the three-phase load are

$$\mathbf{I}_a = 56.6\angle -91.8° \text{ A}$$
$$\mathbf{I}_b = 56.6\angle -211.8° \text{ A}$$
$$\mathbf{I}_c = 56.6\angle 28.2° \text{ A}$$

The load current for the single-phase load is

$$\mathbf{I}_{ca} = 463.0\angle 64.2° \text{ A}$$

The transformer currents are

$$\mathbf{I}'_{ca} = 463.0\angle 64.2° + 56.6\angle 28.2°$$
$$= 251.4 + j443.6$$
$$= 509.9\angle 60.5° \text{ A}$$
$$\mathbf{I}'_{ab} = -56.6\angle -211.8° \text{ A}$$
$$= 56.6\angle -31.8° \text{ A}$$

The apparent power loadings on the transformers are

$$S_{ca} = 509.9 \cdot 240 = 122{,}376 \text{ VA} \quad \text{or} \quad 122.4 \text{ kVA}$$
$$S_{ab} = 56.6 \cdot 240 = 13{,}584 \text{ VA} \quad \text{or} \quad 13.6 \text{ kVA}$$

Therefore, a 167-kVA transformer is needed for the lighting leg, and a 15-kVA transformer is needed for the power leg.

The appropriate winding voltage designation for both transformers is 12,470GrdY/7200–120/240 V. Each transformer would have one high-voltage bushing. As an alternative, a winding voltage designation of 7200/12,470Y V may be used. This transformer would have two high-voltage bushings and would not be as economical as the previous choice.

Open Delta–Open Delta and Open Wye–Open Delta Lagging Connection

The schematic and connection diagrams for the open delta–open delta and open wye–open delta lagging connections are shown in Figs. 6-27 and 6-28. The phasor diagram corresponding to the low-voltage secondary is shown in Fig. 6-29. In the lagging connection, the transformer that supplies the single-phase load is connected to the phase

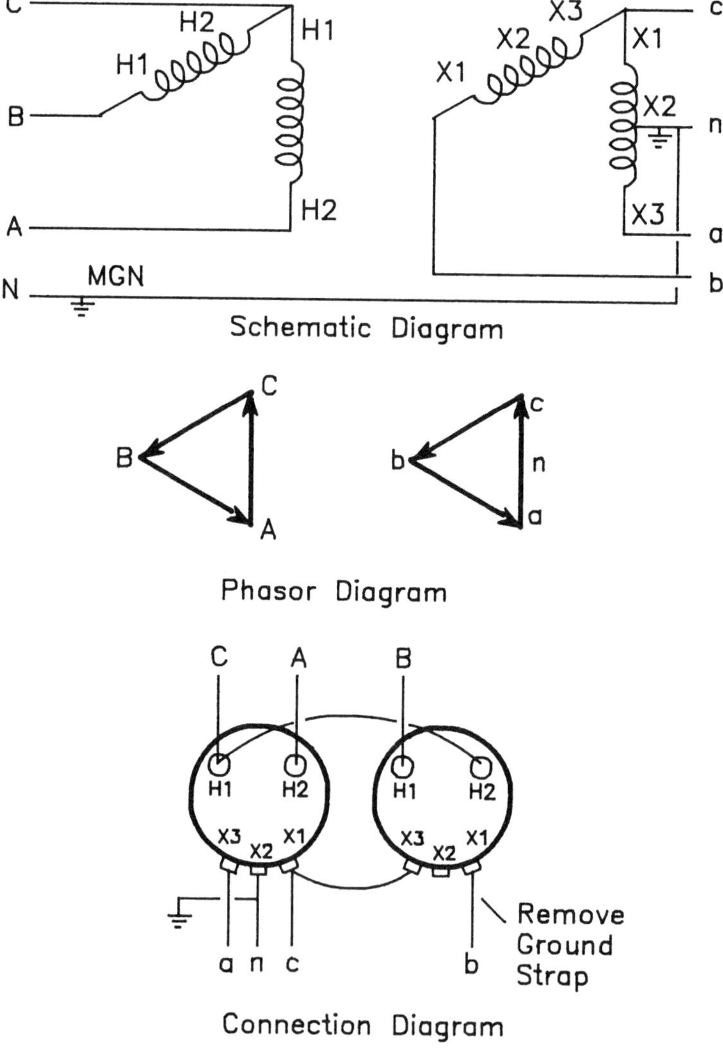

Figure 6-27 Open delta–open delta lagging connection.

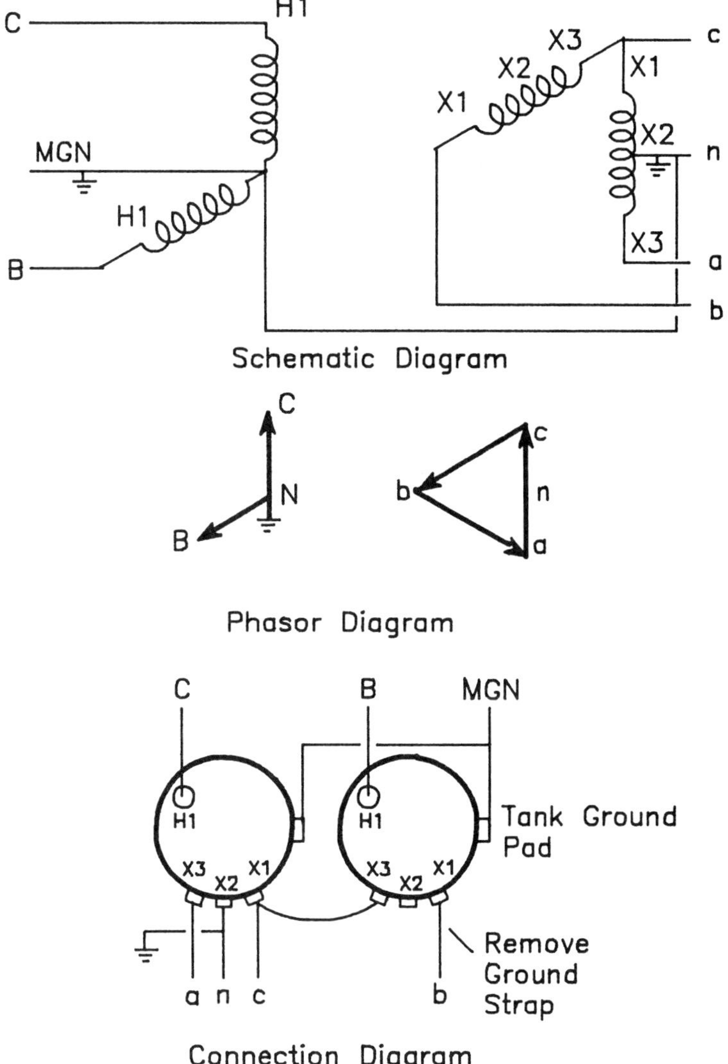

Figure 6-28 Open wye–open delta lagging connection.

voltage that lags the phase voltage supplying the power leg transformer. This is evident from the schematic and phasor diagrams of Fig. 6-29.

In reference to Fig. 6-29 the following results:

$$\mathbf{I}'_{bc} = \mathbf{I}_b \tag{6.55}$$

$$\mathbf{I}'_{ca} = \mathbf{I}_{ca} - \mathbf{I}_a \tag{6.56}$$

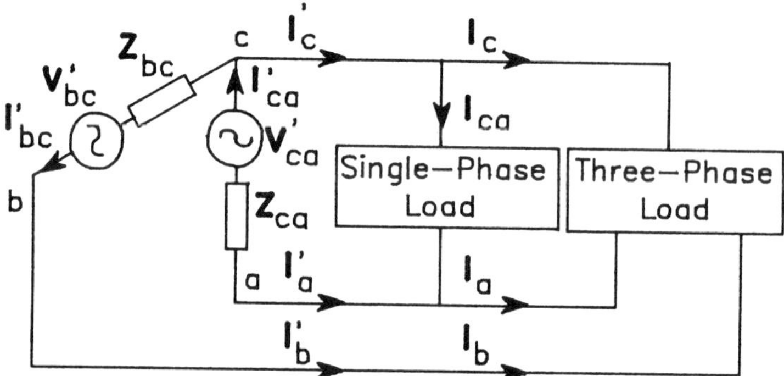

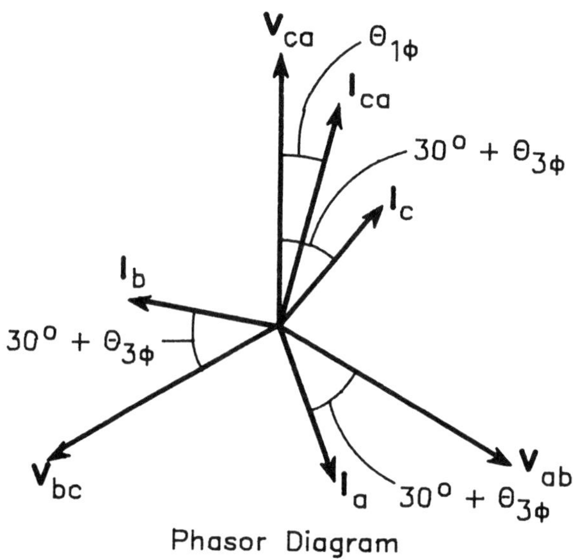

Figure 6-29 Open delta lagging–secondary equivalent circuit.

The apparent power loading on the lighting transformer (between the *a* and *c* phases) is equal to the magnitude of $\mathbf{I}'_{ca}$ multiplied by the magnitude of $\mathbf{V}_{ca}$. The apparent power loading on the power transformer (between the *b* and *c* phases) is equal to the magnitude of $\mathbf{I}'_{bc}$ multiplied by the magnitude of $\mathbf{V}_{bc}$.

EXAMPLE 6-10

Repeat Example 6-9 for the open wye–open delta lagging connection.

Solution The magnitude of the single- and three-phase load currents is the same as in Example 6-9.

$$I_{1\phi} = 463.0 \text{ A}$$

$$I_{3\phi} = 56.6 \text{ A}$$

The power factor angles of the loads are also the same as in Example 6-9.

$$\theta_{1\phi} = 25.8°$$

$$\theta_{3\phi} = 31.8°$$

The line currents for the three-phase load are also the same as in Example 6-9.

$$\mathbf{I}_a = 56.6\angle -91.8° \text{ A}$$

$$\mathbf{I}_b = 56.6\angle -211.8° \text{ A}$$

$$\mathbf{I}_c = 56.6\angle 28.2° \text{ A}$$

From the phasor diagram of Fig. 6-29, the line current for the single-phase load is

$$\mathbf{I}_{ca} = 463.0\angle 64.2° \text{ A}$$

The transformer currents are

$$\mathbf{I}'_{bc} = 56.6\angle -211.8° \text{ A}$$

$$\begin{aligned}\mathbf{I}'_{ca} &= 463.0\angle 64.2° - 56.6\angle -91.8° \text{ A} \\ &= 203.3 + j473.4 \\ &= 515.2\angle 66.8° \text{ A}\end{aligned}$$

The apparent power loadings on the transformers are

$$S_{ca} = 56.6 \cdot 240 = 13{,}584 \text{ VA} \quad \text{or} \quad 13.6 \text{ kVA}$$

$$S_{ab} = 515.2 \cdot 240 = 123{,}648 \text{ VA} \quad \text{or} \quad 123.6 \text{ kVA}$$

Therefore, a 167-kVA transformer is needed for the lighting leg, and a 15-kVA transformer is needed for the power leg, the same as in Example 6-9. Note, however, that there is a slight difference in the loading on the lighting leg transformer compared to the open wye–open delta leading connection.

The appropriate winding voltage designation for both transformers is 12,470GrdY/7200–120/240 V. Each transformer will have one high-voltage bushing. As an alternative, a winding voltage designation of 7200/12,470Y V may be used. This transformer would have two high-voltage bushings and would not be as economical as the previous choice.

Rule of Thumb for Determining Loading on Open-Delta Secondaries When distribution transformers are connected in either the open wye–open delta or open delta–open delta configuration, a rule of thumb can be applied to determine the approximate apparent power loadings on the two transformers in the bank. The lighting leg transformer will carry 100% of the single-phase load plus 58% of the total three-phase load. The power leg transformer will carry approximately 58% of the total three-phase load.

Important Application Note: The use of CSP transformers for either the open delta–open delta or open wye–open delta connections is not recommended. Tripping of the secondary circuit breaker in the lighting leg transformer would create a floating neutral to the load. This floating neutral would most likely lead to overvoltages across the 120-V loads. Conventional transformers are recommended for these connections, with an external high-voltage fuse link and lighting arrester furnished and installed by the user.

EXAMPLE 6-11

Repeat Example 6-9 using the rule of thumb for loading on open-delta secondaries.

Solution The apparent power consumed by the single- and three-phase loads are

$$S_{1\phi} = \frac{100{,}000}{0.9} = 111{,}111 \text{ VA}$$

$$S_{3\phi} = \frac{20{,}000}{0.85} = 23{,}529 \text{ VA}$$

The load on the lighting leg transformer is approximately

$$S_{ca} \approx 111{,}111 + (0.58)(23{,}529) = 124{,}758 \text{ VA} \quad \text{or} \quad 124.8 \text{ kVA}$$

The load on the power leg transformer is

$$S_{ab} \approx (0.58)(23{,}529) = 13{,}647 \text{ VA} \quad \text{or} \quad 13.6 \text{ kVA}$$

Note that the results obtained from applying the rule of thumb agree favorably with the results calculated in Example 6-9. Therefore, a 167-kVA transformer is needed for the lighting leg, and a 15-kVA transformer is needed for the power leg.

6-6 Distribution Substation Transformers

Distribution substation transformers are usually classified as *medium-power transformers* and normally range in size from 3750 kVA to 12 MVA (self-cooled, three-phase OA rating). The transformers are usually delta connected on the high side and grounded wye connected on the low side. The incoming high voltage rating typically ranges anywhere from 23 to 138 kV, while the low voltage rating may range from 4.16 to 34.5 kV.

A typical distribution substation transformer is shown in Fig. 6-30. Note that the transformer is equipped with high- and low-voltage bushings and high- and low-voltage lightning arresters. Usually, no internal overcurrent protective device is supplied with these transformers by the manufacturer. High- and low-side overcurrent protection is normally provided by the end user in the form of power fuses or circuit breakers. Indicating gauges may also be provided to monitor the top oil temperature and oil level in the tank. Bushing mounted current transformers may be supplied for metering and relaying purposes. A control cabinet is provided to house various control apparatus, terminal strips for CT secondary, and station power connections for auxiliary equipment, alarm contacts, and so forth.

Figure 6-30 Distribution substation transformer. (Photo Courtesy of Ohio Edison Company)

Many distribution substation transformers are equipped with a de-energized tap changer that allows selection of a high-voltage tap setting. Typically, taps are available at nominal voltage, $\pm 5\%$, and $\pm 2.5\%$ of nominal.

It is important to note the differences between No-Load tap changing, de-energized tap changing, and load tap changing duties for the tap changing mechanism and contacts. *No-load-tap changing* indicates that the tap changer cannot be operated with a load connected to the transformer. The transformer may be energized, however. *De-energized tap changing* indicates that the tap changer can be operated only when the transformer is completely de-energized. Attempting to operate the tap changer while the transformer is energized may cause chopping of the magnetizing current, resulting in a high transient overvoltage across the tap changer switch contacts. *Load tap changing* indicates that the tap changer can be operated with a load on the transformer.

Distribution substation transformers are normally equipped with side-mounted radiators to allow cooling of the insulating fluid. In many instances, self-cooling by natural air convection over the surface of the radiators will allow for satisfactory operation of the transformer. To increase the rating of the transformer, cooling fans may be installed over the radiator surface to provide for forced-air cooling. Generally, forced-air cooling increases the rating by 25% above the self-cooled rating. Thus, a transformer with a self-cooled rating of 7500 kVA would have a forced-air cooled rating of 9375 kVA. Also, in many large power transformers, oil pumps are used to force circulation of the insulating fluid through the transformer to increase the capacity.

6-7 Autotransformers

Three-phase autotransformers are usually used to transform voltages in a power system when the voltage ratio from high to low is approximately 3:1 or less. A typical example would be when the voltage is transformed from 345 to 138 kV. If the voltage ratio is greater than 3:1, a two-winding transformer is usually employed. A distinct advantage of the au-

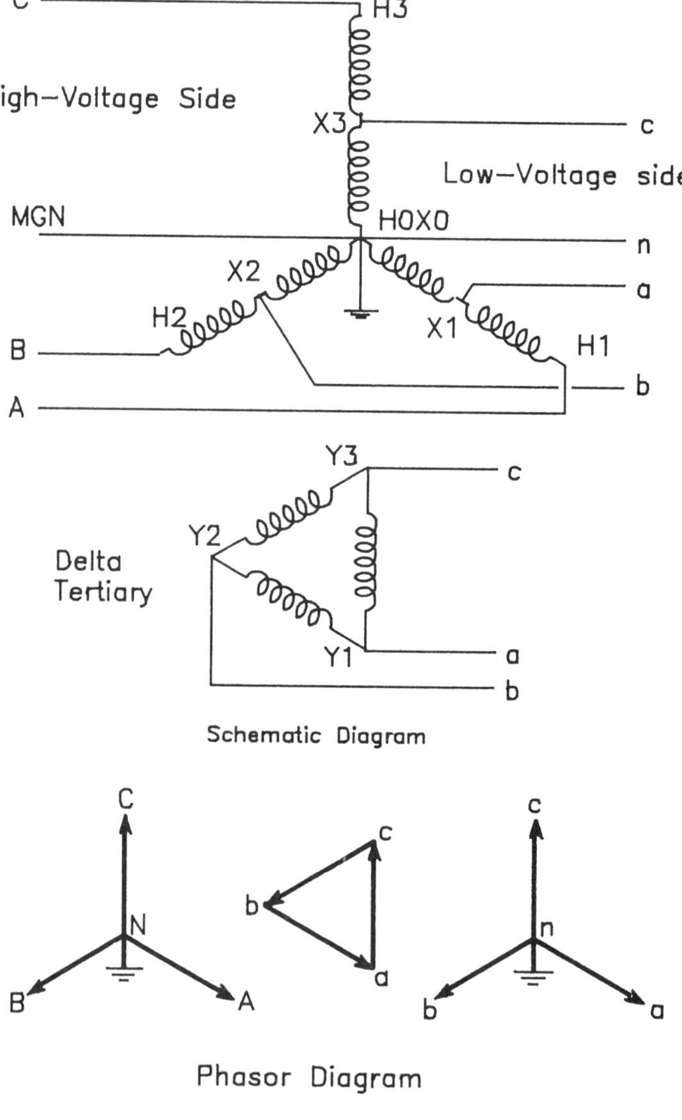

Figure 6-31 Grounded wye–grounded wye connected autotransformer with delta–connected tertiary winding.

totransformer over a two-winding transformer of the same apparent power rating is reduced size, weight, and cost. A major disadvantage, however, is the loss of electrical isolation between the high- and low-voltage sides. Due to this loss of electrical isolation, autotransformers are not used to step down primary voltages to utilization service voltages.

Figure 6-31 shows the schematic and phasor diagrams for a three-phase, grounded wye–grounded wye autotransformer commonly used in transmission systems of 69 kV and above. In addition to the main high- and low-voltage windings, a third winding, referred to as the *tertiary* winding, is usually present on three-phase autotransformers. The voltage rating of the tertiary winding is generally in the medium-voltage range (12.47 to 24.94 kV). The purpose of the tertiary winding is to provide a path for circulation of the third harmonic component of excitation current and to stabilize the neutral. In addition, since the voltage rating of the tertiary winding is usually in the medium-voltage range, a small distribution transformer may be used to step down the tertiary winding voltage to utilization voltage (120 V) for station power requirements.

The winding voltage designation for a grounded wye autotransformer with a delta tertiary is

$$E_{1H}\text{GrdY}/E_H\text{–}E_{1X}\text{GrdY}/E_X\text{–}E_Y$$

As an example, a three-phase grounded wye connected autotransformer is used to connect between the 345- and 138-kV portions of a power system. The delta tertiary is to be rated at 13.8 kV. The appropriate winding voltage designation for this transformer is 345, 000GrdY/199, 200–138, 000GrdY/79, 680–13, 800 V. The three-phase autotrans-

Figure 6-32 Three-phase autotransformer rated at 45 MVA, 140,000GrdY/80,830–22,900Y/13,320–13200 V. (Photo Courtesy of Ohio Edison Company)

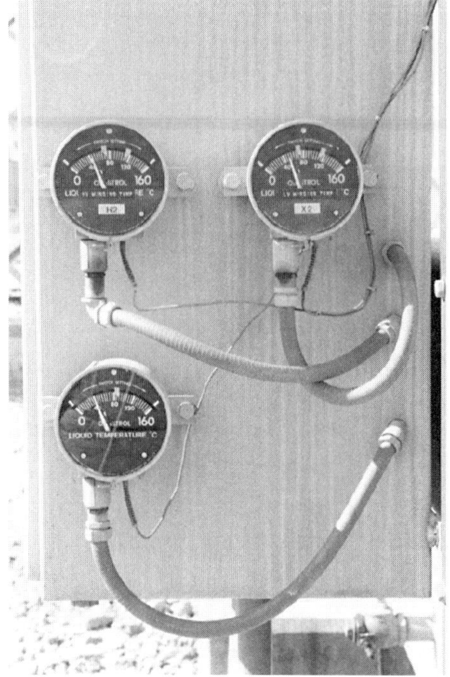

Figure 6-33 Transformer indicating gauges. (Photo Courtesy of Ohio Edison Company)

former shown in Fig. 6-32 has a self-cooled rating of 45 MVA, a forced-air cooled rating of 60 MVA, and a voltage rating of 140,000GrdY/80,830–22,900Y/13320–13,200 V. A close-up of the indicating gauges for this transformer is shown in Fig. 6-33.

6-8 Grounding Transformers

Grounding transformers are typically used to create a grounded neutral on an ungrounded system. An example of this would be a three-phase, three-wire system supplied from the delta secondary of a transformer. Also, a grounding transformer may be used to decrease the impedance to short circuits involving ground in a power system. A grounding transformer bank may consist of either a grounded wye–delta connection or a zigzag configuration. Although either connection may be used, the zigzag is more economical and therefore more common.

The schematic diagram for the grounded wye–delta connection is shown in Fig. 6-34. This connection is the same as a standard grounded wye-delta without a load placed on the secondary. Under normal conditions with balanced three-phase voltages applied

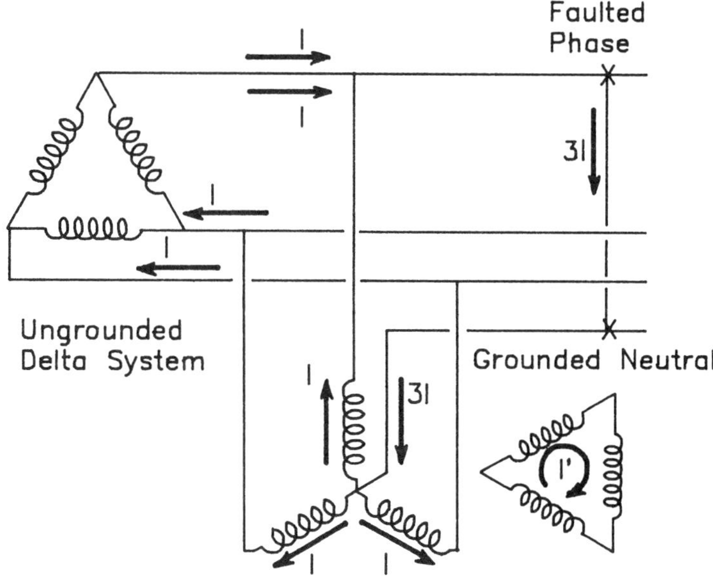

Figure 6-34 Grounded wye–delta-connected grounding transformer.

to the bank, no current will flow other than the transformer excitation current. In addition, since balanced voltages are applied to the primary, the voltages induced in the secondary will also comprise a balanced three-phase set of voltages. The net voltage around the closed delta secondary will therefore be equal to zero.

If a line to ground fault develops on the system, the voltage across one of the transformer windings will be equal to zero. This being the case, the voltage induced in the secondary of the shorted transformer will also be equal to zero. Thus, the net voltage around the closed delta secondary will not be equal to zero, and a large circulating current will flow. This circulating current is reflected to the transformer bank primary and flows to the fault location as shown in Fig. 6-34. The value of the fault current depends on the grounding transformer bank impedance, the source impedance, and the line impedance to the fault point. This topic will be discussed in more detail in Chapter 11.

The schematic diagram for the zigzag grounding transformer connection is shown in Fig. 6-35. Note that coils wound around the same core are shown parallel to one another. Under normal conditions, no current is flowing into the transformer except for transformer excitation current. If a line to ground fault occurs, the voltage across the coils connected to the faulted phase will be equal to zero. The resulting imbalance will cause current to flow through the windings to the fault location as shown in Fig. 6-35. As in the case of the grounded wye–delta grounding transformer, the magnitude of the fault current will depend on the transformer, source, and line impedances.

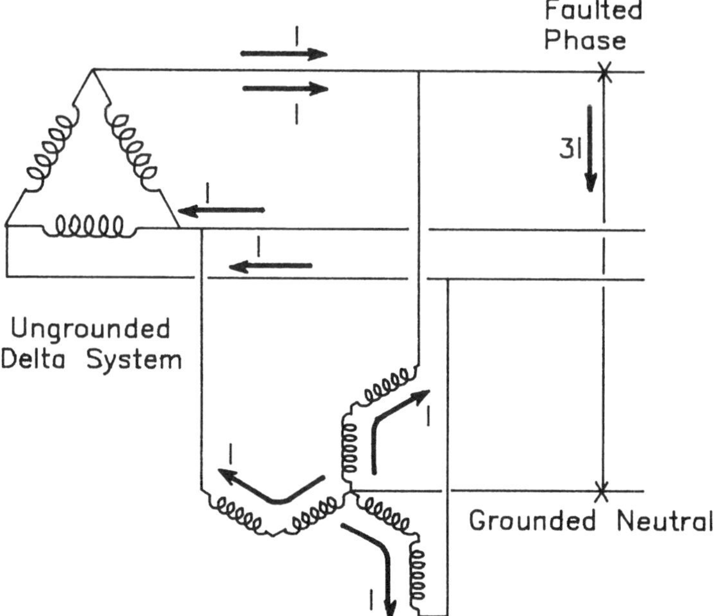

Figure 6-35 Zigzag grounding transformer.

6-9 Network Transformers

Network transformers are three-phase transformers designed for use in underground network systems. Generally, these transformers are installed in an underground vault and are designed for either continuous or occasional submerged operation. The transformers are available in either dry type or liquid filled. Standard winding connections are either delta–wye or wye–wye. In the wye–wye connection, the high- and low-voltage neutrals are connected by means of a removable link. Standard kVA and voltage ratings for liquid-immersed and dry-type network transformers are shown in Table 6-6. The standard percent impedance for network transformers is 5.0% for 300 through 1000 kVA and 7.0% for 1500 through 2500 kVA, self-cooled ratings.

A two- or three-position high-voltage switch is also supplied to disconnect, isolate, and ground the transformer high-voltage side. The three-position switch is provided with three operating positions: open, closed, and ground. The two-position switch is provided with two operating positions: clear and ground. The two-position switch is intended for use as a grounding switch. An electrical interlock prevents the high-voltage switch from being operated when the transformer is energized.

A network protector is supplied to provide short-circuit protection to the network system. Under normal conditions, the flow of active and reactive power is from the high-voltage feeder, through the network transformer, and into the network through the net-

Table 6-6 Standard kVA and Voltage Ratings for Network Transformers

Liquid Filled		*Dry Type*	
55°C	*65°C*	*Self-Cooled*	*Forced-Air Cooled*
300	336	300	400
500	560	500	667
750	840	750	1000
1000	1120	1000	1333
1500	1680	1500	2000
2000	2240	2000	2667
2500	2800	2500	3333

Note: Transformers for 208Y/120-V network available only in 300- to 1000-kVA sizes.

High-Voltage Ratings	*Low-Voltage Ratings*
4160	
4160Y/2400	216Y/125
7200	480Y/277
12,000	
13,200	
13,200Y/7620	
14,400	
22,900	
34,400	

Source: This material is reproduced from American National Standard C57.12.40-1990, copyright 1990, and American National Standard C57.12.57-1987, copyright 1987, with permission by the American National Standards Institute. Copies of these standards may be purchased from American National Standards Institute, 11 West 42nd Street, New York, NY 10036.

work protector. If, for any reason, the flow of active and reactive power is reversed through the network protector, it will trip and isolate the network transformer from the network. The reversal of power flow through the network protector may be caused by several factors.

1. A fault on a primary feeder may cause fault current to flow from the other network transformers through the network and then backfeed through one of the other network transformers. Both the feeder circuit breaker at the substation and the network protector should trip to clear this fault.
2. If the high-voltage source is disconnected from one of the network transformers, the transformer will be energized from the network system on the low-voltage side. This will result in the core losses of the transformer being supplied from the network. The result is a reverse power flow through the network protector.

Although the actual core losses are very small, the network protector is sensitive enough to detect this reverse power condition.

3. Since several primary feeders are connected to the network grid, it is possible to have active and reactive power flow from one primary distribution feeder, through the network, and out to another primary distribution feeder. Again, the network protector that detects a flow of power from the low-voltage network to the high-voltage primary feeder will trip.

Problems

6.1. A single-phase transformer is to be used to supply the following loads:

Load 1: 10 kW, 0.95 lagging power factor
Load 2: 13 kW, 0.80 lagging power factor
Load 3: 22 kW, 0.90 lagging power factor
Load 4: 17 kW, 0.85 lagging power factor

Assume that the demand factor for these four loads is 0.75. The primary distribution feeder is a 12.47-kV, three-phase, MGN system. The load voltage is 120/240 V, single phase, three wire for all four services. Determine the appropriate kVA and winding voltage designations for the transformer supplying these loads.

6.2. Three single-phase transformers are to be connected in a grounded wye–grounded wye configuration to supply a commercial establishment. The estimated loading is

Three-phase load: 80 kW, 0.80 lagging power factor
Single-phase load: 50 kW, 0.92 lagging power factor

The primary distribution feeder is a 4.16-kV, three-phase, MGN system. The load voltage is to be 208 V, three phase, four wire. Calculate the actual apparent power loading on each transformer and select the appropriate kVA ratings and winding voltage designations for each transformer in the bank. Specify the number of high-voltage bushings and lightning arresters required if CSP transformers are used.

6.3. Three single-phase transformers are to be connected floating wye–delta in a bank to supply the following loads:

Three-phase load: 100 kW, 0.85 lagging PF, 240 V, three wire
Single-phase load: 20 kW, 0.92 lagging PF, 120/240V, three wire

The primary distribution feeder is a 12.47-kV, three-phase, MGN system. Calculate the actual apparent power loading on each transformer and select the appropriate kVA ratings and winding voltage designations. Specify the number of high-voltage bushings required.

6.4. Three single-phase transformers are to be connected delta–delta in a bank to supply the following loads:

Three-phase load: 75 kW, 0.80 lagging PF, 240 V, three wire
Single-phase load: 15 kW, 0.95 lagging PF, 120/240 V, three wire

The primary distribution feeder is a 24.94-kV, three-phase, MGN system. Calculate the actual apparent power loading on each transformer and select the appropriate kVA ratings and winding voltage designations. Specify the number of high-voltage bushings required. Assume that the standard impedances for the transformers are $R = 1\%$ and $X = 1.9\%$.

6.5. Two single-phase transformers are to be connected open delta–open delta to supply the following loads:

Three-phase load: 30 kW, 0.80 lagging PF, 240 V, three wire
Single-phase load: 75 kW, 0.95 lagging PF, 120/240 V, three wire

The primary distribution feeder is a 13.8-kV, three-phase, MGN system. Calculate the actual apparent power loading on each transformer and select the appropriate kVA ratings and winding voltage designations. Specify the number of high-voltage bushings required.

6.6. Two single-phase transformers are to be connected open wye–open delta to supply the following loads:

Three-phase load: 20 kW, 0.80 lagging PF, 240 V, three wire
Single-phase load: 100 kW, 0.95 lagging PF, 120/240 V, three wire

The primary distribution feeder is a 34.5-kV, three-phase, MGN system. Calculate the actual apparent power loading on each transformer and select the appropriate kVA ratings and winding voltage designations. Specify the number of high-voltage bushings required.

7

Line and Cable Characteristics

7-1 General

To perform calculations such as voltage drop and short circuit, it is necessary to determine the impedances of overhead and underground lines. Transformer and generator impedances are specified by the manufacturer, and typical values may be found in various reference books. The impedance of overhead lines depends on the conductor type and size and the geometric configuration of pole top construction employed by the utility. Likewise, the impedances of underground cables depend on the conductor size, type, and installation practice. Since there is such a wide variety of installation practices among various utilities, line and cable impedances must be calculated by the utility engineer to suit the particular application.

The capacitance of a line or cable may be a significant factor in voltage regulation, switching surges, and ferroresonance. Line or cable capacitance should not be confused with capacitors used for power factor correction and voltage support. The capacitance of a line or cable is the result of electric charges traveling from one energized conductor, through a dielectric medium, to another energized conductor. In overhead lines, the dielectric medium is the surrounding air. In cables, the dielectric medium is the cable insulation. Generally, the capacitance of overhead lines can be neglected for lines operating at less than 69 kV. Above 69 kV, line charging current can flow into an energized but unloaded line. This line charging current can cause a voltage rise along the line, resulting in excessive voltages at the line terminals. The capacitance of cable circuits is usually high enough to warrant careful consideration.

This chapter begins with a general discussion of the various types of underground cable and overhead wire used by the utilities. Line resistance, inductive reactance, and capacitance are calculated for balanced three-phase conditions. The calculation of impedances for operation under unbalanced conditions is discussed in Chapters 10 and 11. Line and cable terminations are discussed, followed by a section on equivalent circuit line and cable representations.

7-2 Types of Overhead and Underground Cables

Overhead Conductor Types

Several different types of conductor are used for overhead line construction. It is common practice for utility companies to install bare conductor for overhead lines. The most common types of bare conductor used for overhead lines are hard drawn copper, all aluminum conductor (AAC), and aluminum conductor steel reinforced (ACSR). The hard drawn copper conductor may be comprised of a single solid copper conductor or several strands of copper conductors. The AAC conductor is typically made of several strands of aluminum conductors. The ACSR conductor is a stranded conductor that uses an inner stranding of steel conductors surrounded by the aluminum strands. The steel strands add extra strength to the ACSR as compared to AAC and copper conductors. Figure 7-1 shows the different types of overhead conductor.

Overhead Spacer Cable

If the overhead line is to be installed in an area where the phase conductors need to be in close proximity to one another or if a tree condition exists, a special type of overhead cable referred to as *spacer cable* may be installed. Spacer cable consists of insulated aluminum or copper conductor surrounded by an insulating jacket. It is important to note that, although the spacer cable conductor is surrounded by an insulating jacket, the outer surface of the insulation is not considered to be at ground potential. Plastic spacers are used to keep the individual conductors from coming in contact with one another. Figure 7-2 shows a close-up view of a typical spacer cable installation.

Underground Residential Distribution Cable

Underground cables used in distribution circuits from 4.16 to 34.5 kV are typically referred to as underground residential distribution (URD) cables. Figure 7-3a shows a representive view of URD cable used for medium-voltage distribution in the range from 4.16 to 34.5 kV. A cross-sectional view of the cable is shown in Fig. 7-3b. These cables may use either copper or aluminum conductors, although aluminum is far more prevalent in utility systems. The conductors are covered by a thin layer of semiconducting material

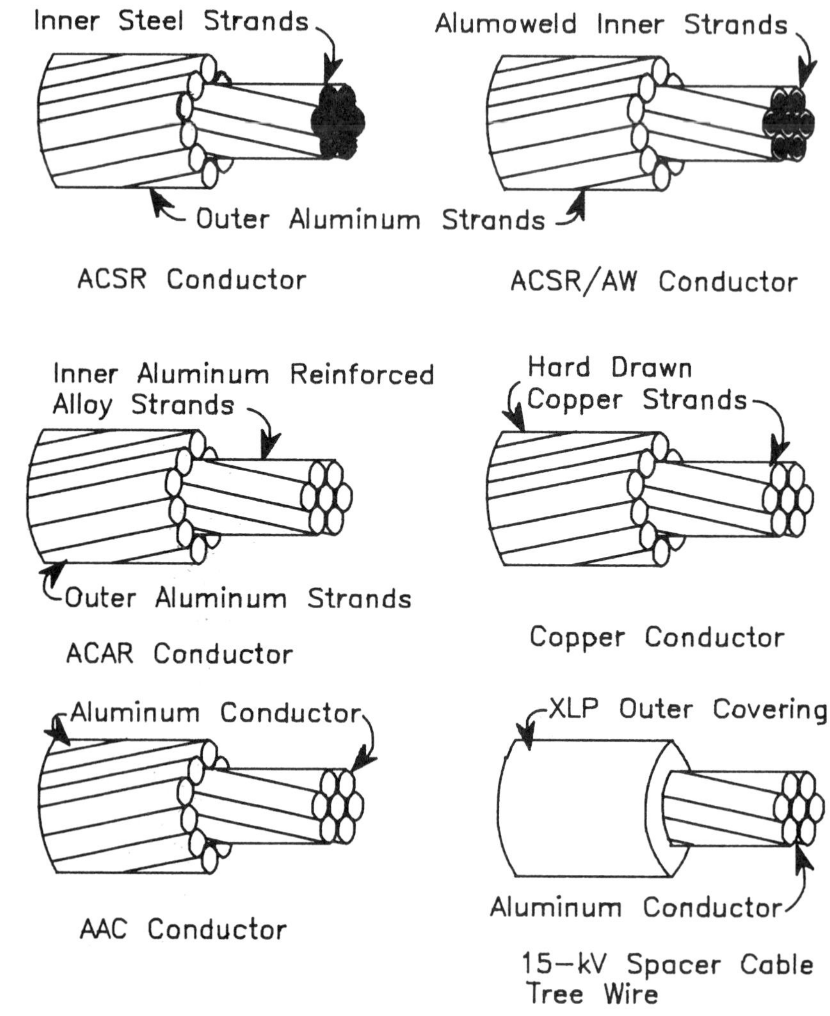

Figure 7-1 Overhead conductor types.

that helps to shape the electric fields around the center conductor and to prevent excessive voltage gradients near the conductor surface. High electrical fields will tend to accelerate the breakdown of the insulation and shorten the life of the cable. Several types of insulation are used, including polyethylene (PE), cross-linked polyethylene (XLP), ethylene propylene rubber (EPR), polyvinyl chloride (PVC), and chlorosulfonated polyethylene (CSP). The outer surface of the insulation is also covered by a layer of semicon. The outer surface of the semicon is covered with a protective outer jacket.

To form the system neutral, concentric neutral conductors are placed around the insulation jacket. These conductors are generally made of tinned copper and may be bare or covered with an outer jacket to prevent corrosion. The common practice among

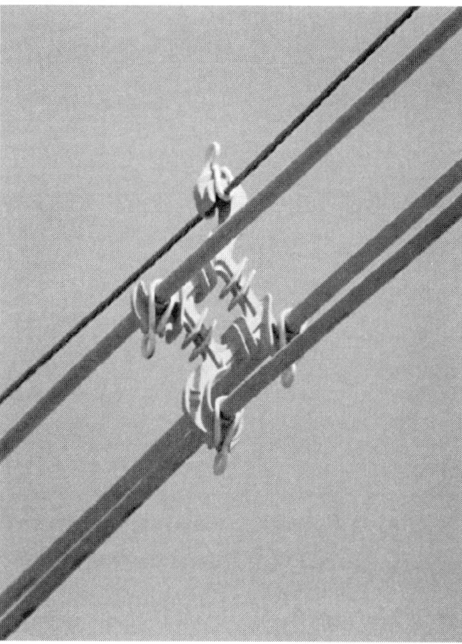

Figure 7-2 Close-up of spacer used in typical spacer cable installation. (Photo Courtesy of Ohio Edison Company)

utilities today is to use jacketed cable to minimize corrosion of the concentric neutral conductors.

In applications where the underground distribution circuit consists of one or two phases of a three-phase system, the cable is typically single conductor with a full concentric neutral. A full concentric neutral implies that the ampacity of the neutral conductors as a whole is equal to the ampacity of the phase conductor. If the distribution circuit consists of all three phases of the three-phase system, either the full size or a one-third reduced neutral may be used. A reduced neutral is permissible in three-phase configurations since the neutral current on the distribution feeder is small under nearly balanced operating conditions. Also, the use of a reduced-size neutral can limit the magnitude of circulating currents in the concentric neutral strands.

Three-Conductor Cables

Three-phase transmission and distribution circuits may also be constructed using a single three-conductor cable. The three-conductor cable may either be belted or shielded. Belted cable may be found in voltages of 15 kV and less. Cables designed to operate at more than 15 kV are usually of the shielded type. The National Electrical Code® requires that all cable designed to operate at 2 kV and above must be of the shielded type, unless specifically designed for nonshielded operation. Shielding reduces the elec-

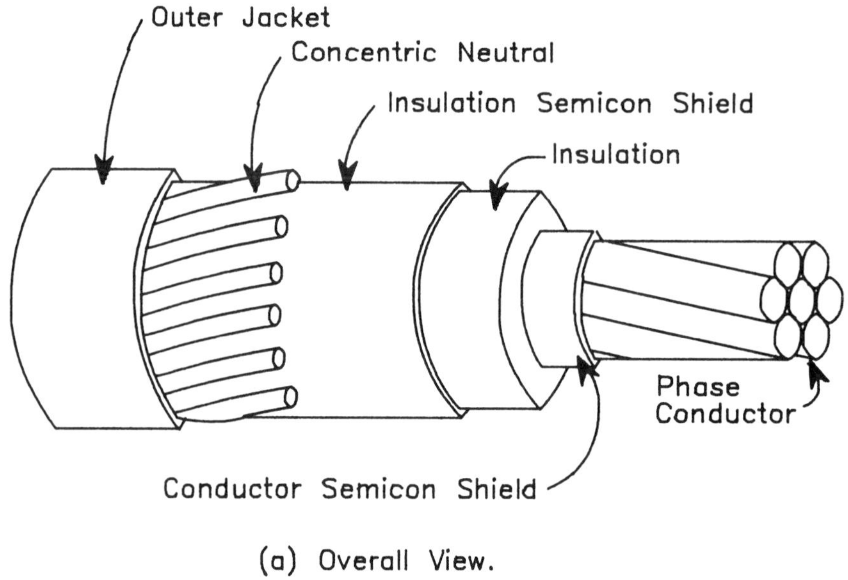

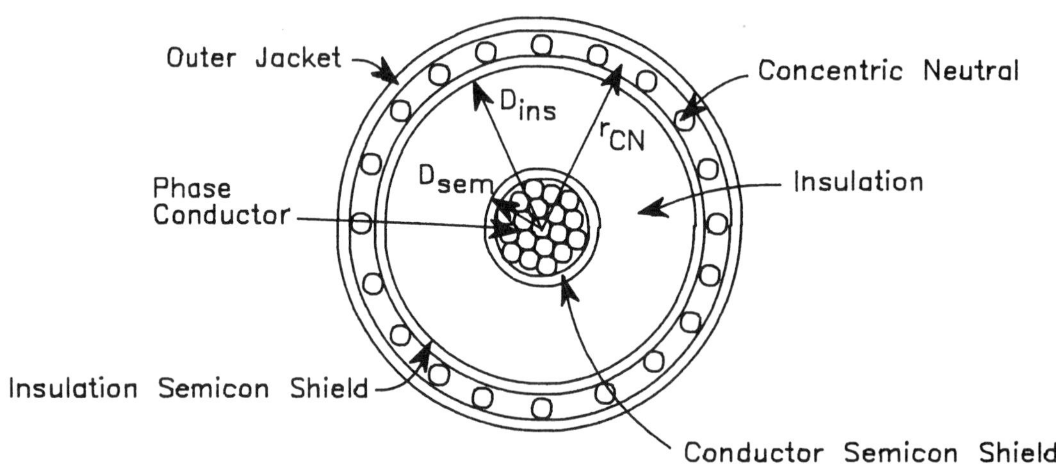

Figure 7-3 Underground residential distribution cable.

trical stresses that may occur at higher voltages. In addition, the shield provides a means to ground the external surface of the cable for personnel protection. Belted three-conductor cable is comprised of three separately insulated phase conductors that are cabled together and covered by a layer of insulation. The outer sheath is then applied over the insulation.

In the shielded three-conductor cable, the individual phase conductors are separately insulated and covered by a thin shielding tape. The three conductors are then cabled together and covered by a layer of insulation. The insulation is covered by another layer of shielding tape and then by an outer sheath.

Service Cables

Single-phase, three-wire, 120/240-V services are usually supplied by triplex cable. The triplex cable consists of two fully insulated phase conductors and either a bare or insulated neutral conductor. A bare neutral conductor is generally used for overhead services, while the insulated neutral is commonly used for underground services to minimize corrosion of the neutral conductors. The neutral conductor size is usually two wire sizes smaller than the phase conductors. For larger single-phase, three-wire services, three single conductor cables may be installed. Three-phase services may be supplied by single conductor cables or quadruplex cable. The quadruplex cable consists of three fully insulated phase conductors and either a bare or insulated neutral conductor.

In the triplex and quadruplex cables, the insulated phase conductors are spiraled around the neutral conductor. Aluminum conductors are commonly used for the phase conductors. For overhead installations, the neutral conductor of the cable also serves as a messenger to support the cable assembly. To provide the extra strength required to support the cable, the neutral is typically constructed of ACSR conductor.

7-3 Three-Phase Overhead Line Characteristics

Resistance and Inductive Reactance

Since the conductors used in overhead line construction are typically stranded and made of composite materials, the resistance is somewhat difficult to calculate directly. It is far more common to use manufacturers' reference material to determine conductor properties. Appendix A shows typical conductor characteristic data available to the user. The actual calculation of resistance for composite, stranded conductors is beyond the scope of this text.

The determination of the series resistance and inductive reactance of a line begins with the application of Carson's equations. Carson's equations give the expressions for the self-impedance of a conductor with ground return and the mutual impedance between two conductors with ground return. For normal power system operation, Carson's equations can be stated in simplified form as follows [1]:

$$\mathbf{Z}_s = R_\phi + 0.0954 \frac{f}{60} + j0.2794 \frac{f}{60} \log_{10}\left(\frac{D_e}{GMR_\phi}\right) \tag{7.1}$$

$$\mathbf{Z}_m = 0.0954 \frac{f}{60} + j0.2794 \frac{f}{60} \log_{10}\left(\frac{D_e}{d_{ab}}\right) \tag{7.2}$$

where

Z_s = self-impedance of conductor in ohms per mile

$\mathbf{Z}_m$ = mutual impedance between conductors in ohms per mile

R_ϕ = resistance of phase conductor in ohms per mile

f = operating frequency (Hz)

GMR_ϕ = geometric mean radius of the phase conductor

d_{ab} = separation distance between conductors a and b

$$D_e = 2160 \left(\frac{\rho}{f}\right)^{1/2} \tag{7.3}$$

where

ρ = earth resistivity in ohm-meters

f = operating frequency

Values for earth resistivity will vary depending on soil conditions. Table 7-1 lists values of earth resistivity for different types of soil conditions [2].

For a three-phase line, the physical location of the phase conductors will have an effect on the mutual impedance between the conductors. When determining the line impedances, it is common to assume that the line is transposed to balance out the effect of unequal conductor spacings. Transposing of the phase conductors means that the phases assume alternate positions on the tower or pole along the length of the line. Figure

Table 7-1 Earth Resistivities (ohm-meters)

Soil Type	*Resistivity*
Average value	100
Seawater	0.01–1.0
Swampy ground	10–100
Dry earth	1000
Pure slate	10^7
Sandstone	10^9

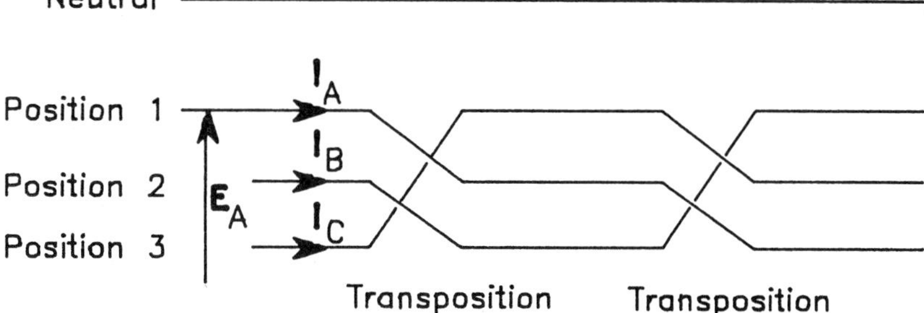

Figure 7-4 Transposed three-phase overhead line.

7-4 shows a three-phase line with the phase conductors transposed along the length of the line. The position of the neutral remains the same, while the phase conductors are transposed. Two transpositions are shown in Fig. 7-4. The third transposition returns the phase conductors to their original locations. It is important to note that transposing of conductors is done only in special instances. Rarely are conductors transposed in distribution circuits or transmission circuits of lower voltage and short line length. The assumption of transposition is for the purpose of calculating the line impedance only.

In reference to Fig. 7-4, assume that the total line length is 1 mile. The voltage drop along the A phase conductor is

$$\begin{aligned} \mathbf{E}_A = \; & \mathbf{I}_A\mathbf{Z}_{11} + \mathbf{I}_B\mathbf{Z}_{12} + \mathbf{I}_C\mathbf{Z}_{13} \\ & + \mathbf{I}_A\mathbf{Z}_{22} + \mathbf{I}_B\mathbf{Z}_{23} + \mathbf{I}_C\mathbf{Z}_{21} \\ & + \mathbf{I}_A\mathbf{Z}_{33} + \mathbf{I}_B\mathbf{Z}_{31} + \mathbf{I}_C\mathbf{Z}_{32} \end{aligned} \tag{7.4}$$

where

$\mathbf{Z}_{ii}$ = self-impedance of the conductor at position i, given by Eq. (7.1)

$\mathbf{Z}_{ij}$ = mutual impedance between the conductors at positions i and j, given by Eq. (7.2)

Due to the symmetry of the line construction, the following equalities result:

$$\mathbf{Z}_{11} = \mathbf{Z}_{22} = \mathbf{Z}_{33}, \qquad \mathbf{Z}_{12} = \mathbf{Z}_{21}, \qquad \mathbf{Z}_{13} = \mathbf{Z}_{31}, \qquad \mathbf{Z}_{23} = \mathbf{Z}_{32}$$

Applying these equalities to Eq. (7.4) and gathering terms results in the following:

$$\begin{aligned} \mathrm{E}_A &= 3\mathbf{I}_A\mathbf{Z}_{11} + (\mathbf{I}_B + \mathbf{I}_C)\mathbf{Z}_{12} + (\mathbf{I}_B + \mathbf{I}_C)\mathbf{Z}_{13} + (\mathbf{I}_B + \mathbf{I}_C)\mathbf{Z}_{23} \\ &= 3\mathbf{I}_A\mathbf{Z}_{11} + (\mathbf{I}_B + \mathbf{I}_C)(\mathbf{Z}_{12} + \mathbf{Z}_{13} + \mathbf{Z}_{23}) \end{aligned} \tag{7.5}$$

Furthermore, for balanced three-phase operation,

$$\mathbf{I}_B + \mathbf{I}_C = -\mathbf{I}_A \tag{7.6}$$

Substituting Eq. (7.6) into (7.5) results in

$$\begin{aligned}\mathbf{E}_A &= 3\mathbf{I}_A\mathbf{Z}_{11} + (-\mathbf{I}_A)(\mathbf{Z}_{12} + \mathbf{Z}_{13} + \mathbf{Z}_{23}) \\ &= \mathbf{I}_A(3\mathbf{Z}_{11} - \mathbf{Z}_{12} - \mathbf{Z}_{13} - \mathbf{Z}_{23})\end{aligned} \qquad \textbf{(7.7)}$$

The bracketed term of Eq. (7.7) is the impedance of the A phase conductor. Equation (7.7) can be rewritten as

$$\mathbf{E}_A = \mathbf{I}_A \cdot \mathbf{Z}_A \qquad \textbf{(7.8)}$$

where

$$\mathbf{Z}_A = 3\mathbf{Z}_{11} - \mathbf{Z}_{12} - \mathbf{Z}_{13} - \mathbf{Z}_{23} \qquad \textbf{(7.9)}$$

Equation (7.9) gives the expression for the impedance of the A phase conductor for balanced three-phase line construction and operation. Notice that both the self-impedance of the A phase conductor and the mutual impedances between the other two phases contribute to the total impedance. It can be shown that the impedances of the B and C phase conductors are identical to that shown in Eq. (7.9).

If Eqs. (7.1) and (7.2) were applied directly to Eq. (7.9), the impedance $\mathbf{Z}_A$ as calculated from Eq. (7.9) would be for a 3-mile length of line. To determine the impedance for a 1-mile length of line, Eqs. (7.1) and (7.2) are applied directly to (7.9), with the resulting equation divided by 3. The following results:

$$\mathbf{Z}_A = R_\phi + j0.2794\,\frac{f}{60}\,\log_{10}\left(\frac{(d_{12}d_{23}d_{31})^{1/3}}{GMR_\phi}\right)\quad \Omega/\text{mile} \qquad \textbf{(7.10)}$$

where

GMR_ϕ = geometric mean radius of phase conductors from manufacturers' tables

R_ϕ = resistance of phase conductor in ohms per mile from manufacturers' tables

d_{12} = distance between conductors at positions 1 and 2

d_{23} = distance between conductors at positions 2 and 3

d_{31} = distance between conductors at positions 3 and 1

f = operating frequency

In Eq. (7.10), the term $(d_{12}d_{23}d_{31})^{1/3}$ is referred to as the *geometric mean distance* between the phase conductors. The geometric mean distance between the phase conductors is often designated GMD_ϕ. Note that both the geometric mean radius and geometric mean distances must have the same units. Typically, manufacturers' data list the conductor GMR_ϕ in units of feet. Therefore, it is common to calculate the GMD_ϕ in units of feet as well. Any other system of units is permissible, with the required unit conversion.

Capacitance

The capacitance per phase of a balanced three-phase overhead line is given by the following:

$$C_1 = \frac{0.0389}{\log_{10}\left(\frac{GMD_\phi}{r_\phi}\right)} \quad \mu\text{F per mile per phase} \tag{7.11}$$

where

GMD_ϕ = geometric mean distance between conductors

r_ϕ = conductor radius, from manufacturers' information

As in the case of the inductive reactance calculation, the units for both the GMD_ϕ and conductor radius must be the same.

Bundled Conductors

On overhead lines above 230 kV, bundled conductors are commonly used to reduce the electric field strength at the conductor surface. These bundled conductors consist of two or more conductors per phase, separated by a spacer. Typical examples of bundled conductor configurations are shown in Fig. 7-5. Determination of the resistance, inductive reactance, and capacitance of the line must be modified to account for the use of more than one conductor per phase.

The individual phase conductors in each bundle are electrically connected at points of attachment to the line supporting structure and also at locations where bundle spacers are used. Therefore, the individual conductors comprising a single bundle are connected in parallel with each other. Since each conductor in a given bundle is of the same size and type, each conductor will have the same resistance. Therefore, the equivalent resistance of the bundle will be equal to the resistance of one of the conductors divided by the number of conductors in the bundle.

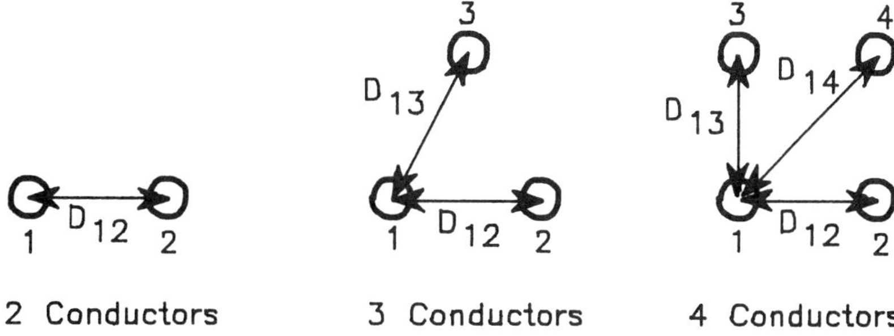

Figure 7-5 Bundled conductor configurations.

The use of bundled conductors also has an effect on the inductive reactance of the line. Specifically, both the GMR_ϕ and the GMD_ϕ are affected by the bundle. In the calculation of the geometric mean distance between the phases, the distances between the centers of each bundle are used. The calculation of the geometric mean radius of each conductor bundle can be calculated from the following:

$$\text{Two-conduction bundle:} \quad GMR_{\phi'} = (GMR_\phi \cdot D_{12})^{1/2} \tag{7.12}$$

$$\text{Three-conduction bundle:} \quad GMR_{\phi'} = (GMR_\phi \cdot D_{12} \cdot D_{13})^{1/3} \tag{7.13}$$

$$\text{Four-conduction bundle:} \quad GMR_{\phi'} = (GMR_\phi \cdot D_{12} \cdot D_{13} \cdot D_{14})^{1/4} \tag{7.14}$$

where GMR_ϕ is the geometric mean radius of the individual conductors in the bundle. The $GMR_{\phi'}$, as calculated from Eqs. (7.12), (7.13), or (7.14) may be substituted into Eq. (7.10) for the impedance calculation.

The use of bundled conductors has the effect of making the conductor appear as a larger-diameter conductor. The equivalent radius of a conductor bundle can be calculated from the following:

$$\text{Two-conductor bundle:} \quad r_{\phi'} = (r_\phi \cdot D_{12})^{1/2} \tag{7.15}$$

$$\text{Three-conductor bundle:} \quad r_{\phi'} = (r_\phi \cdot D_{12} \cdot D_{13})^{1/3} \tag{7.16}$$

$$\text{Four-conductor bundle:} \quad r_{\phi'} = (r_\phi \cdot D_{12} \cdot D_{13} \cdot D_{14})^{1/4} \tag{7.17}$$

where r_ϕ is the radius of the individual conductors in the bundle. The value of $r_{\phi'}$, as calculated from Eqs. (7.15), (7.16), or (7.17) may be substituted into Eq. (7.11) for the capacitance calculation.

EXAMPLE 7-1

Calculate the resistance, inductive reactance, and capacitive reactance per phase and rated current carrying capacity for the overhead line shown in Fig. 7-6. Assume that the line operates at 60 Hz and a conductor temperature of 75°C.

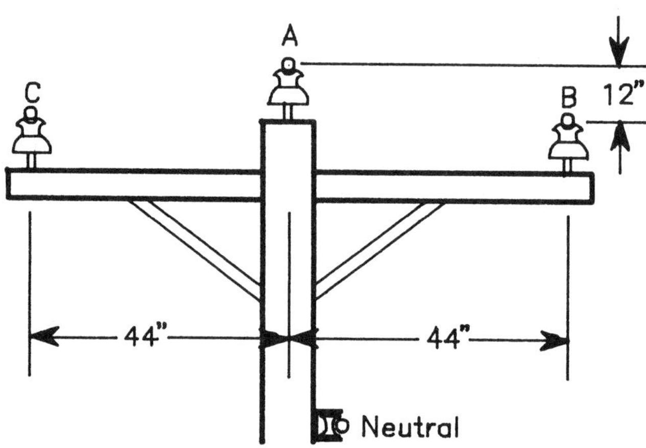

Figure 7-6 Line configuration for Example 7-1.

Solution From the ACSR tables, the conductor resistance is 0.3263 Ω/mile, the conductor GMR_ϕ is 0.0244 ft, and the conductor diameter is 0.720 in. The geometric mean distance between phases is

$$\begin{aligned} GMD_\phi &= [(45.6) \cdot (88) \cdot (45.6)]^{1/3} \\ &= 56.78 \text{ in.} \\ &= 4.7315 \text{ ft} \end{aligned}$$

The impedance is given by Eq. (7.10).

$$\begin{aligned} \mathbf{Z}_A &= 0.3263 + j0.2794 \frac{60}{60} \log_{10} \left(\frac{4.7315}{0.0244}\right) \\ &= 0.3263 + j0.6391 \ \Omega/\text{mile} \end{aligned}$$

To calculate the capacitance, the conductor radius must be expressed in feet:

$$r_\phi = \frac{\text{diameter}}{2} \cdot \frac{1}{12} = \frac{0.720}{2} \cdot \frac{1}{12} = 0.03 \text{ ft}$$

The capacitance is calculated from Eq. (7.11).

$$\begin{aligned} C_1 &= \frac{0.0389}{\log_{10}\left(\frac{4.7315}{0.03}\right)} \\ &= 0.177 \ \mu\text{F/mile/phase} \end{aligned}$$

The capacitive reactance is equal to

$$X_C = \frac{1}{2 \cdot \pi \cdot 60 \cdot 0.0177 \times 10^{-6}} = 149{,}860 \quad \Omega\text{-mile}$$

From the data tables, the rated current carrying capacity is 529 A.

EXAMPLE 7-2

Calculate the resistance, inductive reactance, capacitive reactance, and current carrying capacity of the overhead line shown in Fig. 7-7. Assume that the line operates at 60 Hz, and a conductor temperature of 75°C.

Solution The resistance of each conductor in the bundle is 0.1204 Ω/mile. Since there are four conductors per phase, the resistance per phase is equal to the individual conductor resistance divided by 4.

$$R_\phi = \frac{0.1204}{4} = 0.0301 \ \Omega/\text{mile}$$

The GMD_ϕ for this configuration is

$$\begin{aligned} GMD_\phi &= [(31.62) \cdot (60.0) \cdot (31.62)]^{1/3} \\ &= 39.15 \text{ ft} \end{aligned}$$

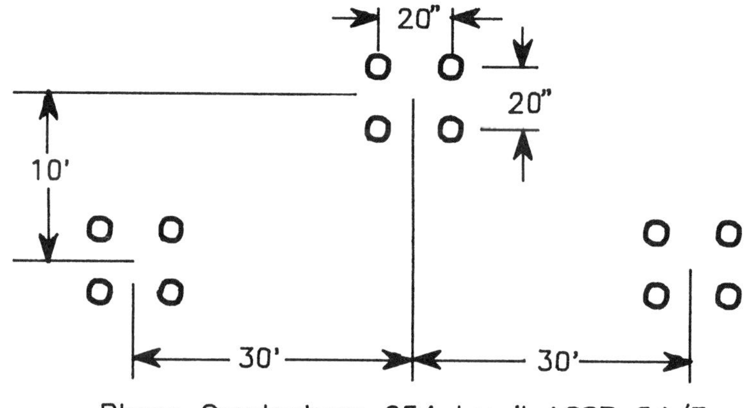

Figure 7-7 Line configuration for Example 7-2.

The GMR_ϕ for the bundle is

$$GMR_\phi = [(0.0403) \cdot (1.67) \cdot (1.67) \cdot (1.414) \cdot (1.67)]^{1/4}$$
$$= 0.7178 \text{ ft}$$

From Eq. (7.10), the impedance is

$$\mathbf{Z}_A = 0.0301 + j0.2794 \frac{60}{60} \log_{10}\left(\frac{39.15}{0.7178}\right)$$
$$= 0.0301 + j0.4852 \ \Omega/\text{mile}$$

From Appendix A, the conductor diameter is 1.196 in. The conductor radius expressed in feet is

$$r_\phi = \frac{1.196}{2} \cdot \frac{1}{12} = 0.0498 \text{ ft}$$

The equivalent radius is given by Eq. (7.17) as follows:

$$r_{\phi'} = [(0.0498) \cdot (1.67) \cdot (1.67) \cdot (1.414) \cdot (1.67)]^{1/4}$$
$$= 0.7568 \text{ ft}$$

The capacitance is

$$C_1 = \frac{0.0389}{\log_{10}\left(\dfrac{39.15}{0.7568}\right)}$$
$$= 0.0227 \ \mu\text{F/mile/phase}$$

The capacitive reactance is equal to

$$X_C = \frac{1}{2 \cdot \pi \cdot 60 \cdot 0.0227 \times 10^{-6}} = 116{,}850 \ \Omega\text{-mile}$$

The rated current carrying capacity for each conductor in the bundle is 996 A. Since there are four conductors per phase in each bundle, the current carrying capacity per phase is equal to four times the rated current of each conductor. Therefore, the rated current carrying capacity is 3984 A.

7-4 Three-Phase Underground Cable Characteristics

In the discussion of overhead lines, the individual phase conductors are separated from one another by a fairly large distance as compared to the diameter of the phase conductors. When considering cable circuits, the phase conductors are located in close proximity to one another. Voltage drops will appear in the phase conductor of each cable due to current flow in the concentric neutral strands or sheaths of the cables in question. This phenomena is referred to as *proximity effect.* Two components of voltage drop are due to this proximity effect, one in phase and one in quadrature with the phase current. The in-phase component of voltage drop will usually result in an increase in the conductor resistance. The quadrature component of voltage drop usually results in a decrease in the inductive reactance of the conductor. In the analysis that follows, the concentric neutral strands are treated as a continuous cable sheath, rather than individually. This assumption will give reasonable results for most applications.

The assumed cable configuration is shown in Fig. 7-8. As in the case of the three-phase overhead line, balanced operation is assumed, as well as full transposition of the cables. The phase conductors of the cables are centered at positions 1, 2, and 3. The concentric neutrals or cable sheaths of the three cables are centered at positions 1′, 2′, and 3′. The phase currents are designated $\mathbf{I}_A$, $\mathbf{I}_B$, and $\mathbf{I}_C$. The neutral currents are designated $\mathbf{I}_a$, $\mathbf{I}_b$, and $\mathbf{I}_c$.

In reference to Fig. 7-8, the voltage drop along the A phase conductor is

$$\begin{aligned}\mathbf{E}_A = {} & \mathbf{I}_A\mathbf{Z}_{11} + \mathbf{I}_B\mathbf{Z}_{12} + \mathbf{I}_C\mathbf{Z}_{13} + \mathbf{I}_a\mathbf{Z}_{11'} + \mathbf{I}_b\mathbf{Z}_{12'} + \mathbf{I}_c\mathbf{Z}_{13'} \\ & + \mathbf{I}_A\mathbf{Z}_{22} + \mathbf{I}_B\mathbf{Z}_{23} + \mathbf{I}_C\mathbf{Z}_{21} + \mathbf{I}_a\mathbf{Z}_{2'2} + \mathbf{I}_b\mathbf{Z}_{3'2} + \mathbf{I}_c\mathbf{Z}_{1'2} \\ & + \mathbf{I}_A\mathbf{Z}_{33} + \mathbf{I}_B\mathbf{Z}_{31} + \mathbf{I}_C\mathbf{Z}_{32} + \mathbf{I}_a\mathbf{Z}_{3'3} + \mathbf{I}_b\mathbf{Z}_{1'3} + \mathbf{I}_c\mathbf{Z}_{2'3}\end{aligned} \tag{7.18}$$

Likewise, the voltage drop along the A phase concentric neutral or sheath is

$$\begin{aligned}0 = {} & \mathbf{I}_A\mathbf{Z}_{1'1} + \mathbf{I}_B\mathbf{Z}_{21'} + \mathbf{I}_C\mathbf{Z}_{31'} + \mathbf{I}_a\mathbf{Z}_{1'1'} + \mathbf{I}_b\mathbf{Z}_{2'1'} + \mathbf{I}_c\mathbf{Z}_{3'1'} \\ & + \mathbf{I}_A\mathbf{Z}_{2'2} + \mathbf{I}_B\mathbf{Z}_{32'} + \mathbf{I}_C\mathbf{Z}_{12'} + \mathbf{I}_a\mathbf{Z}_{2'2'} + \mathbf{I}_b\mathbf{Z}_{3'2'} + \mathbf{I}_c\mathbf{Z}_{1'2'} \\ & + \mathbf{I}_A\mathbf{Z}_{3'3} + \mathbf{I}_B\mathbf{Z}_{13'} + \mathbf{I}_C\mathbf{Z}_{23'} + \mathbf{I}_a\mathbf{Z}_{3'3'} + \mathbf{I}_b\mathbf{Z}_{1'3'} + \mathbf{I}_c\mathbf{Z}_{2'3'}\end{aligned} \tag{7.19}$$

where

$\mathbf{Z}_{ii}$ = self-impedance of the conductor at position i

$\mathbf{Z}_{ij}$ = mutual impedance between the conductors at positions i and j

$\mathbf{Z}_{ij'}$ = mutual impedance between the phase conductor at i and the concentric neutral at j'

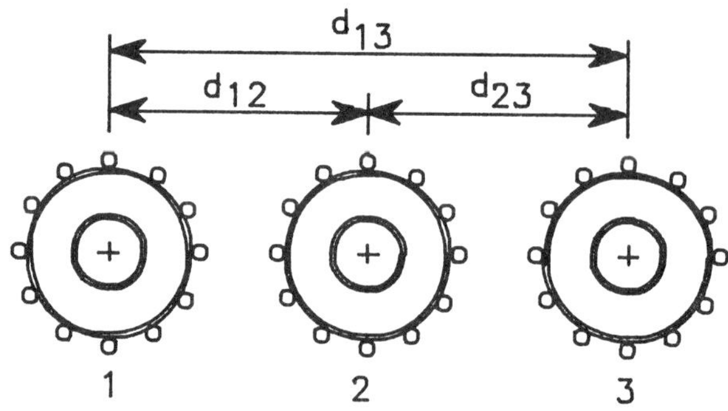

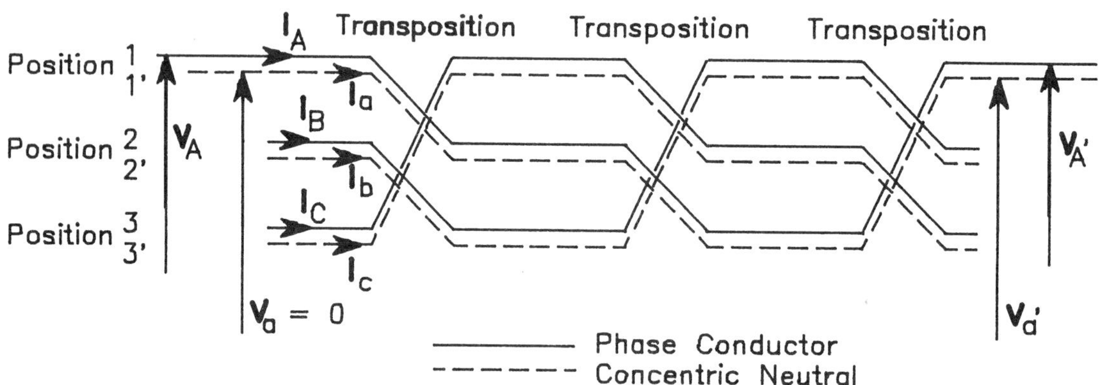

Figure 7-8 Cable configuration for three single-conductor cables.

$\mathbf{Z}_{i'j}$ = mutual impedance between the phase conductor at j and the concentric neutral at i'

$\mathbf{Z}_{i'i'}$ = self-impedance of the neutral at position i'

Due to the symmetry of the cable construction, the following equalities result:

$$\mathbf{Z}_{11} = \mathbf{Z}_{22} = \mathbf{Z}_{33}$$

$$\mathbf{Z}_{1'1'} = \mathbf{Z}_{2'2'} = \mathbf{Z}_{3'3'}$$

$$\mathbf{Z}_{12} = \mathbf{Z}_{21} = \mathbf{Z}_{1'2'} = \mathbf{Z}_{2'1'} = \mathbf{Z}_{1'2} = \mathbf{Z}_{21'} = \mathbf{Z}_{12'} = \mathbf{Z}_{2'1}$$

$$\mathbf{Z}_{13} = \mathbf{Z}_{31} = \mathbf{Z}_{1'3'} = \mathbf{Z}_{3'1'} = \mathbf{Z}_{1'3} = \mathbf{Z}_{31'} = \mathbf{Z}_{13'} = \mathbf{Z}_{3'1}$$

$$\mathbf{Z}_{23} = \mathbf{Z}_{32} = \mathbf{Z}_{2'3'} = \mathbf{Z}_{3'2'} = \mathbf{Z}_{2'3} = \mathbf{Z}_{32'} = \mathbf{Z}_{23'} = \mathbf{Z}_{3'2}$$

$$\mathbf{Z}_{1'1} = \mathbf{Z}_{2'2} = \mathbf{Z}_{3'3}$$

Applying these equalities to Eq. (7.18) and gathering terms results in the following:

$$\begin{aligned}\mathbf{E}_A = {} & 3\mathbf{I}_A\mathbf{Z}_{11} + \mathbf{I}_B(\mathbf{Z}_{12} + \mathbf{Z}_{23} + \mathbf{Z}_{31}) + \mathbf{I}_C(\mathbf{Z}_{31} + \mathbf{Z}_{12} + \mathbf{Z}_{23}) \\ & + 3\mathbf{I}_a\mathbf{Z}_{1'1} + \mathbf{I}_b(\mathbf{Z}_{12'} + \mathbf{Z}_{23'} + \mathbf{Z}_{31'}) + \mathbf{I}_c(\mathbf{Z}_{3'1} + \mathbf{Z}_{1'2} + \mathbf{Z}_{2'3})\end{aligned} \tag{7.20}$$

For balanced three-phase operation, $\mathbf{I}_B + \mathbf{I}_C = -\mathbf{I}_A$ and $\mathbf{I}_b + \mathbf{I}_c = -\mathbf{I}_a$. Therefore, Eq. (7.20) reduces to

$$\begin{aligned}\mathbf{E}_A &= 3\mathbf{I}_A\mathbf{Z}_{11} - \mathbf{I}_A(\mathbf{Z}_{12} + \mathbf{Z}_{23} + \mathbf{Z}_{31}) + 3\mathbf{I}_a\mathbf{Z}_{1'1} - \mathbf{I}_a(\mathbf{Z}_{12'} + \mathbf{Z}_{23'} + \mathbf{Z}_{31'}) \\ &= 3\mathbf{I}_A\left(\mathbf{Z}_{11} - \frac{\mathbf{Z}_{12} + \mathbf{Z}_{23} + \mathbf{Z}_{31}}{3}\right) + 3\mathbf{I}_a\left(\mathbf{Z}_{1'1} - \frac{\mathbf{Z}_{12'} + \mathbf{Z}_{23'} + \mathbf{Z}_{31'}}{3}\right)\end{aligned} \tag{7.21}$$

In a similar manner, applying the equalities to Eq. (7.19) and gathering terms results in the following:

$$\begin{aligned}0 = {} & 3\mathbf{I}_A\mathbf{Z}_{1'1} + \mathbf{I}_B(\mathbf{Z}_{1'2} + \mathbf{Z}_{2'3} + \mathbf{Z}_{3'1}) + \mathbf{I}_C(\mathbf{Z}_{31'} + \mathbf{Z}_{12'} + \mathbf{Z}_{23'}) \\ & + 3\mathbf{I}_a\mathbf{Z}_{1'1'} + \mathbf{I}_b(\mathbf{Z}_{1'2'} + \mathbf{Z}_{2'3'} + \mathbf{Z}_{3'1'}) + \mathbf{I}_c(\mathbf{Z}_{3'1'} + \mathbf{Z}_{1'2'} + \mathbf{Z}_{2'3'})\end{aligned} \tag{7.22}$$

Again, for balanced three-phase operation, $\mathbf{I}_B + \mathbf{I}_C = -\mathbf{I}_A$ and $\mathbf{I}_b + \mathbf{I}_c = -\mathbf{I}_a$. Therefore, Eq (7.22) reduces to

$$\begin{aligned}0 = {} & 3\mathbf{I}_A\mathbf{Z}_{1'1} - \mathbf{I}_A(\mathbf{Z}_{1'2} + \mathbf{Z}_{2'3} + \mathbf{Z}_{3'1}) \\ & + 3\mathbf{I}_a\mathbf{Z}_{1'1'} - \mathbf{I}_a(\mathbf{Z}_{1'2'} + \mathbf{Z}_{2'3'} + \mathbf{Z}_{3'1'})\end{aligned} \tag{7.23}$$

Solving Eq. (7.23) for $\mathbf{I}_a$ results in

$$\mathbf{I}_a = \frac{-\mathbf{I}_A(3\mathbf{Z}_{1'1} - \mathbf{Z}_{1'2} - \mathbf{Z}_{2'3} - \mathbf{Z}_{3'1})}{3\mathbf{Z}_{1'1'} - \mathbf{Z}_{1'2'} - \mathbf{Z}_{2'3'} - \mathbf{Z}_{3'1'}} \tag{7.24}$$

Substituting Eq. (7.24) into (7.21) results in

$$\begin{aligned}\mathbf{E}_A &= 3\mathbf{I}_A\left(\mathbf{Z}_{11} - \frac{\mathbf{Z}_{12} + \mathbf{Z}_{23} + \mathbf{Z}_{31}}{3}\right) \\ &\quad - 3\frac{\mathbf{I}_A(3\mathbf{Z}_{1'1} - \mathbf{Z}_{1'2} - \mathbf{Z}_{2'3} - \mathbf{Z}_{3'1})}{3\mathbf{Z}_{1'1'} - \mathbf{Z}_{1'2'} - \mathbf{Z}_{2'3'} - \mathbf{Z}_{3'1'}}\left(\mathbf{Z}_{1'1} - \frac{\mathbf{Z}_{12'} + \mathbf{Z}_{23'} + \mathbf{Z}_{31'}}{3}\right) \\ &= 3\mathbf{I}_A\left(\mathbf{Z}_{11} - \frac{\mathbf{Z}_{12} + \mathbf{Z}_{23} + \mathbf{Z}_{31}}{3}\right) \\ &\quad - 3\frac{\mathbf{I}_A(3\mathbf{Z}_{1'1} - \mathbf{Z}_{1'2} - \mathbf{Z}_{2'3} - \mathbf{Z}_{3'1})}{3\mathbf{Z}_{1'1'} - \mathbf{Z}_{1'2'} - \mathbf{Z}_{2'3'} - \mathbf{Z}_{3'1'}}\left[\frac{3\mathbf{Z}_{1'1} - (\mathbf{Z}_{12'} + \mathbf{Z}_{23'} + \mathbf{Z}_{31'})}{3}\right] \\ &= 3\mathbf{I}_A\left(\mathbf{Z}_{11} - \frac{\mathbf{Z}_{12} + \mathbf{Z}_{23} + \mathbf{Z}_{31}}{3}\right) \\ &\quad - 3\frac{\mathbf{I}_A(3\mathbf{Z}_{1'1} - \mathbf{Z}_{1'2} - \mathbf{Z}_{2'3} - \mathbf{Z}_{3'1})^2}{3\mathbf{Z}_{1'1'} - \mathbf{Z}_{1'2'} - \mathbf{Z}_{2'3'} - \mathbf{Z}_{3'1'}} \\ &= 3\mathbf{I}_A\left(\mathbf{Z}_{11} - \frac{\mathbf{Z}_{12} + \mathbf{Z}_{23} + \mathbf{Z}_{31}}{3}\right) - \frac{\mathbf{I}_A(3\mathbf{Z}_{1'1} - \mathbf{Z}_{1'2} - \mathbf{Z}_{2'3} - \mathbf{Z}_{3'1})^2}{3\mathbf{Z}_{1'1'} - \mathbf{Z}_{1'2'} - \mathbf{Z}_{2'3'} - \mathbf{Z}_{3'1'}} \\ &= 3\mathbf{I}_A\left[\mathbf{Z}_{11} - \frac{\mathbf{Z}_{12} + \mathbf{Z}_{23} + \mathbf{Z}_{31}}{3} - \frac{(3\mathbf{Z}_{1'1} - \mathbf{Z}_{1'2} - \mathbf{Z}_{2'3} - \mathbf{Z}_{3'1})^2}{3\mathbf{Z}_{1'1'} - \mathbf{Z}_{1'2'} - \mathbf{Z}_{2'3'} - \mathbf{Z}_{3'1'}}\right]\end{aligned} \tag{7.25}$$

The bracketed term on the right-hand side of Eq. (7.25) is equal to the impedance of the line for balanced three-phase operation. Carson's equations must now be substituted into Eq. (7.25) in order to calculate the impedance. To simplify the reduction, the following terms are evaluated:

$$\mathbf{Z}_{11} - \frac{\mathbf{Z}_{12} + \mathbf{Z}_{23} + \mathbf{Z}_{31}}{3} = R_\phi + j0.0529\,\frac{f}{60}\,\log_{10}\left[\frac{(d_{12}d_{23}d_{31})^{1/3}}{GMR_\phi}\right] \tag{7.26}$$

$$(3\mathbf{Z}_{1'1} - \mathbf{Z}_{1'2} - \mathbf{Z}_{2'3} - \mathbf{Z}_{3'1})^2 = \left\{j0.0529\,\frac{f}{60}\,\log_{10}\left[\frac{(d_{12}d_{23}d_{31})^{1/3}}{r_{CN}}\right]\right\}^2 \tag{7.27}$$

$$3\mathbf{Z}_{1'1'} - \mathbf{Z}_{1'2'} - \mathbf{Z}_{2'3'} - \mathbf{Z}_{3'1'} = R_N + j0.0529\,\frac{f}{60}\,\log_{10}\left[\frac{(d_{12}d_{23}d_{31})^{1/3}}{GMR_N}\right] \tag{7.28}$$

where

R_ϕ = resistance of phase conductor

R_N = resistance of neutral conductors

GMD_ϕ = geometric mean distance between phase conductors

$= (d_{12}d_{23}d_{31})^{1/3}$

f = operating frequency

r_{CN} = radius of circle formed by concentric neutral wires (Fig. 7-3)

GMR_N = geometric mean radius of neutral

Since several concentric stands surround the cable, the GMR_N is approximately equal to the radius of the circle formed by the strands. Therefore, $GMR_N \approx r_{CN}$, and the imaginary parts of Eqs. (7.27) and (7.28) are approximately equal. The impedance is therefore equal to

$$\mathbf{Z}_A \approx R_\phi + j0.0529\,\frac{f}{60}\,\log_{10}\left(\frac{GMD_\phi}{GMR_\phi}\right) - \frac{\left[j0.0529\,\frac{f}{60}\,\log_{10}\left(\frac{GMD_\phi}{GMR_N}\right)\right]^2}{R_N + j0.0529\,\frac{f}{60}\,\log_{10}\left(\frac{GMD_\phi}{GMR_N}\right)} \tag{7.29}$$

Define the following:

$$X_a = j0.0529\,\frac{f}{60}\,\log_{10}\left(\frac{GMD_\phi}{GMR_\phi}\right) \tag{7.30}$$

$$X_m = j0.0529\,\frac{f}{60}\,\log_{10}\left(\frac{GMD_\phi}{GMR_N}\right) \tag{7.31}$$

Substituting Eqs. (7.30) and (7.31) into (7.29) results in

$$\mathbf{Z}_A \approx R_\phi + jX_a - \frac{X_m^2}{R_N + jX_m}$$
$$= R_\phi + \frac{X_m^2\, R_N}{R_N^2 + X_m^2} + j\left(X_a - \frac{X_m^3}{R_N^2 + X_m^2}\right) \quad \textbf{(7.32)}$$

In the case of three-conductor cables, the cable impedances are calculated in a manner similar to overhead lines. Impedance information for three-conductor cables is usually obtained from manufacturers' data directly, rather than by calculation.

Capacitance

The capacitance of single-conductor cables can be calculated from the following:

$$C = \frac{0.00736 \cdot K}{\log_{10}(D_{\text{ins}}/D_{\text{sem}})} \quad \mu\text{F}/1000\ \text{ft} \quad \textbf{(7.33)}$$

where

D_{ins} = outer diameter of insulation (Fig. 7-3)

D_{sem} = outer diameter of semicon over conductor (Fig. 7-3)

K = dielectric constant of the insulation (typically 3.0 for XLP and EPR insulation and 2.3 for polyethylene)

EXAMPLE 7-3

Determine the series impedance per phase, capacitive reactance per phase, and rated current carrying capacity for a three-phase distribution circuit consisting of three 15-kV, 350-kcmil aluminum, 37-strand, XLP-insulated, concentric neutral URD cables. The cable has a one-third reduced neutral and 100% insulation level (175 mils). The cables are arranged in a flat horizontal configuration with 6 in. separation between the cable centers. Assume a dielectric constant of 3.0 and that the circuit operates at 60 Hz.

Solution The following data are obtained from Appendix A:

$$R_\phi = 0.0605\ \Omega/1000\ \text{ft}$$
$$R_N = 0.1775\ \Omega/1000\ \text{ft}$$
$$GMR_\phi = 0.2568\ \text{in.}$$
$$r_{CN} = 0.632\ \text{in.}$$

The geometric mean distance between the phase conductors is

$$GMD_\phi = (6 \cdot 6 \cdot 12)^{1/3} = 7.56\ \text{in.}$$

The mutual reactance between the phase and neutral is calculated from Eq. (7.31):

$$X_m = 0.0529 \frac{60}{60} \log_{10} \left(\frac{7.56}{0.632}\right) = 0.0570 \ \Omega/1000 \text{ ft}$$

The self-inductive reactance of the phase conductor is calculated from Eq. (7.30):

$$X_a = 0.0529 \frac{60}{60} \log_{10}\left(\frac{7.56}{0.2568}\right) = 0.0777 \ \Omega/1000 \text{ ft}$$

The impedance is determined by applying Eq. (7.32):

$$\begin{aligned} \mathbf{Z}_A &= 0.0605 + \frac{(0.057)^2(0.1775)}{(0.1775)^2 + (0.057)^2} + j\left[0.0777 - \frac{(0.057)^3}{(0.1775)^2 + (0.057)^2}\right] \\ &= 0.0771 + j0.0724 \ \Omega/1000 \text{ ft} \end{aligned}$$

From Eq. (7.32), the apparent inductive reactance is

$$X_1 = 0.0777 - \frac{(0.057)^3}{(0.1775)^2 + (0.057)^2} = 0.0724 \ \Omega/1000 \text{ ft}$$

To calculate the cable capacitance, it is necessary to determine the outer diameter of the cable insulation and the outer diameter of the semicon over the phase conductor. From the data of Appendix A,

$$\begin{aligned} D_{\text{ins}} &= 1.081 \text{ in.} \\ D_{\text{sem}} &= 0.731 \text{ in.} \end{aligned}$$

The cable capacitance is calculated by applying Eq. (7.33):

$$\begin{aligned} C &= \frac{0.00776K}{\log_{10}(D_{\text{ins}}/D_{\text{sem}})} \\ &= \frac{0.00736 \cdot (3.0)}{\log_{10}(1.081/0.731)} \\ &= 0.1300 \ \mu\text{F}/1000 \text{ ft} \end{aligned}$$

The capacitive reactance is

$$X_C = \frac{1}{2 \cdot \pi \cdot f \cdot C} = \frac{1}{2 \cdot \pi \cdot 60 \cdot 0.1300 \times 10^{-6}} = 20{,}411 \ \Omega\text{-}1000 \text{ ft}$$

Note that the units for capacitive reactance are Ω-1000 ft, as opposed to Ω/1000 ft used for resistance and inductive reactance.

The rated current is 389 A for direct burial and 319 A for duct bank installation. Note that the ampacity is greater for direct burial as opposed to duct bank installation. This is due to greater heat dissipation to the surrounding earth in direct burial cable installations.

7-5 Service Drop Cable Characteristics

When designing low-voltage service installations, the characteristics of the service-drop cable must be calculated. The resistance and inductive reactance for single-conductor, triplex, and quadruplex conductors will be calculated. For low-voltage services less than 600 V, the capacitance of the cable may be neglected.

Single-Phase Three-Wire Services

The conductors used to supply single-phase, three-wire services may be arranged in a triplexed cable or in three separate conductors. In the analysis that follows, it is assumed that the single-phase load is balanced. As such, the neutral current is equal to zero, and the presence of the neutral can be neglected in the calculations. The current in the phase conductors will therefore be equal and opposite to one another.

The total resistance of the phase conductors will be equal to twice the resistance of the individual conductors. Representative data are included in Appendix A. These data are also readily available from manufacturers' data.

The inductive reactance is given by the following:

$$X = 1.0583 \times 10^{-2} \frac{f}{60} \log_{10}\left(\frac{GMD_{\phi}}{GMR_{\phi}}\right) \quad \Omega/100\text{ ft} \qquad \textbf{(7.34)}$$

where

GMD_{ϕ} = geometric mean distance between phase conductors

GMR_{ϕ} = geometric mean radius of phase conductors

Since the cables are in close proximity to one another, it is common to use units of inches for both the separation between the phase conductors and the geometric mean radius.

EXAMPLE 7-4 Calculate the resistance and inductive reactance for a triplexed cable consisting of two #1/0 19-strand aluminum conductors operating at 60 Hz.

Solution The resistance is 0.2 Ω/1000 ft per conductor. The total circuit resistance is

$$R = 2 \cdot (0.2\ \Omega/1000\text{ ft}) = 0.4\ \Omega/1000\text{ ft} = 0.04\ \Omega/100\text{ ft}$$

For the 1/0 cable, the geometric mean distance between phase conductors, GMD_ϕ, is 0.482 in. Also, the conductor GMR_ϕ is 0.1412 in. Therefore, inductive reactance is

$$X = 1.0583 \times 10^{-2}\frac{60}{60}\log_{10}\left(\frac{0.482}{0.1412}\right)$$
$$= 5.643 \times 10^{-3}\ \Omega/100\ \text{ft}$$

EXAMPLE 7-5 Calculate the resistance and inductive reactance for three single conductors installed in a vertical configuration with a separation of 8 in. between the phase conductors. The conductors are 500-kcmil 37-strand copper, and the circuit operates at 60 Hz.

Solution The resistance is 0.0276 Ω/1000 ft per conductor. The total circuit resistance is

$$R = 2 \cdot (0.0276\ \Omega/1000\ \text{ft}) = 0.0552\ \Omega/1000\ \text{ft} = 0.00552\ \Omega/100\ \text{ft}$$

The conductor GMR_ϕ is 0.3120 in. Therefore, the inductive reactance is

$$X = 1.0583 \times 10^{-2}\frac{60}{60}\log_{10}\left(\frac{8.0}{0.3120}\right)$$
$$= 1.4911 \times 10^{-2}\ \Omega/100\ \text{ft}$$

Three-Phase Services

When calculating the impedances of cables used to supply three-phase services, the three-phase load is assumed to be balanced. Therefore, the neutral current is zero, and the presence of the neutral may be neglected. The resistance of the circuit is equal to the resistance of the phase conductors.

The inductive reactance is given by the following:

$$X = 5.29 \times 10^{-3}\,\frac{f}{60}\log_{10}\left(\frac{GMD_\phi}{GMR_\phi}\right)\quad \Omega/100\ \text{ft} \tag{7.35}$$

where

GMD_ϕ = geometric mean distance between phase conductors

GMR_ϕ = geometric mean radius of phase conductors

EXAMPLE 7-6 Calculate the resistance and inductive reactance for a quadruplexed cable consisting of three #4/0 19-strand aluminum conductors operating at 60 Hz.

Solution From data tables, the resistance is

$$R = 0.0999\ \Omega/1000\ \text{ft} = 0.00999\ \Omega/100\ \text{ft}$$

For the #4/0 cable, GMD_ϕ is 0.632 in., and the phase conductor GMR_ϕ is 0.1999 in. Therefore, inductive reactance is

$$\begin{aligned} X &= 5.29 \times 10^{-3} \frac{60}{60} \log_{10}\left(\frac{0.632}{0.1999}\right) \\ &= 2.6445 \times 10^{-3}\ \Omega/100\ \text{ft} \end{aligned}$$

EXAMPLE 7-7

Calculate the resistance and inductive reactance of four single conductors installed in a vertical configuration with a separation of 8 in. between the phase conductors. The conductors are 500-kcmil 37-strand copper, and the circuit operates at 60 Hz.

Solution From the data tables, the resistance is

$$R = 0.0276\ \Omega/1000\ \text{ft} = 0.00276\ \Omega/100\ \text{ft}$$

The conductor GMR_ϕ is 0.3120 in. The geometric distance between the phase conductors is

$$GMD_\phi = (8 \cdot 8 \cdot 16)^{1/3} = 10.08\ \text{in.}$$

Therefore, inductive reactance is

$$\begin{aligned} X &= 5.29 \times 10^{-3} \frac{60}{60} \log_{10}\left(\frac{10.08}{0.3120}\right) \\ &= 7.9842 \times 10^{-3}\ \Omega/100\ \text{ft} \end{aligned}$$

7-6 Cable Splicing and Terminations

Splicing and terminating of cables operating above 1000 V requires special consideration due to the high electrical stresses produced in the cable insulation. If not correctly controlled, these high electrical stresses can cause breakdown of the cable insulation. Eventually, complete failure of the cable insulation will occur.

To understand the need for electrical stress control, consider the cable shown in Fig. 7-9a. Note that the cable insulation has been stripped back to expose the conductor. Recall that the insulation semicon shield is surrounded by the concentric neutral conductors. As such, the semicon is at ground potential throughout the length of the cable. If the cable insulation is stripped back as shown, there will be a region of high

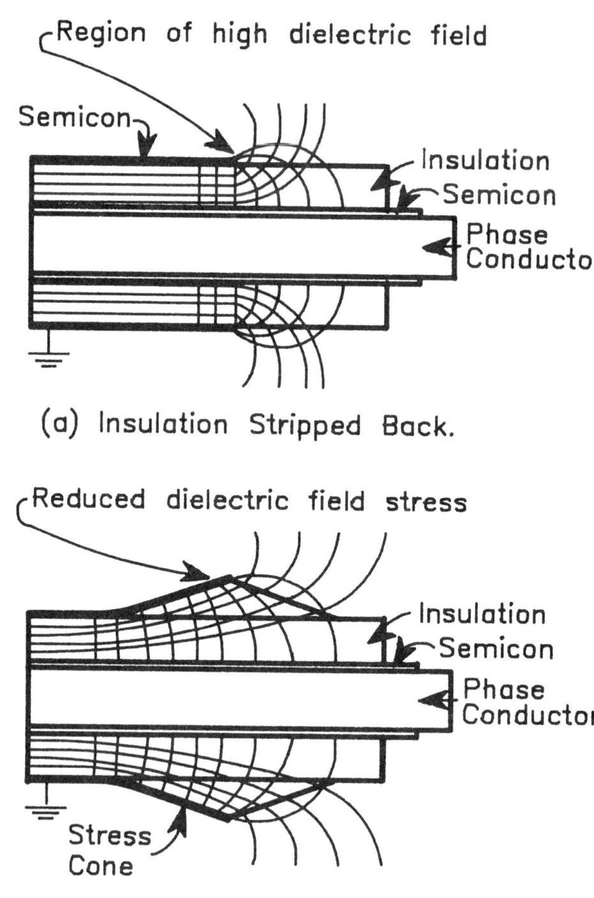

Figure 7-9 Stress cone used to reduce high electrical field stresses.

electrical field stress between the grounded semicon shield and the phase conductor as shown.

The electrical field stress can be controlled by grading the insulation, as shown in Fig. 7-9b. Note that the electrical field has been shaped to produce less electrical stress. All medium- and high-voltage cable terminations must use some form of electrical stress relief to prolong insulation life. Stress cones are used to terminate underground cable to live front transformer terminals and capacitor bushings. Riser pole terminations, or potheads, are used to make the transition from bare overhead conductor to underground cable. A typical three-phase riser pole installation is shown in Fig. 7-10. Loadbreak elbows are used to provide cable termination and disconnecting capability for dead front pad mount transformer terminals. All these devices provide electrical stress relief.

Figure 7-10 Three-phase riser pole on 12.47-kV distribution circuit. (Photo Courtesy of Ohio Edison Company)

7-7 Equivalent Circuits

To perform certain electrical calculations, the equivalent circuit of an overhead line or underground cable is required. Two types of equivalent circuit representations are used, depending on the line or cable characteristics. The length of the line, operating voltage, and whether the line is overhead or underground all influence the choice of which equivalent circuit to use. The type of calculation to be performed will also affect the choice of equivalent circuit. For example, when performing short-circuit calculations, it is common to neglect the capacitance of the line. When performing voltage-drop calculations, the capacitance of the line may have a significant effect on the calculated results.

The short-line representation is typically used for low- and medium-voltage overhead lines, low-voltage cable circuits, and higher-voltage lines of less than 50 miles in length. In the short-line representation, the series resistance and inductive reactance are shown on a per phase equivalent basis. The capacitance and capacitive reactance are

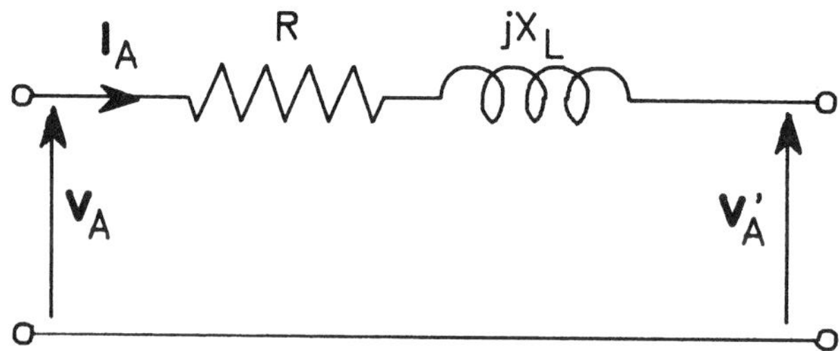

Figure 7-11 Short line per phase equivalent circuit.

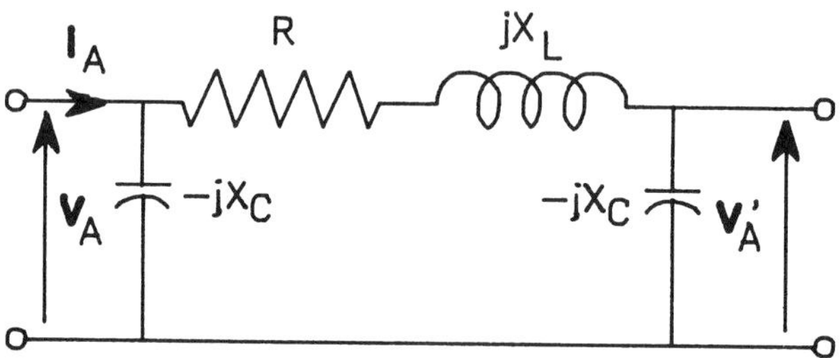

Figure 7-12 Equivalent pi representation.

neglected in the short-line representation. Figure 7-11 shows the per phase equivalent circuit of a short line. The equations for resistance and inductive reactance presented in the preceding sections give the results in terms of ohms per unit length of line per phase. It is therefore necessary to multiply the resistance and inductive reactance by the respective line length to determine the total impedance for a particular section of line. The short-line representation is also used for the single-phase, three-wire system previously discussed.

The equivalent pi representation is used for high-voltage lines longer than 50 miles and for medium- and high-voltage cable circuits. In the equivalent pi representation, the series resistance and inductive reactance are determined as in the short-line representation. However, the capacitive reactance is split equally between the sending end and receiving end of the line. This is equivalent to placing two times the capacitive reactance at each end of the line. The total capacitive reactance is divided by the total length of the line section. The result is then multiplied by 2 to determine the equivalent circuit parameters. The equivalent pi model is shown in Fig. 7-12.

EXAMPLE 7-8 Determine the equivalent pi circuit representations for the overhead line of Example 7-2 assuming a line length of 150 miles.

Solution The total resistance is equal to

$$R = 0.0301\ \Omega/\text{mile} \cdot 150\ \text{miles} = 4.515\ \Omega$$

The total inductive reactance is

$$X_l = 0.4852\ \Omega/\text{mile} \cdot 150\ \text{miles} = 72.78\ \Omega$$

The total capacitive reactance is

$$X_C = 116{,}850\ \Omega\text{-miles} \div 150\ \text{miles} = 779.0\ \Omega$$

The capacitive reactance placed at each end of the line model is

$$X_C' = 779.0 \cdot 2 = 1558.0\ \Omega$$

The equivalent pi model is shown in Fig. 7-13.

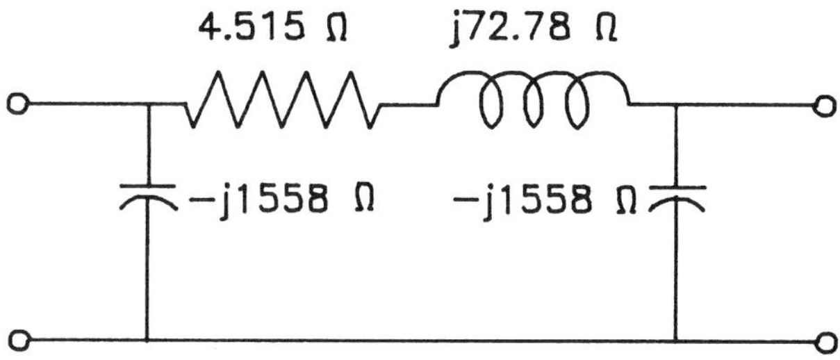

Figure 7-13 Equivalent pi circuit, Example 7-8.

EXAMPLE 7-9 Determine the equivalent pi model for the cable of Example 7-3 assuming a circuit length of 2 miles.

Solution The line length is equal to

$$\text{Length} = 2\ \text{miles} = 10{,}560\ \text{ft}$$

The total resistance is equal to

$$R = (0.0771\ \Omega/1000\ \text{ft}) \cdot 10{,}560\ \text{ft} = 0.8142\ \Omega$$

The total inductive reactance is

$$X_l = (0.0724\ \Omega/1000\ \text{ft}) \cdot 10{,}560\ \text{ft} = 0.7645\ \Omega$$

The total capacitive reactance is

$$X_C = \frac{20{,}411\ \Omega\text{-1000 ft}}{10{,}560\ \text{ft}} = 1932.9\ \Omega$$

The capacitive reactance placed at each end of the line model is

$$X_C' = 1932.9 \cdot 2 = 3865.7\ \Omega$$

The equivalent pi model is shown in Fig. 7-14.

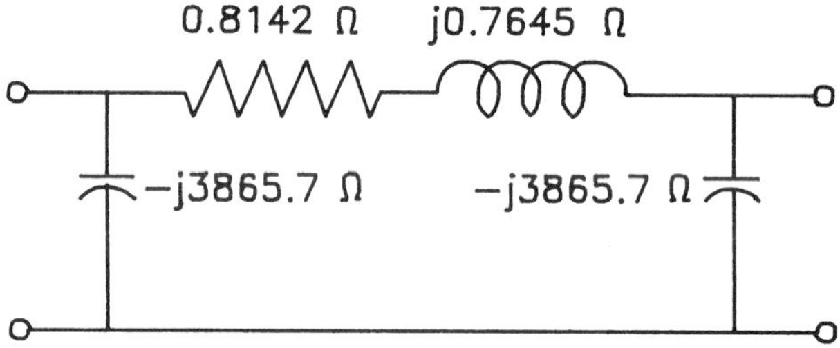

Figure 7-14 Equivalent pi circuit, Example 7-9.

References

[1] *Symmetrical Components,* by C. F. Wagner and R. D. Evans, McGraw-Hill Book Company, New York, 1933, p. 143. Reproduced with permission of McGraw-Hill, Inc.

[2] Ibid., p. 148.

Problems

7.1. Determine the resistance, inductive reactance, capacitive reactance, and rated ampacity for the circuit shown in Fig. 7-15. The phase conductors are 477 kcmil, 26/7 strand, ACSR.

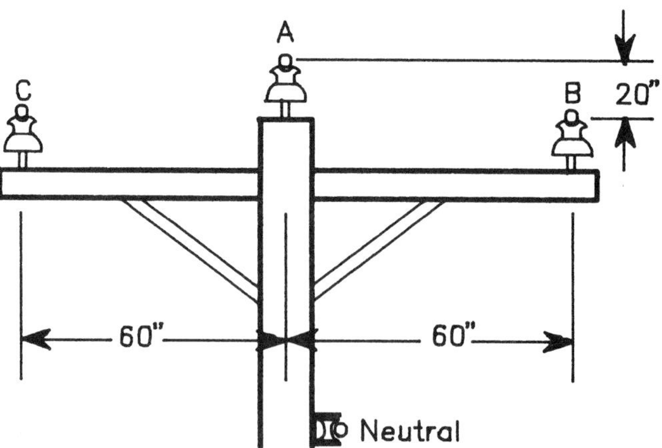

Figure 7-15 Line configuration for Problem 7-1.

7.2. Determine the resistance, inductive reactance, capacitive reactance, and rated ampacity for the circuit shown in Fig. 7-16. The phase conductors are 954 kcmil, 54/7 strand, ACSR.

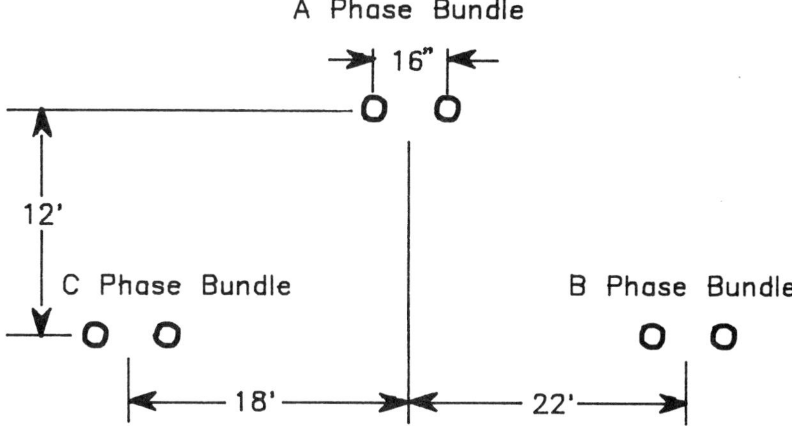

Figure 7-16 Line configuration for Problem 7-2.

7.3. Determine the resistance, inductive reactance, capacitive reactance, and rated ampacity for the circuit shown in Fig. 7-17. The circuit consists of three 750-kcmil, 61-strand, aluminum, 15-kV, one-third-size neutral, URD cables installed in a duct bank.

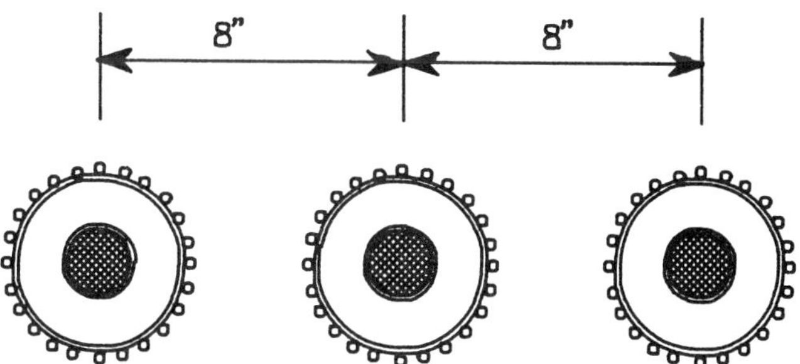

Figure 7-17 Cable configuration for Problem 7-3.

7.4. Determine the resistance, inductive reactance, and rated ampacities for the following triplexed 600-V cables:

a. #4 Aluminum, 7 strand, overhead
b. #1/0 Aluminum, 19 strand, overhead
c. #1/0 Aluminum, 19 strand, underground
d. 350-kcmil aluminum, 37 strand, underground

7.5. Determine the resistance, inductive reactance, and rated ampacities for the following quadruplexed 600-V cables:

a. #1/0 Aluminum, 19 strand, overhead
b. #4/0 AWG Aluminum, 19 strand, overhead
c. #2/0 Aluminum, 19 strand, underground
d. 350-kcmil aluminum, 37 strand, underground

7.6. Determine the resistance, inductive reactance, and rated ampacities for the following single-conductor, 600-V cables used to supply single-phase, three-wire services. Assume an 8-in. separation between the phase conductors.
a. 477-kcmil aluminum, 37 strand, overhead
b. 500-kcmil copper, 37 strand, overhead
c. 300-kcmil aluminum, 37 strand, underground
d. 500-kcmil aluminum, 37 strand, underground

7.7. Determine the resistance, inductive reactance, and rated ampacity for the following single-conductor, 600-V cables used to supply three-phase services. Assume an 8-in. separation between each of the phase conductors.
a. 636-kcmil aluminum, 37 strand, overhead
b. #4/0 AWG copper, 37 strand, overhead
c. #2/0 AWG aluminum, 37 strand, underground
d. 500-kcmil aluminum, 37 strand, underground

7.8. Sketch the equivalent pi circuit representation for the line of Problem 7.1 assuming a circuit length of 3.5 miles.

7.9. Sketch the equivalent pi circuit representation for the line of Problem 7.2 assuming a circuit length of 79.0 miles.

7.10. Sketch the equivalent pi circuit representation for the cable circuit of Problem 7.3 assuming a circuit length of 1.78 miles.

7.11. Sketch the equivalent circuit representation for the cable of Problem 7.4a assuming a circuit length of 175 ft.

7.12. Sketch the equivalent circuit representation for the cable of Problem 7.6c assuming a circuit length of 250 ft.

7.13. Sketch the equivalent circuit representation for the cable of Problem 7.7b assuming a circuit length of 125 ft.

8

Voltage-Drop Calculations and Voltage Regulation

8-1 General

This chapter discusses the problem of voltage regulation on electrical utility systems. Nominal system voltages were discussed in Chapter 3, with typical system voltage levels given in Table 3-1. Normal system voltage is defined to be within a certain tolerance of nominal system voltage. Lower than normal voltage on a system will result in motor failures, dropout of motor starters, and dimming of lamps. Higher than normal system voltage will cause motor failures due to insulation stress, saturation of transformers, and other factors.

The actual voltage present on the power system lines will differ from the nominal values given in Table 3-1 due to voltage drops across line and transformer impedances. The ability to calculate voltage drops in a power system is of prime importance to the utility system engineer. Selection of line and cable size is often dictated with consideration to voltage drop as well as current carrying capability. This is particularly true for the long line lengths encountered in electrical power systems.

In addition to calculating voltage drop, this chapter will address methods of regulating the system voltage to within an acceptable tolerance. These methods include generator terminal voltage regulation and the use of line voltage regulators at various locations in the power system.

8-2 Voltage Ranges

As previously stated, the actual voltage present in any part of a power system will deviate from nominal due to voltage drops on the system. ANSI® standard C84 specifies the allowable tolerances for various nominal voltage levels. For low-voltage systems (<1000 V), the actual service voltage must lie within ±5% of nominal for continuous operation. On medium-voltage systems up to 35 kV, the service voltage must lie within −2.5% and +5% of nominal for continuous operation. Any voltage deviations beyond these tolerances must be corrected. On high-voltage transmission systems, the voltage range is generally the same as for medium-voltage systems.

EXAMPLE 8-1 Calculate the allowable service-voltage range for a 120/240 V, single-phase, three-wire service.

Solution The lower end of the range is

$$V = 240 \cdot 0.95 = 228 \text{ V line to line}$$

$$V = 120 \cdot 0.95 = 114 \text{ V line to neutral}$$

The upper end of the range is

$$V = 240 \cdot 1.05 = 252 \text{ V}$$

$$V = 120 \cdot 1.05 = 126 \text{ V}$$

Therefore, the allowable range for line to neutral voltage is 114 to 126 V. The allowable range for the phase to phase voltage is 228 to 256 V.

EXAMPLE 8-2 Calculate the allowable service-voltage range for a 12.47Y/7.2-kV, three-phase, four-wire service.

Solution The lower end of the range is

$$V = 12{,}470 \cdot 0.975 = 12{,}158 \text{ V line to line}$$

$$V = 7200 \cdot 0.975 = 7020 \text{ V line to neutral}$$

The upper end of the range is

$$V = 12{,}470 \cdot 1.05 = 13{,}094 \text{ V}$$

$$V = 7200 \cdot 1.05 = 7560 \text{ V}$$

Therefore, the allowable range for line to neutral voltage is 7020 to 7560 V. The allowable range for the phase to phase voltage is 12,158 to 13,094 V.

Examples 8-1 and 8-2 illustrated the calculation of allowable voltage ranges for service voltage. The utility engineer is responsible for designing the system to provide service voltage within the specified range. The customer is responsible for maintaining voltages within the premise at acceptable values.

8-3 Distribution System Voltage Drop

Three-Phase Overhead Lines and Underground Cable Circuits

The voltage drop per mile of a three-phase distribution line operating under balanced conditions can be determined by calculating the voltage drop in phase A only. Phases B and C will have an identical voltage drop since balanced conditions were assumed. The voltage drop in phase A is determined by multiplying the line current in phase A by the impedance of the line. Typically, the line to neutral voltage at the source, or sending end, is selected as a reference. The line current is then determined with respect to the reference voltage. The voltage at the receiving end is then equal to the voltage at the sending end minus the **IZ** drop in the line. The equivalent circuit is shown in Fig. 8-1a. Here the line current is designated as $\mathbf{I}_A$, the sending end voltage as $\mathbf{V}_A$, the receiving end voltage as $\mathbf{V}_{A'}$, and the line impedance as $\mathbf{Z}_A$. The voltage at the receiving end of the line is

$$\mathbf{V}_{A'} = \mathbf{V}_A - \mathbf{I}_A \cdot \mathbf{Z}_A \tag{8.1}$$

The magnitude of the voltage drop that occurs along the line is defined as being equal to the magnitude of the sending end voltage minus the magnitude of the receiving end voltage.

$$|\mathbf{V}_{\text{drop}}| = |\mathbf{V}_A| - |\mathbf{V}_{A'}| \tag{8.2}$$

The phasor diagram shown in Fig. 8-1b represents the sending and receiving end conditions. As an approximation, the magnitude of the voltage drop can be determined by subtracting the in-phase component of the voltage drop from the sending end voltage. The result is

$$|\mathbf{V}_{\text{drop}}| \approx |\mathbf{I}_A| \cdot [R \cdot \cos(-\theta) + X \cdot \sin(-\theta)] \tag{8.3}$$

where

R = circuit resistance in ohms

X = circuit reactance in ohms

θ = phase angle of line current, assumed positive for lagging power factor

The voltage drop is usually expressed as a percentage of nominal as follows:

$$\%V_{\text{drop}} = \frac{|\mathbf{V}_{\text{drop}}|}{|\mathbf{V}_A|} \cdot 100 \tag{8.4}$$

It is possible to calculate a voltage-drop factor for a given line configuration. This drop factor is calculated to obtain the percent of drop for a given loading per unit length.

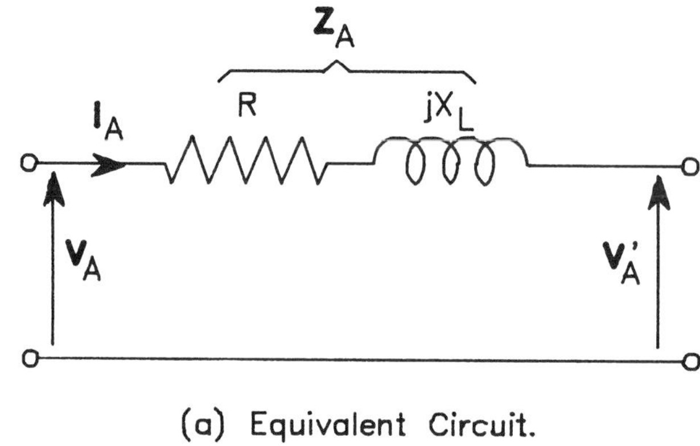

(a) Equivalent Circuit.

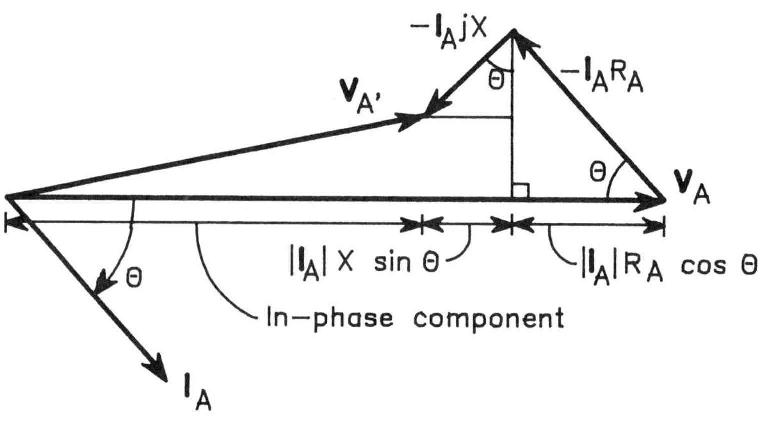

(b) Phasor Diagram.

Figure 8-1 Per phase equivalent circuit for voltage-drop calculations.

For overhead distribution circuits, the drop factor is calculated on a per mile basis, for a loading of 1000 kVA at a selected power factor. For underground cable circuits, the drop factors are calculated for a circuit length of 1000 ft based on a loading of 1000 kVA at a selected power factor. The line impedances to be used are those derived for balanced three-phase operation. A table of drop factors can then be produced for quick reference. The following examples illustrate the procedure.

EXAMPLE 8-3

Calculate the voltage-drop factors of the three-phase overhead line configuration of Example 7-1 for power factors of (**a**) unity and (**b**) 0.8 lagging. Perform the calculations using the exact results of Eq. (8.2), and compare to the approximate results of Eq. (8.3).

Express the results in percent per MVA per mile at a nominal system voltage of 12.47Y/7.2 kV.

Solution The phase A line to neutral voltage is selected as a reference:

$$\mathbf{V}_A = 7200\angle 0° \text{ V}$$

From Example 7-1, the impedance is

$$\mathbf{Z}_A = 0.3263 + j\,0.6391\ \Omega/\text{mile}$$

a. At unity power factor, the line current for a 1-MVA load at 12.47 kV is

$$\mathbf{I}_A = 46.3\angle 0° \text{ A}$$

From Eq. (8.1), the receiving end voltage is

$$\begin{aligned}\mathbf{V}_{A'} &= 7200\angle 0° - (46.3\angle 0°) \cdot (0.3263 + j0.6391)\\ &= 7200\angle 0° - 33.22\angle 63°\\ &= 7184.9 - j29.6\\ &= 7185.0\angle -0.24° \text{ V}\end{aligned}$$

From Eq. (8.2), the magnitude of the voltage drop is

$$|\mathbf{V}_{\text{drop}}| = 7200.0 - 7185.0 = 15.0 \text{ V}$$

The drop factor is

$$\%V_{\text{drop}} = \frac{15.0}{7200} \cdot 100 = 0.208\%/\text{MVA/mile}$$

Using the approximation of Eq. (8.3),

$$\begin{aligned}|\mathbf{V}_{\text{drop}}| &\approx 46.3[0.3263 \cdot \cos(0°) + 0.6391 \cdot \sin(0°)]\\ &= 15.1 \text{ V}\end{aligned}$$

The drop factor is

$$\%V_{\text{drop}} = \frac{15.1}{7200} \cdot 100 = 0.210\%/\text{MVA/mile}$$

b. At 0.8 lagging power factor, the line current is

$$\mathbf{I}_A = 46.3\angle -36.9° \text{ A}$$

From Eq. (8.1), the receiving end voltage is

$$\begin{aligned}\mathbf{V}_{A'} &= 7200\angle 0° - (46.3\angle -36.87°) \cdot (0.3263 + j0.6391)\\ &= 7200\angle 0° - 33.22\angle 26.1°\\ &= 7170.2 - j14.6\\ &= 7170.2\angle -0.117° \text{ V}\end{aligned}$$

From Eq. (8.2), the magnitude of the voltage drop is

$$|\mathbf{V}_{\text{drop}}| = 7200.0 - 7170.2 = 29.8 \text{ V}$$

The drop factor is

$$\%V_{\text{drop}} = \frac{29.8}{7200} \cdot 100 = 0.414\%/\text{MVA/mile}$$

Using the approximation of Eq. (8.3)

$$|\mathbf{V}_{\text{drop}}| \approx 46.3[0.3263 \cdot \cos(36.87°) + 0.6391 \cdot \sin(36.87°)]$$
$$= 29.8 \text{ V}$$

The drop factor is

$$\%V_{\text{drop}} = \frac{29.8}{7200} \cdot 100 = 0.414\%/\text{MVA/mile}$$

Therefore, for unity power factor loading, there will be a voltage drop of approximately 0.21% per MVA per mile of line. At 0.8 lagging power factor, the voltage drop will be approximately 0.41% per MVA per mile. The results using the approximate method agree favorably with the exact results. Also, note that the load power factor has a significant effect on the voltage drop of the line.

EXAMPLE 8-4

Calculate the voltage drop factors of the three-phase underground cable circuit of Example 7-3 for power factors of (**a**) unity and (**b**) 0.8 lagging. Perform the calculations using the exact results of Eq. (8.2), and compare to the approximate results of Eq. (8.3). Express the results in percent per MVA per 1000 ft at a nominal system voltage of 4.16Y/2.4 kV.

Solution The phase A line to neutral voltage is selected as a reference:

$$\mathbf{V}_A = 2400\angle 0° \text{ V}$$

From Example 7-3, the impedance is

$$\mathbf{Z}_A = 0.771 + j0.0724 \ \Omega/1000 \text{ ft}$$

a. At unity power factor, the line current for a three-phase load of 1 MVA at 4.16 kV is

$$\mathbf{I}_A = 138.8\angle 0° \text{ A}$$

The voltage at the receiving end of 1000 ft of circuit is

$$\mathbf{V}_{A'} = 2400\angle 0° - (138.8\angle 0°)(0.0771 + j0.0724)$$
$$= 2400\angle 0° - 14.68\angle 43°$$
$$= 2389.3 - j10.0$$
$$= 2389.3\angle -0.24° \text{ V}$$

From Eq. (8.2), the magnitude of the voltage drop is

$$|\mathbf{V}_{\text{drop}}| = 2400.0 - 2389.3 = 10.7 \text{ V}$$

The drop factor is

$$\%V_{\text{drop}} = \frac{10.7}{2400} \cdot 100 = 0.466\%/\text{MVA/M-ft}$$

Using the approximation of Eq. (8.3),

$$\begin{aligned} |\mathbf{V}_{\text{drop}}| &\approx 138.8[0.0771 \cdot \cos(0°) + 0.0724 \cdot \sin(0°)] \\ &= 10.7 \text{ V} \end{aligned}$$

The drop factor is

$$\%V_{\text{drop}} = \frac{10.7}{2400} \cdot 100 = 0.446\%/\text{MVA/M-ft}$$

b. At 0.8 lagging power factor, the line current is

$$I_A = 138.8\angle -36.9° \text{ A}$$

The voltage at the receiving end of 1000 ft of circuit is

$$\begin{aligned} \mathbf{V}_{A'} &= 2400\angle 0° - (138.8\angle -36.9°)(0.0771 + j0.0724) \\ &= 2400\angle 0° - 14.68\angle 6.1° \\ &= 2385.4 - j1.6 \\ &= 2385.4\angle -0.04° \text{ V} \end{aligned}$$

From Eq. (8.2), the magnitude of the voltage drop is

$$|\mathbf{V}_{\text{drop}}| = 2400.0 - 2385.4 = 14.6 \text{ V}$$

The drop factor is

$$\%V_{\text{drop}} = \frac{14.6}{2400} \cdot 100 = 0.6083\%/\text{MVA/M-ft}$$

Using the approximation of Eq. (8.3),

$$\begin{aligned} |\mathbf{V}_{\text{drop}}| &\approx 138.8[0.0771 \cdot \cos(36.87°) + 0.0724 \cdot \sin(36.87°)] \\ &= 14.6 \text{ V} \end{aligned}$$

The drop factor is

$$\%V_{\text{drop}} = \frac{14.6}{2400} \cdot 100 = 0.6083\%/\text{MVA/M-ft}$$

Therefore, for unity power factor loading, there will be a voltage drop of approximately 0.446% per MVA per 1000 ft of cable. At 0.8 lagging power factor, the voltage drop will be approximately 0.6083% per MVA per 1000 ft of cable. The results using the approximate method agree favorably with the exact results.

The drop factors for other line spacings, conductor sizes and types, and circuit operating voltage levels can be calculated and tabulated for reference in a similar manner.

Open-Wye Overhead Lines

In the determination of the voltage-drop factors for three-phase overhead lines, the voltage drop in each phase was assumed to be identical due to the assumed transposition of the phase conductors. In overhead lines consisting of two phases and the neutral of a three-phase system, the voltage drops in each of the two phases will be different.

The arrangement of conductors for the open-wye overhead line configuration is shown in Fig. 8-2. Here the phase conductors are at positions 1 and 2 and the neutral at position N. The total line length is 1 mile, with the phase conductors assumed to be transposed every ½ mile. The receiving end voltages will be calculated assuming that B and C phases are present. The currents in phases B and C and the neutral will be designated $\mathbf{I}_B$, $\mathbf{I}_C$, and $\mathbf{I}_N$, respectively. The results will be similar regardless of which two phases are actually present.

The receiving end voltages for the phases and neutral are

$$\mathbf{V}_{B'} = \mathbf{V}_B - [\mathbf{I}_B\mathbf{Z}_{11} + \mathbf{I}_C\mathbf{Z}_{12} + \mathbf{I}_N\mathbf{Z}_{1N} + \mathbf{I}_B\mathbf{Z}_{22} + \mathbf{I}_C\mathbf{Z}_{12} + \mathbf{I}_N\mathbf{Z}_{2N}] \tag{8.5}$$

$$\mathbf{V}_{C'} = \mathbf{V}_C - [\mathbf{I}_C\mathbf{Z}_{22} + \mathbf{I}_B\mathbf{Z}_{12} + \mathbf{I}_N\mathbf{Z}_{2N} + \mathbf{I}_C\mathbf{Z}_{11} + \mathbf{I}_B\mathbf{Z}_{12} + \mathbf{I}_N\mathbf{Z}_{1N}] \tag{8.6}$$

$$\mathbf{V}_{N'} = 0 = \mathbf{I}_N\mathbf{Z}_{NN} + \mathbf{I}_B\mathbf{Z}_{1N} + \mathbf{I}_C\mathbf{Z}_{2N} + \mathbf{I}_N\mathbf{Z}_{NN} + \mathbf{I}_C\mathbf{Z}_{1N} + \mathbf{I}_B\mathbf{Z}_{2N} \tag{8.7}$$

where

$$\mathbf{Z}_{11} = \frac{1}{2}\left[R_\phi + 0.0954\frac{f}{60} + j0.2794\frac{f}{60}\log_{10}\left(\frac{D_e}{GMR_\phi}\right)\right] \quad \Omega \tag{8.8}$$

$$\mathbf{Z}_{12} = \frac{1}{2}\left[0.0954\frac{f}{60} + j0.2794\frac{f}{60}\log_{10}\left(\frac{D_e}{d_{12}}\right)\right] \quad \Omega \tag{8.9}$$

$$\mathbf{Z}_{1N} = \frac{1}{2}\left[0.0954\frac{f}{60} + j0.2794\frac{f}{60}\log_{10}\left(\frac{D_e}{d_{1N}}\right)\right] \quad \Omega \tag{8.10}$$

$$\mathbf{Z}_{2N} = \frac{1}{2}\left[0.0954\frac{f}{60} + j0.2794\frac{f}{60}\log_{10}\left(\frac{D_e}{d_{2N}}\right)\right] \quad \Omega \tag{8.11}$$

$$\mathbf{Z}_{NN} = \frac{1}{2}\left[R_N + 0.0954\frac{f}{60} + j0.2794\frac{f}{60}\log_{10}\left(\frac{D_e}{GMR_N}\right)\right] \quad \Omega \tag{8.12}$$

Note that Eqs. (8.8) through (8.12) contain a factor of 1/2. This is due to the fact that there are two transpositions per 1-mile length of line. Each untransposed section of

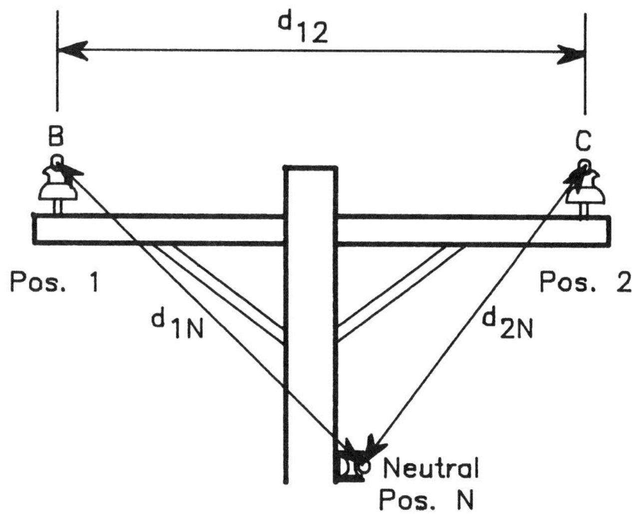

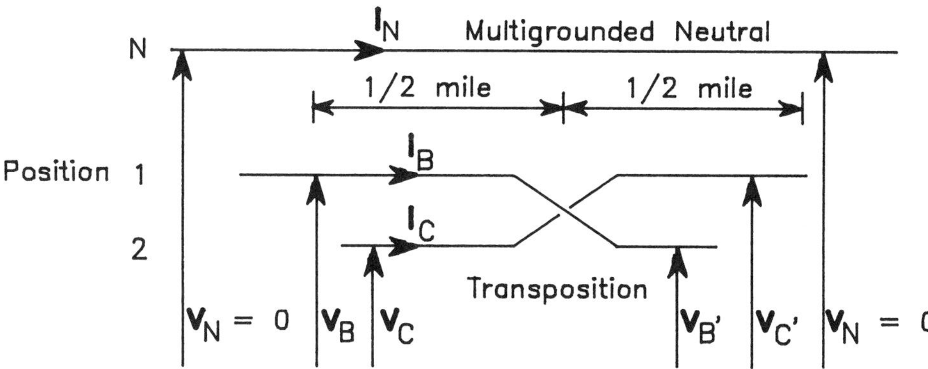

Figure 8-2 Open-wye overhead line configuration.

line is assumed to be ½ mile in length. Therefore, each of the **IZ** drops in Eqs. (8.5), (8.6), and (8.7) are for a 1/2-mile length of line. Solving Eq. (8.7) for $\mathbf{I}_N$ results in

$$\mathbf{I}_N = -\frac{(\mathbf{I}_B + \mathbf{I}_C)(\mathbf{Z}_{1N} + \mathbf{Z}_{2N})}{2\mathbf{Z}_{NN}} \tag{8.13}$$

Due to symmetry, $\mathbf{Z}_{11} = \mathbf{Z}_{22}$. Substituting Eq. (8.13) into (8.5) and (8.6), gathering terms, and simplifying results in

$$\mathbf{V}_{B'} = \mathbf{V}_B - \mathbf{I}_B\left[2\mathbf{Z}_{11} - \frac{(\mathbf{Z}_{1N} + \mathbf{Z}_{2N})^2}{2\mathbf{Z}_{NN}}\right] - \mathbf{I}_C\left[2\mathbf{Z}_{12} - \frac{(\mathbf{Z}_{1N} + \mathbf{Z}_{2N})^2}{2\mathbf{Z}_{NN}}\right] \tag{8.14}$$

$$\mathbf{V}_{C'} = \mathbf{V}_C - \mathbf{I}_B\left[2\mathbf{Z}_{12} - \frac{(\mathbf{Z}_{1N} + \mathbf{Z}_{2N})^2}{2\mathbf{Z}_{NN}}\right] - \mathbf{I}_C\left[2\mathbf{Z}_{11} - \frac{(\mathbf{Z}_{1N} + \mathbf{Z}_{2N})^2}{2\mathbf{Z}_{NN}}\right] \tag{8.15}$$

To simplify Eqs. (8.14) and (8.15), the following are defined:

$$\mathbf{Z}' = \left[2\mathbf{Z}_{11} - \frac{(\mathbf{Z}_{1N} + \mathbf{Z}_{2N})^2}{2\mathbf{Z}_{NN}}\right] \quad \textbf{(8.16)}$$

$$\mathbf{Z}'' = \left[2\mathbf{Z}_{12} - \frac{(\mathbf{Z}_{1N} + \mathbf{Z}_{2N})^2}{2\mathbf{Z}_{NN}}\right] \quad \textbf{(8.17)}$$

Substituting Eqs. (8.16) and (8.17) into Eqs. (8.14) and (8.15) results in

$$\mathbf{V}_{B'} = \mathbf{V}_B - \mathbf{I}_B \cdot \mathbf{Z}' - \mathbf{I}_C \cdot \mathbf{Z}'' \quad \textbf{(8.18)}$$

$$\mathbf{V}_{C'} = \mathbf{V}_C - \mathbf{I}_B \cdot \mathbf{Z}'' - \mathbf{I}_C \cdot \mathbf{Z}' \quad \textbf{(8.19)}$$

Note that $\mathbf{Z}'$ and $\mathbf{Z}''$ are constants that depend only on the physical configuration of the line. Therefore, when determining voltage-drop factors for a particular line configuration, it is necessary to calculate these constants only once. The line currents $\mathbf{I}_B$ and $\mathbf{I}_C$ will vary depending on the assumed power factor of the load. Consequently, the receiving end voltages will change as a function of load power factor.

The magnitude of the voltage drops in phases B and C are determined in a manner similar to the three-phase overhead line. Therefore,

$$|\mathbf{V}_{\text{drop},B}| = |\mathbf{V}_B| - |\mathbf{V}_{B'}| \quad \textbf{(8.20)}$$

$$|\mathbf{V}_{\text{drop},C}| = |\mathbf{V}_C| - |\mathbf{V}_{C'}| \quad \textbf{(8.21)}$$

The magnitude of the voltage drops for the two phases expressed as a percentage of nominal are given by

$$\%V_{\text{drop},B} = \frac{|\mathbf{V}_{\text{drop},B}|}{|\mathbf{V}_B|} \cdot 100 \quad \textbf{(8.22)}$$

$$\%V_{\text{drop},C} = \frac{|\mathbf{V}_{\text{drop},C}|}{|\mathbf{V}_C|} \cdot 100 \quad \textbf{(8.23)}$$

EXAMPLE 8-5

Determine the voltage-drop factors for the line configuration shown in Fig. 8-3. The phase and neutral conductors are #1/0 ACSR, 6/1 stranding. The line operates at 12.47 kV line to line. Assume an earth resistivity of 100 Ω-m and an operating frequency of 60 Hz. Calculate the voltage drop factors per MVA per mile for **(a)** unity and **(b)** 0.8 lagging power factor.

Solution From Appendix A data tables, the resistance and *GMR* of the #1/0 ACSR are

$$R_\phi = R_N = 1.1458\ \Omega/\text{mile}$$

$$GMR_\phi = GMR_N = 0.00446\ \text{ft}$$

The depth of the equivalent earth return is

$$D_e = 2160(100/60)^{1/2} = 2788.5\ \text{ft}$$

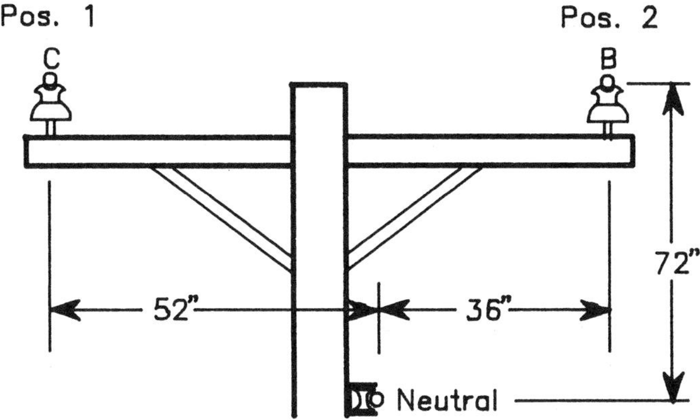

Figure 8-3 Line configuration for Example 8-5.

The distance between the phase conductors is

$$d_{12} = 88 \text{ in.} = 7.33 \text{ ft}$$

The distance from position 1 to neutral is

$$d_{1N} = (52^2 + 72^2)^{1/2} = 88.8 \text{ in.} = 7.4 \text{ ft}$$

The distance from position 2 to neutral is

$$d_{2N} = (36^2 + 72^2)^{1/2} = 80.5 \text{ in.} = 6.71 \text{ ft}$$

Applying Eqs. (8.8) through (8.12) results in

$$\mathbf{Z}_{11} = \frac{1}{2}\left[1.1458 + 0.0954 + j0.2794 \log_{10}\left(\frac{2788.5}{0.00446}\right)\right]$$
$$= 0.6206 + j0.8097\ \Omega$$

$$\mathbf{Z}_{12} = \frac{1}{2}\left[0.0954 + j0.2794 \log_{10}\left(\frac{2788.5}{7.33}\right)\right]$$
$$= 0.0477 + j0.3604\ \Omega$$

$$\mathbf{Z}_{1N} = \frac{1}{2}\left[0.0954 + j0.2794 \log_{10}\left(\frac{2788.5}{7.4}\right)\right]$$
$$= 0.0477 + j0.3599\ \Omega$$

$$\mathbf{Z}_{2N} = \frac{1}{2}\left[0.0954 + j0.2794 \log_{10}\left(\frac{2788.5}{6.71}\right)\right]$$
$$= 0.0477 + j0.3659\ \Omega$$

$$\mathbf{Z}_{NN} = \frac{1}{2}\left[1.1458 + 0.0954 + j0.2794 \log_{10}\left(\frac{2788.5}{0.00446}\right)\right]$$
$$= 0.6206 + j0.8097\ \Omega$$

$\mathbf{Z}'$ and $\mathbf{Z}''$ are calculated from Eqs. (8.16) and (8.17):

$$\mathbf{Z}' = \left[2\mathbf{Z}_{11} - \frac{(\mathbf{Z}_{1N} + \mathbf{Z}_{2N})^2}{2\mathbf{Z}_{NN}}\right]$$

$$= 1.3417 + j1.3768 = 1.9224\angle 45.7^\circ\ \Omega$$

$$\mathbf{Z}'' = \left[2\mathbf{Z}_{12} - \frac{(\mathbf{Z}_{1N} + \mathbf{Z}_{2N})^2}{2\mathbf{Z}_{NN}}\right]$$

$$= 0.1959 + j0.4782 = 0.5168\angle 67.7^\circ\ \Omega$$

Note that $\mathbf{Z}'$ and $\mathbf{Z}''$ are not affected by power factor. The line currents are calculated by assuming a 1-MVA load on the two phases, or 500 kVA per phase.

a. At unity power factor, the line currents are

$$\mathbf{I}_B = \frac{500\ \text{kVA} \cdot 1000}{7.2\ \text{kV}} \angle -120^\circ = 69.44\angle -120^\circ\ \text{A}$$

$$\mathbf{I}_C = \frac{500\ \text{kVA} \cdot 1000}{7.2\ \text{kV}} \angle +120^\circ = 69.44\angle +120^\circ\ \text{A}$$

The voltages at the receiving end of the line are calculated by applying Eqs. (8.18) and (8.19).

$$\mathbf{V}_{B'} = \mathbf{V}_B - \mathbf{I}_B\mathbf{Z}' - \mathbf{I}_C\mathbf{Z}''$$

$$= 7200\angle -120^\circ - (69.44\angle -120^\circ)(1.9224\angle 45.7^\circ)$$

$$-(69.44\angle +120^\circ)(0.5168\angle 67.7^\circ)$$

$$= 7085.2\angle -120.5^\circ\ \text{V}$$

$$\mathbf{V}_{C'} = \mathbf{V}_C - \mathbf{I}_B\mathbf{Z}'' - \mathbf{I}_C\mathbf{Z}'$$

$$= 7200\angle 120^\circ - (69.44\angle -120^\circ)(0.5168\angle 67.7^\circ)$$

$$-(69.44\angle +120^\circ)(1.9224\angle 45.7^\circ)$$

$$= 7142.9\angle 119.3^\circ\ \text{V}$$

The voltage-drop factors are

$$B\ \text{phase:}\quad \%V_{\text{drop}} = \frac{114.8}{7200} \cdot 100 = 1.59\%/\text{MVA/mile}$$

$$C\ \text{phase:}\quad \%V_{\text{drop}} = \frac{57.1}{7200} \cdot 100 = 0.79\%/\text{MVA/mile}$$

b. At 0.8 lagging power factor, the line currents are

$$\mathbf{I}_B = \frac{500\ \text{kVA} \cdot 1000}{7.2\ \text{kV}} \angle(-120^\circ - 36.9^\circ) = 69.44\angle -156.9^\circ\ \text{A}$$

$$\mathbf{I}_C = \frac{500\ \text{kVA} \cdot 1000}{7.2\ \text{kV}} \angle(120^\circ - 36.87^\circ) = 69.44\angle 83.1^\circ\ \text{A}$$

As in part a, the voltage drops are determined by applying Eqs. (8.18) and (8.19).

$$\begin{aligned}\mathbf{V}_{B'} &= \mathbf{V}_B - \mathbf{I}_B\mathbf{Z}' - \mathbf{I}_C\mathbf{Z}'' \\ &= 7200\angle -120° - (69.44\angle -156.9°)(1.9224\angle 45.7°) \\ &\quad -(69.44\angle 83.1°)(0.5168\angle 67.7°) \\ &= 7066.3\angle -119.9° \text{ V} \\ \mathbf{V}_{C'} &= \mathbf{V}_C - \mathbf{I}_B\mathbf{Z}'' - \mathbf{I}_C\mathbf{Z}' \\ &= 7200\angle 120° - (69.44\angle -156.9°)(0.5168\angle 67.7°) \\ &\quad -(69.44\angle 83.1°)(1.9224\angle 45.7°) \\ &= 7099.5\angle 119.7° \text{ V}\end{aligned}$$

The voltage-drop factors are

$$B \text{ phase:} \quad \%V_{\text{drop}} = \frac{133.7}{7200} \cdot 100 = 1.86\%/\text{MVA/mile}$$

$$C \text{ phase:} \quad \%V_{\text{drop}} = \frac{100.5}{7200} \cdot 100 = 1.40\%/\text{MVA/mile}$$

Open-Wye Underground Cable

The arrangement of conductors for an underground concentric neutral cable circuit consisting of two phases is shown in Fig. 8-4. Here the phase conductors are at positions 1 and 2 and the concentric neutrals at positions 1′ and 2′. The total circuit length is 1000 ft, with the cables assumed to be transposed every 500 ft. The receiving end voltages will be calculated assuming that B and C phases are present. The currents in the B and C phases will be designated $\mathbf{I}_B$ and $\mathbf{I}_C$. The currents in the concentric neutrals of the B and C phases will be designated $\mathbf{I}_b$ and $\mathbf{I}_c$ respectively. The results will be similar regardless of which two phases are actually present.

The receiving end voltages for the phases and concentric neutrals are

$$\begin{aligned}\mathbf{V}_{B'} = \mathbf{V}_B - (&\mathbf{I}_B\mathbf{Z}_{11} + \mathbf{I}_C\mathbf{Z}_{12} + \mathbf{I}_b\mathbf{Z}_{1'1} + \mathbf{I}_c\mathbf{Z}_{2'1} \\ &+ \mathbf{I}_B\mathbf{Z}_{22} + \mathbf{I}_C\mathbf{Z}_{21} + \mathbf{I}_b\mathbf{Z}_{2'2} + \mathbf{I}_c\mathbf{Z}_{1'2})\end{aligned} \tag{8.24}$$

$$\begin{aligned}\mathbf{V}_{C'} = \mathbf{V}_C - (&\mathbf{I}_C\mathbf{Z}_{22} + \mathbf{I}_B\mathbf{Z}_{12} + \mathbf{I}_b\mathbf{Z}_{1'2} + \mathbf{I}_c\mathbf{Z}_{2'2} \\ &+ \mathbf{I}_C\mathbf{Z}_{11} + \mathbf{I}_B\mathbf{Z}_{12} + \mathbf{I}_b\mathbf{Z}_{2'1} + \mathbf{I}_c\mathbf{Z}_{1'1})\end{aligned} \tag{8.25}$$

$$\begin{aligned}\mathbf{V}_{b'} = 0 = \; &\mathbf{I}_B\mathbf{Z}_{1'1} + \mathbf{I}_C\mathbf{Z}_{21'} + \mathbf{I}_b\mathbf{Z}_{1'1'} + \mathbf{I}_c\mathbf{Z}_{2'1'} \\ &+ \mathbf{I}_B\mathbf{Z}_{2'2} + \mathbf{I}_C\mathbf{Z}_{12'} + \mathbf{I}_b\mathbf{Z}_{2'2'} + \mathbf{I}_c\mathbf{Z}_{1'2'}\end{aligned} \tag{8.26}$$

$$\begin{aligned}\mathbf{V}_{c'} = 0 = \; &\mathbf{I}_C\mathbf{Z}_{2'2} + \mathbf{I}_c\mathbf{Z}_{2'2'} + \mathbf{I}_B\mathbf{Z}_{12'} + \mathbf{I}_b\mathbf{Z}_{1'2'} \\ &+ \mathbf{I}_C\mathbf{Z}_{1'1} + \mathbf{I}_B\mathbf{Z}_{21'} + \mathbf{I}_c\mathbf{Z}_{1'1'} + \mathbf{I}_b\mathbf{Z}_{2'1'}\end{aligned} \tag{8.27}$$

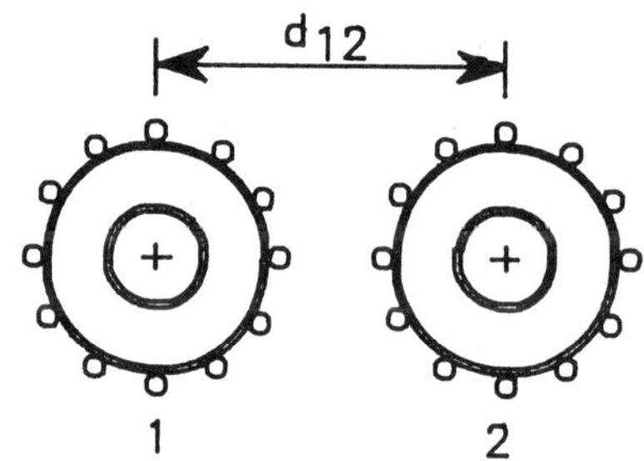

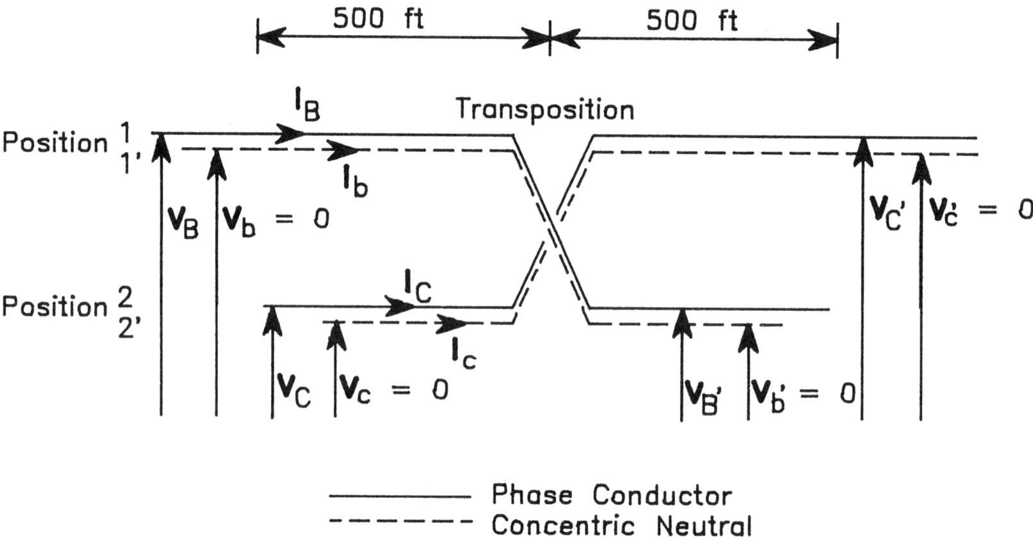

Figure 8-4 Open-wye underground cable configuration.

Due to symmetry, the following equalities exist:

$$\mathbf{Z}_{11} = \mathbf{Z}_{22}, \qquad \mathbf{Z}_{1'1'} = \mathbf{Z}_{2'2'}, \qquad \mathbf{Z}_{1'1} = \mathbf{Z}_{2'2} = \mathbf{Z}_{11'} = \mathbf{Z}_{22'}$$

$$\mathbf{Z}_{12} = \mathbf{Z}_{21} = \mathbf{Z}_{1'2} = \mathbf{Z}_{12'} = \mathbf{Z}_{21'} = \mathbf{Z}_{2'1} = \mathbf{Z}_{1'2'} = \mathbf{Z}_{2'1'}$$

Applying the equalities to Eqs. (8.24), (8.25), (8.26), and (8.27), gathering terms, and simplifying results in

$$\mathbf{V}_{B'} = \mathbf{V}_B - 2(\mathbf{I}_B\mathbf{Z}_{11} + \mathbf{I}_C\mathbf{Z}_{12} + \mathbf{I}_b\mathbf{Z}_{1'1} + \mathbf{I}_c\mathbf{Z}_{12}) \tag{8.28}$$

$$\mathbf{V}_{C'} = \mathbf{V}_C - 2(\mathbf{I}_C\mathbf{Z}_{11} + \mathbf{I}_B\mathbf{Z}_{12} + \mathbf{I}_b\mathbf{Z}_{12} + \mathbf{I}_c\mathbf{Z}_{1'1}) \tag{8.29}$$

$$\mathbf{V}_{b'} = 0 = \mathbf{I}_B\mathbf{Z}_{1'1} + \mathbf{I}_C\mathbf{Z}_{12} + \mathbf{I}_b\mathbf{Z}_{1'1'} + \mathbf{I}_c\mathbf{Z}_{12} \tag{8.30}$$

$$\mathbf{V}_{c'} = 0 = \mathbf{I}_C\mathbf{Z}_{1'1} + \mathbf{I}_c\mathbf{Z}_{1'1'} + \mathbf{I}_B\mathbf{Z}_{12} + \mathbf{I}_b\mathbf{Z}_{12} \tag{8.31}$$

where

$$\mathbf{Z}_{11} = \frac{1}{2}\left[R_\phi + 0.01807\,\frac{f}{60} + j0.0529\,\frac{f}{60}\,\log_{10}\!\left(\frac{D_e}{GMR_\phi}\right)\right]\quad \Omega \tag{8.32}$$

$$\mathbf{Z}_{1'1'} = \frac{1}{2}\left[R_N + 0.01807\,\frac{f}{60} + j0.0529\,\frac{f}{60}\,\log_{10}\!\left(\frac{D_e}{GMR_N}\right)\right]\quad \Omega \tag{8.33}$$

$$\mathbf{Z}_{12} = \frac{1}{2}\left[0.01807\,\frac{f}{60} + j0.0529\,\frac{f}{60}\,\log_{10}\!\left(\frac{D_e}{d_{12}}\right)\right]\quad \Omega \tag{8.34}$$

$$\mathbf{Z}_{1'1} = \frac{1}{2}\left[0.01807\,\frac{f}{60} + j0.0529\,\frac{f}{60}\,\log_{10}\!\left(\frac{D_e}{d_{1'1}}\right)\right]\quad \Omega \tag{8.35}$$

Note that Eqs. (8.32) through (8.35) contain a factor of ½. This is due to the fact that each of the **IZ** drops in Eqs. (8.28) through (8.31) are for a 500-ft length of cable circuit.

For concentric neutral cable and sheathed cable, the geometric mean radius of the neutral is approximately equal to the radius formed by the neutral strands or shield. Therefore,

$$GMR_N \approx r_{CN} \approx d_{1'1}$$

Equations (8.30) and (8.31) can be solved to express the concentric neutral currents, $\mathbf{I}_b$ and $\mathbf{I}_c$, in terms of the phase currents $\mathbf{I}_B$ and $\mathbf{I}_C$. The following results:

$$\mathbf{I}_b = \frac{\mathbf{Z}_{1'1'}(-\mathbf{I}_B\mathbf{Z}_{1'1} - \mathbf{I}_C\mathbf{Z}_{12}) + \mathbf{Z}_{12}(\mathbf{I}_C\mathbf{Z}_{1'1} + \mathbf{I}_B\mathbf{Z}_{12})}{\mathbf{Z}_{1'1'}^2 - \mathbf{Z}_{12}^2} \tag{8.36}$$

$$\mathbf{I}_c = \frac{\mathbf{Z}_{1'1'}(-\mathbf{I}_C\mathbf{Z}_{1'1} - \mathbf{I}_B\mathbf{Z}_{12}) + \mathbf{Z}_{12}(\mathbf{I}_B\mathbf{Z}_{1'1} + \mathbf{I}_C\mathbf{Z}_{12})}{\mathbf{Z}_{1'1'}^2 - \mathbf{Z}_{12}^2} \tag{8.37}$$

Simplifying Eqs. (8.36) and (8.37) results in

$$\mathbf{I}_b = \frac{\mathbf{Z}_{12}^2 - \mathbf{Z}_{1'1'}\mathbf{Z}_{1'1}}{\mathbf{Z}_{1'1'}^2 - \mathbf{Z}_{12}^2}\,\mathbf{I}_B + \frac{\mathbf{Z}_{12}\mathbf{Z}_{1'1} - \mathbf{Z}_{1'1'}\mathbf{Z}_{12}}{\mathbf{Z}_{1'1'}^2 - \mathbf{Z}_{12}^2}\,\mathbf{I}_C \tag{8.38}$$

$$\mathbf{I}_c = \frac{\mathbf{Z}_{12}\mathbf{Z}_{1'1} - \mathbf{Z}_{1'1'}\mathbf{Z}_{12}}{\mathbf{Z}_{1'1'}^2 - \mathbf{Z}_{12}^2}\,\mathbf{I}_B + \frac{\mathbf{Z}_{12}^2 - \mathbf{Z}_{1'1'}\mathbf{Z}_{1'1}}{\mathbf{Z}_{1'1'}^2 - \mathbf{Z}_{12}^2}\,\mathbf{I}_C \tag{8.39}$$

Define the following:

$$\mathbf{Z}' = \frac{\mathbf{Z}_{12}^2 - \mathbf{Z}_{1'1'}\mathbf{Z}_{1'1}}{\mathbf{Z}_{1'1'}^2 - \mathbf{Z}_{12}^2} \tag{8.40}$$

$$\mathbf{Z}'' = \frac{\mathbf{Z}_{12}\mathbf{Z}_{1'1} - \mathbf{Z}_{1'1'}\mathbf{Z}_{12}}{\mathbf{Z}_{1'1'}^2 - \mathbf{Z}_{12}^2} \tag{8.41}$$

Substituting Eqs. (8.40) and (8.41) into Eqs. (8.38) and (8.39) results in

$$\mathbf{I}_b = \mathbf{Z}' \cdot \mathbf{I}_B + \mathbf{Z}'' \cdot \mathbf{I}_C \tag{8.42}$$

$$\mathbf{I}_c = \mathbf{Z}'' \cdot \mathbf{I}_B + \mathbf{Z}' \cdot \mathbf{I}_C \tag{8.43}$$

Equations (8.42) and (8.43) are used to calculate the currents in the concentric neutral conductors or sheath of the cable, given the currents in phases B and C. The resulting neutral currents are then substituted into Eqs. (8.28) and (8.29) to obtain the receiving end voltages in phases B and C.

The magnitudes of the voltage drops in phases B and C are determined in a manner similar to the open-wye overhead line. Therefore, Eqs. (8.20) through (8.23) apply to the open-wye underground URD concentric neutral cable circuit as well.

EXAMPLE 8-6

Determine the voltage-drop factors for the cable circuit shown in Fig. 8-5. The circuit consists of two #1/0, 15-kV, 19-strand, aluminum, 100% insulation level, URD cable. The line operates at 12.47 kV line to line. Assume an earth resistivity of 100 Ω-m and an operating frequency of 60 Hz. Calculate for **(a)** unity and **(b)** 0.8 lagging power factor.

Solution From the cable data of Appendix A, the radius of the circle formed by the neutral conductors is

$$r_{CN} = 0.468 \text{ in.}$$

The geometric mean radius of the neutral strands is

$$GMR_N \approx r_{CN} = 0.468 \text{ in.}$$

The geometric mean radius of the phase conductors is

$$GMR_\phi = 0.1336 \text{ in.}$$

The resistances of the phase and neutral are

$$R_\phi = 0.2097 \ \Omega/1000 \text{ ft}, \qquad R_N = 0.1997 \ \Omega/1000 \text{ ft}$$

The distance between the center of the phase conductor and the neutral conductors is

$$d_{1'1} \approx r_{CN} = 0.468 \text{ in.}$$

The distance between the phase conductors is

$$d_{12} = 6 \text{ in.}$$

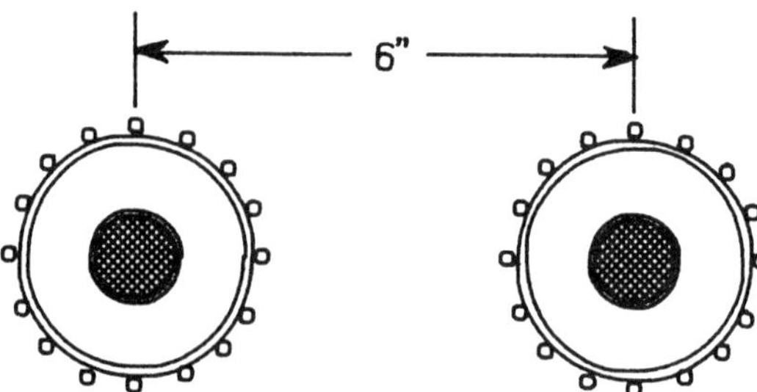

Figure 8-5 Cable configuration for Example 8-6.

The depth of the equivalent ground return conductor is

$$D_e = 2160 \cdot ({}^{100}\!/\!_{60})^{1/2} = 2788.5 \text{ ft} = 33{,}462 \text{ in.}$$

From Eqs. (8.32) through (8.35),

$$\mathbf{Z}_{11} = \frac{1}{2}\left(0.2097 + 0.01807\,\frac{60}{60} + j0.0529\,\frac{60}{60}\,\log_{10}\frac{33{,}462}{0.1336}\right)$$

$$= 0.1139 + j0.1428 = 0.1827\angle 51.4^\circ\ \Omega$$

$$\mathbf{Z}_{1'1'} = \frac{1}{2}\left(0.1997 + 0.01807\,\frac{60}{60} + j0.0529\,\frac{60}{60}\,\log_{10}\frac{33{,}462}{0.468}\right)$$

$$= 0.1089 + j0.1284 = 0.1686\angle 49.7^\circ\ \Omega$$

$$\mathbf{Z}_{12} = \frac{1}{2}\left(0.01807\,\frac{60}{60} + j0.0529\,\frac{60}{60}\,\log_{10}\frac{33{,}462}{6.0}\right)$$

$$= 0.00904 + j0.0991 = 0.0995\angle 84.8^\circ\ \Omega$$

$$\mathbf{Z}_{1'1} = \frac{1}{2}\left(0.01807\,\frac{60}{60} + j0.0529\,\frac{60}{60}\,\log_{10}\frac{33{,}462}{0.468}\right)$$

$$= 0.00904 + j0.1284 = 0.1287\angle 86^\circ\ \Omega$$

Applying Eqs. (8.40) and (8.41),

$$\mathbf{Z}' = \frac{(0.0995\angle 84.8^\circ)^2 - (0.1686\angle 49.7^\circ)(0.1287\angle 86^\circ)}{(0.1686\angle 49.7^\circ)^2 - (0.0995\angle 84.8^\circ)^2}$$

$$= 0.5468\angle -145.6^\circ$$

$$\mathbf{Z}'' = \frac{(0.0995\angle 84.8)(0.1287\angle 86^\circ) - (0.1686\angle 49.7^\circ)(0.0995\angle 84.8^\circ)}{(0.1686\angle 49.7^\circ)^2 - (0.0995\angle 84.8^\circ)^2}$$

$$= 0.3737\angle 186.1^\circ$$

Note that $\mathbf{Z}'$ and $\mathbf{Z}''$ are constants that depend only on cable configuration.

a. The 1-MVA load is assumed to be divided evenly between the B and C phases. Therefore, a loading of 500-kVA per phase is used. At unity power factor, the line currents in the B and C phases are

$$\mathbf{I}_B = \frac{500{,}000}{7200}\angle -120^\circ = 69.44\angle -120^\circ \text{ A}$$

$$\mathbf{I}_C = \frac{500{,}000}{7200}\angle 120^\circ = 69.44\angle 120^\circ \text{ A}$$

The currents in the concentric neutral of each cable are calculated from Eqs. (8.42) and (8.43).

$$\mathbf{I}_b = (0.5468\angle -145.6^\circ)(69.44\angle -120^\circ) + (0.3737\angle 186.1^\circ)(69.44\angle 120^\circ)$$

$$= 20.94\angle 53.8^\circ \text{ A}$$

$$\mathbf{I}_c = (0.3737\angle 186.1^\circ)(69.44\angle -120^\circ) + (0.5468\angle -145.6^\circ)(69.44\angle 120^\circ)$$

$$= 45.35\angle 9.3^\circ \text{ A}$$

The receiving end voltages in phases B and C may be calculated by applying Eqs. (8.28) and (8.29).

$$\begin{aligned}\mathbf{V}_{B'} &= 7200\angle -120° - 2 \cdot [(69.44\angle -120°)(0.1827\angle 51.4°)\\ &\quad + (69.44\angle 120°)(0.0995\angle 84.8°) + (20.94\angle 53.8°)(0.1287\angle 86°)\\ &\quad + (45.35\angle 9.3°)(0.0995\angle 84.8°)]\\ &= 7181.3\angle -120° \text{ V}\\ \mathbf{V}_{C'} &= 7200\angle 120° - 2 \cdot [(69.44\angle 120°)(0.1827\angle 51.4°)\\ &\quad + (69.44\angle -120°)(0.0995\angle 84.8°) + (20.94\angle 53.8°)(0.0995\angle 84.8°)\\ &\quad + (45.35\angle 9.3°)(0.1287\angle 86°)]\\ &= 7182.2\angle 119.9° \text{ V}\end{aligned}$$

The voltage-drop factors are

$$B \text{ phase:} \quad \%V_{\text{drop}} = \frac{18.7}{7200} \cdot 100 = 0.260\%/\text{MVA}/1000 \text{ ft}$$

$$C \text{ phase:} \quad \%V_{\text{drop}} = \frac{17.8}{7200} \cdot 100 = 0.247\%/\text{MVA}/1000 \text{ ft}$$

b. At 0.8 lagging power factor, the line currents are

$$\mathbf{I}_B = \frac{500{,}000}{7200}\angle(-120° - 36.87°) = 69.44\angle -156.9° \text{ A}$$

$$\mathbf{I}_C = \frac{500{,}000}{7200}\angle(120° - 36.87°) = 69.44\angle 83.1° \text{ A}$$

As in part a, the currents in the concentric neutral of each cable are calculated from Eqs. (8.42) and (8.43).

$$\begin{aligned}\mathbf{I}_b &= (0.5468\angle -145.6°)(69.44\angle -156.9°) + (0.3737\angle 186.1°)(69.44\angle 83.1°)\\ &= 20.94\angle 16.9° \text{ A}\\ \mathbf{I}_c &= (0.3737\angle 186.1°)(69.44\angle -156.9°) + (0.5468\angle -145.6°)(69.44\angle 83.1°)\\ &= 45.35\angle -27.6° \text{ A}\end{aligned}$$

The receiving end voltages in phases B and C may be calculated by applying Eqs. (8.28) and (8.29).

$$\begin{aligned}\mathbf{V}_{B'} &= 7200\angle -120° - 2 \cdot [(69.44\angle -156.9°)(0.1827\angle 51.4°)\\ &\quad + (69.44\angle 83.1°)(0.0995\angle 84.8°) + (20.94\angle 16.9°)(0.1287\angle 86°)\\ &\quad + (45.35\angle -27.6°)(0.0995\angle 84.8°)]\\ &= 7184.2\angle -119.9° \text{ V}\end{aligned}$$

$$\mathbf{V}_{C'} = 7200\angle 120° - 2 \cdot [(69.44\angle 83.1°)(0.11827\angle 51.4°) + (69.44\angle -156.9°)(0.0995\angle 84.8°) + (20.94\angle 16.9°)(0.0995\angle 84.8°) + (45.35\angle -27.6°)(0.1287\angle 86°)]$$
$$= 7179.4\angle 120° \text{ V}$$

The voltage-drop factors are

$$B \text{ phase:} \quad \%V_{\text{drop}} = \frac{15.8}{7200} \cdot 100 = 0.219\%/\text{MVA}/1000 \text{ ft}$$

$$C \text{ phase:} \quad \%V_{\text{drop}} = \frac{20.6}{7200} \cdot 100 = 0.286\%/\text{MVA}/1000 \text{ ft}$$

Single-Phase Overhead Lines

The arrangement of conductors for the single-phase overhead line configuration is shown in Fig. 8-6. A line length of 1 mile is assumed for the calculations. The phase conductor is at position 1 and the neutral at position N. The receiving end voltage will be calculated assuming that phase A and the neutral are present. The current in phase A and the neutral will be designated $\mathbf{I}_{A'}$ and $\mathbf{I}_N$, respectively. The results will be similar regardless of which phase is actually present.

The receiving end voltages for the phase and neutral are

$$\mathbf{V}_{A'} = \mathbf{V}_A - [\mathbf{I}_A\mathbf{Z}_{11} + \mathbf{I}_N\mathbf{Z}_{1N}] \tag{8.44}$$

$$\mathbf{V}_{N'} = 0 = \mathbf{I}_N\mathbf{Z}_{NN} + \mathbf{I}_A\mathbf{Z}_{1N} \tag{8.45}$$

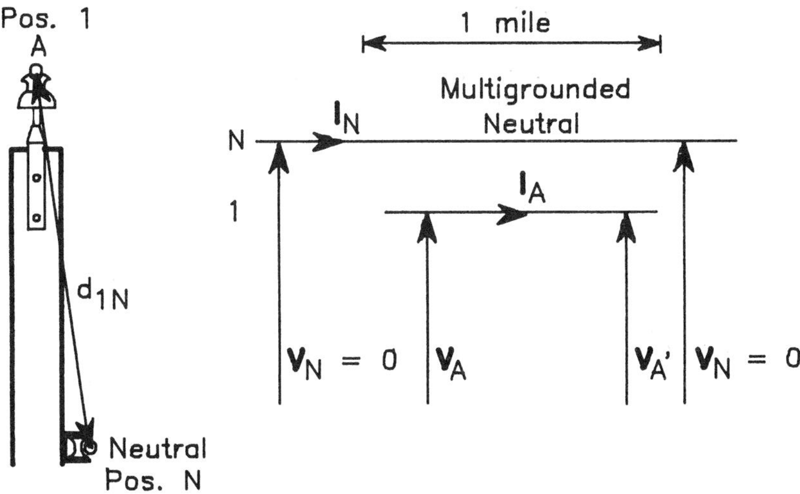

Figure 8-6 Single-phase overhead line.

where

$$\mathbf{Z}_{11} = R_\phi + 0.0954\frac{f}{60} + j0.2794\frac{f}{60}\log_{10}\left(\frac{D_e}{GMR_\phi}\right)\ \Omega \tag{8.46}$$

$$\mathbf{Z}_{1N} = 0.0954\frac{f}{60} + j0.2794\frac{f}{60}\log_{10}\left(\frac{D_e}{d_{1N}}\right)\ \Omega \tag{8.47}$$

$$\mathbf{Z}_{NN} = R_N + 0.0954\frac{f}{60} + j0.2794\frac{f}{60}\log_{10}\left(\frac{D_e}{GMR_N}\right)\ \Omega \tag{8.48}$$

Solving Eq. (8.45) for $\mathbf{I}_N$ results in

$$\mathbf{I}_N = -\frac{\mathbf{I}_A\mathbf{Z}_{1N}}{\mathbf{Z}_{NN}} \tag{8.49}$$

Substituting Eq. (8.49) into (8.44) results in

$$\mathbf{V}_{A'} = \mathbf{V}_A - \mathbf{I}_A\left(\mathbf{Z}_{11} - \frac{\mathbf{Z}_{1N}^2}{\mathbf{Z}_{NN}}\right) \tag{8.50}$$

Equation (8.50) gives the receiving end voltage for a 1-mile section of line.
The magnitude of the voltage drop is

$$|\mathbf{V}_{\text{drop}}| = |\mathbf{V}_A| - |\mathbf{V}_{A'}| \tag{8.51}$$

Expressed as a percentage of nominal, the voltage-drop factor is calculated as

$$\%V_{\text{drop}} = \frac{|\mathbf{V}_A| - |\mathbf{V}_{A'}|}{|\mathbf{V}_A|}\cdot 100 \tag{8.52}$$

EXAMPLE 8-7

Calculate the voltage-drop factor for a single-phase overhead line consisting of a #4 ACSR, 7/1 stranding, phase conductor, and a #4 ACSR, 7/1 stranding, neutral conductor. The line to neutral voltage is 7200 V. The separation between the phase conductor and neutral is 72 in. Assume an earth resistivity of 100 Ω-m and an operating frequency of 60 Hz. Calculate for **(a)** unity and **(b)** 0.8 lagging power factor.

Solution From Appendix A, the resistance and GMR_ϕ of the #4 ACSR are

$$R_\phi = R_N = 2.7403\ \Omega/\text{mile}$$

$$GMR_\phi = GMR_N = 0.00452\ \text{ft}$$

The depth of the equivalent earth return is

$$D_e = 2160\left(\frac{100}{60}\right)^{1/2} = 2788.5\ \text{ft}$$

The distance between the phase conductor and neutral is

$$d_{1N} = 72\ \text{in.} = 6.0\ \text{ft}$$

Applying Eqs. (8.46), (8.48), and (8.49) results in

$$\mathbf{Z}_{11} = 2.7403 + 0.0954 + j0.2794 \log_{10}\left(\frac{2788.5}{0.00452}\right)$$

$$= 2.8357 + j1.6178 \ \Omega/\text{mile}$$

$$\mathbf{Z}_{1N} = 0.0954 + j0.2794 \log_{10}\left(\frac{2788.5}{6.0}\right)$$

$$= 0.0954 + j0.7452 \ \Omega/\text{mile}$$

$$\mathbf{Z}_{NN} = 2.7403 + 0.0954 + j0.2794 \log_{10}\left(\frac{2788.5}{0.00452}\right)$$

$$= 2.8357 + j1.6178 \ \Omega/\text{mile}$$

a. The line current for a 1-MVA, unity power factor load at 7.2 kV is

$$\mathbf{I}_A = 138.9\angle 0° \text{ A}$$

Applying Eq. (8.50) results in

$$\mathbf{V}_{A'} = \mathbf{V}_A - \mathbf{I}_A\left(\mathbf{Z}_{11} - \frac{\mathbf{Z}_{1N}^2}{\mathbf{Z}_{NN}}\right)$$

$$= 7200\angle 0° - (138.9\angle 0°)(3.3165\angle 26.8°)$$

$$= 6792.0\angle -1.75° \text{ V}$$

The voltage-drop factor is

$$\%V_{\text{drop}} = \frac{408}{7200} \cdot 100 = 5.67\%/\text{MVA/mile}$$

b. The line current for a 1-MVA, 0.8 lagging power factor load at 7.2 kV is

$$\mathbf{I}_A = 138.9\angle -36.87° \text{ A}$$

Applying Eq. (8.50) results in

$$\mathbf{V}_{A'} = \mathbf{V}_A - \mathbf{I}_a\left(\mathbf{Z}_{11} - \frac{\mathbf{Z}_{1N}^2}{\mathbf{Z}_{NN}}\right)$$

$$= 7200\angle 0° - (138.9\angle -36.87°)(3.3165\angle 26.8°)$$

$$= 6746.9\angle 0.7° \text{ V}$$

The voltage-drop factor is

$$\%V_{\text{drop}} = \frac{453.1}{7200} \cdot 100 = 6.29\%/\text{MVA/mile}$$

Single-Phase Underground URD Concentric Neutral Cable Circuits

The arrangement of conductors for the single-phase underground line configuration is shown in Fig. 8-7. A circuit length of 1000 ft is assumed for the calculations. The phase conductor is at position 1 and the neutral at position 1′. The receiving end voltages will be calculated assuming that phase A is present. The current in phase A and the neutral will be designated $\mathbf{I}_{A'}$ and $\mathbf{I}_a$, respectively. As in the case of the single-phase overhead line, the results will be similar regardless of which phase is actually present.

The receiving end voltages for the phase and neutral are

$$\mathbf{V}_{A'} = \mathbf{V}_A - (\mathbf{I}_A\mathbf{Z}_{11} + \mathbf{I}_a\mathbf{Z}_{1'1}) \tag{8.53}$$

$$\mathbf{V}_{a'} = 0 = \mathbf{I}_A\mathbf{Z}_{1'1} + \mathbf{I}_a\mathbf{Z}_{1'1'} \tag{8.54}$$

where

$$\mathbf{Z}_{11} = R_\phi + 0.01807\,\frac{f}{60} + j0.0529\,\frac{f}{60}\,\log_{10}\!\left(\frac{D_e}{GMR_\phi}\right)\quad \Omega \tag{8.55}$$

$$\mathbf{Z}_{1'1} = 0.01807\,\frac{f}{60} + j0.0529\,\frac{f}{60}\,\log_{10}\!\left(\frac{D_e}{d_{1'1}}\right)\quad \Omega \tag{8.56}$$

$$\mathbf{Z}_{1'1'} = R_N + 0.01807\,\frac{f}{60} + j0.0529\,\frac{f}{60}\,\log_{10}\!\left(\frac{D_e}{GMR_N}\right)\quad \Omega \tag{8.57}$$

Solving Eq. (8.54) for $\mathbf{I}_a$ results in

$$\mathbf{I}_a = -\frac{\mathbf{I}_A\mathbf{Z}_{1'1}}{\mathbf{Z}_{1'1'}} \tag{8.58}$$

Substituting Eq. (8.58) into (8.53) results in

$$\mathbf{V}_{A'} = \mathbf{V}_A - \mathbf{I}_A\left(\mathbf{Z}_{11} - \frac{\mathbf{Z}_{1'1}^2}{\mathbf{Z}_{1'1'}}\right) \tag{8.59}$$

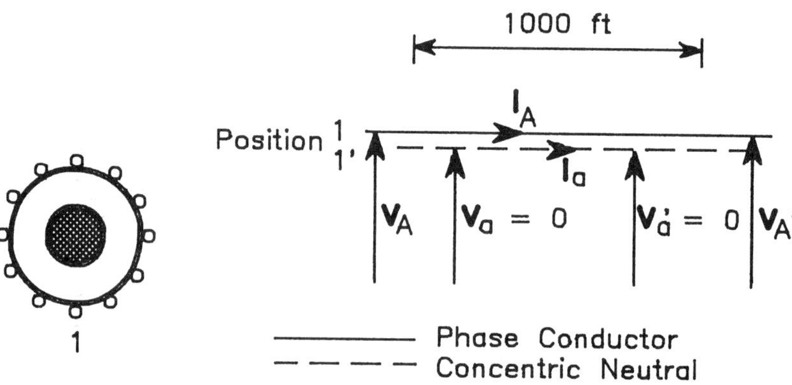

Figure 8-7 Single-phase underground cable.

Equation (8.59) gives the receiving end voltage at the end of the 1000-ft cable section. The magnitude of the voltage drop is

$$|\mathbf{V}_{\text{drop}}| = |\mathbf{V}_A| - |\mathbf{V}_{A'}| \qquad \textbf{(8.60)}$$

Expressed as a percentage of nominal, the voltage-drop factor is calculated as

$$\%V_{\text{drop}} = \frac{|\mathbf{V}_A| - |\mathbf{V}_{A'}|}{|\mathbf{V}_A|} \cdot 100 \qquad \textbf{(8.61)}$$

EXAMPLE 8-8

Calculate the voltage-drop factor for a #2 aluminum, 7-strand, 15-kV, 100% insulation URD cable. The circuit operates at 7.2 kV line to neutral. Express the voltage-drop factor in percent per MVA per 1000 ft.

Solution From the cable data of Appendix A,

$$r_{CN} = 0.429 \text{ in.}$$

The geometric mean radius of the neutral strands is

$$GMR_N \approx r_{CN} = 0.429 \text{ in.}$$

The geometric mean radius of the phase conductor is

$$GMR_\phi = 0.1060 \text{ in.}$$

The resistances of the phase and neutral are

$$R_\phi = 0.3334\ \Omega/1000 \text{ ft}, \qquad R_N = 0.3195\ \Omega/1000 \text{ ft}$$

The distance between the center of the phase conductor and the neutral conductors is

$$d_{1'1} = r_{CN} = 0.429 \text{ in.}$$

The depth of the equivalent ground return conductor is

$$D_e = 2160 \cdot ({}^{100}\!/\!_{60})^{1/2} = = 2788.5 \text{ ft} = 33{,}462 \text{ in.}$$

From Eqs. (8.55), (8.56), and (8.57),

$$\mathbf{Z}_{11} = 0.3334 + 0.01807\,\frac{60}{60} + j0529\,\frac{60}{60}\log_{10}\frac{33{,}462}{0.1060}$$

$$= 0.3515 + j0.2909 = 0.4563\angle 39.6^\circ\ \Omega/1000 \text{ ft}$$

$$\mathbf{Z}_{1'1} = 0.01807\,\frac{60}{60} + j0.0529\,\frac{60}{60}\log_{10}\frac{33{,}462}{0.429}$$

$$= 0.01807 + j0.2588 = 0.2594\angle 86^\circ\ \Omega/1000 \text{ ft}$$

$$\mathbf{Z}_{1'1'} = 0.3195 + 0.01807\,\frac{60}{60} + j0.0529\,\frac{60}{60}\log_{10}\frac{33{,}462}{0.429}$$

$$= 0.3376 + j0.2588 = 0.4254\angle 37.5^\circ\ \Omega/1000 \text{ ft}$$

a. At unity power factor, the line current for a 1 MVA of load at 7.2 kV is

$$\mathbf{I}_A = 138.9\angle 0^\circ \text{ A}$$

Applying Eq. (8.59),

$$\mathbf{V}_{A'} = 7200\angle 0^\circ - 138.9\angle 0^\circ\left[0.4563\angle 39.6^\circ - \frac{(0.2594\angle 86^\circ)^2}{0.4254\angle 37.5^\circ}\right]$$
$$= 7200\angle 0^\circ - (138.9\angle 0^\circ)\cdot(0.4955\angle 21.1^\circ)$$
$$= 7135.8\angle -0.2^\circ \text{ V}$$

The voltage-drop factor is

$$\%V_{\text{drop}} = \frac{64.2}{7200}\cdot 100 = 0.892\%/\text{MVA}/1000 \text{ ft}$$

b. At 1 MVA, 0.8 lagging power factor, the line current is

$$\mathbf{I}_A = 138.9\angle -36.9^\circ \text{ A}$$

Applying Eq. (8.59),

$$\mathbf{V}_{A'} = 7200\angle 0^\circ - (138.9\angle -36.9^\circ)\cdot(0.4955\angle 21.1^\circ)$$
$$= 7133.8\angle 0.15^\circ \text{ V}$$

The voltage-drop factor is

$$\%V_{\text{drop}} = \frac{66.2}{7200}\cdot 100 = 0.919\%/\text{MVA}/1000 \text{ ft}$$

Low-Voltage Services

Voltage-drop factors can also be calculated for low-voltage (less than 600 V) secondaries and services. Since these secondaries and services involve relatively short lengths of cable and small apparent power loads, the voltage-drop factors are calculated in units of percent per kVA per 100 ft of length. The following example illustrates the procedure.

EXAMPLE 8-9

Calculate voltage-drop factors for the service cable of Example 7-4 for **(a)** unity and **(b)** 0.8 lagging power factor. Assume a service voltage of 120/240 V, three phase, three wire.

Solution

a. The load current for a 1-kVA, 240-V, unity power factor load is

$$\mathbf{I} = (1000 \text{ VA}/240 \text{ V})\angle 0^\circ = 4.17\angle 0^\circ \text{ A}$$

From Example 7-4, the cable impedance is

$$\mathbf{Z} = 0.04 + j0.005643\ \Omega/100 \text{ ft}$$

The voltage at the receiving end of the cable is

$$\mathbf{V}' = 240\angle 0° - (4.17\angle 0°)(0.04 + j0.005643) \approx 239.8\angle 0°$$

The voltage-drop factor is

$$\%V_{\text{drop}} = \frac{0.2}{240} \cdot 100 = 0.083\%/\text{kVA}/100 \text{ ft}$$

b. At 0.8 lagging power factor, the current is

$$\mathbf{I} = 4.17\angle -36.9° \text{ A}$$

The voltage at the receiving end is

$$\mathbf{V}' = 240\angle 0° - (4.17\angle -36.9°)(0.04 + j0.005643) \approx 239.9\angle 0°$$

The voltage-drop factor is

$$\%V_{\text{drop}} = \frac{0.1}{240} \cdot 100 = 0.042\%/\text{kVA}/100 \text{ ft}$$

EXAMPLE 8-10

Calculate voltage-drop factors for the service cable of Example 7-6 for **(a)** unity and **(b)** 0.8 lagging power factors. Assume a service voltage of 208Y/120 V, three phase, four wire.

Solution

a. At unity power factor, the load current for a three-phase, 1-kVA load at 208 V is

$$\mathbf{I} = 2.78\angle 0° \text{ A}$$

From Example 7-6, the cable impedance is

$$\mathbf{Z} = 0.00999 + j0.0026445 \ \Omega/100 \text{ ft}$$

The voltage at the receiving end of the cable is

$$\mathbf{V}' = 120\angle 0° - (2.78\angle 0°)(0.00999 + j0.0026445) \approx 119.97\angle 0°$$

The voltage-drop factor is

$$\%V_{\text{drop}} = \frac{0.03}{120} \cdot 100 = 0.025\%/\text{kVA}/100 \text{ ft}$$

b. At 0.8 lagging power factor, the load current is

$$\mathbf{I} = 2.78\angle -36.9° \text{ A}$$

The voltage at the receiving end is

$$\mathbf{V}' = 120\angle 0° - (2.78\angle -36.9°)(0.00999 + j0.0026445) \approx 119.98\angle 0°$$

The voltage-drop factor is

$$\%V_{\text{drop}} = \frac{0.02}{120} \cdot 100 = 0.0167\%/\text{kVA}/100 \text{ ft}$$

8-4 Transformer Voltage Drop

Another significant source of voltage drop in a power system is the voltage drop through transformers. The voltage drop through a transformer can be calculated by using the percent resistance and percent inductive reactance. The resistance and reactance can be referred to either the high- or low-voltage side. Typically, the excitation branch of the transformer equivalent circuit is neglected when performing voltage-drop calculations. Voltage-drop calculations for single- and three-phase transformers will be presented in this section.

Three-Phase Transformers

The voltage drop for a three-phase transformer will be calculated assuming that the resistance and inductive reactance are equal in all three phases. Therefore, the voltage drop can be calculated on a single-phase line to neutral equivalent basis, using the A phase as a reference. The method presented also applies to three identical single-phase transformers connected in a bank to supply balanced three-phase loads. This method will *not* apply to the open or closed delta banks discussed in Chapter 6.

The single-phase equivalent circuit with all parameters referred to the low-voltage side is shown in Fig. 8-8. Assuming a constant current representation for the load and applying Kirchhoff's voltage law around the secondary results in

$$\mathbf{E}_{\mathrm{LS}} = \mathbf{V}_{\mathrm{LS}} + \mathbf{I}_{\mathrm{LS}} \cdot (R_{\mathrm{LS,eq}} + jX_{\mathrm{LS,eq}}) \tag{8.62}$$

where

$\mathbf{E}_{\mathrm{LS}}$ = induced voltage on low-voltage side
$\mathbf{V}_{\mathrm{LS}}$ = terminal voltage on low-voltage side
$\mathbf{I}_{\mathrm{LS}}$ = load current on low-voltage side
$R_{\mathrm{LS,eq}}$ = equivalent resistance referred to low-voltage side
$X_{\mathrm{LS,eq}}$ = equivalent reactance referred to low-voltage side

For the purposes of voltage-drop calculation, the terminal voltage on the low-voltage side will be selected as reference. In addition, the magnitude of the terminal

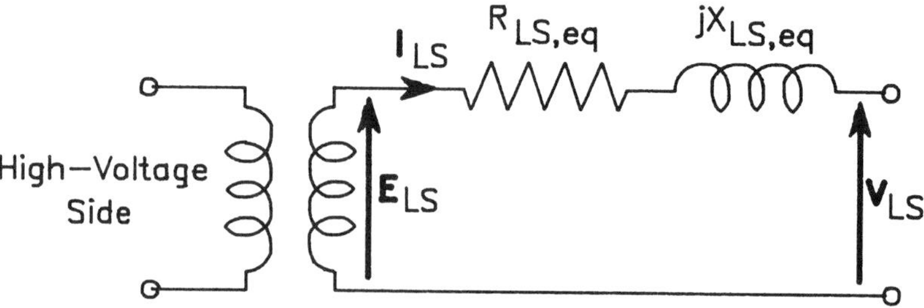

Figure 8-8 Transformer single-phase equivalent circuit.

voltage on the low side will be assumed equal to the rated low voltage of the transformer. The voltage drop through the transformer expressed as a percentage of rated voltage is

$$\%V_{\text{drop}} = \frac{|\mathbf{E}_{\text{LS}}| - |\mathbf{V}_{\text{LS}}|}{|\mathbf{V}_{\text{LS}}|} \cdot 100 \tag{8.63}$$

Note that the voltage drop expressed as a percentage of rated voltage is equal to the percent regulation of the transformer.

EXAMPLE 8-11

Determine the percent of voltage drop for a 500-kVA, 12.47-kV–480Y/277-V, three-phase transformer having a resistance of 1.3% and a reactance of 7%. Calculate for the following load conditions:

a. Full load, unity power factor
b. Full load, 0.8 lagging power factor
c. Full load, 0.8 leading power factor

Solution For all three load conditions, the equivalent resistance and reactance will be expressed in ohms referred to the low-voltage side. The base impedance on the low-voltage side is

$$Z_{\text{Base}} = \frac{480^2}{500{,}000} = 0.4608\ \Omega$$

The resistance and reactance are

$$R_{\text{LS,eq}} = 0.013 \cdot 0.4608 = 0.006\ \Omega$$
$$X_{\text{LS,eq}} = 0.070 \cdot 0.4608 = 0.0323\ \Omega$$

The reference voltage on the low-voltage side is

$$\mathbf{V}_{\text{LS}} = 277\angle 0^\circ\ \text{V}$$

a. The magnitude of the load current on the low-voltage side is

$$|\mathbf{I}_{\text{LS}}| = \frac{500{,}000\ \text{VA}}{\sqrt{3} \cdot 480\ \text{V}} = 601.4\ \text{A}$$

At unity power factor, the current and voltage are in phase. Therefore,

$$\mathbf{I}_{\text{LS}} = 601.4\angle 0^\circ\ \text{A}$$

Applying Eq. (8.62),

$$\begin{aligned}\mathbf{E}_{\text{LS}} &= 277\angle 0^\circ + 601.4\angle 0^\circ(0.006 + j0.0323)\\ &= 277\angle 0^\circ + 19.76\angle 79.5^\circ\\ &= 280.6 + j19.42\\ &= 281.26\angle 3.93^\circ\ \text{V}\end{aligned}$$

The voltage drop is

$$\%V_{drop} = \frac{281.28 - 277}{277} \cdot 100 = 1.545\%$$

b. At full load, 0.8 lagging power factor, the load current is

$$\mathbf{I}_{LS} = 601.4\angle -36.87° \text{ A}$$

Applying Eq. (8.62),

$$\begin{aligned}\mathbf{E}_{LS} &= 277\angle 0° + 601.4\angle -36.87°(0.006 + j0.0323)\\ &= 277\angle 0° + 19.76\angle 42.63°\\ &= 291.54 + j13.38\\ &= 291.85\angle 2.63° \text{ V}\end{aligned}$$

The voltage drop is

$$\%V_{drop} = \frac{291.85 - 277}{277} \cdot 100 = 5.36\%$$

c. At full load, 0.8 leading power factor, the load current is

$$\mathbf{I}_{LS} = 601.4\angle 36.87° \text{ A}$$

Applying Eq. (8.62),

$$\begin{aligned}\mathbf{E}_{LS} &= 277\angle 0° + 601.4\angle 36.87°(0.006 + j0.0323)\\ &= 277\angle 0° + 19.76\angle 116.37°\\ &= 268.2 + j17.7\\ &= 268.8\angle 3.78° \text{ V}\end{aligned}$$

The voltage drop is

$$\%V_{drop} = \frac{268.8 - 277}{277} \cdot 100 = -2.97\%$$

The results of Example 8-11 indicate that the voltage drop is a function of both power factor and load on the transformer. Note also that a negative voltage drop implies that the voltage actually rises as load is applied to the transformer.

Single-Phase Transformers

Voltage-drop calculations for single-phase distribution transformers supplying single-phase services are similar to the voltage-drop calculations for three-phase transformers. The following example illustrates the calculation.

EXAMPLE 8-12

Determine the percent of voltage drop for a 25-kVA, 7.2-kV–120/240-V, single-phase transformer having a resistance of 1.3% and a reactance of 2%. Calculate for the following load conditions:

a. Full load, unity power factor
b. Full load, 0.8 lagging power factor
c. Full load, 0.8 leading power factor

Solution For all three load conditions, the equivalent resistance and reactance will be expressed in ohms referred to the low-voltage side. The base impedance is

$$Z_{\text{Base}} = \frac{240^2}{25{,}000} = 2.304\ \Omega$$

The resistance and reactance are

$$R_{\text{LS,eq}} = 0.013 \cdot 2.304 = 0.03\ \Omega$$

$$X_{\text{LS,eq}} = 0.020 \cdot 2.304 = 0.0461\ \Omega$$

The reference voltage on the low-voltage side is selected as

$$\mathbf{V}_{\text{LS}} = 240\angle 0^\circ\ \text{V}$$

a. The magnitude of the load current on the low-voltage side is

$$|\mathbf{I}_{\text{LS}}| = \frac{25{,}000}{240} = 104.2\ \text{A}$$

At unity power factor, the current and voltage are in phase. Therefore,

$$\mathbf{I}_{\text{LS}} = 104.2\angle 0^\circ\ \text{A}$$

Applying Eq. (8.62),

$$\begin{aligned}\mathbf{E}_{\text{LS}} &= 240\angle 0^\circ + 104.2\angle 0^\circ(0.03 + j0.0461)\\ &= 240\angle 0^\circ + 5.73\angle 56.9^\circ\\ &= 243.1 + j4.8\\ &= 243.1\angle 1.13^\circ\ \text{V}\end{aligned}$$

The voltage drop is

$$\%V_{\text{drop}} = \frac{243.1 - 240}{240} \cdot 100 = 1.3\%$$

b. At full load, 0.8 lagging power factor, the load current is

$$\mathbf{I}_{\text{LS}} = 104.2\angle -36.87^\circ\ \text{A}$$

Applying Eq. (8.62),

$$\mathbf{E}_{LS} = 240\angle 0° + 104.2\angle -36.87°(0.03 + j0.0461)$$
$$= 245.4\angle 0.45° \text{ V}$$

The voltage drop is

$$\%V_{drop} = \frac{245.4 - 240}{240} \cdot 100 = 2.25\%$$

c. At full load, 0.8 leading power factor, the load current is

$$\mathbf{I}_{LS} = 104.2\angle 36.87° \text{ A}$$

Applying Eq. (8.62),

$$\mathbf{E}_{LS} = 240\angle 0° + 104.2\angle 36.87°(0.03 + j0.0461)$$
$$= 240\angle 0° + 5.73\angle 93.74°$$
$$= 239.7\angle 1.4° \text{ V}$$

The voltage drop is

$$\%V_{drop} = \frac{239.7 - 240}{240} \cdot 100 = -0.125\%$$

8-5 Transmission System Regulation and Load Flow

The voltage on the transmission and subtransmission system is regulated primarily through the use of generator terminal voltage regulation. Recall that the terminal voltage of a synchronous generator is adjusted by means of the dc field excitation. Increasing the dc field current will raise the generator terminal voltage and increase the reactive power output of the generator. Consequently, the transmission system bus to which the generator is connected will also experience an increase in voltage. Likewise, decreasing the dc field current will result in a lowering of the transmission system voltage in the vicinity of the plant.

In addition to generator voltage control, power capacitors may be installed at certain buses in the system. These capacitors supply a certain amount of reactive power to the transmission network. The result is an increase in voltage on the transmission system in the vicinity of the capacitor location.

One disadvantage of power capacitors is that the amount of reactive compensation is not continuously adjustable. In the past, synchronous condensers were used to supply a variable amount of reactive power, thereby regulating system voltage. A synchronous condenser is essentially a synchronous motor with no provisions for connecting a mechanical load, that is, no output shaft. The reactive power output and terminal voltage were regulated by adjustment of the dc field in a manner similar to the synchronous generator. Although synchronous condensers are not frequently used, older installations

```
                                        LINE AND TRANSFORMER INPUT DATA

X---FROM BUS---X X---TO BUS---X IMPEDANCE (%) LINE CHRG X-----LOAD TAP CHANGING XFMR-----X X-PHASE SHIFTING XFMR-X  RATINGS
 NO.     NAME     NO.    NAME      R      X       MVA     TAP    TMIN    TMAX  NUM CONT VOLTS  SHIFT  SMIN  SMAX  MW  NORM  EMER
---- ----------- ---- --------- ------ ------ --------- ----- ------ ------ --- ---- -----  -----  ----  ---- ---- ----  ----
 102   MAPLE138  105     OAK138  0.125  0.359      2.56                                                                150   180
 546     OAK138  235    PINE138  0.237  0.765      3.24                                                                100   135
 102   MAPLE138  539   MAPLE69   0.500 14.000      0.00 0.972  0.972  0.972      102 1.000                                45    45

~~~~~~~~~~~~~~~~~~~~~~~~~~~~~~~~~~~~~~~~~~~~~~~~~~~~~~~~~~~~~~~~~~~~~~~~~~~~~~~~~~~~~~~~~~~~~~~~~~~~~~~~~~~~~~~~~~~~~~~~~~~~~~

                                              BUS INPUT DATA

X----BUS IDEN----X    BUS    PHASE  X---BUS LOAD---X X-------------BUS GENERATION-------------X X--STATIC MVAR--X
 NO.     NAME        VOLTS   ANGLE    MW      MVAR     MW     MVAR   MIN--LIMITS--MAX  CONT  VOLTS  VOLTAGE     MVAR
---- ------------  -------  -----  ------  -------- ------ ------ -------- -------- ----  -----  ---------  ------
102      MAPLE138     1.00   -2.5   25.0      10.0
546        OAK138     1.02   -0.7   10.0       5.0  100.0   10.0  -50.0       75.0  546   1.05
269         ASH69     0.98   -3.5   23.0      20.0                                                 69.0        8.4
~~~~~~~~~~~~~~~~~~~~~~~~~~~~~~~~~~~~~~~~~~~~~~~~~~~~~~~~~~~~~~~~~~~~~~~~~~~~~~~~~~~~~~~~~~~~~~~~~~~~~~~~~~~~~~~~~~~~~~~~~~~~~~

~~~~~~~~~~~~~~~~~~~~~~~~~~~~~~~~~~~~~~~~~~~~~~~~~~~~~~~~~~~~~~~~~~~~~~~~~~~~~~~~~~~~~~~~~~~~~~~~~~~~~~~~~~~~~~~~~~~~~~~~~~~~~~

                                              BUS OUTPUT DATA

X---------------------------------BUS DATA----------------------------------------X X------------LINE FLOWS------------X
                                              X---GENERATION---X  X-----LOAD-----X  CAP/REAC   TO
 NO.    NAME           VOLTS       ANGLE        MW       MVAR        MW      MVAR     MVAR     BUS     NAME        MW     MVAR
---- ------------      -----       -----     --------  --------   -------- --------  -------- ------- ---------  -------- --------
 269          ASH69     0.98        -3.5        0.0       0.0       23.0     20.0      8.07    261    CHERRY69      25.9     3.8
                                                                                               262   HEMLOCK69     -12.6    -4.2
                                                                                               263    SPRUCE69      -5.4     1.0
                                                                                               264     CLARK69      25.9     3.9
                                                                                               265    MERCER69     -16.4    -8.5
                                                                                               266     CEDAR69     -17.4     4.0
                                                                                             ====================================
```

Figure 8-9 Example of typical load flow program input and output.

may still exist. The modern approach to variable reactive compensation is through the use of static VAR compensators. These devices use power electronic switching devices to precisely control the amount of reactive power supplied to the system.

Typically, the active power generation and voltage output of the generating units are controlled by *automatic generation control,* or AGC, from a system control center. A voltage schedule is often made available to generating plant personnel so that local dispatching can be made in the event of a loss of communications between the generating plant and system control center.

To calculate the voltage levels on the transmission system, a load flow program is commonly used. The load flow calculation is an iterative solution to a system of nonlinear equations. Several techniques are used including Gauss–Seidel, Newton–Raphson, fast decoupled, and dc equivalent. At each iteration, the results converge toward the final solution. Load flows are commonly used in system planning and operational studies and are usually done off line. Specific details of load flow algorithms and solution techniques are beyond the scope of this text.

Input to the load flow program includes line and transformer impedances, generator active power schedule, generator voltage schedule, bus loading, transformer tap settings, phase angle regulator settings, and capacitor ratings. Output from the load flow program includes the voltage magnitude and phase angle at each bus in the system, line flows, and transformer loading. Figure 8-9 shows representive input and output for a load flow program.

Load flow programs are generally not suitable for real-time control of the power system. A different type of program, referred to as a *state estimator,* processes real-time telemetered data to obtain an estimate of the bus voltages and line flows throughout the power system. The state estimator typically uses a least-squares solution to the nonlinear system equations to minimize the effect of metering errors and to detect bad data points. Results of the state estimator are passed down to the AGC system to facilitate real-time control of the system.

8-6 Distribution System Regulation

The voltage of distribution circuits in the medium-voltage range (5 to 35 kV) is regulated by either induction or, more commonly, step voltage regulators. A step voltage regulator is basically an autotransformer with a common winding and a tapped series winding. A reversing switch enables the series winding to be connected for either raising or lowering of the line voltage. The number of taps depends on the percentage of increment in voltage regulation resolution desired per step. Typically, step voltage regulators have 16 steps of ⅝% per step, for a total regulation range of $\pm 10\%$. Four step auto boosters with four $+2\frac{1}{2}\%$ taps for a regulation range of 0% to +10% are also available. Figure 8-10 shows the schematic diagram of a representive step voltage regulator. Figure 8-11 shows a typical step voltage regulator installation on a 12.47-kV distribution circuit exit.

Standard voltage and kVA ratings for three-phase and single-phase step voltage regulators are shown in Tables 8-1 and 8-2. The kVA rating of a regulator is defined to

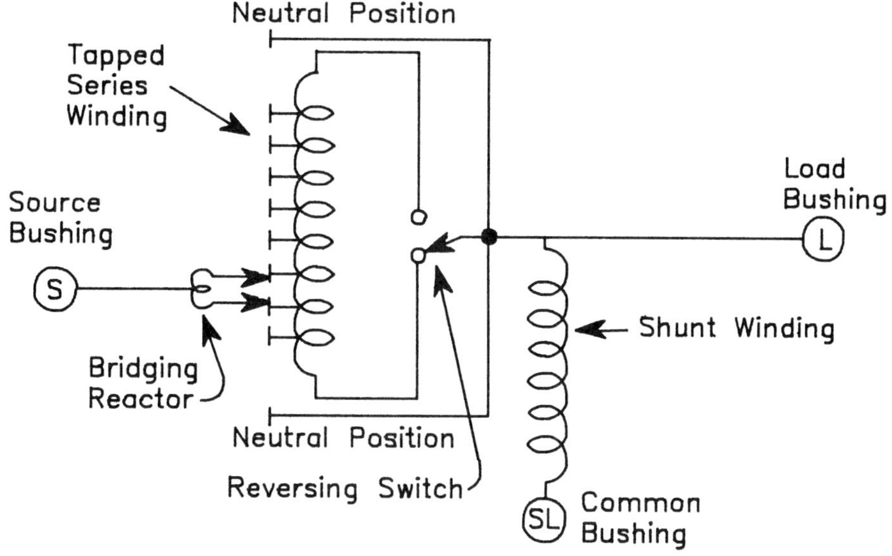

Figure 8-10 Schematic diagram of step voltage regulator.

Figure 8-11 Group of three single-phase step-voltage regulators on 12.47-kV distribution circuit exit. (Photo Courtesy of Ohio Edison Company)

Table 8-1 Standard Voltage and kVA Ratings, Single-Phase Step Voltage Regulators

System Voltage	*kVA*	*Line Amperes*
2400/4160Y	50	200
	75	300
	100	400
	125	500
	167	668
	250	1000
	333	1332
4800/8320Y	50	100
	75	150
	100	200
	125	250
	167	334
	250	500
	333	668
7620/13,200Y	38.1	50
	57.2	75
	76.2	100
	114.3	150
	167	219
	250	328
	333	438
	416	546
	509	668
	667	875
	833	1093
13,800	69	50
	138	100
	207	150
	276	200
	414	300
	552	400
14,400/24,940Y	72	50
	144	100
	216	150
	288	200
	333	231
	432	300
	576	400
	667	463
	833	578
19,920/34,500Y	100	50
	200	100
	333	167
	400	201
	667	334
	833	418

Derived from IEEE Std. C57.15-1986, *IEEE Standard Requirements, Terminology, and Test Code for Step-Voltage and Induction-Voltage Regulators* (Reaff, 1992), © 1986.

Table 8-2 Standard Voltage and kVA Ratings, Three-Phase Step Voltage Regulators

Voltage	*Self-Cooled/ Force-Cooled, kVA*	*Self-Cooled/ Force-Cooled, Amperes*
2400	500/625	1155/1443
	750/937	1732/2165
	1000/1250	2309/2887
2400/4160Y	500/625	667/833
	750/937	1000/1250
	1000/1250	1334/1667
4800	500/625	557/721
	750/937	866/1082
	1000/1250	1155/1443
7620/13,200Y	500/625	219/274
	750/937	328/410
	1000/1250	437/546
	1500/2000	656/874
	2000/2667	874/1166
7970/13,800Y	500/625	209/261
	750/937	313/391
	1000/1250	418/523
	1500/2000	628/837
	2000/2667	837/1166
	2500/3333	1046/1394
14,400/24,940Y	500/625	125.5/156.8
	750/937	188.3/235.4
	1000/1250	251/314
	1500/2000	377/502
	2000/2667	502/669
	2500/3333	628/837
19,920/34,500Y	500/625	83.7/104.6
	750/937	125.5/156.8
	1000/1250	167/209
	1500/2000	251/335
	2000/2667	335/447
	2500/3333	418/557
26,560/46,000Y	500/625	62.8/78.5
	750/937	94.1/117.6
	1000/1250	126/157
	1500/2000	188/251
	2000/2667	251/335
	2500/3333	314/419
39,840/69,000Y	500/625	41.8/52.5
	750/937	62.8/78.5
	1000/1250	83.7/105
	1500/2000	126/167
	2000/2667	167/223
	2500/3333	209/278

Derived from IEEE Std. C57.15-1986, *IEEE Standard Requirements, Terminology, and Test Code for Step-Voltage and Induction-Voltage Regulators* (Reaff, 1992), © 1986.

be equal to the product of the rated load amperes and the regulation voltage range. For example, a single-phase, 7620-V, ±10%, 328-A regulator has a kVA rating of 10% · (7620) · (328)/1000 = 250 kVA. However, if this regulator is applied to a 12.47Y/7.2-kV multigrounded neutral distribution circuit, the maximum circuit loading will be 328 · (7200)/1000 = 2361.6 kVA per phase. It is important to note that the regulator kVA rating is substantially different from the maximum permissible circuit loading.

The single-phase voltage regulator is connected to the line through high-voltage bushings, similar to distribution transformers. The phase conductor on the source side of the regulator is connected to the bushing marked **S**. The phase conductor on the load side is connected to the bushing marked **L**. The multigrounded system neutral is connected to the bushing marked **SL**.

Three-phase voltage regulators are connected to the phase conductors on the source side through bushings $\mathbf{S_1}$, $\mathbf{S_2}$, and $\mathbf{S_3}$. The phase conductors on the load side of the regulator are connected to bushings $\mathbf{L_1}$, $\mathbf{L_2}$, and $\mathbf{L_3}$. If a neutral connection is to be made to the regulator, a bushing labeled $\mathbf{S_0L_0}$ is provided.

To remove a regulator from service for repair or maintenance, it is necessary to bypass the regulator in order to maintain continuity of service. A special switch, referred to as a regulator bypass switch, is available to enable bypassing of the regulator in one-switch operation. Figure 8-12 shows a schematic representation of the bypass switch. It is also possible to use three separate switches to perform the desired switching operation. The bypass switch consists of three sets of contacts: one set on the source side, one set on the load side, and a set to short out the series winding. Normal operation of the regulator requires that the source and load side contacts be closed and the bypass contact open. If it is desired to bypass the regulator, the tap mechanism

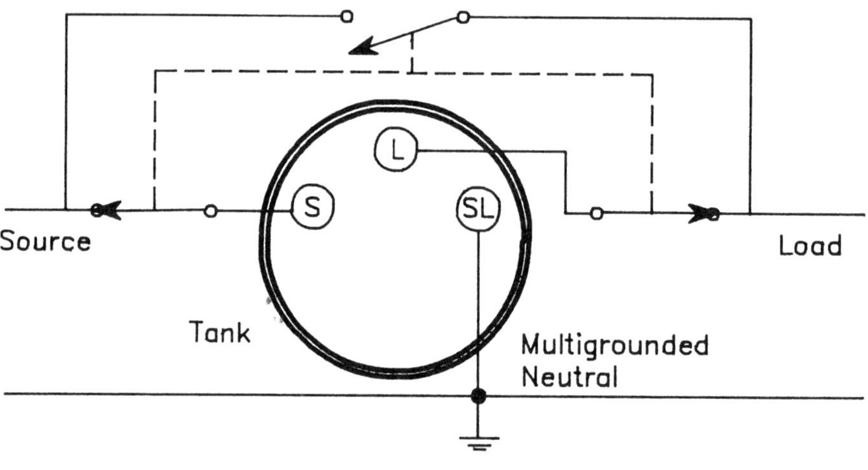

Figure 8-12 Single-phase regulator bypass switches.

must be set to the neutral position. Operating the bypass switch will cause the bypass contact to make *before* the source and load side contacts break. The regulator may now be removed from service.

NOTE: Failure to set the tap mechanism to neutral before operating the bypass switch will result in short circuiting of the series winding. This may cause damage to the regulator, or injury to personnel!

Step voltage regulators are normally equipped with a voltage transformer and current transformer to sense the voltage and current on the load side of the regulator. The voltage transformer turns ratio is selected to provide a 120-V output with nominal system voltage applied. Current transformer ratios are selected to provide a 1-A output with rated current flowing in the primary. The voltage sensing unit will examine the actual voltage on the distribution circuit and compare it to the set point of the control. The set point is typically adjustable from 108 to 132 V. The actual circuit voltage is related to the set point by the voltage transformer ratio. Corrective action is taken to raise or lower the output voltage to the desired value. To prevent excessive hunting of the regulator, an adjustable time delay (15 to 90 sec), and adjustable voltage bandwidth (1.5 to 3 V) are included in most regulator controls.

To regulate the voltage at a point on the distribution circuit remote from the regulator location, a line drop compensator is used. The function of the line drop compensator is to model the voltage drop that occurs on the distribution circuit due to the line impedance between the regulator location and the desired regulation point. The line drop compensator circuitry is shown in Fig. 8-13.

There are typically two adjustable settings on the line drop compensator; the resistance R and reactance X. The settings for both resistance and reactance are specified in terms of volts on a 120-V base. The range of adjustment is typically 0 to +24 V, which corresponds to 0% to +20% voltage. If no loads are tapped off the distribution

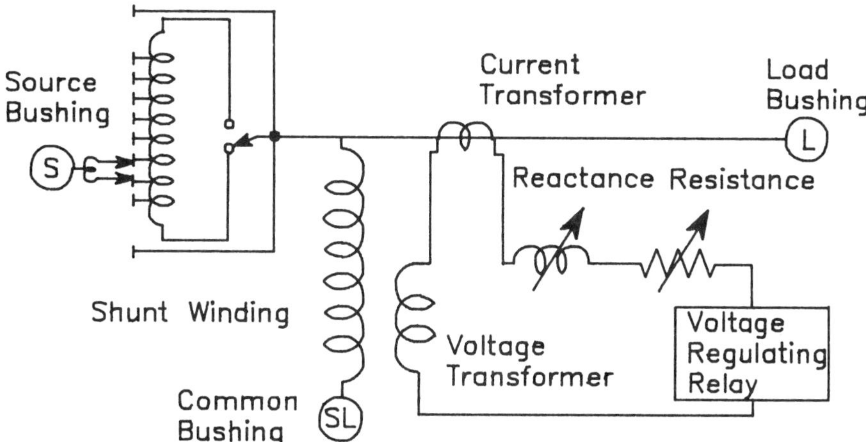

Figure 8-13 Line-drop compensator circuit.

circuit between the regulator location and the regulation point, the line drop compensator settings can be calculated from the following:

$$R_{\text{comp}} = R_{\text{line}} \cdot \frac{CT \text{ ratio}}{VT \text{ ratio}} \tag{8.64}$$

$$X_{\text{comp}} = X_{\text{line}} \cdot \frac{CT \text{ ratio}}{VT \text{ ratio}} \tag{8.65}$$

where

R_{line} = equivalent resistance of line from regulator location to regulation point in ohms

X_{line} = equivalent reactance of line from regulator location to regulation point in ohms

Since the *CT* ratio results in a secondary current of 1 A, Eqs. (8.64) and (8.65) also express the settings in terms of volts.

EXAMPLE 8-13

A three-phase distribution express feeder extends 3 miles from the distribution substation before reaching the first customer. The circuit is a 12.47Y/7.2-kV, multigrounded neutral system. The feeder circuit has a resistance of 0.621 Ω/mile and a reactance of 0.783 Ω/mile. Ammeters in the substation have indicated a peak circuit load of 5000 kVA. The existing regulators are to be replaced with single-phase step voltage regulators connected phase to neutral. Determine the voltage and kVA ratings of the new regulators. Also, determine the voltage set point and resistance and reactance settings of the line drop compensator to regulate the voltage at the regulation point to 126 V. Assume that the following *CT* ratios are available: 50:1, 100:1, 200:1, 300:1, 400:1, and 500:1.

Solution The line current magnitude for 5000 kVA at 12.47 kV is

$$I = \frac{5000 \text{ kVA}}{\sqrt{3} \cdot 12.47 \text{ kV}} = 231.5 \text{ A}$$

From Table 8-1, 250-kVA, 328-A, 7620-V regulators are required. Note that even though the system voltage is 7200 V line to neutral, 7620 V is a standard rating. The voltage transformer ratio is selected to give 120 V with nominal system voltage applied. Therefore,

$$VT \text{ ratio} = \frac{7200}{120} = 60:1$$

For a 328-A regulator, the *CT* ratio is 400:1. The equivalent resistance of the line is

$$R_{\text{line}} = 3 \text{ miles} \cdot 0.621 \ \Omega/\text{mile} = 1.863 \ \Omega$$

The equivalent reactance is

$$X_{\text{line}} = 3 \text{ miles} \cdot 0.783 \ \Omega/\text{mile} = 2.349 \ \Omega$$

The line resistance and reactance referred to the line drop compensator circuit are

$$R_{comp} = 1.863 \cdot \frac{400}{60} = 12.42\ \Omega$$

$$X_{comp} = 2.349 \cdot \frac{400}{60} = 15.66\ \Omega$$

Therefore, the resistance and reactance settings are 12.42 and 15.66 V, respectively. The voltage regulating relay is set at 126 V.

8-7 Transformer Taps

Generator step up, station auxiliary power, transmission, subtransmission, and distribution substation transformers are commonly specified to have taps on either the high- or low-voltage winding. In some instances, three-phase distribution transformers may have taps as well. It is far more common to specify taps on the high-voltage side, rather than the low-voltage side. The tap ratings are usually specified as a percentage above or below the nominal voltage rating of the winding. These taps may be fixed or adjustable by a load tap changing mechanism.

The presence of taps on a transformer winding essentially means that the transformer turns ratio is adjustable to the amount specified by the tap rating. As such, the output voltage of the transformer is adjustable by changing the tap. From Chapter 5, the transformer turns ratio was defined as

$$a = \frac{\text{rated high-side voltage}}{\text{rated low-side voltage}} \tag{5.24}$$

For transformers with tapped windings, the rated high- or low-side voltage will vary depending on the tap setting. The actual voltage on the low-voltage side under no load conditions is

$$V_{LS,act} = V_{HS,act} \cdot \frac{1}{a} \tag{8.66}$$

where $V_{HS,act}$ is the actual voltage applied to the high-voltage side of the transformer.

EXAMPLE 8-14 A 7500/9375 OA/FA, 69,000–12,470Y/7200-V, three-phase distribution substation transformer is equipped with taps on the high side at nominal, ±2.5%, and ±5%. From a transmission system load flow study, the actual voltage on the 69-kV subtransmission system at this location is 65.8-kV. Determine the actual voltage rating of each tap and the low-side voltage at no load (neglect transformer voltage drop) for each of the tap settings.

Solution The actual high-side voltage ratings for each tap are

$$+5\% \text{ Tap: } V = 1.05 \cdot 69 \text{ kV} = 72.5 \text{ kV}$$

$$+2.5\% \text{ Tap: } V = 1.025 \cdot 69 \text{ kV} = 70.7 \text{ kV}$$

$$\text{Nominal: } V = 1.0 \cdot 69 \text{ kV} = 69 \text{ kV}$$

$$-2.5\% \text{ Tap: } V = 0.975 \cdot 69 \text{ kV} = 67.3 \text{ kV}$$

$$-5 \text{ Tap: } V = 0.95 \cdot 69 \text{ kV} = 65.6 \text{ kV}$$

The actual voltages on the low-voltage side for each tap setting are determined by applying Eq. (8.66).

$$+5\% \text{ Tap: } V_{\text{LS}} = 65.8 \text{ kV} \cdot \frac{12.47}{72.5} = 11.32 \text{ kV} = 90.8\%$$

$$+2.5\% \text{ Tap: } V_{\text{LS}} = 65.8 \text{ kV} \cdot \frac{12.47}{70.7} = 11.61 \text{ kV} = 93.1\%$$

$$\text{Nominal: } V_{\text{LS}} = 65.8 \text{ kV} \cdot \frac{12.47}{69} = 11.89 \text{ kV} = 95.4\%$$

$$-2.5\% \text{ Tap: } V_{\text{LS}} = 65.8 \text{ kV} \cdot \frac{12.47}{67.3} = 12.19 \text{ kV} = 97.8\%$$

$$-5\% \text{ Tap: } V_{\text{LS}} = 65.8 \text{ kV} \cdot \frac{12.47}{65.6} = 12.51 \text{ kV} = 100.3\%$$

From Example 8-14, the 65.6-kV tap is probably the most desirable since it results in approximately 100% rated voltage on the low-voltage side. Bear in mind, however, that there will also be a voltage drop through the transformer under various load conditions. It is generally desirable to select the tap that will result in a bus voltage between 100% and 105% of nominal bus voltage under light load conditions.

8-8 Voltage Drop Due to Motor Starting

Special consideration must be given to the voltage drop or flicker that occurs on a power system due to large motor starting. As indicated in Table 2-1, the locked rotor kVA of a motor during starting is several times the normal full-load kVA. This large inrush current will cause a momentary dip in voltage as the motor comes up to speed. Voltage drop is especially large when starting large motors applied to systems having a relatively high source impedance. The voltage drop may be severe enough to cause control relay and motor start coils to drop out, television and CRT flicker, and other problems. Several methods are used to determine the magnitude of voltage drop due to motor starting.

The motor may be represented as a constant impedance load during starting, as shown in Fig. 8-14a. The voltage at any point in the system may be calculated by applying the voltage-divider rule to the equivalent circuit.

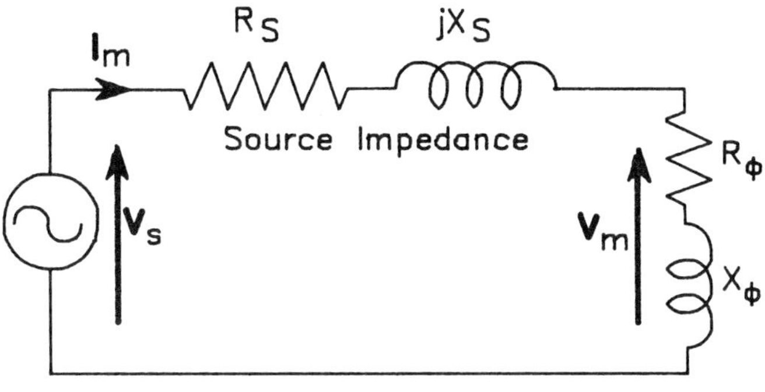

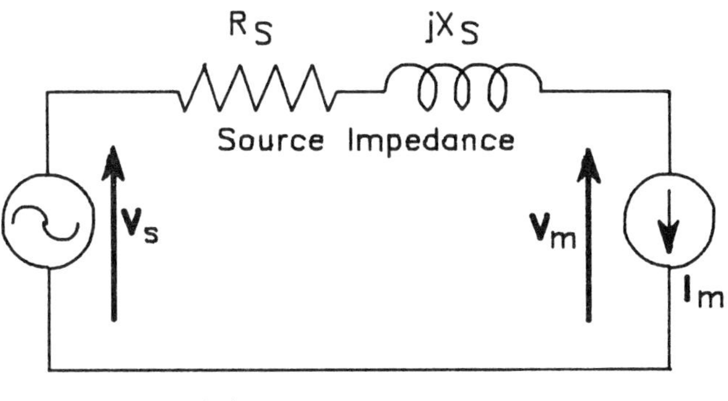

Figure 8-14 Motor representation.

A more common method is to represent the motor as a constant-current load during starting, as shown in Fig. 8-14b. The voltage drop due to starting is then calculated in a manner similar to that discussed in Section 8-3. The following example illustrates the methods previously discussed.

EXAMPLE 8-15 A 50-hp, 460-V, code letter G induction motor is to be started with full voltage applied from a 480Y/277-V system whose equivalent impedance is $0.01 + j0.02\ \Omega$/phase. Assume a locked rotor power factor of 35% lagging. Calculate the percent of voltage drop during starting using **(a)** the constant impedance and **(b)** the constant-current representations.

Solution

a. From Table 2-1, the locked rotor kVA/hp is between 5.6 and 6.3. For worst-case voltage drop, a value of 6.3 will be used. The locked rotor kVA during starting is

$$\text{kVA}_{\text{lr}} = 6.3\ \text{kVA/hp} \cdot 50\ \text{hp} = 315\ \text{kVA}$$

The locked rotor current is

$$I_{lr} = \frac{315\ \text{kVA} \cdot 1000}{\sqrt{3} \cdot 460\ \text{V}} = 395.4\ \text{A}$$

The active and reactive power during starting are

$$P_{3\phi} = 315\ \text{kVA} \cdot 0.35 = 110.25\ \text{kW}$$
$$Q_{3\phi} = 315\ \text{kVA} \cdot (1 - 0.35^2)^{1/2} = 295.1\ \text{kVAR}$$

The constant impedance representation is determined by applying Eqs. (4.3) and (4.4).

$$R_{\phi} = \frac{110.25 \cdot 1000}{3 \cdot (395.4)^2} = 0.2351\ \Omega$$
$$X_{\phi} = \frac{295.1 \cdot 1000}{3 \cdot (395.4)^2} = 0.6292\ \Omega$$

The voltage at the motor terminals is determined by applying the voltage-divider rule.

$$\mathbf{V}_m = 277\angle 0°\left(\frac{0.2351 + j0.6292}{0.2351 + j0.6292 + 0.01 + j0.02}\right)$$
$$= 268.1\angle -0.2°\ \text{V}$$

The percent of voltage drop is

$$\%V_{\text{drop}} = \frac{277 - 268.1}{277} \cdot 100 = 3.213\%$$

b. The constant-current representation of the motor is determined by selecting the A phase line to neutral voltage as a reference. Therefore,

$$\mathbf{I}_m = 395.4\angle -69.7°\ \text{A}$$

The voltage at the motor terminals (receiving end) is

$$\mathbf{V}_{A'} = 277\angle 0° - (395.4\angle -69.5°) \cdot (0.01 + j0.02)$$
$$= 268.2\angle 0.2°\ \text{V}$$

The percent of voltage drop is

$$\%V_{\text{drop}} = \frac{277 - 268.2}{277} \cdot 100 = 3.18\%$$

Note close agreement between parts a and b.

Approximate Method of Voltage Drop Due to Motor Starting

In some instances, the locked rotor power factor of the motor may not be known. In these cases, it is possible to calculate the voltage drop by assuming that the voltage drop is in phase with the source voltage. For the previous example, the magnitude of the **IZ** drop across the source impedance is

$$\mathbf{IZ} = 395.4 \cdot |0.01 + j0.02| = 8.84 \text{ V}$$

This corresponds to a percent voltage drop of

$$\%V_{\text{drop}} = \frac{8.84}{277} \cdot 100 = 3.19\%$$

Note the close agreement with Example 8-15.

Use of Flicker Curve

In addition to the magnitude of the voltage drop produced by motor starting, the frequency of occurrence of the voltage drop will also determine the severity of the drop. For example, a large voltage drop that occurs infrequently may be acceptable. Likewise, smaller voltage drops may be tolerated on a more frequent basis. The flicker curve shown in Fig. 8-15 illustrates the border line of objectionable voltage dips. As shown in the curve, the maximum permissible voltage drop is a function of the frequency of occurrence.

EXAMPLE 8-16

Determine the maximum number of motor starts permitted for the following voltage drops:

a. 2.0%
b. 3.0%
c. 4.0%
d. 5.0%
e. 6.0%

Solution Examination of the flicker curve indicates the following permissible number of motor starts:

a. 45 starts per hour
b. 10 starts per hour
c. 4 starts per hour
d. 2 starts per hour
e. 1 start per hour

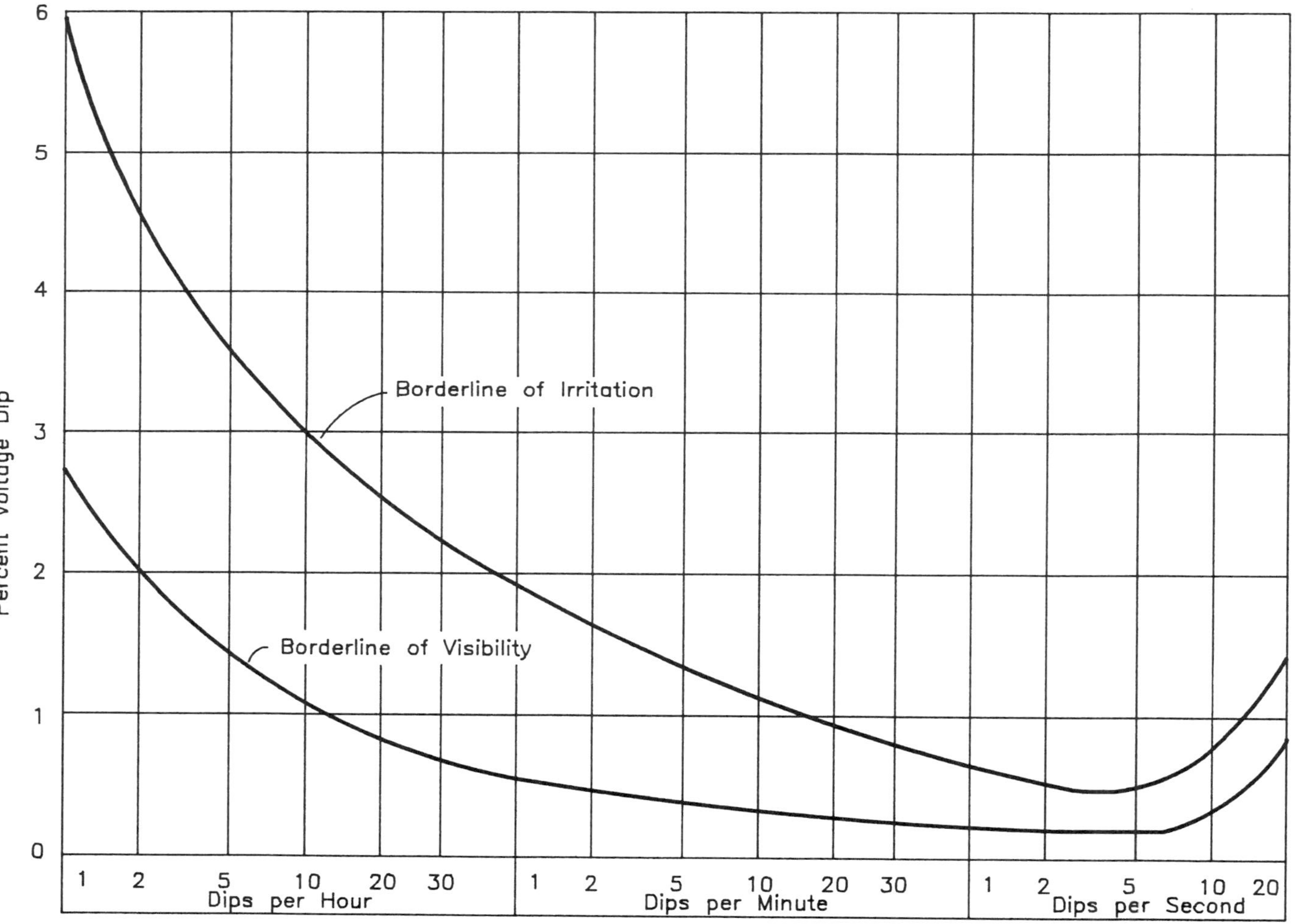

Figure 8-15 Flicker curve. (Derived from IEEE Std 141-1993. *IEEE Recommended Practice for Electric Power Distribution for Industrial Plants,* IEEE Red Book, © 1994.)

8-9 Example of Voltage-Drop Study

As an example of voltage-drop calculations, consider the distribution circuit shown in Fig. 8-16. This circuit could represent a distribution circuit supplying an industrial area. To calculate the voltage drop at various locations, the circuit is divided into segments. The total loading along each line segment is lumped together and placed at the end of each line segment. The voltage drop along each segment can then be calculated using the methods developed in this chapter. The percentage voltage drops are added to keep a running total of the voltage drop in the circuit.

The total circuit loading during peak load conditions is 2415 kVA at 0.8 lagging power factor. The loads of the larger customers have been determined and are indicated on the one-line diagram. The total loading on the smaller distribution transformers is equal to the total circuit loading minus the sum of the loads of the larger customers.

$$\begin{aligned}\text{Loading} &= 2415\ \text{kVA} - 420\ \text{kVA} - 450\ \text{kVA} - 1300\ \text{kVA}\\ &= 245\ \text{kVA}\end{aligned}$$

The total installed capacity of the smaller distribution transformers is 350 kVA. The resulting demand factor for the smaller distribution transformers is therefore

$$\text{Demand factor} = \frac{245}{350} = 0.7$$

This demand factor will be applied to all the smaller distribution transformers to determine an approximate value for the transformer loadings.

The following voltage-drop factors are used:

Conductor Size and Type	*Drop Factor*
3ϕ 336.4 kcmil ASCR, 26/7	0.4%/MVA/mile
2ϕ #1/0 ACSR (worst case)	1.8%/MVA/mile
1ϕ #4 ACSR	6.0%/MVA/mile

Table 8-3 summarizes the results of the calculations to determine the voltage drop at various locations along the line.

If the primary circuit voltage is regulated to 105% of nominal at the substation, the voltage at point 13 will be

$$V = 105\% - 3.262\% = 101.7\%$$

Likewise, the voltage at point 9 will be

$$V = 105\% - 2.673\% = 102.3\%$$

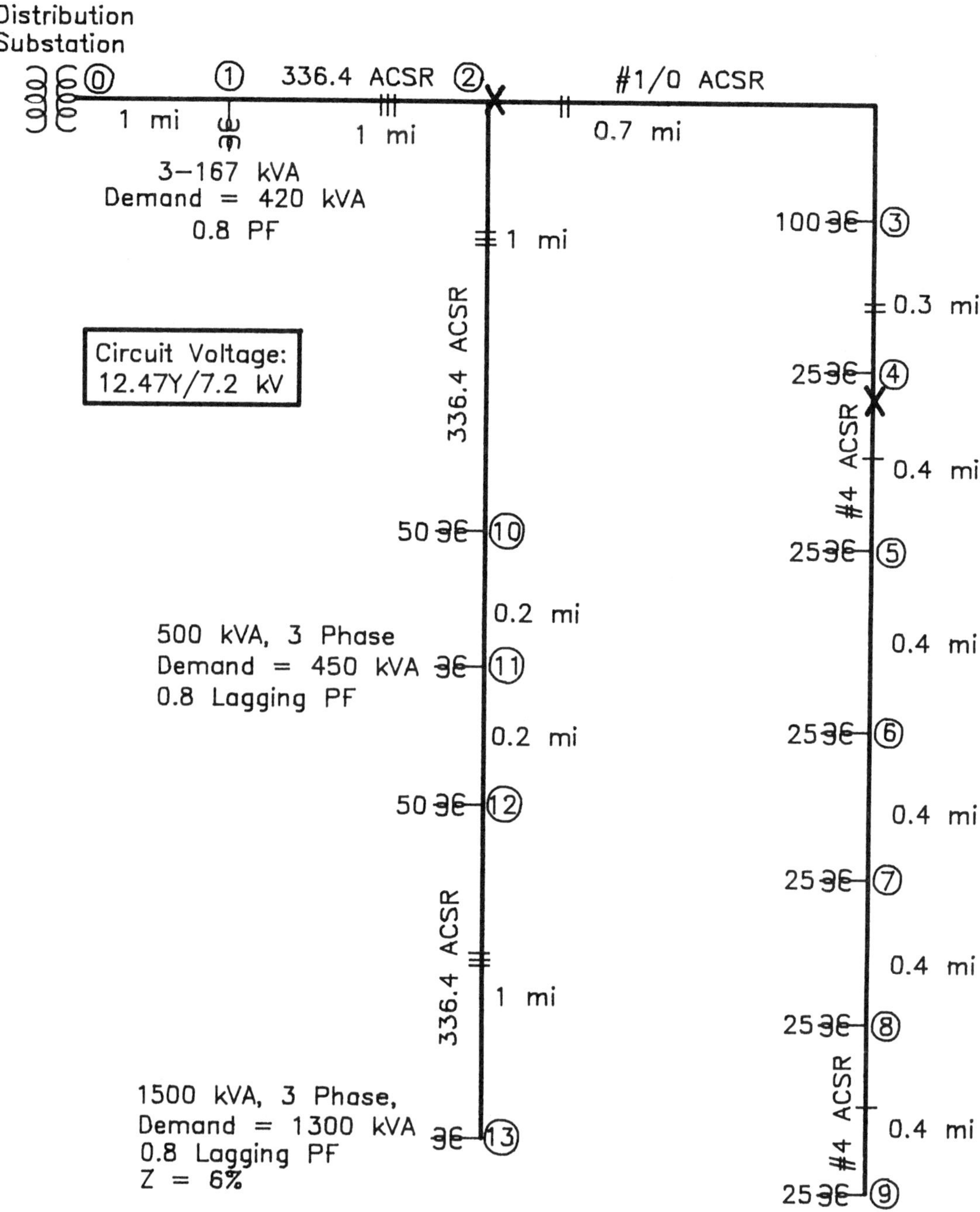

Figure 8-16 Example of voltage-drop study.

Table 8-3

Segment	*Load (kVA)*	*Distance (mile)*	*Segment, %V_{drop}*	*Total %V_{drop}*
0–1	2415	1	0.966	0.966
1–2	1995	1	0.798	1.764
2–3	175	0.7	0.222	1.986
3–4	105	0.3	0.057	2.043
4–5	87.5	0.4	0.210	2.253
5–6	70	0.4	0.168	2.421
6–7	52.5	0.4	0.126	2.547
7–8	35	0.4	0.084	2.631
8–9	17.5	0.4	0.042	2.673
Carry from point 2 →				1.764
2–10	1820	1	0.728	2.492
10–11	1785	0.2	0.143	2.635
11–12	1335	0.2	0.107	2.742
12–13	1300	1	0.520	3.262

Problems

8.1. Calculate the allowable service-voltage range for a 480Y/277-V, three-phase, four-wire service.

8.2. Calculate the allowable service-voltage range for a 208Y/120-V, three-phase, four-wire service.

8.3. Calculate the allowable service-voltage range for a 4.16Y/2.4-kV, three-phase, four-wire, medium-voltage service.

8.4. Repeat Example 8-3 for a circuit voltage of 4.16Y/2.4 kV.

8.5. Calculate voltage-drop factors for unity and 0.8 lagging power factors for three #1/0 aluminum, 15-kV, XLP insulated, 100% insulation level, one-third-size neutral, URD cables arranged in a flat horizontal configuration with 8-in. separation between the cables. The circuit voltage is 12.47 kV phase to phase. Express the results in percent per MVA per 1000 ft.

8.6. Repeat Example 8-5 for a circuit voltage of 4.16Y/2.4 kV.

8.7. Determine voltage-drop factors at unity and 0.8 lagging power factors for an underground cable circuit consisting of two #2 aluminum, 15-kV, XLP insulated, 100% insulation level, full neutral concentric neutral URD cables. The circuit voltage is 12.47 kV phase to phase. Express the results in percent per kVA per 1000 ft.

8.8. Repeat Example 8-7 for a circuit voltage of 4.16Y/2.4 kV.

8.9. Repeat Example 8-8 for a circuit voltage of 2.4 kV phase to neutral.

8.10. Calculate voltage-drop factors for the following 600-V service cables supplying a 120/240-V, single-phase, three-wire service. Calculate for unity and 0.8 lagging power factor, and express the results in terms of percent per kVA per 100 ft.

a. #4 Aluminum triplex
b. #2/0 Aluminum triplex
c. 350 kcmil aluminum triplex
d. 350 kcmil aluminum, three single conductors, 8-in. separation

8.11. Calculate voltage-drop factors for the following 600-V service cables supplying a 480Y/277-V, three-phase, four-wire service. Calculate for unity and 0.8 lagging power factor, and express the results in terms of percent per kVA per 100 ft.
a. #1/0 Aluminum quadruplex
b. 350 kcmil aluminum quadruplex
c. 350 kcmil aluminum, four single conductors, 8-in. separation

8.12. Repeat the voltage-drop study of Section 8-9 for a circuit voltage of 4.16/2.4 kV. How do the results of the lower circuit voltage compare to the results with the higher circuit voltage? What conclusions can be drawn from these results? *Assume that the drop factors vary as a function of the voltage squared.*

8.13. Calculate the percent of voltage drop for a 225-kVA, 4.16-kV–208Y/120-V, three-phase transformer having a resistance of 1.4% and a reactance of 3.5% for **(a)** full-load unity power factor and **(b)** 0.8 lagging power factor.

8.14. Calculate the percent voltage drop for a 10-kVA, 7.2-kV–120/240-V, single-phase distribution transformer having a resistance of 1.4% and a reactance of 1.2% for **(a)** full-load unity power factor and **(b)** 0.8 lagging power factor.

8.15. A three-phase feeder extends 3.2 miles from the substation to the first customer. The feeder has an impedance of $0.756 + j1.2\ \Omega$/mile. Voltage regulators at the substation have a *CT* ratio of 200:1 and a *VT* ratio of 120:1. It is desired to regulate the voltage at the first customer location to 124 V. Determine appropriate voltage regulating relay and line drop compensator settings.

8.16. A 1000-kVA, 24.94 kV–480Y/277 V, three-phase distribution transformer has taps on the high side at nominal, ±2.5%, and 5%. The transformer impedance is $1\% + j6\%$. The actual high-side voltage is 24.2 kV phase to phase. Calculate the following:
a. Percent of voltage drop through the transformer at full-load 0.9 lagging power factor
b. Actual voltages on the low-voltage side under no-load conditions for each tap setting
c. Actual voltage on the low-voltage side at full-load 0.9 lagging power factor for each tap setting

8.17. A 5-hp, 230-V, single-phase motor is to be started with full voltage applied. The service is supplied from a 10-kVA, 7.2 kV–120/240-V, distribution transformer with an impedance of $1.2 + j1.1\%$. The service conductors consist of 125 ft of #4 aluminum, 600-V triplexed cable. Assume a locked rotor kVA/hp of 6.3 and a locked rotor power factor of 50%. Using the constant-current representation of the motor, calculate the following:
a. Transformer impedance in ohms referred to the low side
b. Impedance of the triplexed service conductor in ohms
c. Percent of voltage drop due to motor starting
d. Maximum number of starts permitted

9

Capacitor Applications

9-1 General

The application of capacitors to electrical power systems can produce several desirable effects. Improved voltage regulation, power factor correction, reduced line losses, and released system capacity are a few of the advantages. Capacitors are usually installed on a power system in a three-phase configuration, rather than single phase. The individual capacitor units making up a bank may be either three phase or single phase. Capacitors may be installed on the customer service or on the utility system.

The primary function of capacitors is to supply reactive power to the system. As a result, capacitors supply a portion of the reactive power required by various lagging power factor loads in the system. A reduction in line current magnitude, overall system apparent power loading, and I^2R line losses are obtained. In addition, voltage drop is reduced due to the decrease in line current magnitude and improvement in power factor.

This chapter will discuss the general construction and ratings of capacitors, three-phase connections of single-phase units, switching, and control of capacitor banks. Additional emphasis will be placed on sizing capacitors for power factor improvement and locating capacitors for maximum loss reduction and voltage improvement.

9-2 Capacitor Construction and Standard Ratings

Figure 9-1a shows a view of a single-bushing, single-phase, medium-voltage capacitor unit commonly used on utility power systems. Note that there is only one high-voltage

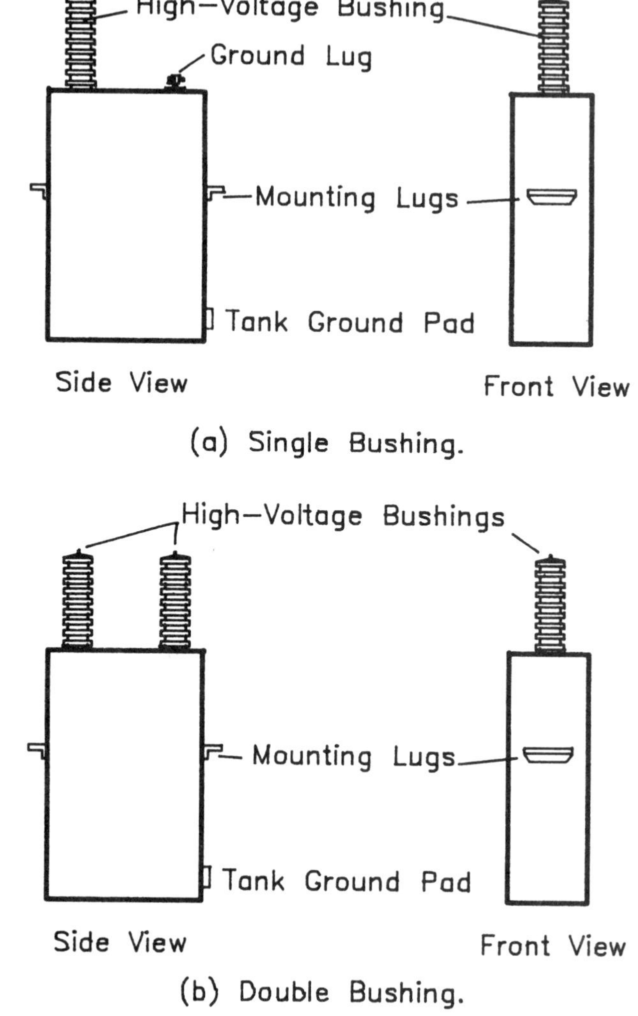

Figure 9-1 Capacitor construction features.

bushing for connection to the phase conductor. These units are suitable for connection in a grounded-wye configuration.

A two-bushing, single-phase, medium-voltage capacitor unit is shown in Fig. 9-1b. These units are typically connected in a delta or floating-wye configuration, in much the same fashion as the distribution transformers discussed in Chapter 6.

Low-voltage (less than 1000 V) capacitor units may be either single phase or three phase. The low-voltage, single-phase units typically have two bushings for connection to the line. Three-phase low-voltage units are typically supplied with three bushings for

Table 9-1 Voltage and kVAR Ratings, Single-Phase, Medium-Voltage Capacitors

Voltage		*kVAR*
2400	12,470	50
2770	13,280	100
4160	13,800	150
4800	14,400	200
6640	15,125	300
7200	19,920	400
7620	20,800	500
7960	21,600	
8320	22,130	
9540	22,800	
9960	23,800	
11,400	24,940	

Courtesy: Cooper Power Systems

connection to all three-phase conductors on a three-phase system. Low-voltage capacitors are usually connected in a delta configuration.

In accordance with the National Electrical Code®, all capacitor units are supplied with an internal discharge resistor. The discharge resistor is connected in parallel with the capacitor unit and provides a path for current to flow in the event that the capacitor is disconnected from the source. For low-voltage capacitors, the residual voltage trapped on the capacitor unit must decrease to less than 50 V within 1 min after de-energizing. For medium-voltage capacitors, the residual voltage must decrease to less than 50 V within 5 min after de-energizing.

Table 9-1 lists standard voltage and kVAR ratings for medium-voltage capacitors. Standard voltage ratings for low-voltage capacitor units are 240, 480, and 600 V. Standard kVAR ratings for low-voltage capacitor units are too numerous to list here. The reader is referred to manufacturers' product literature.

9-3 Connections

Capacitors installed on medium-voltage, multigrounded, neutral utility distribution systems are usually either solidly grounded wye or floating wye connected. Figure 9-2 shows some of the more common capacitor connections. A typical installation of a fixed capacitor bank on a 12.47-kV distribution feeder is shown in Fig. 9-3. A switched capacitor bank installed on a 12.47-kV distribution feeder is shown in Fig. 9-4. These capacitors are switched off and on by the oil switches located next to the capacitor units. In both figures, the capacitors are installed in a grounded-wye configuration.

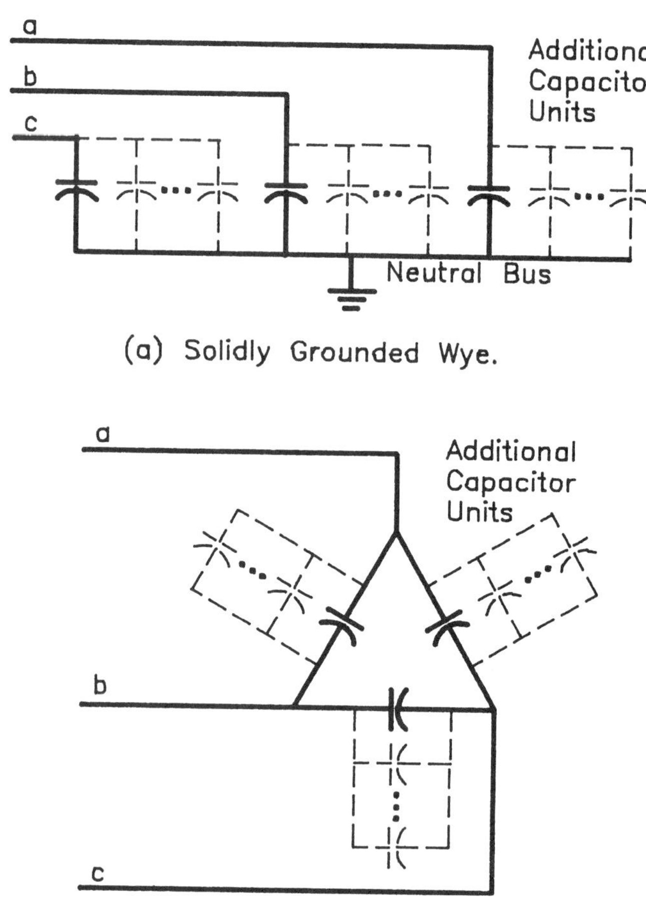

Figure 9-2 Capacitor connections.

Solidly Grounded Wye Connection

The solidly grounded wye connection shown in Fig. 9-2a is typically used on medium-voltage distribution feeders. The voltage rating of the capacitor units in the solidly grounded wye bank must be equal to or greater than the nominal line to neutral voltage of the feeder. The kVAR rating of the capacitor units is selected to provide the desired amount of reactive compensation. Additional single-phase capacitor units may be connected in parallel per phase to increase the rating of the bank. The individual capacitor units in the bank must have the same kVAR and voltage

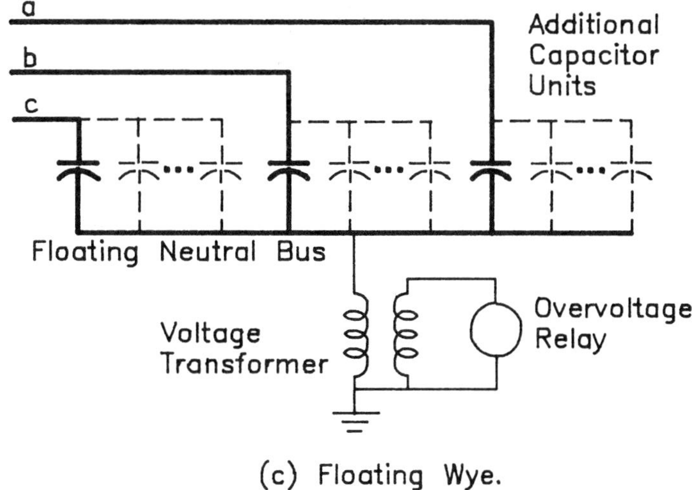

(c) Floating Wye.

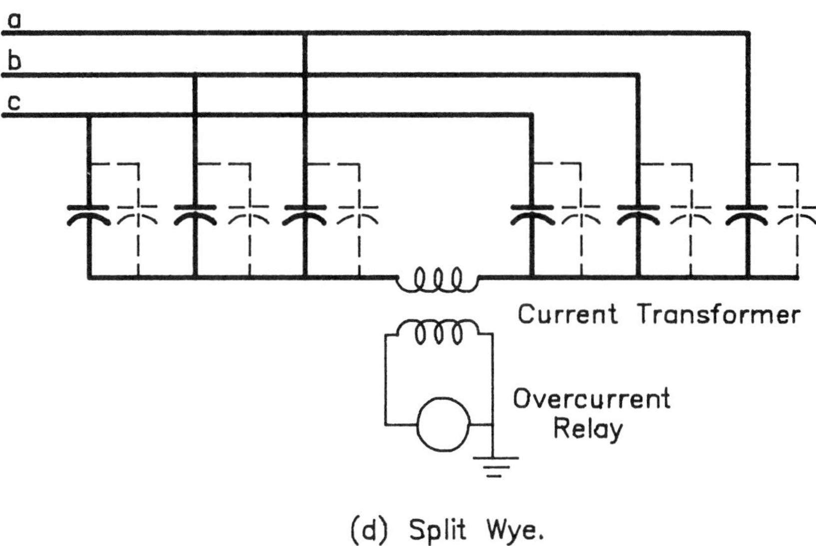

(d) Split Wye.

Figure 9-2 (Cont.)

ratings. Group fusing of the capacitors is typically provided by fused cutouts. Since the capacitor units are solidly connected between line and neutral, the failure of any individual capacitor unit will not result in an overvoltage across the remaining units in the bank.

Figure 9-3 Fixed capacitor bank installation on 12.47-kV distribution feeder. (Photo Courtesy of Ohio Edison Company)

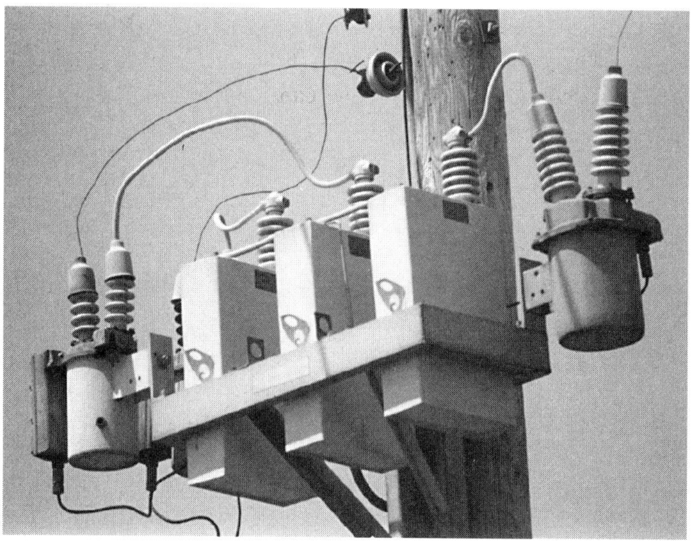

Figure 9-4 Close-up of switched capacitor bank installation on 12.47-kV distribution feeder. (Photo Courtesy of Ohio Edison Company)

EXAMPLE 9-1

Determine the appropriate voltage and kVAR ratings for the capacitor units used to make up a 1800-kVAR, grounded-wye connected capacitor bank to be installed on a 12.47-kV, three-phase, MGN distribution feeder.

Solution The kVAR per phase is equal to

$$\text{kVAR/phase} = 1800 \text{ kVAR/3 phases} = 600 \text{ kVAR/phase}$$

Referring to Table 9-1, the following possible combinations exist:

12–50 kVAR units per phase
6–100 kVAR units per phase
4–150 kVAR units per phase
3–200 kVAR units per phase
2–300 kVAR units per phase

The most practical combination would be two 300-kVAR units per phase, for a total of six units comprising the bank. Therefore, six 300-kVAR, 7200-V capacitor units are needed for this bank. Single- or double-bushing units may be used.

The voltage rating of each capacitor unit is equal to the nominal line to neutral voltage of the system.

$$V_{\text{ln}} = \frac{12{,}470}{\sqrt{3}} = 7200 \text{ V}$$

In larger capacitor banks installed on distribution or subtransmission substation busses, individual fusing of the capacitor units may be employed. Figure 9-5 shows a capacitor bank installed on a 23-kV substation bus. With the solidly grounded wye connection using individual fusing of the capacitor units, a blown fuse detection scheme is needed to detect operation of any of the individual fuse elements. One such blown fuse detection scheme employs a current transformer connected between the neutral point of the bank and ground. Under normal operating conditions with all capacitor units energized, the current flow from the bank neutral to ground is zero. However, if any of the individual capacitor fuse elements operate, an unbalanced current will result. The secondary of the current transformer could be connected to an overcurrent relay to detect the unbalanced current. Tripping of the capacitor bank breaker or switch could be initiated or an alarm condition reported.

EXAMPLE 9-2

A 4800-kVAR, 12.47-kV, solidly grounded wye capacitor bank is made up of eight 200-kVAR, 7200-V capacitor units per phase. A blown fuse detection scheme is to be used to determine the presence of a blown fuse. Assume that one fuse in phase *A* is blown and calculate the current flowing from the neutral of the bank to ground.

Figure 9-5 Capacitor bank installation on 23-kV substation bus. (Photo Courtesy of Ohio Edison Company)

Solution All eight capacitor units are energized in phases B and C. The impedances in these two phases are

$$\mathbf{Z}_B = \mathbf{Z}_C = -j\frac{7200^2}{8 \cdot 200{,}000} = -j32.4\ \Omega$$

The impedance in phase A is equal to

$$\mathbf{Z}_A = -j\frac{7200^2}{7 \cdot 200{,}000} = -j37.0\ \Omega$$

The source voltage references are selected as

$$\mathbf{V}_{AN} = 7200\angle 0^\circ\ \text{V}, \qquad \mathbf{V}_{BN} = 7200\angle -120^\circ\ \text{V}, \qquad \mathbf{V}_{CN} = 7200\angle 120^\circ\ \text{V}$$

The resulting capacitor bank line currents are

$$\mathbf{I}_A = \frac{7200\angle 0^\circ}{37.0\angle -90^\circ} = 194.6\angle 90^\circ\ \text{A}$$

$$\mathbf{I}_B = \frac{7200\angle -120^\circ}{32.4\angle -90^\circ} = 222.2\angle -30^\circ\ \text{A}$$

$$\mathbf{I}_C = \frac{7200\angle 120^\circ}{32.4\angle -90^\circ} = 222.2\angle 210^\circ \text{ A}$$

The neutral current is equal to

$$\begin{aligned}\mathbf{I}_N &= -(\mathbf{I}_A + \mathbf{I}_B + \mathbf{I}_C) \\ &= -(194.6\angle 90^\circ + 222.2\angle -30^\circ + 222.2\angle 210^\circ) \\ &= 27.6\angle 90^\circ \text{ A}\end{aligned}$$

Therefore, with one capacitor unit in the bank de-energized, the neutral current is equal to 27.6 A. A current transformer and overcurrent relay could be used to sense this current in the event of a fuse operation.

Delta Connection

In the delta connection shown in Fig. 9-2b, the individual capacitor units are connected phase to phase. Therefore, the required voltage rating of the capacitor units must be equal to or greater than the nominal line to line voltage of the system. Similarly to the grounded-wye connection, the failure of any of the individual capacitor units will not result in an overvoltage across the remaining units in the bank.

EXAMPLE 9-3

Determine the appropriate voltage and kVAR ratings for the capacitor units used to make up a 2400-kVAR, delta-connected capacitor bank to be installed on a 13.8-kV, three-phase, three-wire feeder.

Solution The kVAR per phase is equal to

$$\text{kVAR/phase} = 2400 \text{ kVAR/3 phases} = 800 \text{ kVAR/phase}$$

The most practical combination would be two 400-kVAR units per phase, for a total of six units comprising the bank. Therefore, six 400-kVAR, 13,800-V capacitor units are needed for this bank. Double-bushing units are required for the delta connection.

The voltage rating of each capacitor unit is equal to the nominal line to line voltage of the system:

$$V_{ll} = 13{,}800 \text{ V}$$

Floating-Wye Connection

The floating-wye connection shown in Fig. 9-2c is commonly used for larger kVAR rated capacitor banks installed on distribution substation and subtransmission substation buses. In this connection, the common or neutral point of the capacitor bank is not directly connected to ground. Since the potential of the bank neutral is allowed to float with respect to ground, the capacitor units should have two bushings. In some installations, however, single-bushing units are used, with the neutral connection made between the individual capacitor units and the capacitor mounting rack. The capacitor mounting rack itself is insulated from ground potential and is allowed to float with respect to ground. With this type of connection, it is possible for the capacitor housings to become energized.

The voltage rating of the capacitor units must be equal to or greater than the nominal line to neutral voltage of the system. Individual capacitor units may be series connected to achieve higher voltage ratings and parallel connected to achieve higher kVAR ratings. Each unit in the bank should have the same kVAR and voltage rating.

EXAMPLE 9-4

Determine the appropriate voltage and kVAR ratings for the capacitor units used to make up a 8400-kVAR, floating-wye connected capacitor bank to be installed on a 69-kV, three-phase, subtransmission substation bus.

Solution The kVAR per phase is equal to

$$\text{kVAR/phase} = 8400 \text{ kVAR/3 phases} = 2800 \text{ kVAR/phase}$$

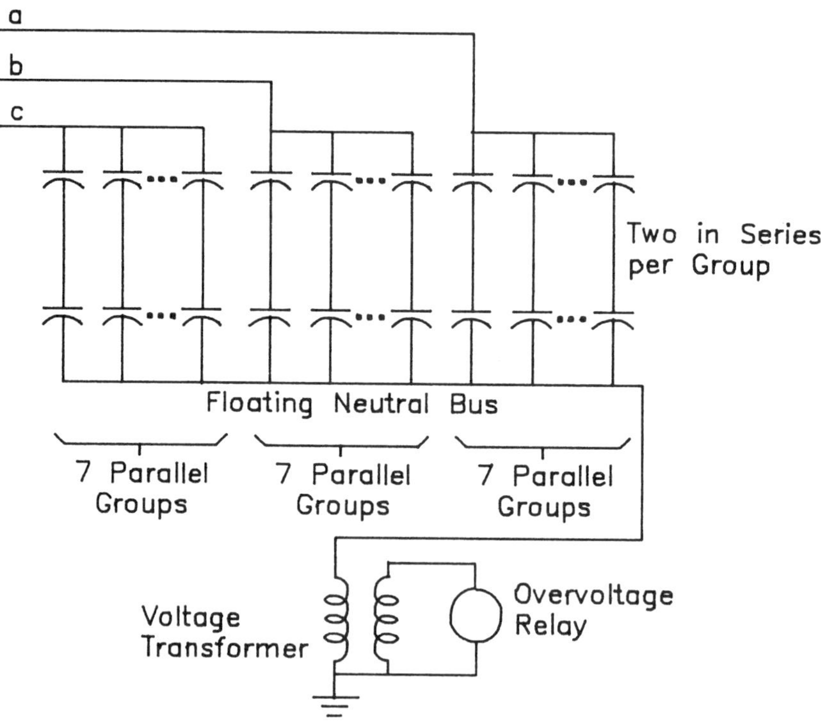

Figure 9-6 Capacitor bank of Example 9-4.

Possible combinations include

Seven 400-kVAR per phase
Fourteen 200-kVAR per phase

The voltage rating per phase is equal to the nominal line to neutral voltage of the system.

$$V_{\text{ln}} = \frac{69{,}000}{\sqrt{3}} = 39{,}840 \text{ V}$$

To achieve the required voltage rating, two 19,920-V capacitor units will be connected in series. Therefore, of the possible combinations listed, fourteen 200-kVAR units are the only practical solution: seven parallel combinations of two in series per phase. Each capacitor will have two bushings. The connection is shown in Fig. 9-6.

Because of the higher current rating of these larger banks, individual capacitor unit fusing is recommended, rather than group fusing of the entire bank. To detect individual blown fuses, a voltage transformer may be connected between the floating neutral point of the bank and the substation ground grid. Under normal operating conditions with all capacitor units energized, the voltage between the floating neutral and ground will be essentially zero. In the event of an individual fuse operation, the voltage between the floating neutral and ground will increase. An overvoltage relay connected to the secondary of the voltage transformer can be set to trip in the event of a capacitor unit failure. This overvoltage relay may cause the circuit breaker or switch protecting the bank to trip or may merely indicate an alarm condition.

The operation of individual fuses will also produce an overvoltage on the remaining capacitors in the phase with the blown fuse. Capacitors are designed to operate satisfactorily at up to 110% of rated voltage. Any voltage higher than this will cause breakdown of the dielectric and subsequent failure. The following example illustrates the method used to calculate the neutral to ground voltage and the voltage across the remaining capacitors in a floating-wye bank.

STP

EXAMPLE 9-5

A 12.47-kV, 3600-kVAR, floating-wye connected capacitor bank is made up of six 200-kVAR, 7200-V capacitor units per phase. The bank is connected to a 12.47-kV, three-phase, MGN system bus. Assume that a fuse element blows on a single unit connected in phase *A*. Calculate the voltage across the remaining capacitor units on all three phases and the voltage between the floating neutral point of the capacitor bank and ground.

Solution The capacitor units will be represented as constant-impedance elements. The impedance of each unit is

$$\mathbf{Z}_{\text{cap}} = -j\,\frac{7200^2}{200{,}000} = -j259.2\ \Omega$$

In the B and C phases, there are six parallel units. The combined impedance is

$$\mathbf{Z}_B = \mathbf{Z}_C = \frac{-j259.2}{6} = -j43.2\ \Omega$$

In the A phase, there are five parallel units due to the blown fuse. The combined impedance is

$$\mathbf{Z}_A = -j51.84\ \Omega$$

The source voltages are selected as

$$\mathbf{V}_{AN} = 7200\angle 0°\ \text{V}, \qquad \mathbf{V}_{BN} = 7200\angle -120°\ \text{V}, \qquad \mathbf{V}_{CN} = 7200\angle 120°\ \text{V}$$

The equivalent circuit model is shown in Fig. 9-7, with mesh currents $\mathbf{I}_1$ and $\mathbf{I}_2$ indicated. Writing loop equations for $\mathbf{I}_1$ and $\mathbf{I}_2$ results in the following:

$$\text{Loop } \mathbf{I}_1\text{:}\quad \mathbf{I}_1(-j43.2) + (\mathbf{I}_1 - \mathbf{I}_2)(-j51.84) = \mathbf{V}_{CN} - \mathbf{V}_{AN} = 12{,}470\angle 150°$$
$$\text{Loop } \mathbf{I}_2\text{:}\quad (\mathbf{I}_2 - \mathbf{I}_1)(-j51.84) + \mathbf{I}_2(-j43.2) = \mathbf{V}_{AN} - \mathbf{V}_{BN} = 12{,}470\angle 30°$$

Gathering terms and arranging in matrix format,

$$\begin{bmatrix} -j95.04 & +j51.84 \\ +j51.84 & -j95.04 \end{bmatrix} \begin{bmatrix} \mathbf{I}_1 \\ \mathbf{I}_2 \end{bmatrix} = \begin{bmatrix} 12{,}470\angle 150° \\ 12{,}470\angle 30 \end{bmatrix}$$

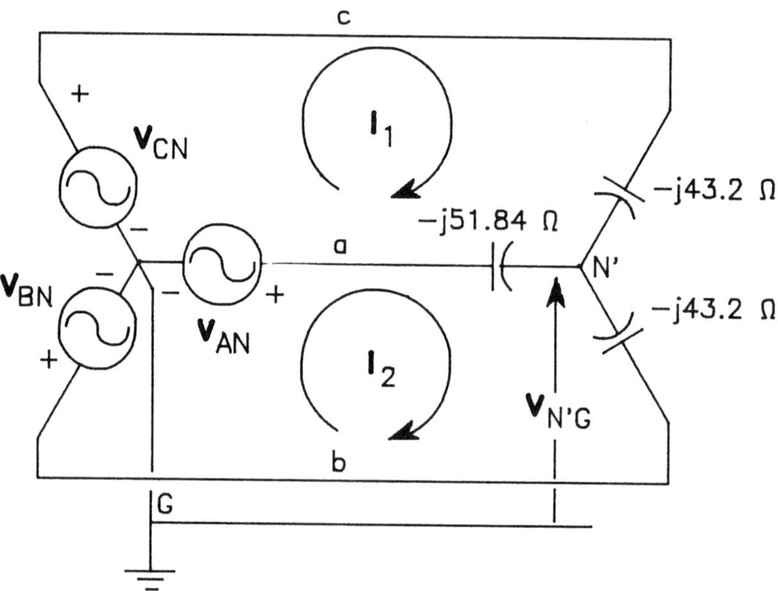

Figure 9-7 Circuit for Example 9-5.

Solving this system of equations for $\mathbf{I}_1$ and $\mathbf{I}_2$ results in the following:

$$\mathbf{I}_1 = 162\angle-153° \text{ A}, \qquad \mathbf{I}_2 = 162\angle-207° \text{ A}$$

From the circuit diagram of Fig. 9-7, the capacitor bank line currents are

$$\mathbf{I}_A = \mathbf{I}_2 - \mathbf{I}_1 = 162\angle-207° - 162\angle-153° = 147.1\angle 90° \text{ A}$$

$$\mathbf{I}_B = -\mathbf{I}_2 = 162\angle-27° \text{ A}$$

$$\mathbf{I}_C = \mathbf{I}_1 = 162\angle-153° \text{ A}$$

The voltages across each capacitor phase group are equal to

$$\mathbf{V}_{AN'} = \mathbf{I}_A \cdot \mathbf{Z}_A = (147.1\angle 90°)(51.84\angle-90°) = 7625.7\angle 0° \text{ V}$$

$$\mathbf{V}_{BN'} = \mathbf{I}_B \cdot \mathbf{Z}_B = (162\angle-27°)(43.2\angle-90°) = 6997.5\angle-117° \text{ V}$$

$$\mathbf{V}_{CN'} = \mathbf{I}_C \cdot \mathbf{Z}_C = (162\angle-153°)(43.2\angle-90°) = 6997.5\angle-243° \text{ V}$$

Expressed as a percentage of rated voltages, the voltages across each capacitor phase group are

$$|\mathbf{V}_{AN'}| = \frac{7625.7}{7200} \cdot 100 = 106\%$$

$$|\mathbf{V}_{BN'}| = |\mathbf{V}_{CN'}| = \frac{6997.5}{7200} \cdot 100 = 97.2\%$$

Note that the voltage across the remaining capacitors in phase group A has increased to 106% of rated voltage, while the voltage in phase groups B and C has decreased to 97.2% of rated. These changes are due to the neutral shift that occurs in a floating-wye connected bank.

The voltage between the floating neutral point of the capacitor bank and ground can be obtained by applying Kirchhoff's voltage law around the A phase loop, resulting in the following equation:

$$\begin{aligned} \mathbf{V}_{N'G} &= \mathbf{V}_{AN} - \mathbf{I}_A \cdot \mathbf{Z}_A = \mathbf{V}_{AN} - \mathbf{V}_{AN'} \\ &= 7200\angle 0° - 7625.7\angle 0° \\ &= 425.7\angle 180° \text{ V} \end{aligned}$$

If a voltage transformer with a 7200–120-V ratio is connected between floating neutral and ground, the voltage on the secondary will be

$$V = 425.7 \cdot \frac{120}{7200} = 7.1 \text{ V}$$

The calculations shown in Example 9-5 are rather cumbersome to perform. A rule of thumb may be applied to limit the overvoltage on the remaining capacitors in the bank to less than 110% of rated voltage. Simply stated, *use either one capacitor unit per phase or at least four units per phase.*

Split-Wye Connection

Two groups of capacitors may be connected in the form of the split-wye connection shown in Fig. 9-2d. Series and parallel combinations of capacitor units may be employed in a manner similar to the floating-wye connection to increase voltage and kVAR ratings. The voltage rating of the capacitor units is selected based on the nominal line to neutral system voltage.

To detect the operation of individual fuses, a current transformer is connected between the floating neutrals of the two groups. Under normal conditions, each group of capacitors represents a balanced three-phase load. The resulting neutral current is therefore equal to zero. In the event of a blown fuse on one or more of the units, an unbalanced current will result. This unbalanced current is detected by the overcurrent relay connected to the current transformer secondary. The overcurrent relay may trip a circuit breaker or switch or merely signal an alarm.

EXAMPLE 9-6

A split-wye capacitor bank is made up of two 3600-kVAR, 12.47-kV sections, for a total installed rating of 7200 kVAR. Each section consists of six 200-kVAR, 7200-V, single-phase capacitor units per phase. Individual fusing is provided on each capacitor unit. A current transformer and overcurrent relay are provided for blown fuse detection. Assume that one capacitor fuse operates in phase A of one of the split-wye sections, and calculate the current flow in the neutral between the two sections.

Solution The circuit in Fig. 9-8a models the condition with one fuse blown on one capacitor unit. The first step in determining the neutral current flow between the two sections is to calculate the neutral to ground voltage present on the floating neutral of the bank. The equivalent parallel impedances per phase are calculated with the modified equivalent circuit shown in Fig. 9-8b. The procedure used to calculate the line currents is similar to that shown in Example 9-5.

The loop equations in matrix format are

$$\begin{bmatrix} -j45.2 & +j23.6 \\ +j23.6 & -j45.2 \end{bmatrix} \begin{bmatrix} \mathbf{I}_1 \\ \mathbf{I}_2 \end{bmatrix} = \begin{bmatrix} 12{,}470\angle 150^\circ \\ 12{,}470\angle 30^\circ \end{bmatrix}$$

Solving this system of equations for $\mathbf{I}_1$ and $\mathbf{I}_2$ results in the following:

$$\mathbf{I}_1 = 328.6\angle -151.5^\circ \text{ A}, \qquad \mathbf{I}_2 = 328.6\angle -208.5^\circ \text{ A}$$

The capacitor bank line currents are

$$\mathbf{I}_A = \mathbf{I}_2 - \mathbf{I}_1 = 328.6\angle -208.5^\circ - 328.6\angle -151.5^\circ = 313.6\angle 90^\circ \text{ A}$$

$$\mathbf{I}_B = -\mathbf{I}_2 = 328.6\angle -28.5^\circ \text{ A}$$

$$\mathbf{I}_C = \mathbf{I}_1 = 328.6\angle -151.5^\circ \text{ A}$$

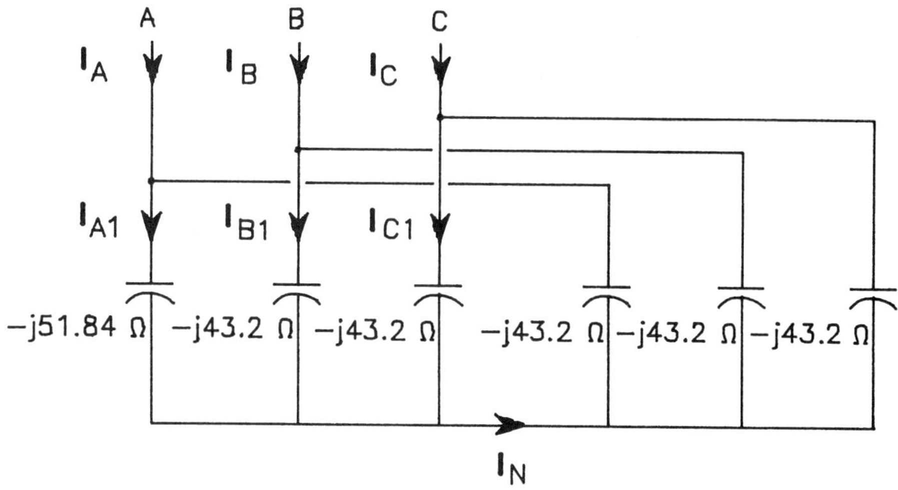

(a) Equivalent Circuit Model.

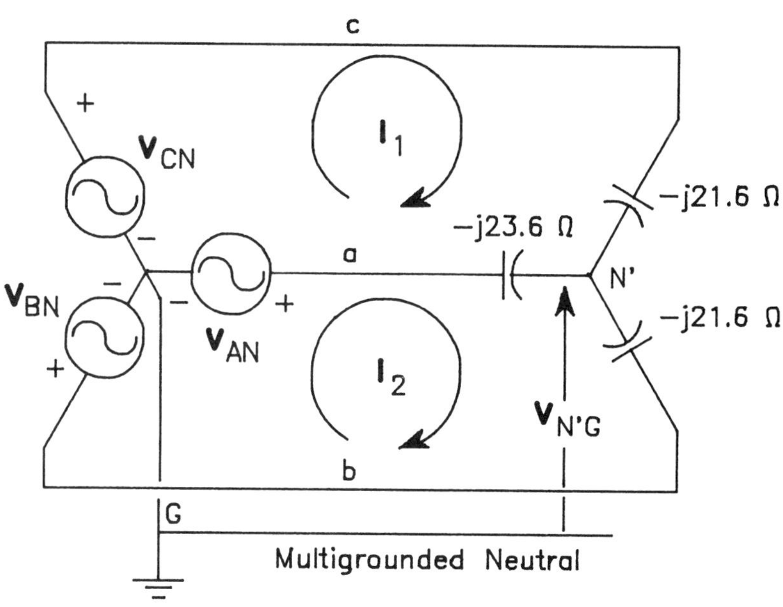

(b) Reduced Equivalent Circuit.

Figure 9-8 Circuit for Example 9-6.

The voltages across each capacitor phase group are equal to

$$\mathbf{V}_{AN'} = \mathbf{I}_A \cdot \mathbf{Z}_A = (313.6\angle 90°)(23.6\angle -90°) = 7401\angle 0° \text{ V}$$

$$\mathbf{V}_{BN'} = \mathbf{I}_B \cdot \mathbf{Z}_B = (328.6\angle -28.5°)(21.6\angle -90°) = 7098\angle -118.5° \text{ V}$$

$$\mathbf{V}_{CN'} = \mathbf{I}_C \cdot \mathbf{Z}_C = (328.6\angle -151.5°)(21.6\angle -90°) = 7098\angle -241.5° \text{ V}$$

Expressed as a percentage of rated voltage, the voltages across each capacitor phase group are

$$|\mathbf{V}_{AN'}| = \frac{7401}{7200} \cdot 100 = 102.8\%$$

$$|\mathbf{V}_{BN'}| = |\mathbf{V}_{CN'}| = \frac{7098}{7200} \cdot 100 = 98.6\%$$

It is interesting to compare the results of this example with Example 9-5. In this example, the voltage across the remaining capacitors in phase group A has increased to 102.8% of rated voltage, while in Example 9-5 the voltage increased to 106% of rated. The difference is that there is less of an imbalance due to the increased number of capacitors per phase in the bank.

The voltage between the floating neutral point of the capacitor bank and ground can be obtained by applying Kirchhoff's voltage law around the A phase loop, resulting in the following equation:

$$\begin{aligned}\mathbf{V}_{N'G} &= \mathbf{V}_{AN} - \mathbf{I}_A \cdot \mathbf{Z}_A = \mathbf{V}_{AN} - \mathbf{V}_{AN'} \\ &= 7200\angle 0° - 7401\angle 0° \\ &= 201\angle 180° \text{ V}\end{aligned}$$

Again, note the comparison between the results of Example 9-5 and this example.

In reference to Fig. 9-8a, the neutral current flowing between the two sections of the split-wye bank is equal to

$$\mathbf{I}_N = \mathbf{I}_{A1} + \mathbf{I}_{B1} + \mathbf{I}_{C1}$$

The currents $\mathbf{I}_{A1'}$, $\mathbf{I}_{B1'}$, and $\mathbf{I}_{C1}$ are given by

$$\mathbf{I}_{A1} = \frac{\mathbf{V}_{AN'}}{51.84\angle -90°} = \frac{7401\angle 0°}{51.84\angle -90°} = 142.8\angle 90° \text{ A}$$

$$\mathbf{I}_{B1} = \frac{\mathbf{V}_{BN'}}{43.2\angle -90°} = \frac{7098\angle -118.5°}{43.2\angle -90°} = 164.3\angle -28.5° \text{ A}$$

$$\mathbf{I}_{C1} = \frac{\mathbf{V}_{CN'}}{43.2\angle -90°} = \frac{7098\angle -241.5°}{43.2\angle -90°} = 164.3\angle -151.5° \text{ A}$$

The neutral current flowing between the split-wye connection is

$$\begin{aligned}\mathbf{I}_N &= 142.8\angle 90° + 164.3\angle -28.5° + 164.3\angle -151.5° \\ &= 14.0\angle 90° \text{ A}\end{aligned}$$

Therefore, under the specified conditions, approximately 14 A of current will flow between the two sections of the capacitor bank through the current transformer.

9-4 Power Factor Improvement

Power capacitors are used to a large extent to improve the power factor of industrial plants and utility power systems. As a result of improved power factor, the apparent power loading and line current are reduced. Reduced line losses are also achieved due to the reduction in line current. Power factor correction capacitors are typically installed in the form of a three-phase bank. Since each phase contains capacitors of equal rating, the result is a balanced three-phase connection.

The ability of capacitors to improve power factor can be understood by examining the one-line diagram for an industrial plant shown in Fig. 9-9. The load is assumed to be operating at a lagging power factor. As such, the load will absorb active power P_{LOAD} and reactive power Q_{LOAD} from the system. A capacitor bank added to the bus will supply reactive power Q_{CAP}. This results in a decrease in the reactive power supplied by the source Q_S and, consequently, an improved power factor. Unity power factor occurs if the reactive power supplied by the capacitor is equal to the reactive power consumed by the load. Under unity power factor conditions, the source does not supply any reactive power to the load.

If the reactive power supplied by the capacitor is less than the reactive power consumed by the load, the overall plant power factor will improve, but remain lagging. If the reactive power supplied by the capacitor bank exceeds the reactive power consumed by the load, a leading power factor will result. This condition is sometimes referred to as *overcompensating*. It is generally undesirable to operate a system at a leading power factor.

From Section 1.13, recall the power concepts for single-phase and balanced three-phase loads. In particular, Eqs. (1.67), (1.68), and (1.69) give expressions for the appar-

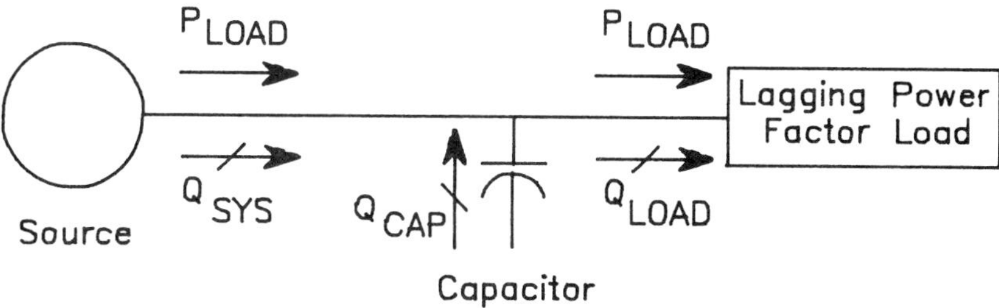

Figure 9-9 One-line diagram illustrating use of capacitor for power factor improvement.

ent, active, and reactive powers for balanced three-phase loads. These equations are repeated here for reference:

$$S_{3\phi} = \sqrt{3}V_{ll}I_l \tag{1.67}$$

$$P_{3\phi} = \sqrt{3}V_{ll}I_l \cos(\theta) \tag{1.68}$$

$$Q_{3\phi} = -\sqrt{3}V_{ll}I_l \sin(\theta) \tag{1.69}$$

The angle θ is the power factor angle of the load and is assumed to be positive for leading power factor loads. The quantity $\cos(\theta)$ is the load power factor (PF), and the term $\sin(\theta)$ is the reactive factor (RF).

Equations (1.67), (1.68), and (1.69) can be used to express the complex form of the apparent power.

$$\mathbf{S}_{3\phi} = P_{3\phi} + jQ_{3\phi} \tag{9.1}$$

For actual and desired load conditions, a power triangle can be constructed based on Eq. (9.1) as shown in Fig. 9-10. Here the following variables are defined:

S_{LOAD} = apparent power consumed by the load before adding capacitors

S_{DES} = apparent power supplied by the source after adding capacitors

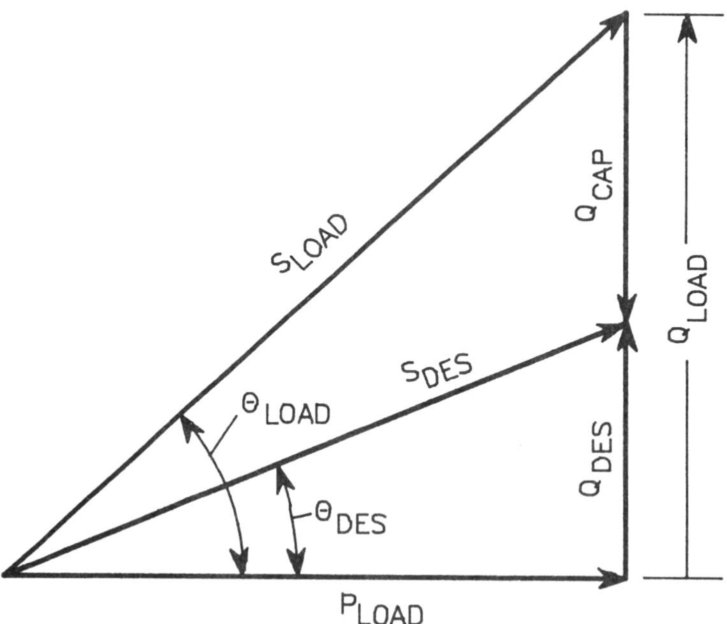

Figure 9-10 Power triangle for system of Fig. 9-9.

$$Q_{\text{LOAD}} = \text{reactive power consumed by the load before adding capacitors}$$
$$Q_{\text{DES}} = \text{reactive power supplied by the source after adding capacitors}$$
$$P_{\text{LOAD}} = \text{active power consumed by the load}$$

In the analysis that follows, it is assumed that the active power consumed by the load will remain constant both before and after addition of capacitors. The amount of reactive compensation supplied by the capacitor bank is

$$Q_{\text{CAP}} = Q_{\text{LOAD}} - Q_{\text{DES}} \tag{9.2}$$

The apparent power for the actual and desired power factor conditions can be expressed in terms of the active power demand and actual and desired power factors as follows:

$$S_{\text{LOAD}} = \frac{P_{\text{LOAD}}}{\text{PF}_{\text{LOAD}}} \tag{9.3}$$

$$S_{\text{DES}} = \frac{P_{\text{LOAD}}}{\text{PF}_{\text{DES}}} \tag{9.4}$$

where PF_{LOAD} and PF_{DES} are the actual load and desired system power factors, respectively.

The reactive power can be expressed in terms of the apparent power and active power for the actual and desired power factor conditions as follows:

$$Q_{\text{LOAD}} = (S_{\text{ACT}}^2 - P_{\text{LOAD}}^2)^{1/2} \tag{9.5}$$

$$Q_{\text{DES}} = (S_{\text{DES}}^2 - P_{\text{LOAD}}^2)^{1/2} \tag{9.6}$$

Substituting Eq. (9.3) into (9.5) and Eq. (9.4) into (9.6) results in the following:

$$Q_{\text{LOAD}} = \left[\left(\frac{P_{\text{LOAD}}}{\text{PF}_{\text{ACT}}}\right)^2 - P_{\text{LOAD}}^2\right]^{1/2} \tag{9.7}$$

$$Q_{\text{DES}} = \left[\left(\frac{P_{\text{LOAD}}}{\text{PF}_{\text{DES}}}\right)^2 - P_{\text{LOAD}}^2\right]^{1/2} \tag{9.8}$$

Substituting Eqs. (9.7) and (9.8) into Eq. (9.2) results in

$$\begin{aligned} Q_{\text{CAP}} &= \left[\left(\frac{P_{\text{LOAD}}}{\text{PF}_{\text{LOAD}}}\right)^2 - P_{\text{LOAD}}^2\right]^{1/2} - \left[\left(\frac{P_{\text{LOAD}}}{\text{PF}_{\text{DES}}}\right)^2 - P_{\text{LOAD}}^2\right]^{1/2} \\ &= P_{\text{LOAD}} \cdot \left[\left(\frac{1}{(\text{PF}_{\text{LOAD}})^2} - 1\right)^{1/2} - \left(\frac{1}{(\text{PF}_{\text{DES}})^2} - 1\right)^{1/2}\right] \end{aligned} \tag{9.9}$$

Equation (9.9) can be used to determine the reactive power rating of a capacitor bank required to improve the power factor to a desired level.

EXAMPLE 9-7

An industrial plant has an active power demand of 500 kW at a power factor of 0.76 lagging. Determine the required amount of capacitance required to raise the power factor to the following:

a. 0.8 lagging
b. 0.85 lagging
c. 0.9 lagging
d. 0.95 lagging
e. Unity

Assume that capacitor steps are available in 50-kVAR increments.

Solution Direct application of Eq. (9.9) results in the following:

a. $$Q_{\text{CAP}} = 500\text{ kW} \cdot \left[\left(\frac{1}{0.76^2} - 1\right)^{1/2} - \left(\frac{1}{0.80^2} - 1\right)^{1/2}\right]$$
$$= 52.6\text{ kVAR} \approx 50\text{ kVAR}$$

b. $$Q_{\text{CAP}} = 500\text{ kW} \cdot \left[\left(\frac{1}{0.76^2} - 1\right)^{1/2} - \left(\frac{1}{0.85^2} - 1\right)^{1/2}\right]$$
$$= 117.7\text{ kVAR} \approx 100\text{ kVAR}$$

c. $$Q_{\text{CAP}} = 500\text{ kW} \cdot \left[\left(\frac{1}{0.76^2} - 1\right)^{1/2} - \left(\frac{1}{0.90^2} - 1\right)^{1/2}\right]$$
$$= 185.4\text{ kVAR} \approx 200\text{ kVAR}$$

d. $$Q_{\text{CAP}} = 500\text{ kW} \cdot \left[\left(\frac{1}{0.76^2} - 1\right)^{1/2} - \left(\frac{1}{0.95^2} - 1\right)^{1/2}\right]$$
$$= 263.2\text{ kVAR} \approx 250\text{ kVAR}$$

e. $$Q_{\text{CAP}} = 500\text{ kW} \cdot \left[\left(\frac{1}{0.76^2} - 1\right)^{1/2} - \left(\frac{1}{1.00^2} - 1\right)^{1/2}\right]$$
$$= 427.6\text{ kVAR} \approx 400\text{ kVAR}$$

Notice that in order to improve the power factor to 0.95 power factor approximately 250 kVAR of capacitors is required. However, to improve the power factor to unity requires 400 kVAR of capacitors.

EXAMPLE 9-8

A large industrial plant is supplied power at 12.47 kV and has a demand of 4000 kW at a power factor of 0.7 lagging. The source impedance is $0.5 + j1.3\ \Omega$/phase. Calculate the amount of capacitors required to improve the power factor to 0.97 lagging. Assume 300-kVAR increments in capacitor size. Also calculate the line current and line I^2R losses before and after addition of the capacitors.

Solution The initial plant load conditions are

$$P_{3\phi} = 4000\text{ kW}$$

$$S_{3\phi} = \frac{4000\text{ kW}}{0.7} = 5714.3\text{ kVAR}$$

$$Q_{3\phi} = (5714.3^2 - 4000^2)^{1/2} = 4080.8\text{ kVAR}$$

The line current magnitude before adding the capacitors is

$$I_1 = \frac{5714.3 \text{ kVA}}{\sqrt{3} \cdot 12.47 \text{ kV}} = 264.6 \text{ A}$$

The I^2R losses per phase in the supply line are

$$P_{1\phi} = 264.6^2 \cdot 0.5 = 35{,}000 \text{ W/phase}$$

For all three phases, the total loss is

$$P_{3\phi} = 3 \cdot P_{1\phi} = 105{,}000 \text{ W} \quad \text{or} \quad 105 \text{ kW}$$

The required capacitor kVAR can be calculated from Eq. (9.9).

$$Q_{\text{CAP}} = 4000 \text{ kW} \cdot \left[\left(\frac{1}{0.7^2} - 1\right)^{1/2} - \left(\frac{1}{0.97^2} - 1\right)^{1/2}\right]$$

$$= 3078 \text{ kVAR} \approx 3000 \text{ kVAR} \quad \text{(1000 kVAR per phase)}$$

The plant load conditions with the addition of 3000 kVAR of capacitors are

$$P_{3\phi} = 4000 \text{ kW}$$

$$Q_{3\phi} = 4080.8 \text{ kVAR} - 3000 \text{ kVAR} = 1080.8 \text{ kVAR}$$

$$S_{3\phi} = (4000^2 + 1080.8^2)^{1/2} = 4143.2 \text{ kVA}$$

The line current is

$$I_1 = \frac{4143.2 \text{ kVA}}{\sqrt{3} \cdot 12.47 \text{ kV}} = 191.8 \text{ A}$$

The I^2R losses per phase in the supply line are

$$P_{1\phi} = 191.8^2 \cdot 0.5 = 18{,}400 \text{ W/phase}$$

For all three phases, the total loss is

$$P_{3\phi} = 3 \cdot P_{1\phi} = 55{,}200 \text{ W} \quad \text{or} \quad 55.2 \text{ kW}$$

Note that the line current has been reduced by 27.5%, while the power loss has been reduced by 47.3 %.

9-5 Voltage Improvement

In addition to improved power factor, capacitors will produce a voltage rise on the bus that they are connected to. This voltage rise is due to the leading current of the capacitor being supplied through the inductive reactance of the source. Consider the circuit shown in Fig. 9-11. The rated capacitor current is given by

$$I_C = \frac{Q_{\text{CAP}}}{\sqrt{3} \cdot V_{\text{LL}}} \tag{9.10}$$

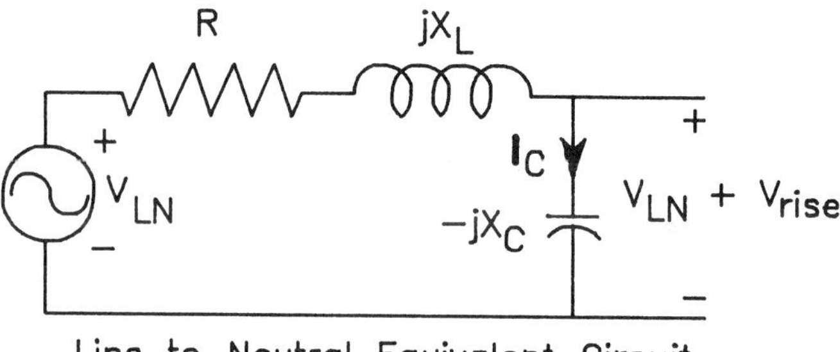

Figure 9-11 Voltage rise due to capacitor.

where

Q_{CAP} = three-phase reactive power rating of the capacitor in volt-amperes reactive (VAR)

V_{LL} = rated line to line voltage of the capacitor bank in volts

The voltage rise produced by the capacitor is equal to

$$V_{\text{rise}} = X_L \cdot I_C \tag{9.11}$$

where X_L is the inductive reactance of the line and I_C is the rated capacitor current. Substituting Eq. (9.10) into (9.11) results in the following:

$$V_{\text{rise}} = X_L \cdot \frac{Q_{\text{CAP}}}{\sqrt{3} \cdot V_{\text{LL}}} \tag{9.12}$$

The percent voltage rise produced by the capacitor is equal to the actual voltage rise in volts, as given by Eq. (9.12), divided by the nominal line to neutral system voltage, multiplied by 100. In the form of an equation,

$$\% V_{\text{rise}} = \frac{V_{\text{rise}}}{V_{\text{LN}}} \cdot 100 \tag{9.13}$$

Substituting Eq. (9.12) into (9.13) results in

$$\% V_{\text{rise}} = X_L \cdot \frac{\left[\dfrac{Q_{\text{CAP}}}{(\sqrt{3} \cdot V_{\text{LL}})}\right]}{V_{\text{LN}}} \cdot 100 \tag{9.14}$$

Recall that for balanced three-phase operation

$$V_{\text{LN}} = \frac{V_{\text{LL}}}{\sqrt{3}} \tag{9.15}$$

Substituting Eq. (9.15) into (9.14) results in a simplified expression for the voltage rise due to capacitor installation.

$$\% V_{\text{rise}} = X_L \cdot \left[\frac{Q_{\text{CAP}}}{V_{\text{LL}}^2}\right] \cdot 100 \tag{9.16}$$

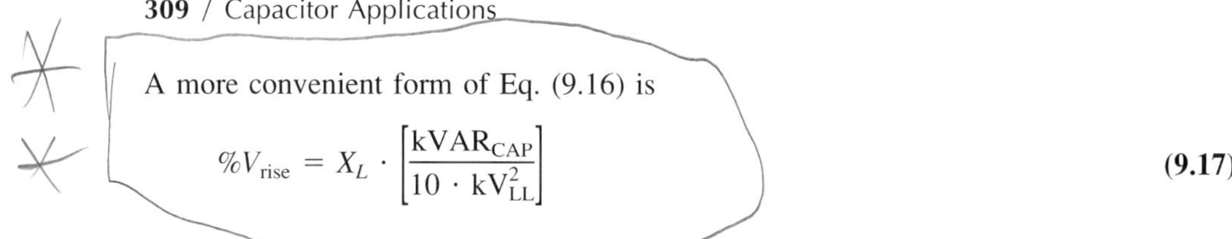

A more convenient form of Eq. (9.16) is

$$\%V_{\text{rise}} = X_L \cdot \left[\frac{\text{kVAR}_{\text{CAP}}}{10 \cdot \text{kV}_{\text{LL}}^2}\right] \tag{9.17}$$

EXAMPLE 9-9 A 1200-kVAR, 12.47-kV, three-phase capacitor bank is to be installed at the end of a three-phase distribution feeder 2 miles in length. The impedance of the feeder is 0.306 + j0.639 Ω/mile. Calculate the percentage of voltage rise due to this capacitor.

Solution The inductive reactance of the line is

$$X_L = (2 \text{ miles}) \cdot (0.639 \ \Omega/\text{mile}) = 1.278 \ \Omega$$

Direct application of Eq. (9.17) results in

$$\%V_{\text{rise}} = 1.278 \cdot \left[\frac{1200}{10 \cdot 12.47^2}\right]$$
$$= 0.986\% \approx 1.0\%$$

Therefore, a voltage rise of approximately 1% will result.

9-6 Location and Sizing for Optimal Line Loss Reduction

In addition to improved power factor and resulting decrease in line current, the installation of capacitors on a distribution circuit will reduce the line losses along the feeder. Example 9-8 illustrated the reduction in I^2R losses due to the installation of a capacitor bank at the end of a 12.47-kV three-phase feeder. It is desirable to determine the optimal size and location of capacitors to maximize reduction in line losses.

As previously discussed, the capacitor bank will absorb a leading current from the source, while inductive lagging power factor loads absorb a lagging current. The magnitude of the line current can be expressed as follows:

$$I_1 = (I_p^2 + I_q^2)^{1/2} \tag{9.18}$$

where

I_p = magnitude of in-phase component of line current

I_q = magnitude of quadrature component of line current

The current absorbed by a capacitor bank will subtract from the quadrature component of line current, resulting in the following:

$$I_1 = (I_p^2 + (I_q - I_c)^2)^{1/2} \tag{9.19}$$

where I_c is the magnitude of the capacitor current. For a constant active power load on the circuit, the in-phase component of line current will remain essentially constant. Therefore, the minimum line current magnitude will occur when I_c is equal to I_q. When this equality is established, the power factor is unity and the line losses will be minimum.

For concentrated loads, the optimum value of capacitor correction will be the value that corrects the power factor to unity. The optimum capacitor location would be at the load bus itself. Since the load has been corrected to unity power factor, the resulting line current supplied by the source, and hence line losses, will be minimized.

Determining the optimum location and size of capacitor banks to be installed on radial distribution feeders is slightly more complicated than determining the requirements for an industrial plant. Unlike industrial plant buses, the loads on radial distribution feeders are distributed along the length of the circuit or circuit segment. The nature of the distributed loads will vary depending on circuit topography. Large concentrated loads in addition to distributed loads are also very common on distribution circuits.

The time-varying nature of the loads will also be a significant factor in determining capacitor requirements. As discussed in Chapter 4, the loads on a power system change depending on time of day, day of the week, season, and the like. The power factor at which these loads operate will fluctuate as well.

Generally, the rating of fixed capacitor banks installed on a distribution feeder will be equal to the minimum reactive power consumed by the loads connected to the feeder at light load conditions. The voltage rise produced by fixed capacitors must be calculated under light load conditions to ensure that the system voltage is not excessive. Various combinations of switched capacitor units can be applied to supply additional amounts of compensation as the load dictates. Recordings of active and reactive load on the distribution feeders are taken at the distribution substation circuit exits. These recordings are then used to determine the correct amount of fixed and switched capacitors to add to the circuit.

EXAMPLE 9-10

Figure 9-12a shows the reactive power load profile characteristic of a 4.16-kV, three-phase, MGN distribution feeder. Determine the amount of fixed and switched capacitor kVAR to be added to correct the circuit power factor.

Solution From Fig. 9-12a, the minimum reactive power occurs at 2:00 AM and is equal to approximately 970 kVAR. Therefore, a fixed capacitor bank of 900 kVAR (300 kVAR per phase) will be added to the circuit. The switched capacitor requirements will be selected to correct the power factor to as close to unity as possible, without producing a leading power factor. An additional bank of 900 kVAR will be switched on at 10:00 AM and off at 8:00 PM to provide reactive compensation during peak load conditions. Figure 9-12a shows the portion of reactive power supplied by the 900-kVAR fixed bank and the 900-kVAR switched bank.

It is also possible to install two steps of switched capacitor banks to provide a more precise control of reactive power requirements. These two banks may consist of one step of 600 kVAR switched on at 8:00 AM and off at 10:00 PM and a 900-kVAR bank switched on at 12:00 PM and off at 6:00 PM. The addition of additional switched steps is more costly than a single switched step. As always, the increased cost must be

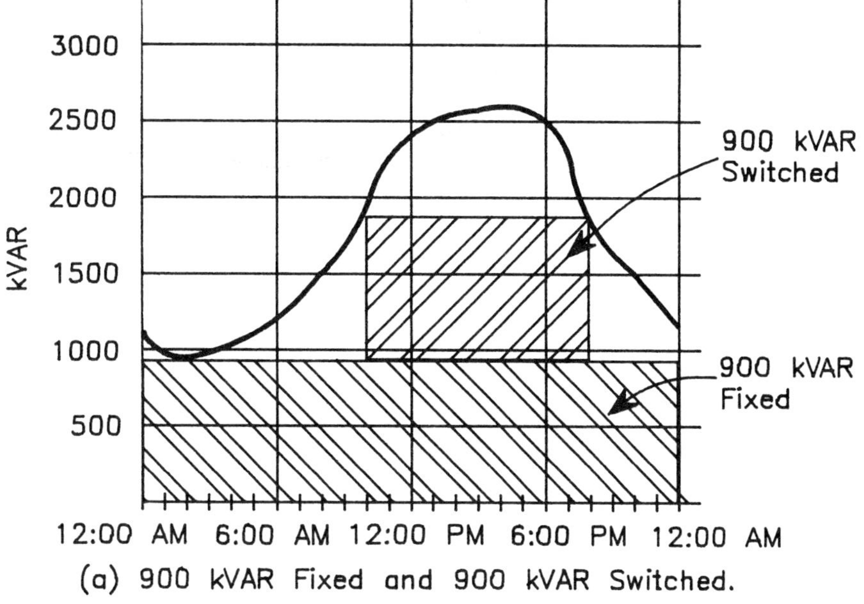

(a) 900 kVAR Fixed and 900 kVAR Switched.

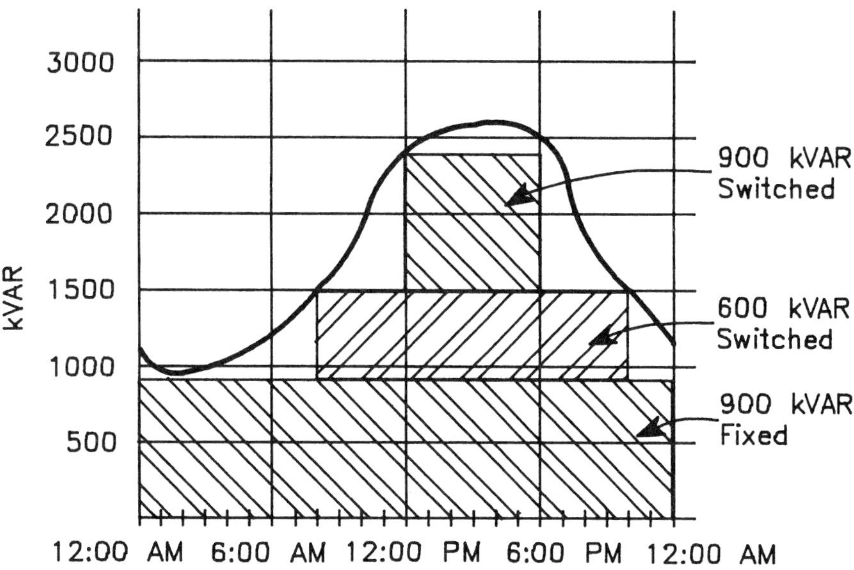

(b) 900 kVAR Fixed, 600 and 900 kVAR Switched.

Figure 9-12 Reactive demand curve, Example 9-10.

balanced against the benefits provided. Figure 9-12b shows the reactive power supplied by one fixed bank and two switched banks.

To determine the most economical size and location of a capacitor bank installed on a radial distribution feeder, consider the circuit segment shown in Fig. 9-13a. The reactive load current is assumed to be uniformly distributed along the length of the line. The reactive current at the beginning of the line segment is designated I_1. The reactive current at the and of the line is considered to be a lumped load and is designated as KI_1. Thus, the reactive current at the end of the line segment is expressed as a multiple of the reactive current at the beginning of the line segment. The length of the line is designated as l. Figure 9-13b shows the reactive load current plotted as a function of distance from the beginning of the line segment.

The equation for the reactive load current as a function of x is

$$i(x) = \frac{KI_1 - I_1}{l} x + I_1 \tag{9.20}$$

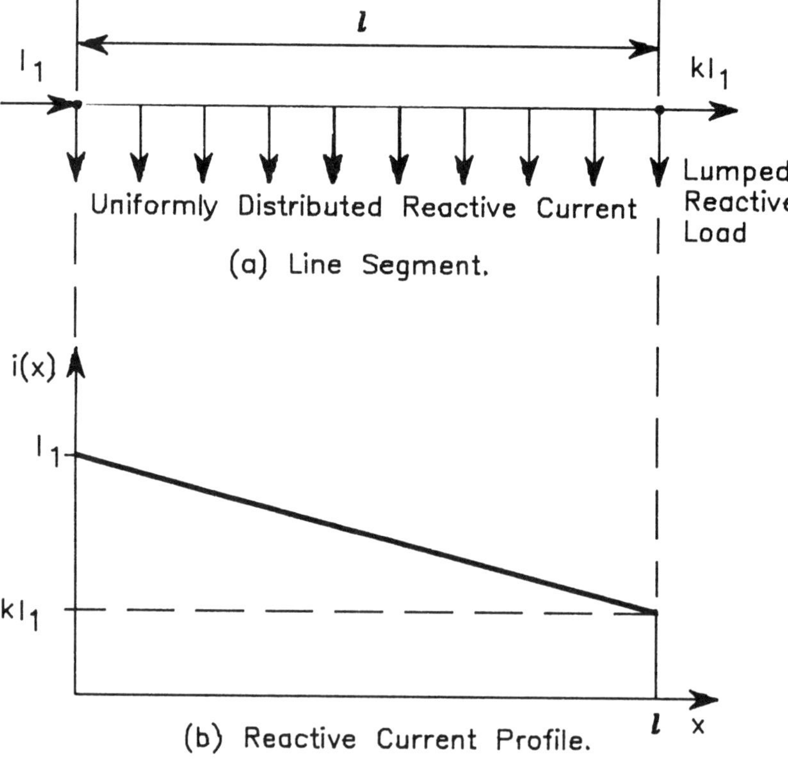

Figure 9-13 Reactive load current distribution.

The active power loss per phase due to the reactive component of load current is

$$P_{\text{loss}} = \int_0^l \left[\frac{KI_1 - I_1}{l}x + I_1\right]^2 R\,dx$$
$$= \frac{l}{3}I_1^2(K^2 + K + 1)R \qquad \textbf{(9.21)}$$

where R is the resistance per unit length of the line.

Note that if the load on the circuit consisted of only a lumped sum load with no uniformly distributed load the value of K would be 1. Applying Eq. (9.20) with $K = 1$ results in

$$P_{\text{loss}} = I_1^2 lR \qquad \textbf{(9.22)}$$

Equation (9.22) is the familiar I^2R relationship for power loss.

If the load on the circuit consisted of a uniformly distributed load with no concentrated load at the end, the value of K would be zero. The power loss per phase due to the reactive component of load current would be

$$P_{\text{loss}} = \frac{l}{3}I_1^2(K^2 + K + 1)R$$
$$= \frac{l}{3}I_1^2R \qquad \textbf{(9.23)}$$

If a single capacitor bank is added to the circuit, the reactive load profile is modified as shown in Fig. 9-14. The reactive current supplied by the capacitor is equal to I_c. The equation for the reactive component of load current must be split up into two parts, depending on which side of the capacitor bank is of interest. The reactive component of load current is given by

$$i(x) = \frac{KI_1 - I_1}{l}x + I_1 - I_c, \qquad \text{for } 0 \le x \le x' \qquad \textbf{(9.24)}$$

and

$$i(x) = \frac{KI_1 - I_1}{l}x + I_1, \qquad \text{for } x' \le x \le l \qquad \textbf{(9.25)}$$

The power loss per phase with the addition of the capacitor is

$$P_{\text{loss}} = \int_0^{x'} \left[\frac{KI_1 - I_1}{l}x + I_1 - I_c\right]^2 R\,dx$$
$$+ \int_{x'}^{l} \left[\frac{KI_1 - I_1}{l}x + I_1\right]^2 R\,dx \qquad \textbf{(9.26)}$$
$$= \left\{\frac{x'^2}{l}(I_1I_c(1 - K)) + x'(I_c^2 - 2I_1I_c) + \frac{l}{3}\left[I_1^2(K^2 + K + 1)\right]\right\} \cdot R$$

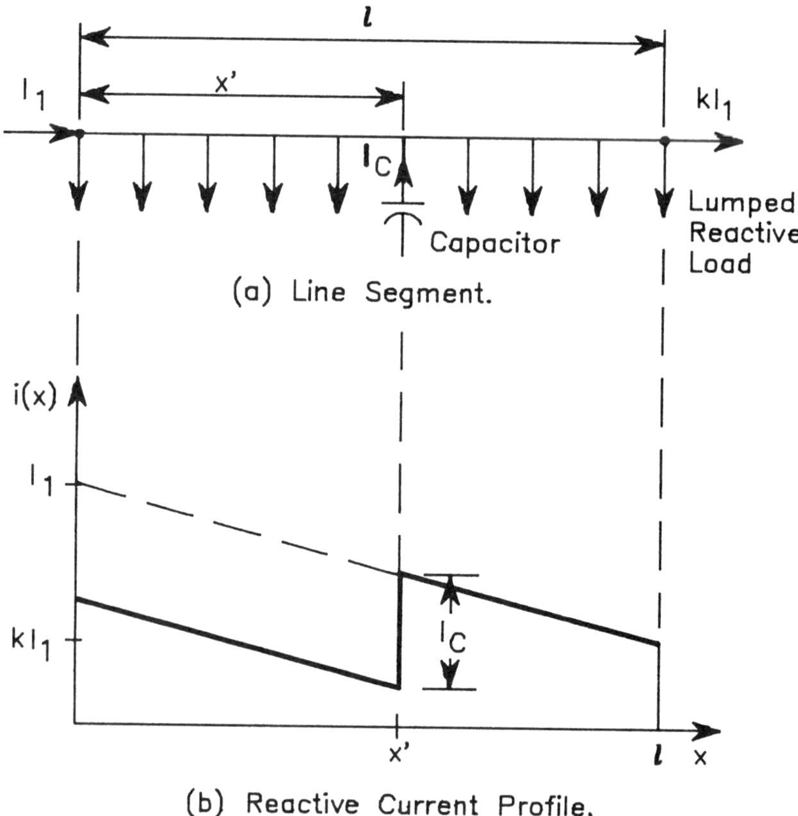

Figure 9-14 Reactive load current distribution with capacitor added.

For a given load profile, line length, and resistance, the quantities K, I_1, R, and l are constant in Eq. (9.26). The only two variables are I_c and x', the capacitor size and location, respectively. To determine the optimum capacitor size and location to minimize circuit losses, the partial derivatives of Eq. (9.26) are taken with respect to the two variables I_c and x' and equated to zero. The following equations result:

$$\frac{\partial P_{\text{loss}}}{\partial x'} = 0 = \frac{2x'}{l}[I_1 I_c(1 - K)] + (I_c^2 - 2I_1 I_c) \tag{9.27}$$

$$\frac{\partial P_{\text{loss}}}{\partial I_c} = 0 = \frac{x'^2}{l}[I_1(1 - K)] + 2x'I_c - 2I_1 x') \tag{9.28}$$

$$= \frac{x'}{l}[I_1(1 - K)] + 2I_c - 2I_1)$$

Equations (9.27) and (9.28) must be solved simultaneously to determine the optimum values of I_c and x'. Solving Eq. (9.27) for x' results in

$$x' = \frac{-(I_c^2 - 2I_1 I_c)}{I_1 I_c(1 - K)} \frac{l}{2} \tag{9.29}$$

It is convenient to express the capacitor current I_c as a function of the reactive load current I_1 as follows:

$$I_c = \alpha I_1 \tag{9.30}$$

Substituting Eq. (9.30) into (9.29) and simplifying results in

$$x' = \frac{l}{2}\left[\frac{2 - \alpha}{1 - K}\right] \tag{9.31}$$

Equation (9.31) gives the optimum location for a given capacitor size and ratio K.

Substituting Eq. (9.30) into (9.28) and simplifying,

$$\begin{aligned}\frac{\partial P_{\text{loss}}}{\partial I_c} &= 0 = \frac{x'}{l}[I_1(1 - K)] + 2\alpha I_1 - 2I_1) \\ &= \frac{x'}{l}(1 - K) + 2\alpha - 2\end{aligned} \tag{9.32}$$

Substituting Eq. (9.31) into (9.32) and simplifying,

$$\begin{aligned}0 &= \frac{\frac{l}{2}\left[\frac{(2 - \alpha)}{(1 - K)}\right](1 - K)}{l} + 2\alpha - 2 \\ &= \frac{2 - \alpha}{2} + 2\alpha - 2 \\ &= \frac{3}{2}\alpha - 1\end{aligned} \tag{9.33}$$

Solving Eq. (9.33) for α results in $\alpha = 2/3$.

From the previous derivation, it would appear that the optimum-sized capacitor would have a current rating equal to two-thirds times the reactive load current at the beginning of the line segment. A capacitor rating of two-thirds times the reactive current at the beginning of the line segment does provide optimum line loss reductions up to a K value of 1/3. This result can be verified by substituting $\alpha = 2/3$ into Eq. (9.31) and solving for x' as a function of K. The result is

$$x' = \frac{2}{3}l\left[\frac{1}{1 - K}\right] \tag{9.34}$$

Examination of Eq. (9.34) indicates that for values of K greater than 1/3 the value of x' exceeds l. This value of x' is of course longer than the line segment itself. As such, the optimum size of 2/3 is only valid for K less than or equal to 1/3.

If K exceeds 1/3, the optimum location is at $x' = l$, which is at the end of the segment. The optimum value of α will no longer be 2/3, but can be calculated by substituting $x' = l$ into Eq. (9.32) and solving for α, as follows:

$$0 = \frac{l}{l}(1 - K) + 2\alpha - 2$$

$$0 = 1 - K + 2\alpha - 2$$

from which

$$\alpha = \frac{K + 1}{2} \tag{9.35}$$

EXAMPLE 9-11

A section of a 12.47-kV distribution line has a length of 3 miles. The reactive power loading was measured as 2000 kVAR at the distribution substation line exit. The reactive power loading at the end of the 3-mile section was estimated as 600 kVAR. Determine the optimum capacitor rating and location to minimize line loss on this section of feeder.

Solution The ratio of reactive power at the end of the line section to the reactive power at the beginning of the line section is

$$K = \frac{600 \text{ kVAR}}{2000 \text{ kVAR}} = 0.3$$

Since the ratio K is less than 1/3, the optimum capacitor rating is two-thirds times the reactive power loading at the beginning of the line section.

$$\text{kVAR}_{\text{CAP}} = \tfrac{2}{3} \cdot 2000 \text{ kVAR} = 1333.3 \text{ kVAR}$$

The optimum capacitor location is given by Eq. (9.34).

$$x' = \frac{2}{3} \text{ (3 miles)} \left(\frac{1}{1 - 0.3}\right) = 2.86 \text{ miles}$$

Therefore, a capacitor bank of approximately 1333.3 kVAR located a distance of approximately 2.86 miles from the substation is required to minimize line losses on this section of feeder. A capacitor bank rating of either 1200 or 1500 kVAR will be appropriate. The bank will be comprised of either four 100-kVAR or five 100-kVAR single-phase units per phase.

EXAMPLE 9-12

An 8.32-kV distribution feeder has two major line sections, as shown in Fig. 9-15. Two capacitor banks are to be installed, one on each line section, to minimize losses. Using the estimated reactive power flows shown, determine the optimum rating and location for each line section.

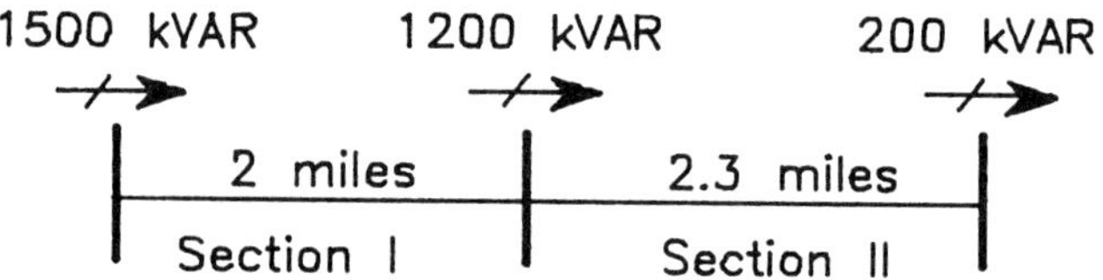

Figure 9-15 Circuit for Example 9-12.

Solution The correct procedure is to locate and size the capacitors at the line section farthest away from the source. Next, the reactive profile of the next line section closer to the source will be modified, and the location and size of capacitors for this line section determined. This procedure will result in the minimizing of losses for each line section of interest. Therefore, line section II will be analyzed first, followed by line section I.

SECTION II: The ratio K is calculated as

$$K = \frac{200 \text{ kVAR}}{1200 \text{ kVAR}} = 0.167$$

Since K is less than 1/3, the optimum capacitor bank rating is two-thirds time the reactive load at the beginning of the line section. The optimum capacitor location is determined by applying Eq. (9.34).

$$x' = \frac{2}{3}\,(2.3 \text{ miles})\left(\frac{1}{1 - 0.167}\right) = 1.84 \text{ miles}$$

$$\text{kVAR}_{\text{CAP}} = \tfrac{2}{3} \cdot 1200 = 800 \text{ kVAR}$$

Therefore, a capacitor bank with a rating of 900 kVAR will be the most practical for this line section. This 900-kVAR bank will be installed approximately 1.84 miles from the beginning of line section II in order to minimize losses in this section of feeder.

SECTION I: With the 900-kVAR capacitor bank installed in line section II, the reactive power flow over line section I needs to be modified. The reactive power flows at the beginning and end of line section I are equal to the initial reactive flows minus the reactive power supplied by the 900-kVAR capacitor bank in line section II. Thus, the reactive power flows at the beginning and end of line section I are equal to 600 and 300 kVAR, respectively.

The ratio K is calculated as

$$K = \frac{300 \text{ kVAR}}{600 \text{ kVAR}} = 0.5$$

Since K is greater than 1/3, the optimum location of the capacitor bank is at the end of line section I. The optimum capacitor bank rating is determined by applying Eq. (9.35).

$$\alpha = \frac{0.5 + 1}{2} = 0.75$$

The capacitor bank rating is

$$\text{kVAR}_{\text{CAP}} = 0.75 \cdot 600 = 450 \text{ kVAR}$$

Therefore, a bank rating of 450 kVAR will be installed at the end of line section I to minimize losses on this section of line.

Summary

If the ratio K is less than or equal to 1/3, then the optimum-sized capacitor has a rating equal to two-thirds times reactive load at the beginning of the line segment. The optimum location can be calculated by applying Eq. (9.34).

If the ratio K is greater than 1/3, the optimum capacitor location is at the end of the feeder segment. The optimum capacitor rating is calculated by applying Eq. (9.35).

On most distribution feeders, the two-thirds rule is commonly used to locate and size capacitor banks. This rule states that a capacitor bank rating equal to two-thirds the reactive load at the beginning of a line section should be located a distance of two-thirds the length of the feeder from the source to minimize line losses.

9-7 Capacitor Switching Considerations

In many instances, it is desirable to install several steps of switched capacitor units, rather than one large fixed bank. This is particularly true if the load reactive power requirements fluctuate by a substantial amount during the day. When a de-energized capacitor is energized, the capacitor essentially behaves as an electrical short. A large current will flow into the capacitor bank under these conditions. The inductance of the source will tend to limit the magnitude of the current flowing into the capacitor bank when energized. Energizing a single bank is referred to as *isolated bank switching*.

Likewise, when energizing one step of a multistepped capacitor bank, a high-magnitude current will result as the energized step discharges into the step being energized. This type of switching is referred to as *back to back switching*. Generally, back to back switching results in higher-magnitude currents than isolated bank switching.

The calculation of currents during capacitor switching is an extremely important consideration in capacitor applications. Contactors and circuit breakers used for capacitor switching are limited in the amount of momentary current the contacts can safely withstand. This momentary current rating is specified by the switch or breaker manufacturer. Failure to limit momentary current below specified values will result in contact welding, increased pitting of the contacts, or severe damage to the switch.

The high-magnitude currents that occur during capacitor switching are also of relatively high frequency compared to the system frequency. These high-frequency currents produce high-frequency voltage spikes on the system that may interfere with the operation of various control circuits. When switching large capacitor banks, it is important to provide overvoltage protection or isolated power supplies for proper operation of the control circuitry.

Isolated Bank Switching

Exact calculations of capacitor switching currents are extremely difficult to perform manually. To provide some basic guidelines, the following assumptions will be made:

1. The system will be analyzed on a single-phase, line to neutral equivalent basis.
2. The source will be modeled as a dc voltage source.
3. The magnitude of the dc voltage source will be constant.
4. The dc voltage source will have a magnitude equal to the peak line to neutral system voltage.
5. Resistance will be neglected.

The validity of these assumptions lies in the fact that the transient period of interest usually occurs in much less than one cycle of the nominal system frequency. As such, the magnitude of the source voltage will not change substantially during the period of interest.

The equivalent circuit based on the preceding assumptions is shown in Fig. 9-16. The magnitude of the source voltage is

$$V_o = \frac{\sqrt{2} \cdot V_{\mathrm{LL}}}{\sqrt{3}} \tag{9.36}$$

An approximate value of source inductance is given by

$$L_s \approx \frac{1}{2 \cdot \pi \cdot f} \cdot \frac{\mathrm{kV}_{\mathrm{LL}}^2}{\mathrm{MVA}_{\mathrm{SC}}} \tag{9.37}$$

where

f = system frequency
$\mathrm{kV}_{\mathrm{LL}}$ = line to line system voltage
$\mathrm{MVA}_{\mathrm{SC}}$ = three phase short circuit MVA

The capacitance per phase of the capacitor bank is given by

$$C = \frac{\mathrm{MVAR}_{\mathrm{rated}}}{2 \cdot \pi \cdot f_{\mathrm{rated}} \cdot (\mathrm{kV}_{\mathrm{LL,rated}})^2} \tag{9.38}$$

To determine the capacitor current, the LaPlace transform method is used. Figure 9-16 shows the equivalent circuit for isolated bank switching in the s domain. In reference to Fig. 9-16, the capacitor current is given by

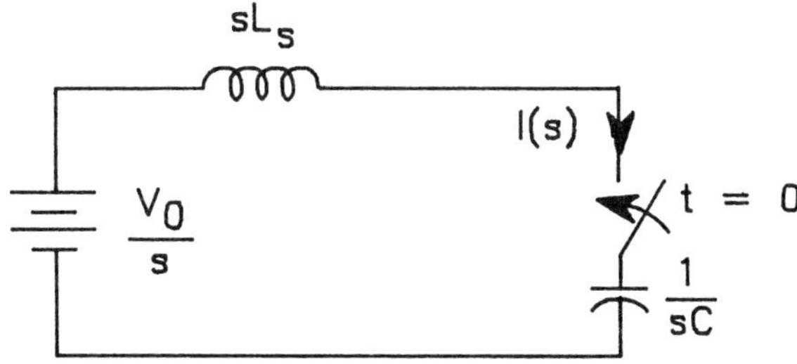

Figure 9-16 Equivalent circuit for isolated bank capacitor switching.

$$I(s) = \frac{V_o/s}{sL_s + (1/sC)} = \frac{V_o/L_s}{s^2 + (1/L_sC)} \tag{9.39}$$

Equation (9.39) must be rearranged to a form suitable for taking the inverse LaPlace transform. The following results:

$$I(s) = V_o\left(\frac{C}{L_s}\right)^{1/2}\left(\frac{\omega_o}{s^2 + \omega_o^2}\right) \tag{9.40}$$

where

$$\omega_o = \frac{1}{(L_sC)^{1/2}} \tag{9.41}$$

Equation (9.41) can be used to determine the frequency of the transient inrush current. The inverse LaPlace transform of Eq. (9.40) is

$$i(t) = \mathcal{L}^{-1}I(s) = V_o\left[\frac{C}{L_s}\right]^{1/2} \sin(\omega_o t) \tag{9.42}$$

The maximum instantaneous value of the inrush current is

$$I_{\max} = V_o \cdot \left[\frac{C}{L_s}\right]^{1/2} \tag{9.43}$$

EXAMPLE 9-13 A 1200-kVAR, 4.16-kV capacitor bank is installed on a plant bus. The plant bus is supplied from a 5000-kVA, 69kV–4.16Y/2.4kV transformer having an impedance of 7%. Neglecting the impedance of the 69kV source and resistance, determine the maximum instantaneous value and the frequency of the inrush current. Also, determine the inductance and current rating of the inductors that must be added to reduce the inrush current to 1000 A.

Solution The transformer inductive reactance is

$$X = 0.07 \cdot \frac{(4.16\ \text{kV})^2}{5\ \text{MVA}} = 0.2422\ \Omega$$

The transformer inductance is

$$L = \frac{0.2422}{2 \cdot \pi \cdot 60} = 6.425 \times 10^{-4}\ \text{H}$$

The capacitance per phase is equal to

$$C = \frac{1.2\ \text{MVAR}}{2 \cdot \pi \cdot 60 \cdot (4.16\ \text{kV})^2} = 1.839 \times 10^{-4}\ \text{F}$$

The peak source voltage is equal to

$$V_o = \frac{\sqrt{2} \cdot 4160}{\sqrt{3}} = 3396 \text{ V}$$

Applying Eq. (9.43) results in

$$I_{\max} = 3396 \left(\frac{1.839 \times 10^{-4}}{6.425 \times 10^{-4}} \right)^{1/2} = 1817 \text{ A}$$

The frequency of the transient inrush current is

$$\omega_o = \frac{1}{(1.839 \times 10^{-4} \cdot 6.425 \times 10^{-4})^{1/2}} = 2909 \text{ rad/sec}$$
$$= 463 \text{ Hz}$$

To determine the amount of inductance to be added in order to limit the inrush current to 1000 A, Eq. (9.43) is solved for L_s as follows:

$$L_s = \frac{V_o^2}{I_{\max}^2} C$$

Substituting in known values,

$$L_s = \frac{3396^2}{1000^2} \cdot 1.839 \times 10^{-4} = 2.1209 \times 10^{-3} \text{ H}$$

The inductance to be added is equal to

$$L_{\text{ind}} = 2.1209 \times 10^{-3} - 6.425 \times 10^{-4}$$
$$= 1.4784 \times 10^{-3} \text{ H}$$
$$\approx 1.5 \text{ mH}$$

Therefore, an inductor of approximately 1.5 mH should be added in each phase of the capacitor bank in order to limit the inrush current to acceptable values. The inductors used for current limiting are typically air core in design. Iron core inductors are not recommended for current-limiting purposes since the iron will saturate under high current conditions. The result of core saturation is a reduction in the inductance of the inductor. Therefore, the effectiveness of the iron core inductor to limit switching currents will be greatly reduced.

The continuous current rating of the inductors must be equal to the continuous current rating of the capacitor bank.

$$I_{\text{ind}} = \frac{1200 \text{ kVAR}}{\sqrt{3} \cdot 4.16 \text{ kV}} = 166.5 \text{ A}$$

Back to Back Switching

The equivalent circuit model for back to back capacitor switching is shown in Fig. 9-17. There are a total of N steps of capacitance that may be switched on and off as reactive power demands dictate. The most severe switching duty will arise when the last step is being energized, with all other steps energized, and the system voltage is at maximum peak value. Under these conditions, the energized steps will discharge into the step being switched on. For the purposes of this analysis, the source contribution will be neglected.

In the circuit model shown in Fig. 9-17, C_{eq} represents the equivalent capacitance of the $N - 1$ capacitor step(s) already energized. Since the energized capacitor steps are in parallel, the equivalent capacitance is

$$C_{eq} = C_1 + C_2 + \cdots + C_{N-1} \tag{9.44}$$

where C_1, C_2, $\cdots$ C_{N-1} are the capacitance values per phase of the $N - 1$ capacitor steps already energized. Each of these capacitance values may be calculated by applying Eq. (9.38) for each step.

Likewise, L_{eq} represents the equivalent inductance of the current-limiting inductors in series with the $N - 1$ capacitor steps already energized. This inductance is given by

$$\frac{1}{L_{eq}} = \frac{1}{L_1} + \frac{1}{L_2} + \cdots + \frac{1}{L_{N-1}} \tag{9.45}$$

where L_1, L_2, $\cdots$, L_{N-1} are the values of inductance for each step.

The voltage present on the energized capacitors is assumed to be equal to the peak value of the nominal line to neutral source voltage, as given by Eq. (9.36). In reference to Fig. 9-17, the transient current flowing into the de-energized capacitor bank is

$$\begin{aligned} I(s) &= \frac{V_o/s}{s(L_{eq} + L_N) + (1/sC_{eq}) + (1/sC_N)} \\ &= \frac{V_o/(L_{eq} + L_N)}{s^2 + \dfrac{1}{C_{eq}(L_{eq} + L_N)} + \dfrac{1}{C_N(L_{eq} + L_N)}} \\ &= \frac{V_o/(L_{eq} + L_N)}{s^2 + \dfrac{1/C_{eq} + 1/C_N}{L_{eq} + L_N}} \end{aligned} \tag{9.46}$$

The natural frequency is

$$\omega_o = \left(\frac{1/C_{eq} + 1/C_N}{L_{eq} + L_N}\right)^{1/2} \tag{9.47}$$

Substituting Eq. (9.47) into (9.46) and simplifying results in the following:

$$I(s) = V_o \frac{1}{[(L_{eq} + L_N)(1/C_{eq} + 1/C_N)]^{1/2}} \cdot \frac{\omega_o}{s^2 + \omega_o^2} \tag{9.48}$$

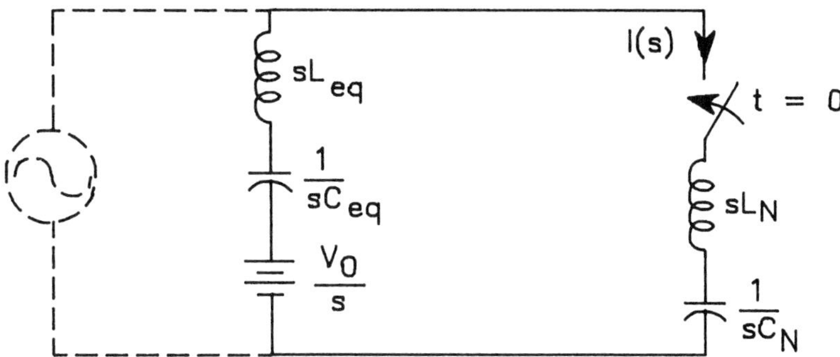

Figure 9-17 Equivalent circuit for back to back capacitor switching.

The inverse LaPlace transform of Eq. (9.48) is

$$\begin{aligned} i(t) &= \mathcal{L}^{-1} I(s) \\ &= V_o \frac{1}{[(L_{eq} + L_N)(1/C_{eq} + 1/C_N)]^{1/2}} \sin(\omega_o t) \end{aligned} \tag{9.49}$$

The maximum instantaneous value of the inrush current is

$$I_{max} = V_o \frac{1}{[(L_{eq} + L_N)(1/C_{eq} + 1/C_N)]^{1/2}} \tag{9.50}$$

Equation (9.49) gives the expression for the transient inrush current flowing into the last step to become energized in a multistep bank. The peak value of the transient inrush current is given by Eq. (9.50) and the frequency by Eq. (9.47).

Equations (9.44) through (9.50) can be simplified when the capacitor bank is made up of equal kVAR-rated steps. The capacitance per phase and the corresponding current-limiting inductors are assumed to have the same value. Let the capacitance and inductance per step be equal to C and L, respectively. For $N - 1$ equal-sized steps, Eqs. (9.44) and (9.45) become

$$C_{eq} = C \cdot (N - 1) \tag{9.51}$$

$$L_{eq} = \frac{L}{N - 1} \tag{9.52}$$

Substituting Eqs. (9.51) and (9.52) into (9.47) and (9.50) results in

$$\omega_o = \frac{1}{(LC)^{1/2}} \tag{9.53}$$

$$I_{max} = V_o \cdot \frac{N - 1}{N} \left(\frac{C}{L}\right)^{1/2} \tag{9.54}$$

To determine the rating of the current-limiting inductors required to limit the maximum peak transient inrush current to a specified value, Eq. (9.54) is solved for the inductance L, as follows:

$$L = C \cdot \frac{V_o^2}{I_{\text{max}}^2} \cdot \frac{(N-1)^2}{N^2} \tag{9.55}$$

Important Application Note

The derivation of the equations for back to back switching were derived by neglecting the source contribution to switching current. This assumption may not be valid for capacitor banks installed on stiff utility system buses where there is a high availability of fault current. The maximum permissible momentary duty can be derated to 80% of rated to provide a more reasonable estimate of transient switching currents expected. However, if a substantial amount of source contribution is expected, a more detailed analysis may be warranted. This detailed analysis may be performed using a transient analysis package such as the Electromagnetic Transient Analysis Program, or EMTP.

EXAMPLE 9-14

A 13.8-kV, three-step capacitor bank is comprised of three steps of 1800 kVAR each. The vacuum contactor used to switch the steps on and off has a momentary current rating of 10 kA. Neglecting the source contribution and derating the momentary switch rating to 80% of rated, determine the amount of inductance needed to limit the transient inrush current to an acceptable value for the following cases:

a. One step energized, second step coming on
b. Two steps energized, third step coming on

Make recommendations as to the proper inductor rating.

Solution The capacitance per step is determined by applying Eq. (9.38).

$$C = \frac{1.8 \text{ MVAR}}{2 \cdot \pi \cdot 60 \cdot (13.8 \text{ kV})^2} = 2.5071 \times 10^{-5} \text{ F}$$

The momentary rating of the switch will be derated to

$$I_{\text{max}} = 0.8 \cdot 10{,}000 \text{ A} = 8000 \text{ A}$$

The maximum peak system voltage is

$$V_o = \frac{\sqrt{2} \cdot 13{,}800}{\sqrt{3}} = 11{,}266.3 \text{ V}$$

a. With one step energized and the second step coming on, the number of steps N is equal to 2. Application of Eq. (9.55) results in the following:

$$\begin{aligned} L &= 2.5071 \times 10^{-5} \cdot \frac{11{,}266.3^2}{8000^2} \cdot \frac{(2-1)^2}{2^2} \\ &= 12.431 \times 10^{-6} \text{ H} \\ &\approx 12.5 \ \mu\text{H} \end{aligned}$$

Therefore, inductors of approximately 12.5μH would be required if this were a two step bank.

b. With two steps energized and the third step coming on, the number of steps N is equal to 3. Direct application of Eq. (9.55) results in

$$L = \frac{11{,}266.3^2}{8000^2} \cdot 2.5071 \times 10^{-5} \cdot \frac{(3-1)^2}{3^2}$$
$$= 22.1 \times 10^{-6} \text{ H}$$
$$\approx 22 \ \mu\text{H}$$

Therefore, an inductor of approximately 22 μH should be installed in each phase of each step in order to limit the transient inrush current to an acceptable level.

The worst-case switching scenario occurs when two steps are energized and the third step is switched on. Comparison of the results of parts a and b indicates that the inductors should have a rating of 22 μH. As in Example 9-13, these inductors will be installed in each phase of each step in series with the capacitor units. Since the inductors are series connected, the continuous current rating of the inductors should be equal to the rated current of each capacitor step.

$$I_{\text{ind}} = \frac{1800 \text{ kVAR}}{\sqrt{3} \cdot 13.8 \text{ kV}} = 75.3 \text{ A}$$

EXAMPLE 9-15

A 12.47-kV capacitor bank consists of the following steps:

Step 1: 2400 kVAR
Step 2: 1200 kVAR
Step 3: 600 kVAR

The three steps may be switched at random to provide the required degree of reactive compensation. Determine suitable current-limiting inductor ratings to limit the maximum transient inrush current to 6000 A.

Solution Since the capacitor bank is comprised of different kVAR-rated step sizes, Eq. (9.55) is not directly applicable. However, a conservative design approach is to assume that all steps of the bank are equal to the kVAR rating of the largest step and then to apply Eq. (9.55). For this example, the inductor design will be based on three equal steps of 2400 kVAR each. The maximum transient inrush current is then calculated based on *actual* kVAR step sizes and all possible switching combinations. The results of the calculations for all possible switching combinations will be checked to ensure that the maximum transient inrush currents are within design specifications.

The capacitance per phase for the 2400-kVAR step is equal to

$$C_1 = \frac{2.4 \text{ MVAR}}{2 \cdot \pi \cdot 60 \cdot (12.47 \text{ kV})^2} = 40.9 \times 10^{-6} \text{ F}$$

Likewise, for the 1200- and 600-kVAR steps,

$$C_2 = 20.5 \times 10^{-6} \text{ F}, \qquad C_3 = 10.2 \times 10^{-6} \text{ F}$$

The peak instantaneous value of the source voltage is

$$V_o = \frac{\sqrt{2} \cdot 12{,}470}{\sqrt{3}} = 10{,}180 \text{ V}$$

The number of steps N is equal to 3. Direct application of Eq. (9.55) results in the following inductance:

$$\begin{aligned} L &= 40.9 \times 10^{-6} \cdot \frac{10{,}180^2}{6000^2} \cdot \frac{(3-1)^2}{3^2} \\ &= 52.3 \times 10^{-6} \text{ H} \\ &\approx 50 \ \mu\text{H} \end{aligned}$$

Therefore, an inductor having an inductance of approximately 50 μH is required in each step.

With the 2400-kVAR step energized and the 1200-kVAR step being switched on, the following relationships apply.

$$L_{eq} = L_1, \qquad L_N = L_2, \qquad C_{eq} = C_1, \qquad C_N = C_2$$

Applying Eq. (9.50) gives the peak transient inrush current.

$$\begin{aligned} I_{max} &= 10{,}180 \cdot \frac{1}{[(100 \times 10^{-6})(7.323 \times 10^4)]^{1/2}} \\ &= 3762 \text{ A} \end{aligned}$$

With the 2400-kVAR step energized and the 600-kVAR step being switched on, the following relationships apply:

$$L_{eq} = L_1, \qquad L_N = L_3, \qquad C_{eq} = C_1, \qquad C_N = C_3$$

Applying Eq. (9.50) gives the peak transient inrush current.

$$\begin{aligned} I_{max} &= 10{,}180 \cdot \frac{1}{[(100 \times 10^{-6})(1.225 \times 10^5)]^{1/2}} \\ &= 2909 \text{ A} \end{aligned}$$

With the 1200-kVAR step energized and the 600-kVAR step being switched on, the following relationships apply:

$$L_{eq} = L_2, \qquad L_N = L_3, \qquad C_{eq} = C_2, \qquad C_N = C_3$$

Applying Eq. (9.50) gives the peak transient inrush current.

$$\begin{aligned} I_{max} &= 10{,}180 \cdot \frac{1}{[(100 \times 10^{-6})(1.468 \times 10^5)]^{1/2}} \\ &= 2657 \text{ A} \end{aligned}$$

With both the 2400- and 1200-kVAR steps energized and the 600-kVAR step being switched on, the following relationships apply:

$$L_{eq} = L_1//L_2 = 25 \times 10^{-6}\ \text{H}, \qquad L_N = L_3 = 50 \times 10^{-6}\ \text{H}$$

$$C_{eq} = C_1 + C_2 = 61.4 \times 10^{-6}\ \text{F}, \qquad C_N = C_3 = 10.2 \times 10^{-6}\ \text{F}$$

Applying Eq. (9.50) gives the peak transient inrush current.

$$\begin{aligned} I_{max} &= 10{,}180 \cdot \frac{1}{[(75 \times 10^{-6})(1.1433 \times 10^{5})]^{1/2}} \\ &= 3477\ \text{A} \end{aligned}$$

The results of this example indicate that the choice of 50-μH current-limiting inductors is indeed conservative. This method of selecting current-limiting inductors can provide an initial starting point in the design. The inductor size may be decreased and the transient currents recalculated until a more realistic inductor size is obtained. This is left as an exercise for the student.

9-8 Operation at Off-Rated Voltage and Frequency

In some instances, it is necessary to operate capacitors at voltages and frequencies other than rated. The result is a change in the actual reactive power rating of the capacitor bank. The actual reactive power rating of the capacitor bank can be determined for any operating voltage or frequency by recognizing that the capacitance of the capacitor bank is constant regardless of the actual applied voltage or frequency. This value of equivalent line to neutral capacitance can be calculated from Eq. (9.38). The capacitive reactance is given by

$$X_{c,\text{act}} = \frac{1}{2 \cdot \pi \cdot f_{\text{act}} \cdot C} \tag{9.56}$$

where f_{act} is the actual operating frequency of the capacitor, and C is the capacitance as given by Eq. (9.38). Substituting Eq. (9.38) into (9.56) results in the following:

$$X_{c,\text{act}} = \frac{f_{\text{rated}}}{f_{\text{act}}} \cdot \frac{(\text{kV}_{\text{LL,rated}})^2}{\text{MVAR}_{\text{rated}}} \tag{9.57}$$

Equation (9.57) indicates that the capacitive reactance is inversely proportional to the actual operating frequency.

The actual line current drawn by the capacitor is

$$\begin{aligned} I_c &= \frac{V_{\text{LN,act}}}{X_{c,\text{act}}} \\ &= \frac{V_{\text{LL,act}}/\sqrt{3}}{X_{c,\text{act}}} \end{aligned} \tag{9.58}$$

where $V_{LL,act}$ is the actual line to line operating voltage. Substituting Eq. (9.57) into (9.58) results in

$$I_{c,act} = \frac{f_{act}}{f_{rated}} \cdot \frac{MVAR_{rated}}{(kV_{LL,rated})^2} \cdot \frac{V_{LL,act}}{\sqrt{3}} \tag{9.59}$$

The actual three-phase reactive power rating of the capacitor bank is

$$MVAR_{act} = \sqrt{3} \cdot (V_{LL,act}) \cdot (I_{c,act}) \times 10^{-6} \tag{9.60}$$

Substituting Eq. (9.59) into (9.60) and simplifying results in

$$MVAR_{act} = MVAR_{rated} \cdot \frac{f_{act}}{f_{rated}} \cdot \frac{(kV_{LL,act})^2}{(kV_{LL,rated})^2} \tag{9.61}$$

A more convenient form of Eq. (9.61) is

$$kVAR_{act} = kVAR_{rated} \cdot \frac{f_{act}}{f_{rated}} \cdot \frac{(kV_{LL,act})^2}{(kV_{LL,rated})^2} \tag{9.62}$$

Equation (9.61) or (9.62) can be used to calculate the actual reactive power output of the capacitor bank at off-nominal voltage and frequency. Keep in mind, however, that capacitors should not be operated at above rated voltage.

EXAMPLE 9-16

A three-phase capacitor bank is made up of six 200-kVAR, 2770-V, 60-Hz, single-phase capacitor units per phase. The capacitors are floating wye connected and will be applied on a 4.16-kV, 60-Hz plant bus. Determine the actual reactive power rating of the capacitor bank under these conditions.

Solution The rated line to line voltage of the capacitor bank is

$$kV_{LL,rated} = 2770 \cdot \sqrt{3} = 4800 \text{ V}$$

The rated reactive power of the capacitor bank is

$$\begin{aligned} kVAR_{rated} &= (6 \text{ units/phase})(200 \text{ kVAR/unit})(3 \text{ phases}) \\ &= 3600 \text{ kVAR} \end{aligned}$$

The actual reactive power of the bank is determined by applying Eq. (9.62).

$$\begin{aligned} kVAR_{act} &= 3600 \text{ kVAR} \cdot \frac{60 \text{ Hz}}{60 \text{ Hz}} \cdot \frac{4160^2}{4800^2} \\ &= 2700 \text{ kVAR} \end{aligned}$$

Therefore, the reactive power output has been reduced to 75% of nameplate value due to operation at reduced voltage.

9-9 Controls

As previously discussed, capacitor banks may be permanently connected (fixed) or switched as reactive power demands dictate. Fixed capacitors are generally sized to supply reactive power equal to the minimum reactive power demands of the system. Switched capacitors are used to supply the variable amount of reactive power needed as the load increases. Switching of the capacitor banks may be done either manually or automatically. Several types of automatic control can be used to initiate switching of capacitor banks. These include time clock, power factor, and voltage. The type of control selected depends on the primary function of the capacitor bank itself.

Time clocks can be used where the reactive power demand is a predictable function of time. Examination of the reactive load profile for a given distribution feeder or substation bus will indicate the desired switching times. The reactive power consumption of industrial plant loads may also be a predictable function of time based on manufacturing and shift schedules. It must be understood that capacitor switching based on time ignores the actual load conditions and may produce undesirable results. However, capacitor switching based on time of day is the most economical of all automatic switching schemes.

If the primary function of the capacitor bank is to control the load power factor to a specified value, a controller that senses the load power factor is the most desirable. This type of control operates independently of time and generally produces the most desirable effect. Typically, a set of current and/or voltage transformers may be needed to provide the appropriate electrical quantities to the controller. The costs associated with controllers based on load power factor are generally higher than time-based control. This is due to the increased complexity of the controller itself, as well as the need for voltage and current transformers.

Control based on voltage is used where the primary function of the capacitor bank is to provide voltage improvement. The capacitor is switched on and off based on the magnitude of the system voltage. An increase in the reactive power demand of a lagging power factor load causes a reduction in the bus voltage. This decrease in voltage is sensed by the controller and switching action is initiated. Conversely, as the reactive power demand of the load decreases, the bus voltage increases. Under these conditions, the controller switches the capacitor steps off to prevent excessive bus voltages from occurring.

Switching of multistep capacitor banks is usually performed one step at a time. A time delay between step switching is often included to allow the system to adjust to the new conditions. The amount of time delay is often adjustable by the user. Also, an adjustable reactive power bandwidth is provided to prevent excessive hunting of the controller, thereby minimizing switching operations. Excessive switching will cause premature wear of the switch contacts and control mechanism.

Problems

9.1. Determine the required voltage and kVAR ratings of the capacitor units used to construct a 2100-kVAR, grounded-wye connected capacitor bank. The bank is to be installed on an

8.32-kV MGN distribution substation bus. Use equal kVAR ratings for all capacitors in the bank. Specify the required number of high-voltage bushings.

9.2. The capacitor units in the bank of Problem 9.1 are protected by individual fuse elements. Determine the resulting neutral current if one of the fuse elements blows.

9.3. Determine the required voltage and kVAR ratings of the capacitor units used to construct a 1800-kVAR, delta-connected capacitor bank. The bank is to be installed on a 13.8-kV plant bus. Use equal kVAR ratings for all capacitors in the bank. Specify the required number of high-voltage bushings.

9.4. Determine the required voltage and kVAR ratings of the capacitor units used to construct a 2700-kVAR, floating-wye connected capacitor bank. The bank is to be installed on a 24.94-kV MGN distribution substation bus. Use equal kVAR ratings for all capacitors in the bank. Specify the required number of high-voltage bushings.

9.5. The capacitor units in the bank of Problem 9.4 are protected by individual fuse elements. Determine the resulting neutral to ground voltage and the voltage across the remaining capacitor elements in the bank if one of the fuse elements blows.

9.6. A floating-wye capacitor bank is constructed of three 200-kVAR, 2400-V capacitor units per phase. The capacitor units are individually fused. Determine the voltages on the remaining capacitor units in the bank and the neutral to ground voltage if one of the fuse elements blows. Is this an acceptable design? If not, recommend an alternative design. Specify quantity, kVAR, and voltage ratings of capacitors used in the new design.

9.7. A split-wye capacitor bank is made up of two 4500-kVAR, 13.8-kV sections, for a total installed rating of 9000 kVAR. Each section consists of five 300-kVAR, 7960-V, single-phase capacitor units per phase. The capacitor units are individually fused. Determine the current flow in the neutral between the two sections if one fuse element blows in one of the sections.

9.8. An industrial plant is supplied service at 4.16 kV. The plant has an active power demand of 1200 kW at a power factor of 0.72 lagging. Determine the following:

a. Apparent power demand
b. Reactive power demand
c. Line current magnitude
d. Amount of capacitors required to improve the plant power factor to 0.95 lagging
e. Active, reactive, and apparent power demands after addition of the capacitors
f. Line current magnitude after addition of the capacitors

9.9. A 12.47-kV, three-phase, MGN, distribution feeder has a length of 3-miles. The impedance is $0.129 + j0.591\ \Omega$/mile. An 1800-kVAR capacitor bank is installed at the end of the feeder. Calculate the percentage of voltage rise due to the installation of this capacitor bank.

9.10. A 4-mile section of 12.47-kV, three-phase distribution feeder has a uniformly distributed load and a concentrated load at the end of the line section. The reactive power loading at the beginning of the line section was measured as 3200 kVAR. The reactive power loading at the end of the line section is estimated to be 600 kVAR. Determine the rating and location of a capacitor bank required to minimize line losses along this section of line.

9.11. A 3600-kVAR, 13.8-kV capacitor bank is installed on a plant bus supplied from a 7500-kVA, 138 kV–13.8 kV transformer having a nameplate impedance of 6.8%. Neglecting the impedance of the 138-kV source and transformer resistance, determine the maximum instantaneous value and frequency of the transient inrush current when the capacitor bank is switched on.

9.12. For the plant in Problem 9.11, it is desired to limit the maximum peak transient inrush current to 1000 A in order to minimize voltage dips during switching. If current-limiting inductors are required, specify the inductance and continuous current rating.

9.13. A four-step, 4.16-kV capacitor bank consists of three steps of 1200 kVAR and one step of 600 kVAR. The maximum momentary rating of the switching device is 5000 A. Determine the inductance and continuous current rating of the current-limiting inductors required for this situation.

9.14. A 2400-kVAR, 60-Hz, floating-wye connected capacitor bank is constructed of four 200-kVAR, 7960-V, single-phase capacitor units per phase. Calculate the actual reactive power rating if connected to a 12.47-kV bus.

10

Introduction to Symmetrical Components

10-1 General

The method of symmetrical components is used extensively in electrical power systems analysis for fault current calculations and protective relay applications. As applied to three-phase power systems, the method of symmetrical components provides a means to transform an unbalanced system into three balanced systems. Since each of these component sets is balanced, it may be analyzed on a single-phase basis, similar to that discussed in Chapter 1. Thus, an unbalanced three-phase system may be analyzed in terms of three balanced systems if the proper transformations are used. Typical causes of unbalanced conditions include faults involving one or two phases and ground and large single-phase loads.

10-2 Transformation of Phase Quantities to Sequence Quantities

The sequence components resulting from the symmetrical component transformation applied to a three-phase system are referred to as the zero sequence, positive sequence, and negative sequence components. Each set of sequence components will have three quantities corresponding to each phase of the actual phase quantities. Thus, the zero sequence components will consist of the zero sequence component of the *A* phase, the zero sequence component of the *B* phase, and the zero sequence component of the *C* phase. The positive sequence components consist of the positive sequence component of the *A* phase, the positive sequence component of the *B* phase, and the positive sequence component of the *C* phase. Finally, the negative sequence components consist of the negative sequence component of the *A* phase, the negative sequence component of the *B* phase, and the negative sequence component of the *C* phase. The components of the sequence sets are shown in Fig. 10-1 for a general case of unbalanced phase voltages. A similar analysis can be done for unbalanced phase currents.

In reference to Fig. 10-1, the phase quantities can be expressed in terms of the sequence quantities, as shown:

$$\mathbf{V}_a = \mathbf{V}_{a0} + \mathbf{V}_{a1} + \mathbf{V}_{a2} \quad \textbf{(10.1)}$$

$$\mathbf{V}_b = \mathbf{V}_{b0} + \mathbf{V}_{b1} + \mathbf{V}_{b2} \quad \textbf{(10.2)}$$

$$\mathbf{V}_c = \mathbf{V}_{c0} + \mathbf{V}_{c1} + \mathbf{V}_{c2} \quad \textbf{(10.3)}$$

where $\mathbf{V}_a$, $\mathbf{V}_b$, and $\mathbf{V}_c$ are the phase quantities. The zero sequence voltages are designated $\mathbf{V}_{a0}$, $\mathbf{V}_{b0}$, and $\mathbf{V}_{c0}$; the positive sequence voltages are designated $\mathbf{V}_{a1}$, $\mathbf{V}_{b1}$, and $\mathbf{V}_{c1}$; and the negative sequence quantities are designated $\mathbf{V}_{a2}$, $\mathbf{V}_{b2}$, and $\mathbf{V}_{c2}$.

The zero sequence components are equal in magnitude and have the same phase angle. Therefore, it is convenient to define the zero sequence voltage, $\mathbf{V}_0$ for all three phases, as follows:

$$\mathbf{V}_0 = \mathbf{V}_{a0} = \mathbf{V}_{b0} = \mathbf{V}_{c0} \quad \textbf{(10.4)}$$

The positive and negative sequence components have equal magnitude and are displaced 120° from one another. The phase sequence of the positive sequence component set is *ABC*, while the phase sequence of the negative sequence component set is *ACB*. To streamline the notation, the **a** operator is introduced as follows:

$$\mathbf{a} = 1.0\angle 120°$$

Some additional properties of the **a** operator are

$$\mathbf{a}^2 = 1.0\angle 240° = 1.0\angle -120°$$

$$\mathbf{a}^3 = 1.0\angle 360° = 1.0\angle 0°$$

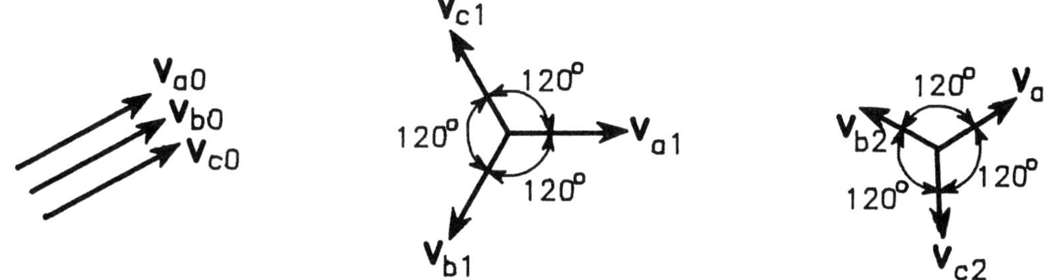

Figure 10-1 Sequence voltages.

Applying the **a** operator to the positive sequence voltages results in the following:

$$\mathbf{V}_{b1} = \mathbf{a}^2\,\mathbf{V}_{a1} = \mathbf{a}^2\,\mathbf{V}_1 \tag{10.5}$$

and

$$\mathbf{V}_{c1} = \mathbf{a}\,\mathbf{V}_{a1} = \mathbf{a}\,\mathbf{V}_1 \tag{10.6}$$

where $\mathbf{V}_1$ is the positive sequence voltage. Likewise, for the negative sequence voltages,

$$\mathbf{V}_{b2} = \mathbf{a}\,\mathbf{V}_{a2} = \mathbf{a}\,\mathbf{V}_2 \tag{10.7}$$

and

$$\mathbf{V}_{c1} = \mathbf{a}^2\,\mathbf{V}_{a2} = \mathbf{a}^2\,\mathbf{V}_2 \tag{10.8}$$

where $\mathbf{V}_2$ is the negative sequence voltage.

Substituting the results of Eqs. (10.4) through (10.8) into Eqs. (10.1), (10.2), and (10.3) results in the following set of equations for the actual phase voltages in terms of the sequence voltages.

$$\mathbf{V}_a = \mathbf{V}_0 + \mathbf{V}_1 + \mathbf{V}_2 \tag{10.9}$$

$$\mathbf{V}_b = \mathbf{V}_0 + \mathbf{a}^2\,\mathbf{V}_1 + \mathbf{a}\,\mathbf{V}_2 \tag{10.10}$$

$$\mathbf{V}_c = \mathbf{V}_0 + \mathbf{a}\,\mathbf{V}_1 + \mathbf{a}^2\,\mathbf{V}_2 \tag{10.11}$$

Arranging Eqs. (10.9), (10.10), and (10.11) in matrix form,

$$\begin{bmatrix} \mathbf{V}_a \\ \mathbf{V}_b \\ \mathbf{V}_c \end{bmatrix} = \begin{bmatrix} 1 & 1 & 1 \\ 1 & \mathbf{a}^2 & \mathbf{a} \\ 1 & \mathbf{a} & \mathbf{a}^2 \end{bmatrix} \begin{bmatrix} \mathbf{V}_0 \\ \mathbf{V}_1 \\ \mathbf{V}_2 \end{bmatrix} \tag{10.12}$$

To calculate the sequence components given the actual phase quantities, Eq. (10.12) is solved for $\mathbf{V}_0$, $\mathbf{V}_1$, and $\mathbf{V}_2$ as follows:

$$\begin{aligned} \begin{bmatrix} \mathbf{V}_0 \\ \mathbf{V}_1 \\ \mathbf{V}_2 \end{bmatrix} &= \begin{bmatrix} 1 & 1 & 1 \\ 1 & \mathbf{a}^2 & \mathbf{a} \\ 1 & \mathbf{a} & \mathbf{a}^2 \end{bmatrix}^{-1} \begin{bmatrix} \mathbf{V}_a \\ \mathbf{V}_b \\ \mathbf{V}_c \end{bmatrix} \\ &= \frac{1}{3} \begin{bmatrix} 1 & 1 & 1 \\ 1 & \mathbf{a} & \mathbf{a}^2 \\ 1 & \mathbf{a}^2 & \mathbf{a} \end{bmatrix} \begin{bmatrix} \mathbf{V}_a \\ \mathbf{V}_b \\ \mathbf{V}_c \end{bmatrix} \end{aligned} \tag{10.13}$$

Expanding the matrix of Eq. (10.13) results in the following set of transformation equations.

$$\mathbf{V}_0 = \tfrac{1}{3}\,(\mathbf{V}_a + \mathbf{V}_b + \mathbf{V}_c) \tag{10.14}$$

$$\mathbf{V}_1 = \tfrac{1}{3}\,(\mathbf{V}_a + \mathbf{a}\,\mathbf{V}_b + \mathbf{a}^2\,\mathbf{V}_c) \tag{10.15}$$

$$\mathbf{V}_2 = \tfrac{1}{3}\,(\mathbf{V}_a + \mathbf{a}^2\,\mathbf{V}_b + \mathbf{a}\,\mathbf{V}_c) \tag{10.16}$$

A similar set of transformation equations results for phase currents.

$$\mathbf{I}_0 = \tfrac{1}{3}\,(\mathbf{I}_a + \mathbf{I}_b + \mathbf{I}_c) \tag{10.17}$$

$$\mathbf{I}_1 = \tfrac{1}{3}\,(\mathbf{I}_a + \mathbf{a}\,\mathbf{I}_b + \mathbf{a}^2\,\mathbf{I}_c) \tag{10.18}$$

$$\mathbf{I}_2 = \tfrac{1}{3}\,(\mathbf{I}_a + \mathbf{a}^2\,\mathbf{I}_b + \mathbf{a}\,\mathbf{I}_c) \tag{10.19}$$

Equations (10.14) through (10.19) can be used to determine the sequence components of a set of phase voltages or phase currents.

From Eq. (1.43), the neutral current for a wye-connected load is equal to

$$\mathbf{I}_n = -(\mathbf{I}_a + \mathbf{I}_b + \mathbf{I}_c) \tag{1.43}$$

Comparing Eq. (1.43) with Eq. (10.17) indicates the following:

$$\mathbf{I}_0 = -\tfrac{1}{3}\,\mathbf{I}_n \tag{10.20}$$

or

$$\mathbf{I}_n = -3\mathbf{I}_0 \tag{10.21}$$

Equation (10.21) indicates that the neutral current is equal to three times the zero sequence current.

In a delta-connected load, there is no neutral connection. Therefore, the following results:

$$\mathbf{I}_a + \mathbf{I}_b + \mathbf{I}_c = 0$$

Therefore, the zero sequence component of current in a delta-connected load is equal to zero.

Also, in any system, delta or wye, the sum of the line to line voltages is equal to zero.

$$\mathbf{V}_{ab} + \mathbf{V}_{bc} + \mathbf{V}_{ca} = 0$$

The resulting zero sequence voltage is

$$\mathbf{V}_0 = \tfrac{1}{3}(\mathbf{V}_{ab} + \mathbf{V}_{bc} + \mathbf{V}_{ca}) = 0$$

Therefore, the zero sequence component of the line to line voltages is always equal to zero. However, the line to neutral voltages may have a zero sequence component.

EXAMPLE 10-1

Determine the zero, positive, and negative sequence voltages present in the event of an *A* phase to ground fault on a 4.16-kV, three-phase, MGN feeder. Assume an *ABC* phase sequence.

Solution The phase *A* to neutral voltage is equal to zero as a result of the short circuit. The phase *B* to neutral voltage is

$$\mathbf{V}_b = \frac{4160}{\sqrt{3}\angle -120^\circ} = 2400\angle -120^\circ \text{ V}$$

Likewise, the phase C to neutral voltage is

$$\mathbf{V}_c = \frac{4160}{\sqrt{3}\angle 120^\circ} = 2400\angle 120^\circ \text{ V}$$

Applying Eqs. (10.14) through (10.16) results in

$$\begin{aligned}\mathbf{V}_0 &= \tfrac{1}{3}(0 + 2400\angle -120^\circ + 2400\angle 120^\circ)\\ &= 800\angle 180^\circ \text{ V}\end{aligned}$$

$$\begin{aligned}\mathbf{V}_1 &= \tfrac{1}{3}[0 + (1\angle 120^\circ)(2400\angle -120^\circ) + (1\angle 240^\circ)(2400\angle 120^\circ)]\\ &= 1600\angle 0^\circ \text{ V}\end{aligned}$$

$$\begin{aligned}\mathbf{V}_2 &= \tfrac{1}{3}[0 + (1\angle 240^\circ)(2400\angle -120^\circ) + (1\angle 120^\circ)(2400\angle 120^\circ)]\\ &= 800\angle 180^\circ \text{ V}\end{aligned}$$

EXAMPLE 10-2

A delta-connected capacitor bank is comprised of three 200-kVAR, 4.16-kV, 60 Hz, single-phase capacitor units per phase. Determine the following:

a. Zero, positive, and negative sequence components of the line current with all capacitors energized

b. Zero, positive, and negative sequence components of the line current with one capacitor removed between phases a and b

Solution The phase sequence is assumed to be ABC. The phase a to b voltage is selected as the reference:

$$\mathbf{V}_{ab} = 4160\angle 0^\circ \text{ V}$$

The other phase to phase voltages are

$$\mathbf{V}_{bc} = 4160\angle -120^\circ \text{ V}$$

$$\mathbf{V}_{ca} = 4160\angle 120^\circ \text{ V}$$

a. The impedance of the capacitor elements connected between the phases is

$$\mathbf{Z}_{ab} = \mathbf{Z}_{bc} = \mathbf{Z}_{ca} = -j\frac{(4160 \text{ V})^2}{3 \cdot (200{,}000 \text{ VA})} = -j28.84\ \Omega$$

The equivalent circuit of the capacitor bank under these conditions is shown in Fig. 10-2a.

The phase currents are

$$\mathbf{I}_{ab} = \frac{\mathbf{V}_{ab}}{\mathbf{Z}_{ab}} = \frac{4160\angle 0^\circ}{28.84\angle -90^\circ} = 144.24\angle 90^\circ \text{ A}$$

$$\mathbf{I}_{bc} = \frac{\mathbf{V}_{bc}}{\mathbf{Z}_{bc}} = \frac{4160\angle -120^\circ}{28.84\angle -90^\circ} = 144.24\angle -30^\circ \text{ A}$$

$$\mathbf{I}_{ca} = \frac{\mathbf{V}_{ca}}{\mathbf{Z}_{ca}} = \frac{4160\angle 120^\circ}{28.84\angle -90^\circ} = 144.24\angle 210^\circ \text{ A}$$

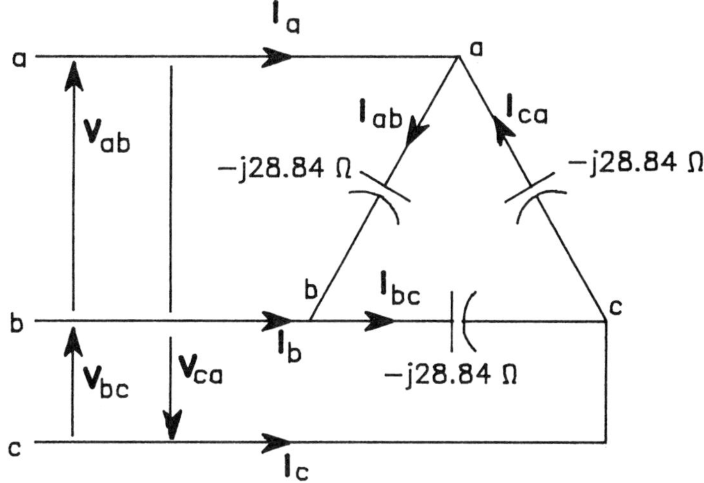

(a) All Capacitors in Each Phase Group Energized.

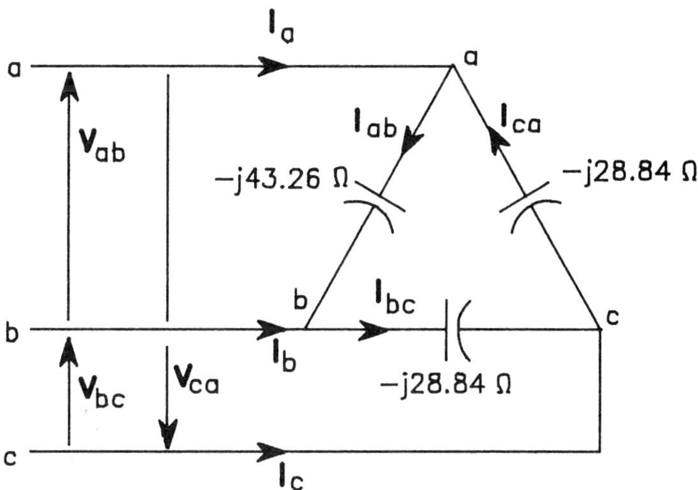

(b) One Capacitor Unit Removed Between Phases a and b.

Figure 10-2 Equivalent circuits for Example 10-2.

The line currents are determined by applying Kirchhoff's current law to each node of the equivalent circuit.

$$\mathbf{I}_a = \mathbf{I}_{ab} - \mathbf{I}_{ca} = 144.24\angle 90° - 144.24\angle 210° = 249.83\angle 60° \text{ A}$$

$$\mathbf{I}_b = \mathbf{I}_{bc} - \mathbf{I}_{ab} = 144.24\angle -30° - 144.24\angle 90° = 249.83\angle -60° \text{ A}$$

$$\mathbf{I}_c = \mathbf{I}_{ca} - \mathbf{I}_{bc} = 144.24\angle 210° - 144.24\angle -30° = 249.83\angle 180° \text{ A}$$

Applying the transformation equations results in the following:

$$\mathbf{I}_0 = \tfrac{1}{3}(249.83\angle 60° + 249.83\angle -60° + 249.83\angle 180°)$$
$$= 0 \text{ A}$$

$$\mathbf{I}_1 = \tfrac{1}{3}[249.83\angle 60° + (\mathbf{a})(249.83\angle -60°) + (\mathbf{a}^2)(249.83\angle 180°)]$$
$$= 249.83\angle 60° \text{ A}$$

$$\mathbf{I}_2 = \tfrac{1}{3}[249.83\angle 60° + (\mathbf{a}^2)(249.83\angle -60°) + (\mathbf{a})(249.83\angle 180°)]$$
$$= 0 \text{ A}$$

Note that both the zero sequence and negative sequence components of current are equal to zero. This is a result of the capacitor bank forming a balanced load.

b. The impedance of the capacitor elements connected between phases *B* and *C* and phases *C* and *A* remains the same as in part a.

$$\mathbf{Z}_{bc} = \mathbf{Z}_{ca} = -j28.84\ \Omega$$

The impedance of the capacitor elements connected between phases *A* and *B* with one capacitor element removed is equal to

$$\mathbf{Z}_{ab} = -j\frac{(4160 \text{ V})^2}{2 \cdot (200{,}000 \text{ VA})} = -j43.26\ \Omega$$

The equivalent circuit of the capacitor bank under these conditions is shown in Fig. 10-2b.

The phase currents are

$$\mathbf{I}_{ab} = \frac{\mathbf{V}_{ab}}{\mathbf{Z}_{ab}} = \frac{4160\angle 0°}{43.26\angle -90°} = 96.16\angle 90° \text{ A}$$

$$\mathbf{I}_{bc} = \frac{\mathbf{V}_{bc}}{\mathbf{Z}_{bc}} = \frac{4160\angle -120°}{28.84\angle -90°} = 144.24\angle -30° \text{ A}$$

$$\mathbf{I}_{ca} = \frac{\mathbf{V}_{ca}}{\mathbf{Z}_{ca}} = \frac{4160\angle 120°}{28.84\angle -90°} = 144.24\angle 210° \text{ A}$$

The line currents are determined by applying Kirchhoff's current law to each node of the equivalent circuit.

$$\mathbf{I}_a = \mathbf{I}_{ab} - \mathbf{I}_{ca} = 96.16\angle 90° - 144.24\angle 210° = 209.58\angle 53.4° \text{ A}$$

$$\mathbf{I}_b = \mathbf{I}_{bc} - \mathbf{I}_{ab} = 144.24\angle -30° - 96.16\angle 90° = 209.58\angle -53.4° \text{ A}$$

$$\mathbf{I}_c = \mathbf{I}_{ca} - \mathbf{I}_{bc} = 144.24\angle 210° - 144.24\angle -30° = 249.83\angle 180° \text{ A}$$

Applying the transformation equations results in the following:

$$\mathbf{I}_0 = \tfrac{1}{3}(209.58\angle 53.4^\circ + 209.58\angle -53.4^\circ + 249.83\angle 180^\circ)$$

$$= 0 \text{ A}$$

$$\mathbf{I}_1 = \tfrac{1}{3}[209.58\angle 53.4^\circ + (\mathbf{a})\,(209.58\angle -53.4^\circ) + (\mathbf{a}^2)(249.83\angle 180^\circ)]$$

$$= 222.1\angle 60^\circ \text{ A}$$

$$\mathbf{I}_2 = \tfrac{1}{3}[209.58\angle 53.4^\circ + (\mathbf{a}^2)(209.58\angle -53.4^\circ) + (\mathbf{a})(249.83\angle 180^\circ)]$$

$$= 27.8\angle -60^\circ \text{ A}$$

Note that the zero sequence component of current is equal to zero, since the capacitors are delta connected. Note also that a negative sequence component of current is present. This is due to the fact that the capacitor bank now represents an unbalanced three-phase load.

10-3 Line and Cable Sequence Impedances

In the previous sections, it was demonstrated that a system of unbalanced voltages and/or currents could be represented by a set of sequence components. A sequence impedance is the impedance of the circuit with respect to a particular sequence component. For example, the positive sequence impedance is the impedance of the circuit to the flow of positive sequence current. Similar statements can be made in regard to the negative sequence and zero sequence impedances as well. The calculation of sequence impedances is an extremely important prerequisite to performing short-circuit calculations.

This section will present equations that can be used to calculate the sequence impedances of overhead lines and underground cables. The equations are limited to application on multigrounded systems. In addition, only the series sequence impedances will be considered, since the series impedances are most commonly used when performing short-circuit calculations. The calculation of sequence impedances for shunt elements is beyond the scope of this text.

Three-Phase Overhead Distribution Circuit

The circuit arrangement for the calculation of the positive, negative, and zero sequence impedances for a three-phase overhead distribution circuit is shown in Fig. 10-3a. The positive and negative sequence impedances are given by the following:

$$\mathbf{Z}_1 = \mathbf{Z}_2 = \mathbf{Z}_S - \mathbf{Z}_M \quad \Omega/\text{mile} \tag{10.22}$$

where

$$\mathbf{Z}_S = R_\phi + 0.0954\frac{f}{60} + j0.2794\frac{f}{60}\log_{10}\left(\frac{D_e}{GMR_\phi}\right)$$

$$\mathbf{Z}_M = 0.0954\frac{f}{60} + j0.2794\frac{f}{60}\log_{10}\left(\frac{D_e}{(d_{AB}d_{BC}d_{CA})^{1/3}}\right)$$

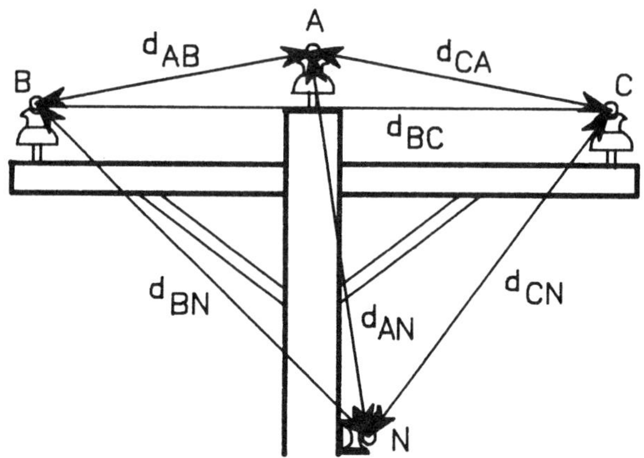

(a) General Configuration.

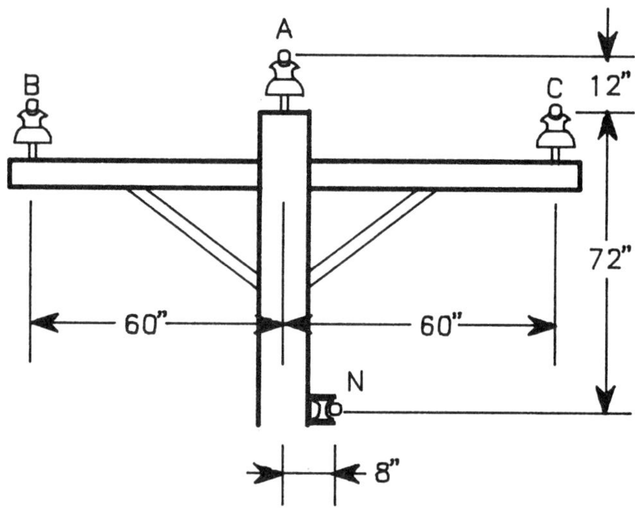

Phase Cond. – 336.4 kcmil ACSR 26/7 Str.
Neutral Cond. – #3/0 ACSR 6/1 Str.

(b) Configuration for Example 10–3.

Figure 10-3 Sequence impedances for three-phase overhead line.

The zero sequence impedance can be calculated from the following:

$$\mathbf{Z}_0 = \mathbf{Z}_S + 2 \cdot \mathbf{Z}_M - 3 \cdot \frac{\mathbf{Z}_{\phi N}^2}{\mathbf{Z}_{NN}} \quad \Omega/\text{mile} \tag{10.23}$$

where

$$\mathbf{Z}_{\phi N} = 0.0954\frac{f}{60} + j0.2794\frac{f}{60}\log_{10}\left(\frac{D_e}{(d_{AN}d_{BN}d_{CN})^{1/3}}\right)$$

$$\mathbf{Z}_{NN} = R_N + 0.0954\frac{f}{60} + j0.2794\frac{f}{60}\log_{10}\left(\frac{D_e}{GMR_N}\right)$$

EXAMPLE 10-3 Calculate the positive, negative, and zero sequence impedances for the distribution line shown in Fig. 10-3b. Assume an earth resistivity of 100 Ω-m and an operating frequency of 60 Hz.

Solution The distances between the phase conductors are

$$d_{AB} = d_{CA} = (60^2 + 12^2)^{1/2} = 61.2 \text{ in.} = 5.1 \text{ ft}$$

$$d_{BC} = 10 \text{ ft}$$

The distances between each phase conductor and neutral are

$$d_{AN} = (84^2 + 8^2)^{1/2} = 84.4 \text{ in.} = 7.03 \text{ ft}$$

$$d_{BN} = (72^2 + 68^2)^{1/2} = 99.0 \text{ in.} = 8.25 \text{ ft}$$

$$d_{CN} = (72^2 + 52^2)^{1/2} = 88.8 \text{ in.} = 7.40 \text{ ft}$$

From manufacturers' data (Appendix A), the following data are obtained:

$$GMR_\phi = 0.0244 \text{ ft}, \qquad GMR_N = 0.006 \text{ ft}$$

$$R_\phi = 0.3263\ \Omega/\text{mile}, \qquad R_N = 0.7603\ \Omega/\text{mile}$$

The depth of the equivalent earth return conductor is

$$D_e = 2160\left(\frac{100}{60}\right)^{1/2} = 2788.5 \text{ ft}$$

The self- and mutual impedances of the phase conductors are given by

$$\mathbf{Z}_s = 0.3263 + 0.0954 + j0.2794\log_{10}\frac{2788.5}{0.0244}$$

$$= 0.4217 + j1.4132\ \Omega/\text{mile}$$

$$\mathbf{Z}_m = 0.0954 + j0.2794\log_{10}\frac{2788.5}{(5.1 \cdot 5.1 \cdot 10)^{1/3}}$$

$$= 0.0954 + j0.7377\ \Omega/\text{mile}$$

The positive and negative sequence impedances are

$$\mathbf{Z}_1 = \mathbf{Z}_2 = 0.3263 + j0.6755\ \Omega/\text{mile}$$

The mutual impedance between the phase conductors and neutral is

$$\mathbf{Z}_{\phi N} = 0.0954 + j0.2794 \log_{10} \frac{2788.5}{(7.03 \cdot 8.25 \cdot 7.4)^{1/3}}$$

$$= 0.0954 + j0.7174\ \Omega/\text{mile}$$

The self-impedance of the neutral conductor is

$$\mathbf{Z}_{NN} = 0.7603 + 0.0954 + j0.2794 \log_{10} \frac{2788.5}{0.006}$$

$$= 0.8557 + j1.5834\ \Omega/\text{mile}$$

The zero sequence impedance is

$$\mathbf{Z}_0 = 0.6125 + j2.886 - 3 \cdot \frac{(0.0954 + j0.7174)^2}{0.8557 + j1.5834}$$

$$= 0.6125 + j2.8886 - \frac{1.5713\angle 164.9^\circ}{1.7998\angle 61.6^\circ}$$

$$= 0.6125 + j2.8886 - 0.8730\angle 103.3^\circ$$

$$= 0.8133 + j2.0390\ \Omega/\text{mile}$$

Open-Wye Overhead Distribution Circuit

In the determination of the sequence impedances for the open-wye case, phases *B* and *C* are assumed to be present. The line configuration is shown in Fig. 10-4a. The positive sequence impedance is given by

$$\mathbf{Z}_1 = \mathbf{Z}_2 = \mathbf{Z}_S - \mathbf{Z}_M \quad \Omega/\text{mile} \tag{10.24}$$

where

$$\mathbf{Z}_S = R_\phi + 0.0954\frac{f}{60} + j0.2794\frac{f}{60}\log_{10}\left(\frac{D_e}{GMR_\phi}\right)$$

$$\mathbf{Z}_M = 0.0954\frac{f}{60} + j0.2794\frac{f}{60}\log_{10}\left[\frac{D_e}{d_{BC}}\right]$$

The zero sequence impedance is given by

$$\mathbf{Z}_0 = \mathbf{Z}_S + 2 \cdot \mathbf{Z}_M - 3 \cdot \frac{\mathbf{Z}_{\phi N}^2}{\mathbf{Z}_{NN}} \quad \Omega/\text{mile} \tag{10.25}$$

where

$$\mathbf{Z}_{\phi N} = 0.0954\frac{f}{60} + j0.2794\frac{f}{60}\log_{10}\left(\frac{D_e}{(d_{BN}d_{CN})^{1/2}}\right)$$

$$\mathbf{Z}_{NN} = R_N + 0.0954\frac{f}{60} + j0.2794\frac{f}{60}\log_{10}\left(\frac{D_e}{GMR_N}\right)$$

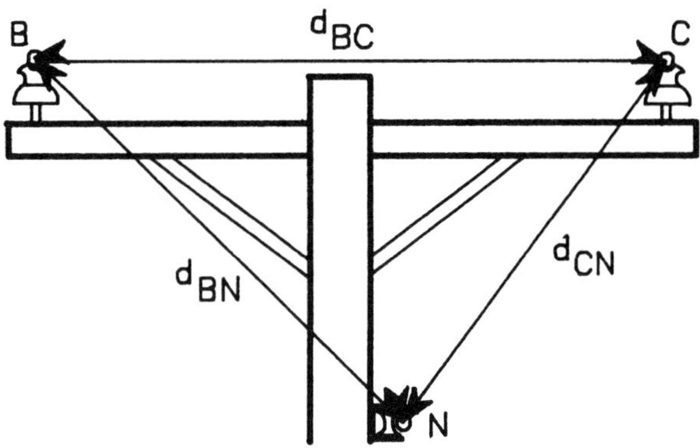

(a) General Configuration.

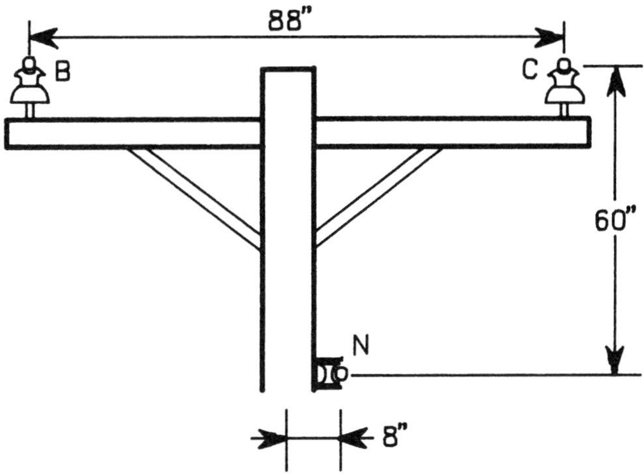

Phase Cond. – #1/0 ACSR 6/1 Str.
Neutral Cond. – #1/0 ACSR 6/1 Str.

(b) Configuration for Example 10–4.

Figure 10-4 Sequence impedances for open-wye overhead line.

EXAMPLE 10-4 Calculate the positive, negative, and zero sequence impedances of the open-wye overhead line shown in Fig. 10-4b. Assume an earth resistivity of 100 Ω-m and an operating frequency of 60 Hz.

Solution The distance between the phase conductors is

$$d_{BC} = 88 \text{ in.} = 7.33 \text{ ft}$$

The distances between each phase conductor and neutral are

$$d_{BN} = (52^2 + 60^2)^{1/2} = 79.4 \text{ in.} = 6.62 \text{ ft}$$
$$d_{CN} = (36^2 + 60^2)^{1/2} = 70.0 \text{ in.} = 5.83 \text{ ft}$$

The following data are obtained from Appendix A.

$$R_N = R_\phi = 1.1458 \ \Omega/\text{mile}$$
$$GMR_N = GMR_\phi = 0.00446 \text{ ft}$$

The depth of the equivalent earth return conductor, D_e, is 2788.5 ft, as in Example 10-3. The self- and mutual impedances of the phase conductors are given by

$$\mathbf{Z}_s = 1.1458 + 0.0954 + j0.2794 \log_{10} \frac{2788.5}{0.00446}$$
$$= 1.2412 + j1.6194 \ \Omega/\text{mile}$$
$$\mathbf{Z}_m = 0.0954 + j0.2794 \log_{10} \frac{2788.5}{7.33}$$
$$= 0.0954 + j0.7209 \ \Omega/\text{mile}$$

The positive and negative sequence impedances are

$$\mathbf{Z}_1 = \mathbf{Z}_2 = 1.1458 + j0.8985 \ \Omega/\text{mile}$$

The mutual impedance between the phase conductors and neutral is

$$\mathbf{Z}_{\phi N} = 0.0954 + j0.2794 \log_{10} \frac{2788.5}{(6.62 \cdot 5.83)^{1/2}}$$
$$= 0.0954 + j0.7410 \ \Omega/\text{mile}$$

The self-impedance of the neutral conductor is

$$\mathbf{Z}_{NN} = 1.1458 + 0.0954 + j0.2794 \log_{10} \frac{2788.5}{0.00446}$$
$$= 1.2412 + j1.6194 \ \Omega/\text{mile}$$

The zero sequence impedance is

$$\mathbf{Z}_0 = 1.4320 + j3.0612 - 3 \cdot \frac{(0.0954 + j0.741)^2}{1.2412 + j1.6194}$$

$$= 1.4320 + j3.0612 - \frac{1.6745\angle 165.3°}{2.0404\angle 52.5°}$$

$$= 1.4320 + j3.0612 - 0.8207\angle 112.8°$$

$$= 1.7500 + j2.3046\ \Omega/\text{mile}$$

Single-Phase Overhead Distribution Circuit

The line configuration for the single-phase overhead line is shown in Fig. 10-5a. The positive, negative, and zero sequence impedances are

$$\mathbf{Z}_0 = \mathbf{Z}_1 = \mathbf{Z}_2 = \mathbf{Z}_S - \frac{\mathbf{Z}_{\phi N}^2}{\mathbf{Z}_{NN}}\ \Omega/\text{mile} \tag{10.26}$$

where

$$\mathbf{Z}_S = R_\phi + 0.0954\frac{f}{60} + j0.2794\frac{f}{60}\log_{10}\left(\frac{D_e}{GMR_\phi}\right)$$

$$\mathbf{Z}_{\phi N} = 0.0954\frac{f}{60} + j0.2794\frac{f}{60}\log_{10}\left(\frac{D_e}{d_{AN}}\right)$$

$$\mathbf{Z}_{NN} = R_N + 0.0954\frac{f}{60} + j0.2794\frac{f}{60}\log_{10}\left(\frac{D_e}{GMR_N}\right)$$

EXAMPLE 10-5

Calculate the positive, negative, and zero sequence impedances for the single-phase overhead circuit shown in Fig. 10-5b. Assume an earth resistivity of 100 Ω-m and an operating frequency of 60 Hz.

Solution The distance between the phase and neutral conductors is

$$d_{AN} = (48^2 + 8^2)^{1/2} = 48.7\text{ in.} = 4.06\text{ ft}$$

The following data are obtained from Appendix A.

$$R_N = R_\phi = 2.7403\ \Omega/\text{mile}$$

$$GMR_\phi = GMR_N = 0.00452\text{ ft}$$

The depth of the equivalent earth return conductor, D_e, is 2788.5 ft.

The self-impedances of the phase and neutral conductors are equal since the same size and type of conductor are used.

$$\mathbf{Z}_S = \mathbf{Z}_{NN} = 2.7403 + 0.0954 + j0.2794 \log_{10} \frac{2788.5}{0.00452}$$

$$= 2.8357 + j1.6178 \ \Omega/\text{mile}$$

(a) General Configuration.

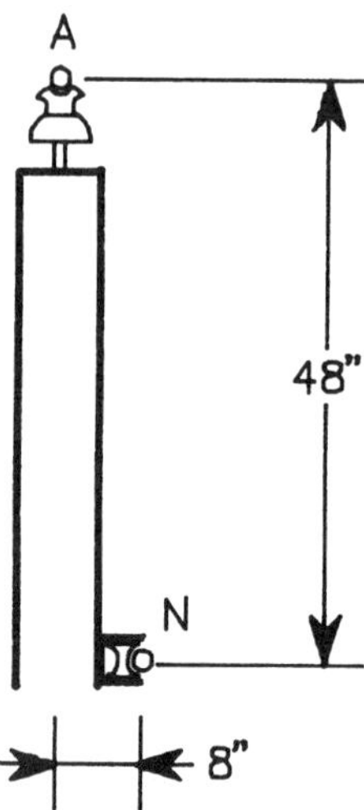

(b) Configuration for Example 10–5.

Figure 10-5 Sequence impedances for single-phase overhead line.

The mutual impedance between phase and neutral is

$$\mathbf{Z}_{\phi N} = 0.0954 + j0.2794 \log_{10} \frac{2788.5}{4.06}$$
$$= 0.0954 + j0.7926 \ \Omega/\text{mile}$$

The positive, negative and zero sequence impedances are

$$\mathbf{Z}_1 = \mathbf{Z}_2 = \mathbf{Z}_0 = 2.8357 + j1.678 - \frac{(0.0954 + j0.7926)^2}{2.8357 + j1.6178}$$
$$= 2.8357 + j1.6178 - \frac{0.6373\angle 166.3°}{3.2647\angle 29.7°}$$
$$= 2.8357 + j1.6178 - 0.1952\angle 136.6°$$
$$= 2.9775 + j1.4837 \ \Omega/\text{mile}$$

Three-Phase Underground Distribution Circuit

The geometry of a three-phase underground cable circuit consisting of three single-phase concentric neutral cables is shown in Fig. 10-6a. The positive, negative, and zero sequence impedances are given by the following [1]:

$$\mathbf{Z}_1 = \mathbf{Z}_2 = \mathbf{Z}_S - \mathbf{Z}_M - \frac{(\mathbf{Z}_{\phi N} - \mathbf{Z}_M)^2}{\mathbf{Z}_{NN} - \mathbf{Z}_M} \quad \Omega/1000 \text{ ft} \tag{10.27}$$

$$\mathbf{Z}_0 = \mathbf{Z}_S + 2 \cdot \mathbf{Z}_M - \frac{(\mathbf{Z}_{\phi N} + 2 \cdot \mathbf{Z}_M)^2}{\mathbf{Z}_{NN} + 2 \cdot \mathbf{Z}_M} \quad \Omega/1000 \text{ ft} \tag{10.28}$$

where

$$\mathbf{Z}_S = R_\phi + 0.01807 \frac{f}{60} + j0.0529 \frac{f}{60} \log_{10}\left(\frac{D_e}{GMR_\phi}\right)$$

$$\mathbf{Z}_{NN} = R_N + 0.01807 \frac{f}{60} + j0.0529 \frac{f}{60} \log_{10}\left(\frac{D_e}{GMR_N}\right)$$

$$\mathbf{Z}_M = 0.01807 \frac{f}{60} + j0.0529 \frac{f}{60} \log_{10}\left[\frac{D_e}{(d_{AB}d_{BC}d_{CA})^{1/3}}\right]$$

$$\mathbf{Z}_{\phi N} = 0.01807 \frac{f}{60} + j0.0529 \frac{f}{60} \log_{10}\left(\frac{D_e}{r_{CN}}\right)$$

EXAMPLE 10-6 Calculate the positive, negative, and zero sequence impedances for the three-phase concentric neutral cable circuit shown in Fig. 10-6b. The cable is 500-kcmil, aluminum, 37-strand, 25-kV, 100% insulation level, XLP insulated URD. Assume an earth resistivity of 100 Ω-m and an operating frequency of 60 Hz.

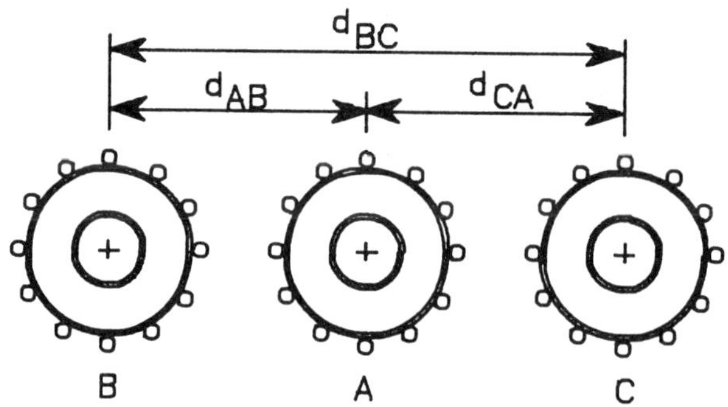

(a) General Configuration.

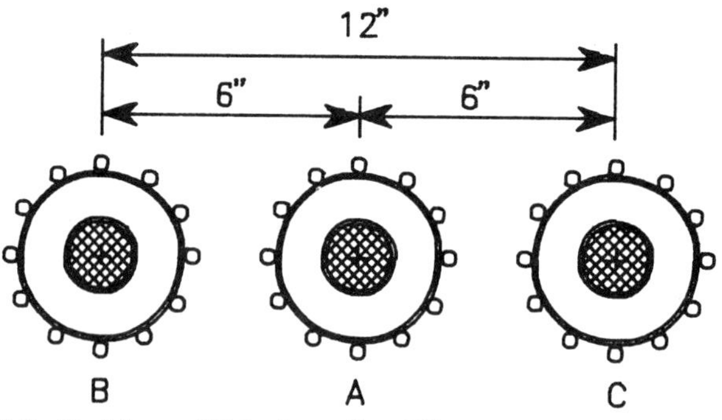

(b) Configuration for Example 10–6.

Figure 10-6 Sequence impedances for three-phase URD concentric neutral cable circuit.

Solution From the cable data of Appendix A,

$$R_\phi = 0.0425\ \Omega/\text{M-ft}, \qquad GMR_\phi = 0.3120\ \text{in.}$$

$$R_N = 0.1287\ \Omega/\text{M-ft}, \qquad r_{CN} = 0.787\ \text{in.}$$

The geometric mean radius of the concentric neutral strands is assumed to be approximately equal to the radius of the circle formed by the neutral stands. Therefore, $GMR_N \approx r_{CN} = 0.787$ in.

The depth of the equivalent earth return conductor is

$$D_e = 2160\left(\frac{100}{60}\right)^{1/2} = 2788.5\ \text{ft} = 33{,}463\ \text{in.}$$

The self-impedances of the phase and neutral conductors are

$$\mathbf{Z}_S = 0.0425 + 0.01807 + j0.0529 \log_{10} \frac{33{,}463}{0.3120}$$

$$= 0.0606 + j0.2661 \ \Omega/\text{M-ft}$$

$$\mathbf{Z}_{NN} = 0.1287 + 0.01807 + j0.0529 \log_{10} \frac{33{,}463}{0.787}$$

$$= 0.1468 + j0.2449 \ \Omega/\text{M-ft}$$

The mutual impedance between the three-phase conductors is

$$\mathbf{Z}_M = 0.01807 + j0.0529 \log_{10} \frac{33{,}463}{(6 \cdot 6 \cdot 12)^{1/3}}$$

$$= 0.01807 + j0.1929 \ \Omega/\text{M-ft}$$

The mutual impedance between the phase conductor and neutral is

$$\mathbf{Z}_{\phi N} = 0.01807 + j0.0529 \log_{10} \frac{33{,}463}{0.787}$$

$$= 0.01807 + j0.2449 \ \Omega/\text{M-ft}$$

The positive and negative sequence impedances are

$$\mathbf{Z}_1 = \mathbf{Z}_2 = 0.0606 + j0.2661 - (0.01807 + j0.1929)$$

$$- \frac{[0.01807 + j0.2449 - (0.01807 + j0.1929)]^2}{0.1468 + j0.2449 - (0.01807 + j0.1929)}$$

$$= 0.0425 + j0.0732 - \frac{(j0.052)^2}{0.1287 + j0.052}$$

$$= 0.0425 + j0.0731 - \frac{0.0027\angle 180^\circ}{0.1388\angle 22.0^\circ}$$

$$= 0.0605 + j0.0658 \ \Omega/\text{M-ft}$$

The zero sequence impedance is

$$\mathbf{Z}_0 = 0.0606 + j0.2661 + 2(0.01807 + j0.1929)$$

$$- \frac{[0.01807 + j0.2449 + 2(0.01807 + j0.1929)]^2}{0.1468 + j0.2449 + 2(0.01807 + j0.1929)}$$

$$= 0.0967 + j0.6519 - \frac{(0.0542 + j0.6307)^2}{0.1829 + j0.6307}$$

$$= 0.0967 + j0.6519 - \frac{0.40\angle 170.2^\circ}{0.6567\angle 73.5^\circ}$$

$$= 0.1678 + j0.0470 \ \Omega/\text{M-ft}$$

Open-Wye Underground Distribution Circuit

The geometry of an open-wye, multigrounded neutral underground cable circuit consisting of two single-phase concentric neutral cables is shown in Fig. 10-7a. The positive, negative, and zero sequence impedances are given by the following [2]:

$$\mathbf{Z}_1 = \mathbf{Z}_2 = \mathbf{Z}_S - \mathbf{Z}_M - \frac{(\mathbf{Z}_{\phi N} - \mathbf{Z}_M)^2}{\mathbf{Z}_{NN} - \mathbf{Z}_M} \quad \Omega/1000 \text{ ft} \tag{10.29}$$

$$\mathbf{Z}_0 = \mathbf{Z}_S + 2 \cdot \mathbf{Z}_M - \frac{3}{2}\frac{(\mathbf{Z}_{\phi N} + \mathbf{Z}_M)^2}{\mathbf{Z}_{NN} + \mathbf{Z}_M} + \frac{1}{2}\frac{(\mathbf{Z}_{\phi N} - \mathbf{Z}_M)^2}{\mathbf{Z}_{NN} - \mathbf{Z}_M} \quad \Omega/1000 \text{ ft} \tag{10.30}$$

where

$$\mathbf{Z}_S = R_\phi + 0.01807\frac{f}{60} + j0.0529\frac{f}{60}\log_{10}\left(\frac{D_e}{GMR_\phi}\right)$$

$$\mathbf{Z}_{NN} = R_N + 0.01807\frac{f}{60} + j0.0529\frac{f}{60}\log_{10}\left(\frac{D_e}{GMR_N}\right)$$

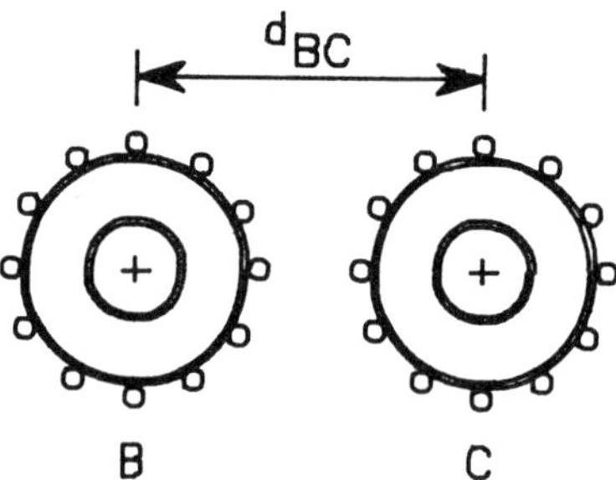

(a) General Configuration.

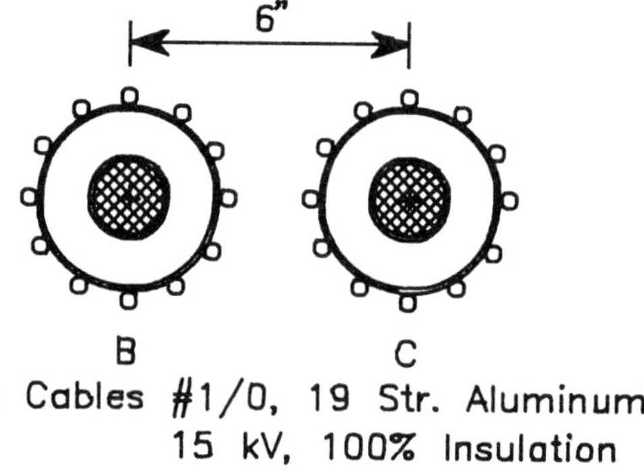

(b) Configuration for Example 10–7.

Figure 10-7 Sequence impedances for open-wye URD concentric neutral cable circuit.

$$\mathbf{Z}_M = 0.01807\frac{f}{60} + j0.0529\frac{f}{60}\log_{10}\left(\frac{D_e}{d_{BC}}\right)$$

$$\mathbf{Z}_{\phi N} = 0.01807\frac{f}{60} + j0.0529\frac{f}{60}\log_{10}\left(\frac{D_e}{r_{CN}}\right)$$

EXAMPLE 10-7 Calculate the positive, negative, and zero sequence impedances for the open-wye concentric neutral cable circuit shown in Fig. 10-7b. The cable is #1/0 AWG, aluminum, 37-strand, 15-kV, 100% insulation level, XLP insulated URD. Assume an earth resistivity of 100 Ω-m and an operating frequency of 60 Hz.

Solution From the cable data of Appendix A,

$$R_\phi = 0.2097\ \Omega/\text{M-ft}, \qquad GMR_\phi = 0.1336\ \text{in.}$$

$$R_N = 0.1997\ \Omega/\text{M-ft}, \qquad r_{CN} = 0.468\ \text{in.}$$

The geometric mean radius of the concentric neutral strands is assumed to be equal to the radius of the circle formed by the neutral strands. Therefore, $GMR_N \approx r_{CN} = 0.468$ in.

The depth of the equivalent earth return conductor is

$$D_e = 2160\left(\frac{100}{60}\right)^{1/2} = 2788.5\ \text{ft} = 33{,}463\ \text{in.}$$

The self-impedances of the phase and neutral conductors are

$$\mathbf{Z}_S = 0.2097 + 0.01807 + j0.0529\ \log_{10}\frac{33{,}463}{0.1336}$$

$$= 0.2278 + j0.2856\ \Omega/\text{M-ft}$$

$$\mathbf{Z}_{NN} = 0.1997 + 0.01807 + j0.0529\ \log_{10}\frac{33{,}463}{0.468}$$

$$= 0.2178 + j0.2568\ \Omega/\text{M-ft}$$

The mutual impedance between the phase conductors is

$$\mathbf{Z}_M = 0.01807 + j0.0529\ \log_{10}\frac{33{,}463}{6.0}$$

$$= 0.01807 + j0.1982\ \Omega/\text{M-ft}$$

The mutual impedance between the phase conductor and neutral is

$$\mathbf{Z}_{\phi N} = 0.01807 + j0.0529\ \log_{10}\frac{33{,}463}{0.468}$$

$$= 0.01807 + j0.2568\ \Omega/\text{M-ft}$$

The positive and negative sequence impedances are

$$\mathbf{Z}_1 = \mathbf{Z}_2 = 0.2278 + j0.2856 - (0.01807 + j0.1982)$$

$$- \frac{[0.01807 + j0.2568 - (0.01807 + j0.1982)]^2}{0.2178 + j0.2568 - (0.01807 + j0.1982)}$$

$$= 0.2097 + j0.0874 - \frac{(j0.0586)^2}{0.1997 + j0.0586}$$

$$= 0.2097 + j0.0874 - \frac{0.0034\angle 180°}{0.2081\angle 16.4°}$$

$$= 0.2254 + j0.0828 \ \Omega/\text{M-ft}$$

The zero sequence impedance is

$$\mathbf{Z}_0 = 0.2278 + j0.2856 + 2(0.01807 + j0.1982)$$

$$- \frac{3}{2}\frac{(0.01807 + j0.2568 + 0.01807 + 0.1982)^2}{0.2178 + j0.2568 + 0.01807 + j0.1982}$$

$$+ \frac{1}{2}\frac{[0.01807 + j0.2568 - (0.01807 + j0.1982)]^2}{0.2178 + j0.2568 - (0.01807 + j0.1982)}$$

$$= 0.2639 + j0.6820 - \frac{3}{2}\frac{(0.03614 + j0.4550)^2}{0.2359 + j0.4550} + \frac{1}{2}\frac{(j0.0586)^2}{0.1997 + j0.0586}$$

$$= 0.2639 + 0.6820 - \frac{3}{2}\frac{0.2083\angle 170.9°}{0.5125\angle 62.6°} + \frac{1}{2}\frac{0.0034\angle 180°}{0.2081\angle 16.4°}$$

$$= 0.4475 + j0.1055 \ \Omega/\text{M-ft}$$

Single-Phase Underground Distribution Circuit

The geometry of a single-phase, multigrounded neutral, underground cable circuit consisting of a single concentric neutral cable is shown in Fig. 10-8a. The positive, negative, and zero sequence impedances are given by the following [3]:

$$\mathbf{Z}_1 = \mathbf{Z}_2 = \mathbf{Z}_0 = \mathbf{Z}_S - \frac{(\mathbf{Z}_{\phi N})^2}{\mathbf{Z}_{NN}} \quad \Omega/1000 \text{ ft} \tag{10.31}$$

where

$$\mathbf{Z}_S = R_\phi + 0.01807\frac{f}{60} + j0.0529\frac{f}{60}\log_{10}\left(\frac{D_e}{GMR_\phi}\right)$$

$$\mathbf{Z}_{NN} = R_N + 0.01807\frac{f}{60} + j0.0529\frac{f}{60}\log_{10}\left(\frac{D_e}{GMR_N}\right)$$

$$\mathbf{Z}_{\phi N} = 0.01807\frac{f}{60} + j0.0529\frac{f}{60}\log_{10}\left(\frac{D_e}{r_{CN}}\right)$$

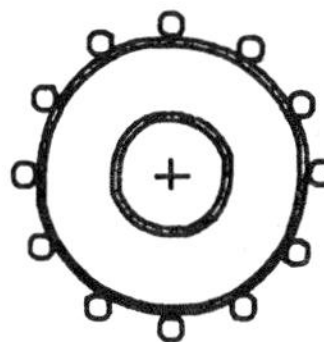

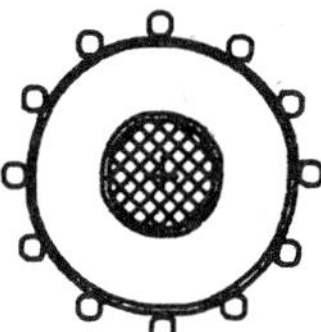

Cable #2 AWG, 7 Str. Aluminum, 15 kV
100% Insulation.
(b) Configuration for Example 10–8.

Figure 10-8 Sequence impedances for single-phase URD concentric neutral cable circuit.

EXAMPLE 10-8

Calculate the positive, negative, and zero sequence impedances for the single-phase concentric neutral cable circuit shown in Fig. 10-8b. The cable is #2 AWG, aluminum, 37-strand, 15-kV, 100% insulation level, XLP insulated URD. Assume an earth resistivity of 100 Ω-m and an operating frequency of 60 Hz.

Solution From the cable data found in Appendix A,

$$R_\phi = 0.3334\ \Omega/\text{M-ft}, \qquad GMR_\phi = 0.1060\ \text{in.}$$

$$R_N = 0.3195\ \Omega/\text{M-ft}, \qquad r_{CN} = 0.429\ \text{in.}$$

In addition, the geometric mean radius of the concentric neutral strands, GMR_N, will be assumed equal to the radius of the circle formed by the neutral strands r_{CN}. Therefore, $GMR_N \approx 0.429$ in.

The depth of the equivalent earth return conductor is

$$D_e = 2160\left(\frac{100}{60}\right)^{1/2} = 2788.5\ \text{ft} = 33{,}463\ \text{in.}$$

The self-impedances of the phase and neutral conductors are

$$\mathbf{Z}_S = 0.3334 + 0.01807 + j0.0529\log_{10}\frac{33{,}463}{0.106}$$

$$= 0.3515 + j0.2909\ \Omega/\text{M-ft}$$

$$\mathbf{Z}_{NN} = 0.3195 + 0.01807 + j0.0529 \log_{10}\frac{33{,}463}{0.429}$$
$$= 0.3376 + j0.2588\ \Omega/\text{M-ft}$$

The mutual impedance between the phase and neutral is

$$\mathbf{Z}_{\phi N} = 0.01807 + j0.0529 \log_{10}\frac{33{,}463}{0.429}$$
$$= 0.01807 + j0.2588\ \Omega/\text{M-ft}$$

The positive, negative, and zero sequence impedances are

$$\mathbf{Z}_1 = \mathbf{Z}_2 = \mathbf{Z}_0 = 0.3515 + j0.2909 - \frac{(0.01807 + j0.2588)^2}{0.3576 + j0.2588}$$
$$= 0.4624 + j0.1781\ \Omega/\text{M-ft}$$

10-4 Transformer Sequence Networks

The positive, negative, and zero sequence impedances of a transformer are equal to the nameplate impedance of the transformer. The ohmic value of the transformer sequence impedance may be referred to either the high- or low-voltage side. If expressed in per unit, the impedance is the same on either the high- or low-voltage side. The sequence networks of transformers depend on the type of transformer connection. This section will develop sequence network representations for the wye–wye, delta–wye, wye–delta, and delta–delta connections.

The sequence network representations for the wye connections are generalized to include a grounding impedance $\mathbf{Z}_g$. This grounding impedance is placed between the common neutral connection of the wye-connected winding and ground. For solidly grounded transformer windings, the value of $\mathbf{Z}_g$ is zero. If the wye-connected winding is ungrounded, $\mathbf{Z}_g$ is infinite. For wye-connected neutral grounded through a finite impedance, three times $\mathbf{Z}_g$ is placed in the zero sequence network representation.

Wye–Wye Connection

In the wye–wye connection, there is no phase shift between the line and phase voltages of the high-voltage side with respect to the low-voltage side. Therefore, the transformer sequence network representation consists of the sequence impedance in series with an ideal transformer. The turns ratio of the ideal transformer is equal to the turns ratio of the actual transformer. If per unit quantities are used, the turns ratio of the ideal transformer must be used in place of the actual turns ratio. The equivalent sequence impedance networks for the wye–wye connection are shown in Fig. 10-9a.

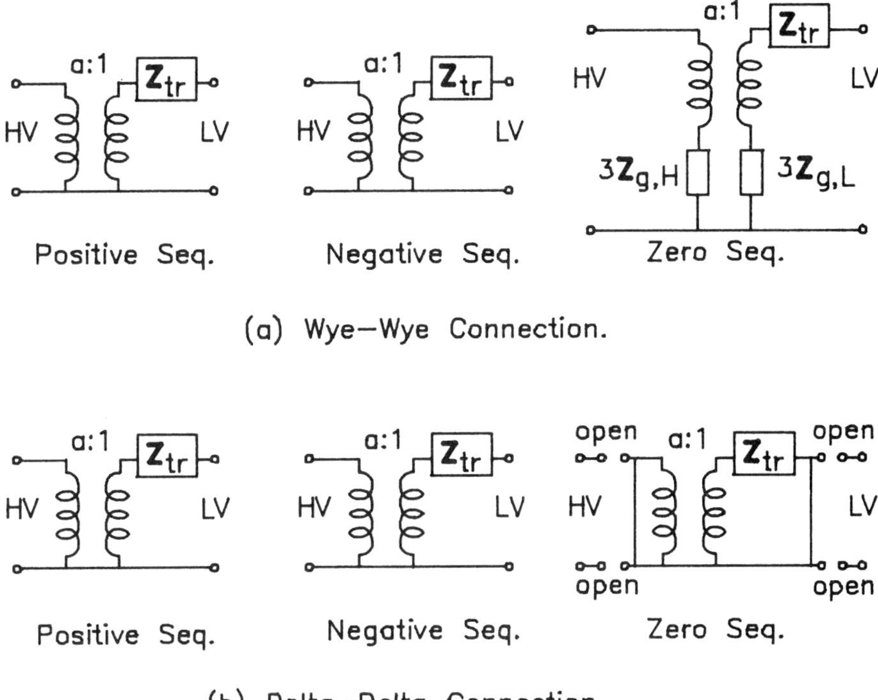

Figure 10-9 Sequence impedance networks for wye–wye and delta–delta connected transformers.

Delta–Delta Connection

Similar to the wye–wye connection, there is no phase shift between high- and low-side voltages in the delta–delta connection. The positive and negative sequence network representations will consist of the sequence impedance in series with an ideal transformer.

Since the transformer high- and low-voltage sides are delta connected, no zero sequence current can flow in the three phases from the source to the transformer primary. Likewise, zero sequence current cannot flow to the load from the transformer secondary. Therefore, when "looking in" to the zero sequence network from either the high- or low-side of the transformer, an open circuit should be seen. Note that, although it is impossible for zero sequence current to flow in the phases from the source or to the load, it is possible for zero sequence current to circulate within the closed delta windings. The equivalent sequence impedance network representations are shown in Fig. 10-9b.

Delta–Wye Connection

In the delta–wye connection, there is a 30° phase shift between the high- and low-side line and phase voltages. In accordance with ANSI standards, the high voltage will lead the low voltage by 30°. In terms of sequence quantities, the high-side positive sequence voltages and currents will lead the low-side positive sequence voltages and currents by 30°. Conversely, the high-side negative sequence voltages and currents will lag the low-side negative sequence voltages and currents by 30°. There will be no phase shift between voltages and currents in the zero sequence network.

To account for the 30° phase shifts in the positive and negative sequence networks, a fictitious transformer with a complex ideal turns ratio will be introduced into the equivalent circuit representations. The complex turns ratio of the transformer will have both magnitude and phase angle. The magnitude of the complex turns ratio will be equal to the high-side voltage divided by the low-side voltage. The phase angle of the complex turns ratio will be selected to produce the desired phase shift. Figure 10-10 shows the sequence network representations for the delta–wye connection.

In the delta–wye connection, it is possible for zero sequence currents to flow into or out of the wye-connected side. Therefore, the zero sequence representation must make provision for the flow of zero sequence current. On the other hand, it is not possible for zero sequence currents to flow into or out of the delta-connected winding. Thus, when looking into the zero sequence network from the delta-connected side, an open circuit should be encountered.

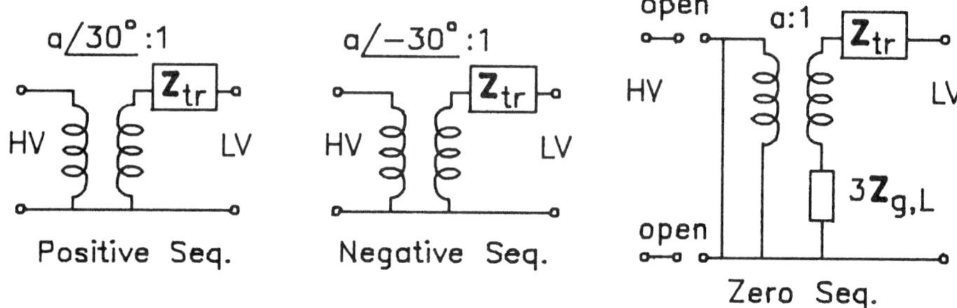

Figure 10-10 Sequence impedance networks for delta–wye connected transformer.

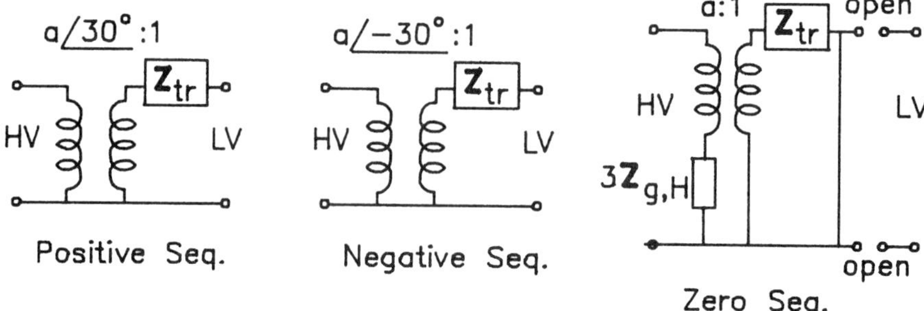

Figure 10-11 Sequence impedance networks for wye–delta connected transformer.

Wye–Delta Connection

The wye–delta connection is essentially the reverse of the delta–wye connection. The major difference between the wye–delta and delta–wye sequence networks is the location of the open circuit in the zero sequence network. The sequence network representations for the wye–delta connection are shown in Fig. 10-11.

EXAMPLE 10-9

Determine the positive, negative, and zero sequence representations for the following transformers. The transformer impedances should be placed on the low-voltage side of the transformer and expressed in ohms.

a. 5000 kVA, 69 kV–2.4 kV, delta–delta, $R = 1\%$, $X = 8\%$
b. 2000 kVA, 12.47Y/7.2 kV–480Y/277 V, wye–wye, $R = 1\%$, $X = 6\%$
c. 7500 kVA, 138 kV–4.16Y/2.4 kV, delta–wye, $R = 1\%$, $X = 7\%$
d. 50 MVA, 138Y/79.7 kV–15 kV, wye–delta, $R = 1\%$, $X = 12\%$

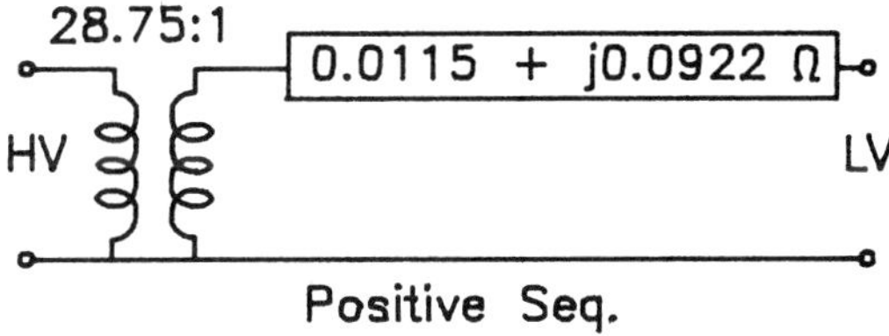

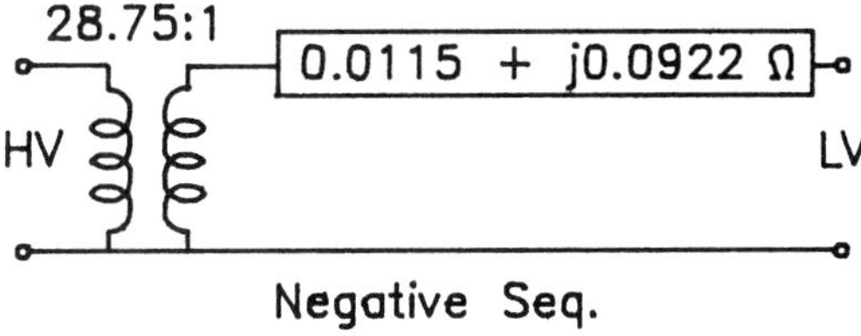

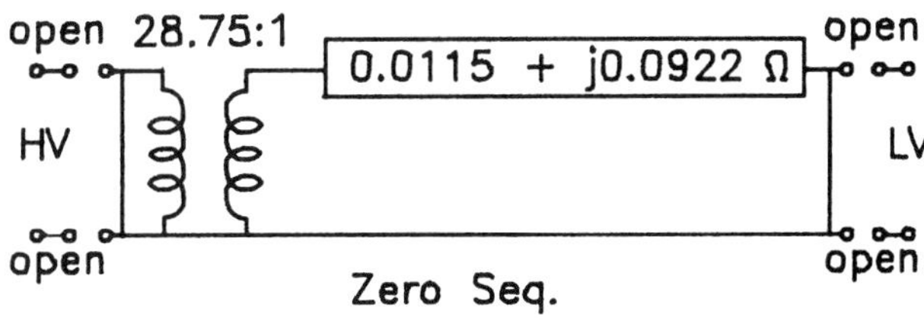

Figure 10-12 Sequence network representations for transformer of Example 10-9a.

Solution

a. The transformer percent impedance is converted to ohms referred to the low-voltage side as follows:

$$\mathbf{Z}_{\text{TR}} = (0.01 + j0.08)\,\frac{(2.4\ \text{kV})^2}{5.0\ \text{MVA}} = 0.0115 + j0.0922\ \Omega$$

The turns ratio is

$$a = \frac{69\ \text{kV}}{2.4\ \text{kV}} = 28.75$$

The sequence networks are shown in Fig. 10-12.

b. $\mathbf{Z}_{\text{TR}} = (0.01 + j0.06)\,\dfrac{(480\ \text{V})^2}{2000\ \text{kVA} \cdot 1000} = 0.0012 + j0.0069\ \Omega$

The turns ratio is

$$a = \frac{12.47\ \text{kV}}{0.48} = 25.98$$

The sequence networks are shown in Fig. 10-13.

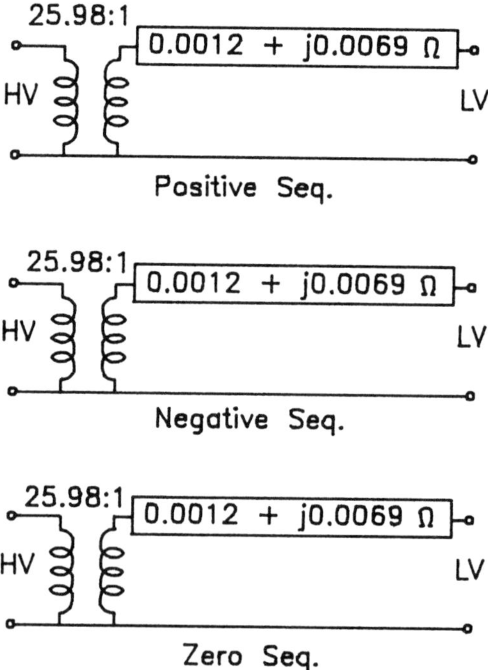

Figure 10-13 Sequence network representations for transformer of Example 10-9b.

c. $\mathbf{Z}_{TR} = (0.01 + j0.07)\dfrac{(4.16\text{ kV})^2}{7.5\text{ MVA}} = 0.0231 + j0.1615\ \Omega$

The magnitude of the complex turns ratio is

$$a = \frac{138\text{ kV}}{4.16\text{ kV}} = 33.17$$

The sequence networks are shown in Fig. 10-14.

d. $\mathbf{Z}_{TR} = (0.01 + j0.12)\dfrac{(15\text{ kV})^2}{50\text{ MVA}} = 0.045 + j0.54\ \Omega$

The magnitude of the complex turns ratio is

$$a = \frac{138\text{ kV}}{15\text{ kV}} = 9.2$$

The sequence networks are shown in Fig. 10-15.

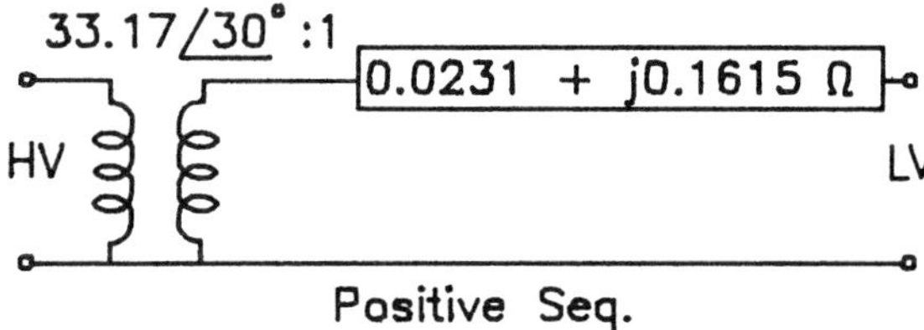

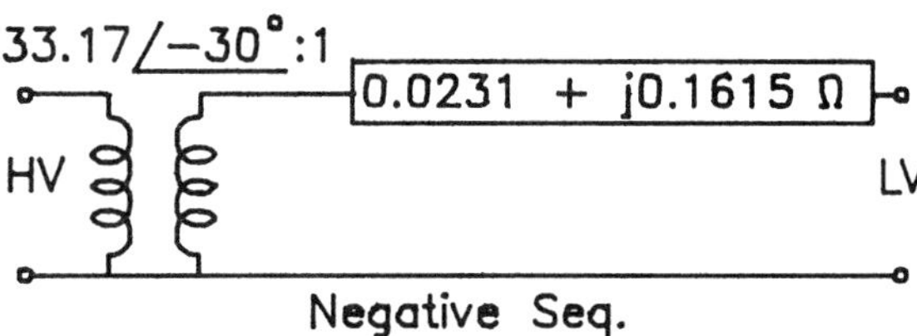

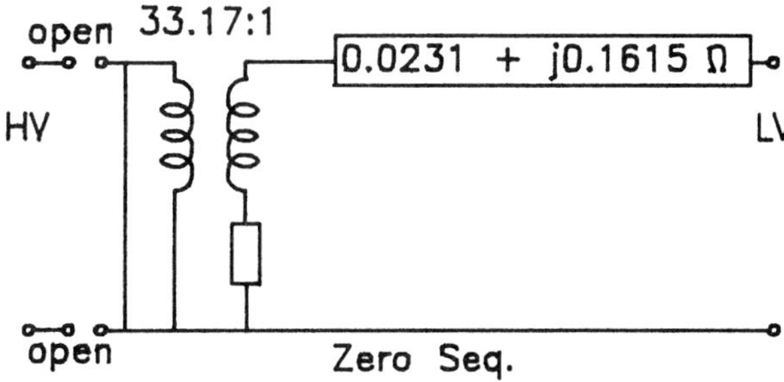

Figure 10-14 Sequence network representations for transformer of Example 10-9c.

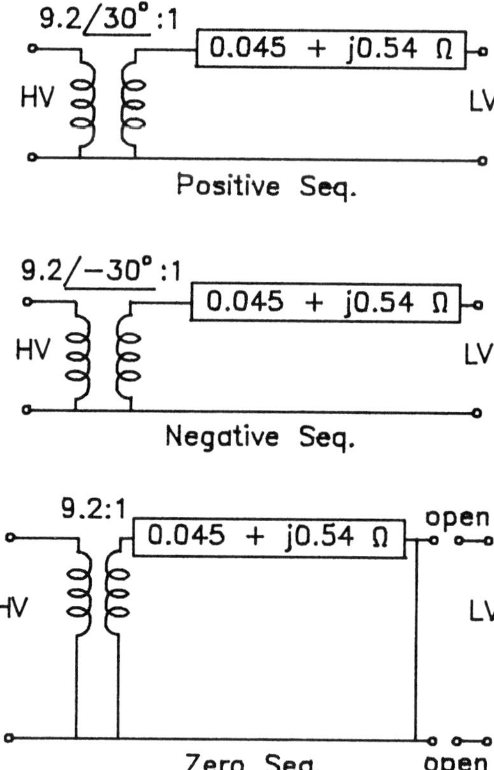

Figure 10-15 Sequence network representations for transformer of Example 10-9d.

10-5 Rotating Machine Sequence Networks

The sequence impedances for rotating machines are difficult to determine analytically. When precise calculations are desired, sequence impedance data should be obtained from the manufacturer of the rotating equipment. These values are expressed in per unit based on the rated voltage and rated power of the machine. Conversion to actual ohmic impedances or conversion to another power base is often necessary.

When converting the per unit impedances to actual ohmic values or to another power base, it is necessary to use the proper base voltage and base power. The voltage base for both motors and generators is the rated line to line voltage of the machine. For generators, the proper base power is the rated apparent power of the generator, usually expressed in terms of kVA or MVA. Conversely, the proper base power for motors is the rated shaft output converted from horsepower to watts.

EXAMPLE 10-10

Determine the sequence impedances expressed in ohms for the following three-phase, wye-connected synchronous generator.

$$30\ \text{MVA}, \quad 18\ \text{kV}, \quad 1800\ \text{rpm}, \quad 60\ \text{Hz}$$

$$X_1 = 15\%, \quad X_2 = 14\%, \quad x_0 = 3\%,$$

$$r_1 = 0.5\%, \quad r_2 = 3\%, \quad r_0 = 1\%$$

Solution The base impedance is calculated using the generator apparent power rating as the base apparent power. Likewise, the generator voltage rating is selected as the base voltage. Therefore,

$$Z_{\text{base}} = \frac{18^2}{30} = 10.8\ \Omega$$

The sequence impedances are calculated as follows:

$$r_1 = (0.005)(10.8) = 0.054\ \Omega, \qquad X_1 = (0.15)(10.8) = 1.62\ \Omega$$

$$r_2 = (0.03)(10.8) = 0.324\ \Omega, \qquad X_2 = (0.14)(10.8) = 1.512\ \Omega$$

$$r_0 = (0.01)(10.8) = 0.108\ \Omega, \qquad X_0 = (0.03)(10.8) = 0.324\ \Omega$$

Synchronous Generators

The positive sequence impedance network representation for synchronous motors and generators will consist of a voltage source in series with the positive sequence impedance of the machine. This is due to the fact that polyphase synchronous generators are designed to produce voltages that are equal in magnitude and displaced by 120°. The negative sequence and zero sequence voltage components of a balanced set of three-phase voltages will be zero. Therefore, a voltage source will not appear in either the negative sequence or zero sequence networks. The negative sequence network will consist of a single series impedance.

The zero sequence network representations will depend on the connection of the generator winding. For ungrounded wye- and delta-connected windings, an infinite impedance (open circuit) should be seen when looking into the zero sequence network. For wye-connected generator windings grounded through an impedance, it is necessary to place three times the grounding impedance in series with the zero sequence impedance of the generator. Figure 10-16 shows the sequence network representations for synchronous generators.

EXAMPLE 10-11

The generator of Example 10-10 is high resistance grounded through an impedance of 100 Ω. Determine the positive, negative and zero sequence networks. Assume that the generator voltage is 110% of rated.

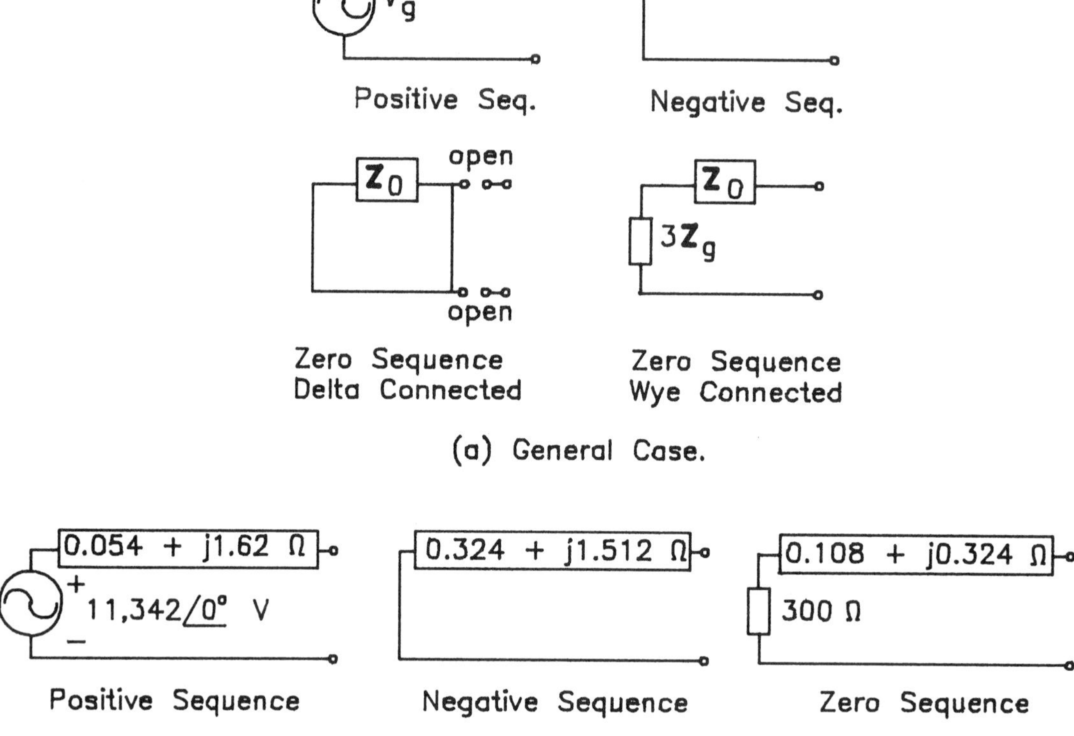

Figure 10-16 Sequence networks for synchronous generators.

Solution Since the generator is grounded through a 100-Ω resistor, a 300-Ω resistor must be placed in the zero sequence network. The generator voltage will appear only in the positive sequence network. This voltage is equal to

$$\mathbf{V}_g = 1.1 \cdot \frac{18{,}000}{\sqrt{3}} \angle 0° = 11{,}432\angle 0° \text{ V}$$

The sequence networks are shown in Fig. 10-16b.

Synchronous Motors

The sequence network representations for the synchronous motor are the same as the representations for the synchronous generator. A voltage source is included in the positive sequence network to model the countervoltage of the motor. This countervoltage will contribute to the total short-circuit current in the event of a short circuit in the vicinity of the motor. Therefore, provisions must be made to model the synchronous motor when performing short-circuit calculations.

Induction Motors

In addition to synchronous motors, the presence of large three-phase induction motors may contribute significant current in the event of a short circuit. It is therefore necessary to properly model these induction motors using sequence network representation. As in the synchronous generator, the positive sequence representation of the three-phase induction motor will include a voltage source. This voltage source represents the countervoltage present in the motor due to interaction between the rotor and stator fluxes. This voltage will decay rapidly following initiation of the short circuit. However, during the initial time period, this countervoltage will act as a source of fault current. It is generally recommended that the presence of large induction motors be taken into account when performing fault current calculations. The general sequence network models for three-phase induction motors are the same as those of the synchronous generator shown in Fig. 10-16a.

10-6 Sequence Filters

Sequence filters are used in protective relay applications to detect the presence of certain sequence components. These sequence filters are used in both voltage and current applications. Some of the more common examples are zero sequence current filters to detect line to ground faults, negative sequence voltage filters used to detect phase (and direction) reversal of ac motors, and zero sequence voltage filters to detect line to ground faults on ungrounded power systems.

Zero Sequence Current Filter

The schematic diagram for a zero sequence current is shown in Fig. 10-17. Each current transformer has the same ratio, designated a : 5. This ratio designation indicates that, when a amperes flows in the primary conductor, 5 A will flow in the secondary of each current transformer. Therefore, the secondary current magnitude in each current transformer will be equal to the primary current magnitude divided by $a/5$. The secondary current in each current transformer will be assumed to be in phase with its respective primary current. In actual practice, there will be a slight phase angle error between primary and secondary currents.

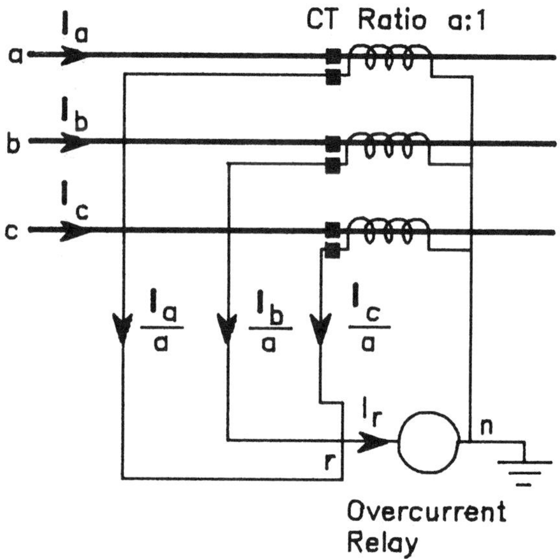

Figure 10-17 Zero sequence current filter.

In reference to Fig. 10-17, the relay current $\mathbf{I}_r$ is determined by applying Kirchhoff's current law at node r. The following results:

$$\begin{aligned} \mathbf{I}_r &= \frac{\mathbf{I}_a}{a/5} + \frac{\mathbf{I}_b}{a/5} + \frac{\mathbf{I}_c}{a/5} \\ &= \frac{1}{a/5}[\mathbf{I}_a + \mathbf{I}_b + \mathbf{I}_c] \end{aligned} \tag{10.32}$$

The line currents can be expressed in terms of sequence components, as follows:

$$\mathbf{I}_a = \mathbf{I}_0 + \mathbf{I}_1 + \mathbf{I}_2 \tag{10.33}$$

$$\mathbf{I}_b = \mathbf{I}_0 + \mathbf{a}^2\,\mathbf{I}_1 + \mathbf{a}\,\mathbf{I}_2 \tag{10.34}$$

$$\mathbf{I}_c = \mathbf{I}_0 + \mathbf{a}\,\mathbf{I}_1 + \mathbf{a}^2\,\mathbf{I}_2 \tag{10.35}$$

Substituting Eqs. (10.33), (10.34), and (10.35) into (10.32) results in the following:

$$\begin{aligned} \mathbf{I}_r &= \frac{1}{a/5}[\mathbf{I}_0 + \mathbf{I}_1 + \mathbf{I}_2 + \mathbf{I}_0 + \mathbf{a}^2\,\mathbf{I}_1 + \mathbf{a}\,\mathbf{I}_2 + \mathbf{I}_0 + \mathbf{a}\,\mathbf{I}_1 + \mathbf{a}^2\,\mathbf{I}_2] \\ &= \frac{1}{a/5}[3\mathbf{I}_0] \end{aligned} \tag{10.36}$$

Inspection of Eq. (10.36) indicates that the relay will carry only a current that is proportional to $3\mathbf{I}_0$ and will not respond to positive or negative sequence currents.

EXAMPLE 10-12

A zero sequence current filter similar to that shown in Fig. 10-17 carries the following line currents:

$$\mathbf{I}_a = 500\angle{-15°}\ \text{A}$$
$$\mathbf{I}_b = 475\angle{-145°}\ \text{A}$$
$$\mathbf{I}_c = 300\angle 120°\ \text{A}$$

Determine the current through the relay $\mathbf{I}_r$ if the *CT* ratio is 800:5.

Solution The zero sequence current is calculated from Eq. (10.17).

$$\begin{aligned}\mathbf{I}_0 &= \tfrac{1}{3}(500\angle{-15°} + 475\angle{-145°} + 300\angle 120°)\\ &= -18.71 - j47.35\\ &= 50.9\angle 248.4°\ \text{A}\end{aligned}$$

The relay current is calculated from Eq. (10.36) as follows:

$$\begin{aligned}\mathbf{I}_r &= \frac{1}{800/5}\,[3\cdot(50.9\angle 248.4°)]\\ &= 0.954\angle 248.4°\ \text{A}\end{aligned}$$

Zero Sequence Voltage Filter

A zero sequence voltage filter can be constructed by connecting three voltage transformers to a three-phase line. The primaries are connected grounded wye and the secondaries in broken delta. The schematic diagram for a zero sequence voltage filter is shown in Fig. 10-18. Each voltage transformer will have an identical turns ratio designated a. The voltage across each transformer secondary coil will be equal to the line to neutral primary voltage divided by a. As in the zero sequence current filter, ratio and phase angle errors will be neglected.

The voltage across the relay V_r is determined by applying Kirchhoff's voltage law around the broken delta secondary. The following results:

$$\begin{aligned}\mathbf{V}_r &= \frac{\mathbf{V}_{ag}}{a} + \frac{\mathbf{V}_{bg}}{a} + \frac{\mathbf{V}_{cg}}{a}\\ &= \frac{1}{a}\cdot(\mathbf{V}_{ag} + \mathbf{V}_{bg} + \mathbf{V}_{cg})\end{aligned} \tag{10.37}$$

Substituting Eqs. (10.9), (10.10), and (10.11) into (10.37) results in

$$\begin{aligned}\mathbf{V}_r = \frac{1}{a}(&\mathbf{V}_0 + \mathbf{V}_1 + \mathbf{V}_2 + \mathbf{V}_0 + \mathbf{a}^2\,\mathbf{V}_1 + \mathbf{a}\,\mathbf{V}_2\\ &+ \mathbf{V}_0 + \mathbf{a}\,\mathbf{V}_1 + \mathbf{a}^2\,\mathbf{V}_2) = \frac{1}{a}(3\mathbf{V}_0)\end{aligned} \tag{10.38}$$

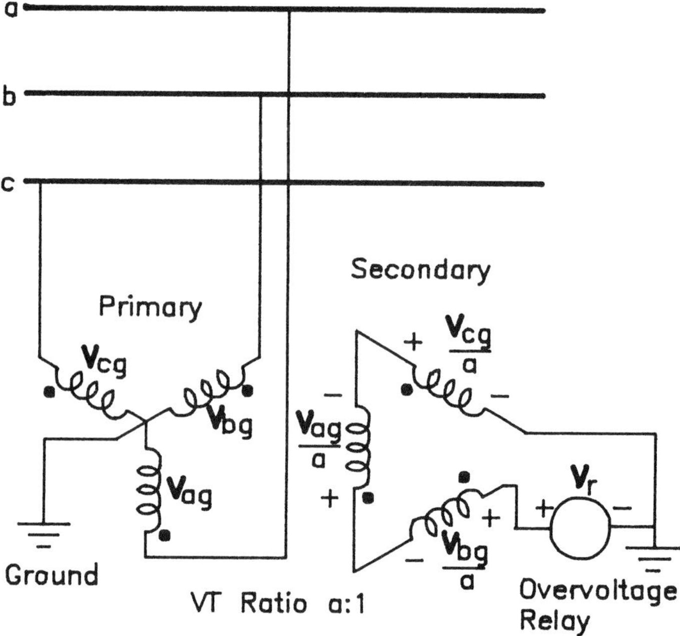

Figure 10-18 Zero sequence voltage filter.

From Eq. (10.38), it is observed that the voltage relay will respond only to zero sequence voltage.

EXAMPLE 10-13

A zero sequence voltage filter is constructed similarly to that of Fig. 10-18. The following line to ground voltages are present as a result of a line to ground fault on an ungrounded, 13.8-kV bus.

$$\mathbf{V}_{ag} = 13{,}800\angle 30° \text{ V}$$
$$\mathbf{V}_{bg} = 0 \text{ V, (faulted phase)}$$
$$\mathbf{V}_{cg} = 13{,}800\ \angle 90° \text{ V}$$

Determine the voltage across the relay if the transformer voltage ratio is 13,800–120 V.

Solution The transformer turns ratio is

$$a = \frac{13{,}800}{120} = 115{:}1$$

The zero sequence voltage is calculated from Eq. (10.14).

$$\begin{aligned}\mathbf{V}_0 &= \tfrac{1}{3}\,(13{,}800\angle 30 + 0 + 13{,}800\angle 90°)\\ &= 3983.7 + j6900\\ &= 7967.4\angle 60° \text{ V}\end{aligned}$$

The voltage across the relay is determined by applying Eq. (10.38).

$$V_r = \frac{1}{115}(3 \cdot 7967.4\angle 60°)$$
$$= 207.8\angle 60° \text{ V}$$

Negative Sequence Voltage Filter

The schematic diagram of a negative sequence voltage filter in common use is shown in Fig. 10-19 [4]. The impedance elements R and X are selected such that the angle of the series connection, $R + jX$, is equal to 60°. The current that flows through the impedance $R + jX$ is given by

$$\mathbf{I} = \frac{\mathbf{V}_{ac}}{R + jX} \tag{10.39}$$

Since the angle of the impedance is 60° by design, the current as given by Eq. (10.39) will lag $\mathbf{V}_{ac}$ by 60°. Furthermore, the voltage across R will be in phase with the current $\mathbf{I}$. Therefore, the voltage from X to Z will lag $\mathbf{V}_{ac}$ by 60°. The voltage $\mathbf{V}_{xz}$ is given by

$$\mathbf{V}_{xz} = \mathbf{I} \cdot R \tag{10.40}$$
$$= \frac{\mathbf{V}_{ac} \cdot R}{R + jX}$$

The autotransformer tap is selected such that the magnitude of the voltage from Y to Z is equal to the magnitude of the voltage from X to Z. In addition, the phase

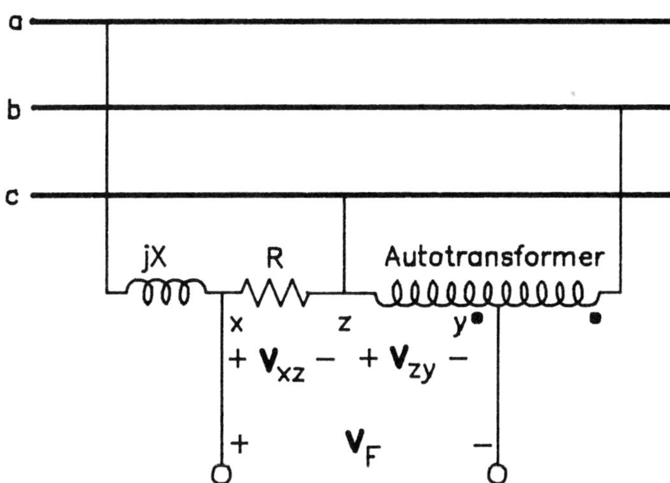

Figure 10-19 Negative sequence voltage filter.

angle of the voltage from Y to Z will be equal to the phase angle of $\mathbf{V}_{bc}$. Therefore, the voltage from Z to Y will be 180° out of phase with $\mathbf{V}_{bc}$. The filter output voltage $\mathbf{V}_F$ is equal to:

$$\mathbf{V}_F = \mathbf{V}_{XZ} + \mathbf{V}_{ZY} \tag{10.41}$$

EXAMPLE 10-14

A negative sequence voltage filter similar in design to the filter shown in Fig. 10-19 has $R = 300\ \Omega$ and $X = 520\ \Omega$. Calculate the filter output voltage for the following:

a. Positive sequence voltages applied:

$$\mathbf{V}_{ab} = 120\angle 0\text{ V},\qquad \mathbf{V}_{bc} = 120\angle -120°\text{ V},\qquad \mathbf{V}_{ca} = 120\angle 120°\text{ V}$$

b. Negative sequence voltages applied:

$$\mathbf{V}_{ab} = 120\angle 0°\text{ V},\qquad \mathbf{V}_{bc} = 120\angle 120°\text{ V},\qquad \mathbf{V}_{ca} = 120\angle -120°\text{ V}$$

Solution

a. The voltage V_{xz} is calculated from Eq. (10.40).

$$\mathbf{V}_{xz} = \frac{-(120\angle 120°)\cdot 300}{300 + j520} = 60.0\angle 240°\text{ V}$$

The voltage $\mathbf{V}_{zy}$ is

$$\mathbf{V}_{zy} = 60.0\angle(-120 + 180)° = 60.0\angle 60°\text{ V}$$

The filter output voltage is calculated by applying Eq. (10.41).

$$\mathbf{V}_f = 60.0\angle 240° + 60.0\angle 60° = 0 + j0\text{ V}$$

Therefore, with positive sequence voltage applied, the filter output is zero.

b. The voltage $\mathbf{V}_{xz}$ is now

$$\mathbf{V}_{xz} = \frac{-(120\angle -120°)\cdot 300}{300 + j520} = 60.0\angle 0°\text{ V}$$

The voltage $\mathbf{V}_{zy}$ is

$$\mathbf{V}_{zy} = 60.0\angle(120 + 180)° = 60.0\angle 300°\text{ V}$$

The filter output voltage is

$$\mathbf{V}_F = 60.0\angle 0° + 60.0\angle 300° = 90.0 - j52.0 = 103.9\angle -30°\text{ V}$$

Therefore, with negative sequence voltage applied, the filter voltage is nonzero.

References

[1] *Symmetrical Component Circuit Constants and Neutral Circulating Currents for Concentric Neutral Underground Distribution Cables,* by W. A. Lewis and G. D. Allen, IEEE PAS-97, No. 1, Jan./Feb. 1978, pp. 191–199.

[2] Ibid.
[3] Ibid.
[4] *Protective Relaying Theory and Applications,* edited by Walter A. Elmore, ABB Power T&D Company, Inc., published by Marcel Dekker, Inc., 1994, p. 44.

Problems

10.1. Calculate the sequence voltages given the following phase voltages:

$$\mathbf{V}_a = 7000\angle 0°\text{V}, \quad \mathbf{V}_b = 7200\angle -110°\text{V}, \quad \mathbf{V}_c = 7300\angle 90°\ \text{V}$$

10.2. Calculate the sequence currents given the following line currents:

$$\mathbf{I}_a = 300\angle 15°\text{A}, \quad \mathbf{I}_b = 350\angle -90°\ \text{A}, \quad \mathbf{I}_c = 325\angle 130°\ \text{A}$$

10.3. A three-phase wye-connected load consists of the following impedances:

$$\mathbf{Z}_{an} = 10.0 + j5.0\ \Omega, \quad \mathbf{Z}_{bn} = 12.0 + j4.0\ \Omega, \quad \mathbf{Z}_{cn} = 11.0 + j6.0\ \Omega$$

The applied voltages are

$$\mathbf{V}_{an} = 277\angle 0°\ \text{V}, \quad \mathbf{V}_{bn} = 285\angle -115°\ \text{V}, \quad \mathbf{V}_{cn} = 260\angle 126°\ \text{V}$$

Calculate the following:

a. Sequence voltages
b. Line currents
c. Sequence currents
d. Neutral current: Does $\mathbf{I}_n = -3\mathbf{I}_0$ as expected?

10.4. A 2400-V, delta-connected capacitor bank consists of four 100-kVAR, 60-Hz, single-phase capacitor units per phase. Determine the following (assume *abc* phase sequence):

a. Sequence components of line currents with all capacitors energized
b. Sequence components of line currents with one capacitor removed between the *b* and *c* phases

10.5. Determine the positive, negative, and zero sequence impedances of the overhead and underground line configurations shown in Fig. 10-20a through f.

10.6. Determine the positive, negative, and zero sequence networks for the following transformers:

a. 1000 kVA, 12.47 kV–480Y/277 V, delta–wye, $R = 1\%$, $X = 6\%$
b. 500 kVA, 4.16Y/2.4 kV–208Y/120 V, wye–wye, $R = 1\%$, $X = 2.5\%$

The transformer impedances should be expressed in ohms referred to the low-voltage side of the transformer.

10.7. A zero sequence current filter similar to that shown in Fig. 10-17 carries the following line currents:

$$\mathbf{I}_a = 1000\angle -85°\ \text{A}, \quad \mathbf{I}_b = 900\angle -140°\ \text{A}, \quad \mathbf{I}_c = 1200\angle 90°\ \text{A}$$

Determine the current through the overcurrent relay if the *CT* ratio is 1200:5.

10.8. A zero sequence voltage relay similar to that shown in Fig. 10-18 has the following voltages on the high-voltage side:

$$\mathbf{V}_{ag} = 0\ \text{V}, \quad \mathbf{V}_{bg} = 2400\angle 180°\ \text{V}, \quad \mathbf{V}_{cg} = 2400\angle 120°\ \text{V}$$

The transformer voltage ratio is 2400–120 V. Determine the voltage across the overvoltage relay.

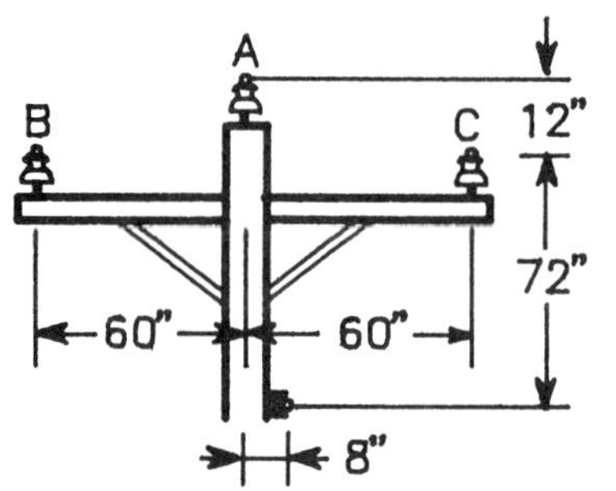

Phase: 636 kcmil AAC, 37 Str.
Neutral: #4/0 AWG AAC, 19 Str.

(a)

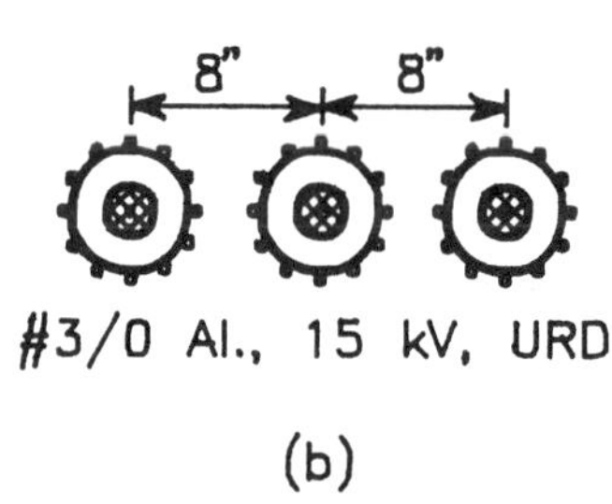

(b)

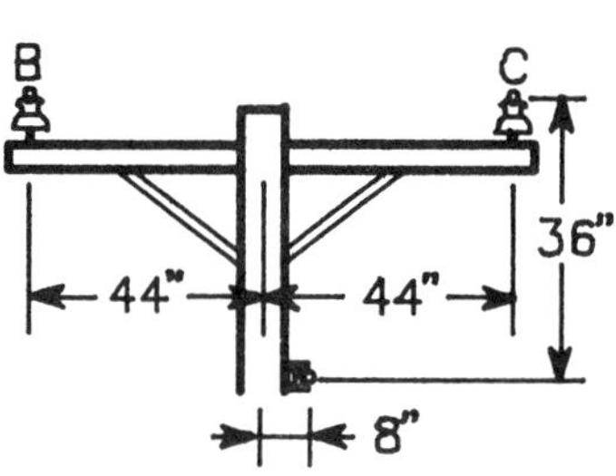

Phase: #4 ACSR 7/1 Str.
Neutral: #4 ACSR 7/1 Str.

(c)

8"

#1/0 Al., 25 kV, URD

(d)

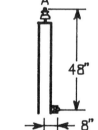

#1/0 Al., 35 kV, URD

(e)

Phase: #3 AWG Cu, 7 Str.
Neutral: #3 AWG Cu, 7 Str.

(f)

Figure 10-20 Line configurations for Problem 10-5.

10.9. A negative sequence voltage filter is constructed similarly to that shown in Fig. 10-19. The filter parameters are $R = 500\ \Omega$ and $X = 866\ \Omega$. The following voltages are applied:

$$\mathbf{V}_{ab} = 480\angle 0°\ \text{V}, \qquad \mathbf{V}_{bc} = 480\angle -120°\ \text{V}, \qquad \mathbf{V}_{ca} = 480\angle 120°\ \text{V}$$

Determine the filter output voltage.

10.10. Repeat Problem 10.9 for reversed phase sequence (*ACB* sequence).

11

Short-Circuit Calculations

11-1 General

This chapter will discuss the methods used to calculate short-circuit currents on electric utility systems. The chapter begins with a discussion of the actual fault current waveform and the effect of system resistance and inductance on the shape of the waveform. Of particular interest is the amount of dc offset present in the waveform immediately after the initiation of the fault. A significant dc offset will result in much higher maximum peak instantaneous current levels than would be encountered if there were no dc offset. Knowledge of the maximum peak instantaneous value of the waveform is necessary when specifying momentary duties of various electrical equipment.

The procedures for calculating short-circuit currents for three-phase, line to line, line to line to ground, line to ground, and line to ground through impedance faults will be discussed. Typically, the line to ground fault is the most prevalent type of fault encountered on utility power systems. The three-phase fault is the least prevalent. The procedures used for calculating fault currents will be based on the method of symmetrical components covered in Chapter 10. The proper connection of the sequence networks will be presented for each type of fault calculation performed. Once the sequence currents have been determined, the actual phase currents may be determined by applying the transformation equations discussed in Chapter 10.

11-2 Symmetrical and Asymmetrical Fault Currents

The actual short-circuit currents that flow in a power system during fault conditions will not be sinusoidal. Rather, the current waveforms will be offset due to the inductance of the system between the source and the location of the fault. In general, the larger the source inductance with respect to the source resistance, the greater the amount of offset. The actual current that flows during a fault condition is referred to as the *asymmetrical* fault current.

When performing power system short-circuit calculations, it is easier to apply sinusoidal steady-state circuit analysis techniques, rather than working in the time domain. The short-circuit currents calculated using sinusoidal steady-state (phasor) analysis will be the steady-state values after all transients have decayed. Since the asymmetrical fault current is a function of the system inductance and resistance, it is convenient to determine the multipliers to be applied to the symmetrical values of fault current in order to determine the asymmetrical values.

To determine the asymmetrical multipliers, consider the circuit shown in Fig. 11-1. The asymmetrical factors will be derived by assuming that a balanced three-phase fault occurs on the system. As such, the three-phase power system can be represented using the line to neutral equivalent circuit. The resistance and inductance of all system components between the source and the fault location are designated as R and L, respectively. The source is represented as a sinusoidal voltage source, with a frequency of ω rad/sec. The angle θ is included to allow the voltage source to have any value at time $t = 0$ sec when the fault occurs.

Applying Kirchhoff's voltage law to the circuit of Fig. 11-1 results in the following:

$$V_m \sin(\omega t + \theta) = R \cdot i(t) + L \cdot \frac{di(t)}{dt} \tag{11.1}$$

Rearranging and simplifying Eq. (11.1) results in

$$\frac{di(t)}{dt} + \frac{R}{L} \cdot i(t) = \frac{V_m}{L} \cdot \sin(\omega t + \theta) \tag{11.2}$$

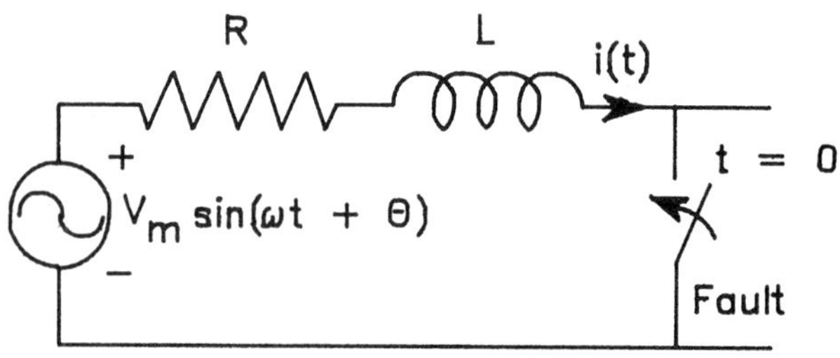

Figure 11-1 Equivalent circuit for determining fault current waveform.

Equation (11.2) is in the standard form required for solution by use of the integrating factor method from differential equations:

$$\frac{di(t)}{dt} + p(t) + i(t) = q(t) \tag{11.3}$$

where $p(t) = R/L$ and $q(t) = (V_m/L) \cdot \sin(\omega t + \theta)$. The integrating factor is given by

$$\begin{aligned} p &= e^{\int p(t)dt} \\ &= e^{\int (R/L)dt} \\ &= e^{(R/L)t} \end{aligned} \tag{11.4}$$

The solution of Eq. (11.2) is given by

$$i(t) = \frac{1}{p}\int p \cdot q(t)\, dt + \frac{C}{p} \tag{11.5}$$

where C is a constant to be determined by applying the initial conditions. Applying Eq. (11.4) and the expression for $q(t)$ into Eq. (11.5) results in the following:

$$\begin{aligned} i(t) &= \frac{1}{e^{(R/L)}}\int e^{(R/L)t} \cdot \frac{V_m}{L} \cdot \sin(\omega t + \theta)\, dt + \frac{C}{e^{(R/L)t}} \\ &= \frac{V_m}{L} \cdot e^{-(R/L)t}\int e^{(R/L)t} \cdot \sin(\omega t + \theta)\, dt + C \cdot e^{-(R/L)t} \\ &= \frac{V_m/L}{(R/L)^2 + \omega^2}\left[\frac{R}{L} \cdot \sin(\omega t + \theta) - \omega \cos(\omega t + \theta)\right] + C \cdot e^{-(R/L)t} \end{aligned} \tag{11.6}$$

The following trigonometric identity will be used to simplify Eq. (11.6).

$$\frac{R}{L}\sin(\omega t + \theta) - \omega\cos(\omega t + \theta) = \left[\left(\frac{R}{L}\right)^2 + \omega^2\right]^{1/2}\sin(\omega t + \theta - \theta_z) \tag{11.7}$$

where $\theta_z = \tan^{-1}(\omega L/R)$. Substituting Eq. (11.7) into (11.6) results in

$$\begin{aligned} i(t) &= \frac{V_m/L}{(R/L)^2 + \omega^2}\left[\left(\frac{R^2}{L} + \omega^2\right)^{1/2}\sin(\omega t + \theta - \theta_z)\right] + C \cdot e^{-(R/L)t} \\ &= \frac{V_m/L}{[(R/L)^2 + \omega^2]^{1/2}} \cdot \sin(\omega t + \theta - \theta_z) + C \cdot e^{-(R/L)t} \end{aligned} \tag{11.8}$$

The constant C in Eq. (11.8) is determined by applying initial conditions to the current that flows in the circuit at the instant the fault occurs. The initial current is designated as I_0 and is equal to the current flowing at time $t = 0$. Substituting $t = 0$ into Eq. (11.8) results in

$$I_0 = i(0) = \frac{V_m/L}{[(R/L)^2 + \omega^2]^{1/2}} \cdot \sin(\theta - \theta_z) + C \tag{11.9}$$

Solving Eq. (11.9) for C,

$$C = I_0 - \frac{V_m/L}{[(R/L)^2 + \omega^2]^{1/2}} \cdot \sin(\theta - \theta_z) \tag{11.10}$$

The final expression for the current that flows in the event of a balanced three-phase fault is found by substituting Eq. (11.10) into (11.8). The following results:

$$\begin{aligned} i(t) &= \frac{V_m/L}{[(R/L)^2 + \omega^2]^{1/2}} \cdot \sin(\omega t + \theta - \theta_z) \\ &\quad + \left[I_0 - \frac{V_m/L}{[(R/L)^2 + \omega^2]^{1/2}} \cdot \sin(\theta - \theta_z)\right] \cdot e^{-(R/L)t} \end{aligned} \tag{11.11}$$

It is convenient to refer to the X/R (X over R) ratio of the system impedance when discussing asymmetrical fault current. The preceding analysis used the inductance rather than the inductive reactance of the source. The inductance and inductive reactance are related by the following:

$$L = \frac{X}{\omega} \tag{11.12}$$

Substituting Eq. (11.12) into (11.11) and simplifying results in

$$\begin{aligned} i(t) &= \frac{(V_m/X)\omega}{[(\omega \cdot R/X)^2 + \omega^2]^{1/2}} \cdot \sin(\omega t + \theta - \theta_z) \\ &\quad + \left[I_0 - \frac{(V_m/X)\omega}{[(\omega \cdot R/X)^2 + \omega^2]^{1/2}} \cdot \sin(\theta - \theta_z)\right] \cdot e^{-(\omega R/X)t} \end{aligned} \tag{11.13}$$

Simplifying,

$$\begin{aligned} i(t) &= \frac{V_m}{(R^2 + X^2)^{1/2}} \cdot \sin(\omega t + \theta - \theta_z) \\ &\quad + \left[I_0 - \frac{V_m}{(R^2 + X^2)^{1/2}} \cdot \sin(\theta - \theta_z)\right] \cdot e^{-(\omega R/X)t} \end{aligned} \tag{11.14}$$

Equation (11.14) gives the expression for the total current that flows when a three-phase fault occurs on a power system. The first part of Eq. (11.14) is the steady-state solution and may be obtained using phasor analysis. The second part is the transient component of the total fault current. Notice that the transient component decays to zero after a period of time. However, the transient component is very significant during the first few cycles after the fault occurs and cannot be neglected.

For given initial values of current I_0 and closing angle θ, it can be seen that the total fault current is a function of system resistance and inductive reactance. It is common to assume that the initial current I_0 is equal to zero and that the closing angle θ is also equal to zero. Equation (11.14) thus reduces to

$$\begin{aligned} i(t) &= \frac{V_m}{(R^2 + X^2)^{1/2}} \cdot [\sin(\omega t - \theta_z) + \sin(\theta_z) \cdot e^{-(\omega R/X)t}] \\ &= V_m/Z_s\,[\sin(\omega t - \theta_z) + \sin(\theta_z) \cdot e^{-(\omega R/X)t}] \end{aligned} \tag{11.15}$$

where $Z_s = (R^2 + X^2)^{1/2}$, the magnitude of the system impedance between the source and the fault.

The term V_m/Z_s in Eq. (11.15) represents the maximum peak value of fault current, I_p, that would be calculated using steady-state phasor analysis. The rms value of fault current is easily calculated by dividing the rms system voltage by the system impedance Z_s. Since the rms value of a sinusoidal waveform is equal to the maximum peak value divided by $\sqrt{2}$, the rms value of fault current will be

$$I_{\text{rms}} = \frac{I_p}{\sqrt{2}} = \frac{V_m}{\sqrt{2} \cdot Z_s} \tag{11.16}$$

Rearranging Eq. (11.16) results in

$$\frac{V_m}{Z_s} = \sqrt{2} \cdot I_{\text{rms}} \tag{11.17}$$

Substituting Eq. (11.17) into (11.15) and simplifying,

$$i(t) = \sqrt{2} \cdot I_{\text{rms}} \left[\sin(\omega t - \theta_z) + \sin(\theta_z) \cdot e^{-(\omega R/X)t}\right] \tag{11.18}$$

A plot of Eq. (11.18) is shown in Fig. 11-2 for X/R equal to infinity and zero. Notice that the dc offset is maximum for an X/R ratio equal to infinity. With X/R equal to zero, there is no dc offset, and the waveform represents a sine wave.

The bracketed term in Eq. (11.18) multiplied by the $\sqrt{2}$ represents a multiplier that can be applied to the rms value of fault current to determine the instantaneous value of fault current at any time t. When specifying the momentary short-circuit withstand ca-

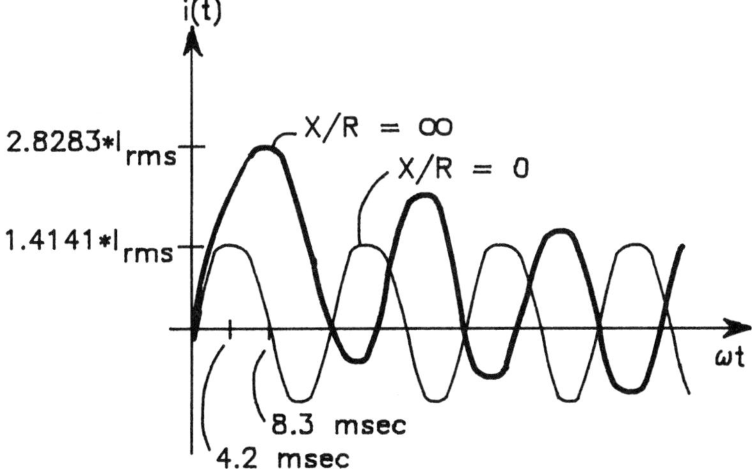

Figure 11-2 Fault current waveforms.

Table 11-1 Asymmetrical Current Factors

System X/R Ratio	*Asymmetrical Factor*	*Time of Peak, t_p (msec)*
0.0	1.4141	4.2
0.1	1.4141	4.4
0.2	1.4142	4.7
0.3	1.4149	4.9
0.4	1.4181	5.2
0.5	1.4250	5.4
0.6	1.4362	5.5
0.7	1.4511	5.7
0.8	1.4692	5.8
0.9	1.4897	5.9
1.0	1.5122	6.1
2.0	1.7560	6.8
3.0	1.9495	7.1
4.0	2.0892	7.4
5.0	2.1924	7.5
6.0	2.2708	7.6
7.0	2.3323	7.7
8.0	2.3817	7.8
9.0	2.4222	7.8
10.0	2.4561	7.9
20.0	2.6256	8.1
30.0	2.6890	8.2
40.0	2.7224	8.2
50.0	2.7427	8.2
100.0	2.7848	8.3
Infinity	2.8283	8.3

pability of electrical equipment, the maximum peak instantaneous value of fault current is of major importance. The multiplying factor that is used to determine the maximum peak instantaneous fault current can be obtained by taking the derivative of the bracketed term of Eq. (11.18) with respect to time and equating to zero. The result is then solved for the time of maximum peak t_p. The time of maximum peak is then substituted into Eq. (11.18) to determine the appropriate multiplying factor. Table 11-1 summarizes the results for various system X/R ratios.

EXAMPLE 11-1 The source impedance at a 12.47-kV distribution substation bus is $0.4 + j1.5\ \Omega$/per phase. Calculate the rms and maximum peak instantaneous value of fault current if a balanced three-phase fault occurs.

Solution The line to neutral equivalent representation is used. The line to neutral voltage is

$$V_{\text{ln}} = \frac{V_{\text{ll}}}{\sqrt{3}} = \frac{12{,}470}{\sqrt{3}} = 7200 \text{ V}$$

The rms symmetrical fault current is

$$I_{\text{rms}} = \frac{7200}{(0.4^2 + 1.5^2)^{1/2}} = 4638 \text{ A}$$

The system X/R ratio is

$$\frac{X}{R} = \frac{1.5}{0.4} = 3.75$$

From Table 11-1, the asymmetrical factor is determined by interpolation.

$$\begin{aligned}\text{Asymmetrical factor} &= (2.0892 - 1.9495) \cdot (3.75 - 3.0) + 1.9495 \\ &= 2.0543\end{aligned}$$

The maximum peak instantaneous value of fault current is

$$I_p = 2.0543 \cdot 4638 = 9528 \text{ A}$$

Note that in this example all substation electrical equipment must be able to withstand a peak current of approximately 9500 A.

11-3 Three-Phase Faults

The procedure used to calculate fault currents for three-phase faults has been discussed in previous sections. Essentially, a three-phase fault represents a balanced condition in which the fault currents in each phase are equal in magnitude and displaced by 120° and 240°, respectively. Assuming an *ABC* phase sequence, the three-phase fault currents can be expressed as

$$\mathbf{I}_a = I\angle 0°$$

$$\mathbf{I}_b = I\angle 240°$$

$$\mathbf{I}_c = I\angle 120°$$

The symmetrical components of these fault currents are determined by applying Eq. (10.17) to (10.19), resulting in the following:

$$\mathbf{I}_0 = \tfrac{1}{3}(I\angle 0° + I\angle 240° + I\angle 120°) = 0$$

$$\mathbf{I}_1 = \tfrac{1}{3}(I\angle 0° + \mathbf{a} \cdot I\angle 240° + \mathbf{a}^2 \cdot I\angle 120°) = I\angle 0°$$

$$\mathbf{I}_2 = \tfrac{1}{3}(I\angle 0° + \mathbf{a}^2 \cdot I\angle 240° + \mathbf{a} \cdot I\angle 120°) = 0$$

Therefore, the negative and zero sequence currents are equal to zero for a balanced three-phase fault. The positive sequence current is equal to the *A* phase fault current.

When performing fault current calculations, the source is usually represented by only a positive sequence voltage source. Negative and zero sequence voltages are not assumed to be present when performing short-circuit calculations. However, when performing voltage unbalance calculations, a zero and/or negative sequence voltage source may be present in addition to the positive sequence voltage source.

Therefore, since the zero and negative sequence currents are equal to zero and there are no zero or negative sequence voltage sources, only the positive sequence network representation need be used to calculate the fault currents for a three-phase fault. The positive sequence network contains a voltage source, and all positive sequence impedance elements between the source and the fault location. The positive sequence network is reduced using Thevenin's theorem to contain a single voltage source and single impedance. This reduced network is shown in Fig. 11-3.

In reference to Fig. 11-3, the positive sequence current is

$$\mathbf{I}_1 = \frac{\mathbf{V}_1}{\mathbf{Z}_1} \qquad \textbf{(11.19)}$$

where

$\mathbf{V}_1$ = positive sequence source voltage

$\mathbf{Z}_1$ = positive sequence Thevenin impedance

The positive sequence source voltage is usually selected as equal to the nominal line to neutral system voltage. If working in the per unit system, a positive sequence source voltage of 1.0 is usually assumed. In addition, the positive sequence source voltage is usually selected as the reference having a phase angle of 0°.

Once the positive, negative, and zero sequence currents have been determined, the actual phase currents can be calculated by applying a set of transformation equations similar to Eqs. (10.9), (10.10), and (10.11), as follows:

$$\mathbf{I}_a = \mathbf{I}_0 + \mathbf{I}_1 + \mathbf{I}_2 \qquad \textbf{(11.20)}$$

$$\mathbf{I}_b = \mathbf{I}_0 + \mathbf{a}^2 \cdot \mathbf{I}_1 + \mathbf{a} \cdot \mathbf{I}_2 \qquad \textbf{(11.21)}$$

$$\mathbf{I}_c = \mathbf{I}_0 + \mathbf{a} \cdot \mathbf{I}_1 + \mathbf{a}^2 \cdot \mathbf{I}_2 \qquad \textbf{(11.22)}$$

$$\mathbf{I}_n = -3 \cdot \mathbf{I}_0 \qquad \textbf{(11.23)}$$

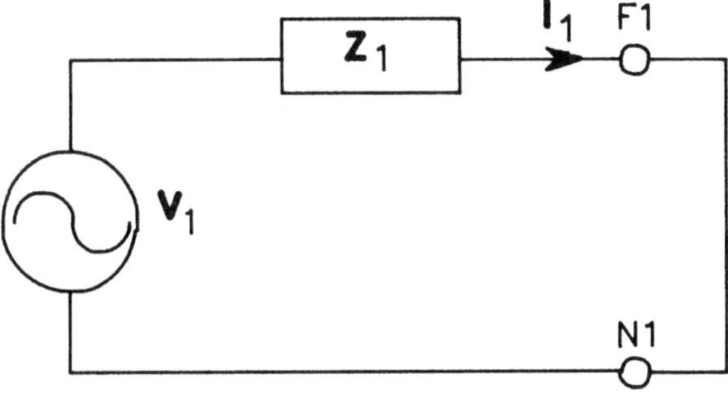

Figure 11-3 Sequence network connections for three-phase fault.

Applying Eqs. (11.20) through (11.23) for a three-phase fault results in the following:

$$\mathbf{I}_a = \mathbf{I}_1, \qquad \mathbf{I}_b = \mathbf{a}^2 \cdot \mathbf{I}_1, \qquad \mathbf{I}_c = \mathbf{a} \cdot \mathbf{I}_1, \qquad \mathbf{I}_n = 0$$

Notice that these equations represent a balanced three-phase set of currents, equal in magnitude and displaced by 120° from each other. In addition, the neutral current $\mathbf{I}_n$ is equal to zero for a balanced three-phase fault.

11-4 Line to Line Faults

The connection of the sequence networks for line to line faults is determined by assuming that the *B* and *C* phases are shorted together. Under these conditions, the fault current in the *A* phase is equal to zero, since the *A* phase is not involved in the fault. Therefore, for a phase *B* to phase *C* fault, $\mathbf{I}_b = -\mathbf{I}_c$, and $\mathbf{I}_a = \mathbf{I}_n = 0$. Applying the symmetrical component transformation equations results in the following:

$$\begin{aligned} \mathbf{I}_0 &= \tfrac{1}{3}(\mathbf{I}_b + \mathbf{I}_c) \\ &= \tfrac{1}{3}(-\mathbf{I}_c + \mathbf{I}_c) \\ &= 0 \end{aligned} \tag{11.24}$$

$$\begin{aligned} \mathbf{I}_1 &= \tfrac{1}{3}(\mathbf{a} \cdot \mathbf{I}_b + \mathbf{a}^2 \cdot \mathbf{I}_c) \\ &= \tfrac{1}{3}(\mathbf{a} \cdot (-\mathbf{I}_c) + \mathbf{a}^2 \cdot \mathbf{I}_c) \\ &= \tfrac{1}{3}\mathbf{I}_c(\mathbf{a}^2 - \mathbf{a}) \end{aligned} \tag{11.25}$$

$$\begin{aligned} \mathbf{I}_2 &= \tfrac{1}{3}(\mathbf{a}^2 \cdot \mathbf{I}_b + \mathbf{a} \cdot \mathbf{I}_c) \\ &= \tfrac{1}{3}(\mathbf{a}^2 \cdot (-\mathbf{I}_c) + \mathbf{a} \cdot \mathbf{I}_c) \\ &= \tfrac{1}{3}\mathbf{I}_c(\mathbf{a} - \mathbf{a}^2) \end{aligned} \tag{11.26}$$

Comparison of Eqs. (11.25) and (11.26) indicates that $\mathbf{I}_1 = -\mathbf{I}_2$. In addition, Eq. (11.24) indicates that the zero sequence network will not be present in the modeling of the fault condition, since the zero sequence current is equal to zero.

Equations (11.25) and (11.26) require that the positive and negative sequence networks be connected in parallel at the point of fault. As with the three-phase fault, a voltage source will be present only in the positive sequence network. In addition, the negative sequence network must be reduced to its Thevenin equivalent at the point of fault. The sequence network interconnections for a line to line fault are shown in Fig. 11-4.

The positive and negative sequence currents are given by

$$\mathbf{I}_1 = -\mathbf{I}_2 = \frac{\mathbf{V}_1}{\mathbf{Z}_1 + \mathbf{Z}_2} \tag{11.27}$$

Equations (11.20) through (11.23) can now be applied to determine the actual phase and neutral currents. In addition, the result of applying Eqs. (11.20) through (11.23) should confirm that both $\mathbf{I}_a$ and $\mathbf{I}_n$ are equal to zero and that $\mathbf{I}_b = -\mathbf{I}_c$.

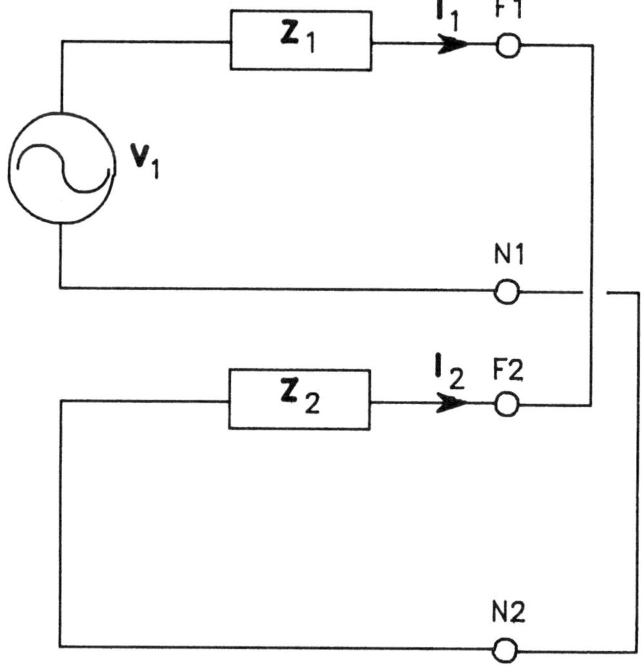

Figure 11-4 Sequence network connections for line to line fault.

11-5 Line to Line to Ground Faults

In the case of the line to line to ground fault, it is assumed that the b and c phases are shorted to ground simultaneously. Therefore, at the point of fault, $\mathbf{V}_b = \mathbf{V}_c = 0$. Applying transformation equations (10.13), the following results:

$$\mathbf{V}_0 = \tfrac{1}{3}(\mathbf{V}_a + \mathbf{V}_b + \mathbf{V}_c) = \tfrac{1}{3} \cdot \mathbf{V}_a \tag{11.28}$$

$$\mathbf{V}_1 = \tfrac{1}{3}(\mathbf{V}_a + \mathbf{a} \cdot \mathbf{V}_b + \mathbf{a}^2 \cdot \mathbf{V}_c) = \tfrac{1}{3} \cdot \mathbf{V}_a \tag{11.29}$$

$$\mathbf{V}_2 = \tfrac{1}{3}(\mathbf{V}_a + \mathbf{a}^2 \cdot \mathbf{V}_b + \mathbf{a} \cdot \mathbf{V}_c) = \tfrac{1}{3} \cdot \mathbf{V}_a \tag{11.30}$$

Therefore, $\mathbf{V}_0 = \mathbf{V}_1 = \mathbf{V}_2$, indicating that the sequence networks are connected in parallel in order to calculate the sequence currents for a line to line to ground fault.

Again, only the positive sequence network will contain a voltage source. The zero sequence network must be reduced to its Thevenin equivalent at the point of fault. The sequence network interconnections for a line to line to ground fault are shown in Fig. 11-5a.

To determine the sequence currents, Fig. 11-5a is redrawn as shown in Fig. 11-5b.

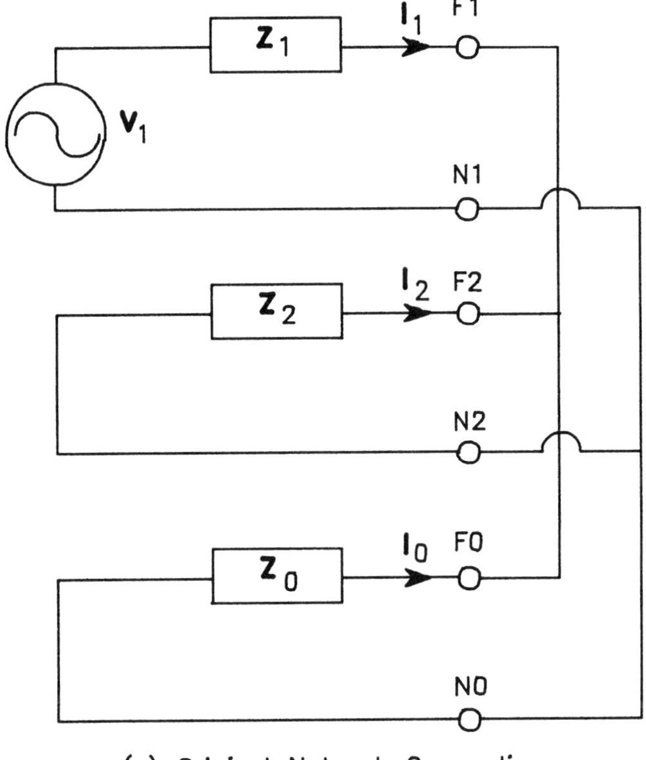

(a) Original Network Connections.

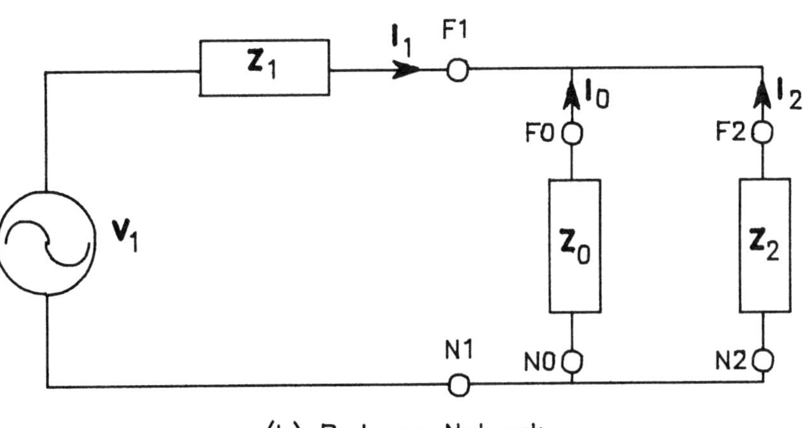

(b) Redrawn Network.

Figure 11-5 Sequence network connections for line to line to ground fault.

Here the sequence currents are given by

$$\mathbf{I}_1 = \frac{\mathbf{V}_1}{\mathbf{Z}_1 + \mathbf{Z}_2 \parallel \mathbf{Z}_0} \tag{11.31}$$

$$\mathbf{I}_2 = -\mathbf{I}_1 \cdot \frac{\mathbf{Z}_0}{\mathbf{Z}_2 + \mathbf{Z}_0} \tag{11.32}$$

$$\mathbf{I}_0 = -\mathbf{I}_1 \cdot \frac{\mathbf{Z}_2}{\mathbf{Z}_2 + \mathbf{Z}_0} \tag{11.33}$$

Equations (11.20) through (11.23) can now be used to calculate the actual phase and neutral currents. Application of these equations should verify that $\mathbf{I}_a = 0$. Also, the neutral current $\mathbf{I}_n$ can be calculated two different ways to verify the results, as follows:

$$\mathbf{I}_n = -(\mathbf{I}_b + \mathbf{I}_c) \tag{11.34}$$

and

$$\mathbf{I}_n = -3 \cdot \mathbf{I}_0 \tag{11.35}$$

If the neutral currents as calculated by Eqs. (11.34) and (11.35) differ from one another, then the calculations should be checked for error.

11-6 Line to Ground Faults

For a line to ground fault, it is assumed that the *A* phase conductor is shorted directly to ground. The resulting currents in the *B* and *C* phases are then equal to zero. Applying the transformation equations, the following results:

$$\mathbf{I}_0 = \tfrac{1}{3}(\mathbf{I}_a)$$

$$\mathbf{I}_1 = \tfrac{1}{3}(\mathbf{I}_a)$$

$$\mathbf{I}_2 = \tfrac{1}{3}(\mathbf{I}_a)$$

Therefore, $\mathbf{I}_0 = \mathbf{I}_1 = \mathbf{I}_2$, indicating that the sequence networks must be connected in series in order to model fault conditions. The sequence network interconnections for a line to ground fault are shown in Fig. 11-6.

The sequence currents are given by

$$\mathbf{I}_1 = \mathbf{I}_2 = \mathbf{I}_0 = \frac{\mathbf{V}_1}{\mathbf{Z}_1 + \mathbf{Z}_2 + \mathbf{Z}_0} \tag{11.36}$$

Application of Eqs. (11.20) through (11.23) should verify that $\mathbf{I}_b$ and $\mathbf{I}_c$ are equal to zero. In addition, for a phase *a* to ground fault, $\mathbf{I}_n = -\mathbf{I}_a$.

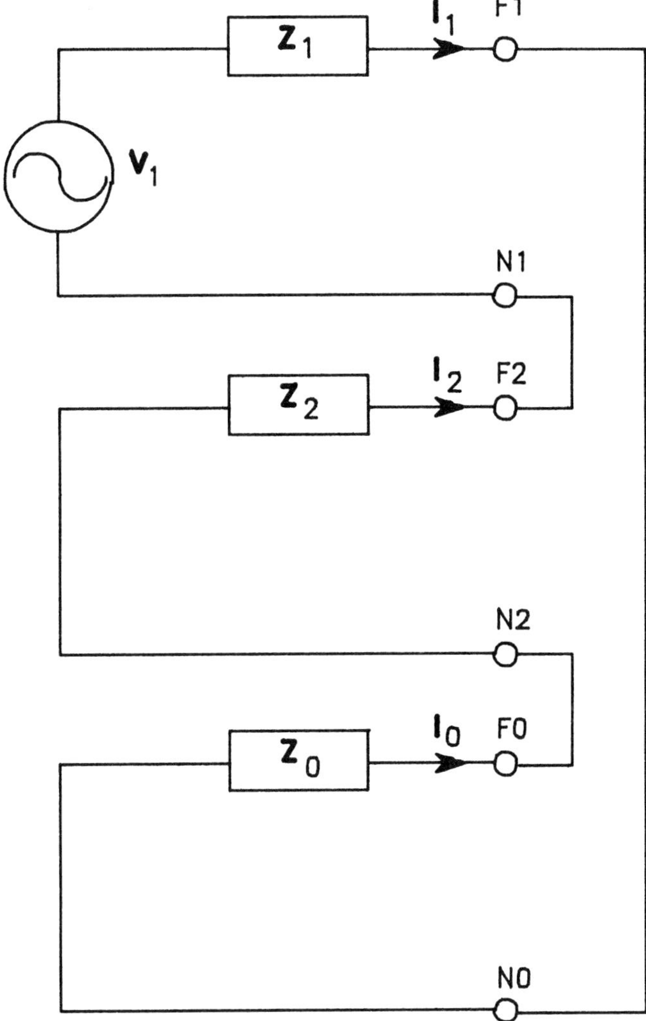

Figure 11-6 Sequence network connections for line to ground fault.

11-7 Line to Ground Faults through Impedance

In many instances, it is desired to determine the line to ground fault current if the phase conductor is not connected solidly to ground. Under these circumstances, an impedance is assumed to be connected between the phase conductor and ground. To determine the location of the fault impedance in the sequence network representation, it will be assumed that phase A is faulted to ground through an impedance $\mathbf{Z}_f$. As in the case of the single line to ground fault, the currents in the *B* and *C* phases will be zero. In addition, the *A* phase voltage at the point of fault will be equal to the following:

$$\mathbf{V}_a = \mathbf{I}_a \cdot \mathbf{Z}_f$$
$$= (\mathbf{I}_0 + \mathbf{I}_1 + \mathbf{I}_2) \cdot \mathbf{Z}_f \quad \textbf{(11.37)}$$

Recall that for a line to ground fault the sequence networks must be connected in series. Therefore, the positive, negative, and zero sequence currents are equal. Equation (11.37) reduces to

$$\mathbf{V}_a = 3 \cdot \mathbf{I}_1 \cdot \mathbf{Z}_f \quad \textbf{(11.38)}$$

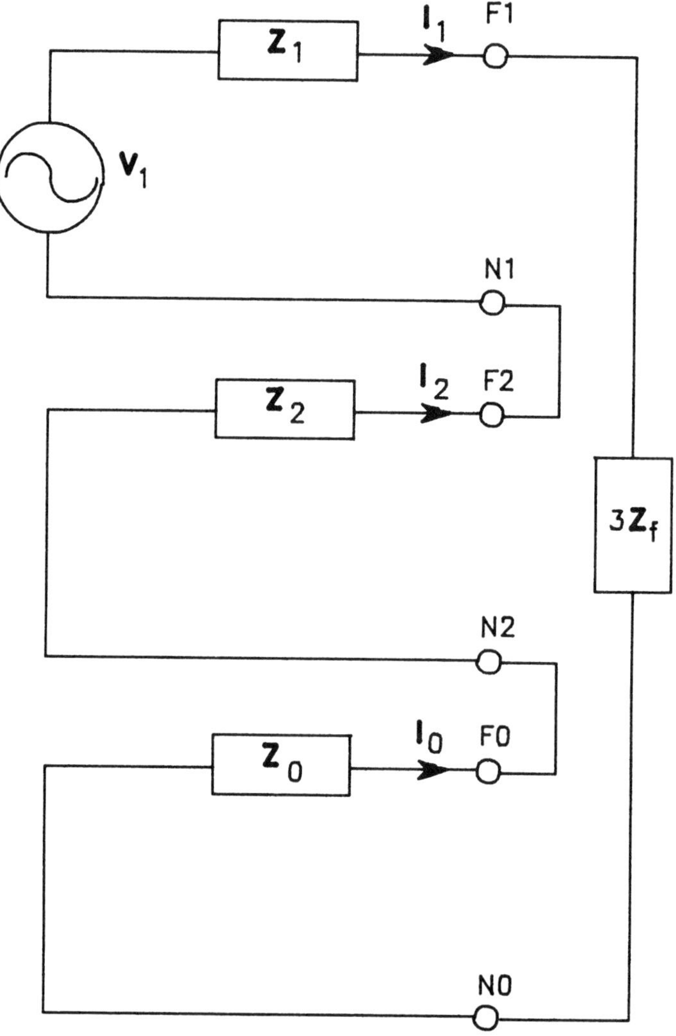

Figure 11-7 Sequence network connections for line to ground fault through impedance.

To satisfy Eq. (11.38), an impedance equal to $3 \cdot \mathbf{Z}_f$ must be inserted into the series-connected sequence networks. The sequence network interconnections for a line to ground fault through the impedance are shown in Fig. 11-7.

The sequence currents are given by

$$\mathbf{I}_1 = \mathbf{I}_2 = \mathbf{I}_0 = \frac{\mathbf{V}_1}{\mathbf{Z}_1 + \mathbf{Z}_2 + \mathbf{Z}_0 + 3\mathbf{Z}_f} \tag{11.39}$$

As in the single line to ground fault, Eqs. (11.20) through (11.23) should verify that $\mathbf{I}_b$ and $\mathbf{I}_c$ are equal to zero. In addition, for a phase A to ground fault through an impedance, $\mathbf{I}_n = -\mathbf{I}_a$.

EXAMPLE 11-2

For the power system shown in Fig. 11-8, calculate the short-circuit currents in amperes at point F for the following types of faults:

a. Three phase
b. Line to line
c. Line to line to ground
d. Line to ground
e. Line to ground plus 10 Ω

Perform all calculations in per unit on a 100-MVA base using a base voltage of 18 kV at the generator terminals. Assume that the generator terminal voltage is actually 19 kV. Calculate line currents in all three-phases for each type of fault specified.

Solution The first step in the calculations is to convert all impedances to per unit on a common base. Starting with a base voltage of 18 kV at the generator terminals, the base voltages for other portions of the power system are determined.

$$\text{Generator:} \quad V_{\text{base}} = 18 \text{ kV} \quad \text{(given)}$$

$$\text{Transmission line:} \quad V_{\text{base}} = 18 \text{ kV} \cdot \frac{69 \text{ kV}}{18 \text{ kV}} = 69 \text{ kV}$$

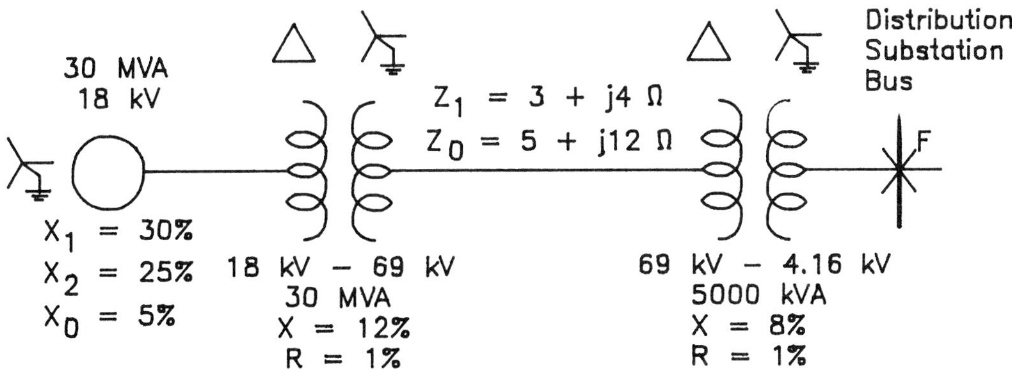

Figure 11-8 System for Example 11-2.

Distribution substation bus: $V_{\text{base}} = 69\text{ kV} \cdot \dfrac{4.16\text{ kV}}{69\text{ kV}} = 4.16\text{ kv}$

The actual terminal voltage of the generator was given as 19 kV. The per unit generator terminal voltage is

$$\mathbf{V}_g = \frac{19.0\angle 0^\circ\text{ kV}}{18.0\text{ kV}} = 1.056\angle 0^\circ\text{ pu}$$

Since all transformer voltage ratings are equal to the respective base voltages, no correction for voltage is necessary when placing all impedances on a common base. The impedances are placed on a common 100-MVA base as follows:

Generator:

$$\mathbf{Z}_{g,1} = j0.30 \cdot \frac{100\text{ MVA}}{30\text{ MVA}} = j1.0\text{ pu}$$

$$\mathbf{Z}_{g,2} = j0.25 \cdot \frac{100\text{ MVA}}{30\text{ MVA}} = j0.833\text{ pu}$$

$$\mathbf{Z}_{g,0} = j0.05 \cdot \frac{100\text{ MVA}}{30\text{ MVA}} = j0.167\text{ pu}$$

Step-up transformer:

$$\mathbf{Z}_0 = \mathbf{Z}_1 = \mathbf{Z}_2 = (0.01 + j0.12) \cdot \frac{100\text{ MVA}}{30\text{ MVA}} = 0.033 + j0.4\text{ pu}$$

Transmission line:

$$Z_{\text{base}} = \frac{(69\text{ kV})^2}{100\text{ MVA}} = 47.61\ \Omega$$

$$\mathbf{Z}_0 = \frac{5.0 + j12.0}{47.61} = 0.105 + j0.252\text{ pu}$$

$$\mathbf{Z}_1 = \mathbf{Z}_2 = \frac{3.0 + j4.0}{47.61} = 0.0.063 + j0.084\text{ pu}$$

Step-down transformer:

$$\mathbf{Z}_0 = \mathbf{Z}_1 = \mathbf{Z}_2 = (0.01 + j0.08) \cdot \frac{100\text{ MVA}}{5\text{ MVA}} = 0.2 + j1.6\text{ pu}$$

The sequence equivalent networks are shown in Fig. 11-9.

Each of the sequence equivalent networks must now be reduced to its Thevenin equivalent ‘‘looking into’’ the system from the point of fault. Since each transformer voltage rating corresponds to the respective base voltage, the per unit turns ratio of both transformers is equal to 1:1. Therefore, the per unit impedances may be reflected from one side of the transformer to the other without taking the actual turns ratio into account.

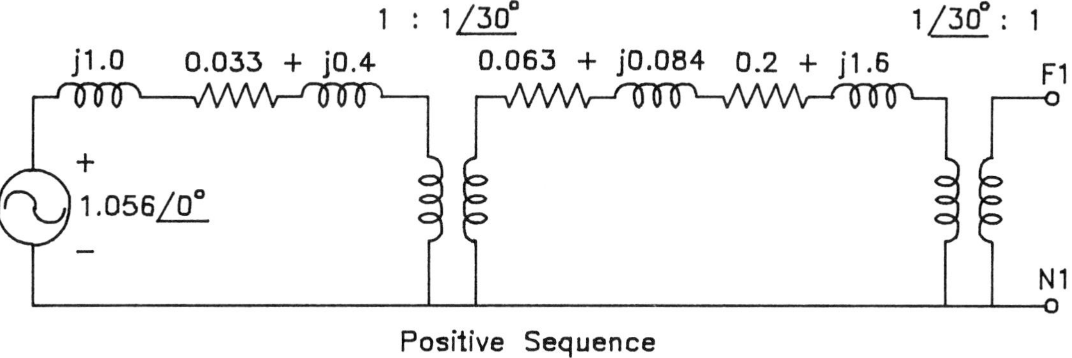

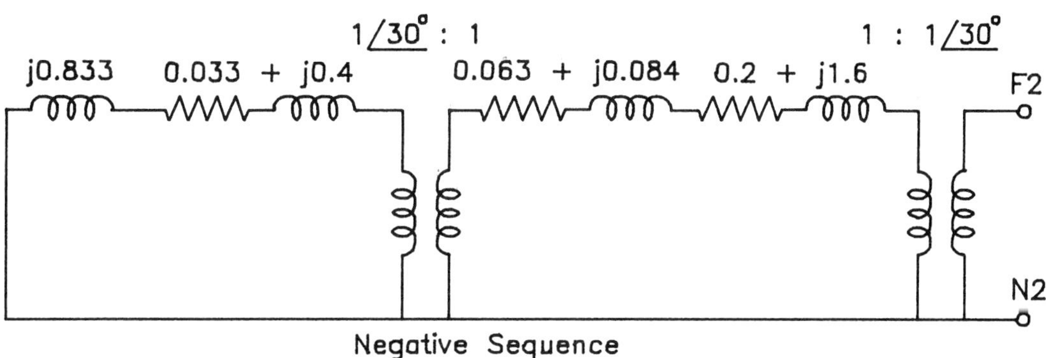

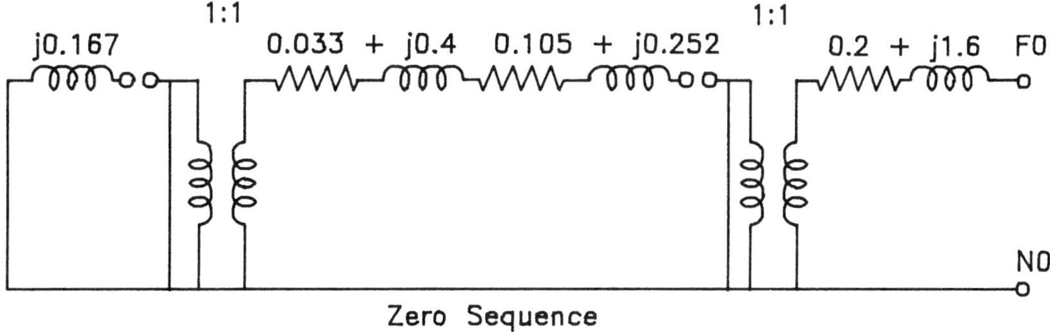

Figure 11-9 Sequence networks for power system of Fig. 11-8.

The per unit impedances in each network are simply added together. The resulting Thevenin equivalent sequence networks are shown in Fig. 11-10.

a. For the three-phase fault, only the positive sequence network is used. The resulting sequence currents are

$$\mathbf{I}_0 = \mathbf{I}_2 = 0$$

$$\mathbf{I}_1 = \frac{1.056\angle 0°}{0.296 + j3.084} = 0.341\angle{-84.5°} \text{ pu}$$

The A phase current is found by multiplying the per unit fault current by the base current at 4.16 kV. The base current is

$$I_{\text{base}} = \frac{100{,}000 \text{ kVA}}{\sqrt{3} \cdot 4.16 \text{ kV}} = 13{,}879 \text{ A}$$

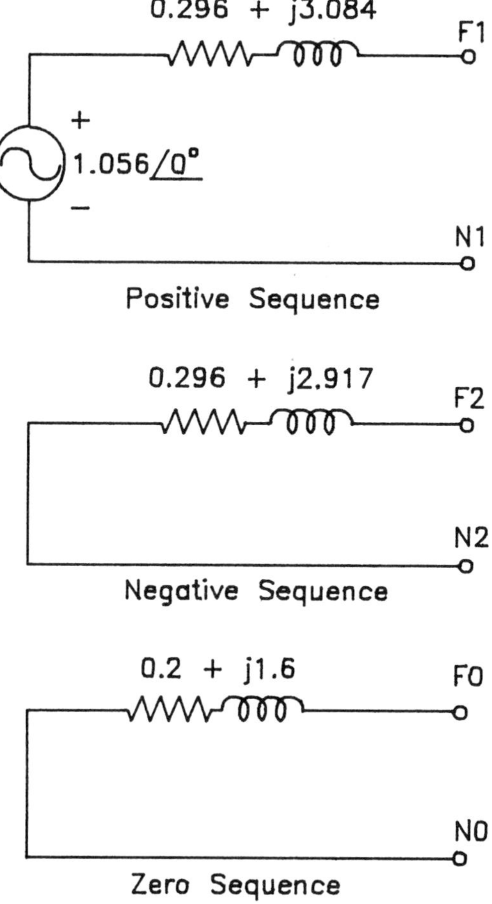

Figure 11-10 Reduced sequence networks of Fig. 11-9.

The sequence currents in amperes for a three-phase fault are

$$\mathbf{I}_1 = I_{\text{base}} \cdot \mathbf{I}_1 = 13{,}879 \cdot (0.341\angle{-84.5^\circ}) = 4733\angle{-84.5^\circ}\ \text{A}$$

The actual phase currents are

$$\begin{aligned}
\mathbf{I}_a &= \mathbf{I}_1 = 4733\angle{-84.5^\circ}\ \text{A} \\
\mathbf{I}_b &= \mathbf{a}^2 \cdot \mathbf{I}_1 = (1\angle 240^\circ) \cdot (4733\angle{-84.5^\circ}) = 4733\angle 155.5^\circ\ \text{A} \\
\mathbf{I}_c &= \mathbf{a} \cdot \mathbf{I}_1 = (1\angle 120^\circ) \cdot (4733\angle{-84.5^\circ}) = 4733\angle 35.5^\circ\ \text{A}
\end{aligned}$$

b. For a line to line fault, the positive and negative sequence networks are connected in parallel. The resulting sequence currents are

$$\begin{aligned}
\mathbf{I}_0 &= 0 \\
\mathbf{I}_1 &= \frac{1.056\angle 0^\circ}{0.296 + j3.084 + 0.296 + j2.917} = 0.1751\angle{-84.4^\circ}\ \text{pu} \\
\mathbf{I}_2 &= -\mathbf{I}_1 = 0.1751\angle 95.6^\circ\ \text{pu}
\end{aligned}$$

The sequence currents in amperes are

$$\begin{aligned}
\mathbf{I}_1 &= (0.1751\angle{-84.4^\circ})(13{,}879) = 2430.2\angle{-84.4^\circ}\ \text{A} \\
\mathbf{I}_2 &= (0.1751\angle 95.6^\circ)(13{,}879) = 2430.2\angle 95.6^\circ
\end{aligned}$$

The actual phase currents are

$$\begin{aligned}
\mathbf{I}_a &= \mathbf{I}_0 + \mathbf{I}_1 + \mathbf{I}_2 = 2430.2\angle{-84.4^\circ} + 2430.2\angle 95.6^\circ = 0\ \text{A} \\
\mathbf{I}_b &= \mathbf{I}_0 + \mathbf{a}^2 \cdot \mathbf{I}_1 + \mathbf{a} \cdot \mathbf{I}_2 \\
&= (1\angle 240^\circ)(2430.2\angle{-84.4^\circ}) + (1\angle 120^\circ)(2430.2\angle 95.6^\circ) \\
&= -4189.1 - j410.7 = 4209.2\angle 185.6^\circ\ \text{A} \\
\mathbf{I}_c &= \mathbf{I}_0 + \mathbf{a} \cdot \mathbf{I}_1 + \mathbf{a}^2 \cdot \mathbf{I}_2 \\
&= (1\angle 120^\circ)(2430.2\angle{-84.4^\circ}) + (1\angle 240^\circ)(2430.2\angle 95.6^\circ) \\
&= 4189.1 + j410.7 = 4209.2\angle 5.6^\circ\ \text{A}
\end{aligned}$$

Notice that $\mathbf{I}_b = -\mathbf{I}_c$ and $\mathbf{I}_a = 0$, as expected.

c. For the line to line to ground fault, the three sequence networks are connected in parallel. The positive sequence current is given by

$$\mathbf{I}_1 = \frac{1.056\angle 0^\circ}{\mathbf{Z}_1 + \mathbf{Z}_2 \parallel \mathbf{Z}_0}$$

$$\begin{aligned}
\mathbf{Z}_2 \parallel \mathbf{Z}_0 &= \frac{(0.296 + j2.917)(0.2 + j1.6)}{(0.296 + j2.917) + (0.2 + j1.6)} \\
&= 0.1195 + j1.0331\ \text{pu} \\
&= 1.040\angle 83.4^\circ\ \text{pu} \\
\mathbf{Z}_1 + \mathbf{Z}_2 \parallel \mathbf{Z}_0 &= 0.4155 + j4.1171\ \text{pu}
\end{aligned}$$

Therefore, the positive sequence current is

$$\mathbf{I}_1 = \frac{1.056\angle 0^\circ}{0.4155 + j4.1171} = 0.2552\angle -84.2^\circ \text{ pu}$$

The negative sequence current is

$$\begin{aligned}\mathbf{I}_2 &= -\mathbf{I}_1 \cdot \frac{\mathbf{Z}_0}{\mathbf{Z}_2 + \mathbf{Z}_0} \\ &= (0.2552\angle 95.8^\circ) \cdot \frac{0.2 + j1.6}{0.296 + j2.917 + 0.2 + j1.6} \\ &= 0.0906\angle 95^\circ \text{ pu}\end{aligned}$$

The zero sequence current is

$$\begin{aligned}\mathbf{I}_0 &= -\mathbf{I}_1 \cdot \frac{\mathbf{Z}_2}{\mathbf{Z}_2 + \mathbf{Z}_0} \\ &= (0.2552\angle 95.8^\circ) \cdot \frac{0.296 + j2.917}{0.296 + j2.917 + 0.2 + j1.6} \\ &= 0.1647\angle 96.3^\circ \text{ pu}\end{aligned}$$

The sequence currents in amperes are

$$\begin{aligned}\mathbf{I}_0 &= (0.1647\angle 96.3^\circ)(13{,}879) = 2285.9\angle 96.3^\circ \text{ A} \\ \mathbf{I}_1 &= (0.2552\angle -84.2^\circ)(13{,}879) = 3541.9\angle -84.2^\circ \text{ A} \\ \mathbf{I}_2 &= (0.0906\angle 95^\circ)(13{,}879) = 1257.4\angle 95^\circ \text{ A}\end{aligned}$$

The actual phase currents are

$$\begin{aligned}\mathbf{I}_a &= \mathbf{I}_0 + \mathbf{I}_1 + \mathbf{I}_2 = 2285.9\angle 96.3^\circ + 3541.9\angle -84.2^\circ + 1257.4\angle 95^\circ \approx 0 \\ \mathbf{I}_b &= \mathbf{I}_0 + \mathbf{a}^2 \cdot \mathbf{I}_1 + \mathbf{a} \cdot \mathbf{I}_2 \\ &= 2285.9\angle 96.3^\circ + (1\angle 240^\circ)(3541.9\angle -84.2^\circ) + (1\angle 120^\circ)(1257.4\angle 95^\circ) \\ &= 2285.9\angle 96.3^\circ + 3541.9\angle 155.8^\circ + 1257.4\angle 215^\circ \\ &= -4511.2 + j3002.8 \\ &= 5419.2\angle 146.4^\circ \text{ A} \\ \mathbf{I}_c &= \mathbf{I}_0 + \mathbf{a} \cdot \mathbf{I}_1 + \mathbf{a}^2 \cdot \mathbf{I}_2 \\ &= 2285.9\angle 96.3^\circ + (1\angle 120^\circ)(3541.9\angle -84.2^\circ) + (1\angle 240^\circ)(1257.4\angle 95^\circ) \\ &= 2285.9\angle 96.3^\circ + 3541.9\angle 35.8^\circ + 1257.4\angle 335^\circ \\ &= 3761.1 + j3812.6 \\ &= 5355.5\angle 45.4^\circ \text{ A}\end{aligned}$$

Note that the *A* phase current is equal to zero as expected. In addition, the neutral current will be calculated using Eqs. (11.34) and (11.35).

$$\mathbf{I}_n = -(\mathbf{I}_b + \mathbf{I}_c)$$
$$= -(5419.2\angle 146.4^\circ + 5355.5\angle 45.4^\circ)$$
$$= -(6853.7\angle 96.3)\ \text{A}$$

and

$$\mathbf{I}_n = -3 \cdot \mathbf{I}_0$$
$$= -3 \cdot (2285.9\angle 96.3^\circ)$$
$$= -(6853.7\angle 96.3^\circ)\ \text{A}$$

Note that the neutral current is the same as calculated using either equation.

d. For the single line to ground fault, the sequence networks are connected in series. The sequence currents are

$$\mathbf{I}_1 = \mathbf{I}_2 = \mathbf{I}_0 = \frac{\mathbf{V}_1}{\mathbf{Z}_1 + \mathbf{Z}_2 + \mathbf{Z}_0}$$
$$= \frac{1.056\angle 0^\circ}{0.792 + j7.601}$$
$$= 0.1382\angle -84.1^\circ\ \text{pu}$$

The sequence currents in amperes are

$$\mathbf{I}_1 = \mathbf{I}_2 = \mathbf{I}_0 = (0.1382\angle -84.1^\circ)(13{,}879) = 1918.1\angle -84.1^\circ\ \text{A}$$

The actual phase currents are

$$\mathbf{I}_a = \mathbf{I}_0 + \mathbf{I}_1 + \mathbf{I}_2 = 3 \cdot (1918.1\angle -84.1^\circ) = 5754.2\angle -84.1^\circ\ \text{A}$$
$$\mathbf{I}_b = \mathbf{I}_0 + \mathbf{a}^2 \cdot \mathbf{I}_1 + \mathbf{a} \cdot \mathbf{I}_2 = 0$$
$$\mathbf{I}_c = \mathbf{I}_0 + \mathbf{a} \cdot \mathbf{I}_1 + \mathbf{a}^2 \cdot \mathbf{I}_2 = 0$$
$$\mathbf{I}_n = -3 \cdot \mathbf{I}_0 = -3 \cdot (1918.1\angle -84.1^\circ) = -5754.2\angle -84.1^\circ\ \text{A}$$

Note that $\mathbf{I}_b$ and $\mathbf{I}_c$ are equal to zero and that $\mathbf{I}_n = -\mathbf{I}_a$ as expected.

e. For the single line to ground fault through an impedance, the sequence networks are connected in series. The sequence currents are

$$\mathbf{I}_1 = \mathbf{I}_2 = \mathbf{I}_0 = \frac{\mathbf{V}_1}{\mathbf{Z}_1 + \mathbf{Z}_2 + \mathbf{Z}_0 + 3 \cdot \mathbf{Z}_f}$$
$$= \frac{1.056\angle 0^\circ}{0.792 + j7.601 + 3 \cdot 10}$$
$$= 0.0333\angle -13.9^\circ\ \text{pu}$$

The sequence currents in amperes are

$$\mathbf{I}_1 = \mathbf{I}_2 = \mathbf{I}_0 = (0.0333\angle -13.9^\circ)(13{,}879) = 462.2\angle -13.9^\circ\ \text{A}$$

The actual phase currents are

$$\mathbf{I}_a = \mathbf{I}_0 + \mathbf{I}_1 + \mathbf{I}_2 = 3 \cdot (462.2\angle -13.9°) = 1386.5\angle -13.9° \text{ A}$$

$$\mathbf{I}_b = \mathbf{I}_0 + \mathbf{a}^2 \cdot \mathbf{I}_1 + \mathbf{a} \cdot \mathbf{I}_2 = 0$$

$$\mathbf{I}_c = \mathbf{I}_0 + \mathbf{a} \cdot \mathbf{I}_1 + \mathbf{a}^2 \cdot \mathbf{I}_2 = 0$$

$$\mathbf{I}_n = -3 \cdot \mathbf{I}_0 = -3 \cdot (462.2\angle -13.9°) = -1386.5\angle -13.9° \text{ A}$$

As in the single line to ground fault, $\mathbf{I}_b$ and $\mathbf{I}_c$ are equal to zero and $\mathbf{I}_n = -\mathbf{I}_a$, as expected.

11-8 Equivalent System Impedance

When performing short-circuit calculations on distribution feeders or industrial plants, it is common practice to obtain the short circuit availability at the substation bus. These short-circuit data are usually specified in terms of an apparent power at a certain voltage level for three-phase faults. In addition, the system X/R ratio at the point of fault is also specified. The line to ground short-circuit current magnitude and X/R ratio may also be specified. These data can be used to calculate the positive, negative, and zero sequence impedances of the source.

Recall that for a three-phase fault only the positive sequence network is involved. Therefore, the A phase fault current is equal to the positive sequence current. If the three-phase short-circuit MVA and reference voltage are specified, the fault current magnitude can be calculated as

$$I_f = I_1 = \frac{\text{MVA}_{\text{sc}} \times 10^6}{\sqrt{3} \cdot V_{\text{ll}}} \tag{11.40}$$

Also, from Eq. (11.19), the magnitude of the positive sequence current is

$$I_1 = \frac{V_1}{Z_1} \tag{11.19}$$

Equating Eq. (11.19) and (11.40),

$$\frac{V_1}{Z_1} = \frac{\text{MVA}_{\text{sc}} \times 10^6}{\sqrt{3} \cdot V_{\text{ll}}} \tag{11.41}$$

Solving Eq. (11.41) for Z_1,

$$Z_1 = \frac{\sqrt{3} \cdot V_{\text{ll}} \cdot V_1}{\text{MVA}_{\text{sc}} \times 10^6} \tag{11.42}$$

Furthermore, since the symmetrical component equations were developed on a line to neutral equivalent basis, the positive sequence voltage is equal to

$$V_1 = \frac{V_{ll}}{\sqrt{3}} \quad \textbf{(11.43)}$$

Substituting Eq. (11.43) into (11.42) and simplifying results in

$$Z_1 = \frac{V_{ll}^2}{\text{MVA}_{sc} \times 10^6} \quad \textbf{(11.44)}$$

Equation (11.44) can be used to calculate the magnitude of the positive sequence impedance given the short-circuit MVA and the system voltage.

The system X/R ratio for a three-phase fault is used to determine the positive sequence impedance angle as follows:

$$\theta_z = \tan^{-1}\frac{X}{R} \quad \textbf{(11.45)}$$

Having determined the positive sequence impedance angle, the positive sequence resistance and reactance can be calculated as follows:

$$R_1 = Z_1 \cos(\theta_z) \quad \textbf{(11.46a)}$$

$$X_1 = Z_1 \sin(\theta_z) \quad \textbf{(11.46b)}$$

The positive sequence impedance is therefore

$$\mathbf{Z}_1 = R_1 + jX_1 = Z_1 \cos(\theta_z) + jZ_1 \sin(\theta_z) \quad \textbf{(11.47)}$$

The line to ground fault current magnitude and system voltage can be used to determine the zero sequence impedance of the system. Recall that for a line to ground fault the sequence networks are connected in series. The resulting fault impedance is equal to

$$\mathbf{Z}_f = \mathbf{Z}_1 + \mathbf{Z}_2 + \mathbf{Z}_0 \quad \textbf{(11.48)}$$

With the exception of rotating electrical machinery, it is generally assumed that the positive and negative sequence impedances of electrical power system equipment are equal. Equation (11.48) can be rewritten as

$$\mathbf{Z}_f = \mathbf{Z}_1 + \mathbf{Z}_2 + \mathbf{Z}_0 = 2\mathbf{Z}_1 + \mathbf{Z}_0 \quad \textbf{(11.49)}$$

The A phase fault current for a line to ground fault is

$$\mathbf{I}_a = 3 \cdot \mathbf{I}_1 = \frac{3\mathbf{V}_1}{2\mathbf{Z}_1 + \mathbf{Z}_0} \quad \textbf{(11.50)}$$

Solving Eq. (11.50) for the zero sequence impedance,

$$\mathbf{Z}_0 = \frac{3\mathbf{V}_1}{\mathbf{I}_a} - 2\mathbf{Z}_1 \quad \textbf{(11.51)}$$

Substituting Eq. (11.43) into (11.51) results in

$$\mathbf{Z}_0 = \frac{3(\mathrm{V}_{ll}/\sqrt{3})}{\mathbf{I}_a} - 2\mathbf{Z}_1 \quad \textbf{(11.52)}$$

where $\mathbf{Z}_1$ is the positive sequence impedance as calculated from Eq. (11.47). The magnitude of $\mathbf{I}_a$ in Eq. (11.52) is generally available from a system short-circuit study. The phase angle of $\mathbf{I}_a$ is determined from the X/R ratio of the system for a line to ground fault. Note that the X/R ratio for a line to ground fault will, in general, differ from the X/R ratio for a three-phase fault. The phase angle of $\mathbf{I}_a$ can be determined as

$$\theta_a = -\tan^{-1}\frac{X}{R} \qquad \textbf{(11.53)}$$

EXAMPLE 11-3

The following system short-circuit data are available for the high-voltage bus of a 138-kV–12.47GrdY/7.2-kV distribution substation transformer.

$$\text{Three-phase fault} = 1000 \text{ MVA}, \qquad \frac{X}{R} = 3.1 \text{ at } 138 \text{ kV}$$

$$\text{Line to ground fault} = 3 \text{ kA}, \qquad \frac{X}{R} = 4.7 \text{ at } 138 \text{ kV}$$

Determine the positive, negative, and zero sequence system impedances.

Solution From Eq. (11.45), the positive sequence system impedance angle is

$$\theta_z = \tan^{-1}(3.1) = 72.1°$$

The magnitude of the positive sequence impedance is

$$Z_1 = \frac{138{,}000^2}{1000 \times 10^6} = 19.044\ \Omega$$

The positive sequence resistance and reactance are

$$R_1 = 19.044 \cos(72.1°) = 5.853\ \Omega$$

$$X_1 = 19.044 \sin(72.1°) = 18.122\ \Omega$$

In complex form, the positive sequence impedance is

$$\mathbf{Z}_1 = \mathbf{Z}_2 = R_1 + jX_1 = 5.853 + j18.122 = 19.044\angle 72.1°\ \Omega$$

The phase angle of the line to ground fault current is

$$\theta_a = -\tan^{-1}(4.7) = -78°$$

The line to ground fault current in complex form is

$$\mathbf{I}_a = 3000\angle -78°\ \text{A}$$

The zero sequence impedance is determined by direct application of Eq. (11.52).

$$\mathbf{Z}_0 = \frac{3(138{,}000/\sqrt{3})}{3000\angle -78°} - 2 \cdot (5.853 + j18.122)$$
$$= 4.859 + j41.687\ \Omega$$

11-9 Current-Limiting Inductors

In certain instances it is desired to limit the available short-circuit current to a certain value. Transformer windings and switchgear busbars installed in locations where there is a high fault current availability may not be able to withstand the mechanical stresses produced by such current. In addition, the electrical insulation on power cables may be subjected to higher than rated temperatures during high fault current conditions.

The high levels of fault current may be reduced to acceptable limits by adding impedance to the circuit. Practically, the added impedance may be either a resistor or inductor. Resistors are seldom used due to the high active power (I^2R) losses incurred. Low-resistance inductors are preferred since the active power losses are kept to a minimum, while achieving the desired current-limiting effect.

Inductors may be of either iron core or air core construction. Iron core inductors used for current-limiting purposes are not desirable, since the iron will saturate under high-current conditions. Saturation of the iron core will substantially decrease the inductance value, thereby reducing the impedance of the inductor.

Air core inductors are the common choice for current-limiting applications. Saturation under high-current conditions does not exist with air core inductors. However, care must be taken to ensure that the flux produced by the air core inductors does not induce substantial eddy currents in adjacent metal enclosures, structural steel, concrete reinforcing bar, and the like. These induced eddy currents may be of sufficient magnitude to cause excessive heating and possibly severe damage to these adjacent structures.

To determine the amount of inductance required for current-limiting purposes, the sequence networks must be modified to include the additional inductive reactance. The equations for calculating fault currents can then be developed using the modified sequence networks. The inductive reactance of the current-limiting inductors must be added in all three sequence networks.

For a three-phase fault, the positive sequence current with the added current-limiting inductor is

$$\mathbf{I}_1 = \frac{\mathbf{V}_1}{\mathbf{Z}_1 + jX_l} \tag{11.54}$$

where X_l is the inductive reactance of the current-limiting inductor. Recall that the A phase current is equal to the positive sequence current for a three-phase fault. The magnitude of the fault current is

$$I_a = I_1 = \frac{V_1}{[R_1^2 + (X_1 + X_l)^2]^{1/2}} \tag{11.55}$$

Solving Eq. (11.55) for X_l,

$$X_l = \left[\left(\frac{V_1}{I_a}\right)^2 - R_1^2\right]^{1/2} - X_1 \tag{11.56}$$

Equation (11.56) can be used to calculate the inductive reactance of the current-limiting inductor required to limit the three-phase fault current to a certain value.

The analysis is similar for a line to ground fault. The sequence currents for a line to ground fault with a current-limiting inductor added are

$$\mathbf{I}_0 = \mathbf{I}_1 = \mathbf{I}_2 = \frac{\mathbf{V}_1}{(\mathbf{Z}_0 + jX_l) + (\mathbf{Z}_1 + jX_l) + (\mathbf{Z}_2 + jX_l)} = \frac{\mathbf{V}_1}{\mathbf{Z}_0 + \mathbf{Z}_1 + \mathbf{Z}_2 + 3(jX_l)} \quad \textbf{(11.57)}$$

The phase A line current is

$$\mathbf{I}_a = 3\mathbf{I}_1 = \frac{3\mathbf{V}_1}{\mathbf{Z}_0 + \mathbf{Z}_1 + \mathbf{Z}_2 + 3(jX_l)} \quad \textbf{(11.58)}$$

The magnitude of the fault current is

$$I_a = \frac{3V_1}{[(R_0 + R_1 + R_2)^2 + (X_0 + X_1 + X_2 + 3X_l)^2]^{1/2}} \quad \textbf{(11.59)}$$

where

V_1 = magnitude of prefault voltage

R_0 = zero sequence system resistance

R_1 = positive sequence system resistance

R_2 = negative sequence system resistance

X_0 = zero sequence system reactance

X_1 = positive sequence system reactance

X_2 = negative sequence system reactance

Solving Eq. (11.59) for X_l results in

$$X_l = \frac{1}{3}\left\{\left[\left(\frac{3V_1}{I_a}\right)^2 - (R_0 + R_1 + R_2)^2\right]^{1/2} - X_0 - X_1 - X_2\right\} \quad \textbf{(11.60)}$$

Equations (11.56) and (11.60) give the value of inductive reactance required to limit the fault current to a specified level. The inductance can be determined from the following:

$$L = \frac{X_l}{2 \cdot \pi \cdot f} \quad \textbf{(11.61)}$$

When determining the required inductance, it is usually sufficient to consider only the three-phase and single line to ground faults. The magnitude of the line to line and line to line to ground fault currents will typically lie somewhere in between the three-phase and single line to ground fault current magnitudes. The actual inductance required will be the larger of the two values calculated by Eqs. (11.56) and (11.60). The following example illustrates the procedure.

EXAMPLE 11-4 Determine the necessary inductance of current-limiting reactors installed on the 4.16-kV side of the distribution substation transformer of Example 11-2 to limit the maximum fault current to 3000 A.

Solution The solution will use per unit values when applying Eqs. (11.56) and (11.50). The maximum fault current in per unit is

$$I_a = \frac{3000}{13{,}879} = 0.2162 \text{ pu}$$

Applying Eq. (11.56) for a three-phase fault results in

$$X_l = \left[\left(\frac{1.056}{0.2162}\right)^2 - 0.296^2\right]^{1/2} - 3.084 = 1.7914 \text{ pu}$$

Applying Eq. (11.60) for a single line to ground fault results in

$$X_l = \frac{1}{3}\left\{\left[\left(\frac{3 \cdot 1.056}{0.2162}\right)^2 - (0.296 + 0.296 + 0.2)^2\right]^{1/2} - 1.6 - 2.917 - 3.084\right\}$$
$$= 2.3436 \text{ pu}$$

Note that the value of required current-limiting inductive reactance calculated for the single line to ground fault exceeds that required for the three-phase fault. Therefore, an inductive reactance of 2.3436 pu will be necessary to reduce fault currents to 3000 A.

The inductive reactance must now be converted from per unit to ohms by multiplying by the base impedance, as follows:

$$X_\Omega = X_{l,\text{pu}} \cdot Z_{\text{base}}$$
$$= 2.3436 \cdot \frac{(4.16 \text{ kV})^2}{100 \text{ MVA}}$$
$$= 0.4056\ \Omega$$

The inductance is determined by applying Eq. (11.61).

$$L = \frac{0.4056}{2 \cdot \pi \cdot 60} = 1.076 \times 10^{-3} \text{ H}$$

The continuous current rating of the current-limiting inductor equals the full-load current rating of the transformer.

$$I = \frac{5000 \text{ kVA}}{\sqrt{3} \cdot (4.16 \text{ kV})} = 694 \text{ A}$$

11-10 Example Short-Circuit Study

This section presents a step-by-step procedure that can be used to calculate the short-circuit currents for various fault conditions at different locations on a radial distribution circuit. Short-circuit currents for three-phase, phase to phase, single line to ground, and single line to ground plus 10-Ω faults will be considered.

Consider the distribution circuit shown in Fig. 11-11. The three-phase fault MVA on the transformer high-voltage side is 400 MVA, with an X/R ratio of 2.5. The distribution substation transformer has a self-cooled rating of 5000 kVA, the voltage rating is 69 kV–12.47Y/7.2 kV, delta grounded wye connected. The transformer nameplate impedances are $R = 1\%$ and $X = 7\%$.

Procedure

Step 1 Determine the equivalent system impedance and refer to transformer low-voltage side.

$$Z_1 = \frac{(69\ \text{kV})^2}{400\ \text{MVA}} = 11.903\ \Omega$$

$$\theta_z = \tan^{-1}(2.5) = 68.2°$$

$$R_1 = 11.903\cos(68.2°) = 4.421\ \Omega$$

$$X_1 = 11.903\sin(68.2°) = 11.052\ \Omega$$

Reflected to the low-voltage side, the equivalent system impedances are

$$R_1 = \left[\frac{12.47\ \text{kV}}{69\ \text{kV}}\right]^2 \cdot 4.421 = 0.144\ \Omega$$

$$X_1 = \left[\frac{12.47\ \text{kV}}{69\ \text{kV}}\right]^2 \cdot 11.052 = 0.361\ \Omega$$

There is no need to determine the zero sequence system impedances since the transformer is delta connected on the high-voltage side. Recall that the zero sequence equivalent circuit for a delta–wye connected transformer has an open circuit on the delta side of the transformer.

Step 2 Determine the transformer sequence impedances.

$$R_0 = R_1 = R_2 = \frac{(12.47\ \text{kV})^2}{5\ \text{MVA}} \cdot 0.01 = 0.311\ \Omega$$

$$X_0 = X_1 = X_2 = \frac{(12.47\ \text{kV})^2}{5\ \text{MVA}} \cdot 0.07 = 2.177\ \Omega$$

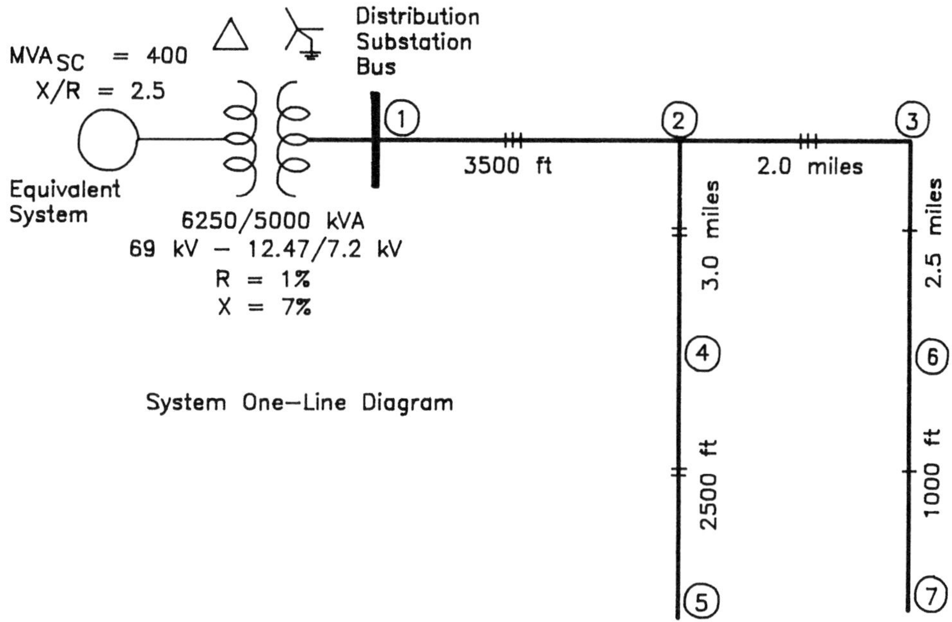

Impedance Data			
Line Segment	Conductor and Cable	Positive Sequence Impedance	Zero Sequence Impedance
1–2	Three 500 kcmil Al. 15 kV URD	0.2135 + j0.2331 Ω	0.1691 + j0.0476 Ω
2–3	Phase: Three 336.4 kcmil ACSR Neutral: One #3/0 ACSR	0.6120 + j1.3510 Ω	1.5770 + j4.0538 Ω
2–4	Phase: Two #1/0 ACSR Neutral: One #1/0 ACSR	3.3600 + j2.7192 Ω	5.1492 + j6.9159 Ω
4–5	Two #1/0 Al. 15 kV URD	0.5635 + j0.2045 Ω	1.1430 + j0.2823 Ω
3–6	Phase: One #4 ACSR Neutral: One #4 ACSR	6.9763 + j3.6805 Ω	6.9763 + j3.6805 Ω
6–7	One #2 Al. 15 kV URD	0.4625 + j0.1839 Ω	0.4625 + j0.1839 Ω

Figure 11-11 Example of short-circuit study.

Step 3 Calculate the three-phase fault current at all applicable points. The positive sequence voltage will be selected as 105% the nominal line to neutral system voltage:

$$V_1 = 7200 \cdot 1.05 = 7560 \text{ V}$$

(*Note:* The prefault voltage is typically selected as 105% of nominal.) The magnitude of the three-phase fault current is given by

$$|\mathbf{I}_{3\phi}| = \frac{|\mathbf{V}_1|}{|\text{Total } \mathbf{Z}_1|}$$

Table 11-2 is prepared as an aid in calculating and tabulating three-phase fault currents.

Step 4 Calculate the line to line fault currents. The magnitude of the line to line fault current is given by

$$|\mathbf{I}_{\phi\phi}| = \frac{\sqrt{3} \cdot |\mathbf{V}_1|}{|\text{Total } \mathbf{Z}_1 + \mathbf{Z}_2|}$$

The line to line fault currents are tabulated in Table 11-3.

Step 5 Calculate the single line to ground fault currents. The magnitude of the line to ground fault current is

$$|\mathbf{I}_{\phi G}| = \frac{3 \cdot |\mathbf{V}_1|}{|\text{Total } \mathbf{Z}_1 + \mathbf{Z}_2 + \mathbf{Z}_0|}$$

The line to ground fault currents are tabulated in Table 11-4.

Step 6 Calculate the single line to ground plus 10-Ω fault currents. The magnitude of the line to ground plus 10-Ω fault current is

$$|\mathbf{I}_{\phi G+10}| = \frac{3 \cdot |\mathbf{V}_1|}{|\text{Total } \mathbf{Z}_1 + \mathbf{Z}_2 + \mathbf{Z}_0 + 3 \cdot 10|}$$

Table 11-2

	Section $\mathbf{Z}_1$ (Ω)	*Total* $\mathbf{Z}_1$ (Ω)	$\|\mathbf{I}_{3\phi}\|$ (A)
System	0.1440 + j0.3610	0.1440 + j0.3610	N/A
Transformer	0.3110 + j2.1770	0.4550 + j2.5380	2932
1–2	0.2135 + j0.2331	0.6685 + j2.7711	2652
2–3	0.6120 + j1.3510	1.2805 + j4.1221	1751

Three-phase faults are not possible at other circut locations.

Table 11-3

	Section $\mathbf{Z}_1 + \mathbf{Z}_2$ (Ω)	*Total* $\mathbf{Z}_1 + \mathbf{Z}_2$ (Ω)	$\|\mathbf{I}_{\phi\phi}\|$ (A)
System	0.2880 + j0.7220	0.2880 + j0.7220	N/A
Transformer	0.6220 + j4.3540	0.9100 + j5.0760	2539
1–2	0.4270 + j0.4662	1.3370 + j5.5422	2297
2–3	1.2240 + j2.7020	2.5610 + j8.2442	1517
Carry over pt. 2		1.3370 + j5.5422	2297
2–4	6.7200 + j5.4384	8.0507 + j10.9806	961
4–5	1.1270 + j0.4090	9.1840 + j11.3896	895

Table 11-4

	Section $\mathbf{Z}_1 + \mathbf{Z}_2 + \mathbf{Z}_0$ (Ω)	*Total* $\mathbf{Z}_1 + \mathbf{Z}_2 + \mathbf{Z}_0$ (Ω)	$\lvert\mathbf{I}_{\phi G}\rvert$ (A)
System	0.2880 + *j*0.7220	0.2880 + *j*0.7220	N/A
Transformer	0.9330 + *j*6.5310	1.2210 + *j*7.2530	3084
1–2	0.5961 + *j*0.5138	1.8171 + *j*7.7668	2843
2–3	2.7810 + *j*6.7558	4.5981 + *j*14.5226	1489
3–6	20.9289 + *j*11.0415	25.5270 + *j*25.5641	628
6–7	1.3875 + *j*0.5517	26.9145 + *j*26.1158	605
Carry over pt. 2		1.8171 + *j*7.7668	2843
2–4	11.8692 + *j*12.3543	13.6869 + *j*20.1211	932
4–5	2.2700 + *j*0.6913	15.9563 + *j*20.8124	865

Table 11-5

	Section $\mathbf{Z}_1 + \mathbf{Z}_2 + \mathbf{Z}_0 + 3\mathbf{Z}_F$ (Ω)	*Total* $\mathbf{Z}_1 + \mathbf{Z}_2 + \mathbf{Z}_0 + 3\mathbf{Z}_F$ (Ω)	$\lvert\mathbf{I}_{\phi G+10}\rvert$ (A)
System	30.2880 + *j*0.7220	30.2880 + *j*0.7220	N/A
Transformer	0.9330 + *j*6.5310	31.2210 + *j*7.2530	708
1–2	0.5961 + *j*0.5138	31.8171 + *j*7.7668	692
2–3	2.7810 + *j*6.7558	34.5981 + *j*14.5226	604
3–6	20.9289 + *j*11.0415	55.5270 + *j*25.5641	371
6–7	1.3875 + *j*0.5517	56.9145 + *j*26.1158	362
Carry over pt. 2		31.8171 + *j*7.7668	692
2–4	11.8692 + *j*12.3543	43.6863 + *j*20.1211	472
4–5	2.2700 + *j*0.6913	45.9563 + *j*20.8124	450

The line to ground plus 10-Ω fault currents are tabulated in Table 11-5.

The circuit of Fig. 11-11 is redrawn as Fig. 11-12 with all fault current magnitudes indicated.

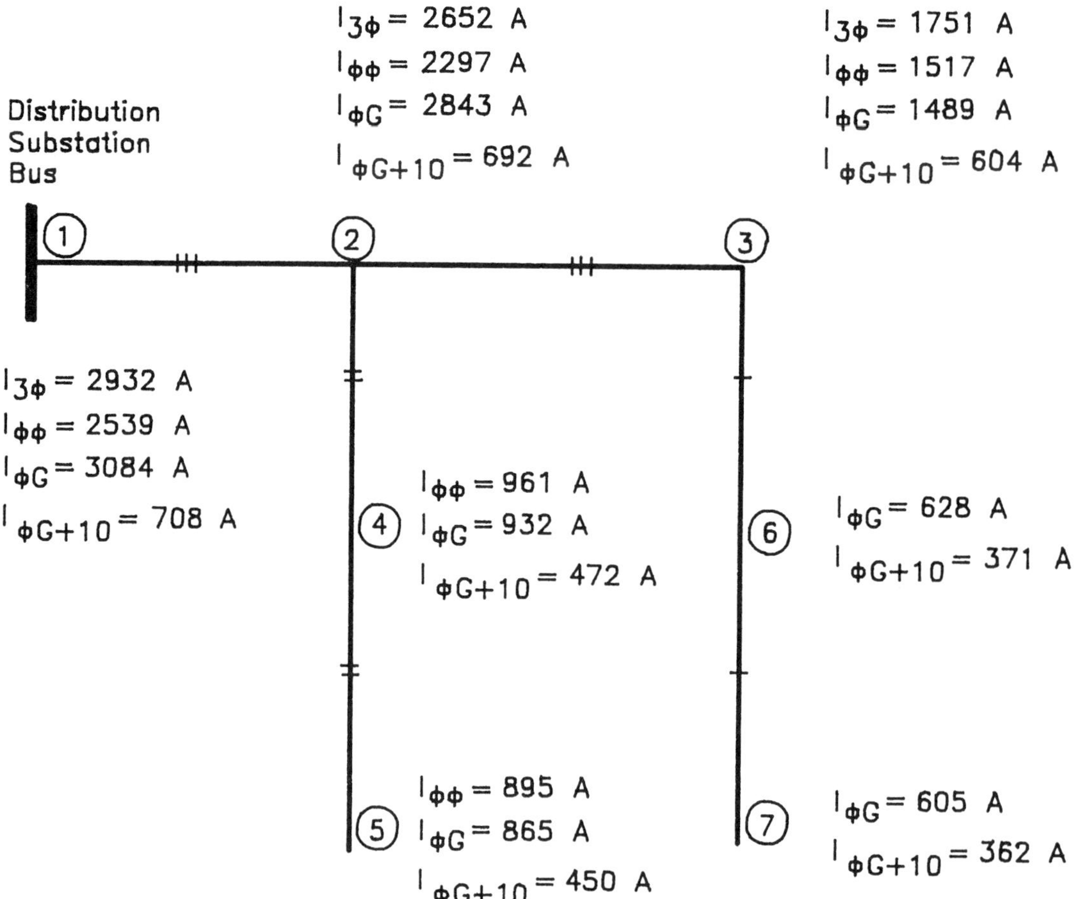

Figure 11-12 System of Fig. 11-11 with short-circuit currents indicated at each point.

Problems

11.1. The source impedance at a 4.16-kV distribution substation bus is $0.1 + j0.375$ Ω-phase. Calculate the rms and maximum peak instantaneous values of fault current for balanced three-phase fault conditions.

11.2. For the power system shown in Fig. 11-13, calculate the short-circuit currents at points $F1$ and $F2$ for the following faults:

a. Three phase
b. Line to line
c. Line to line to ground
d. Line to ground
e. Line to ground plus 20 Ω

11.3. A 13.8-kV distribution substation bus is supplied from the utility 69-kV subtransmission system. The distribution substation transformer has delta-connected high-voltage windings and grounded wye-connected low-voltage windings. The following short-circuit data are available for short-circuits occurring on the high-voltage side of the transformer.

Three-phase fault: 570 MVA, $X/R = 2.4$ at 69 kV
Line to ground fault: 3.3 kA, $X/R = 3.2$ at 69 kV

Determine the positive, negative, and zero sequence equivalent system impedances in ohms

a. Referred to the high-voltage side.
b. Referred to the low-voltage side.

11.4. The distribution substation transformer of Problem 11.3 is rated 20 MVA and has a nameplate impedance of 8%. Calculate the short-circuit current magnitudes for the following:

a. Three-phase fault on the 13.8-kV bus
b. Line to ground fault on the 13.8-kV bus

11.5. For the distribution substation bus of Problems 11.3 and 11.4, determine the rating of the current-limiting inductors required to limit the maximum fault current to 5000 A symmetrical.

11.6. Perform a short-circuit study similar to that of Section 11.10 for the power system shown in Fig. 11-14.

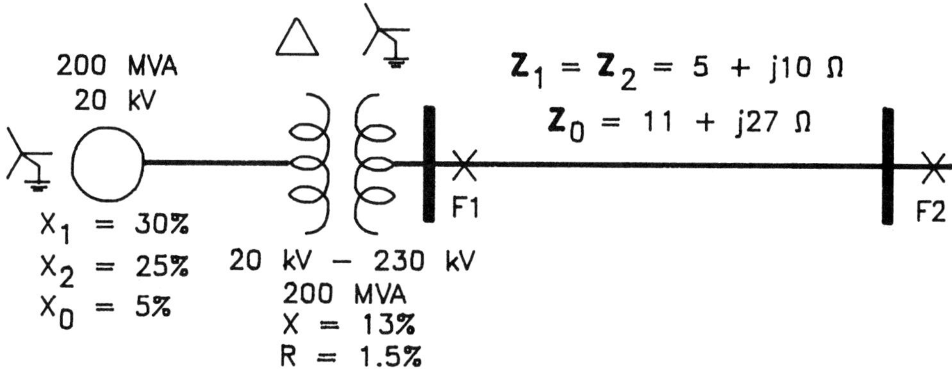

Figure 11-13 System for Problem 11.2.

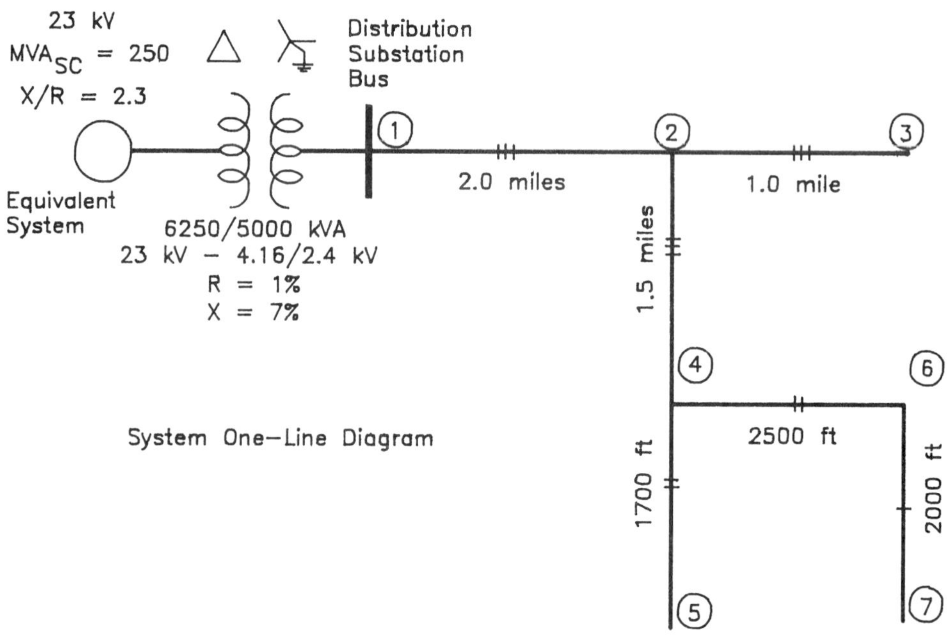

Impedance Data			
Line Segment	Conductor and Cable	Positive Sequence Impedance	Zero Sequence Impedance
1–2	Phase: Three 336.4 kcmil ACSR Neutral: One #3/0 ACSR	0.6120 + j1.3510 Ω	1.5770 + j4.0538 Ω
2–3	Phase: Three 336.4 kcmil ACSR Neutral: One #3/0 ACSR	0.3060 + j0.6755 Ω	0.7885 + j2.0269 Ω
2–4	Phase: Three 336.4 kcmil ACSR Neutral: One #3/0 ACSR	0.4590 + j1.0133 Ω	1.1828 + j3.0404 Ω
4–5	Two #1/0 Al. 15 kV URD	0.3832 + j0.1391 Ω	0.7772 + j0.1920 Ω
4–6	Two #1/0 Al. 15 kV URD	0.5635 + j0.2045 Ω	1.1430 + j0.2823 Ω
6–7	One #2 Al. 15 kV URD	0.9650 + j0.3676 Ω	0.9650 + j0.3676 Ω

Figure 11-14 System for Problem 11.6.

12

Distribution System Overcurrent Protection

12-1 General

This chapter presents an introduction to the apparatus and techniques used to protect utility distribution systems against short-circuit currents. The systems discussed are generally classified as medium voltage, within the range of 2.4 to 35 kV nominal.

The most common form of short-circuit protection applied to utility distribution systems is time–overcurrent. The operation of devices that employ a time–overcurrent operating characteristic depends on both the magnitude and the time duration of the short-circuit current. The operation of an overcurrent device for current flow in either direction is referred to as a nondirectional overcurrent device. If the overcurrent device is designed to operate for current flow in one direction only, it is referred to as a directional overcurrent device. Since the vast majority of utility distribution systems have a radial configuration, they are particularly suited for nondirectional time–overcurrent protection. Recall that on a radial system the short-circuit currents will flow in one direction, from the source to the load, for all types of fault conditions.

The chapter begins with a discussion of the various overcurrent devices that are used to protect radial distribution circuits. These devices include fuses, reclosers, sectionalizers, overcurrent relays, and breakers. The application of these devices to radial distribution lines, capacitors, and transformers is covered next. Finally, the subject of coordination between various overcurrent devices is discussed, followed by an example of a coordination study on a radial distribution circuit.

12-2 Fuses

The fuses typically used for distribution circuit protection are either expulsion type or current limiting. Both types of fuses are one-time devices that will operate in the event of an overcurrent condition through the fuse. Expulsion-type fuses mount in either a distribution cutout or power fuse support. Current-limiting fuses are typically mounted in a nonexpulsion-type fuse support.

Distribution Cutouts

Figure 12-1 shows the basic construction of a distribution cutout. These cutouts are typically of the open-type construction and are mounted on overhead distribution poles or crossarms. A replaceable fuse element or link is mounted inside the fuse holder. The

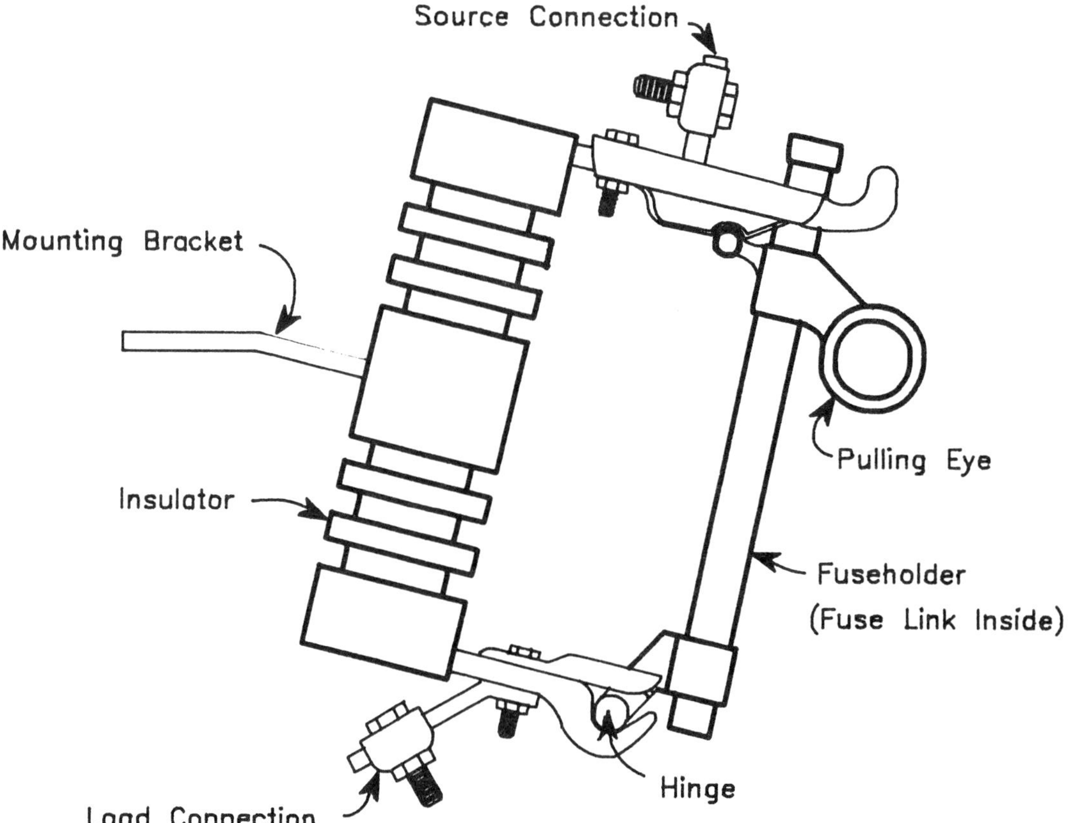

Figure 12-1 Distribution cutout.

fuse holder is hinged at the bottom and is held closed by the fuse link mounted inside the fuse holder. When a short circuit occurs, the fuse link melts, permitting the fuse holder to drop open. The fuse holder now provides a visible indication that the fuse link has blown. The fuse holder can now be removed from the cutout, the fuse link replaced, and the fuse holder reinserted into the fuse cutout. In addition, the open fuse holder will provide a physical means of disconnection from the source. Figure 12-2 shows a fused cutout used to protect a capacitor bank on a 12.47-kV distribution feeder.

Open-type distribution cutouts are generally available in voltage ratings of 7.8, 15, 27, and 38 kV. The voltage rating selected should exceed the nominal line to line voltage of the system. Dual voltage rated cutouts are available for application on a multigrounded neutral system only. If dual voltage rated cutouts are used, the voltage rating selected depends on the application. If a slant voltage rated cutout is applied to a single-phase multigrounded circuit consisting of a phase conductor and grounded neutral conductor, the voltage rating of the cutout should exceed the rating to the left of the slant. If the cutout is to be applied to an open-wye or three-phase portion of a multigrounded neutral circuit, then the voltage rating of the cutout should exceed the rating to the right of the slant.

Current ratings for distribution cutouts vary by manufacturer. Typical current ratings for fused cutouts are either 100 or 200 A. Fuse holder ratings for fused cutouts are typically rated at 100 or 200 A. Cutouts used only for disconnecting purposes may be rated at 300 A and are equipped with a 300-A blade instead of a fuse holder.

Current ratings for fuse links used in distribution cutouts are generally available in the ratings shown in Table 12-1. The fuse links are available with either a **K** or **T** rating. Fuse links with a **K** rating have a faster response time than **T**-rated fuse links of the same current rating. For example, a 25K link fuse has a melting current of between 350 to 420 A at 0.1 sec, while a 25T link fuse has a melting current of between 635 and

Figure 12-2 Fused cutouts protecting a capacitor bank on a 12.47-kV distribution feeder. (Photo Courtesy of Ohio Edison Company)

Table 12-1 Ratings for **K-** and **T-** Rated Fuse Links

Preferred Ratings	*Intermediate Ratings*	*Ratings below 6 Amperes*
6, 10, 15 25, 40, 65 100, 140 200	8, 12, 20 30, 50, 80	1, 2, 3

762 A at 0.1 sec. The melting currents are specified by ANSI® standards at the following times: 300 sec for fuse links rated 100 A and less, 600 sec for fuse links rated above 100 A, 10 sec for all fuse sizes, and 0.1 sec for all fuse sizes.

Expulsion-Type Power Fuses

High-voltage, expulsion-type power fuses are used more often in higher-voltage applications than the open distribution cutout. A typical application would be the high-voltage side of a distribution substation transformer. Similarly to the distribution cutout, the power fuse support provides for expulsion of the fuse element and dropping out of the fuse support, in the event of a fuse operation. The fuse element may then be replaced and the fuse reinstalled. Figure 12-3 shows the general construction features of a power fuse support. Figure 12-4 shows a group of three power fuses used to protect the high-voltage side of a distribution substation transformer.

The fuse elements used in high-voltage power fuses generally have an **E** or **R** current rating. The **R** rating is generally used for medium-voltage motor circuits and the **E** rating for power transformers and distribution systems. According to ANSI standards, the current responsive element for **E**-rated fuses rated at 100 A and below shall melt in 300 sec at a current between 200% to 240% of the continuous rating of the fuse. For **E**-rated fuses rated above 100 A, the current responsive element shall melt in 600 sec at a current within the range of 220% to 264% of the continuous current rating of the fuse.

Ratings for **E**-rated, high-voltage power fuses are shown in Table 12-2. When selecting a power fuse, the voltage rating of the fuse support must exceed the voltage rating of the system to which it is applied. The voltage ratings shown in Table 12-2 are line to line voltages. The fuse support rating must exceed the rating of the fuse element to be installed. Fuse element ratings other than those shown in Table 12-2 are available from various manufacturers.

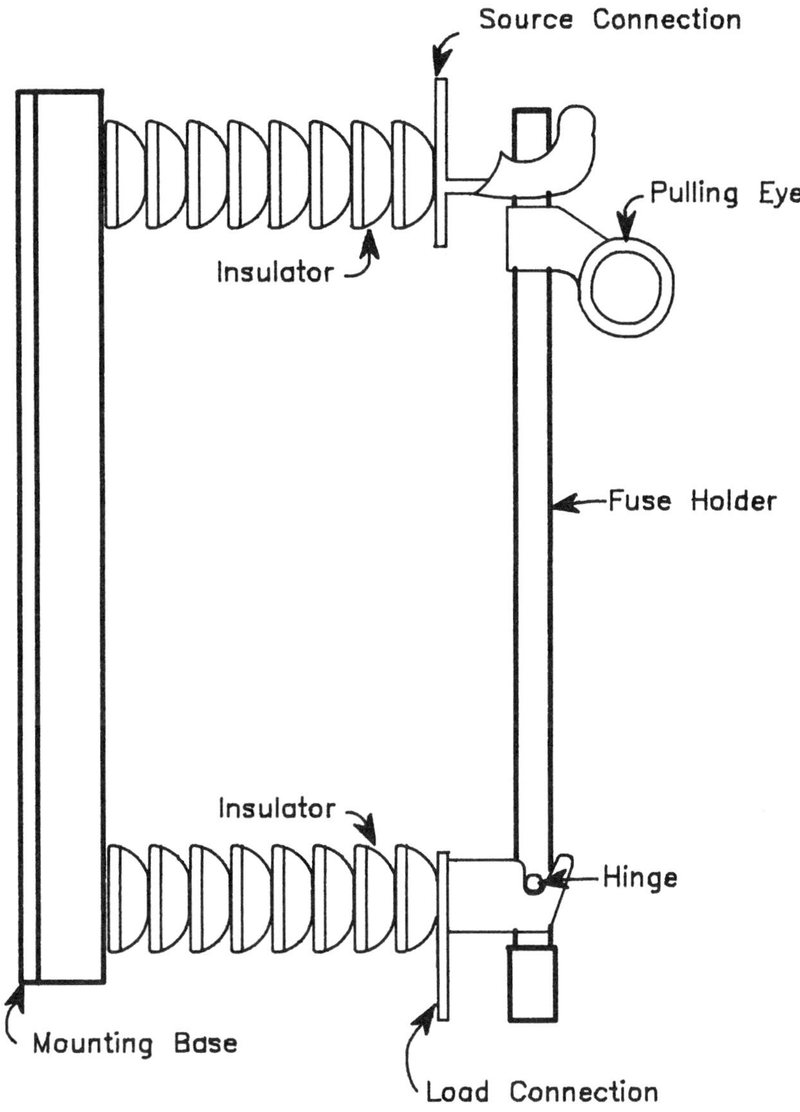

Figure 12-3 High-voltage, expulsion-type power fuse.

Figure 12-4 Group of three power fuses protecting a distribution substation transformer. (Photo Courtesy of Ohio Edison Company)

Table 12-2 Ratings for **E-** Rated Fuses

Voltage Ratings (kV)	*Fuse Support Ratings (A)*	*Fuse Element Ratings (A)*
2.8, 8.3	10, 25, 100	0.5, 1, 2, 3
15.5, 25.8	200, 300, 400	5, 7, 10, 15
38.0, 48.3	450, 700	20, 25, 30, 40
72.5, 121.0		50, 65, 80, 100
145.0, 169.0		125, 150, 200
		250, 300, 400

Current-Limiting Fuses

Current-limiting fuses are used where the available short-circuit current exceeds the momentary rating of the equipment to be protected. Distribution current-limiting fuses have a **C** rating to indicate that they are current limiting. According to ANSI standards, the fuse element shall melt at 1000 sec for currents between 170% to 240% of the continuous current rating of the fuse. Table 12-3 shows standard voltage and current ratings for current-limiting power fuses.

The current-limiting fuse differs from the expulsion-type power fuses previously discussed in that the current-limiting fuse limits the amount of current allowed to pass

Table 12-3 Ratings for Current-Limiting Power Fuses

Voltage Ratings (kV)	*Fuse Support Ratings (A)*	*Fuse Element Ratings (A)*
2.8, 5.5	50, 100, 200	6, 8, 10, 12
8.3, 15.5		15, 18, 20, 25
22.0, 27.0		30, 40, 50, 65
		80, 100, 125
		150, 200

through to the load. Expulsion-type fuses do not have current-limiting capabilities built in and will allow the maximum available fault current to pass through. Current-limiting fuses may be applied to distribution transformers located close to distribution substations, where the available short-circuit current exceeds the withstand capability of the transformer.

The ability of a current-limiting fuse to limit the peak let through current can be understood by examining the fault current waveform shown in Fig. 12-5. The waveform is shown from inception of the fault to the first current zero. A noncurrent-limiting fuse will allow the first half-cycle of current to pass before interrupting at the first current zero. The fuse element in a current-limiting fuse begins to melt when the current exceeds a certain percent of rated. As the fuse element melts, an arc voltage is produced that opposes the applied system voltage. This arc voltage will therefore force the current to zero before the normal expected current zero. The maximum peak let through current is designated I_p and the time of the maximum peak is t_p. Notice that in the current-limiting mode the maximum peak let through current is less than the normally expected peak current of the waveform had no current-limiting action occurred. Also, the time required for the current-limiting fuse to interrupt the short-circuit current is less than the time required for the fault current waveform to pass through the first current zero.

Time–Current Characteristics

The time–current characteristic, or TCC of a fuse, is a plot of the response time of the fuse element as a function of current. Time–current characteristics are usually plotted on a log–log scale. These characteristics are readily available from the fuse manufacturer for different types of fuses. Representive time–current characteristics for a 25T link fuse are shown in Fig. 12-6. Time–current characteristics for other T link fuses are given in Appendix B.

In reference to Fig. 12-6, the TCC for a given fuse rating and type actually consists of two curves. The lower curve is the minimum melt characteristic, and the upper curve

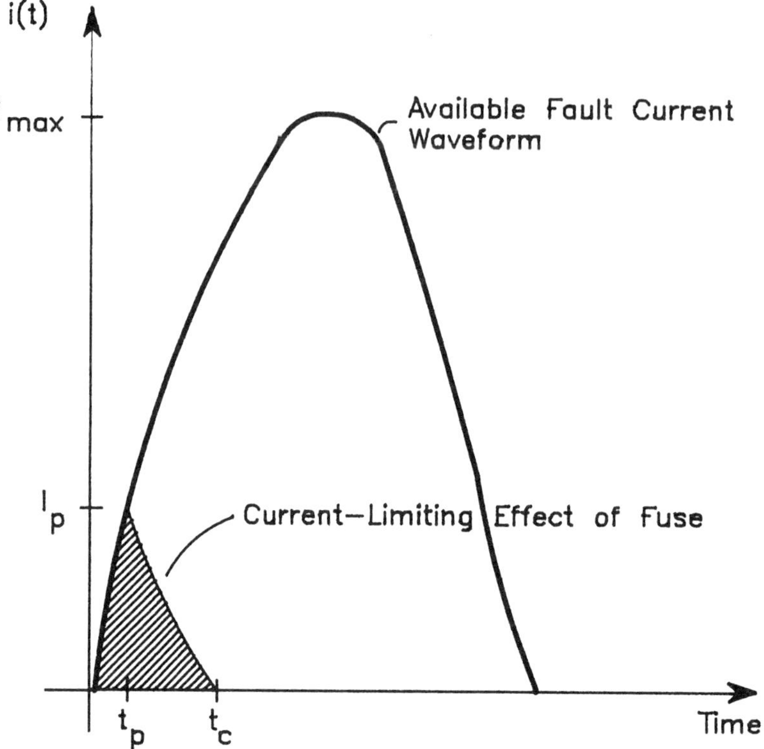

Figure 12-5 Current-limiting fuse operation.

is the total clear characteristic. The minimum melt curve indicates the time required for the fuse element to begin to melt for a given current. The total clear curve indicates the time necessary for the fuse link to completely clear for a given current.

EXAMPLE 12-1

Determine the minimum melt and total clearing times for a 25T link fuse for the following currents:

a. 80 A
b. 200 A
c. 1000 A

Solution The minimum melt and total clearing times are read directly from the TCC shown in Fig. 12-6.

a. Minimum melt at 9.5 sec, total clear at 18.0 sec
b. Minimum melt at 0.95 sec, total clear at 1.2 sec
c. Minimum melt at 0.035 sec, total clear at 0.06 sec

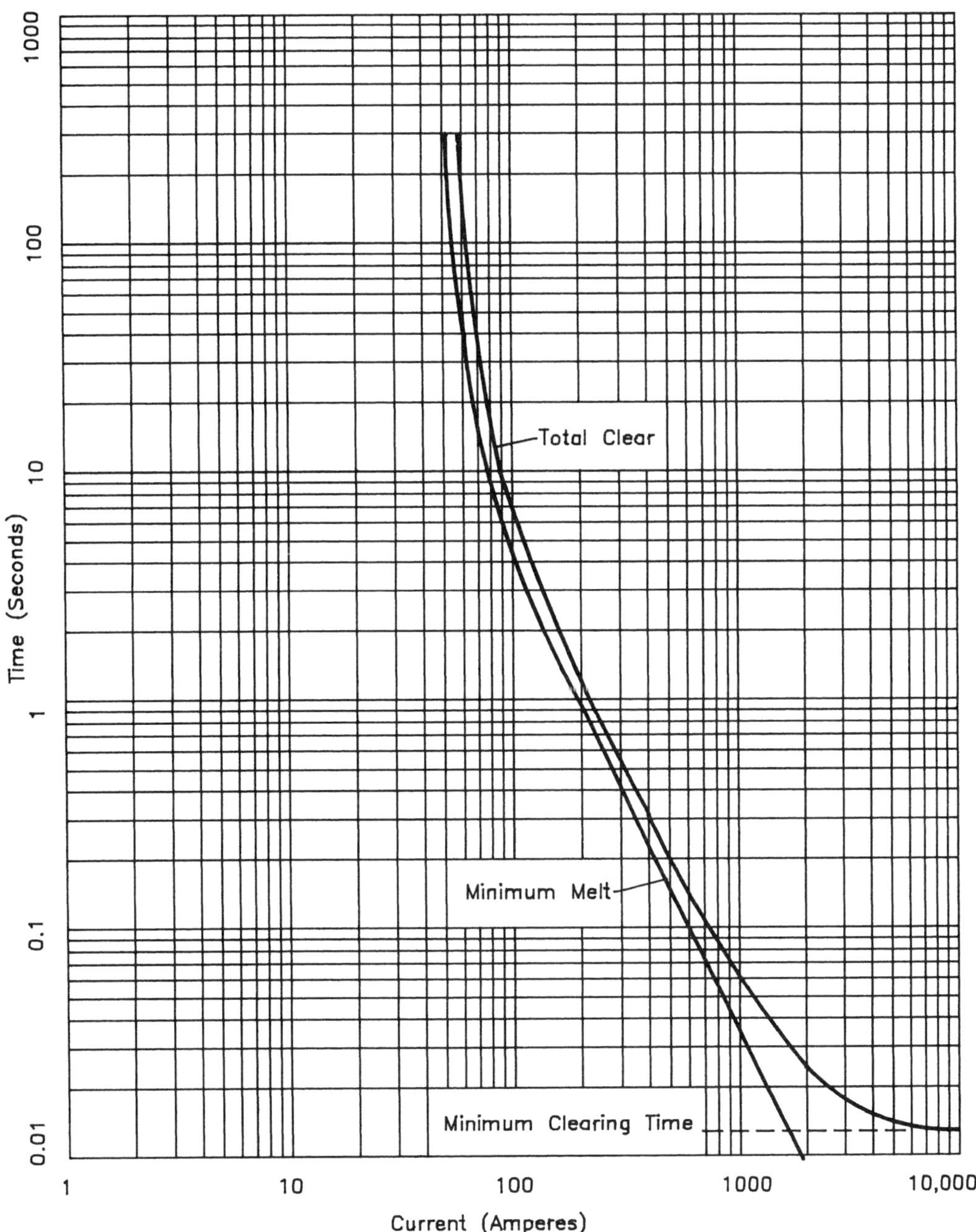

Figure 12-6 Time–current characteristics of 25T link fuse.

I^2t Energy Let Through

The ability of current-limiting fuses to limit the amount of current to a certain level is quantified by the use of peak let through curves and published I^2t values. The peak let through curve of a current-limiting fuse shows the peak let through current as a function of the available symmetrical short-circuit current. A representive peak let through curve for a given fuse is shown in Fig. 12-7. Peak let through curves for other current-limiting fuses are given in Appendix B. Since the peak current is a function of the system X/R

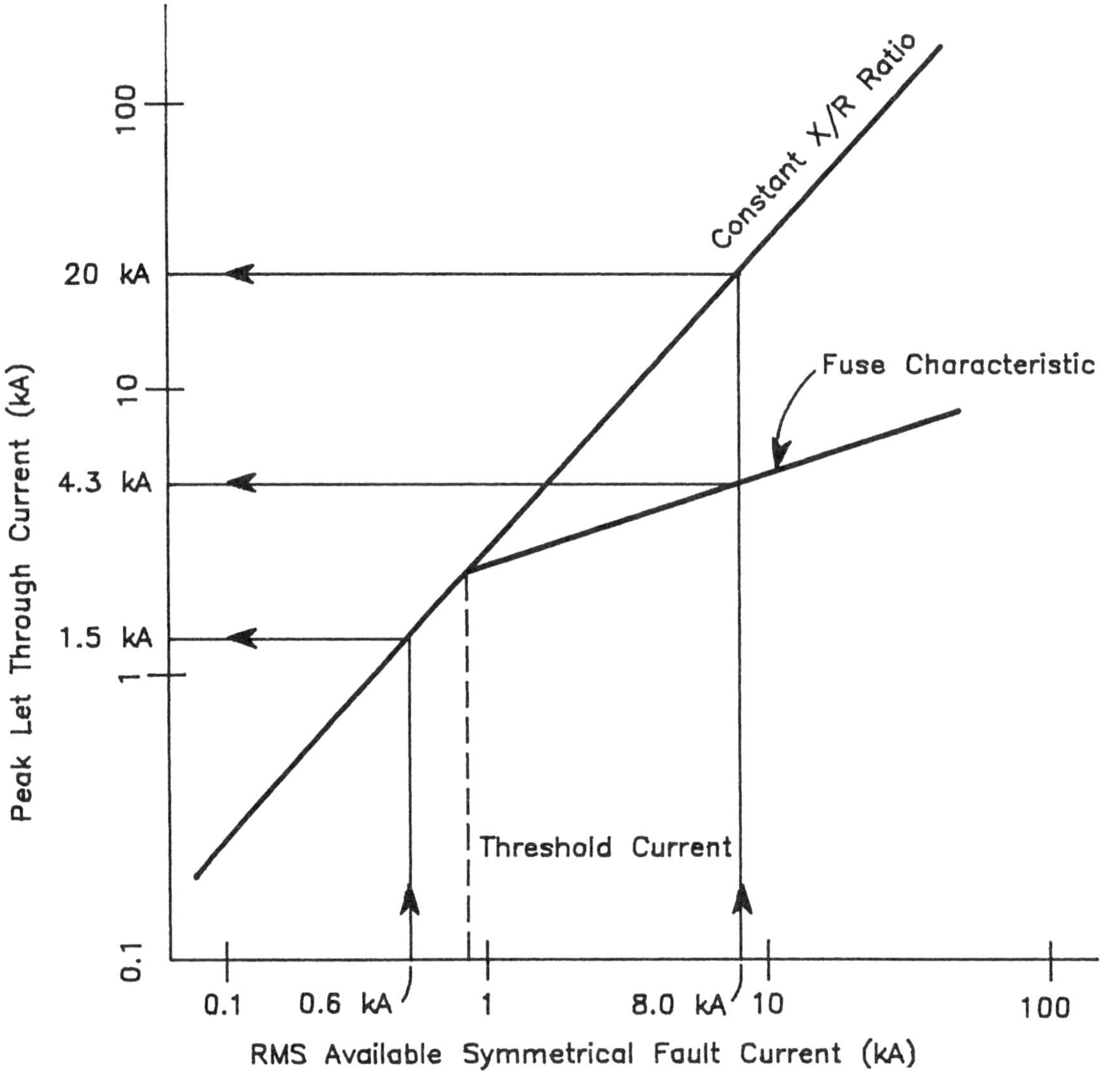

Figure 12-7 Peak let through curve of 50E, 8.3-kV current-limiting fuse.

ratio, the peak let through characteristic will be published for a given X/R ratio. Generally, an X/R ratio not exceeding 15 is used in the determination of the fuse characteristics. The fuse manufacturer should be consulted when X/R ratios higher than 15 are encountered.

EXAMPLE 12-2

Determine the peak let through currents of a 50E, 8.3-kV, current-limiting fuse for the following rms available fault currents. Also, specify what the peak let through currents would be if a current-limiting fuse were not used. The curve of Fig. 12-7 applies.

a. 600 A
b. 8000 A

Solution

a. The peak let through current with the current-limiting fuse is approximately 1500 A. Without the current-limiting fuse, the peak let through is also 1500 A. This is because the available fault current is less than the threshold current of the fuse.
b. With the current-limiting fuse the peak let through current is approximately 4300 A. Without the current-limiting fuse, the peak let through current is 20,000 A. Thus, the use of a current-limiting fuse has resulted in a considerable reduction in peak current.

12-3 Reclosers

Reclosers are self-contained devices used for interrupting short-circuit currents. As the name implies, a recloser will automatically reclose after tripping, thereby restoring power to the circuit it is protecting. All the tripping and reclosing logic is contained in one packaged unit. The primary application of reclosers is on radial distribution circuits. The reclosers may be installed either in the distribution substation or on the distribution circuit.

Figure 12-8a shows the general construction features of a single-phase recloser. Figure 12-9 shows an installation consisting of three single-phase reclosers installed on a 12.47-kV distribution feeder. Three-phase reclosers are also available from several manufacturers. Connection to the distribution circuit is made through high-voltage bushings. An operating handle is provided to manually open and close the recloser as desired. In addition, a nonreclosing handle is provided to set the recloser to trip and lock out without reclosing after one operation.

The operation of the recloser can be understood by examining the simplified circuit diagram shown in Fig. 12-8b. Under normal operating conditions, load current flows through the series trip coil or sensing relay. When the current through the series trip coil or sensing relay exceeds the value of minimum trip current, the trip solenoid is energized.

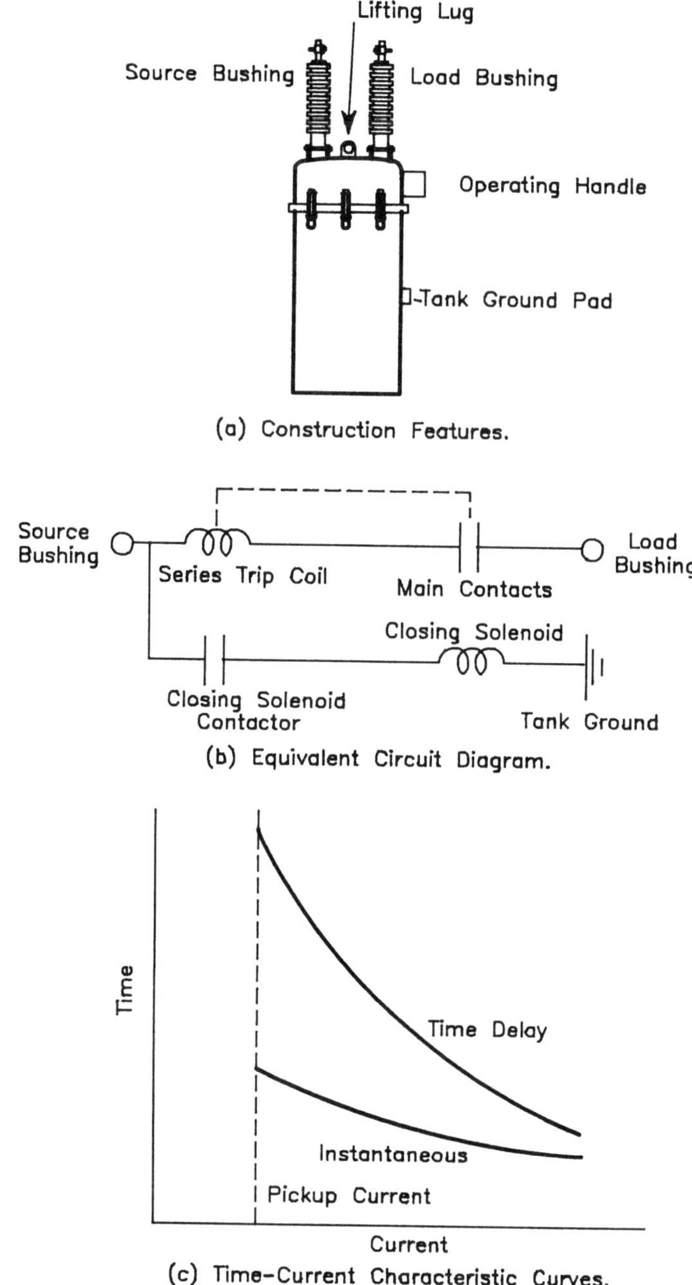

Figure 12-8 Distribution recloser characteristics.

Figure 12-9 Three single-phase reclosers installed on a 12.47-kV distribution feeder. (Photo Courtesy of Ohio Edison Company)

Movement of the trip solenoid operates a latch that releases the charged operating springs and causes the contacts to open. Once the recloser contacts are open, the contacts on the closing solenoid contactor are closed, thereby energizing the closing solenoid. Energizing the closing solenoid causes recloser contacts to close and recharge the opening springs. The recloser is now reset, ready for the next tripping operation, if needed to clear the fault. The main interrupter may use oil, vacuum, or SF_6 gas as the fault interrupting medium.

The time delay characteristics, tripping sequence, and reclosing sequence may be controlled either hydraulically (oil) or electronically. The tripping characteristics of the recloser are described by use of time–current characteristics as shown in Fig. 12-8c. Time–current characteristics for other reclosers are given in Appendix B. In general, there are two groups of time–current trip characteristics, instantaneous and time delay. Initially, upon the occurrence of a short circuit, the recloser will trip at a time specified by the instantaneous time–current characteristic curve. As previously discussed, the recloser will then reclose in an attempt to restore service. If the fault is cleared, the recloser will remain closed, and the controller will reset to the initial trip reclose sequence.

If the fault is still present, the recloser will trip again. The time–current characteristic for the second recloser trip can be selected by the user as either the instantaneous or time delay characteristic curve. After tripping the second time, the recloser will again reclose. If the fault has not been cleared, a third trip and subsequent reclosure will occur. Generally, the third recloser trip will be in accordance with the time delay characteristic.

If the fault is still present after the third reclosure, the recloser will trip for the fourth time and lock out. The recloser will need to be manually reclosed after lockout occurs.

Single-phase reclosers have tripping and locking out characteristics independent of the other phases. For example, one recloser in an installation of three single-phase reclosers may trip and lock out, while the reclosers in the other two phases remain closed. Similarly, three-phase reclosers typically have individual pole tripping and reclosing. However, if any one of the phases operates to lockout, all three poles may be set to trip and lock out as required.

Reclosers are generally available in voltage ratings from 2.4 to 34.5 kV and continuous current ratings up to 1200 A rms. The maximum interrupting current ratings vary as a function of the system voltage and continuous current rating of the recloser. Generally, interrupting ratings range from 1250 to 20,000 A rms symmetrical. Specific voltage, current, and interrupting ratings can be obtained from manufacturers' literature.

EXAMPLE 12-3

Determine the operating times of a 50A type L recloser on both the instantaneous *A* and time delay *B* curves for fault currents equal to **(a)** 200 A and **(b)** 2000 A

Solution The time–current characteristics are given in Appendix B.

a. Instantaneous curve at 0.1 sec, time delay curve at 1.0 sec
b. Instantaneous curve at 0.03 sec, time delay curve at 0.08 sec

---

12-4 Sectionalizers

Sectionalizers are generally used with reclosers or circuit breakers to provide system protection. The physical appearance of the sectionalizer is similar to that of the recloser previously discussed. However, unlike reclosers, sectionalizers do not have the capability to interrupt short-circuit currents. Therefore, any tripping of the sectionalizer must be done while the line is de-energized. In addition, sectionalizers do not have time–current tripping characteristics as do reclosers and fuses. Rather, the operation of the sectionalizer commences after the detection of current in excess of the sectionalizer's actuation current setting.

On radial distribution circuits, a sectionalizer is installed on the load side of a recloser or circuit breaker. If a fault occurs, short-circuit current will flow through both the sectionalizer and source side recloser or breaker. If the magnitude of the fault current exceeds the sectionalizer's actuation setting, the sectionalizer is "armed," or made ready to count. Once armed, the sectionalizer begins to count the number of times the line is de-energized by the source side recloser or circuit breaker. After a preset number of counts is reached, the sectionalizer will trip and lock out. Tripping of the sectionalizer occurs while the line is de-energized by the opening of the source side breaker or recloser.

12-5 Time–Overcurrent Relays

Time–overcurrent (TOC) relays are used in conjunction with current transformers and circuit breakers to sense the current flowing on a line. Upon detection of an overcurrent, the relay will operate, thereby opening or closing its contacts. These relay contacts are used to energize the trip coil of the circuit breaker and possibly a reclosing or timing relay. Figure 12-10a and b show the one-line and schematic diagrams of a typical time–overcurrent relay used to control the tripping of a circuit breaker.

Relay operation begins when the current flowing through the relay exceeds the pickup tap setting. The tap setting is adjustable either by means of plugs in electromechanical relays or electronically in solid-state relays. When current transformers are used, the relay current is equal to the actual primary short-circuit current divided by the *CT* ratio. For example, if a current transformer with a ratio of 400:5 is used, a fault current of 3000 A will be reflected to the *CT* secondary as

$$I_{relay} = \frac{300\text{ A}}{400:5} = 37.5\text{ A}$$

If the relay tap is set at a 5 A, then the actual relay current corresponds to 7.5 times the pickup of the relay.

The actual time that elapses between initiation and actual relay contact closure is adjustable by means of the time dial setting. Figure 12-10c shows a typical time–current characteristic for a time–overcurrent relay. Additional time–current curves for time–overcurrent relays are given in Appendix B. Note that the current axis is labeled in multiples of the pickup value. The time axis may be specified in either seconds or cycles on a 60-Hz basis.

EXAMPLE 12-4

A circuit breaker equipped with bushing mounted current transformers having a ratio of 600:5 is protecting a 4.16-kV distribution feeder. The time–overcurrent relay characteristic is given in Appendix B. The relay is to operate when the load current on the feeder is 500 A. In addition, the available short-circuit current is 5000 A at the breaker location and 2000 A at the far end of the circuit. Determine **(a)** the appropriate tap setting required for the relay to pick up at 500 A and **(b)** the required time dial setting to allow a time delay of 0.3 sec at maximum fault current levels.

Solution

a. The relay current for 500-A load current is

$$I_{relay} = \frac{500}{600:5} = 4.167\text{ A}$$

Therefore, a tap setting of 4.0 is required.

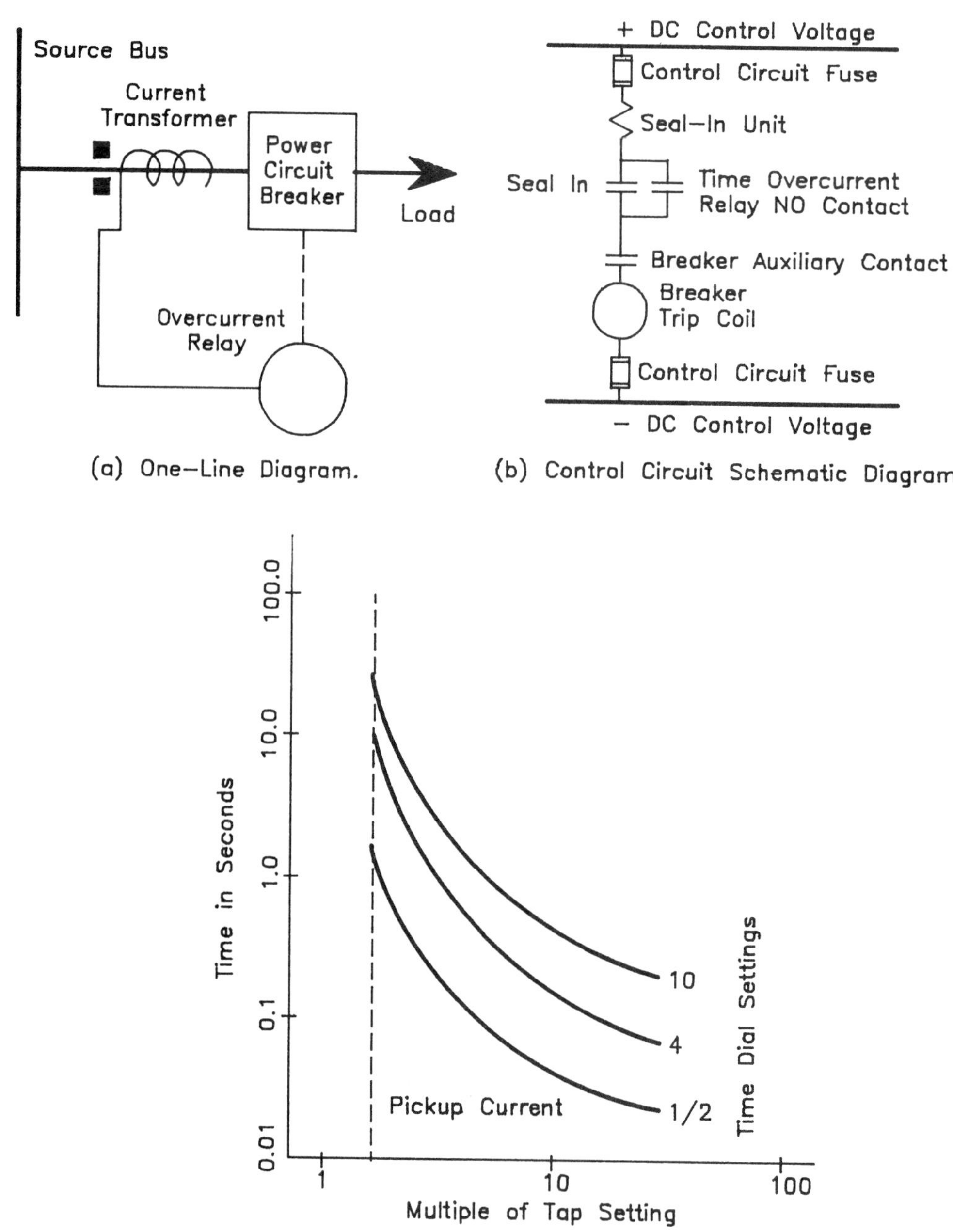

Figure 12-10 Time–overcurrent relay characteristics.

b. The relay current for a fault current of 5000 A on the primary is equal to

$$I_{\text{relay}} = \frac{5000}{600:5} = 41.67 \text{ A}$$

This relay current corresponds to a multiple of tap setting equal to 41.67/4 = 10.4. To obtain a time delay of 0.3 sec, a time dial setting of approximately 5 is necessary.

12-6 Breakers

In some instances, circuit reclosers may not be of sufficient continuous current carrying capacity or interrupting capacity to meet system requirements. Power circuit breakers may be used in these types of situations. Unlike reclosers, the power circuit breaker has no built-in tripping or reclosing logic. Tripping of the breaker is done by energizing the breaker trip coil through some auxiliary means. Likewise, the breaker close coil is energized to close the breaker. Typically, the circuit breaker is equipped with a set of auxiliary contacts that either open or close in conjunction with the main breaker contacts. Figure 12-11

Figure 12-11 Feeder breaker installed on a 12.47-kV distribution circuit exit. (Photo Courtesy of Ohio Edison Company)

shows a feeder breaker installed in a 12.47-kV distribution substation for feeder protection.

The voltage rating of the circuit breaker must exceed the nominal line to line voltage rating of the system to which it is applied. Likewise, the continuous current rating of the breaker must exceed the expected load current of the circuit at the point of application. The momentary and interrupting rating of the breaker must be greater than the maximum expected rms short-circuit current. The minimum interrupting rating of the circuit breaker is generally expressed in terms of rms symmetrical current. Table 12-4 shows standard ratings for indoor circuit and outdoor circuit breakers rated 72.5 kV and below.

The voltage range *K* factor is used to determine the interrupting capacity at voltages between 1/*K* times rated and the rated voltage of the circuit breaker. The symmetrical interrupting capability of a circuit breaker operating at a voltage between 1/*K* times rated and a voltage equal to rated is given by the following:

$$I_{\mathrm{SC,act}} = I_{\mathrm{SC,rated}} \cdot \frac{V_{\mathrm{rated}}}{V_{\mathrm{act}}} \tag{12.1}$$

where

$I_{\mathrm{SC,rated}}$ = rated short-circuit current of the breaker
V_{rated} = rated line to line voltage of the breaker
V_{act} = actual line to line operating voltage of the breaker

The maximum symmetrical interrupting ratings shown in the last column of Table 12-4 must not be exceeded under any circumstances.

EXAMPLE 12-5

A 4.76-kV, 1200-A breaker having a *K* factor of 1.36 and a rated short-circuit current of 8.8 kA is applied to a 4.16-kV bus. The available short-circuit current at the bus is 11.0 kA. Determine if this is a suitable application.

Solution The actual short-circuit current rating at 4.16 kV is given by Eq. (12.1).

$$I_{\mathrm{SC,act}} = I_{\mathrm{SC,rated}} \cdot \frac{V_{\mathrm{rated}}}{V_{\mathrm{act}}}$$

$$= 8.8 \cdot \frac{4.76}{4.16} = 10.1 \text{ kA}$$

The available fault current is 11.0 kA, which exceeds the rated short-circuit rating of the breaker at a voltage of 4.16 kV. Therefore, this is not a suitable application, and a breaker with a higher short-circuit rating must be used.

Unlike medium- and high-voltage power circuit breakers, the circuit breakers used in low-voltage applications have built-in tripping logic. Some low-voltage breakers have

Table 12-4 Standard Ratings for Indoor and Outdoor Circuit Breakers

Voltage Ratings (kV)	*Voltage Range, K Factor*	*Rated Continuous Current (A, rms)*	*Rated Short-Circuit Current (kA, rms)*	*Maximum Symmetrical Interrupting Ratings (kA, rms)*
		Indoor		
4.76	1.36	1200	8.8	12.0
4.76	1.24	1200, 2000	29.0	36.0
4.76	1.19	1200, 2000, 3000	41.0	49.0
8.25	1.25	1200, 2000	33.0	41.0
15.0	1.3	1200, 2000	18.0	23.0
15.0	1.3	1200, 2000	28.0	36.0
15.0	1.3	1200, 2000, 3000	37.0	48.0
38.0	1.65	1200, 2000, 3000	21.0	35.0
38.0	1.0	1200, 3000	40.0	40.0
		Outdoor		
15.5	1.0	600,1200	12.5	12.5
15.5	1.0	1200, 2000	20.0	20.0
15.5	1.0	1200, 2000	25.0	25.0
15.5	1.0	1200, 2000, 3000	40.0	40.0
25.8	1.0	1200, 2000	12.5	12.5
25.8	1.0	1200, 2000	25.0	25.0
38.0	1.0	1200, 2000	16.0	16.0
38.0	1.0	1200, 2000	20.0	20.0
38.0	1.0	1200, 2000	25.0	25.0
38.0	1.0	1200, 2000	31.5	31.5
38.0	1.0	1200, 2000, 3000	40.0	40.0
48.3	1.0	1200, 2000	20.0	20.0
48.3	1.0	1200, 2000	31.5	31.5
48.3	1.0	1200, 2000, 3000	40.0	40.0
72.5	1.0	1200, 2000	20.0	20.0
72.5	1.0	1200, 2000	31.5	31.5
72.5	1.0	1200, 2000, 3000	40.0	40.0

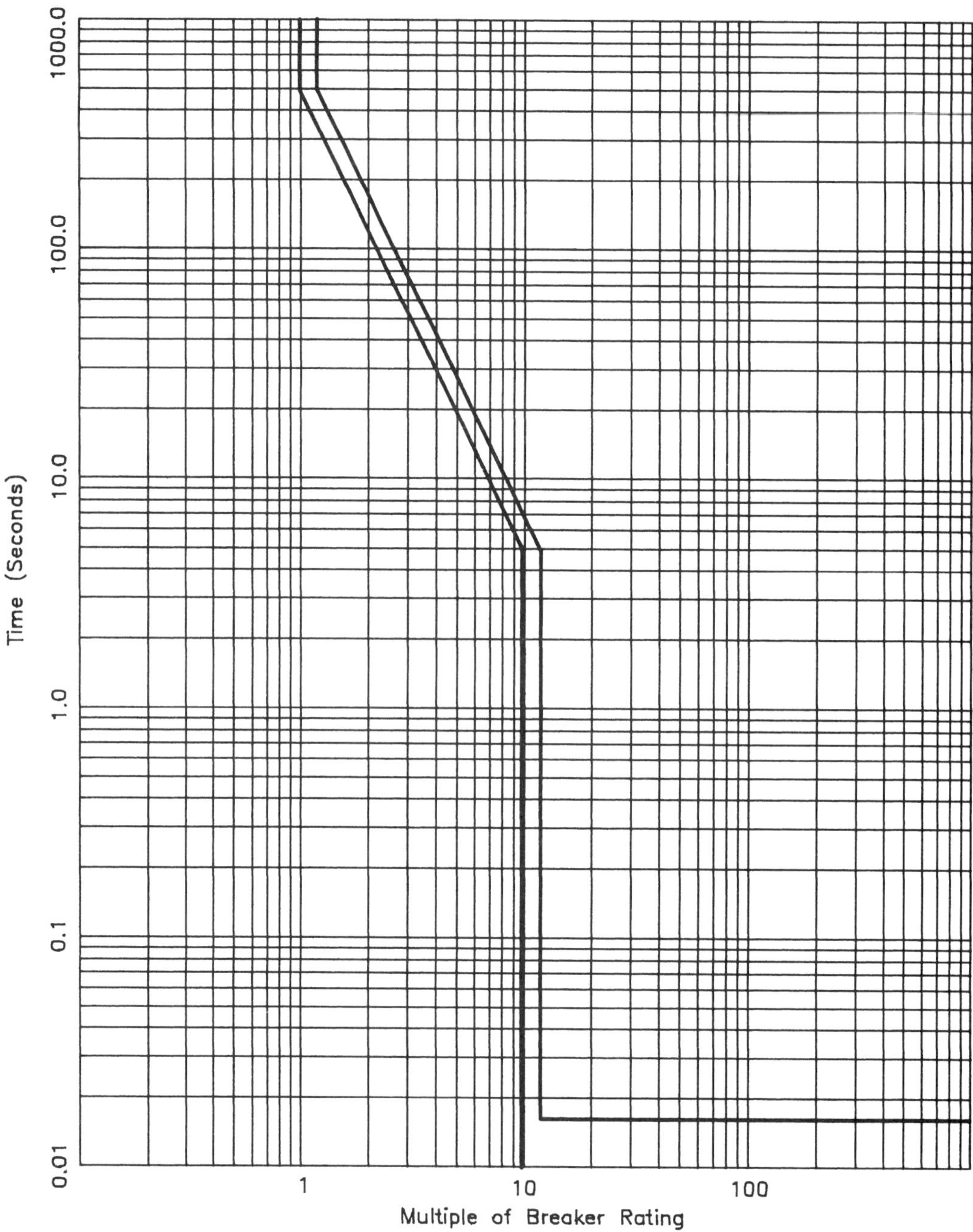

Figure 12-12 Low-voltage breaker time–current characteristics.

adjustable long time and instantaneous trip current settings, as well as adjustable time delay settings. Standard molded case low-voltage breakers have fixed tripping characteristics. A typical time–current characteristic of a low-voltage breaker is shown in Fig. 12-12. Notice that the current axis is labeled in terms of multiples of breaker current rating.

12-7 Protection of Distribution Lines

The protection of distribution lines is based on the philosophy of providing for protection of the general public, protection of equipment from damage, and minimization of outages on a line. Faults may occur on a distribution feeder due to lightning, tree limbs coming in contact with energized conductors, broken poles or crossarms, excavation of underground lines, and so on. Whatever the cause of the fault, the protective devices should operate to clear the fault or de-energize the circuit to provide protection.

To understand the different protection philosophies, it is first necessary to understand the nature of faults. The faults that occur on an electrical power system can be classified as either temporary or permanent. The best example of a temporary fault is the flashing over of an insulator due to a lightning-induced surge. When lightning strikes a line, a voltage surge is produced on the line. This voltage surge travels along the line in an attempt to find ground. As the voltage surge approaches a supporting structure, an insulator on the structure may flash over due to the overvoltage produced. Once the insulator flashes over, a low impedance path to ground is formed, resulting in a line to ground fault. The current that flows under these conditions is equal to the line to ground fault current. If the circuit is momentarily de-energized, the arc across the insulator is extinguished and the fault is removed. The circuit can now be re-energized and service restored.

Permanent faults require repair or removal of the faulted equipment. Examples of permanent faults are downed conductors and underground cable dig-ins. Incidentally, most if not all of the faults that occur on underground cable circuits are permanent in nature.

The general objective of distribution system protection is to select device types and ratings to allow clearing of temporary faults and to isolate faulted sections due to permanent faults. To accomplish these objectives, a combination of reclosers, reclosing circuit breakers, sectionalizers, and line fuses is employed.

Generally, reclosers or reclosing circuit breakers are installed in the distribution substation at each circuit exit. Since these reclosers or breakers supply the entire distribution circuit, they are generally of high continuous current rating. Consequently, the minimum trip rating of these devices is rather high and may not trip for faults toward the end of the circuit. Therefore, it is not uncommon to place line reclosers out on the line itself. These line reclosers have lower continuous current and minimum trip ratings. As a result, the entire distribution circuit is protected by reclosers or reclosing circuit breakers. The protection philosophy in this case is to allow the reclosers to trip initially on their instantaneous trip curve, thereby allowing for temporary de-energization of the

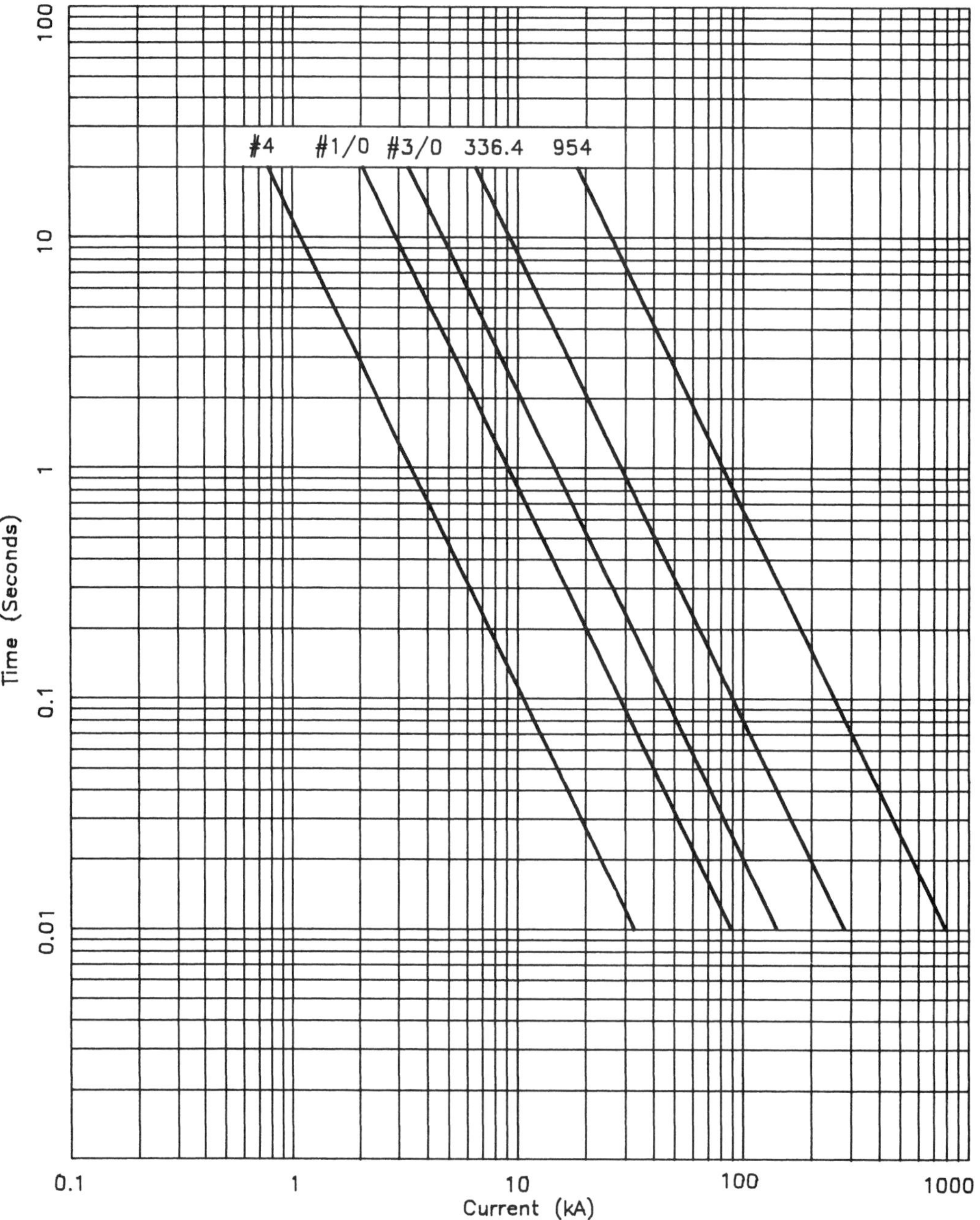

Figure 12-13 ACSR conductor fault current withstand curves. (*Source:* ALCOA Aluminum Overhead Conductor Engineering Databook Section 7)

line and subsequent clearing of temporary faults. When the recloser recloses, the system is restored to normal.

Fuses are typically installed on portions of the circuit that are isolated from the rest of the circuit in the event of a permanent fault. Typical examples are lateral taps made from the main feeder section. If a permanent fault develops on a tap or section of line that serves a small number of customers, it is desirable to isolate only that small section of line. Thus, only a small number of customers will be affected by the fault.

When selecting fuse and recloser sizes, it is important to coordinate the time–current characteristics of these devices with the conductor threshold of damage characteristic curve. Typically, conductors can withstand a certain I^2t value. When plotted on a log–log scale, a constant I^2t becomes a straight line. Figure 12-13 shows the threshold of melting curves for various sizes of ACSR conductors.

It is generally desirable to limit the current levels to 50% of the values shown by the conductor melting curves. This results in a shifting of the conductor withstand curve to the left. The characteristic of the overcurrent protective device must lie below and to the left of the adjusted conductor withstand characteristic.

EXAMPLE 12-6

Determine the maximum short-circuit withstand current of a #4 ACSR conductor at times of **(a)** 0.01 sec and **(b)** 10 sec.

Solution The conductor threshold of melting curves of Fig. 12-13 will be used.

a. $I_{max} \approx 32{,}000$ A for 0.01 sec
b. $I_{max} \approx 1000$ A for 10 sec

Note: If the current levels are to be limited to 50% of the values shown in Fig. 12-13, the following will result:

a. $I_{max} \approx 16{,}000$ A for 0.01 sec
b. $I_{max} \approx 500$ A for 10 sec

12-8 Protection of Transformers

Distribution transformers need to be protected against both internal and through faults. Internal faults are considered to be permanent and will not clear by simply de-energizing the transformer. Examples of internal transformer faults include insulation failures, bushing failures, and tap changer contact welding. Through faults are faults that occur externally to the transformer. An example would be a 7500-kVA distribution transformer supplying a 12.47-kV bus from the 138-kV subtransmission system. If a fault develops on the 12.47-kV bus, fault current will flow through the transformer from the 138-kV system. Thus, while there is no internal transformer fault, the transformer does carry fault current. The maximum fault current that can possibly flow is equal to the system prefault voltage divided by the transformer impedance.

As in the case of distribution lines, it is necessary to consider the short-circuit withstand capability of the transformer. The withstand capability of transformers is specified according to the kVA rating of the transformer. ANSI C37.91-1985 lists four categories of transformer ratings:

Category	*Single-Phase kVA*	*Three-Phase kVA*
I	5–500	15–500
II	501–1667	501–5000
III	1668–10,000	5001–30,000
IV	>10,000	>30,000

Time–current withstand curves are given for each category. Representive withstand curves are shown in Fig. 12-14 for the various transformer categories. The withstand curves indicate the ability of the transformer windings to withstand short-circuit currents for varying intervals of time after inception of the fault. For the primary overcurrent device to protect the transformer, its time–current characteristic curve must lie below and to the left of the transformer withstand curve.

Generally, the rating of fuses or setting of overcurrent relay protecting the transformer primary is approximately 150% to 200% of the full-load line current rating of the primary of the transformer. This range of percentages allows the overcurrent device to carry inrush currents due to magnetizing inrush and load pickup after an outage occurs. To account for the heating effects of inrush currents, a value of 12 to 15 times the transformer full-load current rating for 0.1 sec is typically assumed. This point is plotted on the transformer withstand curve. The primary overcurrent device characteristic must lie above the inrush point so that nuisance fuse blowing or relay operation will not occur during normal energization of the transformer.

With the primary overcurrent protection device (OCPD) sized at 150% to 200% of the full-load primary current rating of the transformer, overload protection is not provided by the primary overcurrent device. Therefore, the primary overcurrent device will provide protection against short circuits only. Overload protection is typically provided by the overcurrent device on the transformer secondary. The rating or setting of the overcurrent device on the transformer secondary is typically in the range of 125% to 250% of the full-load current rating of the secondary.

In reference to Fig. 12-14, note that the abscissa is specified in terms of multiples of the transformer normal base current. When applying protection to the primary side of the transformer, the OCPD characteristic must be expressed as a multiple of the primary current rating of the transformer. Likewise, if the OCPD device is applied to the secondary side of the transformer, the characteristic of the OCPD device must be expressed as a multiple of the secondary current rating of the transformer. Typically, overcurrent protection is located in series with the line terminations of the transformer. As such, the OCPD devices carry the line current of the transformer primary or secondary. In the discussion that follows, the transformers will be assumed to be connected for step-down

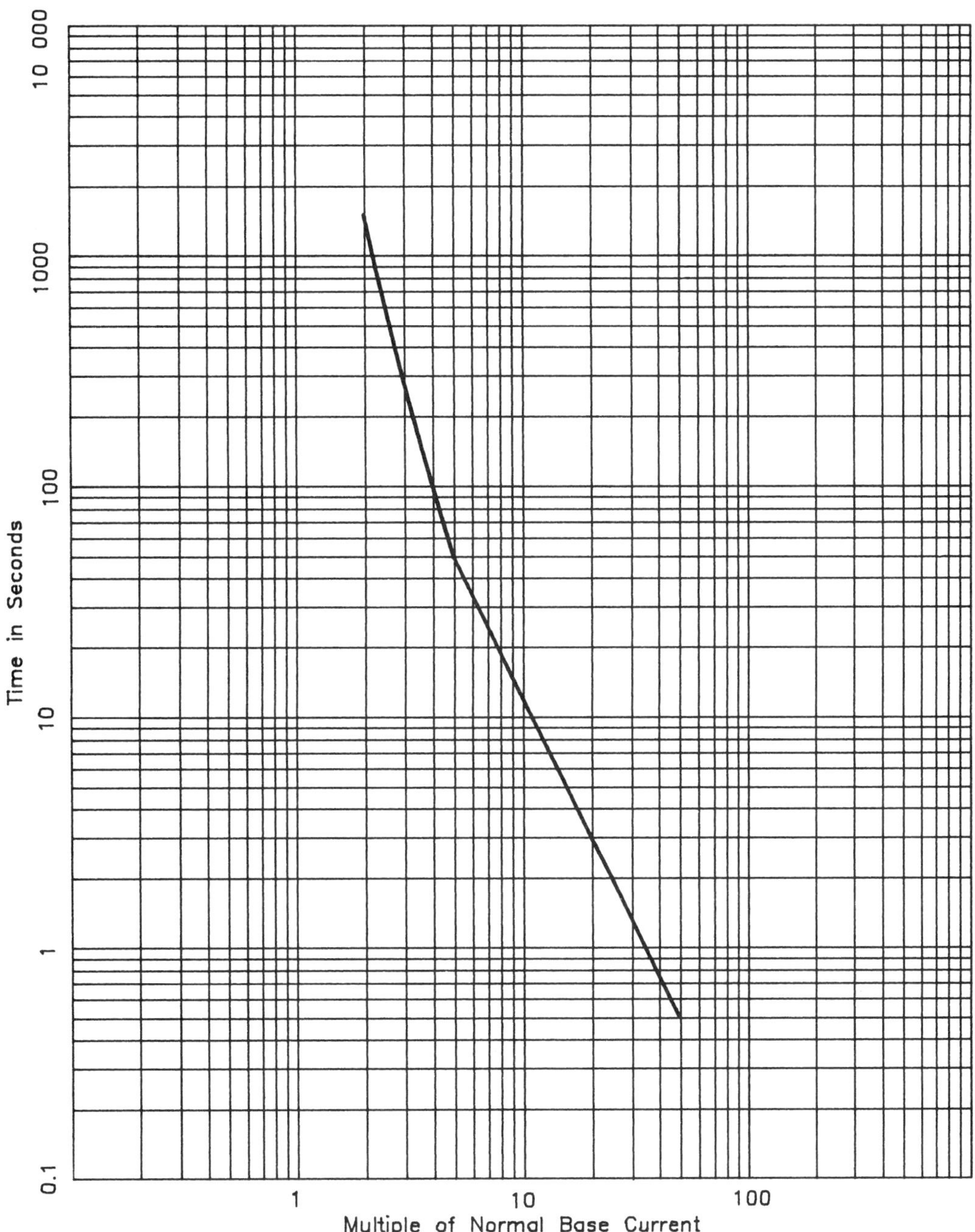

Figure 12-14 (a) Category I transformer withstand curve. (Derived from IEEE C37.91-1985, *IEEE Guide for Protective Relay Applications to Power Transformers,* Reaff, 1991; © 1985)

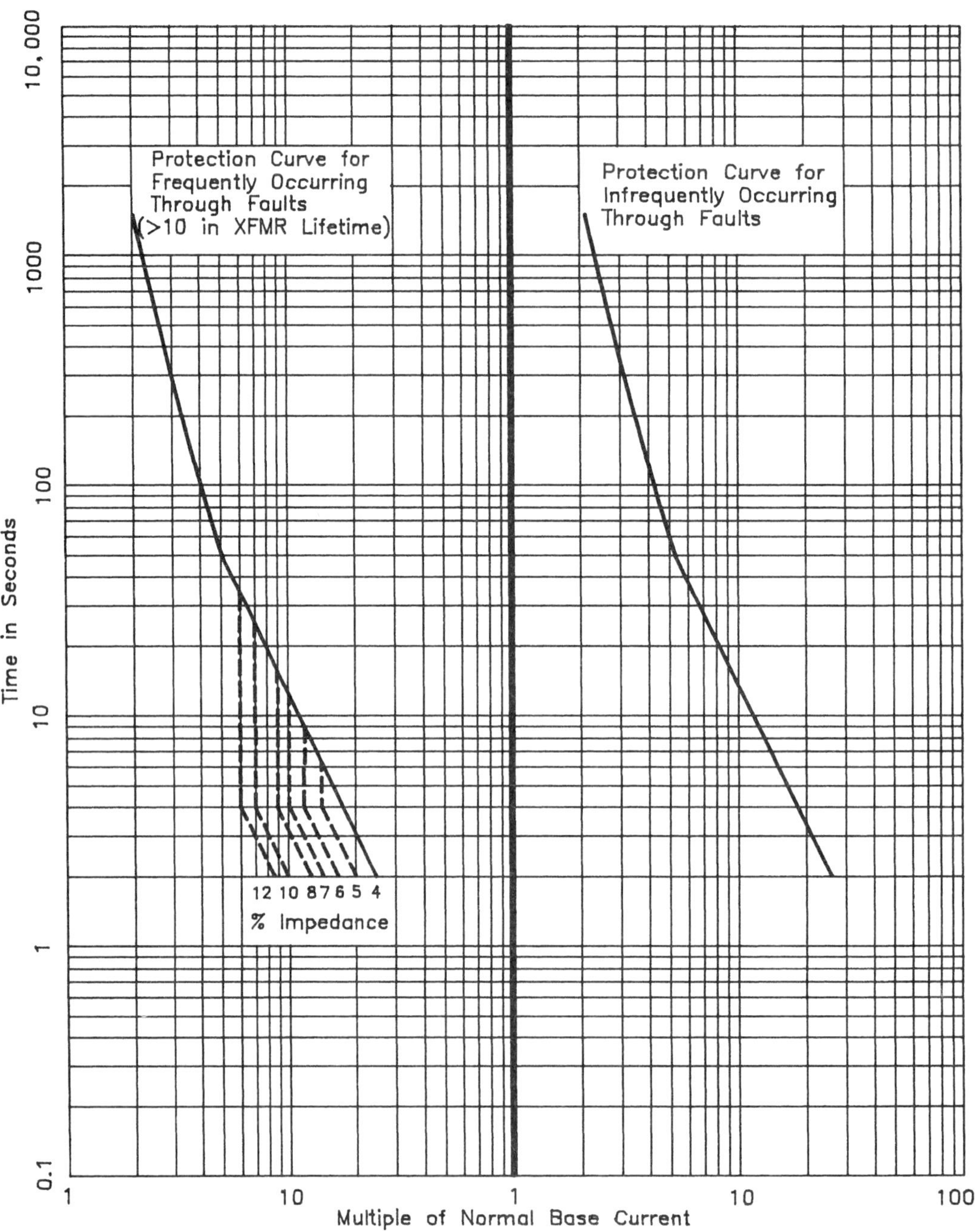

Figure 12-14 (b) Category II transformer withstand curves. (Derived from IEEE C37.91-1985, *IEEE Guide for Protective Relay Applications to Power Transformers,* Reaff 1991; © 1985)

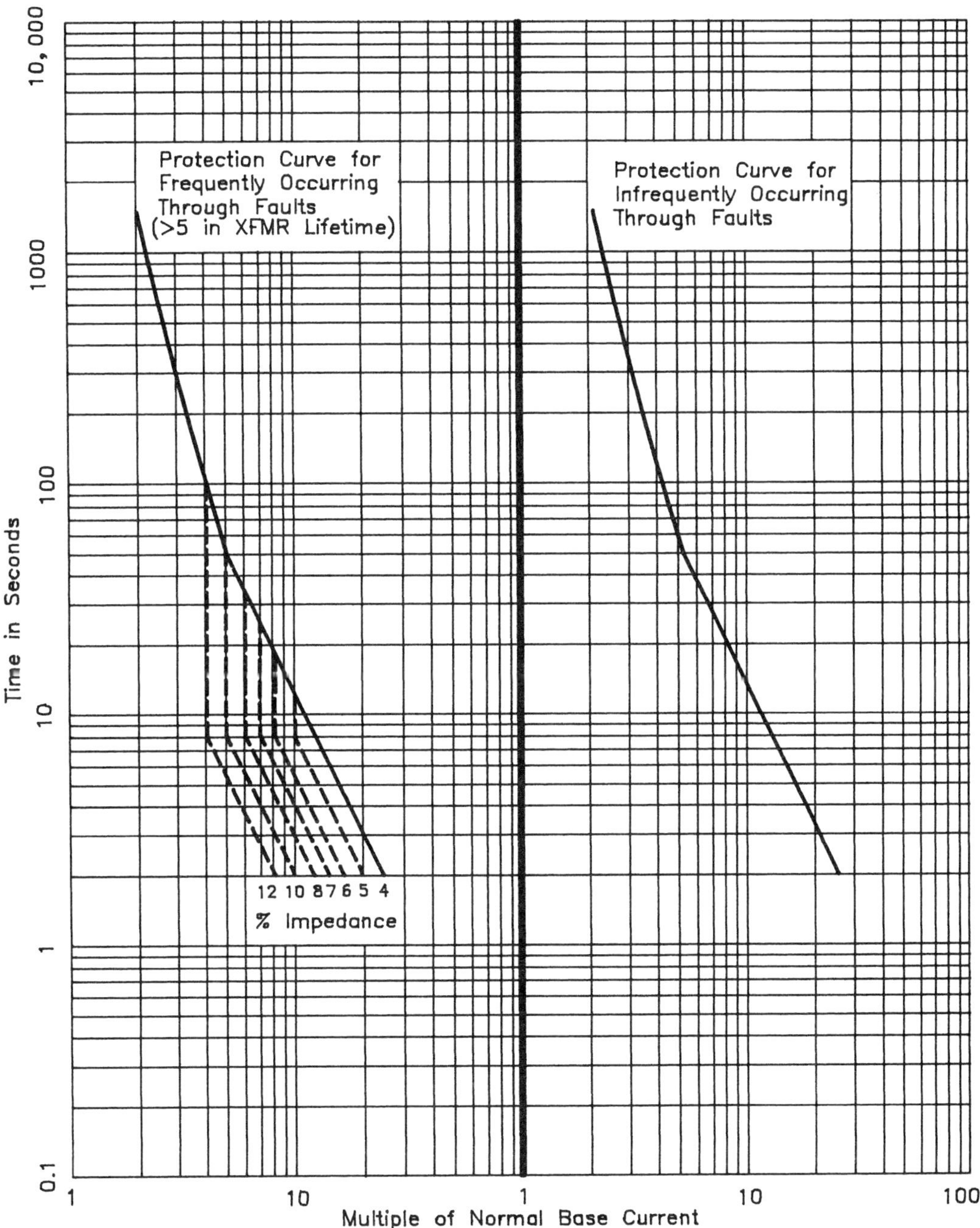

Figure 12-14 (c) Category III transformer withstand curves. (Derived from IEEE C37.91-1985, *IEEE Guide for Protective Relay Applications to Power Transformers,* Reaff 1991; © 1985)

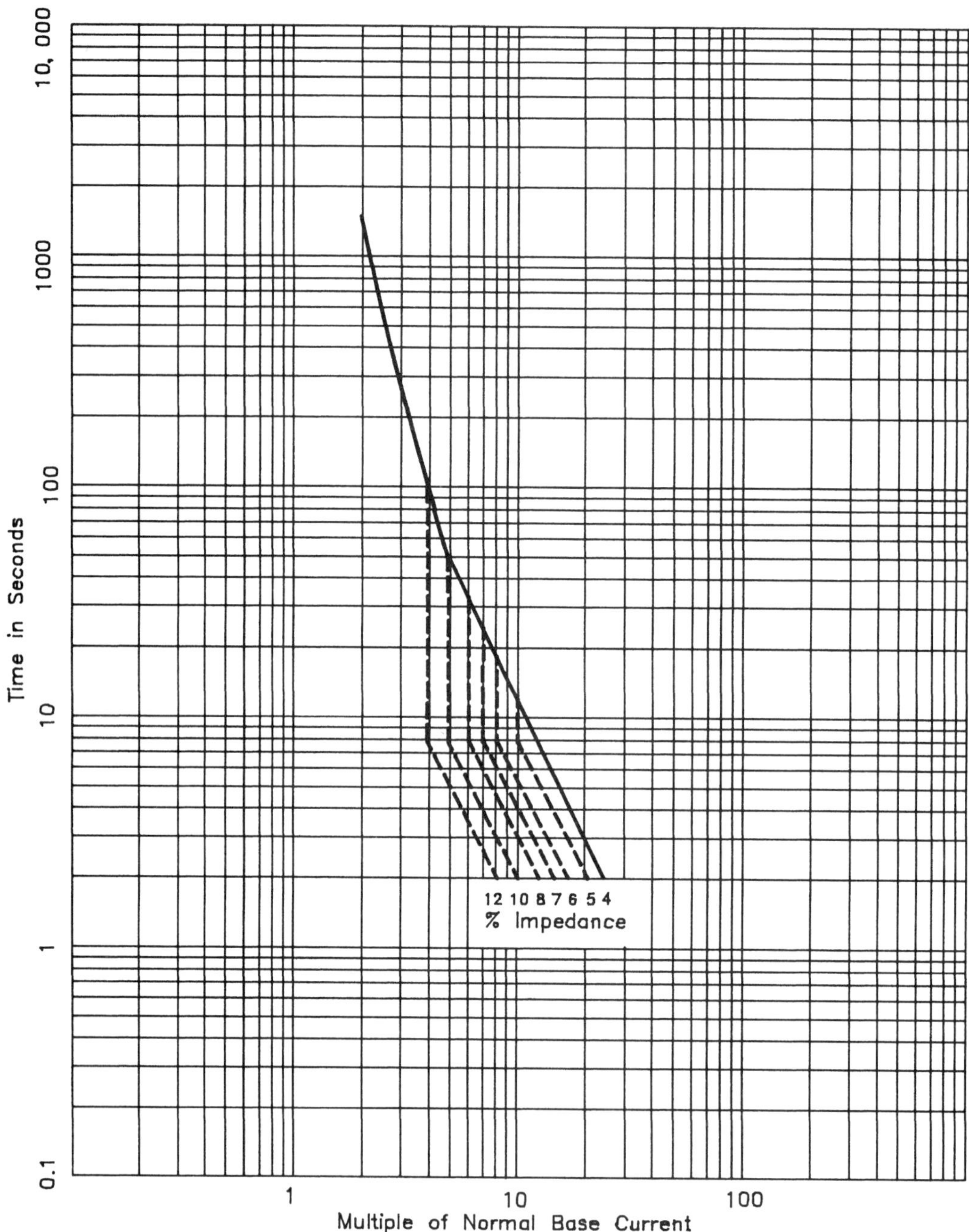

Figure 12-14 (d) Category IV transformer withstand curves. (Derived from IEEE C37.91-1985, *IEEE Guide for Protective Relay Applications to Power Transformers,* Reaff 1991; © 1985)

operation on a radial system, with transformer overcurrent protection provided on the high-voltage side.

As an initial starting point in the selection of fuse rating, a fuse rating equal to at least 150% of the transformer rated full-load primary current is selected. Since the transformer withstand curves are plotted as a multiple of the transformer rated current, the fuse characteristic must also be expressed as a multiple of the transformer rated current. This is accomplished by dividing each current on the fuse time–current characteristic curve by the transformer rated high–side current. The fuse characteristic is then plotted on the same graph as the transformer withstand curve. The resulting graph is then inspected to determine if the protection criteria have been met. If the protection criteria have not been met, then it may be necessary to select the next higher or lower rated device. This process is repeated until the proper fuse size is selected.

Single-Phase Transformers

For single-phase transformers, the withstand curves shown in Fig. 12-14 can be used directly without modification. The fuse characteristic is plotted on the withstand curve to ensure that the fuse characteristic lies below and to the left of the withstand curve and above the inrush point. The inrush point is generally assumed to be 12 times rated current for 0.1 sec.

Grounded Wye–Grounded Wye Connection

The schematic diagrams for the grounded wye–grounded wye connection are shown in Fig. 12-15. Since the transformer withstand curves apply to the transformer windings, it is necessary to determine the relationship between the transformer winding currents and line currents for all possible fault conditions on the transformer secondary.

Figure 12-15a shows the conditions for a three-phase fault on the transformer secondary. Since the three-phase fault represents a balanced fault condition, the transformer winding and line currents are equal. The transformer line and phase currents for phase to phase and phase to ground faults are shown in Fig. 12-15b and c, respectively.

Note that for all fault conditions on the secondary the transformer winding currents are equal to the line currents. Therefore, it is not necessary to adjust or modify the withstand characteristic for a grounded wye–grounded wye connected transformer. The withstand curve can be used directly without modification.

Delta–Delta Connection

The schematic diagrams for the delta–delta connection are shown in Fig. 12-16. As a result of the delta connection, the magnitude of the transformer winding currents is in general different than the magnitude of the line currents. The relationship between the transformer winding currents and line currents depends on the type of fault.

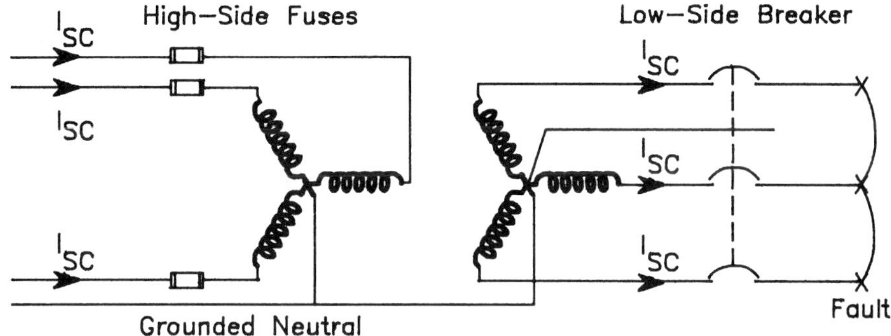

(a) Three–Phase Fault.

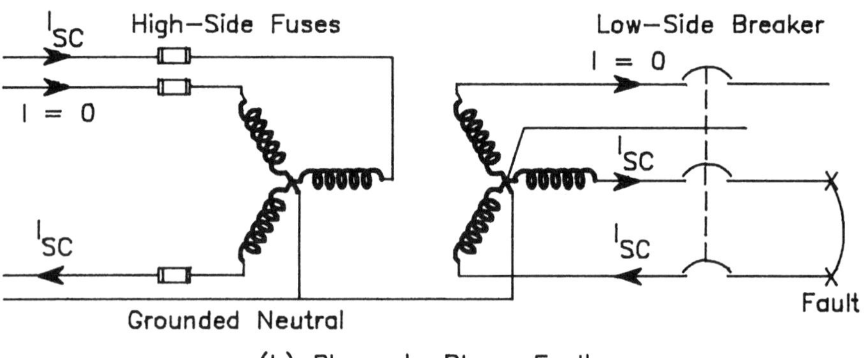

(b) Phase to Phase Fault.

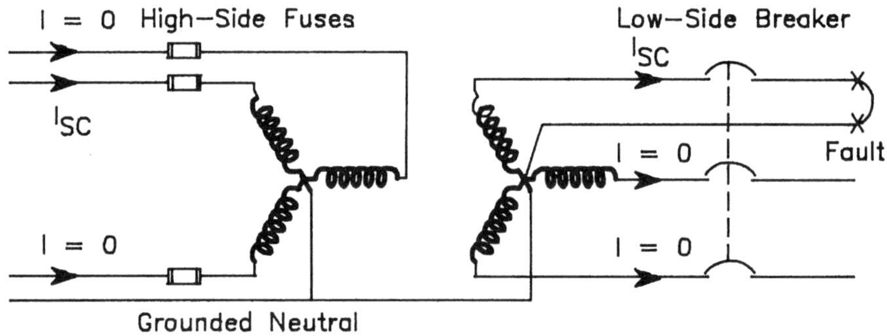

(c) Phase to Ground Fault.

Figure 12-15 Protection of grounded wye–grounded wye transformer.

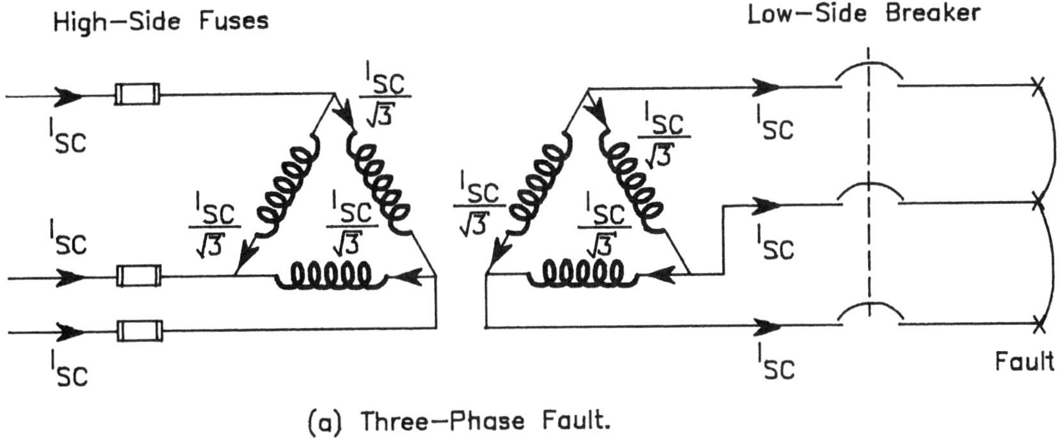

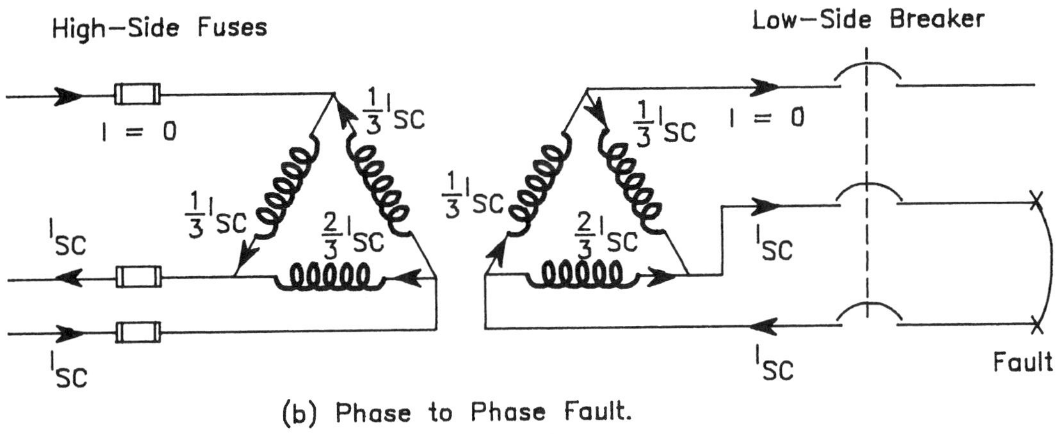

Figure 12-16 Protection of delta–delta transformer.

For the three-phase fault conditions shown in Fig. 12-16a, the magnitude of the transformer winding currents is equal to the magnitude of the line current divided by $\sqrt{3}$. This is the same as the relation between line and phase currents for a balanced three-phase system. Therefore, the transformer withstand curve can be used directly, as in the case of the single-phase and grounded wye–grounded wye connections previously discussed.

The conditions for a phase to phase secondary fault are shown in Fig. 12-16b. This type of fault represents a single-phase condition on the transformer secondary. Since the impedance of each transformer winding is equal, the current in each winding will divide according to the current-divider rule. The fault current flowing through the faulted winding is equal to two-thirds times the short-circuit current. Likewise, the fault current flowing through the other two windings is equal to one-third times the short-circuit current. These secondary currents are reflected to the primary by means of the transformer turns ratio.

The ratio of winding current for the phase to phase fault to winding current for the three-phase fault is

$$\text{Ratio} = \frac{(2/3)I_{SC}}{(1/\sqrt{3})I_{SC}} = \frac{0.6667}{0.5774} = 1.1547$$

The correction factor to be applied to the transformer withstand curve is obtained by dividing the magnitude of the highest line current by the ratio just defined. The result is

$$\text{Correction factor} = \frac{1.0}{1.1547} = 0.866$$

The transformer withstand curve is modified by multiplying each value of current on the curve by the correction factor given previously. The fuse characteristic should lie below and to the left of the modified withstand curve for all probable values of short-circuit current. Note that by multiplying each current on the withstand curve by 0.866 the curve will shift to the left. The result may be a lower-rated fuse for a delta–delta connected transformer as compared to a grounded wye–grounded wye connected transformer of the same ratings.

Delta–Grounded Wye Connection

The schematic diagrams for the delta–grounded wye connection are shown in Fig. 12-17 for the three-phase, phase to phase, and phase to ground fault conditions. As in the case of the delta–delta connection, the relation between the transformer winding currents and line currents must be determined.

Figure 12-17a shows conditions for a three-phase fault. The magnitude of the transformer winding currents on the high-side delta are equal to the magnitude of the line currents divided by $\sqrt{3}$. On the low-voltage side, the transformer winding currents are equal to the line currents. Again, since the three-phase fault represents a balanced fault condition, the transformer withstand curve does not need to be adjusted for the three-phase fault condition.

For the phase to phase secondary fault, the circuit shown in Fig. 12-17b applies. The transformer winding currents on the low-voltage side are equal to the short-circuit current. On the high-voltage side, current will flow in only two of the three transformer windings due to the nature of the fault. The high-side line currents in two of the phases are equal to the transformer winding currents, as shown. However, the line current in the other phase is equal to two times the current in the transformer windings.

The ratio of winding current for the phase to phase fault to winding current for the three-phase fault is

$$\text{Ratio} = \frac{I_{SC}}{(1/\sqrt{3})I_{SC}} = \sqrt{3}$$

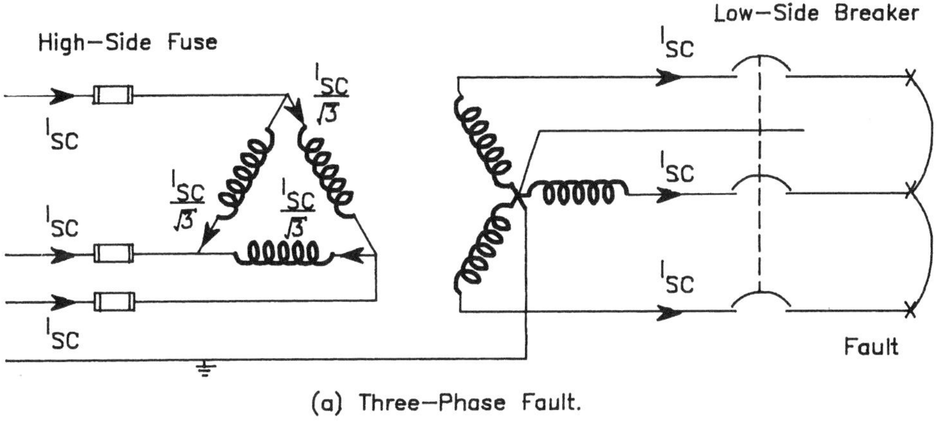

(a) Three–Phase Fault.

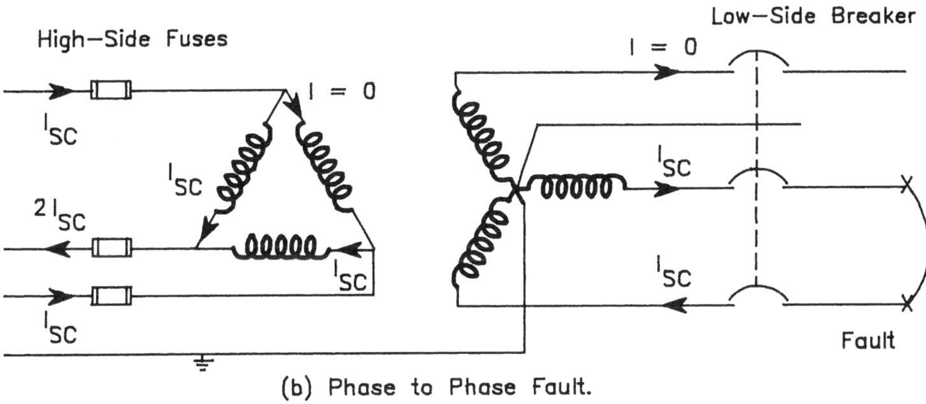

(b) Phase to Phase Fault.

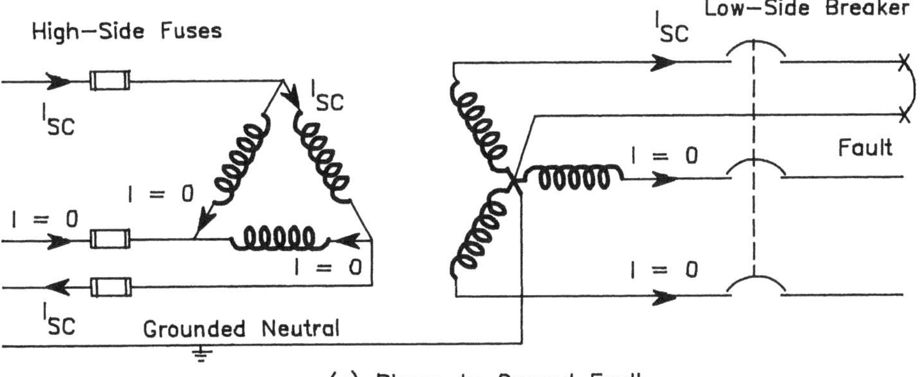

(c) Phase to Ground Fault.

Figure 12-17 Protection of delta–grounded wye transformer.

The correction factor to be applied to the transformer withstand curve is obtained by dividing the magnitude of the highest line current by the ratio just defined. The result is

$$\text{Correction factor} = \frac{2}{\sqrt{3}} = 1.1547$$

The transformer withstand curve is modified by multiplying each point on the curve by 1.1547 for the phase to phase fault. This will result in the transformer withstand curve shifting toward the right.

Conditions for the phase to ground fault are shown in Fig. 12-17c. On both the high- and low-voltage sides, only one transformer winding carries fault current, with the other two windings carrying no fault current. However, due to the delta connection on the high-voltage side, fault current equal to the transformer winding current will flow in two of the lines.

The ratio of winding current for the phase to ground fault to winding current for the three-phase fault is

$$\text{Ratio} = \frac{I_{SC}}{(1/\sqrt{3})I_{SC}} = \sqrt{3}$$

The correction factor to be applied to the transformer withstand curve is obtained by dividing the magnitude of the highest line current by the ratio just defined. The result is

$$\text{Correction factor} = \frac{1}{\sqrt{3}} = 0.5774$$

The transformer withstand curve is modified by multiplying each point on the curve by 0.5774 for the phase to phase fault. This will result in the transformer withstand curve shifting toward the left.

The worst-case condition for the delta–grounded wye connected transformer is for a phase to ground fault on the secondary. This will result in the withstand curve being shifted to the left, typically resulting in a smaller fuse size than for a grounded wye–grounded wye or delta–delta connected transformer having the same ratings.

EXAMPLE 12-7

Determine a suitable E-rated fuse size to protect a 5000-kVA, 69-kV–12.47Y/7.2-kV, delta–grounded wye connected, 7% impedance, distribution substation transformer. Assume that faults will occur infrequently in the transformer lifetime.

Solution As an initial selection, a fuse size equal to 150% of the transformer full-load rated current will be used. The full-load current rating of the transformer is

$$I_{\text{rated}} = \frac{5000 \text{ kVA}}{\sqrt{3} \cdot 69 \text{ kV}} = 41.84 \text{ A}$$

The fuse rating is selected as

$$I_{\text{fuse}} = 150\% \cdot 41.84 \text{ A} = 62.75 \text{ A}$$

Therefore, a 65E fuse is selected.

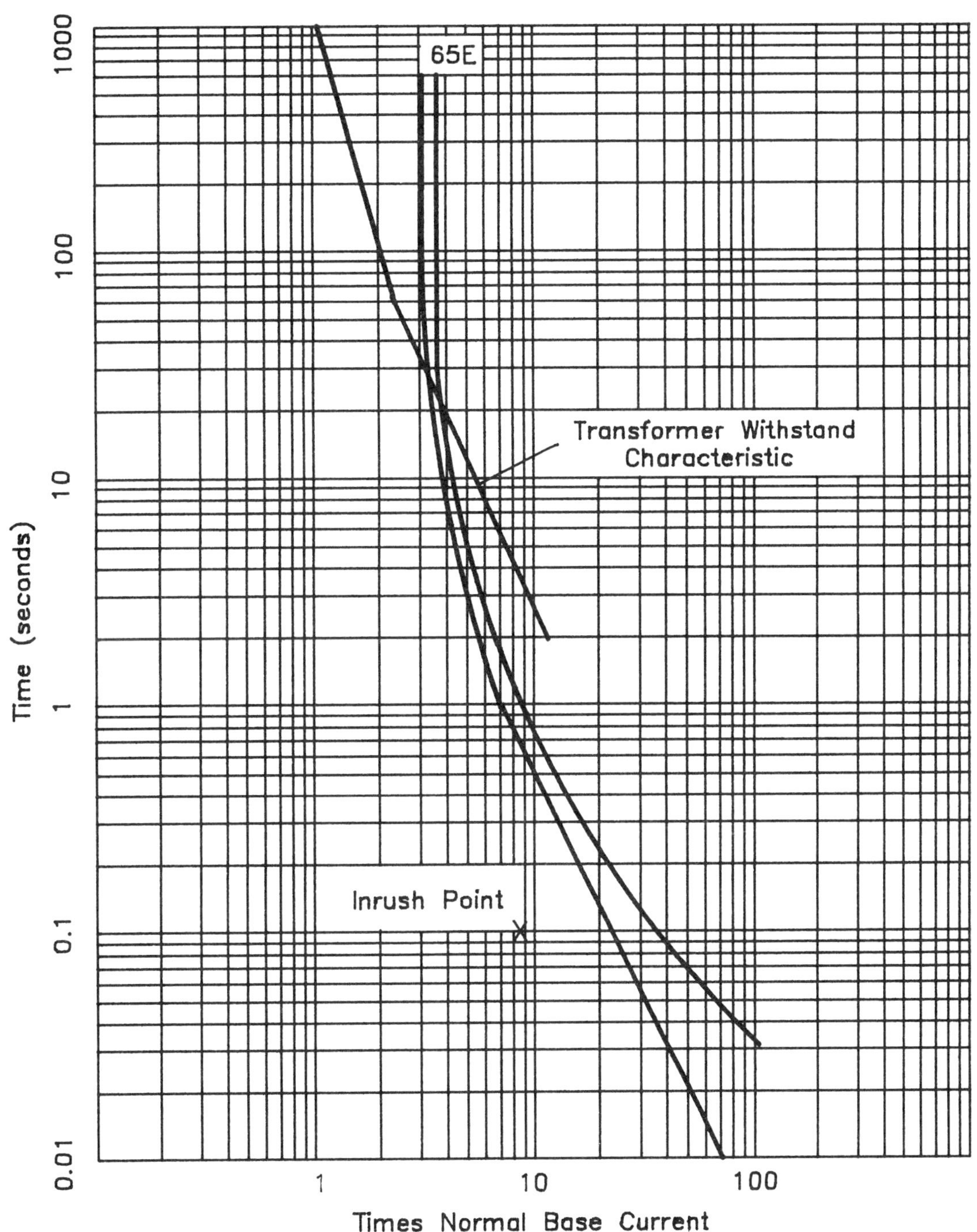

Figure 12-18 Example 12-7.

Since this is a delta–grounded wye connection, the transformer withstand curve must be adjusted to account for worst-case conditions. Recall that worst-case conditions are for a phase to ground fault on the secondary, resulting in a correction factor of 0.5774 to be applied to values of current on the withstand curve.

To plot the fuse and transformer withstand characteristics on the same graph, each current value of the fuse characteristic must be expressed as a multiple of the transformer normal base current. For example, at 0.1 sec, the minimum melting current of the 65E fuse is 1000 A. This value of current corresponds to 1000/41.84 or 23.9 times the normal base current of the transformer.

The adjusted transformer withstand curve, inrush point, and 65E fuse characteristic are plotted in Fig. 12-18. Note that the fuse characteristic lies between the inrush point and the adjusted withstand curve for currents greater than approximately 3.5 times rated. Therefore, a 65E rated fuse is satisfactory in this case.

12-9 Protection of Capacitors

The objective of capacitor protection is to prevent damage to the individual capacitor units in a bank and to prevent damage to adjacent units. Typically, individual capacitor units are protected with either expulsion or current-limiting fuses. To provide proper protection, the time–current characteristic of the protecting fuse must lie below and to the left of the capacitor tank rupture characteristic curve. The capacitor tank rupture characteristic is a plot of the time versus current required to cause tank rupture. A representive tank rupture time–current characteristic curve is shown in Fig. 12-19.

As required by standards, capacitors are required to operate continuously at currents of up to 135% of rated, when rated voltage is applied. Therefore, fuse sizes should be sized with a continuous current-carrying capability equal to approximately 135% of capacitor rated full-load current. (Note that the continuous current-carrying capabiltity of a fuse link differs from the current rating of the fuse.) Larger percentages may be required to prevent nuisance fuse blowing during capacitor energization and switching. Typically, individual capacitor fuses are sized at anywhere between 135% and 165% of the capacitor rated current.

EXAMPLE 12-8

Determine a suitable T link fuse rating required to protect a 900-kVAR, 12.47-kV, grounded-wye connected capacitor bank comprised of three 100-kVAR, 7.2-kV, capacitor units per phase.

Solution As an initial selection, a fuse with a continuous current-carrying capability equal to 135% of the full-load current rating of the capacitor bank is selected. The full-load current rating of the bank is

$$I_{\text{rated}} = \frac{900 \text{ kVAR}}{\sqrt{3} \cdot 12.47 \text{ kV}} = 41.67 \text{ A}$$

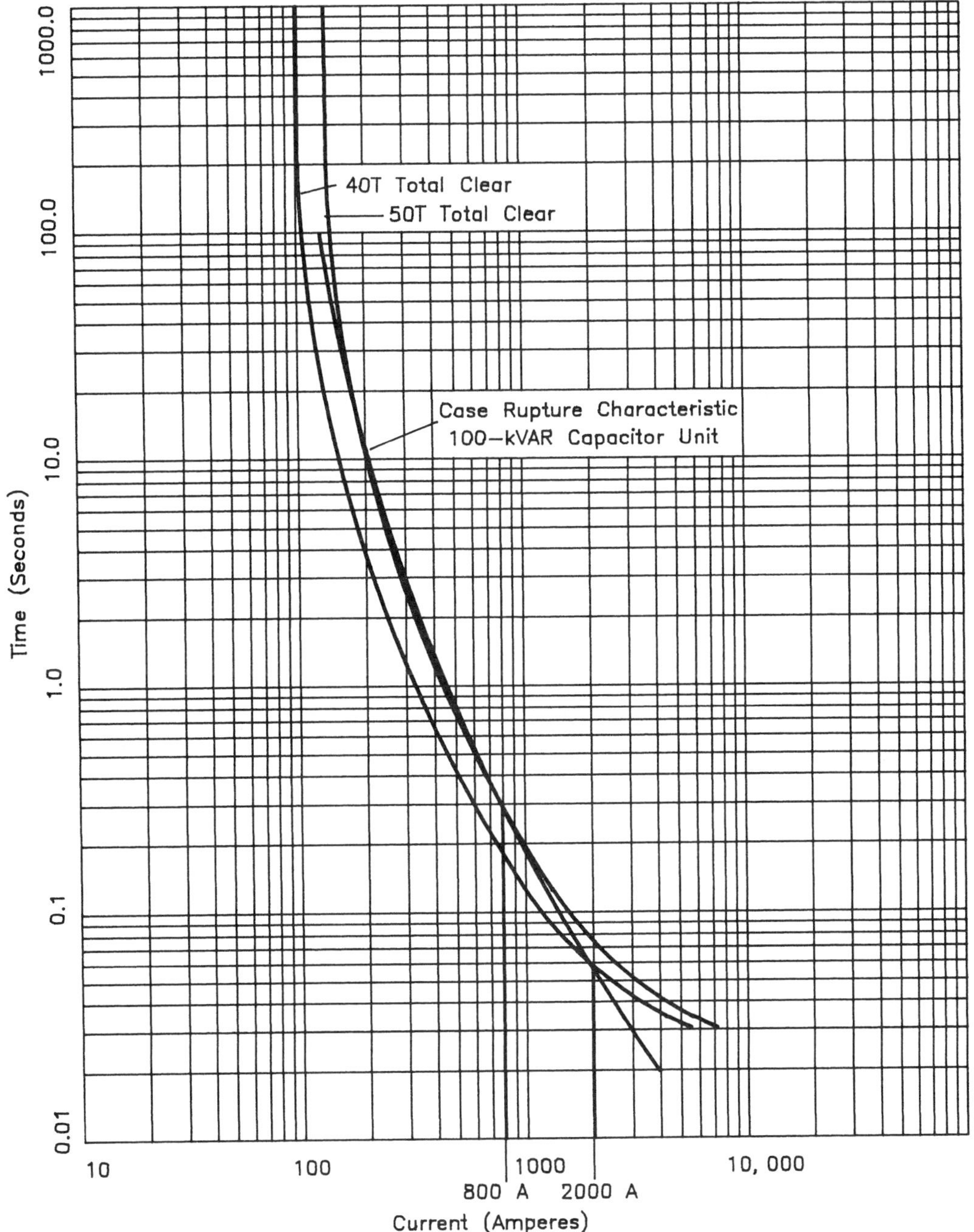

Figure 12-19 Capacitor protection.

The fuse is selected as

$$I_{fuse} = 135\% \cdot 41.67 = 56.3 \text{ A}$$

Therefore, a 40T link fuse with a continuous current-carrying capability of 80 A is selected. The next lower standard-sized fuse link is a 25T, with a continuous current-carrying capability of 50 A, which is too small for this application.

The 40T total clearing time–current characteristic is plotted on the same graph as the tank rupture characteristic in Fig. 12-19. Note that the maximum fault current for proper protection is approximately 2000 A. This level of fault current occurs at the intersection of the tank rupture curve and the fuse total clearing curve. The total clearing time–current characteristic of a 50T fuse is also plotted for comparison.

12-10 Overcurrent Device Coordination

The purpose of overcurrent device coordination is to ensure that the device nearest to the fault operates to permanently isolate only the faulted section of line or equipment. This section deals with coordination of overcurrent devices applied on radial distribution feeders.

Fuse–Fuse Coordination

Coordination exists for two fuses installed in series if the fuse closest to the fault clears for permanent faults. The fuse that is closest to the fault on the source side is referred to as the *protecting* fuse. The next upstream fuse located on the source side of the protecting fuse is referred to as the *protected* fuse. To determine whether coordination exists, the minimum melt and total clearing curves for both the protecting and protected fuse are plotted. In addition, the protected fuse minimum melt characteristic is replotted at 75% of the minimum melting time to allow for preload currents and high ambient temperatures. These characteristics are shown in Fig. 12-20.

In reference to Fig. 12-20, the current where 75% of the minimum melt time of the protected fuse intersects the total clearing curve of the protecting fuse is designated I_{max}. Coordination exists for currents up to the level of I_{max}. If the actual fault current magnitude on the load side of the protecting fuse exceeds I_{max}, both fuses will blow.

If the fault current magnitudes are high, it may be desirable to install current-limiting fuses. Coordination between two current-limiting fuses in series is achieved if the total clearing I^2t of the protecting fuse is greater than the minimum melt I^2t of the protected fuse. This generally applies for high current levels when the fuses are operating in the current-limiting mode. For operation outside the current-limiting region, the coordination is determined by plotting the time–current characteristics as before.

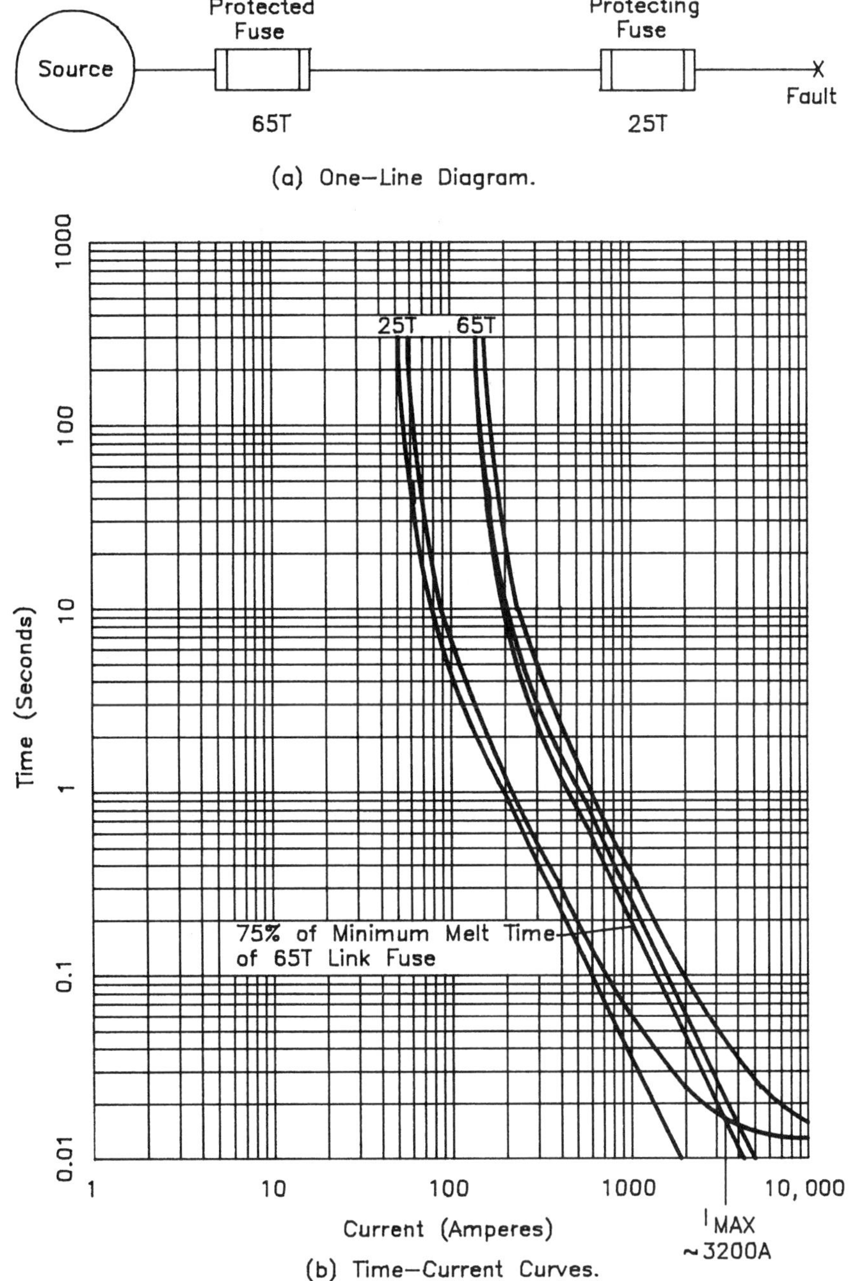

Figure 12-20 Fuse–fuse coordination.

EXAMPLE 12-9

Determine the maximum fault current for coordination between a 25T and a 65T link fuse.

Solution The time–current characteristics of the two fuses are plotted on the same graph as shown in Fig. 12-20. In addition, the TCC of the 65T link fuse has been adjusted by 75% of the time values to allow for preload and ambient temperature. The intersection of the total clearing time of the 25T link fuse and 75% of the minimum melt time of the 65T link fuse occurs at approximately 3200 A, as shown in Fig. 12-20.

Recloser–Recloser Coordination

The time–current characteristics of two reclosers in series is shown in Fig. 12-21. Since reclosers operate on two curves, it is difficult to obtain coordination. However, for the conditions shown in Fig. 12-21, recloser B will lockout for permanent faults at point F. For levels of fault current greater than the pickup value of recloser A, the following sequence of tripping will occur for a *permanent* fault at F.

1. Recloser B trips on its instantaneous curve.
2. Recloser B recloses.
3. Recloser B trips again on its instantaneous curve.
4. Recloser B recloses.
5. Recloser A trips on its instantaneous curve.
6. Recloser A recloses.
7. Recloser A trips again on its instantaneous curve.
8. Recloser A recloses.
9. Recloser B trips on its time delay curve.
10. Recloser B recloses.
11. Recloser B trips and locks out, isolating the fault.

From the preceding scenario, it can be seen that an excessive number of tripping and reclosing operations takes place. This can be avoided by placing recloser B at a point in the circuit where the fault current is slightly *greater* than the minimum pickup of recloser A. By so doing, recloser A will not trip at all for most faults located beyond recloser B.

Fuse–Recloser Coordination

The coordination of a fuse with a recloser is shown in Fig. 12-22. The basic protection philosophy for temporary faults on the load side of the fuse is to have the recloser trip on its instantaneous curve *before* the fuse blows. By temporarily de-energizing the circuit, the fault will be cleared. The recloser then recloses to restore the system. In the event of a permanent fault on the load side of the fuse, the fuse should clear before the recloser

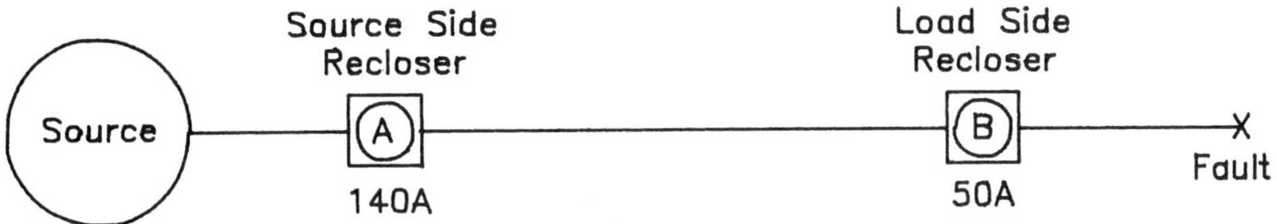

(a) One–Line Diagram.

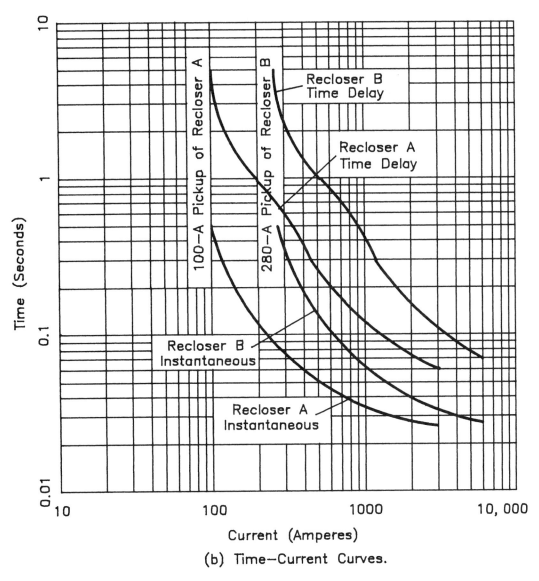

(b) Time–Current Curves.

Figure 12-21 Recloser–recloser coordination.

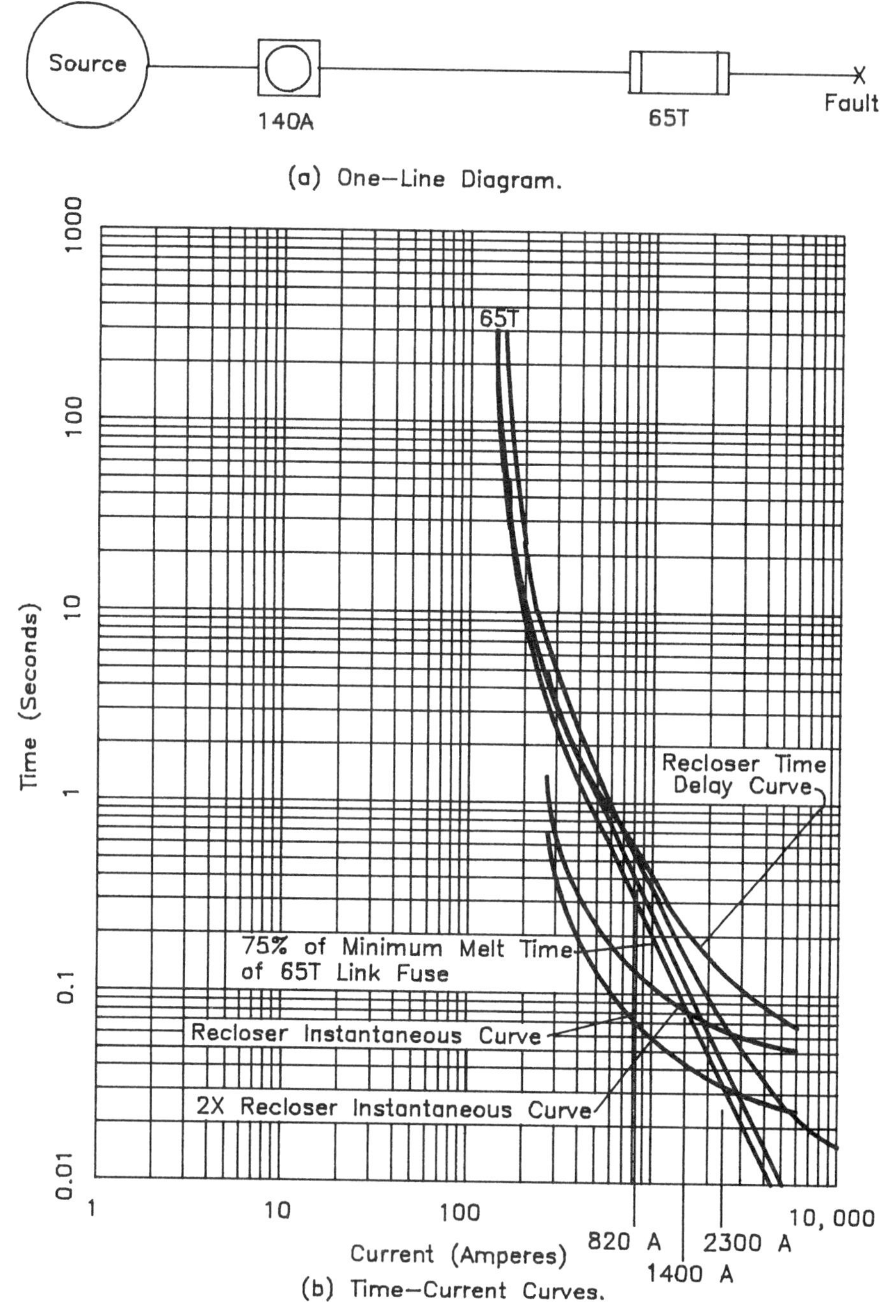

Figure 12-22 Fuse–recloser coordination.

trips on its time delay curve. To accomplish this, the fuse characteristic should lie between the recloser instantaneous and time delay curves.

Several adjustments to the fuse and recloser curves are made to account for preloading and heating of the fuse element. First, it is customary to plot 75% of the minimum melt characteristic of the fuse. Second, if the recloser is set for two trips on its instantaneous curve, two times the instantaneous curve is plotted. If the recloser is set to trip once on its instantaneous curve, then no adjustment is necessary. The maximum current for coordination occurs where the 75% minimum melt curve of the fuse intersects either the instantaneous or two times the instantaneous curve of the recloser. The minimum current for coordination occurs at the intersection of the fuse total clearing and recloser time delay curves. If the fuse total clear and recloser time delay curve do not intersect, then the minimum fault current for coordination is equal to the pickup current of the recloser.

EXAMPLE 12-10

Determine the range of current for which coordination between a 140 A type L recloser and a 65T link fuse will be attained. Assume that the recloser is set for two instantaneous and two time delay operations.

Solution The TCCs of the fuse and recloser are plotted in Fig. 12-22. In addition, 75% of the fuse minimum melt time and two times the recloser instantaneous trip curve are plotted.

The minimum current for coordination occurs at the intersection of the fuse total clear and the recloser time delay curves. This minimum current is read as approximately 820 A. The maximum current for coordination occurs where two times the recloser instantaneous curve intersects 75% of the fuse minimum melt curve. This maximum current is read as approximately 1400 A.

If the recloser had been set for one instantaneous operation and three time delay operations, the maximum current for coordination would have been at the point where the recloser instantaneous curve intersects 75% of the fuse minimum melt characteristic. In this instance, the maximum current for coordination would be read as approximately 2300 A.

Reflecting OCPD Characteristics: Single-Phase Transformers

When overcurrent coordinating protection devices are on opposite sides of a transformer, it is necessary to reflect all overcurrent protection device characteristics to a common voltage. Often, the characteristics of the devices on the low-voltage side are reflected to the high-voltage side to determine if coordination exists. Reflecting of device characteristics is accomplished by dividing each current of the low-side device characteristic by the transformer turns ratio. The following results:

$$I'_{\text{HS}} = I_{\text{LS}} \cdot \left[\frac{\text{transformer rated LS voltage}}{\text{transformer rated HS voltage}}\right] \tag{12.2}$$

where

I'_{HS} = low-side current reflected to high side

I_{LS} = actual low-side current

Equation (12.2) is applied to several points on the low-side device characteristic in order to reflect the characteristic to the high side. The characteristic curves for the high-side device are then plotted directly without modification.

For selective coordination, the high-side device characteristic should lie between the reflected low-side device characteristic and the transformer withstand curve. Backup protection should be provided by the high-side device in the event that the low-side device fails to clear the fault.

If the reflected low-side device characteristic is found to lie above and to the right of the high-side device characteristic, then the high-side device will operate before the low-side device. The result is operation of the high-side device for virtually all low-side faults on the load side of the low-side protective device. Obviously, this example of miscoordination is unacceptable.

Likewise, if either the reflected low-side device characteristic or high-side device characteristic is found to lie above and to the right of the transformer withstand curve, the transformer will not be protected against through faults. Under these circumstances, the transformer will be severely damaged for all faults on the low side. Obviously, this is unacceptable.

Consider the single-phase transformer shown in Fig. 12-23a. The transformer is rated 50 kVA, 7200–120/240 V. The high-voltage side is protected by a 10T link fuse, and the low-voltage side is connected to a low-voltage bus through a 250-A secondary main breaker. In addition, three 100-A feeder breakers are connected to the bus. If a fault occurs on the load side of one of the feeder breakers, only the feeder breaker should trip. The primary high-side fuse, or secondary main breaker, should not operate for any feeder faults. However, the secondary main breaker or transformer high-side fuse should provide backup protection in the event the feeder breaker fails. To selectively coordinate, the time–current characteristic of the feeder breakers must lie below and to the left of the high-side fuse characteristic.

Selective coordination between secondary main overcurrent devices and high-side devices may be difficult to obtain. For example, if a fault occurs on the secondary bus, the secondary main breaker will trip before the primary fuse operates. Tripping of the secondary main breaker results in the de-energization of the entire low-voltage bus. Likewise, if the transformer high-side fuse blows, the transformer will be de-energized, resulting in the de-energization of the entire low-voltage bus as well. Thus, the consequences of either the high-side device or low-side main device operating in the event of a fault are the same. The important point to remember is that coordination must be obtained between the highest ampere rated secondary feeder overcurrent protection device and the high-side primary overcurrent protection device.

Figure 12-23b shows the transformer withstand, 10T minimum melt, and reflected low-voltage breaker trip curves plotted on the same log–log scale. Note that selective coordination is achieved between the low-voltage feeder breakers and the high-side fuse.

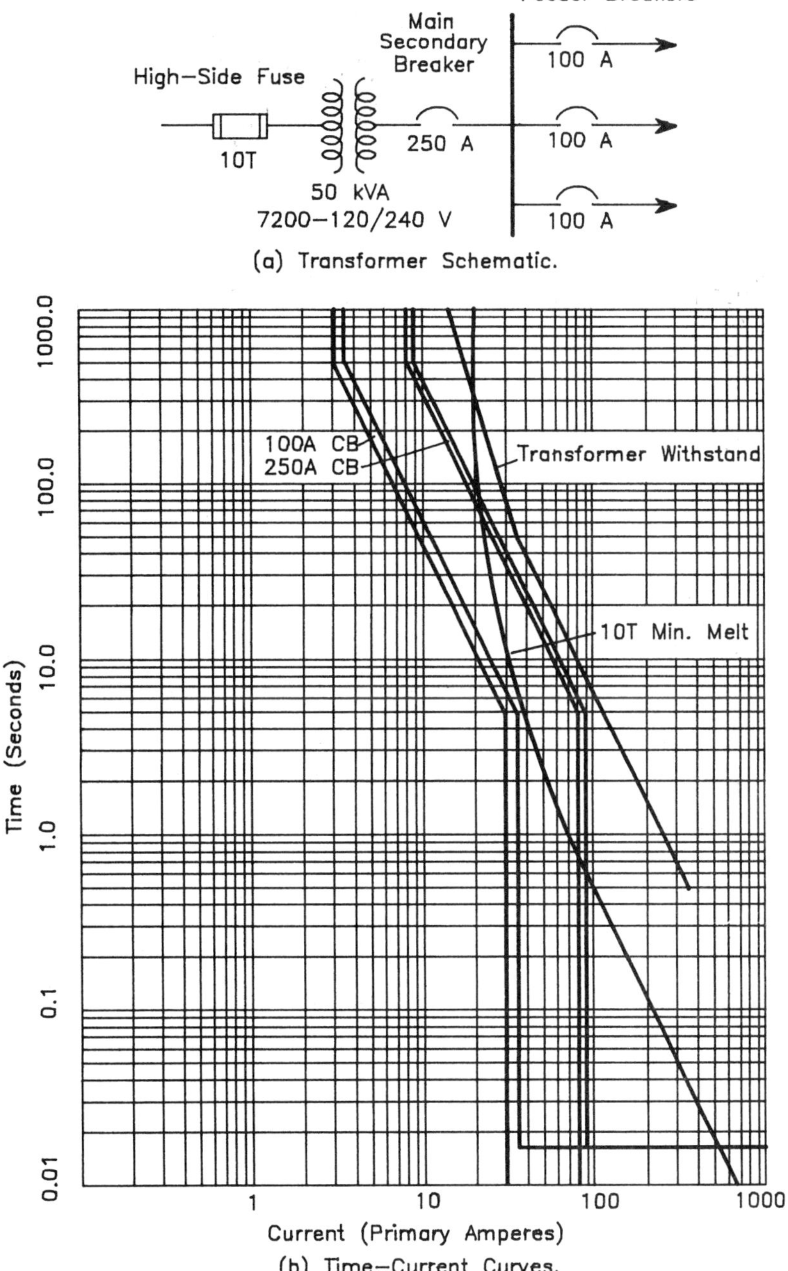

Figure 12-23 Reflecting OCPD characteristics, single-phase transformers.

However, note that the feeder breaker and high-side fuse curves almost overlap each other for fault current between 25 and 35 A reflected to the high side. For this reason, it may be advisable to use a 12T or 15T fuse link to protect the high-voltage side of the transformer. When increasing the primary fuse size, it must be remembered that the fuse curve must lie below and to the left of the transformer withstand curve. Also, increasing the transformer primary fuse size will reduce the protection margin that the fuse provides.

As Fig. 12-23b shows, selective coordination is not achieved between the secondary main breaker and the high-side fuse for faults between 20 and 90 A referred to the high-voltage side. Thus, for fault currents on the low-voltage bus between 20 and 90 A, it is likely that the transformer high-side fuse will blow before the secondary main breaker trips.

Note also from Fig. 12-23b that, since both the 10T fuse and 250-A secondary main breaker characteristics lie below the transformer withstand characteristic, the transformer is properly protected.

Although the previous discussion involved coordination between high-side fuses and low-voltage breakers, the same basic procedures are followed for other types of overcurrent protection devices.

Reflecting OCPD Characteristics on Wye–Wye and Delta–Delta Connected Transformers

When reflecting the low-side overcurrent protective device characteristics on wye–wye or delta–delta connected transformers, the following equation is used:

$$I'_{\mathrm{HS}} = I_{\mathrm{LS}} \cdot \left[\frac{\text{transformer rated LS line voltage}}{\text{transformer rated HS line voltage}}\right] \tag{12.3}$$

where I'_{HS} and I_{LS} are the same as previously defined. Equation (12.3) may be used for all types of faults that may occur on the low-voltage side.

Reflecting OCPD Characteristics on Delta-Grounded, Wye-Connected Transformers

The delta–wye three-phase transformer connection requires special consideration when reflecting low-side OCPD characteristics to the high side for coordination purposes. In particular, the type of fault plays a significant factor in determining the multiplier to be used.

For a three-phase fault, the results of Eq. (12.3) may be used directly. Recall that a three-phase fault represents a balanced fault condition.

To determine the appropriate multiplier to be applied in the event of a phase to phase fault, consider the equivalent circuit shown in Fig. 12-24a. A phase b to phase c fault is assumed. The voltage rating of each high-side coil is equal to the line to line

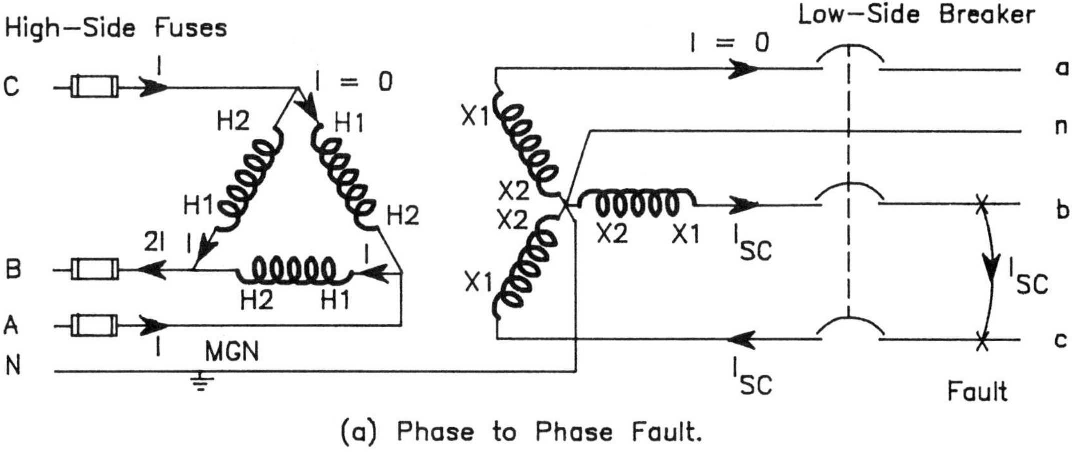

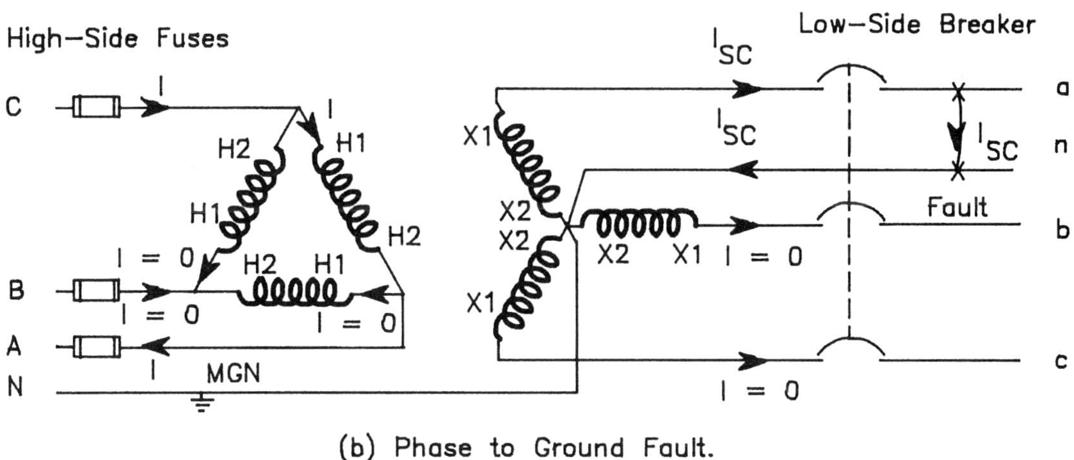

Figure 12-24 Reflecting OCPD characteristics on delta–wye connected three-phase transformer.

voltage of the transformer high-voltage side. On the low-voltage side, the voltage rating of each coil is equal to the line to line voltage of the transformer low-voltage side divided by $\sqrt{3}$.

For the phase to phase fault shown in Fig. 12-24a, assume that the short-circuit current is given as I_{SC}. The current I that flows in the high-voltage coils is given by

$$I = I_{SC} \cdot \left[\frac{\text{transformer rated LS line voltage}/\sqrt{3}}{\text{transformer rated HS line voltage}}\right] \qquad \textbf{(12.4)}$$

The line current magnitudes on the high-voltage side are given by

$$|I_a| = I \tag{12.5a}$$

$$|I_b| = 2I \tag{12.5b}$$

$$|I_c| = I \tag{12.5c}$$

The largest line current magnitude occurs in phase b.

Substituting Eq. (12.4) into (12.5b) and simplifying results in

$$|I_b| = 2I = I_{SC}\,\frac{2}{\sqrt{3}}\left[\frac{\text{transformer rated LS line voltage}}{\text{transformer rated HS line voltage}}\right] \tag{12.6}$$

Therefore, when reflecting the low-side characteristic to the high side for phase to phase faults on the low side, the following equation is used:

$$I'_{HS} = I_{LS}\,\frac{2}{\sqrt{3}}\left[\frac{\text{transformer rated LS line voltage}}{\text{transformer rated HS line voltage}}\right] \tag{12.7}$$

Note that Eq. (12.7) is similar to Eq. (12.3) with the exception of the $2/\sqrt{3}$ factor.

For single line to ground faults, the circuit of Fig. 12-24b applies. Here, a phase to ground fault on phase a is assumed to occur. The fault current on the low side is designated I_{SC}. The current I on the high side is given by

$$I = I_{SC}\left[\frac{\text{transformer rated LS line voltage}/\sqrt{3}}{\text{transformer rated HS line voltage}}\right] \tag{12.8}$$

The line current magnitudes on the high-voltage side are

$$|I_a| = I \tag{12.9a}$$

$$|I_b| = 0 \tag{12.9b}$$

$$|I_c| = I \tag{12.9c}$$

Note that the magnitudes of the line currents in phases a and c are equal. Substituting Eq. (12.8) into (12.9a) and (12.9c) results in

$$|I_a| = |I_c| = I_{SC}\,\frac{1}{\sqrt{3}}\left[\frac{\text{transformer rated LS line voltage}}{\text{transformer rated HS line voltage}}\right] \tag{12.10}$$

Therefore, when reflecting the low-side characteristic to the high side for phase to ground faults on the low-voltage side, the following equation is used:

$$I_{HS'} = I_{LS}\,\frac{1}{\sqrt{3}}\left[\frac{\text{transformer rated LS line voltage}}{\text{transformer rated HS line voltage}}\right] \tag{12.11}$$

Again, note the similarities between Eq. (12.11) and (12.3).

EXAMPLE 12-11

A 5000-kVA, 69-kV–12.47Y/7.2-kV, delta–grounded wye connected, 7% impedance distribution substation transformer is protected on the high-voltage side by a 65E rated power fuse. The low-voltage side is connected to a distribution substation bus through a

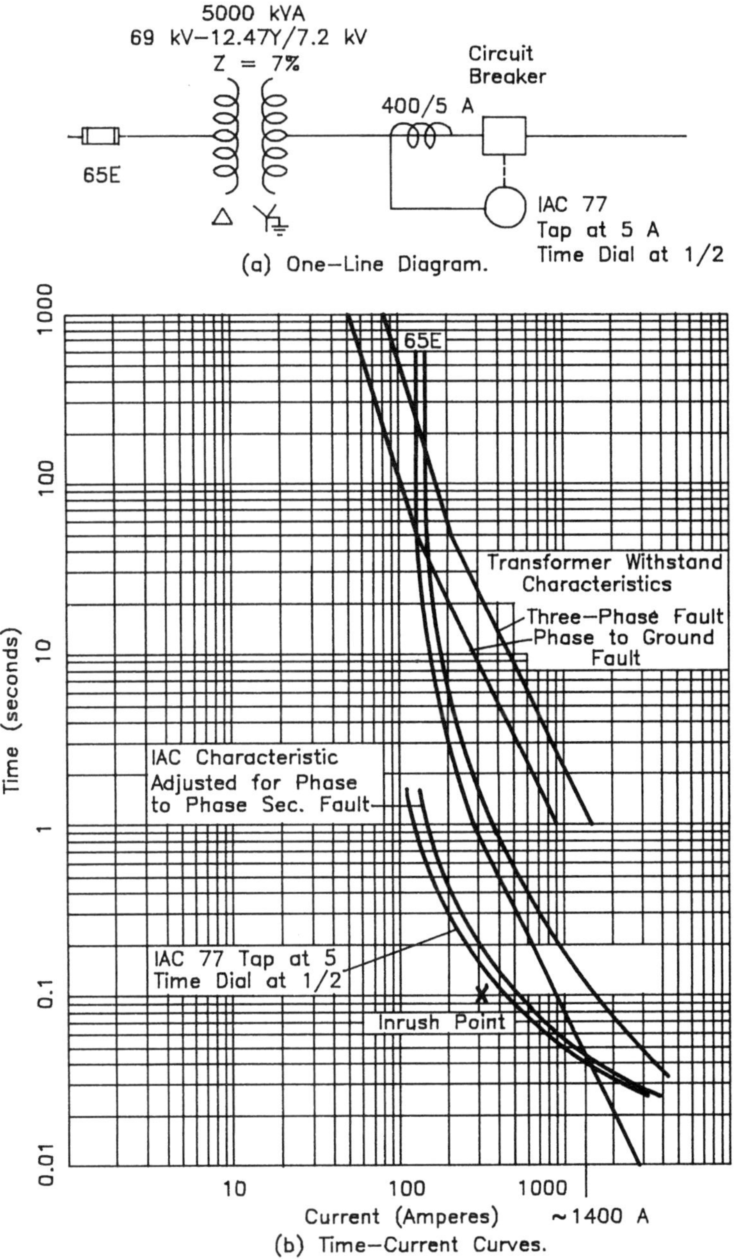
5000 kVA
69 kV–12.47Y/7.2 kV
Z = 7%
Circuit
Breaker
400/5 A
65E
IAC 77
Tap at 5 A
Time Dial at 1/2
(a) One–Line Diagram.
1000
100
10
1
0.1
0.01
Time (seconds)
65E
Transformer Withstand
Characteristics
Three–Phase Fault
Phase to Ground
Fault
IAC Characteristic
Adjusted for Phase
to Phase Sec. Fault
IAC 77 Tap at 5
Time Dial at 1/2
Inrush Point
10
100
1000
Current (Amperes)
~1400 A
(b) Time–Current Curves.

Figure 12-25 Example 12-11.

power circuit breaker. The power circuit breaker has bushing-mounted current transformers with a *CT* ratio of 400:5. The time–overcurrent relay is a type IAC 77, with a pickup tap setting of 5 and a time dial setting of ½. The one-line diagram for the system is shown in Fig. 12-25a. On the same graph, sketch the transformer withstand characteristics, power fuse characteristics, and low-voltage relay characteristics in terms of actual high-voltage side amperes.

Solution To plot the transformer withstand curves in terms of amperes, the rated line current of the transformer must be calculated.

$$I_{\text{line}} = \frac{5000 \text{ kVA}}{\sqrt{3} \cdot 69 \text{ kV}} = 41.8 \text{ A}$$

The transformer withstand characteristic can now be plotted for both three-phase and phase to ground faults on the secondary. Recall that the phase to ground fault on the secondary is the worst-case condition and results in a shifting of the transformer withstand curve to the left by a factor of 0.5774. In addition, the inrush point is also plotted. The 65E power fuse characteristic may be plotted directly on the graph without modification. The high-voltage power fuse characteristic should lie between the adjusted transformer withstand curve for the phase to ground secondary fault and the inrush point.

To plot the low-voltage relay characteristic, it is necessary to convert the relay characteristics from multiples of pickup to actual secondary amperes. The secondary amperes will then be referred to the high-voltage side for three-phase and phase to phase secondary faults. Since the relay pickup is set on the 5.0-A tap and the *CT* ratio is 400:5, a multiple of 1.0 times the relay pickup corresponds to 400 secondary amperes, a multiple of 3.0 times the relay pickup corresponds to 1200 secondary amperes, and so on. These values of secondary amperes are then referred to the primary by multiplying by the transformer line voltage turns ratio. The results for several values of current are tabulated in Table 12-5.

The primary amperes tabulated in Table 12-5 represent the relay characteristic for a three-phase secondary fault. Recall that the worst-case condition to consider when

Table 12-5

Multiple of Pickup	*Secondary Amperes*	*Primary Amperes*	*Time Delay (sec)*
1.0	400	72.3	Infinity
2.0	800	144.6	1.6
10.0	4,000	722.9	0.05
20.0	8,000	1445.8	0.028
30.0	12,000	2168.7	0.024
40.0	16,000	2891.6	0.022

Note: The time delays listed are the relay trip times and do not include the trip time of the breaker. The trip time of the breaker must be added to the trip time of the relay in order to establish the total trip time.

reflecting overcurrent characteristics on a delta–wye transformer bank is for a phase to phase fault on the secondary. Therefore, the currents tabulated here must be multiplied by a factor of $2/\sqrt{3}$ in order to represent the worst-case condition.

The transformer withstand characteristics, 65E power fuse characteristic, and low-voltage relay trip characteristic are plotted in Fig. 12-25b. Note that the 65E power fuse characteristic lies below the transformer withstand curve for a phase to ground fault for fault currents greater than approximately 150 A referred to the primary. In addition, the 65E power fuse characteristic lies above the inrush point. Therefore, the 65E power fuse should not blow due to inrush currents during energization of the transformer.

The low-voltage relay characteristic referred to the high-voltage side lies below and to the left of the 65E power fuse characteristic for fault currents up to 1400 A for three-phase secondary faults and 1200 A for phase to phase secondary faults referred to the primary.

The maximum expected through fault current is determined by neglecting the system impedance and using only the transformer impedance in the calculation. The fault current expressed in primary amperes for a three-phase secondary fault is approximately 600 A. Therefore, the system is selectively coordinated within the range of expected fault current levels.

Problems

12.1. Determine the minimum melt and total clearing times of a 100T fuse link at the following currents:

a. 300 A
b. 500 A
c. 3000 A

12.2. Determine the minimum melt and total clearing times of a 30E power fuse at the following currents:

a. 70 A
b. 100 A
c. 700 A

12.3. Determine the peak let through currents of a 20E, 8.3-kV current-limiting fuse at the following levels of rms symmetrical fault current levels. Also, specify the maximum peak let through current that would be present if a current-limiting fuse had not been used.

a. 100 A
b. 2000 A
c. 20,000 A

12.4. Determine the operating times of a 100 A, type D recloser for the following:

a. 600 A, instantaneous and *C* time delay curves
b. 3000 A, instantaneous and *C* time delay curves

12.5. A power circuit breaker is equipped with bushing-mounted current transformers having a ratio of 800:5. The breaker is protecting a 12.47-kV MGN distribution feeder. The available short-circuit current is 6500 A. IAC 77 time–overcurrent relays are connected to the *CT* secondary to provide short-circuit detection. The relay is to pick up when the current on the *CT* primary is approximately 600 A. Determine the appropriate tap setting of the relay to pick up at 600 A, and the required time dial setting to allow a time delay of 0.1 sec at maximum fault current levels.

12.6. Determine the maximum T link fuse rating permitted to protect a #4 ACSR conductor. Assume that the maximum permissible currents are 50% of the maximum fault current withstand values shown in Fig. 12-13. (It will be necessary to plot the adjusted conductor withstand characteristics and the fuse characteristics on the same log–log scale.)

12.7. Determine the appropriate T link fuse required to protect a 167-kVA, 7200–120/240-V, single-phase distribution transformer.

12.8. Determine the appropriate E-rated power fuse required to protect a 7500-kVA, 69-kV–4.16Y/2.4-kV, delta–grounded wye connected distribution substation transformer. The transformer impedance is 8%, and the faults are assumed to occur infrequently.

12.9. Determine the maximum fault current for proper coordination between the following fuse links:

a. 10T and 25T

b. 40T and 65T

12.10. Determine the range of current for which coordination between a 100 A, type D recloser and a 25T link fuse is attained. Assume two instantaneous and two D operations.

12.11. A 100 kVA, 4800–120/240-V, single-phase transformer is to be protected on the high-voltage side by a T link fuse. The low-voltage side of the transformer supplies a single-phase service. The main secondary breaker is rated at 400 A, and the largest feeder breaker is rated at 60 A. Assume that the breaker trip characteristics are as shown in Fig. 12-12. The maximum fault current availability is 9000 A on the low-voltage side. Plot the breaker and transformer withstand characteristics, with all values referred to the high-voltage side, on the same log–log scale. Determine the appropriate T link fuse rating to protect the transformer and to selectively coordinate with the 60-A, low-side feeder breaker and the 400-A main secondary breaker, if possible. Coordination should be obtained for secondary faults up to the maximum fault current available.

12.12. A 3750-kVA, 69-kV–4.16Y/2.4-kV, delta–grounded wye connected distribution substation transformer supplies two distribution feeders. Each distribution feeder is protected by three single-phase, 400-A, type D reclosers. The reclosers are set to operate once on the instantaneous curve and three times on the *D* time delay curve. The maximum available fault current on the 4.16-kV bus is 7000 A. In the event of a fault on either of the 4.16-kV distribution feeders, the recloser should operate to lockout before the transformer high-side fuse blows. On the same log–log scale, plot the following:

a. Recloser trip characteristics referred to the high-voltage side for worst-case fault conditions on the low-voltage side of the transformer

b. The adjusted transformer withstand characteristic for worst-case fault conditions

Determine the proper E-rated fuse to selectively coordinate with the low-side reclosers and protect the transformer against through faults.

13

Power System Harmonics

13-1 General

The topic of power system harmonics has received increased attention over the past several years. Although the presence of harmonic currents and voltages is not a new phenomenon, the increased use of harmonic-producing equipment has led to an increase in the amount of harmonic currents and voltages present. Advances in power electronic technology have made it possible to control larger amounts of power than previously possible. While the power electronic control equipment is more efficient than previous methods of power control, the increased use of this equipment has created new problems due to increased harmonic current levels. In addition, it is characteristic of this power electronic control equipment to operate at relatively low power factors. To improve the power factor, capacitors are often installed. The installation of these capacitors can result in a parallel resonance condition with the utility supply, thereby amplifying the harmonic currents. Amplification of the harmonic currents results in increased voltage distortion, nuisance fuse blowing and breaker tripping, and overheating of equipment, to name a few of the problems.

This chapter begins with a discussion of the nature of harmonic currents and voltages and some of the more common sources of harmonic-producing equipment. Typical harmonic current levels for various equipment will be presented. Problems related to system resonance and the determination of resonance conditions are also discussed. The design and specification of a detuned capacitor bank used for power factor correction and harmonic filtering are discussed, followed by an example of harmonic analysis and filter design.

13-2 Sources of Harmonics

To fully understand the problems created by harmonic currents and voltages, it is first necessary to understand what is meant by the term *harmonic*. Any periodic, nonsinusoidal time varying waveform may be expressed as the sum of several sinusoidal waveforms referred to as harmonic components. Each of these harmonic components has a certain amplitude, frequency, and phase shift. The amplitude and phase shift of the individual harmonic components are determined by means of Fourier analysis applied to the original waveform. The details of Fourier analysis are beyond the scope of this text.

Generally, the fundamental component of the waveform will have the same frequency as the waveform itself. The frequency of the other harmonic components is expressed as an integer multiple of the fundamental frequency. For example, if the fundamental frequency is 60 Hz, the 5th harmonic frequency will be 5 times 60 Hz, or 300 Hz. Likewise, the 7th harmonic frequency is 420 Hz, and so on. For typical harmonic voltages and currents encountered in electrical power systems, it is sufficient to consider up to about the 25th harmonic frequency when representing nonsinusoidal periodic waveforms. If the waveform of the voltage or current is a pure sinusoid, the waveform will contain only a fundamental component, with the higher-order harmonic terms being equal to zero.

A listing of the frequency, amplitude, and phase angle of the individual harmonic components is referred to as the harmonic spectrum of the waveform. This information is critical in the design specifications of harmonic filtering equipment. Table 13-1 represents the harmonic spectrum of a typical square-wave current waveform up to the 13th harmonic order. The actual waveform becomes more like a square wave in appearance as additional higher-order harmonic terms are added to the waveform expression. The actual waveform is shown in Fig. 13-1.

In addition to the harmonic spectrum of the waveform, several terms are used to quantify the nature of harmonic waveforms. The root of the sum of the squares, or rss, value of the waveform represents the effective rms value of the waveform. The rss value is given by

$$\text{rss} = (V_1^2 + V_2^2 + V_3^2 + \cdots + V_i^2)^{1/2} \tag{13.1}$$

Table 13-1

Frequency	*Harmonic Order*	*Magnitude*	*Phase Shift*
60	Fundamental	1.000	0°
180	3	0.333	0°
300	5	0.200	0°
420	7	0.143	0°
660	11	0.091	0°
780	13	0.077	0°

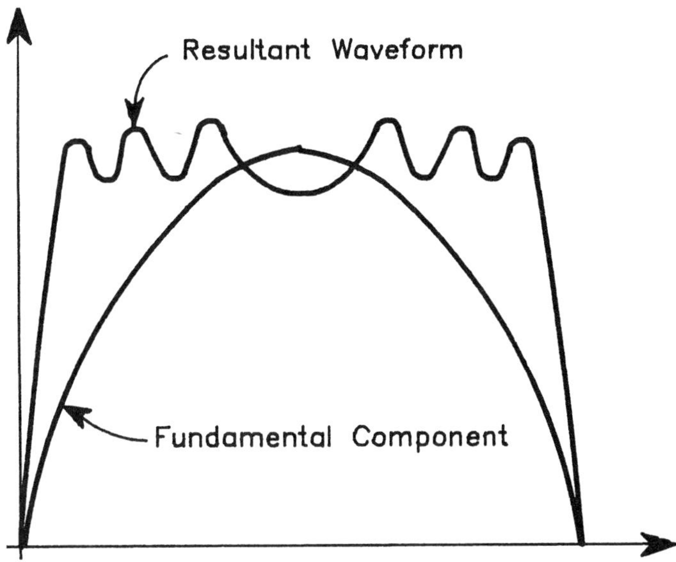

Figure 13-1 Harmonic composition of square wave.

where

V_1 = rms magnitude of the fundamental component

V_2 = rms magnitude of the 2nd harmonic component

V_3 = rms magnitude of the 3rd harmonic component

V_i = rms magnitude of the ith harmonic component

The percent total harmonic distortion, or THD, of the waveform is a measure of how badly a waveform is distorted with respect to a pure sine wave. IEEE Standard 519-1992 specifies the maximum percentage THD permitted for both current distortion and voltage distortion. This standard is discussed in more detail in Section 13-5. The THD is given by

$$\mathrm{THD} = \frac{(V_2^2 + V_3^2 + \cdots + V_i^2)^{1/2}}{V_1} \cdot 100 \tag{13.2}$$

where the V_i are as defined previously. Note that if a waveform is a pure sine wave the rss value of the waveform is equal to the rms value of the fundamental component. Also, the THD of a pure sine wave is zero.

EXAMPLE 13-1 Determine the rss and THD for a voltage waveform with the harmonic spectrum shown in Table 13-2.

All other harmonic components are equal to zero.

Table 13-2 Voltage Harmonic Spectrum

Frequency	*Harmonic Order*	*Voltage Magnitude*
60	1	277.0
300	5	25.0
420	7	12.0
660	11	5.0
780	13	2.0

Solution The rss value is given by Eq. (13.1).

$$\text{rss} = (277^2 + 25^2 + 12^2 + 5^2 + 2^2)^{1/2} = 278.44 \text{ V}$$

The THD is given by Eq. (13.2).

$$\text{THD} = \frac{(25^2 + 12^2 + 5^2 + 2^2)^{1/2}}{277} \cdot 100 = 10.2\%$$

It is characteristic of power electronic control equipment to draw line currents that are nonsinusoidal. As such, the most common representation for harmonic-producing loads is the current source or current sink models. Several sources of harmonic currents that may be found on electrical power systems are listed in Table 13-3. Typical harmonic spectrums of line current drawn from the supply by some three-phase variable speed motor drives and three-phase full wave rectifiers are listed in Table 13-4. Note that the percentages of harmonic content listed in Table 13-4 are typical values only and may be used only as a rough approximation to the actual harmonic currents that may be present. The manufacturer of the specific equipment should be consulted when precise information is desired in the planning stage of a filter design. In an already existing installation, harmonic power analyzers should be used to sample the line currents to determine the actual harmonic content.

The magnitudes of the harmonic components listed in Table 13-4 are expressed in percent of the rated fundamental current of the device. To determine the actual harmonic

Table 13-3 Sources of Harmonics

Variable-speed motor drives
Rectifiers
Arc furnaces
Welders
Uninterruptible power supplies
Computer switched mode power supplies
HID lighting ballasts

Table 13-4 Typical Harmonic Current Spectrum for Three-Phase Variable-Speed Motor Drives and Three-Phase Full-Wave Rectifiers

Harmonic Order	*Amplitude (rms amperes)*
1	100.0%
5	20.0%
7	14.3%
11	9.1%
13	7.7%
17	5.9%
19	5.3%
23	4.3%
25	4.0%

currents, it is necessary to multiply the fundamental current by the respective percentages shown in Table 13-4.

EXAMPLE 13-2 Using the typical values shown in Table 13-4, determine the following for a 500-kW, 480-V, three-phase, full-wave (six pulse) rectifier.

a. Harmonic current spectrum
b. RSS of the current waveform
c. THD of the current waveform

Solution The fundamental component of the line current is

$$I_L = \frac{500{,}000}{\sqrt{3} \cdot 480} = 601.4 \text{ A}$$

a. The individual harmonic currents are calculated and tabulated next.

$$I_1 = 601.4 \text{ A}$$

$$I_5 = (0.20) \cdot (601.4) = 120.3 \text{ A}$$

$$I_7 = (0.143) \cdot (601.4) = 86.0 \text{ A}$$

$$I_{11} = (0.091) \cdot (601.4) = 54.7 \text{ A}$$

$$I_{13} = (0.077) \cdot (601.4) = 46.3 \text{ A}$$

$$I_{17} = (0.059) \cdot (601.4) = 35.5 \text{ A}$$

$$I_{19} = (0.053) \cdot (601.4) = 31.9 \text{ A}$$

$$I_{23} = (0.043) \cdot (601.4) = 25.9 \text{ A}$$

$$I_{25} = (0.040) \cdot (601.4) = 24.1 \text{ A}$$

b. The RSS value of the waveform is

$$\text{RSS} = (601.4^2 + 120.3^2 + 86.0^2 + 54.7^2 + 46.3^2 + 35.5^2 + 31.9^2 + 25.9^2 + 24.1^2)^{1/2} = 626.2 \text{ A}$$

c. The THD of the waveform is

$$\text{THD} = \frac{(120.3^2 + 86.0^2 + 54.7^2 + 46.3^2 + 35.5^2 + 31.9^2 + 25.9^2 + 24.1^2)^{1/2}}{601.4} \cdot 100$$

$$= 29.0\%$$

13-3 Resonance Problems

When applying power factor correction capacitors to a power system bus that has harmonic-producing equipment connected to it, a resonance condition will be created. This resonance takes place between the inductive reactance of the source and the capacitive reactance of the power factor correction capacitor bank. Since the power factor correction capacitor is connected in parallel with the source, an infinite parallel impedance will occur when the inductive reactance of the source is equal to the capacitive reactance of the capacitor bank. The parallel resonant frequency is the frequency at which the inductive and capacitive reactances are equal. If this parallel resonance frequency occurs at or near a harmonic current produced by the load, severe voltage distortion and harmonic current amplification will result. The increase in harmonic current is often enough to cause nuisance fuse blowing and false breaker tripping. It is important to note that the application of capacitors to a bus will not create these harmonic currents, but may cause amplification of these harmonic currents.

To determine the frequency at which parallel resonance will occur, consider the one-line diagram of a typical industrial plant substation shown in Fig. 13-2. This one-line diagram is representive of the majority of industrial plant substations encountered. The plant is supplied from the utility distribution or subtransmission system through a step-down transformer. The total plant load consists of nonharmonic-producing and harmonic-producing loads. A capacitor bank is added to improve the overall plant power factor.

The equivalent system impedance, transformer impedance, and capacitor impedance must be calculated and referred to the transformer low-voltage side. The equivalent system resistance R_{sys} and reactance X_{sys} referred to the high-voltage side of the transformer are given by the following:

$$R_{sys} = \frac{\text{kV}_{LL}^2}{\text{MVA}_{sc}} \cdot \cos\left\{\tan^{-1}\left(\frac{X}{R}\text{ ratio}\right)\right\} \quad \textbf{(13.3)}$$

$$X_{sys} = \frac{\text{kV}_{LL}^2}{\text{MVA}_{sc}} \cdot \sin\left\{\tan^{-1}\left(\frac{X}{R}\text{ ratio}\right)\right\} \quad \textbf{(13.4)}$$

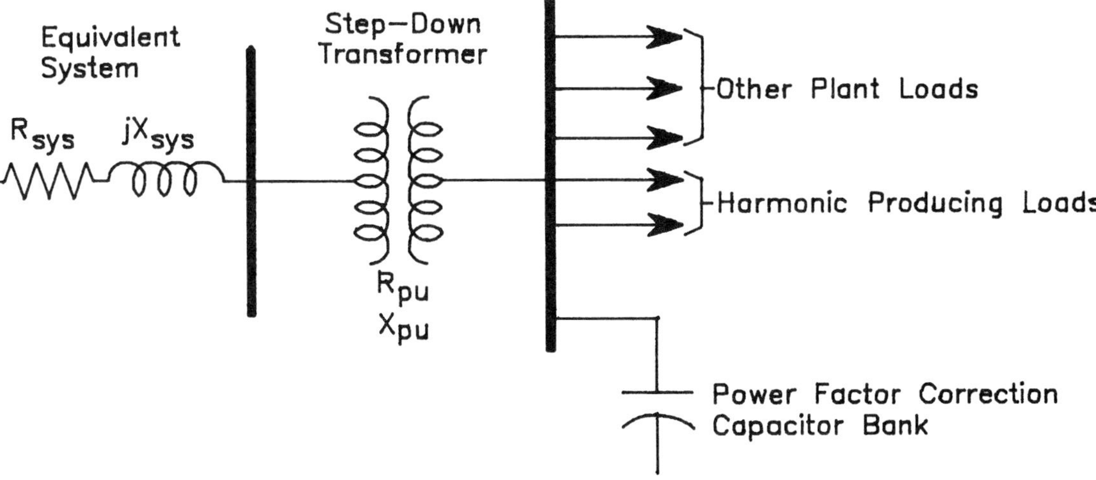

Figure 13-2 Typical industrial plant one-line diagram.

The equivalent system resistance and reactance referred to the low-voltage side are determined by dividing the values referred to the high-voltage side by the transformer turns ratio, as follows:

$$R'_{sys} = \frac{R_{sys}}{a^2} \qquad (13.5)$$

$$X'_{sys} = \frac{X_{sys}}{a^2} \qquad (13.6)$$

The equivalent transformer resistance and reactance referred to the low-voltage side are given by the following:

$$R_{tr} = R_{pu} \cdot \frac{1000 \cdot \text{kV}^2}{\text{kVA}_{tr}} \qquad (13.7)$$

$$X_{tr} = X_{pu} \cdot \frac{1000 \cdot \text{kV}^2}{\text{kVA}_{tr}} \qquad (13.8)$$

where

R_{pu} = per unit transformer resistance

X_{pu} = per unit transformer reactance

kVA_{tr} = transformer rated apparent power

kV = transformer rated line to line low voltage

The total system resistance is the sum of the equivalent system resistance plus the transformer resistance.

$$R_{\text{tot}} = R'_{\text{sys}} + R_{\text{tr}} \tag{13.9}$$

Likewise, the total system reactance is the sum of the equivalent system reactance plus the transformer reactance.

$$X_{\text{tot}} = X'_{\text{sys}} + X_{\text{tr}} \tag{13.10}$$

The equivalent reactance of the capacitor bank is given by the following:

$$X_{\text{cap}} = \frac{1000 \cdot \text{kV}_{\text{cap}}^2}{\text{kVA}_{\text{cap}}} \tag{13.11}$$

where

kV_{cap} = line to line voltage rating of the capacitor

kVA_{cap} = three phase reactive power rating of the capacitor

The inductance of the total source impedance is given by

$$L_{\text{tot}} = \frac{X_{\text{tot}}}{2 \cdot \pi \cdot f_{\text{sys}}} = \frac{X_{\text{tot}}}{\omega_{\text{sys}}} \tag{13.12}$$

where f_{sys} is the normal operating frequency of the system. The total system inductance as given by Eq. (13.12) is constant. The inductive reactance at any other frequency is given by.

$$X_L = 2 \cdot \pi \cdot f_{\text{act}} \cdot L_{\text{tot}} = \omega_{\text{act}} \cdot L_{\text{tot}} \tag{13.13}$$

where f_{act} is the actual operating frequency of the system.

Likewise, the capacitance of the capacitor bank is

$$C = \frac{1}{2 \cdot \pi \cdot f_{\text{sys}} \cdot X_{\text{cap}}} = \frac{1}{\omega_{\text{sys}} \cdot X_{\text{cap}}} \tag{13.14}$$

The capacitance of the capacitor bank is constant regardless of frequency. The capacitive reactance at other frequencies is given by

$$X_C = \frac{1}{2 \cdot \pi \cdot f_{\text{act}} \cdot C} = \frac{1}{\omega_{\text{act}} \cdot C} \tag{13.15}$$

The resulting equivalent circuit for the power system shown in Fig. 13-2 is shown in Fig. 13-3. The impedance $\mathbf{Z}_{\text{in}}$ looking into the system from the load bus consists of the source impedance connected in parallel with the capacitor impedance. Since both the inductive reactance of the system and the capacitive reactance of the capacitor bank are functions of frequency, the impedance $\mathbf{Z}_{\text{in}}$ will also be a function of frequency. This parallel impedance is given by the following:

$$\mathbf{Z}_{\text{in}} = \frac{(R_{\text{tot}} + j\omega_{\text{act}}L_{\text{tot}}) \cdot (-j/\omega_{\text{act}}C)}{R_{\text{tot}} + j\omega_{\text{act}}L_{\text{tot}} - (j/\omega_{\text{act}}C)} \tag{13.16}$$

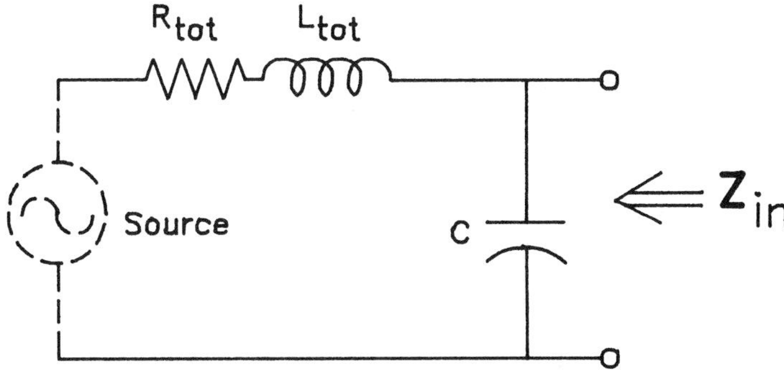

Figure 13-3 Equivalent circuit of power system shown in Fig. 13-2.

Equation (13.16) can be used to determine the system impedance at any value of frequency. A frequency scan of the system may be performed by varying the frequency between the fundamental up to the 50th harmonic and calculating the magnitude of the system impedance. The magnitude of the impedance is then plotted as a function of frequency to locate the parallel resonant frequency.

Parallel resonance occurs when the inductive reactance and capacitive reactance are equal. The frequency at which parallel resonance occurs is designated ω_0 (rad/sec) or f_0 (Hz). Designating the parallel resonant frequency by ω_0 and equating the inductive and capacitive reactances results in the following:

$$\omega_0 L_{tot} = \frac{1}{\omega_0 C} \tag{13.17}$$

Solving Eq. (13.17) for ω_0 results in the following:

$$\omega_0 = \frac{1}{(L_{tot}C)^{1/2}} \tag{13.18}$$

Likewise, the parallel resonant frequency in hertz is given by

$$f_0 = \frac{1}{2 \cdot \pi \cdot (L_{tot}C)^{1/2}} \tag{13.19}$$

EXAMPLE 13-3

An industrial plant is supplied from the utility-12.47 kV, three-phase multigrounded neutral distribution feeder. The short-circuit data from the utility indicate a three-phase short-circuit MVA of 200 MVA and an X/R ratio of 2.4. The transformer supplying the plant is rated 1000 kVA, 12.47 kV–480Y/277 V, R = 1.0%, X = 6.0%. The system frequency is 60 Hz. Determine the parallel resonant frequencies for the following values of power factor correction capacitors.

a. 200 kVAR
b. 400 kVAR
c. 600 kVAR
d. 800 kVAR

The system one-line diagram is shown in Fig. 13-4.

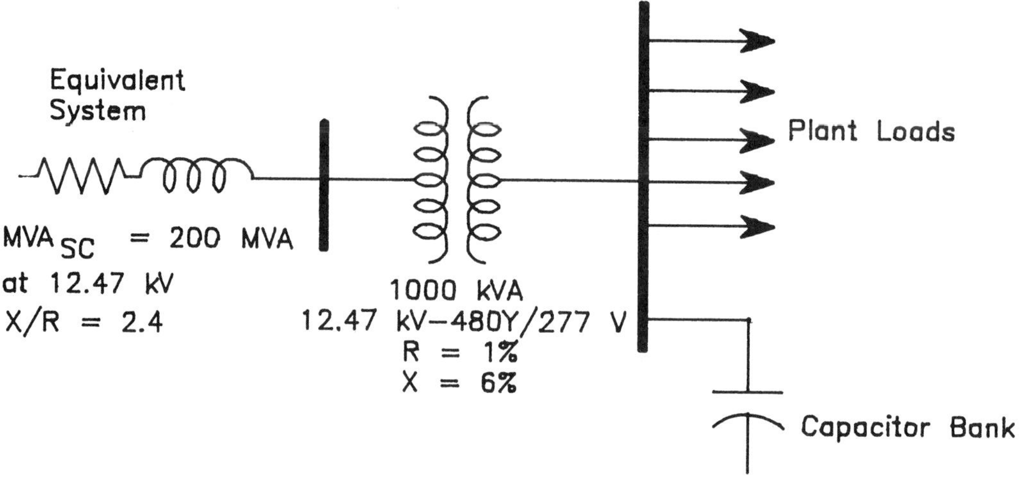

Figure 13-4 One-line diagram for Example 13-3.

Solution The equivalent system resistance and reactance are calculated by applying Eqs. (13.3) and (13.4).

$$R_{\text{sys}} = \frac{12.47^2}{200} \cdot \cos\{\tan^{-1}(2.4)\} = 0.2990\ \Omega$$

$$X_{\text{sys}} = \frac{12.47^2}{200} \cdot \sin\{\tan^{-1}(2.4)\} = 0.7177\ \Omega$$

The transformer turns ratio a is equal to.

$$a = 12{,}470 \div 480 = 25.98$$

The equivalent system resistance and reactance referred to the low-voltage side are

$$R'_{\text{sys}} = 0.2990 \div 25.98^2 = 0.000443\ \Omega$$

$$X'_{\text{sys}} = 0.7177 \div 25.98^2 = 0.001063\ \Omega$$

The transformer resistance and reactance referred to the low-voltage side are

$$R_{\text{tr}} = 0.01 \cdot \frac{1000 \cdot (0.48)^2}{1000} = 0.002304\ \Omega$$

$$X_{\text{tr}} = 0.06 \cdot \frac{1000 \cdot (0.48)^2}{1000} = 0.013824\ \Omega$$

The total system resistance and inductance referred to the low-voltage side of the transformer are:

$$R_{\text{tot}} = 0.000443 + 0.002304 = 0.002747\ \Omega$$

$$X_{\text{tot}} = 0.001063 + 0.013824 = 0.014887\ \Omega$$

The inductance of the system is given by Eq. (13.12).

$$L_{tot} = \frac{0.014887}{2 \cdot \pi \cdot 60} = 39.5 \times 10^{-6}\ \text{H}$$

a. The capacitive reactance for 200 kVAR, 480 V is equal to

$$X_{cap} = \frac{1000 \cdot (0.48)^2}{200} = 1.152\ \Omega$$

The capacitance is calculated from Eq. (13.14).

$$C = \frac{1}{2 \cdot \pi \cdot 60 \cdot 1.152} = 2.3026 \times 10^{-3}\ \text{F}$$

The parallel resonant frequency is

$$f_0 = \frac{1}{2 \cdot \pi \cdot (39.5 \times 10^{-6} \cdot 2.3026 \times 10^{-3})^{1/2}} = 527.73\ \text{Hz}$$

The harmonic order at which parallel resonance occurs is

$$h = 527.73 \div 60 = 8.8$$

b. The capacitive reactance for 400 kVAR, 480 V is equal to

$$X_{cap} = \frac{1000 \cdot (0.48)^2}{400} = 0.576\ \Omega$$

The capacitance is calculated from Eq. (13.14).

$$C = \frac{1}{2 \cdot \pi \cdot 60 \cdot 0.576} = 4.6052 \times 10^{-3}\ \text{F}$$

The parallel resonant frequency is

$$f_0 = \frac{1}{2 \cdot \pi \cdot (39.5 \times 10^{-6} \cdot 4.6052 \times 10^{-3})^{1/2}} = 373.2\ \text{Hz}$$

The harmonic order at which parallel resonance occurs is

$$h = 373.2 \div 60 = 6.22$$

c. The capacitive reactance for 600 kVAR, 480 V is equal to

$$X_{cap} = \frac{1000 \cdot (0.48)^2}{600} = 0.384\ \Omega$$

The capacitance is calculated from Eq. (13.14)

$$C = \frac{1}{2 \cdot \pi \cdot 60 \cdot 0.384} = 6.9076 \times 10^{-3}\ \text{F}$$

The parallel resonant frequency is

$$f_0 = \frac{1}{2 \cdot \pi \cdot (39.5 \times 10^{-6} \cdot 6.9076 \times 10^{-3})^{1/2}} = 304.7 \text{ Hz}$$

The harmonic order at which parallel resonance occurs is

$$h = 304.7 \div 60 = 5.08$$

d. The capacitive reactance for 800 kVAR, 480 V is equal to

$$X_{\text{cap}} = \frac{1000 \cdot (0.48)^2}{800} = 0.288\ \Omega$$

The capacitance is calculated from Eq. (13.14).

$$C = \frac{1}{2 \cdot \pi \cdot 60 \cdot 0.288} = 9.2101 \times 10^{-3} \text{ F}$$

The parallel resonant frequency is

$$f_0 = \frac{1}{2 \cdot \pi \cdot (39.5 \times 10^{-6} \cdot 9.2101 \times 10^{-3})^{1/2}} = 263.9 \text{ Hz}$$

The harmonic order at which parallel resonance occurs is

$$h = 263.9 \div 60 = 4.4$$

Note from Example 13-3 that there exists a parallel resonant frequency very close to the 5th harmonic order if 600 kVAR of capacitors is placed on the system. If a harmonic load that produces a significant 5th harmonic current were to be connected to the bus, severe voltage distortion would result. The following example illustrates the calculation of voltage and current distortion for the power system of Example 13-3 with and without the 600-kVAR capacitor bank connected.

EXAMPLE 13-4

The power system of Example 13-3 supplies a 200-kVA, 480-V, harmonic-producing load that has the harmonic spectrum shown in Table 13-5. Determine the following:

a. The rss and THD of the source current and bus voltage without the 600-kVAR capacitor connected

b. The rss and THD of the bus voltage with the 600-kVAR capacitor connected

c. The rss and THD of the capacitor current with the capacitor connected

Solution The magnitude of the fundamental load current is

$$I_1 = \frac{200{,}000}{\sqrt{3} \cdot 480} = 240.6 \text{ A}$$

Table 13-5 Harmonic Spectrum for 200-kVA Load

Frequency	*Harmonic Order*	*Line Current Magnitude*
300	5	50.0
420	7	30.0
660	11	15.0
780	13	7.0
1020	17	3.0

a. Without the capacitor connected, the system representation is a series *RL* circuit. The inductive reactance of the system is computed at each harmonic frequency according to Eq. (13.13). The resulting inductive reactance is then combined with the system resistance to obtain the magnitude of the system impedance at each harmonic frequency. The voltage drop due to the harmonic load currents will be computed at each harmonic frequency by multiplying the harmonic load current magnitude by the magnitude of the system impedance. The following table summarizes the results:

Frequency	R_{tot}	X_{tot}	$\lvert Z_{tot}\rvert$	I_1	V_1
300	0.002747	0.074455	0.074486	50.0	3.72
420	0.002747	0.104209	0.104245	30.0	3.13
660	0.002747	0.163757	0.163780	15.0	2.46
780	0.002747	0.193531	0.193551	7.0	1.35
1020	0.002747	0.253079	0.253094	3.0	0.76

The rss and THD of the line current are

$$\text{rss current} = (240.6^2 + 50.0^2 + 30.0^2 + 15.0^2 + 7.0^2 + 3.0^2)^{1/2}$$
$$= 248.1 \text{ A}$$
$$\text{THD current} = \frac{(50.0^2 + 30.0^2 + 15.0^2 + 7.0^2 + 3.0^2)^{1/2}}{240.6} \cdot 100$$
$$= 25.22\%$$

The rss and THD of the load voltage are determined with respect to the nominal line to neutral voltage of the system.

$$\text{rss voltage} = (277.0^2 + 3.72^2 + 3.13^2 + 2.46^2 + 1.35^2 + 0.76^2)^{1/2}$$
$$= 277.05 \text{ V}$$
$$\text{THD voltage} = \frac{(3.72^2 + 3.13^2 + 2.46^2 + 1.35^2 + 0.76^2)^{1/2}}{277.0} \cdot 100$$
$$= 2.045\%$$

b. With the capacitor bank added, the magnitude of the system impedance includes the parallel combination of the capacitor and the system. Equation (13.16) can be used to calculate the magnitude of the parallel impedance at each harmonic-order frequency. The voltage drop at each harmonic is equal to the harmonic load current multiplied by the magnitude of the impedance. The results are tabulated next:

Frequency	$\lvert Z_{in} \rvert$	I_1	V_1
300	1.5787	50.0	78.94
420	0.1157	30.0	3.47
660	0.0444	15.0	0.67
780	0.0349	7.0	0.24
1020	0.0248	3.0	0.07

The rss value of the bus voltage is

$$\begin{aligned} \text{rss voltage} &= (277.0^2 + 78.94^2 + 3.47^2 + 0.67^2 + 0.24^2 + 0.07^2)^{1/2} \\ &= 288.1 \text{ V} \end{aligned}$$

The percent of THD of the bus voltage is

$$\begin{aligned} \text{THD voltage} &= \frac{(78.94^2 + 3.47^2 + 0.67^2 + 0.24^2 + 0.07^2)^{1/2}}{277.0} \cdot 100 \\ &= 28.5\% \end{aligned}$$

Note that the percent of THD of the bus voltage is 25.8% with the capacitor bank added, as opposed to 2.045% without the capacitor bank. In this instance, the capacitor bank has combined with the source inductance to create a parallel resonance condition very near the 5th harmonic. The amplification of the 5th harmonic has lead to an increase in the THD of the bus voltage to an unacceptable value.

c. The current through the capacitor bank at each harmonic frequency can be calculated by applying Ohm's law to the capacitor element. The bus voltage at each harmonic frequency has been calculated and tabulated previously. The capacitive reactance of the 600-kVAR, 480-V capacitor bank at 60 Hz is determined by applying Eq. (13.11).

$$X_c = \frac{1000 \cdot (0.48)^2}{600} = 0.384\ \Omega$$

The capacitance of the 600-kVAR, 480-V capacitor bank is determined by applying Eq. (13.14).

$$C = \frac{1}{2 \cdot \pi \cdot 60 \cdot 0.384} = 6.9078 \times 10^{-3} \text{ F}$$

The impedance of the capacitor can be calculated by applying Eq. (13.15) for the harmonic frequencies of interest. The results are tabulated next:

Frequency	X_c	V_1	I_c
300	0.0768	78.94	1027.9
420	0.0549	3.47	63.2
660	0.0349	0.67	19.2
780	0.0295	0.24	8.1
1020	0.0226	0.07	3.1

The fundamental value of the capacitor current is

$$I_1 = \frac{600{,}000}{\sqrt{3} \cdot 480} = 721.7 \text{ A}$$

The rss value of the capacitor current is:

$$\begin{aligned}\text{rss capacitor current} &= (721.7^2 + 1027.9^2 + 63.2^2 + 19.2^2 + 8.1^2 + 3.1^2)^{1/2}\\ &= 1257.6 \text{ A}\end{aligned}$$

Note that the capacitor current is approximately 175% of rated! This magnitude of current will likely cause the capacitor fuses to blow or the capacitor breaker to trip. If the fuse or circuit breaker protecting the capacitor bank does not operate due to this overcurrent, damage to the capacitor will likely result.

13-4 Harmonic Filter Design

Example 13-4 has illustrated the special consideration that must be given to the application of power factor correction capacitors to a power system that contains harmonic-producing equipment. Even though the actual harmonic currents produced by the load may be small, these currents can be amplified to unacceptable levels due to parallel resonance conditions.

The parallel resonance condition discussed in the previous section occurs at a frequency at which the capacitive reactance of the capacitor bank equals the inductive reactance of the system. If this resonance frequency occurs at or near one of the harmonics produced by the load equipment, severe amplification of the harmonic voltages and currents will result. If the parallel resonance frequency could be shifted or made to occur at a value less than the lowest-order harmonic term of the load equipment, then the amplification of the harmonic load currents could be minimized or eliminated.

Shifting of the parallel resonance frequency is accomplished by placing an inductor in series with the capacitor bank. The series inductor–capacitor combination is referred to as a harmonic filter bank, or detuned capacitor bank. These harmonic filter banks may use capacitors that are delta connected, as in Fig. 13-5a, or wye connected, as in Fig. 13-5b. In either the delta or wye connection, the analysis is based on the single-phase line to neutral equivalent circuit representation. The single-phase line to neutral equivalent representation of a harmonic filter bank is shown in Fig. 13-5c. The series resonant frequency or tuning frequency of the filter bank is generally selected to be about 3% to 10% less than the lowest-order harmonic produced by the load equipment. For a typical six-pulse power converter, the lowest-order harmonic term is the 5th harmonic, which corresponds to a frequency of 300 Hz on a 60-Hz system. A filter bank applied to this system will have a tuning frequency of between 270 and 290 Hz. Typically, the tuning frequency for a filter of this nature is 282 Hz, corresponding to the 4.7th harmonic term.

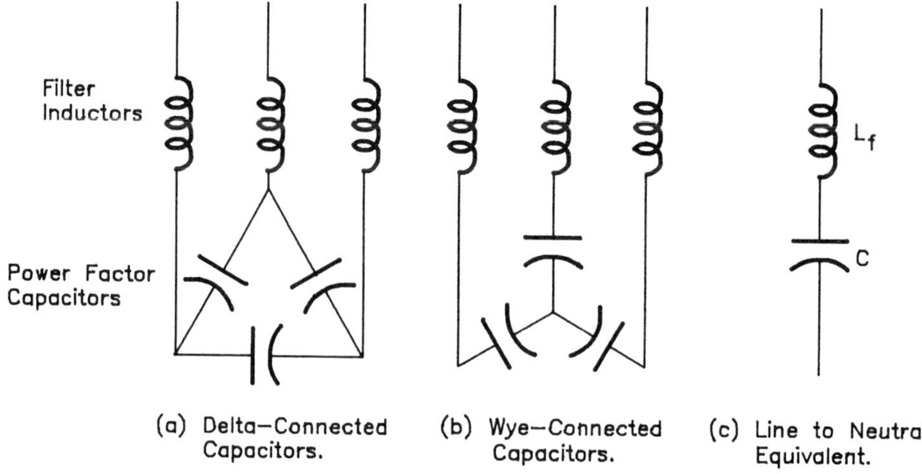

Figure 13-5 Filter configurations.

In addition to shifting the parallel resonant frequency, the filter will supply a portion of the harmonic current demanded by the load. The most significant portion of harmonic load current supplied by the filter occurs at the harmonic order closest to the tuning order of the filter. For example, a harmonic filter tuned to the 4.7th harmonic supplies a major portion of the 5th harmonic current demanded by the load. The filter also supplies a significantly lower amount of the higher-order harmonic load currents. Therefore, since the filter bank supplies some of the load harmonic current, less harmonic current needs to be supplied by the source. This will result in a reduction in the THD of the load bus voltage.

The series resonant frequency of the filter element is given by

$$f_0 = \frac{1}{2 \cdot \pi \cdot (L_f C)^{1/2}} \quad \text{Hz} \tag{13.20}$$

where

L_f = inductance of the tuning inductor

C = capacitance of the capacitor bank

Solving Eq. (13.20) for L_f results in

$$L_f = \frac{1}{C \cdot (2 \cdot \pi \cdot f_0)^2} \tag{13.21}$$

Substituting Eq. (13.14) into (13.21) results in

$$\begin{aligned} L_f &= \frac{2 \cdot \pi \cdot f_{\text{sys}} \cdot X_{\text{cap}}}{(2 \cdot \pi \cdot f_0)^2} \\ &= \frac{f_{\text{sys}} \cdot X_{\text{cap}}}{2 \cdot \pi \cdot (f_0)^2} \end{aligned} \tag{13.22}$$

Substituting Eq. (13.11) into (13.22) results in

$$L_f = \frac{f_{sys} \cdot 1000 \cdot (\mathrm{kV_{cap}})^2}{2 \cdot \pi \cdot (f_0)^2 \cdot \mathrm{kVA_{cap}}} \tag{13.23}$$

Equation (13.23) can be used to determine the filter inductance required to tune the filter to a particular frequency.

EXAMPLE 13-5

Determine the value of filter inductance required to tune the following capacitor banks to 282 Hz (4.7th harmonic). The nominal system frequency is 60 Hz.

a. 50 kVAR, 480 V
b. 1200 kVAR, 12.47 kV

Solution

a. Direct application of Eq. (13.23) results in the following:

$$L_f = \frac{60 \cdot 1000 \cdot (0.48)^2}{2 \cdot \pi \cdot (282)^2 \cdot 50} = 5.533 \times 10^{-4}\ \mathrm{H} \quad \text{or} \quad 553.3\ \mu\mathrm{H}$$

b. $$L_f = \frac{60 \cdot 1000 \cdot (12.47)^2}{2 \cdot \pi \cdot (282)^2 \cdot 1200} = 1.5561 \times 10^{-2}\ \mathrm{H} \quad \text{or} \quad 15.561\ \mathrm{mH}$$

The amount of load harmonic current supplied by the filter and the resulting bus voltage THD can be determined by analyzing the equivalent circuit shown in Fig. 13-6. The input impedance looking into the source from the harmonic load consists of the filter in parallel with the source. The input impedance is a function of frequency and is given by the following:

$$\begin{aligned} \mathbf{Z}_{in} &= \frac{(R_{tot} + j\omega K_{tot}) \cdot [j\omega L_f - j/(\omega C)]}{R_{tot} + j\omega L_{tot} + j\omega L_f - j/(\omega C)} \\ &= \frac{(R_{tot} + j\omega L_{tot}) \cdot [j\omega L_f - j/(\omega C)]}{R_{tot} + j(\omega L_{tot} + \omega L_f - 1/(\omega C)} \end{aligned} \tag{13.24}$$

Parallel resonance occurs when the imaginary part of the denominator of Eq. (13.24) is equal to zero.

$$\omega_0 L_{tot} + \omega_0 L_f - \frac{1}{(\omega_0 C)} = 0 \tag{13.25}$$

Solving Eq. (13.25) for ω_0,

$$\omega_0 = \frac{1}{[(L_{tot} + L_f)C]^{1/2}} \tag{13.26}$$

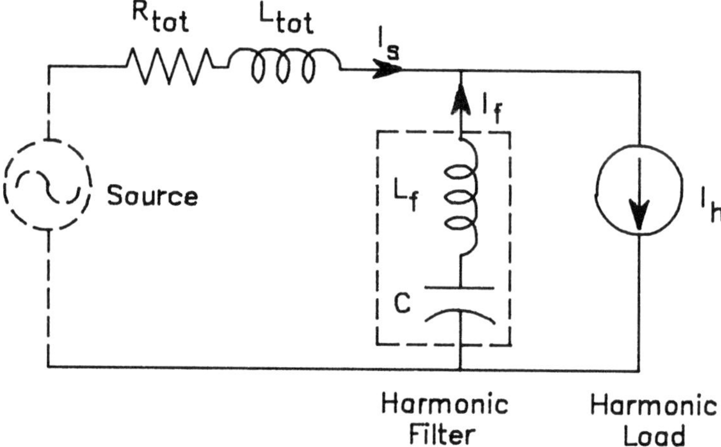

Figure 13-6 Application of current-divider rule to determine filter harmonic duty.

Likewise, the parallel resonant frequency in hertz is given by

$$f_0 = \frac{1}{2 \cdot \pi \cdot [(L_{tot} + L_f)C]^{1/2}} \tag{13.27}$$

Note the similarities between Eqs. (13.26) and (13.18).

EXAMPLE 13-6

The power factor correction capacitors of Example 13-3 have harmonic filter tuning inductors installed in series with the capacitor units. The resulting harmonic filter will be tuned to the 4.7th harmonic order. For each of the capacitor sizes listed in Example 13-3, determine the following:

a. Tuning inductance required

b. Parallel resonant frequency between the source and the filter bank with the tuning inductors installed

c. Tabulate the resonant frequencies with and without the tuning inductors installed.

Solution

a. The required inductance is determined by direct application of Eq. (13.23). The results are tabulated as follows:

200 kVAR: $L_f = 1.3830 \times 10^{-4}$ H

400 kVAR: $L_f = 6.9166 \times 10^{-5}$ H

600 kVAR: $L_f = 4.6100 \times 10^{-5}$ H

800 kVAR: $L_f = 3.4580 \times 10^{-5}$ H

b. The parallel resonant frequencies are determined by applying Eq. (13.27). The total system inductance was determined in Example 13-3 as 39.5×10^{-6} H. The results are tabulated in Table 13-6.

Table 13-6

kVAR	*Capacitance (F)*	*Filter Inductance (H)*	*Parallel Resonant Frequency (Hz)*	*Harmonic Order*
200	2.3026×10^{-3}	1.3830×10^{-4}	248.7	4.14
400	4.6052×10^{-3}	6.9166×10^{-5}	225.0	3.75
600	6.9076×10^{-3}	4.6100×10^{-5}	207.0	3.45
800	9.2101×10^{-3}	3.4580×10^{-5}	193.0	3.21

c. The parallel resonant frequencies with and without the tuning inductors are shown in Table 13-7.

Table 13-7 Parallel Resonant Frequencies

Capacitance (kVAR)	*Without Filter Inductors*	*With Filter Inductors*
200	8.80	4.14
400	6.22	3.75
600	5.08	3.45
800	4.40	3.21

Notice that the parallel resonant frequency has been shifted to a value below the tuning frequency of the filter.

To calculate the bus voltage distortion and filter harmonic duty, it is necessary to calculate the harmonic load current supplied from both the source and the harmonic filter bank. The division of current can be determined by applying the current-divider rule to the circuit of Fig. 13-6. The current supplied by the harmonic filter bank is given by the following:

$$I_f = I_h \cdot \frac{R_{\text{tot}} + j\omega L_{\text{tot}}}{R_{\text{tot}} + j[\omega L_{\text{tot}} + \omega L_f - 1/(\omega C)]} \quad \textbf{(13.28)}$$

In a similar manner, the current supplied by the source is given by

$$I_s = I_h \cdot \frac{j[\omega L_f - 1/(\omega C)]}{R_{\text{tot}} + j[\omega L_{\text{tot}} + \omega L_f - 1/(\omega C)]} \tag{13.29}$$

The bus voltage at each harmonic is determined by multiplying the source current by the source impedance as follows:

$$V_h = I_s \cdot (R_{\text{tot}} + j\omega L_{\text{tot}}) \tag{13.30}$$

Equations (13.28), (13.29), and (13.30) are evaluated at each harmonic frequency of interest to determine the harmonic duty of the filter and the resulting percent of THD bus voltage distortion with the filter capacitors installed. Equations (13.28), (13.29), and (13.30) are applicable to all frequencies except the fundamental.

The magnitude of the fundamental component of the source current is equal to

$$I_{s,1} = \frac{\text{total three-phase load kVA}}{\sqrt{3} \cdot \text{nominal line to line bus voltage}} \tag{13.31}$$

The magnitude of the fundamental component of the filter bank line current is equal to

$$I_{f,1} = \frac{\text{nominal line to neutral bus voltage}}{\omega_{\text{sys}} L_f - 1/(\omega_{\text{sys}} C)} \tag{13.32}$$

The magnitude of the fundamental component of bus voltage is assumed to be equal to the nominal line to neutral bus voltage magnitude.

EXAMPLE 13-7

A 600-kVAR harmonic filter bank has been installed on the power system of Example 13-3. The harmonic spectrum of the load current is given in Ex. 13-4. Determine the following:

a. Filter harmonic current spectrum and rss of the filter current
b. Bus voltage harmonic spectrum
c. Percent of THD and rss of the bus voltage

Solution From Example 13-3, the source resistance and inductance are

$$R_{\text{tot}} = 0.002747\ \Omega, \qquad L_{\text{tot}} = 39.5 \times 10^{-6}\ \text{H}$$

From Example 13-6, the tuning inductor required to tune a 600-kVAR, 480-V, three-phase capacitor bank to the 4.7th harmonic was

$$L_f = 4.61 \times 10^{-5}\ \text{H}$$

The equivalent line to neutral capacitance for the 600-kVAR, 480-V capacitor bank is $C = 6.9076 \times 10^{-3}$ F. The fundamental component of the load harmonic current was determined to be 240.6 A. The load harmonic current spectrum is repeated in Table 13-8 for reference.

Table 13-8 Harmonic Spectrum for 200-kVA Load

Frequency	Harmonic Order	Line Current Magnitude
300	5	50.0
420	7	30.0
660	11	15.0
780	13	7.0
1020	17	3.0

a. The magnitude of the fundamental component of the filter bank current is determined by direct application of Eq. (13.32).

$$I_{f,1} = \left| \frac{480/\sqrt{3}}{377.0 \cdot 4.61 \times 10^{-5} - 1/(377 \cdot 6.9076 \times 10^{-3})} \right| = 756.0 \text{ A}$$

To determine the harmonic current spectrum of the filter, Eq. (13.28) is evaluated at each of the load harmonic frequencies listed previously. The results are tabulated as follows:

Frequency (Hz)	Harmonic Order	Filter Line Current
300	5	44.02
420	7	18.28
660	11	7.68
780	13	3.47
1020	17	1.44

The rss value of the filter bank line current is

$$\begin{aligned} \text{rss current} &= (756^2 + 44.02^2 + 18.28^2 + 7.68^2 + 3.47^2 + 1.44^2)^{1/2} \\ &= 757.5 \text{ A} \end{aligned}$$

The rated current of the capacitor bank is

$$I = \frac{600{,}000}{\sqrt{3} \cdot 480} = 721.7 \text{ A}$$

The rss filter current expressed as a percentage of rated current is

$$I = \frac{757.5}{721.7} \cdot 100 = 105\%$$

b. The bus voltage harmonic distortion is determined by first calculating the harmonic currents supplied from the source. This involves application of Eq. (13.29) at each harmonic frequency of interest. The results are tabulated next:

Frequency (Hz)	*Harmonic Order*	*Source Line Current*
300	5	5.98
420	7	11.72
660	11	7.33
780	13	3.53
1020	17	1.56

The harmonic components of the bus voltage are determined by applying Eq. (13.30) at each harmonic load frequency. The results are

Frequency (Hz)	*Harmonic Order*	*Bus Voltage*
300	5	0.45
420	7	1.22
660	11	1.20
780	13	0.68
1020	17	0.39

The fundamental component of the bus voltage is

$$V_1 = \frac{480}{\sqrt{3}} = 277.0 \text{ V}$$

c. The percent of THD and rss values of the bus voltage are

$$\begin{aligned}\text{THD voltage} &= \frac{(0.45^2 + 1.22^2 + 1.2^2 + 0.68^2 + 0.39^2)^{1/2}}{277.0} \cdot 100\\ &= 0.7\%\\ \text{rss voltage} &= (277.0^2 + 0.45^2 + 1.22^2 + 1.2^2 + 0.68^2 + 0.39^2)^{1/2}\\ &= 277.01 \text{ V}\end{aligned}$$

Note from Example 13-7 that the THD bus voltage distortion has been reduced from 2.045% without the capacitor–filter bank to 0.7% with the capacitor–filter bank. Also, the THD bus voltage has been reduced from 25.8% with 600 kVAR of capacitors

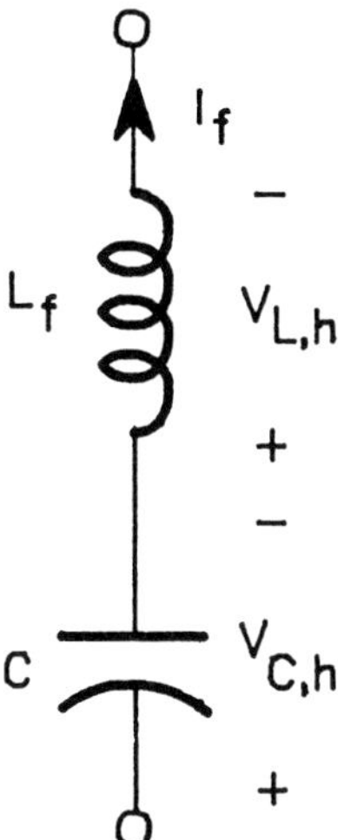

Figure 13-7 Equivalent circuit for determining voltage duty of filter components.

installed to 0.7% with the 600-kVAR capacitor–filter bank. This reduction in THD bus voltage distortion has occurred because the parallel resonant frequency has been shifted to a value less than the lowest-order harmonic component of load current.

When tuning inductors are applied to a capacitor bank to create a harmonic filter, an overvoltage occurs on the individual capacitor units. This overvoltage may cause excessive stress in the dielectric of the capacitor units and lead to premature failure. To determine the voltage on the capacitor unit of a harmonic filter, consider the line to neutral equivalent circuit shown in Fig. 13-7. Here the magnitude of the voltage across the capacitor is given by

$$V_{C,h} = I_f \frac{1}{\omega \cdot C} \tag{13.33}$$

Likewise, the magnitude of the voltage across the filter inductor is

$$V_{L,h} = I_f\,(\omega L_f) \tag{13.34}$$

where I_f is the filter current at the desired frequencies of interest. These currents are obtained by analyzing the system according to Eq. (13.28).

EXAMPLE 13-8 For the harmonic filter of Example 13-7, determine the magnitude of the harmonic voltages across the capacitor units and filter inductor.

Solution Direct application of Eqs. (13-33) and (13-34) results in the following:

Frequency (Hz)	I_f	$V_{L,h}$	Line to Neutral $V_{C,h}$
300	44.02	3.83	3.38
420	18.28	2.22	1.00
660	7.68	1.47	0.27
780	3.47	0.79	0.10
1020	1.44	0.43	0.03

If the capacitor units are delta connected, the equivalent line to neutral voltages must be multiplied by $\sqrt{3}$ to determine the actual voltage across the capacitor units.

The fundamental voltage across the capacitor units is

$$V_{C,1} = 756.0 \cdot \frac{1}{377 \cdot 6.9076 \times 10^{-3}} = 290.3 \text{ V}$$

The rss value of voltage across the capacitor cells is

$$\begin{aligned}\text{rss voltage} &= (290.3^2 + 3.38^2 + 1.00^2 + 0.27^2 + 0.10^2 + 0.03^2)^{1/2} \\ &= 290.32 \text{ V}\end{aligned}$$

Expressed as a percentage of rated capacitor voltage,

$$V_{\text{cap}} = \frac{290.32}{277} \cdot 100 = 104.8\%$$

As Example 13-8 illustrates, an overvoltage of about 5% above nominal will occur across the capacitor units of a capacitor bank tuned to operate as a harmonic filter. For example, if the system bus voltage is 5% above nominal, an overvoltage of approximately 110% will appear across the capacitor units. For this reason, it is common to specify the next higher standard voltage rating for the capacitor units used in a harmonic filter bank. Some capacitor manufacturers have ''low voltage stress'' capacitor units available for harmonic filter applications. If the voltage ratings of the capacitors are higher than the nominal bus voltage, the reactive power rating must be derated according to Eq. (9.62).

13-5 IEEE Standard 519

The maximum allowable voltage and current distortion is specified in IEEE Standard 519-1992. The limits on current distortion apply to the amount of harmonic current to be supplied by the utility source to the harmonic load. By limiting the amount of harmonic current supplied by the utility source, the voltage THD at the point of common coupling (PCC) with the utility can be kept within specified limits. For most industrial power systems, the maximum permitted voltage THD is 5.0%, with the maximum percentage for any one harmonic component equal to 3%.

Table 13-9 Current Distortion Limits for General Distribution Systems

I_{SC}/I_1	<11	$11 \le h < 17$	$17 \le h < 23$	$23 \le h < 35$	$35 \le h$	THD
<20	4.0	2.0	1.5	0.6	0.3	5.0
20<50	7.0	3.5	2.5	1.0	0.5	8.0
50<100	10.0	4.5	4.0	1.5	0.7	12.0
100<1000	12.0	5.5	5.0	2.0	1.0	15.0
>1000	15.0	7.0	6.0	2.5	1.4	20.0

Table 13-9 shows the maximum percentages of current distortion for general distribution systems (120 V to 69 kV) at the point of common coupling with the utility. Note from the table that the maximum permitted current THD is a function of the I_{SC}/I_1 or short-circuit ratio (SCR). I_{SC} is the magnitude of the short-circuit current at the point of common coupling (PCC) with the utility, and I_1 is the rated fundamental current of the total load at the point of common coupling. A high short-circuit ratio indicates a low system impedance as compared to the load. This type of system is able to supply a higher amount of harmonic current than a system with a low SCR ratio.

Table 13-9 specifies limits on the total harmonic current distortion and maximum distortion for the individual harmonic components. These THD limits are given for specific ranges of harmonic currents. For example, a system with an SCR of 75 would be permitted to have a THD of 10.0% for harmonics less than the 11th harmonic order, a THD of 4.5% for harmonic currents between the 11th and 17th harmonic orders, and so on. The THD within a specified range is calculated by taking the square root of the sum of the squares of the harmonic currents within that range and dividing by the maximum fundamental load current at the PCC.

EXAMPLE 13-9

A load containing harmonic generating equipment is connected through a step-down transformer to a 12.47-kV utility distribution feeder. A 5th harmonic filter has been added to the plant bus to filter out the majority of the 5th harmonic current. The point of common coupling is considered to be the 12.47-kV connection to the step-down transformer. The short-circuit availability at the PCC is 55 MVA at 12.47 kV. The maximum fundamental load current is 40 A at 12.47 kV. The following harmonic currents are present on the utility system as a result of this load:

Frequency (Hz)	*Harmonic Order*	*Source Line Current*
300	5	2.5
420	7	3.8
660	11	1.6
780	13	0.6
1020	17	0.4

Determine whether the requirements of IEEE 519 are met for this harmonic load.

Solution The short-circuit current at 12.47 kV is

$$I_{SC} = \frac{55\ \text{MVA} \cdot 1000}{\sqrt{3} \cdot 12.47\ \text{kV}} = 2546.5\ \text{A}$$

The SCR ratio is calculated as

$$\text{SCR} = 2546.5 \div 40 = 63.7$$

The THD for the harmonic current range less than the 11th is

$$\text{THD}_{<11} = \frac{(2.5^2 + 3.8^2)^{1/2}}{40.0} \cdot 100 = 11.4\%$$

According to Table 13-9, the maximum permissible THD for harmonics less than the 11th harmonic order is 10.0%. Therefore, IEEE 519 is violated in this range.

The THD for the harmonic current range between the 11th and 17th harmonic is

$$\text{THD}_{11\text{–}17} = \frac{(1.6^2 + 0.6^2)^{1/2}}{40.0} \cdot 100 = 4.3\%$$

The maximum permissible THD for harmonics between the 11th and 17th harmonic order is 4.5%. Therefore, the requirements of IEEE Standard 519 are met within this range.

The THD for the harmonic current range between the 17th and 23rd harmonic is

$$\text{THD}_{17\text{–}23} = \frac{(0.4^2)^{1/2}}{40.0} \cdot 100 = 1.0\%$$

The maximum permissible THD for harmonics between the 17th and 23rd harmonic order is 4.0%. Therefore, the requirements of IEEE Standard 519 are met within this range.

The THD including all harmonic terms is

$$\text{THD current} = \frac{(2.5^2 + 3.8^2 + 1.6^2 + 0.6^2 + 0.4^2)^{1/2}}{40.0} \cdot 100 = 12.2\%$$

This value of THD slightly exceeds the maximum of 12.0% as specified by IEEE 519.

Example 13-9 has illustrated a situation where the requirements of IEEE 519 have not been met. The large amount of 7th harmonic current is most likely the cause of the violation. To reduce the amount of 7th harmonic current on the system, it may be necessary to install both a 5th and a 7th harmonic filter to the plant bus.

The details of the design and analysis of multiple tuned filters is beyond the scope of this text. However, when applying multiple tuned filters to a power system, it must be remembered that the lowest-order step must be energized first, followed by successively higher-order steps. Likewise, when de-energizing steps, the highest-order step is switched off first, followed by successively lower-order steps. For example, in a filter bank consisting of 5th-, 7th-, and 11th-order steps, the 5th-order step is energized first, followed by the 7th-order, and then the 11th-order steps. With all steps energized, the 11th-order step is de-energized first, followed by the 7th- and then the 5th-order steps in succession.

13-6 Summary of Harmonic Filter Design and Analysis

The examples of Section 13.4 have presented an introduction to the fundamental concepts of harmonic filter design. The basic procedure can be summarized by the following steps:

1. Determine the amount of reactive compensation (kVAR) required.
2. Select a capacitor voltage rating equal to the next higher standard voltage rating available, or use ''low stress'' capacitor design.
3. Determine the actual amount of reactive power supplied by the capacitors after derating.
4. Calculate the rating of the filter inductor required to tune the capacitor–filter to the desired harmonic order frequency.
5. Calculate the harmonic current spectrum of the filter bank.
6. Calculate the harmonic spectrum, THD, and rss of the bus voltage after application of the harmonic filter.
7. Calculate the harmonic spectrum, THD, and rss of the source current.
8. Determine if the requirements of IEEE 519 are met.

Problems

13.1. Determine the THD and rss values of a current waveform having the following harmonic spectrum:

Frequency (Hz)	*Harmonic Order*	*Current (A)*
60	Fundamental	100.0
300	5	17.0
420	7	12.0
660	11	7.5
780	13	4.8
1020	17	3.0
1140	19	2.3
1380	23	1.4
1500	25	0.8

13.2. Determine the THD and rss values of a voltage waveform having the following harmonic spectrum:

Frequency (Hz)	*Harmonic Order*	*Voltage (V)*
60	Fundamental	120.0
300	5	5.0
420	7	2.3
660	11	1.2
780	13	0.3
1020	17	0.1

13.3. Determine a typical harmonic current spectrum for a 100-hp, 460-V, six-pulse, variable-speed motor drive. Assume 1 kVA per hp.

13.4. Determine the rss and THD of the current waveform for the variable-speed motor drive of Problem 13.3.

13.5. An industrial plant is supplied from the utility 24.94-kV, three-phase, MGN distribution feeder. The short-circuit data on the 24.94-kV system indicate a three-phase short-circuit availability of 105 MVA at 24.94 kV, with an X/R ratio of 2.2. The step-down transformer is rated at 2000 kVA, 24.94 kV–480Y/277 V, $R = 1.1\%$, $X = 6.5\%$. Determine the parallel resonant frequencies with the following capacitors connected to the 480-V bus.
a. 400 kVAR
b. 800 kVAR
c. 1200 kVAR

13.6. The industrial plant of Problem 13.5 supplies a total three-phase load of 1700 kVA. Included in the 1700 kVA of total load is a harmonic load having the harmonic spectrum shown in Table 13.10.

Table 13-10 Harmonic Spectrum

Frequency	*Harmonic Order*	*Line Current Magnitude*
300	5	250.0
420	7	130.0
660	11	60.0

It is proposed that a 1200-kVAR capacitor bank be added to the 480-V bus to improve the plant power factor. Determine the following:
a. rss and THD of the line current and bus voltage without the capacitor bank connected
b. rss and THD of the line current and bus voltage with the capacitor bank connected
c. rss and THD of the capacitor current with the capacitor bank connected

13.7. For the power system of Problems 13.5 and 13.6, it is now proposed that a 1200-kVAR, 480-V, capacitor–5th harmonic filter be installed. Assume that "low stress" capacitors are available at a voltage rating of 480 V. Determine the following:

a. Value of tuning inductor required to tune the bank to the 4.7th harmonic order

b. rss and THD of the line current and bus voltage with the filter installed

c. rss and THD of the filter current with the filter connected

13.8. Determine if the requirements of IEEE 519 are met for the filter installation of Problem 13.7. Assume that the PCC is at the high side of the 2000-kVA step-down transformer.

Appendix A

Conductor and Cable Data

The conductor and cable data and all other data contained in this appendix are representive of actual values. These data are to be used solely for the purpose of solving problems in this text. For actual power system design and analysis, the manufacturer should be consulted for exact data.

Table A-1 Bare Hard-Drawn Copper Conductor Characteristics

Size	*Strands*	R_ϕ *Ω/mile*	GMR_ϕ *(ft)*	*Outer Diameter (in.)*	*Ampacity (A)*
1000 kcmil	61	0.0762	0.0368	1.152	1240
750 kcmil	61	0.0992	0.0319	0.998	1040
500 kcmil	37	0.1455	0.0260	0.813	810
350 kcmil	19	0.2061	0.0214	0.678	650
300 kcmil	19	0.2402	0.01987	0.629	590
250 kcmil	19	0.2871	0.01813	0.574	530
#4/0 AWG	19	0.3384	0.01668	0.528	480
#3/0 AWG	7	0.4267	0.01404	0.464	410
#2/0 AWG	7	0.5373	0.01252	0.414	355
#1/0 AWG	7	0.6780	0.01113	0.368	310
#1 AWG	7	0.8545	0.00995	0.328	265
#2 AWG	7	1.0768	0.00883	0.292	230
#3 AWG	7	1.3583	0.00787	0.260	200
#4 AWG	7	1.6956	0.00717	0.232	170
#6 AWG	7	2.6919	0.00568	0.184	130

Source: Southwire Power Cable Manual and Product Catalog, Southwire Company.
Ampacities shown for 75°C conductor temperature, 25°C ambient, 2 ft/sec wind velocity. Resistance shown for 75°C conductor temperature and 60-Hz operating frequency.

Table A-2 Bare All-Aluminum Conductor (AAC) Characteristics

Size	*Strands*	R_ϕ Ω/*mile*	GMR_ϕ (*ft*)	*Outer Diameter (in.)*	*Ampacity (A)*
954 kcmil	37	0.1193	0.03596	1.124	982
795 kcmil	37	0.1426	0.03283	1.026	878
636 kcmil	37	0.1874	0.02936	0.918	765
477 kcmil	19	0.2350	0.02501	0.793	639
336.4 kcmil	19	0.3326	0.02135	0.666	513
#4/0 AWG	7	0.5275	0.01666	0.522	383
#3/0 AWG	7	0.6653	0.01483	0.464	331
#2/0 AWG	7	0.8395	0.01321	0.414	286
#1/0 AWG	7	1.0560	0.01177	0.368	247
#1 AWG	7	1.3306	0.00992	0.328	214
#2 AWG	7	1.6790	0.00883	0.292	185
#3 AWG	7	2.1173	0.00787	0.260	160
#4 AWG	7	2.6717	0.00700	0.232	138
#6 AWG	7	4.2504	0.00556	0.184	103

Source: Southwire Power Cable Manual and Product Catalog, Southwire Company.
Ampacities shown for 75°C conductor temperature, 25°C ambient, 2 ft/sec wind velocity. Resistance shown for 75°C conductor temperature and 60-Hz operating frequency.

Table A-3 Bare ACSR Conductor Characteristics

Size	*Strands*	R_ϕ Ω*/mile*	GMR_ϕ *(ft)*	*Outer Diameter (in.)*	*Ampacity (A)*
1272 kcmil	54/19	0.0913	0.0465	1.382	1187
954 kcmil	54/7	0.1204	0.0403	1.196	996
795 kcmil	54/7	0.1436	0.0368	1.092	889
636 kcmil	26/7	0.1732	0.0329	0.990	789
477 kcmil	26/7	0.2302	0.0290	0.858	659
336.4 kcmil	26/7	0.3263	0.0244	0.720	529
266.8 kcmil	26/7	0.4113	0.0217	0.642	475
#3/0 AWG	6/1	0.7603	0.0060	0.502	315
#1/0 AWG	6/1	1.1458	0.00446	0.398	242
#4 AWG	7/1	2.7403	0.00452	0.257	140

Source: Southwire Power Cable Manual and Product Catalog, Southwire Company.
Ampacities shown for 75°C conductor temperature, 25°C ambient, 2 ft/sec wind velocity. Stranding indicates number of aluminum–steel strands. Resistance shown for 75°C conductor temperature and 60-Hz operating frequency.

Table A-4 15-kV Primary Underground Residential Distribution Concentric Neutral Cable

Phase Conductor				Neutral Conductor			Insulation		Ampacity	
Size	Strands	R_{ϕ} Ω/M-ft	GMR_{ϕ} (in.)	Size	R_N Ω/M-ft	r_{CN} (in.)	D_{INS} (in.)	D_{SEM} (in.)	Direct Burial	Duct
Aluminum Phase Conductor, 100% Insulation Level (175 mils)										
1000 kcmil	61	0.0216	0.4448	20 #10*	0.0632	0.905	1.547	1.197	642	542
750 kcmil	61	0.0286	0.3828	25 #12*	0.0808	0.800	1.398	1.048	569	468
500 kcmil	37	0.0425	0.3120	25 #14*	0.1278	0.696	1.209	0.859	468	384
350 kcmil	37	0.0605	0.2568	18 #14*	0.1775	0.632	1.081	0.731	389	319
#3/0 AWG	19	0.1321	0.1685	25 #14	0.1278	0.515	0.866	0.516	284	201
#1/0 AWG	19	0.2097	0.1336	16 #14	0.1997	0.468	0.772	0.422	218	155
#2 AWG	7	0.3334	0.1060	10 #14	0.3195	0.429	0.693	0.343	168	119
Copper Phase Conductor, 100% Insulation Level (175 mils)										
750 kcmil	37	0.0197	0.3828	15 #8*	0.0530	0.823	1.398	1.048	649	532
500 kcmil	37	0.0289	0.3120	26 #12*	0.0773	0.705	1.209	0.859	577	472
350 kcmil	37	0.0409	0.2568	18 #12*	0.1117	0.641	1.081	0.731	489	400
#3/0 AWG	19	0.0847	0.1685	25 #12	0.0804	0.507	0.866	0.516	358	255
#1/0 AWG	19	0.1346	0.1336	25 #14	0.1278	0.468	0.772	0.422	273	194
#2 AWG	7	0.2138	0.1060	16 #14	0.1997	0.429	0.693	0.343	210	150

Source: Southwire Power Cable Manual and Product Catalog, Southwire Company.
*Reduced (one-third) size neutral. Ampacities shown for 100% load factor, 60-Hz, 36-in. burial depth, 20°C ambient, 90°C conductor temperature, and earth *RHO* = 90. Resistances shown for 90°C phase conductor temperature, 75°C neutral conductor temperature, 60-Hz operating frequency.

Table A-5 25-kV Primary Underground Residential Distribution Concentric Neutral Cable

Phase Conductor				Neutral Conductor			Insulation		Ampacity	
Size	*Strands*	R_ϕ Ω/M-ft	GMR_ϕ (in.)	*Size*	R_N Ω/M-ft	r_{CN} (in.)	D_{INS} (in.)	D_{SEM} (in.)	*Direct Burial*	*Duct*
Aluminum Phase Conductor, 100% Insulation Level (260 mils)										
750 kcmil	61	0.0286	0.3828	24 #12*	0.0837	0.910	1.578	1.058	567	475
500 kcmil	37	0.0425	0.3120	25 #14*	0.1278	0.787	1.389	0.869	466	386
350 kcmil	37	0.0605	0.2568	18 #14*	0.1775	0.723	1.261	0.741	387	320
#3/0 AWG	19	0.1321	0.1685	25 #14	0.1278	0.610	1.036	0.516	278	197
#1/0 AWG	19	0.2097	0.1336	16 #14	0.1997	0.553	0.942	0.422	214	152
#1 AWG	7	0.2642	0.1190	13 #14	0.2457	0.533	0.902	0.382	189	134
Copper Phase Conductor, 100% Insulation Level (260 mils)										
500 kcmil	37	0.0289	0.3120	26 #12*	0.0773	0.795	1.389	0.869	575	475
350 kcmil	37	0.0409	0.2568	18 #12*	0.2227	0.731	1.261	0.741	487	403
#3/0 AWG	19	0.0847	0.1685	25 #12	0.0804	0.619	1.036	0.516	351	250
#1/0 AWG	19	0.1346	0.1336	25 #14	0.1278	0.553	0.942	0.422	268	190
#1 AWG	7	0.1697	0.1190	20 #14	0.1597	0.533	0.902	0.382	235	168

Source: Southwire Power Cable Manual and Product Catalog, Southwire Company.
*Reduced (one-third) size neutral. Ampacities shown for 100% load factor, 60-Hz, 36-in. burial depth, 20°C ambient, 90°C conductor temperature, and earth *RHO* = 90. Resistances shown for 90°C phase conductor temperature, 75°C neutral conductor temperature, 60-Hz operating frequency.

Table A-6 35-kV Primary Underground Residential Distribution Concentric Neutral Cable

	Phase Conductor			Neutral Conductor			Insulation		Ampacity	
Size	*Strands*	R_ϕ Ω/M-ft	GMR_ϕ (in.)	*Size*	R_N Ω/M-ft	r_{CN} (in.)	D_{INS} (in.)	D_{SEM} (in.)	*Direct Burial*	*Duct*
Aluminum Phase Conductor, 100% Insulation Level (345 mils)										
1000 kcmil	61	0.0216	0.4448	20 #10*	0.0632	1.082	1.902	1.212	645	550
750 kcmil	61	0.0286	0.3828	24 #12*	0.0837	0.997	1.753	1.063	565	483
500 kcmil	37	0.0425	0.3120	25 #14*	0.1278	0.894	1.564	0.874	463	389
350 kcmil	37	0.0605	0.2568	18 #14*	0.1775	0.810	1.437	0.747	384	323
#3/0 AWG	19	0.1321	0.1685	25 #14	0.1278	0.695	1.206	0.516	270	187
#1/0 AWG	19	0.2097	0.1336	16 #14	0.1997	0.648	1.112	0.422	209	149
Copper Phase Conductor, 100% Insulation Level (345 mils)										
750 kcmil	61	0.0197	0.3828	15 #8*	0.0530	1.021	1.753	1.063	675	574
500 kcmil	37	0.0289	0.3120	26 #12*	0.0773	0.903	1.564	0.874	573	480
350 kcmil	37	0.0409	0.2568	18 #12*	0.1117	0.819	1.436	0.746	485	406
#3/0 AWG	19	0.0847	0.1685	25 #12	0.0804	0.704	1.206	0.516	340	238
#1/0 AWG	19	0.1346	0.1336	25 #14	0.1278	0.648	1.112	0.422	262	186

Source: Southwire Power Cable Manual and Product Catalog, Southwire Company.

*Reduced (one-third) size neutral. Ampacities shown for 100% load factor, 60-Hz, 36-in. burial depth, 20°C ambient, 90°C conductor temperature, and earth *RHO* = 90. Resistances shown for 90°C phase conductor temperature, 75°C neutral conductor temperature, 60-Hz operating frequency.

Table A-7 600-V Overhead Aluminum Triplex Secondary–Service Cable

Size	*Strands*	R_ϕ Ω/M-ft	GMR_ϕ (in.)	GMD_ϕ (in.)	*Ampacity*
#4/0 AWG	19	0.0999	0.1999	0.632	315
#3/0 AWG	19	0.1260	0.1780	0.576	275
#2/0 AWG	19	0.1590	0.1585	0.526	235
#1/0 AWG	19	0.2000	0.1412	0.482	205
#2 AWG	7	0.3180	0.1060	0.403	150
#4 AWG	7	0.5060	0.0840	0.345	115

Source: Southwire Power Cable Manual and Product Catalog, Southwire Company.

Table A-8 600-V Overhead Aluminum Quadruplex Secondary–Service Cable

Size	*Strands*	R_ϕ Ω/M-ft	GMR_ϕ (in.)	GMD_ϕ (in.)	*Ampacity*
#4/0 AWG	19	0.0999	0.1999	0.632	275
#3/0 AWG	19	0.1260	0.1780	0.576	235
#2/0 AWG	19	0.1590	0.1585	0.526	205
#1/0 AWG	19	0.2000	0.1412	0.482	180
#2 AWG	7	0.3180	0.1060	0.403	135
#4 AWG	7	0.5060	0.0840	0.345	100

Source: Southwire Power Cable Manual and Product Catalog, Southwire Company.

Note (Tables A-7 and A-8): Ampacities shown for cross-linked polyethylene insulation, 90°C conductor temperature, 40°C ambient, 2 ft/sec wind velocity. Resistance shown for 75°C conductor temperature and 60-Hz operating frequency.

Table A-9 600-V Overhead Aluminum Single Conductor Cable

Size	*Strands*	R_ϕ Ω/M-ft	GMR_ϕ (in.)	*Ampacity*
636 kcmil	61	0.0355	0.3523	720
477 kcmil	37	0.0445	0.3001	610
336.4 kcmil	19	0.0630	0.2520	495
#4/0 AWG	19	0.0999	0.1999	370
#2/0 AWG	7	0.1590	0.1501	280
#1/0 AWG	7	0.2000	0.1336	240

Source: Southwire Power Cable Manual and Product Catalog, Southwire Company.

Table A-10 600-V Overhead Copper Single Conductor Cable

Size	*Strands*	R_ϕ Ω/M-ft	GMR_ϕ (in.)	*Ampacity*
750 kcmil	61	0.0188	0.3828	995
500 kcmil	37	0.0276	0.3120	785
350 kcmil	19	0.0390	0.2568	640
250 kcmil	19	0.0544	0.2178	520
#4/0 AWG	19	0.0641	0.2002	465

Source: Southwire Power Cable Manual and Product Catalog, Southwire Company.

Note (Tables A-9 and A-10): Ampacities shown for cross-linked polyethylene insulation, 75°C conductor temperature, 25°C ambient, 2 ft/sec wind velocity. Resistance shown for 75°C conductor temperature and 60-Hz operating frequency.

Table A-11 Underground Aluminum Triplex Secondary–Service Cable

Size	Strands	R_ϕ Ω/M-ft	GMR_ϕ (in.)	GMD_ϕ (in.)	Direct Burial	In Duct
500 kcmil	37	0.0449	0.3121	0.979	495	395
350 kcmil	37	0.0637	0.2614	0.851	415	320
250 kcmil	37	0.0888	0.2209	0.748	345	265
#4/0 AWG	19	0.1048	0.1999	0.672	315	240
#3/0 AWG	19	0.1322	0.1780	0.616	280	205
#2/0 AWG	19	0.1663	0.1585	0.566	245	180
#1/0 AWG	19	0.2099	0.1412	0.522	215	160
#2 AWG	7	0.3344	0.1060	0.403	165	120
#4 AWG	7	0.5306	0.0840	0.345	125	90

Source: Southwire Power Cable Manual and Product Catalog, Southwire Company.
Ampacities shown for 100% load factor, 60-Hz, 36-in. burial depth, 20°C ambient, 90°C conductor temperature, and earth *RHO* = 90. Resistance shown for 90°C conductor temperature and 60 Hz-operating frequency.

Table A-12 Underground Aluminum Quadruplex Secondary–Service Cable

Size	Strands	R_ϕ Ω/M-ft	GMR_ϕ (in.)	GMD_ϕ (in.)	Direct Burial	In Duct
350 kcmil	37	0.0637	0.2614	0.851	385	305
#4/0 AWG	19	0.1048	0.1999	0.672	290	225
#3/0 AWG	19	0.1322	0.1780	0.616	250	195
#2/0 AWG	19	0.1663	0.1585	0.566	225	170
#1/0 AWG	19	0.2099	0.1412	0.522	200	150
#2 AWG	7	0.3344	0.1060	0.403	155	115
#4 AWG	7	0.5306	0.0840	0.345	120	85

Source: Southwire Power Cable Manual and Product Catalog, Southwire Company.
Ampacities shown for 100% load factor, 60-Hz, 36-in. burial depth, 20°C ambient, 90°C conductor temperature, and earth *RHO* = 90. Resistance shown for 90°C conductor temperature and 60 Hz-operating frequency.

Table A-13 600-V Underground Aluminum Single-Conductor Cable

Size	*Strands*	R_ϕ $\Omega/M\text{-}ft$	GMR_ϕ *(in.)*	*Direct Burial*	*In Duct*
500 kcmil	37	0.0449	0.3121	465	370
350 kcmil	37	0.0637	0.2614	385	305
300 kcmil	37	0.0740	0.2420	355	280
#4/0 AWG	37	0.0888	0.2209	320	250
#4/0 AWG	19	0.1048	0.1999	290	225
#3/0 AWG	19	0.1322	0.1780	250	195
#2/0 AWG	19	0.1663	0.1585	225	170
#1/0 AWG	19	0.2099	0.1412	200	150
#2 AWG	7	0.3344	0.1060	155	115
#4 AWG	7	0.5306	0.0840	120	85

Source: Southwire Power Cable Manual and Product Catalog, Southwire Company.
Ampacities shown for 100% load factor, 60-Hz, 36-in. burial depth, 20°C ambient, 90°C conductor temperature, and earth *RHO* = 90. Resistance shown for 90°C conductor temperature and 60-Hz operating frequency.

Appendix B

Typical Time–Current Characteristics

The time–current characteristic data and all other data contained in this appendix are representive of actual values. These data are to be used solely for the purpose of solving problems in this text. For actual power system design and analysis, the manufacturer should be consulted for exact data.

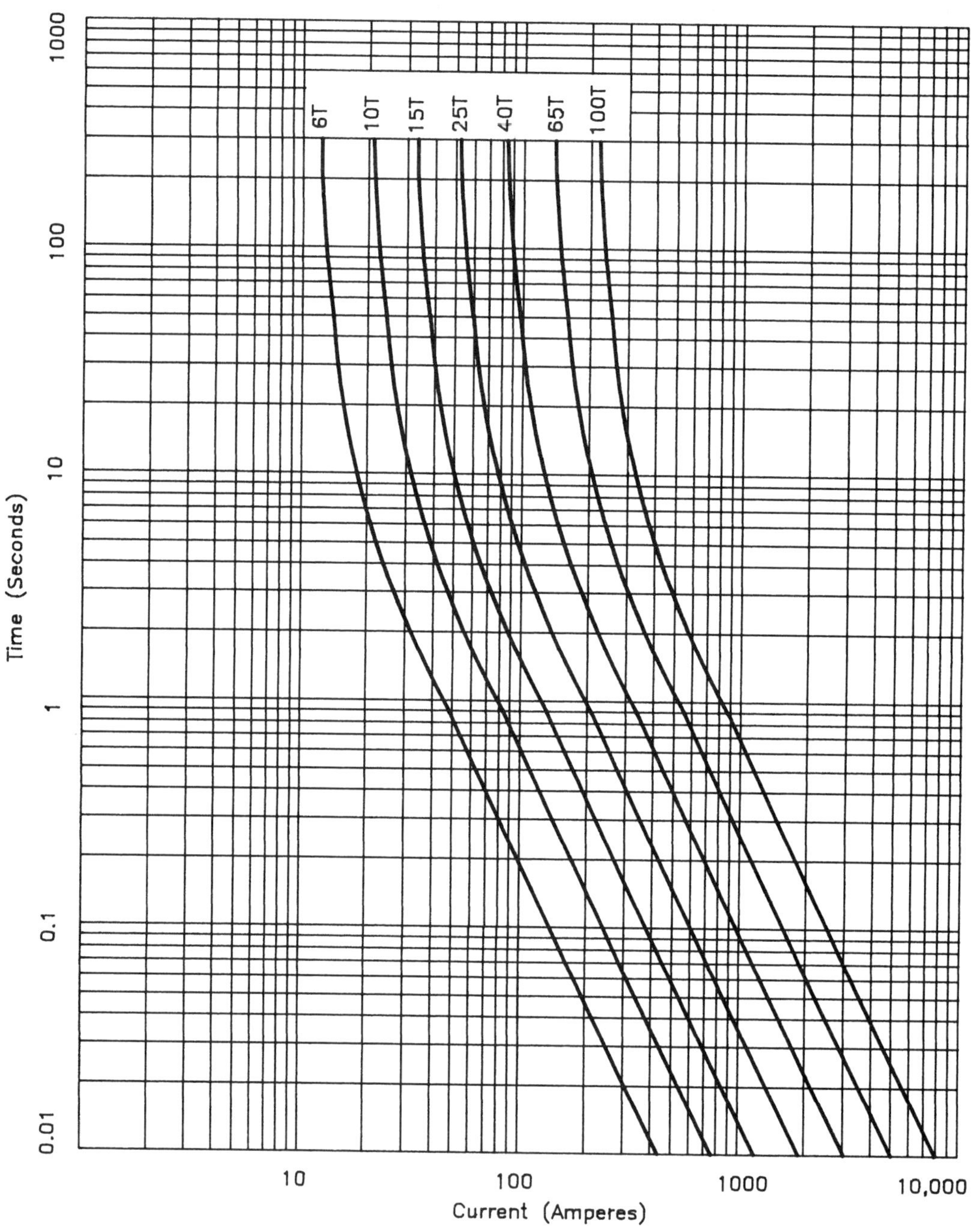

Figure B-1 Minimum melt characteristics of T link fuses. (*Source:* S&C Electric Company TCC# 170-6)

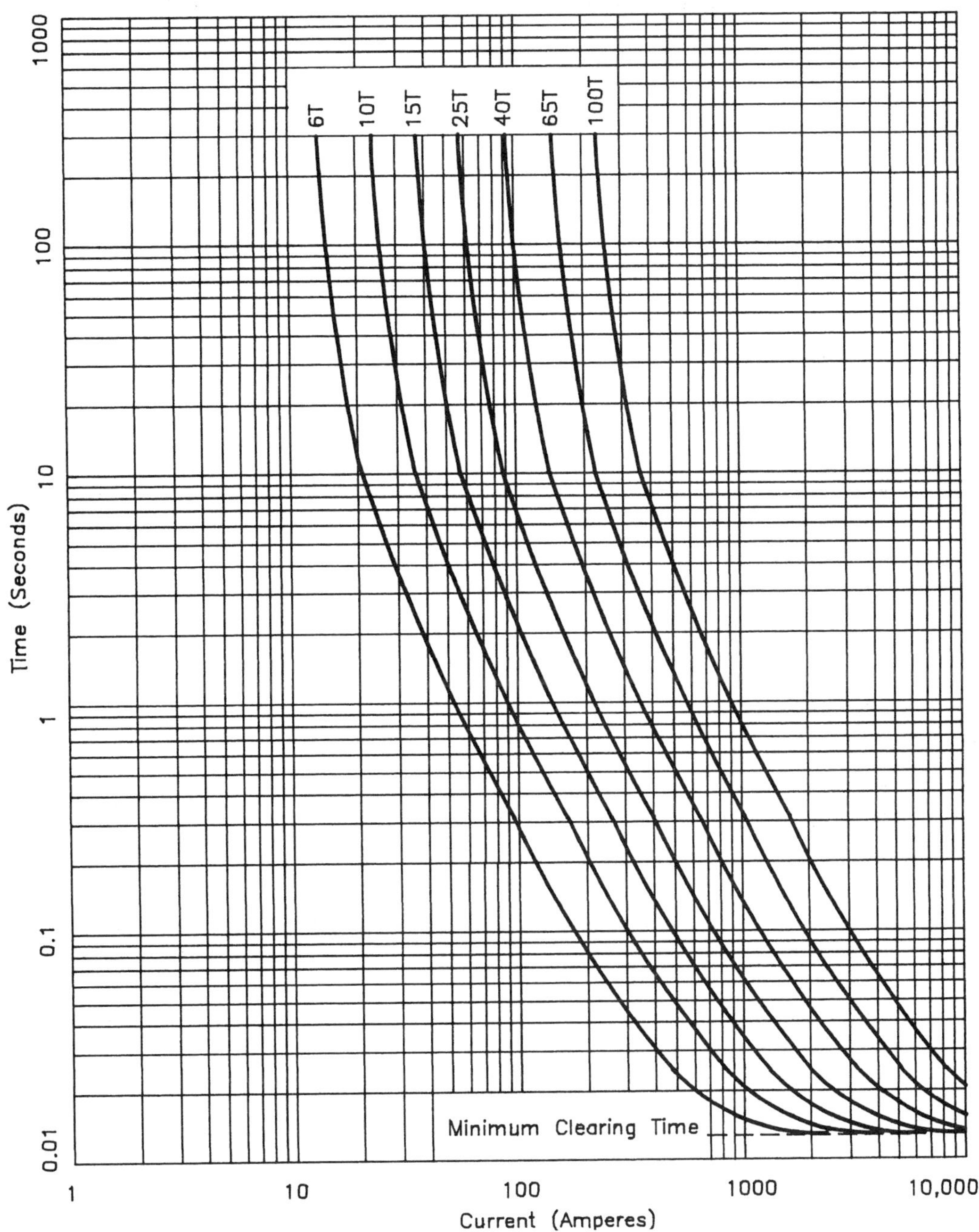

Figure B-2 Total clearing time characteristics of T link fuses. (*Source:* S&C Electric Company TCC# 170-6-2)

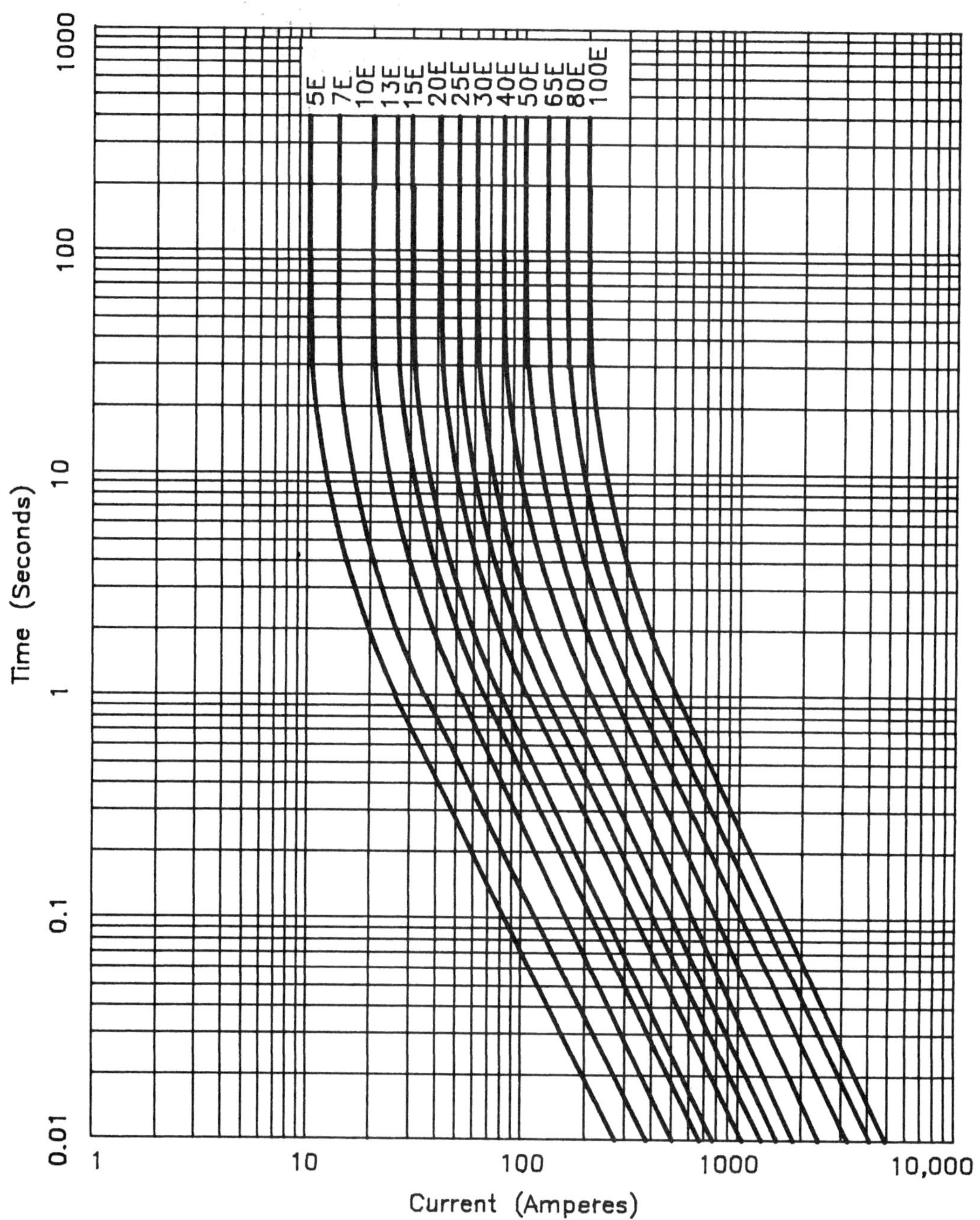

Figure B-3 Minimum melt characteristics of E-rated fuses. (*Source:* S&C Electric Company TCC# 153-1)

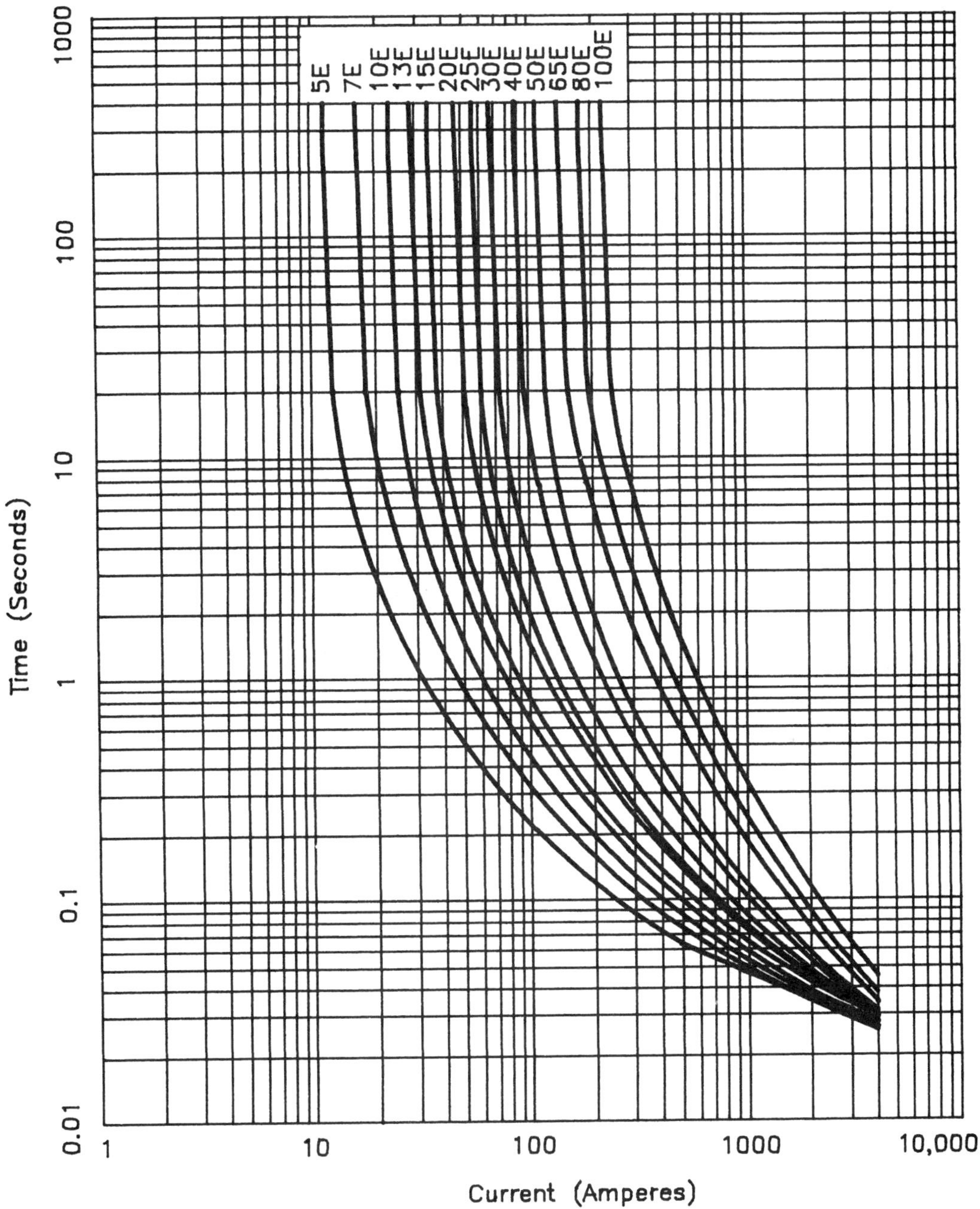

Figure B-4 Total clearing time characteristic of E-rated fuses. (*Source:* S&C Electric Company TCC# 153-1-6-5)

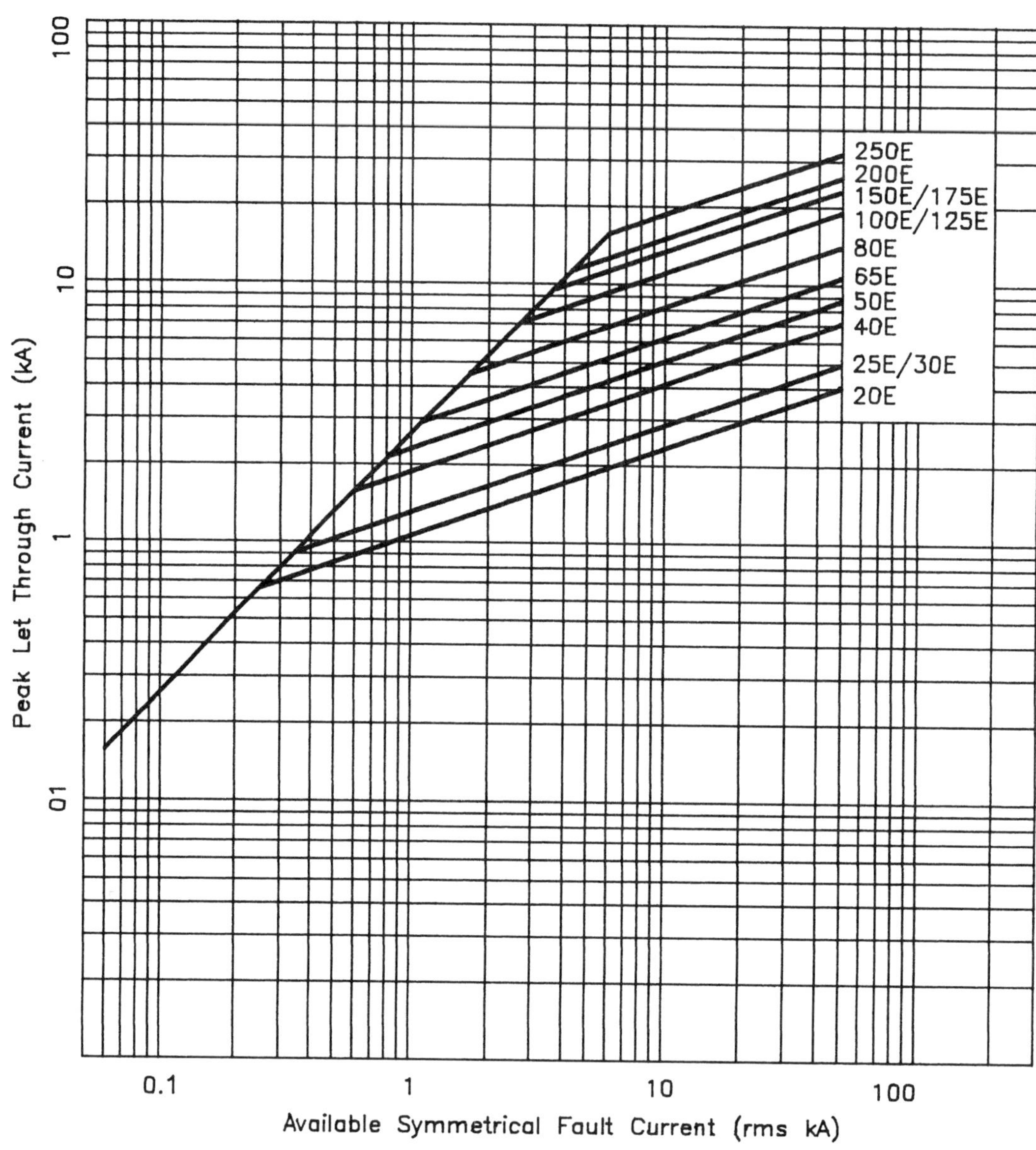

Figure B-5 Peak let through characteristics. (*Source:* General Electric Company Curve # GET-6777)

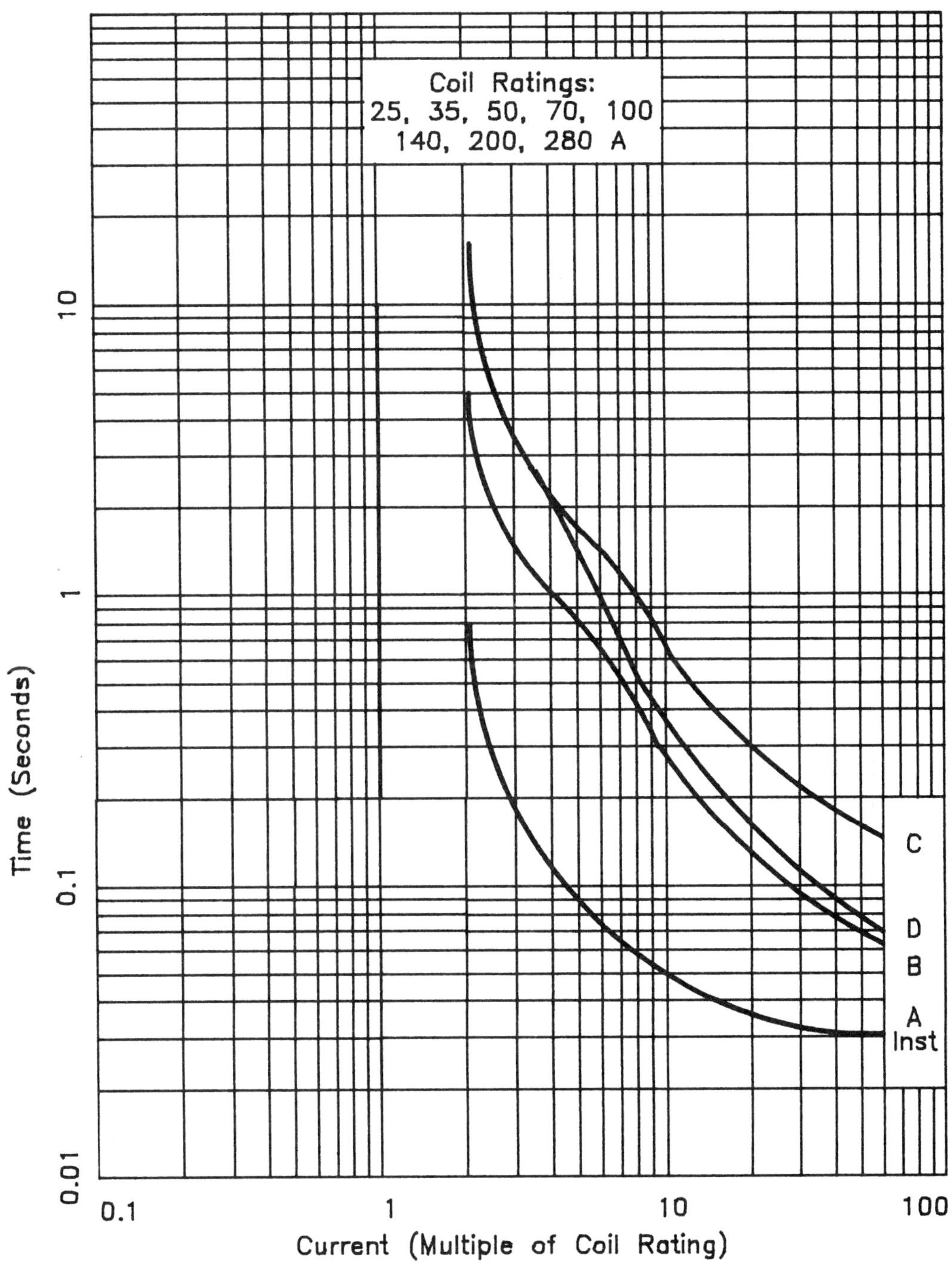

Figure B-6 Type L recloser time–current characteristics. (*Source:* Cooper Power Systems)

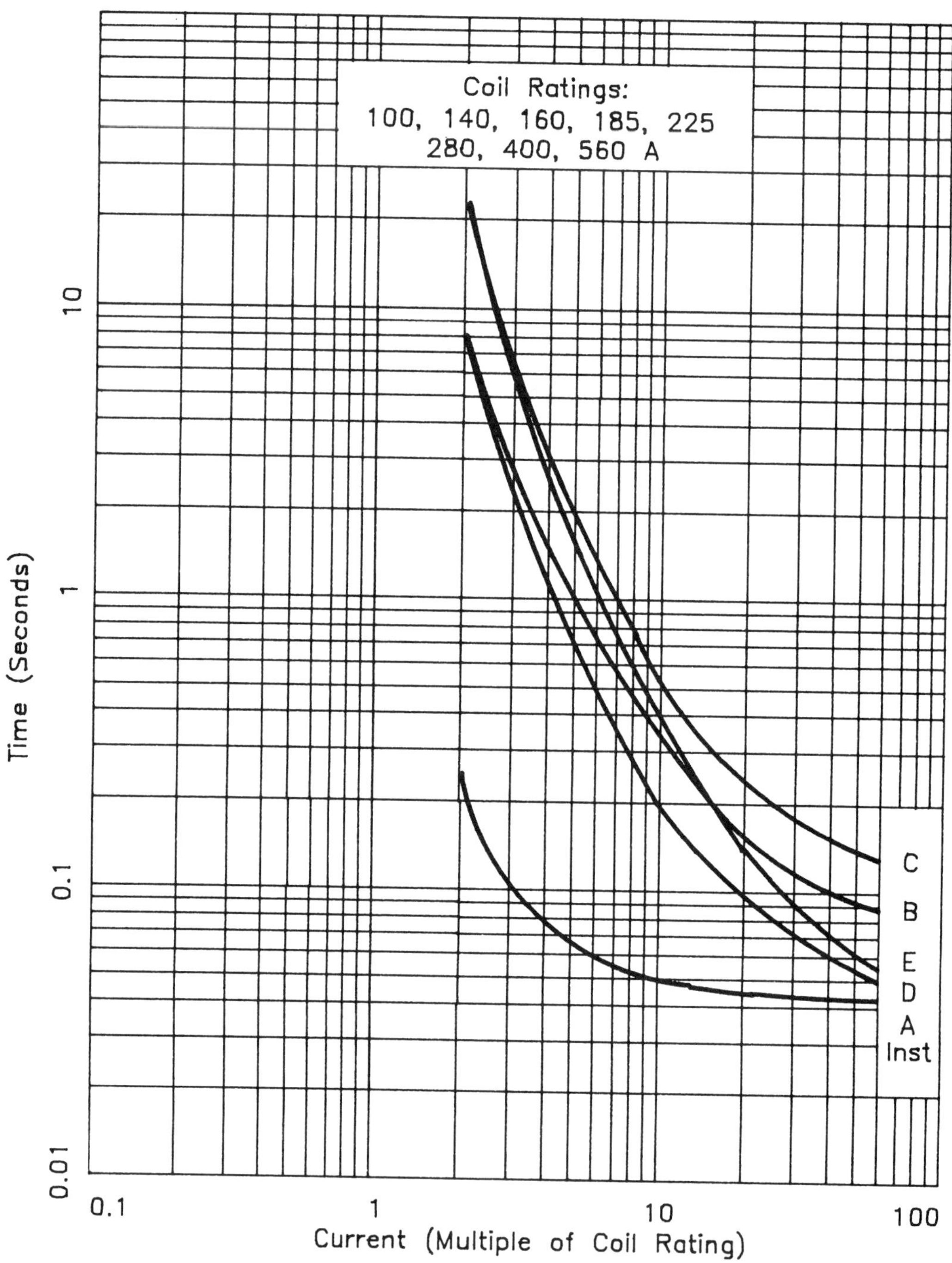

Figure B-7 Type D recloser time–current characteristics. (*Source:* Cooper Power Systems)

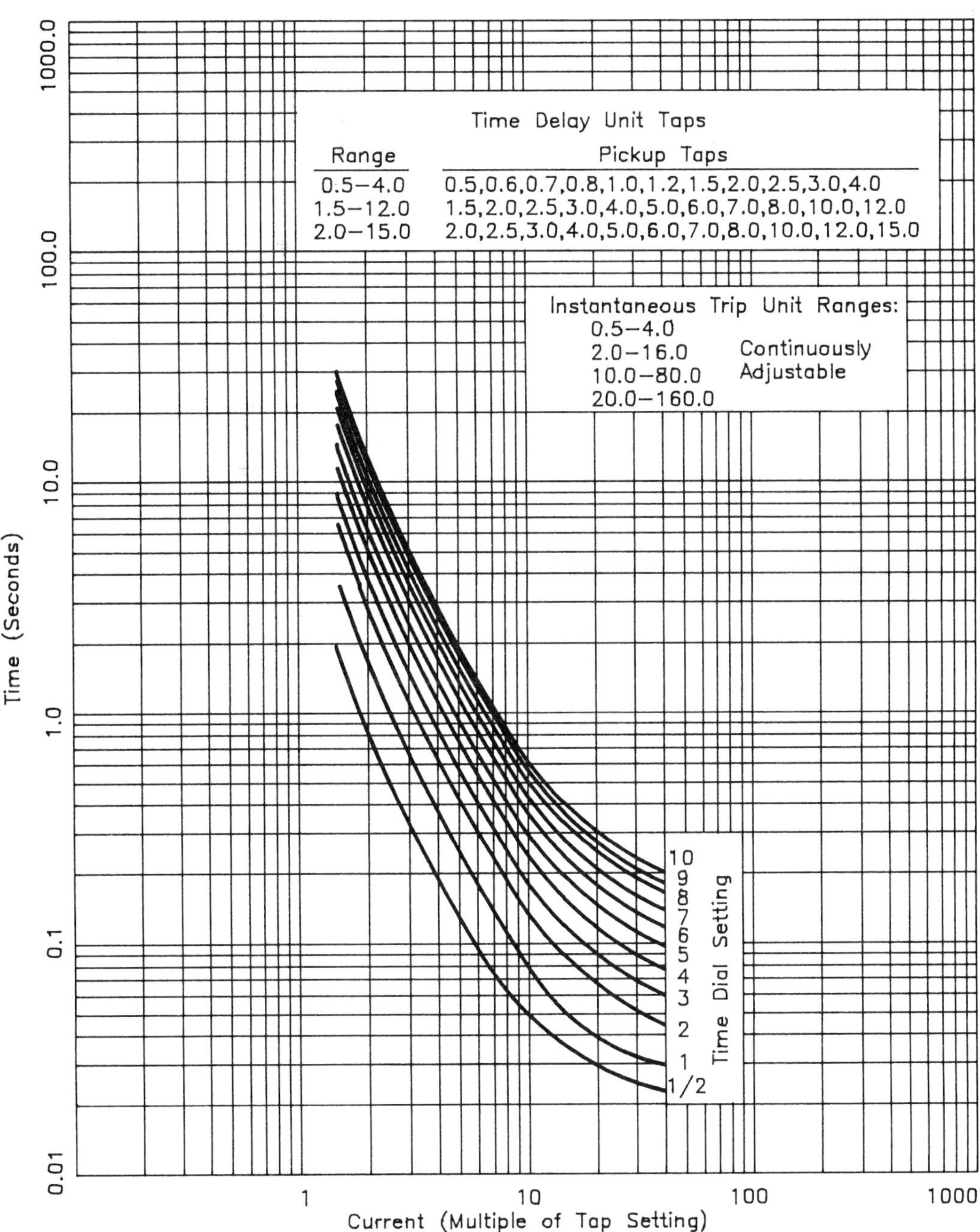

Figure B-8 IAC77 time–current characteristics. (*Source:* General Electric Company Curve # GEK-34055)

Index